# AMERICAN WOMEN ARTISTS
# PAST AND PRESENT
## Volume II

GARLAND REFERENCE LIBRARY
OF THE HUMANITIES
(VOL. 1123)

# AMERICAN WOMEN ARTISTS
## PAST AND PRESENT
### Volume II
### *A Selected Bibliographical Guide*

## Eleanor Tufts

GARLAND PUBLISHING, INC. • NEW YORK & LONDON
1989

Library of Congress Cataloging-in-Publication Data

(Revised for vol. 2)
Tufts, Eleanor
    American women artists, past and present.
    (Garland  reference library of the humanities;
vol. 185, 1123)
    Bibliography: v. 1, p.
    Women artists—United States—Bibliography.
    I. Title.  II. Series: Garland reference library of the
humanities ; v. 185, etc.
Z7963.A75T84    1984      016.704'042'0973      83-48201
ISBN 0-8240-9070-5 (v. 1 : alk. paper)
ISBN 0-8240-1511-8 (v. 2 : alk. paper)

Cover design based on one by Laurence Walczak

Printed on acid-free, 250-year-life paper
Manufactured in the United States of America

To HELEN TUFTS KREGER, pianist and teacher,
and
ANNE B. TUFTS, writer and teacher,
now respectively 92 and 103 years old

# CONTENTS

v

INTRODUCTION


When Garland Publishing asked me to bring out a second volume
of American Women Artists, Past and Present:  A Selected
Bibliographic Guide, I was in the midst of curating the Inaugural
Exhibition for the National Museum of Women in the Arts, a
124-piece show entitled "American Women Artists, 1830-1930"  that
opened the new museum in Washington on 5 April 1987.  During the
two years spent in preparing this exhibition, one-fourth of which
was devoted to miniatures and to sculptures, I discovered
additional women artists who were celebrated in their day with
periodic showings, and I have included them in this book.
The purpose of volume two is to add more artists on whom
information has now been found as well as to supplement (not
replace) the first volume by augmenting the entries of the women
previously listed.  The basis for inclusion remains the same as
stated in the earlier volume:  continuity and visibility.  The
consistency of being represented in national (and international)
exhibitions and magazines has been almost without exception a major
criterion in my choices of living artists.
Two important changes in this new volume are (1) I have
extended the age limit forward to include one more decade of
contemporary women artists:  those born in the 1950's, and (2) I
have added many more photographers and ceramic sculptors.
The number of artists covered has grown to over one thousand
two hundred.  Almost all of the five hundred artists who appeared
in volume one are continued in this volume, even if there might be
only a single new entry.
Concerning the standard reference books listed in the
Introduction to volume one, I should like to call attention to two
more:

Igoe, Lynn Moore, with James Igoe. <u>250 Years of Afro-American Art: An Annotated Bibliography</u>. New York: R.R. Bowker, 1981.

Petteys, Chris. <u>Dictionary of Women Artists: An International Dictionary of Women Artists Born Before 1900</u>. Boston: G.K. Hall & Co., 1985.

Chris Petteys's dictionary, which was published after volume one of this book appeared in 1984, has been enormously helpful in enriching the entries for women artists born before 1900. Since she has included practically all of the artists on whom I have also been working, I have not repeatedly listed her book, but every scholar should check Petteys's comprehensive dictionary for nineteenth-century American women painters and sculptors.

It is my fervent wish that this new book in tandem with the earlier volume will be helpful to students and scholars in their research and that the many references will unlock not only visual surprises but whole oeuvres of talented artists.

Eleanor Tufts
Southern Methodist University
Dallas, 1 June 1988

Sarah Peale, *Congressman Henry A. Wise*, c. 1842, oil on canvas, $29^1/2''$ x $24^1/2''$.
Virginia Museum of Fine Arts, Richmond.

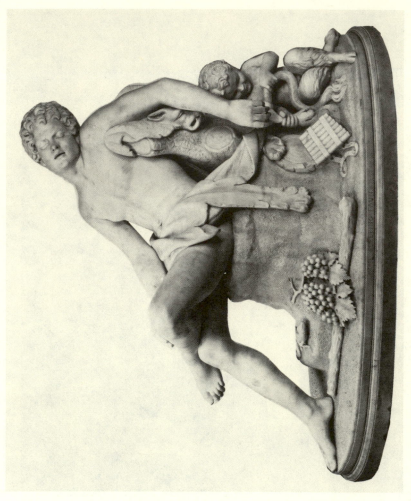

Harriet Hosmer, *Sleeping Faun*, 1865, 50" x 62" x 26". The Forbes Magazine Collection, New York.

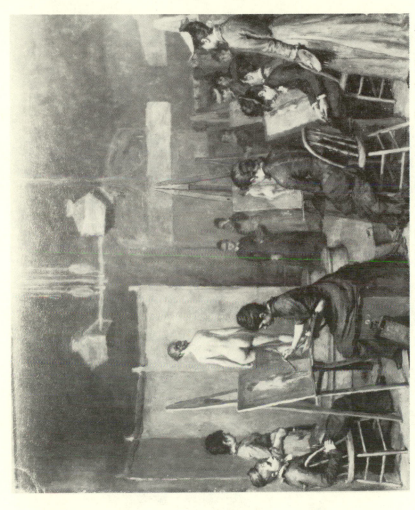

Alice Barber Stephens, *The Woman's Life Class*, 1879, oil on cardboard, 12" x 14". Pennsylvania Academy of the Fine Arts, Philadelphia.

Cecilia Beaux, *Les Derniers Jours d'Enfance*, 1883–1885, oil on canvas, 43³/₄" x 54". Private Collection.

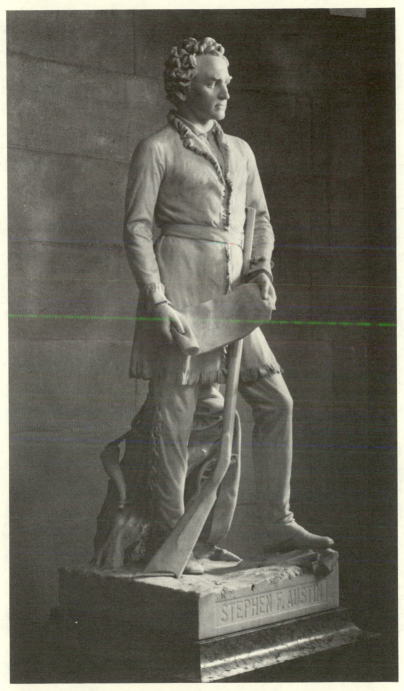

Elisabet Ney, *Stephen F. Austin*, 1904, marble, 6'2". United States Capitol Art Collection. Courtesy of Architect of the Capitol.

Marion Boyd Allen, *Portrait of Anna Vaughn Hyatt*, 1915, oil on canvas, 65" x 40". Maier Museum of Art, Randolph-Macon Woman's College, Lynchburg, Virginia.

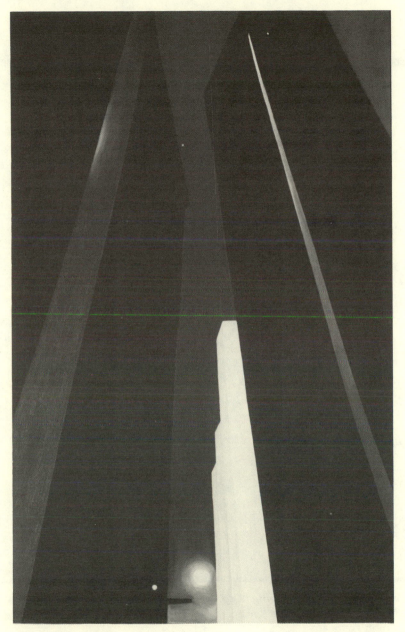

Georgia O'Keeffe, *City Night*, 1926, oil on canvas, 48" x 30". The Minneapolis Institute of Art.

Laura Wheeler Waring, *Anna Washington Derry*, 1927, oil on canvas, 20" x 16". National Museum of American Art, Smithsonian Institution, Gift of the Harmon Foundation.

Jean MacLane, *Seaside Situation*, late 1920's, oil on canvas, 36" x 46". Private Collection, Connecticut. (Photo, courtesy of Balogh Gallery).

Margaret Fitzhugh Browne, *Blessé de Guerre*, 1935, oil on canvas, 37" x 31".
Childs Gallery, New York and Boston.

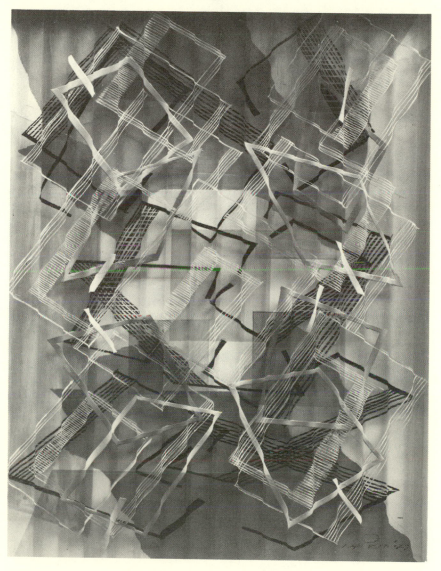

Irene Rice Pereira, *Undulating Arrangement*, 1947, oil on masonite and glass, $23^3/8$" x $17^1/4$". Wadsworth Atheneum, Hartford. The Ella Gallup Sumner and Mary Catlin Sumner Collection.

Joanne Leonard, *Romanticism Is Ultimately Fatal*, 1972, photograph with collage, 10" x 12".

Audrey Flack, *World War II*, 1976–1977, oil over acrylic on canvas, 96" x 96".
Collection of Mr. and Mrs. David Pincus, Wynnewood, Pennsylvania.

Sue Fuller, *String Composition #1-252*, 1980, aluminum frame and plastic thread, ca. 14' x 9'. Unitarian Church of All Souls, New York. Photo credit: Jay Hoops.

Debora Hunter, *Self-Portrait with Tall Man*, 1984, photograph (silver gelatin print), 15" x 15".

American Women Artists
Past and Present
Volume II

BERENICE ABBOTT (1898-    )    Photographer

See volume 1 of this book.

Berenice Abbott. New York:  Marlborough Gallery, 1976.

Levin, Helen.  "Berenice Abbott:  The Beauty of Physics."  Women
     Artists News 12, no. 3 (Summer 1987):  29.

Lyons, Nathan.  Photographers on Photography.  Englewood Cliffs:
     Prentice-Hall, 1966.

National Museum of Women in the Arts.  Washington, D.C.:  Harry N.
     Abrams, Inc., 1987:  76-77, 148-49.

Szarkowski, John.  Looking at Photographs:  100 Pictures from the
     Collection of the Museum of Modern Art.  New York:  The Museum
     of Modern Art, 1973.


               KIM WRIGHT ABELES (1952-    )    Sculptor

Associated Artists of Pittsburgh Annual Exhibition.  Pittsburgh:
     Carnegie Institute Museum of Art, 1977.

Bedient, Calvin.  "Los Angeles:  Kim Abeles at Pepperdine
     University and Karl Bornstein."  Art in America 73, no. 5 (May
     1985):  178, 181.

Clarke, Orville O., Jr.  "Exhibitions:  Reliquaries for the Lost."
     Artweek 14, no. 37 (5 November 1983):  4.

Rubin, Edward.  "New York Reviews:  Breaking and Entering."
     Art News 82, no. 6 (Summer 1983):  196.

Watson-Jones, Virginia.  Contemporary American Women Sculptors.
     Phoenix:  Oryx Press, 1986.

Wortz, Melinda.  "Artists the Critics are Watching, Report from Los
     Angeles:  Kim Abeles, Kimonos Floating in Space."  Art News
     80, no. 5 (May 1981):  88-89.


               GERTRUDE ABERCROMBIE (1909-1977)   Painter

See volume 1 of this book.

Descriptive Catalogue of Painting and Sculpture in the National
     Museum of American Art.  Boston:  G.K. Hall & Co., 1983.

CECILE ABISH (20th Century)    Sculptor

See volume 1 of this book.

Keeffe, Jeffrey. "Cecile Abish: Building from the Ground Up."
Artforum 17, no. 2 (October 1978):   35-39.

Kunst mit Eigen-Sinn. Aktuelle Kunst von Frauen. Vienna and
Munich: Locher Verlag, 1985.

Land Marks. Annandale-on-Hudson, New York:   Edith C. Blum Art
Institute, Bard College, 1984.

Natur-Skulptur, Nature-Sculpture. Stuttgart: Württembergische
Kunstverein, 1981.

Other Ideas. Detroit:  Detroit Institute of Arts, 1969.

Watson-Jones, Virginia. Contemporary American Women Sculptors.
Phoenix: Oryx Press, 1986.


MARY ELIZABETH MICHAEL ACHEY (1832-1886)    Painter

See volume 1 of this book.

Samuels, Peggy and Harold.  The Illustrated Biographical
Encyclopedia of Artists of the American West. Garden City,
New York:  Doubleday, 1976.


ALICE ADAMS (1930-    )    Ceramic Sculptor

See volume 1 of this book.

Citywide Contemporary Sculpture Exhibition. Toledo, Ohio:  Crosby
Gardens, 1984.

Dwellings. Philadelphia:  Institute of Contemporary Art,
University of Pennsylvania, 1978.

Four Sculptors. Williamstown, Massachusetts:  Williams College,
1976.

An International Survey of Recent Painting and Sculpture. New
York:  The Museum of Modern Art, 1984.

3

<u>Painting and Sculpture Today 1974</u>.  Indianapolis:  Indianapolis
     Museum of Art, 1974.

Watson-Jones, Virginia.  <u>Contemporary American Women Sculptors</u>.
     Phoenix:  Oryx Press, 1986.


                    PAT ADAMS (1928-    )  Painter

See volume 1 of this book.

<u>Adams at Zabriskie:  25th Anniversary Exhibition, 1954-1979</u>.  New
     York:  Zabriskie Gallery, 1979.

"Album:  Pat Adams.  Zabriskie Gallery, April 8-May 17."  <u>Arts
     Magazine</u> 60, no. 8 (April 1986):  124-25.

Donadio, Emmie.  "Night Flight to Byzantium:  The New Work of Pat
     Adams."  <u>Arts Magazine</u> 60, no. 10 (Summer 1986):  38-39.

Heartney, Eleanor.  "Pat Adams at Zabriskie."  <u>Art News</u> (Summer
     1984):  186.

Meyer, Ruth K.  <u>Pat Adams Paintings:  A Survey 1954-1979</u>.
     Cincinnati:  Contemporary Arts Center, 1979.

<u>Pat Adams:  Circles, Spheres and Other Correspondences</u>.  New York:
     The New York Academy of Sciences, 1988.

<u>Pat Adams, Works on Paper</u>.  New York:  Zabriskie Gallery, 1986.

Yau, John.  "Pat Adams at Zabriskie."  <u>Art in America</u> 67, no. 3
     (May-June 1979):  142.


               ELEANOR CURTIS AHL (1875-1953)   Painter

<u>The Ahls</u>.  Marietta, Georgia:  Knoke Galleries, 1985.

Falk, Peter Hastings, ed.  <u>Who was Who in American Art</u>.  Madison,
     Connecticut:  Sound View Press, 1985.


               ADELA AKERS (1933-    )   Fiber artist

Creager, Clara.  <u>Weaving</u>.  New York:  Van Nostrand Reinhold, 1980.

Held, Shirley.  <u>Weaving:  A Handbook for the Fiber Artist</u>.  New
     York:  Holt, Rinehart and Winston, 1980.

Scheinman, Pamela.  "Adela Akers:  The Loomed Plane."  <u>Craft
     Horizons</u> 37, no. 1 (February 1977):  24-25, 61-62.

<u>Wood</u>. Roslyn, New York: Nassau County Museum of Fine Arts, 1977.

Znamierowski, Nell. <u>Fiber: The Artist's View</u>. Greenvale, New
     York: Hillwood Art Gallery, Long Island University, 1983.


          ANNI ALBERS (1899-     )   Weaver and Printmaker

See volume 1 of this book.

Anscombe, Isabelle. <u>A Woman's Touch: Women in Design from 1860 to
     the Present Day</u>. New York: Viking Penguin, 1984.

Manhart, Marcia and Tom, eds. <u>The Eloquent Object</u>. Tulsa,
     Oklahoma: Philbrook Museum of Art, 1987.

<u>The Woven and Graphic Art of Anni Albers</u>. Washington, D.C.:
     National Museum of American Art, Smithsonian Institution,
     1985.


     GERTRUDE PARTINGTON ALBRIGHT   (1874-1959)   Painter and Etcher

<u>American Art Annual</u>, vol. 28. Washington, D.C.:  American
     Federation of Arts, 1932.

Dawdy, Doris Ostrander. <u>Artists of the American West</u>, vol 1.
     Chicago: Swallow Press, 1974.

Fielding, Mantle. <u>Dictionary of American Painters, Sculptors and
     Engravers</u>. Enlarged ed. Greens Farms, Connecticut:
     Modern Books and Crafts, 1974.

Porter, Bruce, et al. <u>Art in California: A Survey of American Art
     with Special Reference to California Painting, Sculpture and
     Architecture, Past and Present, Particularly as those Arts
     were Represented at the Panama-Pacific International
     Exposition</u>. San Francisco: R.L. Bernier, 1916: 120, pl. 253.

<u>A Selection of American Prints. A Selection of Biographies
     of Forty Women Artists Working Between 1904-1979</u>. Santa Rosa,
     California: The Annex Galleries, 1987: 1.

<u>Who's Who in American Art</u>, vol. 1. Washington, D.C.:
     American Federation of Arts, 1935.

<u>A Woman's Vision: California Painting Into the 20th Century</u>. San
     Francisco: Maxwell Galleries, 1983.

MAXINE ALBRO (1903-1966)    Painter and Printmaker

"Maxine Albro at California Palace of the Legion of Honor." Art
    News 29 (14 March 1936):  26.

"Maxine Albro at Delphic Studios." Art News 30 (12 December 1931):
    14.

"Maxine Albro in New York." Art Digest 6, no. 6 (15 December
    1931):  11.

"Maxine Albro Exhibition." Arts & Architecture 62 (October 1945):
    22.

"May Destroy Murals." Art Digest 9, no. 15 (May 1935):  11.

Morsell, Mary.  "California Mosaics." Magazine of Art 30, no. 10
    (October 1937):  620-25.

"New York Criticism." Art Digest 6, no. 7 (1 January 1932):  19.

A Selection of American Prints.  A Selection of Biographies
    of Forty Women Artists Working Between 1904-1979.  Santa
    Rosa, California:  The Annex Galleries, 1987:  1.

"A Spanish Hacienda in California with Frescoed Walls." Arts and
    Decoration 37, no. 1 (May 1932):  25.


LITA ALBUQUERQUE (1946-    )  Painter

See volume 1 of this book.

Schipper, Merle.  "Los Angeles:  Lita Albuquerque [at] Saxon-Lee."
    Art News  85, no. 10 (December 1986):  27.

Watson-Jones, Virginia. Contemporary American Women Sculptors.
    Phoenix:  Oryx Press, 1986.


MAY ALCOTT [NIERIKER] (1840-1879)  Painter

See volume 1 of this book.

Bedell, Madelon. The Alcotts:  A Biography of American Family.
    New York:  Clarkson N. Potter, 1980.

Fielding, Mantle. Dictionary of American Painters, Sculptors, and
    Engravers.  Enlarged ed.  Greens Farms, Connecticut:
    Modern Books & Crafts, 1974.

6

Willard, Frances, and Livermore, Mary A., eds. American Women.
    Reprint of 1897 ed., Detroit: Gale Research, 1973.


FRANCESCA ALEXANDER (1837-1917)    Painter

See volume 1 of this book.

Clement, Clara Erskine. Women in the Fine Arts. Boston:
    Houghton, Mifflin and Co., 1904.

Groce, George C., and Wallace, David H. The New-York Historical
    Society of Artists in America 1564-1860. New Haven,
    Connecticut: Yale University Press, 1957.

Spielmann, M. H. "The Roadside Songs of Tuscany." The Magazine
    of Art 18 (June 1895): 295-98.

Swett, Lucia Gray. John Ruskin's Letters to Francesca and Memoirs
    of the Alexanders. Boston: Lothrop, Lee & Shepard, 1931.


MARTHA ALF (1930-    )    Painter

See volume 1 of this book.

Martha Alf Retrospective. Los Angeles: Los Angeles Municipal Art
    Gallery, and San Francisco: San Francisco Art Institute,
    1984.

Perlmutter, Elizabeth. "300 Years of Drawings," Art News 74, no.
    9 (November 1975):  85.

Schipper, Merle. "Martha Alf." Art News 86, no. 2 (February
    1987):  24, 27.

Sources of Light, Contemporary American Luminism. Seattle:  Henry
    Art Gallery, University of Washington, 1953.


LOUISE ALLEN [ATKINS]  (d. 1953)    Sculptor

American Art Annual, vol. 30.  Washington, D.C.:  American
    Federation of Arts, 1934.

Archives of American Art. A Checklist of the Collection.
    Washington, D.C.:  Smithsonian Institution, 1975, 2nd ed.,
    rev., 1977.

Kohlman, Rena Tucker. "America's Women Sculptors." International
    Studio 76 (1922):  225-35.

National Sculpture Society. Exhibition of American Sculpture. San
     Francisco: California Palace of the Legion of Honor, 1929.


               MARION BOYD ALLEN (1862-1941)    Painter

American Art Annual, vol. 28. Washington, D.C.: American
     Federation of Arts, 1932.

"At 67, Mrs. Allen Braves Wilds to Paint." The Art Digest 8, no. 9
     (1 February 1934): 16.

Dawdy, Doris Ostrander. Artists of the American West:  A
     Biographical Dictionary, vol. 2. Chicago: Sage Books, 1980.

Fairbrother, Trevor J. The Bostonians, Painters of an Elegant Age,
     1870-1930. Boston: Museum of Fine Arts, 1986.

Fielding, Mantle. Dictionary of American Painters, Sculptors, and
     Engravers. Enlarged ed. Greens Farms, Connecticut: Modern
     Books and Crafts, 1974.

Fortieth Annual Exhibition. New York: National Association of
     Women Painters and Sculptors, 1931.

Obituary, The New York Times, 29 December 1941: 15.

Tufts, Eleanor. American Women Artists, 1830-1930. Washington,
     D.C.: National Museum of Women in the Arts, 1987.

Williams, Mary Frances. Catalogue of the Collection of American
     Art at Randolph-Macon Women's College. Charlottesville,
     Virginia: Randolph-Macon Women's College, 1977.

Young, William. A Dictionary of American Artists, Sculptors and
     Engravers. Cambridge, Massachusetts: Arno Press, 1968.


          BLANCHE AMES AMES   (1878-1969)   Botanical Illustrator

See volume 1 of this book.

American Art Annual, vol. 20. Washington, D.C.: American
     Federation of Arts, 1923.

Obituary. The New York Times, 3 March 1969: 35.

Women's Who's Who of America. New York: American Commonwealth
     Co., 1914.

8

SARAH FISHER CLAMPITT AMES (1817-1901)   Sculptor

See volume 1 of this book.

Holzer, Harold, and Ostendorf, Lloyd.  "Sculptures of Abraham
    Lincoln from Life."  Antiques 113 (February 1978):  382-93.


LAURIE ANDERSON (1947-    )   Performance Artist

See volume 1 of this book.

Anderson, Laurie.  "'Hi, We Need $1 Million for a Film.'" The New
    York Times,  20 April 1986, "Arts and Leisure":  1, 16.

Cokes, Tony.  "Laurie Anderson at the 57th Street Playhouse." Art
    in America (July 1986):  120.

Howell, John.  "Laurie Anderson." Artforum 24, no. 10 (Summer
    1986):  127.

Jarmusch, Ann.  "Laurie Anderson [at Institute of Contemporary Art,
    Philadelphia]." Art News 83, no. 5 (May 1984):  128-31.


RUTH A. ANDERSON (1884-1939)   Painter

See volume 1 of this book.

American Art Annual, vol. 28.  Washington, D.C.:  American
    Federation of Arts, 1932.

Vose Winter 1987-88.  Boston:  Vose Galleries, 1987:  4.

Who's Who in American Art, vol. 1.  Washington, D.C.:
    American Federation of Arts, 1935.


SOPHIE GENGEMBRE ANDERSON [WALTER] (1823-1903)   Painter

See volume 1 of this book.

Groce, George C., and Wallace, David H.  The New-York Historical
    Society's Dictionary of Artists in America 1564-1860.  New
    Haven:  Yale University Press, 1957.

Jackson-Stups, Gervase, ed.  Treasure Houses of Britain.  New
    Haven:  Yale University Press for National Gallery of Art,
    1985.

EDNA WRIGHT ANDRADE (1917-    )   Painter

See volume 1 of this book.

In This Academy.  The Pennsylvania Academy of the Fine Arts,
     1805-1976.  Philadelphia:  The Pennsylvania Academy of the
     Fine Arts, 1976.

Philadelphia:  Three Centuries of American Art.  Introduction by
     Darrel Sewell.  Philadelphia:  Philadelphia Museum of Art,
     1976.

Who's Who in American Art.  New York:  R.R. Bowker, 1978.


          MARRIETTA MINNIGERODE ANDREWS (1869-1931)   Painter

Andrews, Marietta M.  My Studio Window.  New York:  E.P. Dutton,
     1928.

Cosentino, Andrew J., and Glassie, Henry H.  The Capital Image,
     Painters in Washington, 1800-1915.  Washington, D.C.:
     National Museum of American Art, Smithsonian, 1983.

Fielding, Mantle.  Dictionary of American Painters, Sculptors and
     Engravers.  Enlarged ed.  Greens Farms, Connecticut:  Modern
     Books and Crafts, 1974.

Obituary.  American Art Annual, vol. 28.  Washington, D.C.:
     American Federation of Arts, 1932.

Obituary.  The New York Times, 8 August 1931:  13.


          RIFKA ANGEL (1899-    )   Painter

Aber, Ita.  "Rifka Angel."  Woman's Art Journal 7, no. 2 (Fall
     1986/Winter 1987):  32-35.

Archives of American Art.  Collection of Exhibition Catalogues.
     Boston:  G.K. Hall and Co., 1979.

Jacobson, J.Z.  Art of Today, Chicago--1933.  Chicago:  L.M.
     Stein, 1932.

10

CAROL ANTHONY (1943- ) Sculptor

See volume 1 of this book.

Mann, Virginia. "Carol Anthony: Secret Things." Arts Magazine
58, no. 6 (February 1984): 80-81.


ELEANOR ANTIN (1935- ) Performance Artist and Filmmaker

See volume 1 of this book.

Andre, Michael. "Eleanor Antin." Art News 74, no. 3 (March
1975): 111-112.

Crary, Jonathon. "Eleanor Antin." Arts Magazine 50, no. 7 (March
1976): 8.

intimate/Intimate. Curated by Charles S. Mayer and Bert Brouwer.
Terre Haute: Indiana State University, 1986.

Johnston, Laurie. "100 Boots to End Cross-Country March at
Museum." The New York Times, 16 May 1973: 49.

Lippard, Lucy. Six Years: The Dematerialization of the Art Object
from 1966 to 1972. New York: Praeger Publishers, 1973.

Matrix 34. Hartford: Wadsworth Atheneum, 1977.

Raven, Arlene. Crossing Over: Feminism and Art of Social Concern.
Ann Arbor: U.M.I. Research Press, 1988.

Zelevansky, Lynn. "Eleanor Antin." Art News 83, no. 3 (March
1984): 218, 220.


IDA APPLEBROOG (1929- ) Painter

See volume 1 of this book.

Bass, Ruth. "Ordinary People." Art News 87, no. 5 (May 1988):
151-154.

El Bienal de la Havana. Havana, Cuba, 1986.

Casademont, Joan. "Ida Applebroog, Ronald Feldman Fine Arts."
Artforum 19, no. 9 (May 1981): 72-73.

Cohen, Ronny H. "Ida Applebroog: Her Books." The Print
Collector's Newsletter 15, no. 2 (May-June 1984): 49-51.

Cotter, Holland. "Ida Applebroog." Arts Magazine 60, no. 8 (April
1986): 143.

Directions '83. Text by Phyllis Rosenzwieg. Washington, D.C.: Hirshhorn Museum and Sculpture Garden, 1983.

Documenta 8. Kassel, West Germany, 1987.

Drawing in Situ. Carol Becker Davis, Curator. Greenvale, New York: Hillwood Art Gallery, Long Island University, 1986.

Erotik in der Kunst. Bonn, West Germany: Bonner Kunstverein, 1982.

Frank, Elizabeth. "Ida Applebroog at Feldman (Downtown)." Art in America 69, no. 5 (May 1981): 137.

Gambrell, Jamey. "Ida Applebroog at Feldman." Art in America 73, no. 1 (January 1985): 141-142.

Gill, Susan. "Ida Applebroog at Ronald Feldman." Art News 85, no. 4 (April 1986): 154.

Heartney, Eleanor. "Ida Applebroog [at Ronald Feldman]." Art in America 82, no. 1 (January 1988): 151-52.

Ida Applebroog. New York: Ronald Feldman Fine Arts, 1987.

intimate/Intimate. Curated by Charles S. Mayer and Bert Brouwer. Terre Haute: Indiana State University, 1986.

Matrix 96. Essay by Andrea Keller. Hartford: Wadsworth Atheneum, 1987.

McGreevy, Linda F. "Ida Applebroog's Latest Paradox: Dead-Ends=New Beginnings." Arts Magazine 60, no. 8 (April 1986): 29-31.

_____. "Under Current Events: Ida Applebroog's Intimates and Others." Arts Magazine 59, no. 2 (October 1984): 128-31.

Phillips, Deborah. "Ida Applebroog." Art News 85, no. 2 (February 1985): 141.

Princenthal, Nancy. "Ida Applebroog at Ronald Feldman." Art in America 76, no. 2 (February 1988): 137.

Raven, Arlene. Crossing Over: Feminism and Art of Social Concern. Ann Arbor: U.M.I. Research Press, 1988.

Saunders, Wade. "Ida Applebroog at Ellen Sragow." Art in America 67, no. 3 (May-June 1979): 144.

Sokolowski, Thomas. Morality Tales: History Painting in the 1980's. New York: Grey Art Gallery, New York University, 1987.

12

Tannenbaum, Judith. Investigations 1986. Philadelphia: Institute of Contemporary Art, University of Pennsylvania, 1986.

Walker, Barry. The American Artist as Printmaker. Brooklyn: Brooklyn Museum, 1983.


DIANE ARBUS (1923-1971)    Photographer

See volume 1 of this book.

Kuspit, Donald B. "Diane Arbus at Helios." Art in America 65, no. 4 (July-August 1977): 95.

Sontag, Susan. "Freak Show." New York Review of Books, 15 November 1973: 13-19.

Szarkowski, John. Looking at Photographs: 100 Pictures from the Collection of the Museum of Modern Art. New York: The Museum of Modern Art, 1973.


ANNA MARGARETTA ARCHAMBAULT (1856-1956)    Miniaturist

American Art Annual, vol 28. Washington, D.C.: American Federation of Arts, 1932.

Fielding, Mantle. Dictionary of American Painters, Sculptors and Engravers. Enlarged ed. Greens Farms, Connecticut: Modern Books and Crafts, 1974.

Obituary. The New York Times, 1 July 1956: 56.

Wainwright, Nicholas B. Paintings and Miniatures at The Historical Society of Pennsylvania. Philadelphia: The Historical Society of Pennsylvania, 1974: 315.


RUTH ARMER (1898-1977)    Painter

American Painting Today 1950. New York: Metropolitan Museum of Art, 1950.

Art: USA: 58. New York: Madison Square Garden, 1958.

Painting and Sculpture in California: The Modern Era. San Francisco: San Francisco Museum of Modern Art, 1976.

Ruth Armer Retrospective. San Francisco: San Francisco Art Institute, 1979.

III Bienal. São Paulo, Brazil: Museu de Arte Moderna, 1955.

ANNELI MUSCHENHEIM ARMS (1935-    )   Sculptor

Buonagurio, Edgar.  "Arts Reviews:  Anneli Arms, Rela Banks, Nancy
    Brown."  Arts Magazine 52, no. 2 (October 1977):  26-27.

Caldwell, John.  "Chairs and More 'Chairs.'" The New York Times, 13
    December 1981:  WC26.

Ness, Wilhelmina Van.  "Anneli Arms."  Arts Magazine 55, no. 6
    (February 1981):  12.

Shiro, Anne-Marie.  "Furniture as Art:  To See and to Sit On."  The
    New York Times, 21 December 1978:  C6.

Vaughan, Mary.  "Anneli Arms."  Arts Magazine 52, no. 6 (February
    1978):  18.

Watson-Jones, Virginia.  Contemporary American Women Sculptors.
    Phoenix:  Oryx Press, 1986.

JANE BOTSFORD ARMSTRONG (1921-    )   Sculptor

Allied Artists of America Annual Exhibition.  New York:  National
    Academy of Design, 1976.

Annual Exhibition.  New York:  National Sculpture Society, 1976.

Armstrong, Jane B.  Discovery in Stone.  New York:  East Woods
    Press, 1974.

_____.  "From the Mountains of Vermont."  National Sculpture Review
    23, no. 2 (Summer 1974):  23-25.

Forty-Eighth Annual Exhibition.  New York:  National Sculpture
    Society, 1981.

Loercher, Diane.  "Jane Armstrong--Late-Blooming Sculptor."
    Christian Science Monitor, 19 December 1977:  15.

National Association of Women Artists Annual Exhibition.  New York:
    National Academy of Design, 1972.

National Association of Women Artists Annual Exhibition.  New York:
    National Academy of Design, 1985.

Watson-Jones, Virginia.  Contemporary American Women Sculptors.
    Phoenix:  Oryx Press, 1986.

HELEN MAITLAND ARMSTRONG (1869-1948)    Painter and Designer of
                                         Stained Glass

See volume 1 of this book.

DeKay, Charles. "The Quarter's Art." Quarterly Illustrator 2
     (April-June 1894): 189-208.

Obituary. The New York Times, 27 November 1948: 17.

Who's Who in American Art, vol. 2 (1938-39). Washington, D.C.:
     American Federation of Arts, 1937.


                    ANNE ARNOLD (1925-    )    Sculptor

See volume 1 of this book.

The Animal Image: Contemporary Object and The Beast. Washington,
     D.C.: Renwick Gallery of the National Museum of American Art,
     Smithsonian, 1981.

Campbell, Lawrence. "The Animal Kingdom of Anne Arnold." Art News
     63, no. 8 (December 1964): 32-33, 64-65.

Myers, John Bernard. "The Other." Artforum 21, no. 7 (March
     1983): 44-49.

Painting and Sculpture Today 1974. Indianapolis: Indianapolis
     Museum of Art, 1974.

Ratcliff, Carter. "Anne Arnold." Craft Horizons 31, no. 3 (June
     1971): 18-21, 69-70.

Schwartz, Sanford. The Art Presence. New York: Horizon Press,
     1982.

Sixty-Seventh Annual Exhibition of American Paintings and Sculpture.
     Chicago: Art Institute of Chicago, 1964.

Thirtieth Sculptors Guild Annual. New York: Lever House, 1967.

Watson-Jones, Virginia. Contemporary American Women Sculptors.
     Phoenix: Oryx Press, 1986.


                    EVE ARNOLD (1913-    )    Photographer

See volume 1 of this book.

Auer, Michèle, and Auer, Michel. Encyclopédia Internationale des
     Photographes de 1839 à nos Jours. Hermance, Switzerland:
     Editions Camera Obscura, 1985.

Browne, Turner, and Partnow, Elaine.  Macmillan Biographical
    Encyclopedia of Photographic Artists & Innovators.  New York:
    Macmillan, 1983.


SANDA ARONSON (1940-    )   Assemblage Artist

American Herstory.  Curated by Eleanor Tufts.  Atlanta:  Atlanta
    College of Art, 1988.

The Nine/Plus or Minus.  West Point, New York:  U.S. Military
    Academy Library, 1977.

1987 Artists' Society International Exhibition.  San Francisco:
    ASI Galleries, 1987.

North Carolina Print and Drawing Society's 10th Annual U.S. Print
    and Drawing Exhibition.  Greenville, N.C.:  Greenville Museum
    of Art, 1987.

Works on Paper--Women Artists.  (June Blum, Curator).  Brooklyn:
    The Brooklyn Museum, 1975.


RUTH ASAWA (1926-    )   Sculptor

See volume 1 of this book.

The Art of California.  Oakland, California:  The Oakland Museum,
    1984.

Hopkins, Henry.  50 West Coast Artists.  San Francisco:  Chronicle
    Books, 1981.

Nordland, Gerald.  Ruth Asawa:  A Retrospective View.  San
    Francisco:  San Francisco Museum of Art, 1973.

Painting and Sculpture in California:  The Modern Era.  San
    Francisco:  San Francisco Museum of Modern Art, 1976.

Public Sculpture/Urban Environment.  Oakland, California:  The
    Oakland Museum 1974.

Recent Sculpture USA.  New York:  The Museum of Modern Art, 1959.


DOTTY ATTIE (1938-    )   Drawer

See volume 1 of this book.

National Museum of Women in the Arts.  New York: Harry N. Abrams,
    Inc., 1987.

16

ANNA HELD AUDETTE   (1938-     )    Printmaker

See volume 1 of this book.

Who's Who in American Art. New York:   R.R. Bowker Company, 1986.


VIVIEN LOUISE AUNSPAUGH   (1869-1960)    Painter

American Art Annual, vol. 28.   Washington, D.C.:   American
      Federation of Arts, 1932.

Church, Diana.  Guide to Dallas Artists 1890-1917.  privately
      printed, Plano, Texas, 1987.

Fisk, Frances Battaile.  A History of Texas Artists and Sculptors.
      Abilene, privately printed, 1928:   58-59.


ALICE AUSTEN   (1866-1952)    Photographer

See volume 1 of this book.

Gover, C. Jane.  The Positive Image.  Albany:   State University of
      New York, 1988.


AMANDA PETRONELLA AUSTIN (1859-1917)    Painter and Sculptor

Bénézit, Emmanuel.  Dictionnaire critique et documentaire des
      peintres, sculpteurs et graveurs de tous les temps et de tous
      les pays.  Paris:  Librairie Gründ, 1976.

Exhibition of American Sculptures.  Buffalo, New York:   Albright
      Gallery, 1916.

Geeting, Corinne.  "Amanda Austin's Rescue from Oblivion."  Second
      Spring (April-May 1979):   16-19.

_____.  "The Rediscovery of Amanda Austin."  Westart, 9 June 1978:
      2.

"Missouri Women in History:  Amanda P. Austin."  Missouri
      Historical Review,  July 1972.

Peterson, Margaret.  "Rescued from Oblivion."  The Sacramento Bee,
      10 September 1978:  Scene Section:  1, 3.

Samuels, Peggy and Harold.  The Illustrated Biographical
      Encyclopedia of Artists of the American West.  Garden City,
      New York:  Doubleday, 1976.

Tufts, Eleanor. _American Women Artists, 1830-1930_. Washington,
     D.C.: National Museum of Women in the Arts, 1987.

_29th Annual Exhibition of American Painting and Sculpture_.
     Chicago: Art Institute of Chicago, 1916.


                MAYNA TREANOR AVENT (1868-1959)  Painter

_American Art Annual_, vol. 28. Washington, D.C.: American
     Federation of Arts, 1932.

_Who's Who in American Art_, vol. 3. Washington, D.C.: American
     Federation of Arts, 1940.


                ALICE AYCOCK (1946-    )  Sculptor

See volume 1 of this book.

_Alice Aycock, Retrospective of Projects and Ideas, 1972-1983_.
     Stuttgart: Württembergischer Kunstverein, 1983.

_Artpark: The Program in Visual Arts_. Lewiston, New York:
     Artpark, 1977.

Bourgeois, Jean-Louis. "Alice Aycock at 112 Greene Street." _Art in
     America_ 65, no. 4 (July-August 1977): 94.

Brenson, Michael. "The City as a Sculpture Garden: Seeing the New
     and the Daring." _The New York Times_, 17 July 1987: Y15, 18.

_Contemporary Sculpture: Selections from the Collection of the
     Museum of Modern Art_. New York: The Museum of Modern Art,
     1979.

Davies, Hugh M., and Onorato, Ronald J. _Sitings: Alice
     Aycock/Richard Fleischner/Mary Miss/George Trakas_. La Jolla,
     California: La Jolla Museum of Contemporary Art, 1986.

_The Decade in Review: Selections from the 1970s_. New York:
     Whitney Museum of American Art, 1979.

Denton, Monroe, ed. _'after years of ruminating on the events that
     led up to his misfortune. . .,' Alice Aycock Projects and
     Proposals 1971-1978_. Essays by Stuart Morgan and Edward F.
     Fry. Allentown, Pennsylvania: The Center for the Arts,
     Muhlenberg College, 1978.

_Documenta 6_. Kassel, West Germany: Neue Gallerie, 1977.

_Dwellings_. Philadelphia: Institute of Contemporary Art,
     University of Pennsylvania, and Purchase, New York: Neuberger
     Museum, 1978-79.

18

Environment and Sculpture. Lake Biwa, Japan: International
Contemporary Sculpture Symposium, 1984.

Fading Bounds in Sculpture. Amsterdam: Stedelijk Museum, 1978.

Fry, Edward F. Alice Aycock: Projects 1979-1981. Tampa:
University of South Florida, 1980.

Hauser, Reine. "Alice Aycock." Art News 83, no. 9 (November
1984): 145.

Kardon, Janet. Projects for PCA: Alice Aycock: History of a
Beautiful May Rose Garden in the Month of January.
Philadelphia: Philadelphia College of Art, 1978.

Kwinter, Sanford. "Alice Aycock at John Weber." Art in America
71, no. 4 (April 1983): 180-81.

Lippard, Lucy R. Overlay: Contemporary Art and the Art of
Prehistory. New York: Pantheon Books, 1983.

Metaphor, New Projects by Contemporary Sculptors. Washington,
D.C.: Hirshhorn Museum, 1982.

Myth and Ritual. Zurich: Kunsthaus, 1981.

National Museum of Women in the Arts. New York: Harry N. Abrams,
Inc., 1987: 112-13.

1981 Biennial. New York: Whitney Museum of American Art, 1981.

1979 Biennial. New York: Whitney Museum of American Art, 1979.

Poirier, Maurice. "The Ghost in the Machine." Art News 85, no. 8
(October 1986): 78-85, cover.

Price, Aimee Brown. "Artist's Dialogue: A Conversation with Alice
Aycock." Architectural Digest (April 1983): 54, 58, 60.

Shepard, Ileen. Sculpture of the 80's. Essay by Lowery S. Sims.
Queens, New York: Queens Museum, 1987.

Venice Biennale. Venice, 1978.

Warren, Ron. "Alice Aycock." Arts Magazine 59, no. 4 (December
1984): 40.

Watson-Jones, Virginia. Contemporary American Women Sculptors.
Phoenix: Oryx Press, 1986.

HELENE AYLON (1931-    )  Painter and Performance Artist

See volume 1 of this book.

Roth, Moira, ed.  Connecting Conversations: Interviews with 28 Bay
    Area Women Artists.  Oakland, California:  Eucalyptus Press,
    Mills College, 1988.


NANCY AZARA (1939-    )   Sculptor

La Rose, Elise.  "Nancy Azara."  Arts Magazine 59, no. 1 (September
    1984):  18.

Melf, Terry Hope.  "Women's Autobiographical Artists' Books."  New
    Art Examiner 15, no. 5 (January 1988):  64-65.

Rosser, Phyllis.  "Nancy Azara at Soho 20."  Women Artists News 12,
    no. 3 (Summer 1987):  29-30.


ALICE BABER (1928-1982)   Painter

See volume 1 of this book.

Alice Baber.  New York:  Fine Arts Museum/Women's Interart Center.

McCoy, Ann.  "Alice Baber:  Light as Subject."  Art International
    24, no. 1-2 (September-October 1980):  135-40.

Russo, Alexander.  Profiles on Women Artists.  Frederick, Maryland:
    University Publications of America, 1985.


JUDITH F. BACA (1949-    )   Mural Painter

See volume 1 of this book.

Hicks, Emily.  "The Artist as Citizen."  High Performance 9, no.
    3 (1986):  32-38.


PEGGY BACON (1895-1987)   Painter and Graphic Artist

See volume 1 of this book.

American Art Annual, vol. 28.  Washington, D.C.:  American
    Federation of Arts, 1932.

American Prints in the Library of Congress:  A Catalog of the
    Collection.  Baltimore:  Johns Hopkins Press, 1970.

20

Bacon, Peggy. Animosities. New York: Harcourt, Brace & Co.,
1931.

_____. The Terrible Nuisance and Other Tales. New York: Junior
Literary Guild, 1931.

Brown, Milton W. American Painting from the Armory Show to the
Depression. Princeton: Princeton University Press, 1955:
187-88, 220.

Cary, E. L. "Peggy Bacon and Wanda Gag, Artists." Prints 1
(March 1931): 13-24.

Demuth, Charles. Peggy Bacon. New York: Intimate Gallery, 1928.

First Biennial Exhibition of Contemporary American Sculpture,
Watercolors and Prints. New York: Whitney Museum of American
Art, 1933-34.

Lubowsky, Susan. The Social Graces: 1904-1944. New York:
Phillip Morris Branch of Whitney Museum of American Art, 1987.

McBride, Henry. "Peggy Bacon." Arts 17 (May 1931): 583-85.

Murrell, William, ed. Peggy Bacon. Woodstock, New York: William
M. Fisher, 1922.

"Peggy Bacon, Kindly Humorist, Has a Show." Art Digest 8, no. 11
(1 March 1934): 8.

"Peggy Bacon, 91, Illustrator and Author of Gentle Satires," The
New York Times, 7 January 1987.

"Peggy Bacon--Who Laughs at Life." Art Digest 11, no. 15 (1 May
1937): 9.

Women Pioneers in Maine Art 1900-1945. Portland: Westbrook
College, 1985.

JO BAER (1929-    )   Painter

See volume 1 of this book.

Poirier, Maurice, and Necol, Jane. "The '60s in Abstract: 13
Statements and an Essay." Art in America 71, no. 9 (October
1983): 129, 136-37.

Who's Who in American Art. New York: R.R. Bowker, Company, 1986.

FRANCES STEVENS BAGLEY (1946-    )    Sculptor

American Women Artists 1980. São Paulo, Brazil:  Museu de Arte
      Contemporanea da Universidad de São Paulo, 1980.

Fifth Texas Sculpture Symposium. Dallas:  Connemara Conservancy,
      1985.

Glueck, Grace.  "Guide to What's New in Outdoor Sculpture."  The
      New York Times, 12 September 1980:  C1, C20.

Kutner, Janet.  "The Southwest Texas Ranges:  Dallas, Acquisitions
      are only part of the action."  Art News 81, no. 10 (December
      1982):  86-88.

McFadden, Sarah.  "Going Places, Part II:  The Outside Story,
      Creedmoor Psychiatric Center."  Art in America 68, no. 6
      (Summer 1980):  51-55, 57-59.

Moore, Sylvia, ed.  No Bluebonnets, No Yellow Roses:  Essays on
      Texas Women in the Arts.  New York:  Midmarch Arts Press,
      1988.

Taylor, Elmer.  "An Apprenticeship in England."  Ceramics Monthly
      21, no. 1 (January 1973):  28-29.

Watson-Jones, Virginia.  Contemporary American Women Sculptors.
      Phoenix:  Oryx Press, 1986.

MARTHA SUSAN BAKER (1871-1911)    Miniaturist

Burnett, Mary Q.  Art and Artists of Indiana.  New York:  Century
      Company, 1921.

Champney, Elizabeth.  "Women in Art."  The Quarterly Illustrator 2
      (April-June 1894):  116.

Lounsbery, Elizabeth.  "American Miniature Painters."  Mentor 4,
      no. 23 (5 January 1917).

SARAH BAKER (1899-1983)    Painter

American Art Annual, vol. 28.  Washington, D.C.:  American
      Federation of Arts, 1932.

Archives of American Art.  Collection of Exhibition Catalogs.
      Boston:  G.K. Hall and Company, 1979.

The Phillips Collection, A Summary Catalogue. Washington, D.C.:
    The Phillips Collection, 1985.


            ANNI VON WESTRUM BALDAUGH (1881-1953)   Painter

American Art Annual, vol. 28. Washington, D.C.: American
    Federation of Arts, 1932.

Kamerling, Bruce. "Painting Ladies: Some Early San Diego Women
    Artists." Journal of San Diego History 32, no. 3 (Summer
    1986): 152-54.

Moure, Nancy D. Dictionary of Artists in Southern California
    Before 1950. Los Angeles: Dustin Publications, 1975.

A Selection of Painting by Early San Diego California Artists. San
    Diego: San Diego Museum of Art, 1987.


            ELEANOR CUNNINGHAM BANNISTER (1858-1939)   Painter

American Art Annual, vol. 20. Washington, D.C.: American
    Federation of Arts, 1923.

Catalogue of American Portraits in the New-York Historical Society,
    vol. 2. New Haven: Yale University, 1974: 675.

Fielding, Mantle. Dictionary of American Painters, Sculptors
    Engravers. Enlarged ed. Greens Farms, Connecticut: Modern
    Books and Crafts, 1974.

Harding, Jonathan P. The Boston Athenaeum Collection. Boston:
    The Boston Athenaeum, 1984.

Obituary. Who's Who in American Art, vol. 3. Washington, D.C.:
    American Federation of Arts, 1940.


            BELLE BARANCEANU (1902-1988)   Painter

"Belle Baranceanu Paints La Jolla High School Auditorium Murals."
    San Diego Union, 3 March 1940.

Belle Baranceanu--A Retrospective. Essays by Bram Dijksha and Anne
    Weaver. La Jolla: University of California, San Diego,
    Mandeville Gallery, 1985.

Brown, Suzanne Blair. "The Prime of Belle Baranceanu." San Diego
    Magazine 37, no. 9 (July 1985): 126-31.

Bruce, Edward, and Forbes, Watson. Art in Federal Buildings: An Illustrated Record of the Treasury Department's New Program in Painting and Sculpture. Washington, D.C.: 1936.

Fisk, Karen. "The Annual American Exhibition at the Art Institute of Chicago." The American Magazine of Art 17, no. 12 (December 1926): 621-25.

Gillmon, Rita. "The Seven Arts: Painter Outlasts Painting." San Diego Union, 30 August 1973: A19, A22.

Kamerling, Bruce. "Court Honors Local Artist Baranceanu." San Diego History News 16, no. 3 (March 1980): 2.

_____. "Painting Ladies: Some Early San Diego Women Artists." The Journal of San Diego History 32, no. 3 (Summer 1986): 154-57.

Loring, Marg. "Work of Belle Baranceanu Accepted by Chicago Art Institute Show." The San Diego Sun, 5 December 1937: B3.

Park, Marlene, and Markowitz, Gerald E. Democratic Vistas: Post Offices and Public Art in the New Deal. Philadelphia: Temple University Press, 1984.

"Seven Arts Depicted in Highly Praised Painting: Majestic Mural at La Jolla High School to be Dedicated." Los Angeles Times, 25 January 1941.

Vitale, Lydia Modi, O'Conner, Francis V., et al. New Deal Art California. Santa Clara: De Saisset Art Gallery and Museum, University of Santa Clara, 1976.


ELIZA ROSANNA BARCHUS (1857-1959)   Painter

See volume 1 of this book.

Barchus, Agnes. Eliza R. Barchus: The Oregon Artist, 1857-1959. Portland, Oregon: Binford and Mort, New York: Macmillan Company, 1974.

A Woman's Vision: California Painting into the 20th Century. San Francisco: Maxwell Galleries, 1983.


LUCY HAYWARD BARKER (1872-1948)   Painter

Havlice, Patricia. Index to Artistic Biography, vol. 1. Metuchen, New Jersey: Scarecrow Press, 1973.

Who's Who in American Art, vol. 2. Washington, D.C.: American Federation of Arts, 1937.

24

*Women Pioneers in Maine Art 1900-1945*. Portland, Maine: Joan
Whitney Payson Gallery of Art, Westbrook College, 1985.


LORETTA S. WONACOTT BARNETT (1951-    )    Sculptor

*Fourteenth Annual National Painting and Sculpture Exhibition*.
Fort Myers, Florida:  Edison Community College Gallery, 1980.

*Mainstreams '73, Eighth Annual Marietta College International
Competitive Exhibition for Painting and Sculpture*.  Marietta,
Ohio:  Marietta College, 1973.

*New Hampshire Arts Biennial*.  Manchester:  Manchester Institute of
Arts and Sciences, 1978.

*Regional Selection 1982*.  Hanover, New Hampshire:  Jaffe-Friede
Gallery, Hood Museum of Art, 1982.

Watson-Jones, Virginia.  *Contemporary American Women Sculptors*.
Phoenix:  Oryx Press, 1986.


ALICE PIKE BARNEY  (1857-1931)    Painter

See volume 1 of this book.

*American Art Annual*, vol. 1.  New York:  Macmillan, 1899.

Cosentino, Andrew J., and Glassie, Henry H.  *The Capital Image,
Paintings in Washington, 1800-1915*.  Washington, D.C.:
National Museum of American Art, Smithsonian Institution,
1983.

Hall, Delight.  *Catalogue of the Alice Pike Barney Memorial Lending
Collection*.  Washington, D.C.:  National Collection of Fine
Arts, 1965.


TINA BARNEY (1945-    )    Photographer

Bolt, Thomas.  "Tina Barney."  *Arts Magazine*  59, no. 9 (May 1985):
25.

Edwards, Owen.  "Summer Snapshots."  *American Photographer* 15
(September 1985):  33, 35.

Grundberg, Andy.  "Big Pictures that Say Little."  *The New York
Times*, 8 May 1983:  H31, 36.

*1987 Biennial Exhibition*.  New York:  Whitney Museum of American
Art, 1987.

CORNELIA BAXTER BARNS (1888-1941)    Illustrator

American Art Annual, vol. 28.  Washington, D.C.:  American
    Federation of Arts, 1932.

Fielding, Mantle.  Dictionary of American Painters, Sculptors and
    Engravers.  Enlarged ed.  Greens Farms, Connecticut:  Modern
    Books and Crafts, 1974.

Zurier, Rebecca.  Art for the Masses (1911-1917):  A Radical
    Magazine and its Graphics.  New Haven:  Yale University Art
    Gallery, 1985:  19, 163.

HANNELORE BARON (1926-1987)    Collage Artist

Brenson, Michael.  "Two Artists Tempered in the Crucible of War."
    The New York Times, 29 November 1987, Arts and Leisure
    Section:  37, 43.

Brown, Betty Ann.  "Dark Prophecies."  Artweek 17, no. 13 (5 April
    1986):  6.

Gardner, Colin.  "Illuminating the Human Condition."  Artweek 15,
    no. 12 (24 March 1984):  4.

Grimes, Nancy.  "Hannelore Baron (Schlesinger-Boisanté)."  Art News
    85, no. 2 (February 1986):  125.

Hammond, Pamela.  "Hannelore Baron (Jack Rutberg Gallery)."  Art
    News  87, no. 4 (April 1988):  162.

Henry, Gerrit.  "Hannelore Baron (Schlesinger-Boisanté)."  Art News
    84, no. 2 (February 1985):  151.

Obituary."  The New York Times, 1 May 1987:  Y13.

Obituary "Hannelore Baron, 60."  Art in America 75, no. 7 (July
    1987):  142.

EDITH CLEAVES BARRY (1884-1969)    Painter

American Art Annual, vol. 28.  Washington, D.C.:  American
    Federation of Arts, 1932.

Fielding, Mantle.  Dictionary of American Painters, Sculptors and
    Engravers.  Enlarged ed.  Greens Farms, Connecticut:  Modern
    Books and Crafts, 1974.

Who's Who in American Art, vol. 1.  Washington, D.C.:  American
    Federation of Arts, 1935.

JENNIFER BARTLETT (1941-    )    Painter

See volume 1 of this book.

At the Lake; Up the Creek; In the Garden. Jennifer Bartlett.
     Essay by Richard Francis. London:   Tate Gallery, 1982.

Bartlett, Jennifer.  The History of the Universe.  New York:   Moyer
     Bell, Nimbus Books, 1985.

_____. In the Garden.  Intro. by John Russell.  New York:   Harry
     N. Abrams, Inc., 1982.

Brenson, Michael.  "Art:  Jennifer Bartlett Retrospective."   The
     New York Times, 30 November 1985.

Cotter, Holland, "The Bartlett Variations."  Art in America 74, no.
     5 (May 1986):   124-31.

Field, Richard S., and Fine, Ruth E.  A Graphic Muse.  New York:
     Hudson Hills Press, 1987.

Galligan, Gregory.  "Jennifer Bartlett:  In and Out of the Garden."
     Arts Magazine 60, no. 3 (November 1985):   89-91.

_____. "Jennifer Bartlett:  Recent Pastels."  Arts Magazine  61,
     no. 10 (Summer 1987):   69-71.

Goldwater, Marge; Smith, Roberta; and Tomkins, Calvin.  Jennifer
     Bartlett.  New York:   Abbeville Press, 1985.

Heartney, Eleanor.  "Jennifer Bartlett at Paula Cooper."  Art News
     84, no. 7 (September 1985):   131.

Hughes, Robert.  "Fluent, Electric, Charming."  Time, 30 December
     1985:   79-80.

_____. "Revelations in a Dark Garden."  Time, 31 October 1983:
     106.

Moorman, Margaret.  "Jennifer Bartlett (Paula Cooper)."  Art News
     86, no. 6 (Summer 1987):   201, 202.

Perrone, Jeff.  "Jennifer Bartlett:  New Paintings."  Arts Magazine
     58, no. 4 (December 1983):   68-69.

Robertson, Nan.  "In the Garden with Jennifer Bartlett."  Art News
     82, no. 9 (November 1983):   72-77, cover.

Russell, John.  "Archetypes in Jennifer Bartlett's Pastels."  The
     New York Times, 27 February 1987:   25, 29.

_____. "A Ferocious and Gleeful Intelligence at Work." The New York Times, 19 May 1985, Arts and Leisure Section: 35.

_____. "Jennifer Bartlett Brings a Siberian Prism to Paris." The New York Times, 20 March 1988, Arts and Leisure Section: 33, 38.

Silverthorne, Jeanne. "Jennifer Bartlett." Artforum 24, no. 8 (April 1986): 107-108.

Tomkins, Calvin. "Profiles: Getting Everything In." The New Yorker, 15 April 1985: 50-68.

Van Wagner, Judy K. Collischan. Reflections, New Conceptions of Nature. Greenvale, New York: Hillwood Art Gallery, Long Island University, 1984.

ELIZABETH HOWARD BARTOL (1842-1927)   Painter

See volume 1 of this book.

"Boston Exhibition." Art Journal 5 (1879): 190.

Fielding, Mantle. Dictionary of American Painters, Sculptors and Engravers. Enlarged ed. Greens Farms, Connecticut: Modern Books and Crafts, 1974.

LOREN BARTON (1893-1975)   Painter

American Art Annual, vol. 28. Washington, D.C.: American Federation of Arts, 1932.

Fielding, Mantle. Dictionary of American Painters, Sculptors and Engravers. Enlarged ed. Greens Farms, Connecticut: Modern Books and Crafts, 1974.

"Loren Barton and Rome." Art Digest 6, no. 11 (1 March 1932): 6.

Moure, Nancy Dustin Wall. Dictionary of Art and Artists in Southern California Before 1930. Los Angeles: privately printed, 1975: 13-14, illus. 291.

_____. Los Angeles Painters of the Nineteen Twenties. Claremont, California: Pomona College Gallery, 1972.

Samuels, Peggy and Harold. The Illustrated Biographical Encyclopedia of Artists of the American West. Garden City, New York: Doubleday, 1976.

Southern California Artists, 1890-1940. Laguna Beach, California: Laguna Beach Museum of Art, 1979.

RUTH HENSHAW MILES BASCOM (1772-1848)    Painter

See volume 1 of this book.

The American Folk Art Collection of Frank and Karen Miele.  New
     York:  Sotheby's, 28 January 1984, Lot 3.

Bachmann, Donna G., and Piland, Sherry.  Women Artists.  Metuchen,
     New Jersey:  Scarecrow Press, 1978.

Reutlinger, Dagmar E.  "American Folk Art:  Two Groups of Family
     Portraits by Ruth Henshaw Bascom and Erastus Salisbury Field."
     Worcester Art Museum Bulletin 5 (May 1976):  1-12.


BERTHA CORSON DAY BATES (1875-1968)    Illustrator

American Art Annual, vol. 28.  Washington, D.C.:  American
     Federation of Arts, 1932.

Bertha Corson Day Bates:  Illustrator in the Howard Pyle Tradition.
     Wilmington:  Delaware Art Museum, 1978.

Fielding, Mantle.  Dictionary of American Painters, Sculptors and
     Engravers.  Enlarged ed.  Greens Farms, Connecticut:  Modern
     Books and Crafts, 1974.

Mayer, Anne E.  Women Artists in the Howard Pyle Tradition.  Chadds
     Ford, Pennsylvania:  Brandywine River Museum, 1975.

Who's Who in American Art, vol. 3.  Washington, D.C.:  American
     Federation of Arts, 1940.


MARY BAUERMEISTER (1934-    )   Painter

See volume 1 of this book.

Mary Bauermeister, Paintings and Constructions.  New York:  Galeria
     Bonino, 1967.

Rosenthal, Nan.  "New York Gallery Notes."  Art in America 53, no.
     2 (April 1965):  122.

Who's Who in American Art.  New York:  R.R. Bowker, 1978.


LEILA T. BAUMAN (active c. 1855-1870)    Painter

American Naive Painting of the 18th and 19th Centuries.  111
     Masterpieces from the Collection of Edgar William and Bernice
     Chrysler Garbish.  Washington, D.C.:  American Federation of
     Arts, 1969.

Dewhurst, C. Kurt; MacDowell, Betty; and MacDowell, Marsha.
Artists in Aprons. New York: E.P. Dutton, 1979.

Peterson, Karen, and Wilson, J.J. Women Artists. New York:
Harper & Row, 1976.

Tufts, Eleanor. American Women Artists, 1830-1930. Washington,
D.C.: National Museum of Women in the Arts, 1987.


MARTHA WHEELER BAXTER (1869-1955)   Miniaturist

American Art Annual, vol. 28. Washington, D.C.: American
Federation of Arts, 1932.

Fielding, Mantle. Dictionary of American Painters, Sculptors and
Engravers. Enlarged ed. Greens Farms, Connecticut: Modern
Books and Crafts, 1974.

Moure, Nancy. Los Angeles Painters of the Nineteen Twenties.
Claremont, California: Pomona College, 1972.

Woman's Who's Who of America. New York: American Commonwealth
Company, 1914.


LUCIE BAYARD (c. 1900-    )   Painter

American Art Annual, vol. 17. Washington, D.C.: American
Federation of Arts, 1920.

Breuning, Margaret. "Lucie Bayard." Art Digest 19, no. 15 (1 May
1945): 18.

"Lucie Bayard." Art News 44, no. 6 (1 May 1945): 27.


CAROLINE VAN HOOK BEAN (1879-1980)   Painter

New York City in Wartime (1918-1919). New York: Chapellier
Galleries, 1970.

Cosentino, Andrew J., and Glassie, Henry H. The Capital Image,
Painters in Washington, 1800-1915. Washington, D.C.:
National Museum of American Art, Smithsonian Institution
Press, 1983.

CECILIA BEAUX (1855-1942)   Painter

See volume 1 of this book.

American Art Annual, vol. 28. Washington, D.C.: American
Federation of Arts, 1932.

30

Artists by Themselves. New York:  National Academy of Design, 1983.

Bailey, Elizabeth Graham.  "The Cecilia Beaux Papers."  Archives of American Art Journal, vol. 13, no. 4 (1973):  14-19.

Barnard, Susan B.  "Cecilia Beaux Rediscovered:  An Annotated Bibliography with Introductory Essay."  Bulletin of Bibliography 45, no. 1 (March 1988)  3-7, cover.

Bell, Mrs. Arthur.  "The Work of Cecilia Beaux."  The Studio 17 (September 1899):  215-22.

Bowen, Catherine Drinker.  Family Portrait.  Boston:  Little, Brown and Company, 1970.

Catalogue of the Exhibits of the State of Pennsylvania and Pennsylvanians at the World's Columbian Exposition. Pennsylvania:  State Printer, 1893.

Gray, Allison.  "The Extraordinary Career of Cecilia Beaux."  The American Magazine 96 (October 1923):  61-63, 195-98.

In This Academy.  The Pennsylvania Academy of the Fine Arts, 1805-1976.  Philadelphia:  The Pennsylvania Academy of the Fine Arts, 1976.

Lee, Cuthbert.  Contemporary American Portrait Painters.  New York:  W.W. Norton and Company, 1929:  14-15.

Mechlin, Leila.  "War Portraits by Eminent Artists."  American Magazine of Art 12, no. 3 (March 1921):  76-88.

National Museum of Women in the Arts.  New York:  Harry N. Abrams, Inc., 1987.

Platt, Frederick.  "The War Portraits."  Antiques 26, no. 1 (July 1984):  142-53.

Tufts, Eleanor.  American Women Artists, 1830-1930.  Washington, D.C.:  National Museum of Women in the Arts, 1987.

ROSEMARIE BECK [PHELPS] (1925-    )    Painter

See volume 1 of this book.

Who's Who in American Art.  New York:  R.R. Bowker Company, 1978.

ALICE BECKINGTON (1868-1942)   Painter

American Art Annual, vol. 28.  Washington, D.C.:  American
     Federation of Arts, 1932.

Fielding, Mantle.  Dictionary of American Painters, Sculptors and
     Engravers.  Enlarged ed.  Greens Farms, Connecticut  Modern
     Books and Crafts, 1974.

Fuller, Lucia Fairchild.  "Modern American Miniature Painters."
     Scribner's Magazine 67 (March 1920):  381-84.

Lounsbery, Elizabeth.  "American Miniature Painters."  Mentor 4,
     no. 23 (15 January 1917).

Merrick, Lula.  "The Miniature in America."  International Studio
     76, no. 310 (March 1923):  509-14.

Obituary.  Who's Who in American Art, vol. 4.  Washington, D.C.:
     American Federation of Arts, 1947.

Woman's Who's Who of America.  New York:  American Commonwealth
     Co., 1914.


ZOE BEILER (1884-1969)   Painter

Contemporary Art of the United States.  Washington, D.C.:  Corcoran
     Gallery of Art, 1940.

Kovinick, Phil.  The Woman Artist in the American West 1860-1960.
     Fullerton, California:  Muckenthaler Cultural Center, 1976.

Who's Who in American Art, vol. 8.  Washington, D.C.:  American
     Federation of Arts, 1962.


ROSALIND BENGELSDORF [BROWNE] (1916-1979)   Painter

See volume 1 of this book.

Van Wagner, Judy Collischan.  American Abstract Artists, 50th
     Anniversary Celebration.  Greenvale, New York:  Hillwood Art
     Gallery, Long Island University, C.W. Post Campus, 1986.


LYNDA BENGLIS (1941-    )   Sculptor

See volume 1 of this book.

"Album:  Lynda Benglis."  Arts Magazine 61, no. 8 (April 1987):
     100-101.

32

Bell, Tiffany. "Lynda Benglis." Arts Magazine 58, no. 10 (Summer
    1984): 2.

Contemporary Sculpture: Selections from the Collection of the
    Museum of Modern Art. New York: The Museum of Modern Art,
    1979.

Content: A Contemporary Focus 1974-1984. Washington, D.C.:
    Hirshhorn Museum and Sculpture Garden, 1984.

Cotter, Holland. "Lynda Benglis at Paula Cooper." Art in America
    75, no. 7 (July 1987): 124.

Davis, Douglas. Artculture: Essays on the Post-Modern. New York:
    Harper & Row, 1977.

Developments in Recent Sculpture. New York: Whitney Museum of
    American Art, 1981.

Directions 1983. Washington, D.C.: Hirshhorn Museum and Sculpture
    Garden, 1983.

Floored. Curated by John Perreault. Greenvale, New York:
    Hillwood Art Gallery, Long Island University, 1983.

Handy, Ellen. "Lynda Benglis." Arts Magazine 58, no. 10 (Summer
    1984): 36, 37.

New York Now. Hannover, Germany: Kestner-Gesellschaft, 1982.

Selections from The Frito-Lay Collection. Plano, Texas: The
    Frito-Lay Collection, Inc., 1987: 8.

Watson-Jones, Virginia. Contemporary American Women Sculptors.
    Phoenix: Oryx Press, 1986.

Welch, Douglas. "Lynda Benglis." Arts Magazine 55, no. 3
    (November 1980): 35.

Wooster, Ann-Sargent. "Lynda Benglis at Cooper." Art in America
    62, no. 5 (September-October 1974): 106.

Wortz, Melinda. "Los Angeles. Lynda Benglis." Art News 84, no. 6
    (Summer 1985): 101.


MARY PARK SEAVY BENTON (1815-1910)    Painter

Groce, George C., and Wallace, David H. The New-York Historical
    Society's Dictionary of Artists in America 1564-1860. New
    Haven: Yale University Press, 1957.

Van Nostrand, Jeanne.  The First Hundred Years of Painting in
     California 1775-1875.  San Francisco:  John Howell Books,
     1980.

A Woman's Vision:  California Painting into the 20th Century.  San
     Francisco:  Maxwell Galleries, 1983.


          DOROTHY ALPHENA BERGE (1923-    )  Sculptor

Artists in Georgia.  Atlanta:  High Museum of Art, 1978.

Baur, John I. H.  "New Talent in the U.S."  Art in America 45, no.
     1 (March 1957):  10-11.

Biennial of Paintings, Prints and Sculpture.  Minneapolis:  Walker
     Art Center, 1956 and 1958.

Recent Sculpture U.S.A.  New York:  The Museum of Modern Art, 1959.

Rood, John.  Sculpture with a Torch.  Minneapolis:  University of
     Minnesota Press, 1963.

Torbert, Donald R.  A Century of Art and Architecture in Minnesota.
     Minneapolis:  University of Minnesota Press, 1958.

"Two Level Shopping Centers."  Architectural Forum 105, no. 6
     (December 1956):  114-26.

Watson-Jones, Virginia.  Contemporary American Women Sculptors.
     Phoenix:  Oryx Press, 1986.


          RUTH BERNHARD (1905-    )  Photographer

See volume 1 of this book.

Auer, Michèle, and Auer, Michel.  Encyclopédia Internationale des
     Photographes de 1839 à Nos Jours.  Hermance, Switzerland:
     Editions Camera Obscura, 1985.

Browne, Turner, and Partnow, Elaine.  Macmillan Biographical
     Encyclopedia of Photographic Artists and Innovators.  New
     York:  Macmillan, 1983.


          JUDITH BERNSTEIN (1942-    )  Painter

See volume 1 of this book.

Stranyon, Susan.  "Judith Bernstein."  Arts Magazine 59, no. 1
     (September 1984):  8.

Drawing in Situ. Carol Becker Davis, Curator. Hillwood Art
    Gallery, Long Island University, Greenvale, New York, 1986.


        THERESA F. BERNSTEIN [MEYEROWITZ] (1890-    )  Painter

American Art Annual, vol. 28. Washington, D.C.:  American
    Federation of Arts, 1932.

Catalogue of an Exhibition of Paintings by Theresa F. Bernstein
    and a Group of Colored Etchings by William Meyerowitz,
    Theresa F. Bernstein, Ellen Day Hale, Gabriella De V.
    Clements. Syracuse:  Syracuse Museum of Fine Arts, 1921.

Catalogue, First Exhibition of Original Paintings Held under the
    Auspices of the Young Women's Christian Association. Dallas,
    Texas:  YWCA, 1924.

Fiftieth Annual Exhibition. New York:  National Association of
    Women Painters and Sculptors, 1942.

First Biennial Exhibition of Contemporary American Sculpture,
    Watercolors, and Prints. New York:  Whitney Museum of
    American Art, 1933-34.

Huntsinger, Laura M.  Harvard Portraits, A Catalogue of Portrait
    Paintings at Harvard University. Cambridge:  Harvard
    University Press, 1936.

Keyes, Norman, Jr.  "Documenting the Gloucester Art Colony."  The
    Boston Globe, 11 July 1986.

Masterson, Siobhan.  "At 96, Theresa Bernstein has only just
    begun."  Gloucester Daily Times, 3 July 1986:  Cape Ann
    section:  3, 5-7.

Meyerowitz, Theresa Bernstein.  The Poetic Canvas, A Book of
    Poetry.  Illustrations by William Meyerowitz and Teresa
    Bernstein Meyerowitz. Cranbury, New Jersey:  Cornwall Books,
    1988.

_____.  William Meyerowitz, The Artist Speaks. Cranbury, New
    Jersey:  Cornwall Books, 1986.

Nelson, W. H. de B.  "Theresa F. Bernstein."  The International
    Studio vol. 66, no. 265 (February 1919):  97-102.

The Paintings and Etchings of William Meyerowitz and Theresa
    Bernstein. Gloucester, Massachusetts:  Cape Ann Historical
    Association, 1986.

Theresa Bernstein. Stamford, Connecticut:  Smith-Girard, 1985.

Wolf, Amy J.  New York Society of Women Artists 1925.  New York:
ACA Galleries, 1987.


ELECTRA WAGGONER BIGGS (1916-    )   Sculptor

Broder, Patricia Janis.  Bronzes of the American West.  New York:
Harry N. Abrams, 1974.

National Museum of Women in the Arts.  New York:  Harry N. Abrams,
Inc., 1987.

Watson-Jones, Virginia.  Contemporary American Women Sculptors.
Phoenix:  Oryx Press, 1986.


ILSE BING (1899-    )   Photographer

Auer, Michèle, and Auer, Michel.  Encyclopédia International des
Photographes de 1839 à nos Jours.  Hermance, Switzerland:
Editions Camera Obscura, 1985.

Autoportraits Photographiques.  Paris:  Centre Georges Pompidou,
1981.

Barrett, Nancy C.  Ilse Bing:  Three Decades of Photography.  New
Orleans:  New Orleans Museum of Art, 1985.

Browne, Turner, and Partnow, Elaine.  Macmillan Biographical
Encyclopedia of Photographic Artists and Innovators.  New
York:  Macmillan, 1983.

Julian Levy Collection.  Chicago:  Art Institute of Chicago, 1976.

Kramer, Hilton.  "Ilse Bing."  The New York Times, 7 January 1977.

Newhall, Beaumont.  Photography 1839-1937.  New York:  The Museum
of Modern Art, 1937.

Osterman, Gladys.  "Ilse Bing, A Groundbreaking Photographer."
Women Artists News 8, no. 3 (Spring 1983):  15-16.

Sturman, John.  "Ilse Bing (International Center of Photography)."
Art News 85, no. 7 (September 1986):  135, 137.


ILSE BISCHOFF (1903-    )   Painter and Illustrator

American Art Annual, vol. 28.  Washington, D.C.:  American
Federation of Arts, 1932.

36

_The Intimate Realism of Ilse Bischoff, Paintings and Drawings_
    _1964-1976_. Hanover, New Hampshire:  Carpenter Galleries,
    Dartmouth College, 1976.

Viguers, Ruth Hill, compiled by.  _Illustrators of Children's Books:_
    _1946-1956_. Boston:  The Horn Book, 1958.


                ISABEL BISHOP (1902-1988)    Painter

See volume 1 of this book.

"The Drawings of Isabel Bishop."  _American Artist_ 13, no. 126 (June
    1949):  49-51.

_First Biennial Exhibition of Contemporary American Sculpture,_
    _Watercolors and Prints_. New York:  Whitney Museum of American
    Art, 1933.

Galligan, Gregory.  "Isabel Bishop: Early Drawings. _Arts Magazine_
    61, no. 8 (April 1987):  42-43.

Glueck, Grace.  "The 20th Century Artists Most Admired by Other
    Artists."  _Art News_ 76, no. 9 (November 1977):  80.

Mecklenburg, Virginia M.  _Modern American Realism:  The Sara Roby_
    _Foundation Collection_. Washington, D.C.:  National Museum of
    American Art, 1987.

_National Museum of Women in the Arts_. New York:  Harry N. Abrams,
    1987:  90-91.

Obituary.  _Art in America_ 76, no. 4 (April 1988):  230.

Obituary.  _The New York Times_, 22 February 1988:  Y15.

St. John, Bruce.  _Isabel Bishop:  The Affectionate Eye_. Los
    Angeles:  Laband Art Gallery, Loyola Marymount University,
    1985.

_Second Biennial Exhibition of Contemporary American Painting_.
    New York:  Whitney Museum of American Art, 1934.

Teller, Susan.  _Isabel Bishop:  Etchings and Aquatints:  A_
    _Catalogue Raisonné_. New York:  Associated American Artists,
    1981.

Yglesias, Helen.  _Isabel Bishop_. New York:  Rizzoli, 1988.

OLIVE PARKER BLACK (1868-1948)    Painter

<u>American Art Annual</u>, vol. 28.  Washington, D.C.:  American
    Federation of Arts, 1932.

<u>An Exhibition of Women Students of William Merritt Chase</u>.  New
    York:  Marbella Gallery, 1973.

Fielding, Mantle.  <u>Dictionary of American Painters, Sculptors and
    Engravers</u>.  Enlarged ed.  Greens Farms, Connecticut:  Modern
    Books and Crafts, 1974.

<u>Vose Winter 1987-1988</u>.  Boston:  Vose Galleries, 1987.


HARRIET BLACKSTONE (1864-1939)    Painter

<u>American Art Annual</u>, vol. 28.  Washington, D.C.:  American
    Federation of Arts, 1932.

<u>The Brooklyn Museum, American Paintings</u>.  Brooklyn, New York:  The
    Brooklyn Museum, 1979:  21.

Cuthbert, Lee.  <u>Contemporary American Portrait Painters</u>.  New York:
    W.W. Norton and Co., 1929:  67-68.

D'Unger, Giselle.  "Harriet Blackstone--Portrait Painter."  <u>Fine
    Arts Journal</u> (February 1912):  97-101.

Fielding, Mantle.  <u>Dictionary of American Painters, Sculptors and
    Engravers</u>.  Enlarged ed.  Greens Farms, Connecticut:  Modern
    Books and Crafts, 1974.

<u>A Mystical Vision:  The Art of Harriet Blackstone</u>.  Bennington,
    Vermont:  Bennington Museum, 1984.

<u>National Portrait Gallery, Permanent Collection Illustrated
    Checklist</u>.  Washington, D.C.:  Smithsonian Institution Press,
    1987.

Obituary.  <u>Who's Who in American Art</u>, vol 3.  Washington, D.C.:
    American Federation of Arts, 1940.

P., F. L. H.  "Harriet Blackstone."  <u>The Magazine of Art</u> 9, no. 10
    (August 1918):  396-405.

<u>Woman's Who's Who in America</u>.  New York:  American Commonwealth
    Co., 1914.


NELL BLAINE (1922-    )    Painter

See volume 1 of this book.

38

Ashbery, John. "Nell Blaine." Art News 65, no. 2 (April 1966):
14.

Bass, Ruth. "Nell Blaine (Fishbach)." Art News 82, no. 7
(September 1983): 193.

Bryant, Edward. Nell Blaine. Hamilton, New York: Picker Gallery,
Colgate University, 1974.

Campbell, Lawrence. "Nell Blaine." Art News 69, no. 5 (September
1970): 10.

"Cape Ann Master on Display Again." Gloucester Daily Times, 26
March 1987: B1.

Canaday, John. "Art: Sparkling Vigor in Blaine Work." The New
York Times, 2 December 1972.

Dickinson, Sue. "Handicaps Overcome/Nell Blaine Returns to Art."
Richmond Times-Dispatch, 11 September 1960.

Durden, Sue. "Richmond Artist Honored." Richmond Times-Dispatch,
18 May 1986.

Henry, Gerrit. "Nell Blaine at Fischbach." Art in America 71, no.
10 (November 1983): 222-23.

Nell Blaine: An Exhibition of Recent Paintings, 1964-1965. New
York: Poindexter Gallery, 1966.

Nell Blaine: Recent Paintings. New York: Fischbach Gallery,
1979.

Nell Blaine Sketchbook. Preface by John Ashbery. New York: The
Arts Publisher, Inc., 1986.

Perl, Jed. "The Shows Must Go On." The New Criterion 6, no. 1
(September 1987): 65-66.

Raynor, Vivien. "Nell Blaine." The New York Times, 12 April 1985.

Shirey, David L. "Nell Blaine's Cheerful Palette at the Parrish
Museum." The New York Times, 21 July 1974.

Women's Caucus for Art Honor Awards. New York: National Women's
Caucus for Art, 1986.

Zaferatos, Olga. Painting the Still Life. New York:
Watson-Guptill, 1985.

LUCILE BLANCH (1895-1981)    Painter

See volume 1 of this book.

American Art Annual, vol. 28.  Washington, D.C.:  American
    Federation of Arts, 1932.

First Biennial Exhibition of Contemporary American Sculpture,
    Watercolors and Prints.  New York:  Whitney Museum of American
    Art, 1933-34.

Park, Marlene, and Markowitz, Gerald E.  Democratic Vistas:  Post
    Offices and Public Art in the New Deal.  Philadelphia:  Temple
    University Press, 1984.

Second Biennial Exhibition of Contemporary American Painting.  New
    York:  Whitney Museum of American Art, 1934.

Wolf, Amy J.  New York Society of Women Artists 1925.  New York:
    ACA Galleries, 1987.

Woodstock's Art Heritage;  The Permanent Collection of the
    Woodstock Artists Association.  Essay by Tom Wolf.  Woodstock,
    New York:  Overlook Press, 1987.

Zaidenberg, Arthur, compiled by.  The Art of the Artist.  Theories
    and Techniques of Art by the Artists Themselves.  New York:
    Crown Publishers, 1951:  157-60.

ANNA CAMPBELL BLISS (1923-    )    Painter

Appelhof, Ruth Ann.  "Review."  Syracuse New Times, 6 November
    1976.

Bliss, Anna Campbell.  "Art, Color, Architecture:  Their Synergy
    Explored."  American Institute of Architecture Journal 71, no.
    2 (February 1982):  48-55.

_____.  "Color Selection as a Design Decision."  American Institute
    of Architecture Journal 67, no. 12 (October 1978):  60-65.

_____.  "New Technologies of Art--Where Art and Science Meet."
    Leonardo 19, no. 4 (1986):  311-16.

Dibble, George.  "Exploring the Fascination of Color."  Salt Lake
    Tribune, 15 February 1981.

Groseclose, Barbara.  "Color in the Art of Anna Campbell Bliss."
    Dialogue (March-April 1980).

Morrison, Don. "Review." Minneapolis Star, 24 October 1974.


RITA COPAKEN BLITT (1931-    )    Sculptor

Barnes, Valerie. "Sculpture: A Listing for Morris County." The
    New York Times, 10 December 1978: NJ26-27.

Bostick, Virginia L. The History of Public Monuments and Sculpture
    of Morris County, New Jersey. Trenton: New Jersey State
    Council of the Arts, 1978.

Thirty-Seventh Annual Exhibition. Springfield, Massachusetts:
    Springfield Art Museum, 1967.

Twelfth Biennial Exhibition. Omaha, Nebraska: Joslyn Art Museum,
    1972.

Twenty-First Annual Delta Art Exhibition. Little Rock: Arkansas
    Arts Center, 1978.

Watson-Jones, Virginia. Contemporary American Women Sculptors.
    Phoenix: Oryx Press, 1986.

Wooster, Ann-Sargent. "Rita Blitt (Harkness House)." Art News 77,
    no. 2 (February 1978): 146-47.


LUCIENNE BLOCH (1909-    )    Painter

See volume 1 of this book.

Bloch, Lucienne. "On Location with Diego Rivera." Art in America
    74, no. 2 (February 1986): 237-38.

Nochlin, Linda. "Some Women Realists: Part I." Arts Magazine 48,
    no. 5 (February 1974): 46-51.


JUNE BLUM (1939-    )    Painter

See volume 1 of this book.

Who's Who in American Art. New York: R.R. Bowker Co., 1986.


MARY SHEPARD GREENE BLUMENSCHEIN (1869-1958)    Painter

American Art Annual, vol. 28. Washington, D.C.: American
    Federation of Arts, 1932.

Blumenschein, Helen Greene. Recuerdos: Early Days of the Blumenschein Family. Silver City, New Mexico: Tecolote Press, 1979.

Clement, Clara Erskine. Women in the Fine Arts. Boston: Houghton, Mifflin and Co., 1904.

Nelson, Mary Carroll. The Legendary Artists of Taos. New York: Watson-Guptill Publications, 1980.

Obituary. Who's Who in American Art, no. 7. Washington, D.C.: American Federation of Arts, 1959.

Period Gallery West. Scottsdale, Arizona: Period Gallery West, 1979.

Picturesque Images from Taos and Santa Fe. Denver: Denver Art Museum, 1974.

Samuels, Peggy and Harold. The Illustrated Biographical Encyclopedia of Artists of the American West. Garden City, New York: Doubleday, 1976.

Woman's Who's Who of America. New York: American Commonwealth Co., 1914.


LEE BONTECOU (1931-    )    Sculptor

See volume 1 of this book.

Annual Exhibition of American Paintings and Sculpture. Chicago: Art Institute of Chicago, 1962 and 1963.

Annual Exhibition of Contemporary American Sculpture. New York: Whitney Museum of American Art, 1966 and 1968.

Annual Exhibition of Sculpture and Prints. New York: Whitney Museum of American Art, 1963 and 1964.

Mellow, James R. "Art: Bontecou's Well-Fed Fish and Malevolent Flowers." The New York Times, 6 June 1971: D19.

Prints and Drawings by Lee Bontecou. Essay by Richard S. Fields. Middletown, Connecticut: Davison Art Center, Wesleyan University, 1975.

Seitz, William Chapin. The Art of Assemblage. New York: The Museum of Modern Art, 1961.

Twenty-Eighth Biennial Exhibition. Washington, D.C.: Corcoran Gallery of American Art, 1963.

42

Watson-Jones, Virginia. <u>Contemporary American Women Sculptors</u>.
    Phoenix: Oryx Press, 1986.


            ELIZABETH OTIS LYMAN BOOTT (1846-1888)    Painter

See Elizabeth Otis Lyman Duveneck and volume 1 of this book.


                ISABEL CASE BORGATTA (1921-    )    Sculptor

See volume 1 of this book.

Brown, Gordon.  "Isabel Case Borgatta."  <u>Arts Magazine</u> 51, no. 10
    (June 1977):  39-40.

Olson, Roberta J. M.  "Isabel Case Borgatta."  <u>Arts Magazine</u> 48,
    no. 8 (May 1974):  65-66.

Watson-Jones, Virginia.  <u>Contemporary American Women Sculptors</u>.
    Phoenix:  Oryx Press, 1986.

<u>Who's Who in American Art</u>.  New York:  R.R. Bowker, 1978.


        JESSIE ARMS BOTKE (1883-1971)    Painter and Printmaker

<u>American Art Annual</u>, vol. 28.  Washington, D.C.:  American
    Federation of Arts, 1932.

Fielding, Mantle.  <u>Dictionary of American Painters, Sculptors and
    Engravers</u>.  Enlarged ed.  Greens Farms, Connecticut:  Modern
    Books and Crafts, 1974.

<u>Fiftieth Annual Exhibition</u>.  New York:  National Association of
    Women Painters and Sculptors, 1942.

Hughes, Edan Milton.  <u>Artists in California 1786-1940</u>.  San
    Francisco:  Hughes Publishing Co., 1986.

"Jessie Arms Botke (Grand Central Galleries)."  <u>Art News</u> 47, no. 3
    (May 1948):  53-54.

"Jessie Arms Botke, A Painting Career that has revolved around
    Peacocks."  <u>American Artist</u> 13, no. 126 (June 1949):  26-30.

Moure, Nancy Dustin Wall.  <u>Publications in Southern California Art</u>.
    Los Angeles:  Dustin Publications, 1984.

Obituary.  <u>Los Angeles Times</u>, 4 October 1971.

Ransom, Jay Ellis.  "Beauty from her Brush."  PC, The Weekly
     Magazine of Ventura County, 2 July 1967:  3-5.

A Selection of American Prints.  A Selection of Biographies of
     Forty Women Artists Working Between 1904-1979.  Santa Rosa,
     California:  The Annex Galleries, 1987:  2.

Southern California Artists, 1890-1940.  Laguna Beach, California:
     Laguna Beach Museum of Art, 1979.

Spangenberg, Helen.  Yesterday's Artists on the Monterey Peninsula.
     Monterey, California:  Monterey Peninsula Museum of Art, 1976.

Watson, Ernest W.  Twenty Painters and How They Work.  New York:
     Watson-Guptill Publications, Inc., 1950.

A Woman's Vision:  California Painting into the 20th Century.  San
     Francisco:  Maxwell Galleries, 1983.


ALICE BOUGHTON (1869-1943)    Photographer

See volume 1 of this book.

"Alice Boughton, Photographer, 77."  The New York Times, 23 June
     1943:  21.

Boughton, Alice.  "Season's Pictures."  American Magazine 61
     (January 1906):  325-28.

Gover, C. Jane.  The Positive Image:  Women Photographers in Turn
     of the Century America.  Albany:  State University of New York
     Press, 1988.

Naef, Weston J.  The Collection of Alfred Stieglitz.  New York:
     Viking Press, 1978.


ELIZABETH JANE GARDNER BOUGUEREAU (1837-1922)    Painter

See volume 1 of this book.

"Art Today and Yesterday, Dealer's Choice:  Underrated Artists."
     Art Today (Winter 1987-88):  47-48.

Fidell-Beaufort, Madeline.  "Elizabeth Jane Gardner Bouguereau:  A
     Parisian Artist from New Hampshire."  Archives of American Art
     Journal 24, no. 2 (1984):  2-9.

National Museum of Women in the Arts.  New York:  Harry N. Abrams,
     Inc., 1987.

44

Obituary. The Exeter Newsletter (New Hampshire) 92, no. 5 (3 February 1922): 1.

Tufts, Eleanor. American Women Artists 1830-1930. Washington, D.C.: National Museum of Women in the Arts, 1987.

Wein, Jo Ann. "The Parisian Training of American Women Artists." Woman's Art Journal 2, no. 1 (Spring/Summer 1981): 41-44.

William Bouguereau. "Biography" by Mark Steven Walker. Montreal: Montreal Museum of Art, 1984: 39-59.

LOUISE BOURGEOIS (1911-    )   Sculptor

See volume 1 of this book.

"Album: Louise Bourgeois." Arts Magazine 59, no. 1 (September 1984): 48-49.

Content: A Contemporary Focus, 1974-1984. Washington, D.C.: Hirshhorn Museum and Sculpture Garden, 1984.

Forms in Wood: American Sculpture of the 1950s. Philadelphia: Philadelphia Art Alliance, 1985.

Gallati, Barbara E. "Louise Bourgeois (Robert Miller)." Arts Magazine 57, no. 7 (March 1983): 33-34.

Gorovoy, Jerry. Louise Bourgeois. New York: The Bellport Press, 1986.

Lamont, Rosett C. "Louise Bourgeois: Sculpture as Happening." The Massachusetts Review 24, no. 1 (1983): 229-36.

Linker, Kate. "Louise Bourgeois (Robert Miller Gallery)." Artforum 26, no. 8 (April 1988): 138-39.

Louise Bourgeois Drawings. Introduction by Robert Storr. New York: Robert Miller Gallery, 1988.

Malen, Lenore. "Louise Bourgeois (Robert Miller)." Art News 87, no. 4 (April 1988): 140, 144.

1987 Biennial Exhibition. New York: Whitney Museum of American Art, 1987.

Primitivism in 20th Century Art: Affinity of the Tribal and the Modern. New York: The Museum of Modern Art, 1984.

Princenthal, Nancy. "Louise Bourgeois at Robert Miller." Art in America 74, no. 10 (October 1986): 157-58.

Robins, Corinne. "Louise Bourgeois: Primordial Environments."
    Arts Magazine 50, no. 10 (June 1976): 81-83.

Rose, Barbara. "Two American Sculptors: Louise Bourgeois and
    Nancy Graves." Vogue (January 1983): 222-23.

Russell, John. "New Met Roof Tests Sculpture." The New York
    Times, 31 July 1987: Y13, 16.

200 Years of American Sculpture. New York: Whitney Museum of
    American Art, 1976.

Watson-Jones, Virginia. Contemporary American Women Sculptors.
    Phoenix: Oryx Press, 1986.

Wye, Deborah. Louise Bourgeois. New York: The Museum of Modern
    Art, 1984.

MARGARET BOURKE-WHITE (1904-1971)   Photographer

See volume 1 of this book.

Baigell, Matthew, and Williams, Julia, eds. Artists Against War
    and Fascism: Papers of the First American Artists' Congress.
    New Brunswick, New Jersey: Rutgers University Press, 1986.

Goldberg, Vicki. Margaret Bourke-White, A Biography. New York:
    Harper and Row, 1986.

Grundberg, Andy. "Her Magazine Images brought the World Hope."
    The New York Times, 3 April 1988, Arts & Leisure Section: 37.

Silverman, Jonathan. For the World to See: The Life of Margaret
    Bourke-White. New York: Studio, Viking Press, 1983.

Szarkowski, John. Looking at Photographs: 100 Pictures from the
    Collection of The Museum of Modern Art. New York: The Museum
    of Modern Art, 1973.

CLIO HINTON BRACKEN (1870-1925)   Sculptor

American Art Annual, vol. 14. Washington, D.C.: American
    Federation of Arts, 1917.

Bracken, Clio. "Free hand modeling." The Touchstone 5 (July
    1919): 346-347.

Fanton, Mary Annable. "Clio Hinton Bracken, Woman Sculptor and
    Symbolist of the New Art." The Craftsman 8 (July 1905):
    472-481.

Fielding, Mantle. Dictionary of American Painters, Sculptors and Engravers. Enlarged ed. Greens Farms, Connecticut: Modern Books and Crafts, 1974.

Proske, Beatrice Gilman. Brookgreen Gardens Sculpture, vol. II. Brookgreen, South Carolina: Brookgreen Gardens, 1955, pp. 9-11.

"Six Women Sculptors at Work in Their Studios." Arts and Decoration 16 (November 1921): 26.

Woman's Who's Who of America. New York: American Commonwealth Co., 1914.

MARY E. (HARTZ) BRADLEY (1942-    )   Sculptor

New Hampshire Arts Biennial. Manchester: Manchester Institute of Arts and Sciences, 1978.

Watson-Jones, Virginia. Contemporary American Women Sculptors. Phoenix: Oryx Press, 1986.

Zucker, Barbara. "Museum News: Sculpture, New Hampshire." Art Journal 42, no. 1 (Spring 1982): 64-65.

SUSAN H. BRADLEY (1851-1929)   Painter

Archives of American Art. Collection of Exhibition Catalogs. Boston: G.K. Hall and Co., 1979.

An Exhibition of Women Students of William Merritt Chase. New York: Marbella Gallery, 1973.

Fielding, Mantle. Dictionary of American Painters, Sculptors and Engravers. Enlarged ed. Greens Farms, Connecticut: Modern Books and Crafts, 1974.

Obituary. American Art Annual, vol. 26. Washington, D.C.: American Federation of Arts, 1929.

Richards, Laura E. "Susan H. Bradley." American Magazine of Art 15 (July 1924): 370-74.

CAROLYN BRADY (1937-    )   Painter

See volume 1 of this book.

Ffrench-Frazier, Nina. "Carolyn Brady." Art International 24, nos. 1-2 (September-October 1980): 183-89.

Le Clair, Charles.  "Carolyn Brady."  <u>Arts Magazine</u> 59, no. 7
    (March 1985):  14.

Martin, Alvin.  <u>American Realism, 20th-Century Drawings and
    Watercolors from the Glenn C. Janss Collection</u>.  San
    Francisco:  San Francisco Museum of Modern Art, 1985.

McManus, Irene.  "'The Ultimate Risk':  New Watercolors by Carolyn
    Brady."  <u>Arts Magazine</u> 61, no. 10 (Summer 1987):  86-87.

"Prints & Photographs Published... Carolyn Brady."  <u>Print
    Collector's Newsletter</u> 14, no. 4 (September-October 1983):
    143.

Singer, Alan D.  "Carolyn Brady."  <u>American Artist</u> 49, no. 514
    (May 1985):  36-41, 93-95.

### JOAN BRADY (1934-    )    Painter

Martin, Alvin.  <u>American Realism, 20th-Century Drawings and
    Watercolors from the Glenn C. Janss Collection</u>.  San
    Francisco:  San Francisco Museum of Modern Art, 1985.

Singer, Alan D.  "Carolyn Brady."  <u>American Artist</u> 49, no. 514 (May
    1985):  36-41, 93-95.

Wilmerding, Joannah.  "Joan Brady."  <u>Arts Magazine</u> 60, no. 4
    (December 1985):  107.

### PHYLLIS BRAMSON (1941-    )    Painter

Butera, Virginia Fabbri.  "Phyllis Bramson."  <u>Arts Magazine</u> 56, no.
    9 (May 1982):  32.

Henry, Gerrit.  "Phyllis Bramson."  <u>Art News</u> 80, no. 9 (November
    1981):  196, 199.

<u>intimate/Intimate</u>.  Curated by Charles S. Mayer and Bert Brouwer.
    Terre Haute:  Turman Gallery, Indiana State University, 1986.

Peters, Lisa Nicol.  "Phyllis Bramson."  <u>Arts Magazine</u> 56, no. 9
    (May 1982):  9.

<u>Self-Portraits by Women Artists</u>.  Los Angeles:  Gallery of the
    Plaza, Security Pacific National Bank, 1985.

<u>Who's Who in American Art</u>.  New York:  R.R. Bowker Co., 1978.

48

HELENE (BLAIN) BRANDT (1936-    )    Sculptor

Bridges. Brooklyn, New York:  Pratt Institute, 1983.

Brenson, Michael.  "Sculpture of Summer is in Full Bloom:
  'Bridges.'"  The New York Times, 8 July 1983:  C1, C18.

Brenson, Michael.  "Art:  Welded Sculptures by Helene Brandt."  The
  New York Times, 6 April 1984:  C29.

Discovery Room.  Roslyn, New York:  Nassau County Museum of Fine
  Arts, 1982.

Olejarz, Harold.  "Bridges."  Arts Magazine 58, no. 1 (September
  1983):  17.

Roustayi, Mina.  "Helene Brandt."  Arts Magazine 59, no. 2 (October
  1984):  13.

Shepard, Richard F.  "Going Out Guide:  Pickup Art."  The New York
  Times, 13 June 1983:  C16.

Watson-Jones, Virginia.  Contemporary American Women Sculptors.
  Phoenix:  Oryx Press, 1986.


ANNE BREMER (1868-1923)    Painter

The Art of California.  Oakland:  The Oakland Museum, 1984.

Baird, Joseph Armstrong, ed.  From Exposition to Exposition:
  Progressive and Conservative Northern California Painting,
  1915-1939.  Sacramento:  Crocker Art Museum, 1981.

Hailey, Gene, ed.  California Art Research Monographs, vol. 7.
  San Francisco:  Works Progress Administration, 1937:  88-128.

Impressionism, The California View, Paintings 1890-1930.  Oakland:
  The Oakland Museum, 1981, p. 84.

Porter, Bruce, et al.  Art in California:  A Survey of American Art
  with Special Reference to California Painting, Sculpture and
  Architecture, Past and Present, Particularly as Those Arts
  were Represented at the Pan-Pacific International Exposition.
  San Francisco:  R.L. Bernier, 1916.

Spangenberg, Helen.  Yesterday's Artists on the Monterey Peninsula.
  Monterey, California:  Monterey Peninsula Museum of Art, 1976.

A Woman's Vision:  California Painting into the 20th Century.  San
  Francisco:  Maxwell Galleries, 1983:  7, 11, 13, 21, cover.

ANNA MARY RICHARDS BREWSTER (1870-1952)    Painter

See volume 1 of this book.

*American Art Annual*, vol. 28.  Washington, D.C.:  American
Federation of Arts, 1932.

*An Exhibition of Women Students of William Merritt Chase*.  New
York:  Marbella Gallery, 1973.

Fielding, Mantle.  *Dictionary of American Painters, Sculptors, and
Engravers*.  Enlarged ed.  Greens Farms, Connecticut:  Modern
Books and Crafts, 1974.


FIDELIA BRIDGES (1835-1923)    Painter

See volume 1 of this book.

*American Art Annual*, vol. 1.  New York:  Macmillan, 1899.

Gerdts, William H.  *Down Garden Paths*.  Montclair, New Jersey:
Montclair Art Museum, 1983.

Gerdts, William H., and Burke, Russell.  *American Still-Life
Painting*.  New York:  Praeger, 1971.

Ferber, Linda S.  "Ripe for Revival:  Forgotten American Artists."
*Art News* 79, no. 10 (December 1980):  68-73.

_____, and Gerdts, William H.  *The New Path:  Ruskin and the
American Pre-Raphaelites*.  Brooklyn, New York:  The Brooklyn
Museum, 1985.

Foshay, Ella M.  *Reflections of Nature:  Flowers in American Art*.
New York:  Whitney Museum of American Art, 1984.

McClinton, Katharine M.  *The Chromolithographs of Louis Prang*.  New
York:  Crown Publishers, 1973.

Miles, Ellen G.  "Fidelia Bridges."  *Women Artists in Washington
Collections*.  Edited by Josephine Withers.  College Park:
University of Maryland Art Gallery and Women's Caucus for Art,
1979.

*Paintings from the Cooley Gallery*.  Simsbury, Connecticut:  Cooley
Gallery, 1986.

Rutledge, Anna Wells, ed.  *Cumulative Record of Exhibition
Catalogues, The Pennsylvania Academy of the Fine Arts
1807-1870*.  Philadelphia:  American Philosophical Society,
1955.

50

Skelding, Susie Barstoe, ed. Familiar Birds and What the Poets Sing of Them. Illustrated by Fidelia Bridges. New York: White, Stokes & Allen, 1886.

Tufts, Eleanor. American Women Artists, 1830-1930. Washington, D.C.: National Museum of Women in the Arts, 1987.

ANNE W. BRIGMAN (1869-1950)    Photographer

See volume 1 of this book.

The Art of California. Oakland: The Oakland Museum, 1984.

Gover, C. Jane. The Positive Image. Albany: State University of New York, 1988.

Le Japanisme. Paris: Grand Palais, Editions de la Réunion des musées nationaux, 1988.

Naef, Weston J. The Collection of Alfred Stieglitz. New York: Viking Press, 1978.

MARGARET BRISBINE (1901-1970)    Painter

Fisk, Frances Battaile. A History of Texas Artists and Sculptors. Abilene, Texas: privately printed, 1928.

Moore, Sylvia, ed. No Bluebonnets, No Yellow Roses: Essays on Texas Women in the Arts. New York: Midmarch Arts Press, 1988.

Smith, Goldie Capers. The Creative Arts in Texas, A Handbook of Biography. Nashville and Dallas: Cokesbury Press, 1926.

MARIA BRITO-AVELLANA (1947-    )    Sculptor

Aqui: Twenty-Seven Latin-American Artists Living and Working in the U.S.. Los Angeles: Fisher Gallery, University of Southern California, and Santa Cruz: Mary Porter Sesnon Gallery, University of California, Santa Cruz, 1984.

Artists of Florida. Miami: Miami-Dade Community College, 1983.

Blum, June. Women's Art/ Miles Apart. New York: Aaron Berman Gallery; Orlando: Valencia Community College, 1982.

Forgey, Benjamin. "Arts Galleries: The Cuban Evolution." Washington Post, 14 June 1984: B7.

Hispanics U.S.A. 1982:  Twenty-Seventh Annual Contemporary Art
     Exhibition.  Bethlehem, Pennsylvania:  Lehigh University,
     1982.

Inception.  (Eleanor Tufts, Juror).  Miami Beach:  Jewish Community
     Center of Southern Florida and Woman's Caucus for Art, Florida
     Chapter, 1981.

Kohen, Helen L.  "Open Season in Miami."  Art News 81, no. 2
     (February 1982):  114-16.

Latin-American Art:  A Woman's View.  Miami:  Miami-Dade Community
     College, 1981.

The Miami Generation.  Miami:  Cuban Museum of Arts and Culture,
     and Washington, D.C.:  Meridian House International, 1983.

¡Mira!  The Canadian Club Hispanic Art Tour III.  Farmington Hills,
     Michigan:  Canadian Club, 1988.

Muchnic, Suzanne.  "Art Review:  Latino Work Escapes Ethnicity."
     Los Angeles Times, 12 November 1984, Calendar section:  1, 6.

Watson-Jones, Virginia.  Contemporary American Women Sculptors.
     Phoenix:  Oryx Press, 1986.

Young Collectors of Latin-American Art.  Miami:  Metropolitan
     Museum and Art Center, 1984.

## ANN BROCKMAN (1896-1943)   Painter

Bénézit, E.  Dictionnaire critique et documentaire des peintres,
     sculpteurs, dessinateurs et graveurs de tous les temps et de
     tous les pays.  New ed.  Paris:  Librairie Gründ, 1976.

Falk, Peter Hastings.  Who Was Who in American Art.  Madison,
     Connecticut:  Sound View Press, 1985.

Memorial Exhibition of Paintings and Water Colors by Ann Brockman.
     New York:  Kraushaar Galleries, 1946.

## JUDITH KAPSTEIN BRODSKY (1933-    )   Printmaker

See volume 1 of this book.

Who's Who in American Art.  New York:  R.R. Bowker Co., 1986.

52

CAROLINE SHAWK BROOKS (1840-after 1900)   Sculptor

See volume 1 of this book.

Fielding, Mantle.  Dictionary of American Painters, Sculptors and
    Engravers.  Enlarged ed.  Greens Farms, Connecticut:  Modern
    Books and Crafts, 1974.


ROMAINE BROOKS (1874-1970)   Painter

See volume 1 of this book.

Breeskin, Adelyn D.  "The Rare, Subtle Talent of Romaine Brooks."
    Art News 79, no. 8 (October 1980):  156-59.

_____.  Romaine Brooks in the National Museum of American Art.
    Washington, D.C.:  Smithsonian Institution, 1986.

Morand, Paul, et al.  Romaine Brooks.  Paris:  Pauvert, 1968.

Tufts, Eleanor.  American Women Artists, 1830-1930.  Washington,
    D.C.:  National Museum of Women in the Arts, 1987.

Young, Mahonri S.  "Thief of Souls."  Apollo 93 (May 1971):
    425-27.


ANNA WOOD BROWN (active 1880-1910)   Painter

American Art Annual, vol. 1.  New York:  Macmillan, 1899.

American Impressionism:  The Second Generation.  Washington, D.C.:
    Taggart, Jorgensen and Putnam, 1983.

Five American Women Impressionists.  Santa Fe:  Santa Fe East,
    1982.

Wolf, Amy J.  New York Society of Women Artists, 1925.  New York:
    ACA Galleries, 1987.


CAROL KAPELOW BROWN (1945-    )   Sculptor

American Portraits.  Hollywood, Florida:  Art and Culture Center of
    Hollywood, 1977.

Annual Hortt Memorial Exhibition.  Fort Lauderdale:  Fort
    Lauderdale Museum of Art, 1976.

*Front Range: Women in the Visual Arts*. Chicago: ARC Gallery;
     Boulder: Boulder Center for the Visual Arts; Moorhead,
     Minnesota: Plains Art Museum; and Denver: Arapahoe Community
     College, 1981-1982.

*National Endowment for the Arts Fellowship Artists, Florida, 1984*.
     Tallahassee: F. A. Gallery, School of Visual Arts, Florida
     State University, 1984.

Watson-Jones, Virginia. *Contemporary American Women Sculptors*.
     Phoenix: Oryx Press, 1986.

*A Woman's Place*. Sheboygan, Wisconsin: John Michael Kohler Arts
     Center, 1981.


            CHARLOTTE HARDING BROWN (1873-1951)   Illustrator

*American Art Annual*, vol. 28. Washington, D.C.: American
     Federation of Arts, 1932.

*The American Personality: The Artist-Illustrator of Life in the
     United States, 1860-1930*. Los Angeles: The Grunewald Center
     for the Graphic Arts, University of California at Los Angeles,
     1976.

Brown, Ann Barton. *Charlotte Harding, An Illustrator in
     Philadelphia*. Chadds Ford, Pennsylvania: Brandywine River
     Museum, 1982.

Fallows, Alice Katharine. "Working One's Way through Women's
     Colleges," with pictures by Charlotte Harding. *The Century
     Magazine* 62, no. 3 (July 1901): 323-41.

Fielding, Mantle. *Dictionary of American Painters, Sculptors, and
     Engravers*. Enlarged ed. Greens Farms, Connecticut: Modern
     Books and Crafts, 1974.

Goodman, Helen. "Women Illustrators of the Golden Age of American
     Illustration." *Woman's Art Journal* 8, no. 1 (Spring/Summer
     1987): 13-22.

Mayer, Anne E. *Women Artists in the Howard Pyle Tradition*. Chadds
     Ford, Pennsylvania: Brandywine River Museum, 1975.

Reed, Walt, ed. *The Illustrator in America 1900-1960's*. New York:
     Reinhold Publishing Corp., 1966: 26.

*Woman's Who's Who of America*. New York: American Commonwealth
     Co., 1914.

ETHEL ISADORE BROWN (b. 1871)    Painter

American Art Annual, vol. 1.  New York:  Macmillan, 1899.

Champney, Elizabeth W.  "Woman in Art."  Quarterly Illustrator 2
    (April-June 1894):   113, 115.

Eldredge, Charles C.  American Imagination and Symbolist Painting.
    New York:  Grey Art Gallery, New York University, 1979.


JOAN BROWN (1938-    )   Painter

See volume 1 of this book.

Art as a Muscular Principle.  South Hadley, Massachusetts:  John
    and Norah Warbeke Gallery, Mount Holyoke College, 1975.

Berman, Greta, and Wechsler, Jeffrey.  Realism and Realities.  New
    Brunswick, New Jersey:  Rutgers University Art Gallery, 1982.

The Art of California.  Oakland:  The Oakland Museum, 1984.

Funk.  Berkeley:  University Art Museum, University of California,
    1967.

Hopkins, Henry.  50 West Coast Artists.  San Francisco:  Chronicle
    Books, 1981.

Joan Brown:  The Golden Age.  San Diego:  San Diego State
    University Gallery, 1986.

Painting and Sculpture in California:  The Modern Era.  San
    Francisco:  San Francisco Museum of Art, 1976.

Roth, Moira, ed.  Connecting Conversations:  Interview with 28 Bay
    Area Women Artists.  Oakland, California:  Eucalyptus Press,
    Mills College, 1988.

Self-Portraits by Women Artists.  Los Angeles:  Gallery at the
    Plaza, Security Pacific National Bank, 1985.

Young America 1960.  New York:  Whitney Museum of American Art,
    1960.


SONIA GORDON BROWN (1890-late 1960's)    Sculptor

American Art Annual, vol. 28.  Washington, D.C.:  American
    Federation of Arts, 1932.

First Biennial Exhibition of Contemporary American Sculpture, Watercolors and Prints. New York: Whitney Museum of American Art, 1933.

National Sculpture Society and California Palace of the Legion of Honor. Contemporary American Sculpture. New York: Kalkhoff Co., 1929.

Wolf, Amy J. New York Society of Women Artists, 1925. New York: ACA Galleries, 1987.

MARGARET FITZHUGH BROWNE (1884-1972)   Painter

American Art Annual, vol. 28. Washington, D.C.: American Federation of Arts, 1932.

Browne, Margaret Fitzhugh. Portrait Painting. New York: Isaac Pitman and Sons, 1933.

Crouse, Timothy. "The Wax Works." The New Yorker, 30 July 1984: 60-63.

Fiftieth Annual Exhibition. New York: National Association of Women Painters and Sculptors, 1942.

Fortieth Annual Exhibition. New York: National Association of Women Painters and Sculptors, 1931.

Forty-Sixth Annual Exhibition. New York: National Association of Women Painters and Sculptors, 1937.

Lee, Cuthbert. Contemporary American Portrait Painters. New York: W.W. Norton and Co., 1929: 96-97.

Memorial Exhibition and Sale of Flower Compositions and a Few Portraits by Margaret Fitzhugh Browne. Boston: Copley Society, 1974.

Pierce, Paticia Jobe. Edmund C. Tarbell and the Boston School of Painting, 1889-1980. Hingham, Massachusetts: Pierce Galleries, 1980.

Portraits by Distinguished American Artists. New York: Grand Central Art Galleries, 1942: 46-47.

Tufts, Eleanor. American Women Artists, 1830-1930. Washington, D.C.: National Museum of Women in the Arts, 1987.

COLLEEN BROWNING (1929-    )   Painter

See volume 1 of this book.

56

_Colleen Browning: Recent Paintings_. New York: Kennedy Galleries, 1979.

_Colleen Browning: Recent Paintings_. New York: Kennedy Galleries, 1982.

Fort, Ilene Susan. "Colleen Browning." _Arts Magazine_ 56, no. 9 (May 1982): 30, 31.

_Other Worlds: Paintings by Collen Browning_. New York: Kennedy Galleries, 1986.


JENNIE AUGUSTA BROWNSCOMBE (1850-1936)    Painter

See volume 1 of this book.

_American Art Annual_, vol. 28. Washington, D.C.: American Federation of Arts, 1932.

Callaway, Edwin B. "Thrilling Scenes in American History, Vividly Told in Brush, Stories by Miss Jennie Brownscombe, Internationally Known Artist." _The Wayne Independent_, (Honesdale, Pennsylvania), 11 December 1934.

Clement, Clara Erskine. _Women in the Fine Arts_. Boston: Houghton, Mifflin and Co., 1904.

McClinton, Katharine. _The Chromolithographs of Louis Prang_. New York: Crown Publishers, 1973.

_National Museum of Women in the Arts_. New York: Harry N. Abrams, Inc., 1982, 52-53.

Naylor, Maria. _The National Academy of Design Exhibition Record, 1861-1900_, vol. 1. New York: Kennedy Galleries, 1973: 115-16.

Obituary. _Who's Who in American Art_, vol. 2. Washington, D.C.: American Federation of Arts, 1937.

Tufts, Eleanor. _American Women Artists, 1830-1930_. Washington, D.C.: National Museum of Women in the Arts, 1987.


LOUISE UPTON BRUMBACK (1872-1929)    Painter

_American Art at The Newark Museum_. Newark: Newark Museum, 1981.

_The Brooklyn Museum, American Paintings_. Brooklyn: Brooklyn Museum, 1979: 27.

An Exhibition of Women Students of William Merritt Chase. New York: Marbella Gallery, 1973.

Obituary. American Art Annual, vol. 26. Washington, D.C.: American Federation of Arts, 1929.

Seachrest, Effie. "Louise Upton Brumback." American Magazine of Art 10, no. 9 (July 1919): 336-337.

Wolf, Amy J. New York Society of Women Artists 1925. New York: ACA Galleries, 1987.

## ESTHER BRUTON (1896-    )    Etcher and Painter

Dawdy, Doris Ostrander. Artists of the American West, vol. 1. Chicago: Swallow Press, 1974.

Spangenberg, Helen. Yesterday's Artists on the Monterey Peninsula. Monterey, California: Monterey Peninsula Museum of Art, 1976.

Who's Who in American Art, vol. 1. Washington, D.C.: American Federation of Arts, 1935.

A Woman's Vision: California Painting with the 20th Century. San Francisco: Maxwell Galleries, 1983.

## HELEN BRUTON (1898-    )    Painter

Dawdy, Doris Ostrander. Artists of the American West, vol. 1. Chicago: Swallow Press, 1974.

Snipper, Marin. A Survey of Art Work in the City and County of San Francisco. San Francisco: Art Commission of the City and County, 1975.

Spangenberg, Helen. Yesterday's Artists on the Monterey Peninsula. Monterey, California: Monterey Peninsula Museum of Art, 1976.

Who's Who in American Art, vol. 3. Washington, D.C.: American Federation of Arts, 1940.

A Woman's Vision: California Painting into the 20th Century. San Francisco: Maxwell Galleries, 1983.

## MARGARET BRUTON (1894-    )    Painter

Dawdy, Doris Ostrander. Artists of the American West, vol. 1. Chicago: Swallow Press, 1974.

58

Samuels, Peggy and Harold. The Illustrated Biographical
Encyclopedia of Artists of the American West. Garden City,
New York: Doubleday, 1976.

Spangenberg, Helen. Yesterday's Artists on the Monterey Peninsula.
Monterey, California: Monterey Peninsula Museum of Art, 1976.

Who's Who in American Art, vol. 2. Washington, D.C.: American
Federation of Arts, 1937.

A Woman's Vision: California Painting into the 20th Century. San
Francisco: Maxwell Galleries, 1983.


EDITH BRY (1898-    )    Painter and Printmaker

See volume 1 of this book.

American Prints in the Library of Congress: A Catalog of the
Collection. Baltimore: Johns Hopkins Press, 1970.

Who's Who in American Art, vol. 8. Washington, D.C.: American
Federation of Arts, 1962.


NANNA MATTHEWS BRYANT (1871-1933)    Painter and Sculptor

American Art Annual, vol. 28. Washington, D.C.: American
Federation of Arts, 1932.

Archives of American Art. Collection of Exhibition Catalogs.
Boston: G.K. Hall and Co., 1979.

Fielding, Mantle. Dictionary of American Painters, Sculptors and
Engravers. Enlarged ed. Greens Farms, Connecticut: Modern
Books and Crafts, 1974.

Obituary. American Art Annual, vol. 30. Washington, D.C.:
American Federation of Arts, 1934.

"Pictures Painted in Marble." International Studio 76, no. 308
(January 1923): 338-41.


JOY FLINSCH BUBA (1904-    )    Sculptor

See volume 1 of this book.

National Portrait Gallery, Permanent Collection Illustrated
Checklist. Washington, D.C.: Smithsonian Institution Press,
1982.

Who's Who in American Art. New York:  R.R. Bowker Co., 1978.


ELLA BUCHANAN (d. 1951)   Sculptor

American Art Annual, vol. 28.  Washington, D.C.:  American
    Federation of Arts, 1932.

Fielding, Mantle.  Dictionary of American Painters, Sculptors and
    Engravers.  Enlarged ed.  Greens Farms, Connecticut:  Modern
    Books and Crafts, 1974.

Moure, Nancy.  Dictionary of Artists in Southern California Before
    1950.  Los Angeles:  Dustin Publications, 1975.

National Sculpture Society.  Contemporary American Sculpture.  San
    Francisco:  California Palace of the Legion of Honor, 1929.

Obituary.  The New York Times, 17 July 1951:  27.


HELEN BULLARD (1902-    )   Sculptor

Bullard, Helen.  My People in Wood.  Cumberland, Maryland:  Hobby
    House Press, 1984.

Helen Bullard.  Nashville:  Tennessee State Museum, 1972.

Watson-Jones, Virginia.  Contemporary American Women Sculptors.
    Phoenix:  Oryx Press, 1986.


AUDREY BULLER (1902-    )   Painter

See volume 1 of this book.

McBride, Henry.  "Reviews."  Art News 51, no. 3 (May 1952):  48.

R., C.  "Audrey Buller."  Art Digest 26, no. 15 (May 1952):  19.

Sayre, Ann Hamilton.  "Audrey Buller (Ferargil)."  Art News 34 (2
    May 1936):  8.

Who's Who in American Art, vol. 4.  Washington, D.C.:  American
    Federation of Arts, 1947.


SELMA BURKE (1900-    )   Sculptor

See volume 1 of this book.

60

Harlem Renaissance:  Art of Black America.  Intro. by Mary Schmidt
     Campbell.  New York:  The Studio Museum in Harlem and Harry N.
     Abrams, Inc., 1987.


                    DIANE BURKO (1945-    )    Painter

See volume 1 of this book.

Diane Burko, 1985-1987.  Essays by Lawrence Alloway and Lenore
     Malen.  Philadelphia:  Marian Locks Gallery, 1988.

Donohoe, Victoria.  "A Lofty View of Pennsylvania."  Philadelphia
     Inquirer, 4 February 1983.

Ledger, Marshall  "Her Art is Wide Open."  Today Magazine,
     Philadelphia Inquirer, 7 September 1980.

Marter, Joan.  "Diane Burko."  Arts Magazine 53, no. 7 (March
     1979):  6.

Meyer, Susan.  Twenty Landscape Painters and How They Work.  New
     York:  Watson Guptill, 1977.

Objects &:  8 Women Realists.  Essays by Anne Mochon and Miriam
     Levin.  Amherst:  University of Massachusetts, 1973.

Shafto, Sally Gately.  "Diane Burko:  Drawings."  Arts Magazine
     55, no. 4 (December 1980):  118-19.

Waterways of Pennsylvania:  Drawings and Prints by Diane Burko.
     College Park, Pennsylvania:  Museum of Art, Pennsylvania State
     University, 1983.

Who's Who in American Art.  New York:  R.R. Bowker Co., 1986.


              MILDRED GIDDINGS BURRAGE (1890-1983)   Painter

American Art Annual, vol. 28.  Washington, D.C.:  American
     Federation of Arts, 1932.

Archives of American Art.  A Checklist of the Collection.
     Washington, D.C.:  Smithsonian Institution, 1975; 2nd ed.,
     rev., 1977.

Fielding, Mantle.  Dictionary of American Painters, Sculptors and
     Engravers.  Enlarged ed.  Greens Farms, Connecticut:  Modern
     Books and Crafts, 1974.

Who's Who in American Art, vol. 8.  Washington, D.C.:  American
     Federation of Arts, 1962.

EDITH WOODMAN BURROUGHS (1871-1916)    Sculptor

See volume 1 of this book.

Neuhaus, Eugene.  The Art of the Exposition.  San Francisco:  Paul
    Elder and Co., 1915.


MARGARET T. G. BURROUGHS (1917-    )    Painter

Bontemps, Arna Alexander, ed.  Forever Free:  Art by African-
    American Women.  Normal:  Illinois State University, 1980.

Driskell, David C.  Two Centuries of Black American Art.  New York:
    Alfred A. Knopf and Los Angeles County Museum of Art, 1976.

Dover, Cedric.  American Negro Art.  Greenwich, Connecticut:  New
    York Graphic Society, 1960.

Fine, Elsa Honig.  The Afro-American Artist:  A Search for
    Identity.  New York:  Holt, Rinehart and Winston, 1971.

Margaret Burroughs, Marion Perkins, A Retrospective.  Washington,
    D.C.:  Evans-Tibbs Collection, 1982.

Who's Who in American Art.  New York:  R.R. Bowker Co., 1978.

Women's Caucus for Art Honor Awards.  Houston:  National Women's
    Caucus for Art, 1988.


MARGARET LESLEY BUSH-BROWN (1857-1944)    Painter

See volume 1 of this book.

American Art Annual, vol. 1.  New York:  Macmillan, 1899.

Catalogue of the Exhibits of the State of Pennsylvania and of
    Pennsylvanians at the World's Columbian Exposition.
    [Harrisburg]:  Clarence M. Busch, State Printer of
    Pennsylvania, 1893.

Cosentino, Andrew J., and Glassie, Henry H.  The Capital Image,
    Painters in Washington, 1800-1915.  Washington, D.C.:
    National Museum of American Art, Smithsonian Press, 1983.

Exhibition of Portraits and Pictures by Mrs. Henry K. Bush-Brown.
    Washington, D.C.:  Corcoran Gallery of Art, 1911.

In This Academy.  The Pennsylvanian Academy of the Fine Arts,
    1805-1976.  Philadelphia:  The Pennsylvania Academy of the
    Fine Arts, 1976:  180, 182, and 301.

"Mrs. H. Bush-Brown Portrait Painter, 87." The New York Times, 18
    November 1944:  13.

Peet, Phyllis. American Women of the Etching Revival. Atlanta:
    High Museum of Art, 1988.

Portrait Drawings by M. Lesley Bush-Brown.  Boston:  Doll &
    Richards Gallery, 1923.

Tufts, Eleanor. American Women Artists, 1830-1930. Washington,
    D.C.:  National Museum of Women in the Arts, 1987.

                 DEBORAH BUTTERFIELD (1949-    )   Sculptor

See volume 1 of this book.

The Animal Image:  Contemporary Objects and the Beast. Washington,
    D.C.:  Renwick Gallery of National Museum of American Art,
    Smithsonian Institution, 1981.

Bass, Ruth.  "Deborah Butterfield." Art News 86, no. 3 (March
    1987):  149.

A Celebration of American Women Artists Part II:  The Recent
    Generation. New York:  Sidney Janis Gallery, 1984.

Clothier, Peter.  "Deborah Butterfield at ARCO Center." Art in
    America 70, no. 3 (March 1982):  155.

Concentrations VII:  Deborah Butterfield. Dallas:  Dallas Museum
    of Fine Arts, 1982.

Crowe, Ann Glenn.  "Deborah Butterfield." Artspace 6, no. 4 (Fall
    1982):  13-15, cover.

Gedo, Mary Mathews.  "Deborah Butterfield." Arts Magazine 58, no.
    3 (November 1983):  9.

Graze, Sue.  "Concentrations VII:  Deborah Butterfield." Dallas
    Museum of Fine Arts Bulletin, Fall 1982, pp.  [11-12].

Guenther, Bruce.  50 Northwest Artists:  A Critical Selection of
    Painters and Sculptors Working in the Pacific Northwest.  San
    Francisco:  Chronicle Books, 1983.

Kuspit, Donald.  "Deborah Butterfield." Artforum 25, no. 7 (March
    1987):  123.

Lucie-Smith, Edward. Art in the Seventies. Ithaca, New York:
    Cornell University Press, 1980.

Martin, Richard. "A Horse Perceived by Sighted Persons: New Sculptures by Deborah Butterfield." Arts Magazine 61, no. 5 (January 1987): 73-75, cover.

Morrison, C. L. "Reviews Chicago: Deborah Butterfield, Zolla/Lieberman Gallery." Artforum 18, no. 2 (October 1979): 68.

100 Years of California Sculpture. Oakland: The Oakland Museum, 1982.

"Portrait of the Artist, 1987. Who Supports Him/Her." Artsreview (National Endowment for the Arts) 4, no. 3 (Spring 1987): 93-94.

Schwabsky, Barry. "Deborah Butterfield (Edward Thorp Gallery)." Arts Magazine 61, no. 6 (February 1987): 107.

Westfall, Stephen. "Deborah Butterfiled at Edward Thorp." Art in America 75, no. 4 (April 1987): 218.

LIDYA BUZIO (1948-    )    Potter

Beardsley, John, and Livingston, Jane. Hispanic Art in the United States. Houston: Museum of Fine Arts, and New York: Abbeville Press, 1987.

Buzio, Lidya. "Line and Rhythm." Studio Potter 14 (December 1985): 44.

Ceramic Echoes: Historical References in Contemporary Ceramics. Kansas City, Missouri: Nelson-Atkins Museum of Art, 1983.

Contemporary American Ceramics/Twenty Artists. Newport Beach, California: Newport Harbor Art Museum, 1985.

Lebow, Edward. "Lidya Buzio: In Perspective." American Ceramics 2, no. 2 (Spring 1983): 34-35.

EMMA CADWALADER-GUILD (1843-ca. 1911)    Sculptor

Art in the United State Capitol. Washington, D.C.: U.S. Government Printing Office, 1976.

Clement, Clara Erskine. Women in the Fine Arts. Boston: Houghton, Mifflin and Co., 1904. (under Guild).

Earle, Helen L., comp. Biographical Sketches of American Artists. Lansing: Michigan State Library, 1912.

EMMA CADY (1854-1933)    Painter

See volume 1 of this book.

Dewhurst, C. Kurt; MacDowell, Betty; and MacDowell, Marsha.
    Artists in Aprons. New York:  E.P. Dutton, 1979.

Gerdts, William H., and Burke, Russell. American Still Life
    Painting. New York:  Praeger, 1971.

Groce, George C., and Wallace, David H. The New-York Historical
    Society's Dictionary of Artists in American 1564-1860. New
    Haven:  Yale University Press, 1957.


DORIS PORTER CAESAR (1892-1971)    Sculptor

See volume 1 of this book.

Doris Caesar, Philip Evergood. Hartford:  Wadsworth Athenaeum,
    1960.

"Doris Caesar's Sixth." Art Digest 14, no. 10 (15 February 1940):
    31.


BESSIE STOUGH CALLENDER (1889-1951)    Sculptor

See volume 1 of this book.

Obituary. Art Digest 25 (August 1951):  28.


MARY CALLERY (1903-1977)    Sculptor

See volume 1 of this book.

Mary Callery:  Sculpture. New York:  Wittenborn and Co., 1961.


GRETNA CAMPBELL (1923-1987)    Painter

See volume 1 of this book.

Mainardi, Patricia. "Gretna Campbell, 1922-1987:  Early and Late
    Paintings." Arts Magazine 62, no. 3 (November 1987):  66-67.

Obituary. Art in America 75, no. 10 (October 1987):  208.

Obituary. Women Artists News 12, nos. 4-5 (Fall/Winter 1987):  43.

LOUISE PRESCOTT CANBY (active 1874-1903)   Painter and Etcher

Peet, Phyllis. American Women of the Etching Revival. Atlanta,
     Georgia:  High Museum of Art, 1988.

Weimann, Jeanne Madeline. The Fair Women. Chicago:  Academy
     Chicago, 1981.

The Work of Women Etchers of America. New York:  Union League
     Club, 1988.


RHYS CAPARN (1909-    )   Sculptor

American Sculpture. New York:  Metropolitan Museum of Art, 1951.

Annual Exhibition of Painting and Sculpture. Philadelphia:
     Pennsylvania Academy of the Fine Arts, 1952-1964.

Brummé, C. Ludwig. Contemporary American Sculpture. New York:
     Crown, 1948.

Hale, Robert Beverly. Rhys Caparn. Danbury, Connecticut:
     Retrospective Press, 1972.

Hill, M. Brawley. Women:  A Historical Survey of Works by Women
     Artists. Winston-Salem:  Fine Arts Center; Raleigh:  North
     Carolina Museum of Art, 1972.

Longman, Robin. "Rhys Caparn: The Eloquence of Form." American
     Artist 45, no. 469 (August 1981):  60-65, 86-88, 92-93.

National Association of Women Artists Annual Exhibition. New York:
     National Academy of Design, 1943, 1960, 1961.

Rhys Caparn. New York:  Meltzer Gallery, 1956.

Watson-Jones, Virginia. Contemporary American Women Sculptors.
     Phoenix:  Oryx Press, 1986.


BERTA CAREW (1878-1956)   Miniaturist

American Art Annual, vol. 28. Washington, D.C.:  American
     Federation of Arts, 1932.

Moure, Nancy D. Dictionary of Artists in Southern California
     Before 1950. Los Angeles:  Dustin Publications, 1975.

Who's Who in American Art, vol. 4. Washington, D.C.:  American
     Federation of Arts, 1947.

ELAINE CARHARTT (1951-    )   Ceramic Sculptor

Ceramic Echoes:  Historical References in Contemporary Ceramics.
    Kansas City, Missouri:  Nelson-Atkins Museum of Art, 1983.

McCloud, Mac.  "Elaine Carhartt."  American Ceramics 2, no. 1
    (Winter 1983):  50-51.

"Portfolio:  Elaine Carhartt."  American Craft 41, no. 3 (June-July
    1981):  41.

Watson-Jones, Virginia.  Contemporary American Women Sculptors.
    Phoenix:  Oryx Press, 1986.

Wortz, Melinda.  "White Writing and Pink Horses."  Art News 79, no.
    9 (November 1980):  163.

Pacific Currents/Ceramics.  San Jose, California:  San Jose Museum
    of Art, 1982.


KATHARINE AUGUSTA CARL (ca. 1865-1938)   Painter

See volume 1 of this book.

American Art Annual, vol. 28.  Washington, D.C.:  American
    Federation of Arts, 1932.

Obituary.  Who's Who in American Art, vol. 3.  Washington, D.C.:
    American Federation of Arts, 1940.

Woman's Who's Who of America.  New York:  American Commonwealth
    Co., 1914.


ANNE CARLETON (1878-1968)   Painter

Anne Carleton, 1878-1968:  Artists, Beaches, the Depression,
    Ogunquit, W.P.A., Days in Portsmouth, New Hampshire.
    Hingham, Massachusetts:  Pierce Galleries, 1982.

Anne Carleton, 1878-1968:  Beach Scenes.  North Abbington,
    Massachusetts:  Pierce Galleries, 1979.

Weber, Nicholas Fox.  American Painters of the Impressionist Period
    Rediscovered.  Waterville, Maine:  Colby College Press, 1975.

Women Pioneers in Maine Art 1900-1945.  Portland, Maine:  Joan
    Whitney Payson Gallery of Art, Westbrook College, 1985.

ELLEN MARIA CARPENTER (1836-1909?)    Painter

See volume 1 of this book.

Fielding, Mantle. Dictionary of American Painters, Sculptors and
      Engravers. Enlarged ed. Greens Farms, Connecticut: Modern
      Books and Crafts, 1974.


MARY CASSATT (1844-1926)    Painter

See volume 1 of this book.

American Art Annual, vol. 20. Washington, D.C.: American
      Federation of Arts, 1923.

Broude, Norma. "Will The Real Impressionists Please Stand Up?"
      Art News 85, no. 5 (May 1986):  84-89.

Garb, Tamar. Women Impressionists. New York: Rizzoli, 1986.

Gerdts, William H. American Impressionism. New York: Abbeville,
      1984.

Grafly, Dorothy. "In Retrospect--Mary Cassatt." The American
      Magazine of Art 18, no. 6 (June 1927):  305-12.

Hyslop, Francis E., Jr. "Berthe Morisot and Mary Cassatt."
      Art Journal 13, no. 3 (Spring 1954):  179-84.

In This Academy. The Pennsylvania Academy of the Fine Arts, 1805-
      1976. Philadelphia: The Pennsylvania Academy of the Fine
      Arts, 1976.

Lindsay, Suzanne G. Mary Cassatt and Philadelphia. Philadelphia:
      Philadelphia Museum of Art, 1985.

Mathews, Nancy Mowll, ed. Cassatt and her Circle, Selected
      Letters. New York: Abbeville Press, 1984.

_____. Mary Cassatt. New York: Harry N. Abrams, Inc., 1987.

Moffett, Charles S. The New Painting, Impressionism 1874-1886.
      San Francisco: The Fine Arts Museums, 1986.

National Museum of Women in the Arts. New York: Harry N. Abrams,
      Inc., 1987:  48-49, 166-67.

Neuhaus, Eugen. The Galleries of the Exposition. A Critical
      Review of the Paintings, Statuary and the Graphic Arts in the
      Palace of Fine Arts at the Panama-Pacific International
      Exposition. San Francisco: Paul Elder and Co., 1915.

Peet, Phyllis. American Women of the Etching Revival. Atlanta, Georgia: High Museum of Art, 1988.

Segard, Achille. Un Peintre des Enfants et des Mères: Mary Cassatt. Paris: Librairie Paul Ollendorf, 1913.

Tufts, Eleanor. American Women Artists, 1830-1930. Washington, D.C.: National Museum of Women in the Arts, 1987.

Walton, William. "Miss Mary Cassatt." Scribner's 19 (March 1896): 353-361.

Weitzenhoffer, Frances. The Havemeyers: Impressionism Comes to America. New York: Harry N. Abrams, Inc., 1986.

MURIEL CASTANIS (1926-    )    Sculptor

See volume 1 of this book.

The Classic Tradition in Recent Painting and Sculpture. Ridgefield, Connecticut: Aldrich Museum of Contemporary Art, 1985.

Robertson, David. Content and Collaboration for Contemporary Art: The Sculptural Program for 580 California Street. Carlisle, Pennsylvania: Dickinson, College, 1986.

Staroba, Krisitn. "Muriel Castanis: Fiberglassing." The Classics 12, no. 1 (February/March 1987): 20-21.

Watson-Jones, Virginia. Contemporary American Women Sculptors. Phoenix: Oryx Press, 1986.

ROSEMARIE CASTORO (1939-    )    Sculptor

See volume 1 of this book.

Mahoney, Robert. "Rosemarie Castoro." Arts Magazine 60, no. 4 (December 1985): 111.

Shere, Charles. "San Francisco. Rosemarie Castro." Art News 84, no. 1 (January 1985): 117-18.

ELIZABETH CATLETT (1919-    )    Sculptor and Printmaker

See volume 1 of this book.

Driskell, David C. Hidden Heritage: Afro-American Art, 1800-1950. Bellevue, Washington: Bellevue Art Museum, and San Francisco: The Art Museum Association of America, 1985: 76.

Lewis, Samella S. The Art of Elizabeth Catlett. Claremont, California: Hancraft Studios, 1984.

_____, and Waddy, Ruth, eds. Black Artists on Art. Los Angeles: Contemporary Arts, 1976.

Plástica Mexicana. Mexico City: Galeria Metropolitana, Universidad Autónoma Metropolitana, 1980.

20th Century Black Artists. San Jose, California: San Jose Museum of Art, 1976.

Watson-Jones, Virginia. Contemporary American Women Sculptors. Phoenix: Oryx Press, 1986.

VIJA CELMINS (1939-    )    Painter

See volume 1 of this book.

American Drawings 1963-1973. New York: Whitney Museum of American Art, 1973.

Field, Richard S., and Fine, Ruth E. A Graphic Muse. New York: Hudson Hills Press, 1987.

Hopkins, Henry. 50 West Coast Artists. San Francisco: Chronicle Books, 1981.

Kozloff, Max. "Vija Celmins." Artforum 12, no. 6 (March 1974): 52-53.

Martin, Alvin. American Realism, 20th-Century Drawings of Watercolors from the Glenn C. Janss Collection. San Francisco: San Francisco Museum of Modern Art, 1985: 209.

Painting and Sculpture in California: The Modern Era. San Francisco: San Francisco Museum of Modern Art, 1976.

Vija Celmins. New York: Whitney Museum of American Art, 1973.

Vija Celmins: A Survey Exhibition. Newport Beach, California: Newport Harbor Art Museum, 1980.

NANCY CHAMBERS (1952-    )    Sculptor

Kutner, Janet. "The Ordinary Made Into Art." The Dallas Morning News, 20 November 1984, Section E: 1.

70

Nancy Chambers. Amarillo, Texas:  Amarillo Art Center, 1979.

Nancy Chambers:  Sculpture. Waco, Texas:  The Art Center, 1981.

Paperworks:  An Exhibition of Texas Artists. San Antonio:  San
     Antonio Museum Association, 1979.


               CLYDE GILTNER CHANDLER (1879-1961)    Sculptor

American Art Annual, vol. 12.  Washington, D.C.:  American
     Federation of Arts, 1915.

Burnet, Mary Q. Art and Artists of Indiana. New York:  Century
     Co., 1921.

Church, Diana. Guide to Dallas Artists 1890-1917.  Plano, Texas:
     privately printed, 1987.


          LUCRETIA ANN WAITE CHANDLER (1820-1868)    Painter

Groce, George C., and Wallace, David H.  The New-York Historical
     Society's Dictionary of Artists in America 1564-1860.  New
     Haven:  Yale University Press, 1957.


          CORNELIA VAN AUKEN CHAPIN (1893-1972)    Sculptor

Archives of American Art.  A Checklist of the Collection.
     Washington, D.C.:  Smithsonian Institution, 1975; 2nd ed.,
     rev., 1977.

Fairmount Park Association. Sculpture of a City:  Philadelphia's
     Treasures in Bronze and Stone.  New York:  Walker Publishing
     Co., 1974.

Proske, Beatrice Gilman. Brookgreen Gardens Sculpture, vol. II.
     Brookgreen, South Carolina:  Brookgreen Gardens, 1955:  91-94.

Schnier, Jacques. Sculpture in Modern America. Berkeley:
     University of California Press, 1948.

Who's Who in American Art, vol. 8.  Washington, D.C.:  American
     Federation of Arts, 1962.


        JANE CATHERINE LOUISE VALUE CHAPIN (1814-1891)    Painter

Groce, George C., and Wallace, David H.  The New-York Historical
     Society's Dictionary of Artists in America 1564-1860.  New
     Haven:  Yale University Press, 1957.

CHRISTINE CHAPLIN (b. 1842)    Watercolorist

American Art Annual, vol. 14.  Washington, D.C.:  American
     Federation of Arts, 1917.

Clement, Clara Erskine, and Hutton, Laurence.  Artists of the
     Nineteenth Century and Their Works, vol. 1.  Boston:
     Houghton, Mifflin and Co., 1894.

McClinton, Katharine M.  The Chromolithographs of Louis Prang.
     New York:  Crown, 1973.


MINERVA J. CHAPMAN (1858-1947)    Painter

See volume 1 of this book.

American Art Annual, vol. 28.  Washington, D.C.:  American
     Federation of Arts, 1932.

Hughes, Edan Milton.  Artists in California 1786-1940.  San
     Francisco:  Hughes Publishing Co., 1986.

Staiti, Paul J., and Falk, P. Hastings.  Minerva J. Chapman.
     South Hadley, Massachusetts:  Mount Holyoke College Art
     Museum, 1986.

A Woman's Vision:  California Painting into the 20th Century.  San
     Francisco:  Maxwell Galleries, 1983.

JESSIE CHARMAN (1895-1986)    Painter

Who's Who in American Art, vol. 3.  Washington, D.C.:  American
     Federation of Arts, 1940.


ADELAIDE COLE CHASE (1868-1944)    Painter

American Art Annual, vol. 28.  Washington, D.C.:  American
     Federation of Arts, 1932.

Clement, Clara Erskine.  Women in the Fine Arts.  Boston:
     Houghton, Mifflin and Co., 1904.

Fairbrother, Trevor J.  The Bostonians, Painters of an Elegant Age,
     1870-1930.  Boston:  Museum of Fine Arts, 1986.

Gammell, R.H. Ives.  The Boston Painters 1900-1930.  Orleans,
     Massachusetts:  Parnassus Imprints, 1986.

"Mrs. Adelaide Cole Chase."  The Century Magazine 62, no. 4 (August
     1901):  frontispiece, 635.

72

Obituary. Who's Who in American Art, vol. 4. Washington, D.C.: American Federation of Arts, 1947.

Pierce, Patricia Jobe. Edmund C. Tarbell and the Boston School of Painting. Hingham, Massachusetts: Pierce Galleries, 1980.


LOUISA CHASE (1951-    )    Painter

Cotter, Holland. "Louisa Chase at Robert Miller." Art in America 74, no. 6 (June 1986): 123.

Field, Richard S., and Fine, Ruth E. A Graphic Muse. New York: Hudson Hills Press, 1987.

Heartney, Eleanor. "Images and Impressions at the Walker Art Center." Arts Magazine 59, no. 4 (December 1984): 118-21.

Karmel, Pepe. "Louisa Chase at Robert Miller." Art in America 72, no. 9 (October 1984): 191.

Louisa Chase. New York: Robert Miller, 1984.

Moorman, Margaret. "New editions." Art News 83, no. 8 (October 1984): 100.

Peters, Lisa Nicol. "Louisa Chase." Arts Magazine 57, no. 3 (November 1982): 8.

Schwartz, Ellen. "Artists the critics are watching." Art News 80, no. 5 (May 1981): 81-2.

Woodville, Louisa. "Louisa Chase." Arts Magazine 58, no. 10 (Summer 1984): 11.

Yourgrau, Barry. "Louisa Chase at Robert Miller." Art in America 69, no. 4 (April 1981): 143-44.


BARBARA CHASE-RIBOUD (1935-    )    Sculptor

See volume 1 of this book.

Bevlin, Marjorie Elliott. Design through Discovery. New York: Holt, Rinehart and Winston, 1984.

Chase-Riboud. Berkeley: University Art Museum, 1973.

Contemporary Black Artists in America. New York: Whitney Museum of American Art, 1971.

East/West: Contemporary American Art. Los Angeles: Museum of
      African American Art, 1984.

Lanser, Fay. "Barbara Chase-Riboud." Craft Horizons 32, no. 2
      (April 1972): 22-25, 65.

1971 Annual Exhibition: Contemporary American Sculpture. New
      York: Whitney Museum of American Art, 1971.

The Object as Poet. Washington, D.C.: Renwick Gallery of National
      Collection of Fine Arts, Smithsonian Institution, 1977.

Slivka, Rose. "The Object as Poet." Craft Horizons 37, no. 1
      (February 1977): 26-39, 62-63.

Waller, Irene. Textile Sculpture. London: Studio Vista, 1977.

Watson-Jones, Virginia. Contemporary American Women Sculptors.
      Phoenix: Oryx Press, 1986.


                HARRIET ELIZABETH CHENEY (1838-1913)   Painter

Groce, George C., and Wallace, David H. The New-York Historical
      Society's Dictionary of Artists in America 1564-1860. New
      Haven: Yale University Press, 1957.


                    JUDY CHICAGO (1939-    )   Painter

See volume 1 of this book.

American Sculpture of the Sixties. Los Angeles: Los Angeles
      County Museum of Art, 1967.

Bass, Ruth. "Judy Chicago at ACA." Art News 83, no. 8 (October
      1984): 182.

Chicago, Judy. The Birth Project. Garden City, New York:
      Doubleday, 1985.

Hopkins, Henry. 50 West Coast Artists. San Francisco: Chronicle
      Books, 1981.

Painting and Sculpture in California: The Modern Era. San
      Francisco: San Francisco Museum of Modern Art, 1976.

Public Sculpture/Urban Environment. Oakland: The Oakland Museum,
      1974.

Raven, Arlene. Crossing Over: Feminism and Art of Social Concern.
      Ann Arbor: U.M.I. Press, 1988.

74

Robinson, Hilary, ed. Visible Female, Feminism and Art: An Anthology. London: Camden Press, 1987.

Roth, Moira, ed. Connecting Conversations: Interviews with 28 Bay Area Women Artists. Oakland, California: Eucalyptus Press, Mills College, 1988.

Withers, Josephine. "Judy Chicago's 'Birth Project': A Feminist Muddle?" New Art Examiner 13, no. 5 (January 1986): 28-30.

ALICE B. CHITTENDEN (1860-1934)    Painter

American Art Annual, vol. 28. Washington, D.C.: American Federation of Arts, 1932.

Fielding, Mantle. Dictionary of American Painters, Sculptors and Engravers. Enlarged ed. Greens Farms, Conncecticut: Modern Books and Crafts, 1974.

Who's Who in American Art, vol. 3. Washington, D.C.: American Federation of Arts, 1940.

A Woman's Vision: California Painting into the 20th Century. San Francisco: Maxwell Galleries, 1983.

VARDA CHRYSSA (1933-    )    Sculptor in Neon

See volume 1 of this book.

Chryssa: Selected Prints and Drawings, 1959-1962. New York: Whitney Museum of American Art, 1972.

MINNA CITRON (1896-    )    Painter and Printmaker

See volume 1 of this book.

Citron, Minna. "Communication between Spectator and Artist." The Art Journal 14, no. 2 (Winter 1955): 147-53.

From the 80 Years of Minna Citron. New York: Wittenborn Art Books, 1976.

The Graphic Work of Minna Citron 1945-1950. New York: New School for Social Research, 1950.

Greengard, Stephen Neil. "Ten Crucial Years: A Panel Discussion by Six WPA Artists." The Journal of Decorative and Propaganda Arts 1, no. 1 (Spring 1986): 52-53.

Marxer, Donna.  "Minna Citron at Ninety."  Women Artists News 12,
     no. 1 (February/March 1987):  13.

Minna Citron at 90.  New Brunswick, New Jersey:  Mabel Smith
     Douglass Library, Douglass College, 1986.

Women's Caucus for Art Honor Awards.  6th Annual Exhibition, Los
     Angeles, 1985.


KATE FREEMAN CLARK (1875-1957)    Painter

See volume 1 of this book.

American Art Annual, vol. 28.  Washington, D.C.:  American
     Federation of Arts, 1932.


ROSE CLARK (1852-1942)    Painter and Photographer

American Art Annual, vol. 18.  Washington, D.C.:  American
     Federation of Arts, 1921.

Caffin, Charles H.  "Exhibition of Prints by Miss Rose Clark and
     Mrs. Elizabeth Flint Wade, October 9-20, 1900."  Camera Notes
     4 (January 1901):  186.

"Miss Rose Clark, Artist is Dead at Age 90."  Buffalo Evening News,
     30 November 1942.

Naef, Weston J.  The Collection of Alfred Stieglitz.  New York:
     Viking Press, 1978.

Second Biennial Exhibition of Contemporary American Painting.  New
     York:  Whitney Museum of American Art, 1934.


SARAH ANNE FREEMAN CLARKE (1808-after 1888)    Painter

See volume 1 of this book.

Harding, Jonathan P.  The Boston Athenaeum Collection.
     Pre-Twentieth Century American and European Painting and
     Sculpture.  Boston:  The Boston Athenaeum, 1984.

Swan, Mabel Munson.  The Athenaeum Gallery 1827-1873.  Boston:  The
     Boston Athenaeum, 1940.

76

ALICE CLEAVER (1878-1944)    Painter

American Art Annual, vol. 28.  Washington, D.C.:  American
    Federation of Arts, 1932.

Bucklin, Clarissa.  Nebraska Art and Artists.  Lincoln:  University
    of Nebraska, 1932:  31.

Geske, Norman A.  Art and Artists in Nebraska.  Lincoln:  Sheldon
    Memorial Gallery, 1982:  34.

GABRIELLE DE VEAUX CLEMENTS (1858-1948)    Painter and Etcher

American Art Annual, vol. 28.  Washington, D.C.:  American
    Federation of Arts, 1932.

American Prints in the Library of Congress:  a Catalog of the
    Collection.  Baltimore:  Johns Hopkins Press, 1970.

Catalogue of the Exhibits of the State of Pennsylvania and of
    Pennsylvanians at the World's Columbian Exposition.
    Harrisburg:  Clarence M. Busch, State Printer of Pennsylvania,
    1893.

Hale, Nancy.  The Life in the Studio.  Boston:  Little, Brown and
    Co., 1969.

National Museum of Women in the Arts.  New York:  Harry N. Abrams,
    Inc., 1987:  169.

Obituary.  The New York Times, 28 March 1948:  2.

Peet, Phyllis.  American Women of the Etching Revival.  Atlanta,
    Georgia:  High Museum of Art, 1988.

Woman's Who's Who in America.  New York:  American Commonwealth
    Co., 1914.

The Work of Women Etchers of America.  New York:  Union League
    Club, 1888.

GRACE CLEMENTS (1905-    )    Painter

Between Two Wars.  New York:  Whitney Museum of American Art, 1942.

Grace Clements.  Los Angeles:  Los Angeles Museum, 1931.

Painting and Sculpture in California:  The Modern Era.  San
    Francisco:  San Francisco Museum of Modern Art, 1976.

Post-Surrealist Exhibition. San Francisco: San Francisco Museum of Art, 1935.

Southern California Art Project. Los Angeles: Los Angeles Museum, 1939.

Third Group Show. Los Angeles: Los Angeles Museum, 1944.

E. VARIAN COCKCROFT (b. 1881)   Painter

American Art Annual, vol. 15. Washington, D.C.: American Federation of Arts, 1918.

Fielding, Mantle. Dictionary of American Painters, Sculptors and Engravers. Enlarged ed. Greens Farms, Connecticut: Modern Books and Crafts, 1974.

Fiftieth Anniversary Exhibition, 1889-1939. New York: National Association of Women Painters and Sculptors, 1939.

Wolf, Amy J. New York Society of Women Artists 1925. New York: ACA Galleries, 1987.

SUE COE (1952-    )   Painter

Bass, Ruth. "New Editions." Art News 83, no. 8 (October 1984): 106.

Coe, Mandy. Police State. Essays by Donald Kuspit and Marilyn Zeitlin. Richmond, Virginia: Anderson Gallery, Virginia Commonwealth University, 1987.

Coe, Sue. How to Commit Suicide in South Africa. New York: Raw Books and Graphics, 1986.

_____. X. New York: Raw Books and Graphics, 1986.

Cotter, Holland. "Sue Coe: Witness." Arts Magazine 59, no. 8 (April 1985): 124-25.

Gill, Susan. "Sue Coe's Inferno." Art News 86, no. 8 (October 1987): 110-15, cover.

Kass, Ray. "Sue Coe (Anderson Gallery, Virginia Commonwealth University)." Artforum 25, no. 10 (Summer 1987): 124-25.

Kuspit, Donald B. "Sue Coe (at PPOW)." Artforum 24, no. 1 (September 1985): 129.

McGreevy, Linda F. "Policing the State: The Art of Sue Coe." Arts Magazine 61, no. 6 (February 1987): 18-21.

78

O'Brien, Glenn. "New York. Sue Coe, PPOW Gallery." Artforum 22, no. 6 (February 1984): 75.

Porges, M. "The Dictates of Conscience." Artweek 18 (18 April 1987): 7.

Princenthal, Nancy. "Sue Coe (at PPOW)." Art News 84, no. 7 (September 1985): 135-36.

Scala, Mark. "The Dictates of Conscience: An Interview with Sue Coe." New Art Examiner 14 (April 1987): 21-23.

Yau, John. "Interview with Sue Coe." Flash Art 128 (May/June 1986): 46-47.

KATHERINE M. COHEN (1859-1914)    Sculptor

Clement, Clara Erskine. Women in the Fine Arts. Boston: Houghton, Mifflin and Co., 1904.

Fairmont Park Art Association Fiftieth Anniversary of the Fairmont Park Art Association 1871-1921. Philadelphia: Fairmont Park Art Association, 1922.

Fielding, Mantle. Dictionary of American Painters, Sculptors and Engravers. Enlarged ed. Greens Farms, Connecticut: Modern Books and Crafts, 1974.

Nineteenth Century American Women Artists. New York: Whitney Museum of Art Downtown Branch, 1976.

Obituary. American Art Annual, vol. 12. Washington, D.C.: American Federation of Arts, 1915.

Woman's Who's Who of America. New York: American Commonwealth Co., 1914.

HANNAH HARRISON COHOON (1788-1864)    Painter

See volume 1 of this book.

Peterson, Karen, and Wilson, J.J. Women Artists. New York: Harper Colophon Books, 1976.

SARAH COLE (1805-1857)    Painter and Etcher

Ellet, Elizabeth. Women Artists in All Ages and Countries. New York: Harper Brothers, 1859.

Gerdts, William H. Women Artists of America 1707-1964. Newark: Newark Museum, 1965.

Groce, George C., and Wallace, David H. The New-York Historical Society's Dictionary of Artists in America 1564-1860. New Haven: Yale University Press, 1957.

Peet, Phyllis. American Women of the Etching Revival. Atlanta: High Museum of Art, 1988.

The Work of Women Etchers of America. New York: Union League Club, 1888.


ANN CADWALLADER COLES (1882-1969)    Painter

Chambers, Bruce. Art and Artists of the South: The Robert P. Coggins Collection. Columbia, South Carolina: University of South Carolina Press, 1984: 126.

"Columbian Paints Portrait of Bishop." The State, 22 February 1948.

Fielding, Mantle. Dictionary of American Painters, Sculptors and Engravers. Enlarged ed. Greens Farms, Connecticut: Modern Books and Crafts, 1974.

"Miss Coles, Artist, Dies in Columbia." The State, 31 March 1969.

Parris, Nina G. South Carolina Collection 1779-1985. Columbia, South Carolina: Columbia Museum, 1985: 36.

Who's Who in American Art, vol. 8. Washington, D.C.: American Federation of Arts, 1962.


MARY-RUSSELL FERRELL COLTON (1889-1971)    Painter

American Art Annual, vol. 28. Washington, D.C.: American Federation of Arts, 1932.

Catalogue, First Exhibition of Original Paintings Held Under the Auspices of the Young Women's Christian Association. Dallas: YWCA, 1924.

Dawdy, Doris Ostrander. Artists of the American West. Chicago: Swallow Press, 1974.

Kovinick, Phil. The Woman Artists in the American West, 1860-1960. Fullerton, Califronia: Muckenthaler Cultural Center, 1976.

"Laurels for Ten." The Art Digest 8, no. 9 (1 Febraury 1934): 16.

Samuels, Peggy and Harold. The Illustrated Biographical
    Encyclopedia of Artists of the American West. Garden City,
    New York: Doubleday, 1976.

Tufts, Eleanor. American Women Artists, 1830-1930. Washington,
    D.C.: National Museum of Women in the Arts, 1987.


CHARLOTTE BUELL COMAN (1833-1924)    Painter

See volume 1 of this book.

Obituary. American Art Annual, vol. 22. Washington, D.C.:
    American Federation of Arts, 1925.

Obituary. Art News (15 November 1924): 6.

Sparrow, W. Shaw. Women Painters of the World. London: Hodder
    and Stoughton, 1905: 76, 78.


LUCY SCARBOROUGH CONANT (1867-1920)    Painter

Clark, Henry Hunt. "Lucy Scarborough Conant--Her Work." American
    Magazine of Art 12, no. 8 (August 1921): 274-76.

Oakley, Thornton. "Lucy Scarborough Conant--Artist." American
    Magazine of Art 12, no. 8 (August 1921): 269-73.

Obituary. American Art Annual, vol. 18. Washington, D.C.:
    Federation of Arts, 1921.

Pierce, Patricia Jobe. Edmund C. Tarbell and the Boston School of
    Paintings, 1889-1980. Hingham, Massachusetts: Pierce
    Galleries, 1980.


MABEL HARRIS CONKLING (b. 1871)    Sculptor

American Art Annual, vol. 28. Washington, D.C.: American
    Federation of Arts, 1932.

Famous Small Bronzes. New York: The Gorham Co., 1928.

Fielding, Mantle. Dictionary of American Painters, Sculptors and
    Engravers. Enlarged ed. Greens Farms, Connecticut: Modern
    Books and Crafts, 1974.

National Sculpture Society. Exhibition of American Sculpture.
    New York, 1923: 35.

National Sculpture Society. Exhibition of American Sculpture. San
     Francisco: California Palace of the Legion of Honor, 1929:
     56-57.


SARAH WARD CONLEY (1861-1944)    Painter, Sculptor, Illustrator
                                          and Architect

American Art Annual, vol. 28.  Washington, D.C.:  American
     Federation of Arts, 1932.

Fielding, Mantle. Dictionary of American Painters, Sculptors and
     Engravers. Enlarged ed. Greens Farms, Connecticut:  Modern
     Books and Crafts, 1974.

Who's Who in American Art, vol. 13.  Washington, D.C.:  American
     Federation of Arts, 1940.


               CLYDE CONNELL (1901-    )  SCULPTOR

See volume 1 of this book.

Collage and Assemblage. Jackson, Mississippi:  Mississippi Museum
     of Art, 1981.

Louisiana Major Works, 1980.  New Orleans:  Contemporary Arts
     Center, 1980.

Moser, Charlotte. Clyde Connell:  The Art and Life of a Louisiana
     Woman. Austin:  University of Texas Press, 1988.

Randolph, Lynn M.  "Clyde Connell." Woman's Art Journal 6, no. 2
     (Fall 1985/Winter 1986):  30-34.

Sculpture 1980.  Baltimore:  Maryland Institute College of Art,
     1980.

Vetrocq, Marcia E.  "New Orleans.  Clyde Connell at University Art
     Museum." Art in America 74, no. 4 (May 1986):  167-68.

Watson-Jones, Virginia. Contemporary American Women Sculptors.
     Phoenix:  Oryx Press, 1986.

Women's Caucus for Art Honor Awards, Sixth Annual Exhibition.  Los
     Angeles:  University of Southern California, 1985.


          MAUREEN CONNER (20th Century)    Fabric Sculptor

Alloway, Lawrence.  "The Sculpture of Maureen Connor." Arts
     Magazine 57, no. 1 (September 1982):  126-28.

Heartney, Eleanor. "Maureen Connor (Acquavella)." Art News 83, no. 4 (April 1984): 160.

Klein, Ellen Lee. "Maureen Connor." Arts Magazine 58, no. 7 (March 1984): 42.

Malarcher, Patricia. "On the Edge: Maureen Connor, Shaping a Response to the Past." Fiberarts 9 (July/August 1982): 61-63.

Mascheck, Joseph. "Constructive Issues in Relief." Artforum 21, no. 3 (November 1982): 69-70.

Stein, Judith. "The Artists' New Clothes." Portfolio 5, no. 1 (January/February 1983): 62-67.


                    LIA COOK (1942-    )  Weaver

Alexander, J. "Lia Cook: Exploring the Territory Where Painting and Textiles Meet." Fiberarts 9 (September-October 1982): 28-31.

Connor, Maureen. "The Tapestries of Lia Cook." Arts Magazine 59, no. 6 (February 1985): 94-95.

Cook, Lia. "Old Traditions/New Directions." Fiberarts 8 (November-December 1981): 67.

Manhart, Marcia and Tom, eds. The Eloquent Object. Tulsa, Oklahoma: Philbrook Museum of Art, 1987.

Papa, Nancy. "Lia Cook: An Interview." Interweave (Fall 1979): 2.

The Presence of Light. Dallas: Meadows Gallery, Southern Methodist University, 1984.

6th International Biennal of Tapestry. Lausanne, Switzerland: Musée Cantonal des Beaux-Arts, 1973.

7th International Biennal of Tapestry. Lausanne, Switzerland: Musée Cantonal des Beaux-Arts, 1975.

Staroba, Kristin. "Lia Cook and Helena Hernmarck." Women Artists News 12, nos. 4-5 (Fall/Winter 1987): 14-15.

"Washington Perspective." Shuttle, Spin & Dyepot 15, no. 3 (Summer 1984): 55.

Znamierowski, Nell. Fiber: The Artist's View. Greenvale, New York: Hillwood Art Gallery, Long Island University, 1983.

FANNY YOUNG CORY COONEY (1877-1972)    Illustrator

The American Personality:  The Artist-Illustrator of Life in the
     United States, 1860-1930.  Los Angeles:  The Grunewald Center
     for the Graphic Arts, University of California at Los Angeles,
     1976.

Dawdy, Doris Ostrander.  Artists of the American West:  A
     Biographical Dictionary, vol. 2.  Chicago:  Sage Books, 1980.


EMMA LAMPERT COOPER (1860-1920)    Painter

American Art Annual, vol. 1.  New York:  Macmillan, 1899.

A Century of Women Artists in Cragsmoor.  Cragsmoor, New York:
     Cragsmoor Free Public Library, 1979.

Champney, Elizabeth.  "Woman in Art."  Quarterly Illustrator 2
     (April-June 1894):  119-20.

Clement, Clara Erskine.  Women in the Fine Arts from the Seventh
     Century B.C. to the Twentieth Century A.D.  Boston:  Houghton
     Mifflin Co., 1904.

"Studio-Talk."  The Studio 30 (1903):  81.

Woman's Who's Who of America.  New York:  American Commonwealth
     Co., 1914.


GAIL SHERMAN CORBETT (1871/72-1952)    Sculptor

See volume 1 of this book.

American Art Annual, vol. 28.  Washington, D.C.:  American
     Federation of Arts, 1932.

Fielding, Mantle.  Dictionary of American Painters, Sculptors and
     Engravers.  Enlarged ed.  Greens Farms, Connecticut:  Modern
     Books and Crafts, 1974.

Freeman, Robert, and Lasky, Vivienne.  Hidden Treasures:  Public
     Sculpture in Providence.  Providence, Rhode Island:  Rhode
     Island Bicentennial Foundation, 1980.

Obituary.  Who's Who in American Art, vol. 5.  Washington, D.C.:
     American Federation of Arts, 1953.

Woman's Who's Who of America.  New York:  American Commonwealth
     Co., 1914.

CARLOTTA CORPRON (1901-1988)    Photographer

See volume 1 of this book.

Browne, Turner, and Partnow, Elaine. Macmillan Biographical
    Encyclopedia of Photographic Artists and Innovators. New
    York: Macmillan Publishing Co., 1983.

Walsh, George; Naylor, Colin; and Held, Michael; eds. Contemporary
    Photographers. New York: St. Martin's Press, 1982.


HELEN CORSON [HOVENDEN] (1846-1935)    Painter

See volume 1 of this book.

American Art Annual, vol. 1. New York: Macmillan, 1899.

Obituary. Who's Who in American Art, vol. 1. Washington, D.C.:
    American Federation of Arts, 1936.


MARIE COSINDAS (1925-    )    Photographer

Browne, Turner, and Partnow, Elaine. Macmillan Biographical
    Encyclopedia of Photographic Artists and Innovators. New
    York and London: Macmillan, 1983.

Marie Cosindas, Color Photographs. Essay by Tom Wolfe. Boston:
    New York Graphic Society, 1978.

Photographing Children. New York: Time-Life, 1971.

Photographs: Sheldon Memorial Art Gallery Collection. Lincoln:
    University of Nebraska, 1977.

Pollack, Peter. The Picture History of Photography. New York:
    Abrams, 1969.

Szarkowski, John. Marie Cosindas, Polaroid Color Photographs. New
    York: The Museum of Modern Art, 1966.

_____. Mirrors and Windows, American Photography since 1960. New
    York: The Museum of Modern Art, 1978.

Walsh, George; Naylor, Colin; and Held, Michael. Contemporary
    Photographs. New York: Saint Martin's Press, 1982.


AMALIA KUSSNER COUDERT (1873-1932)    Miniaturist

Burnet, Mary Q. Art and Artists of Indiana. New York: Century
    Co., 1921.

Clement, Clara Erskine. Women in the Fine Arts. Boston:
      Houghton, Mifflin and Co., 1904.

Fielding, Mantle. Dictionary of American Painters, Sculptors and
      Engravers. Enlarged ed. Greens Farms, Connecticut: Modern
      Books and Crafts, 1974.

Logan, Mary S. The Part Taken by Women in American History.
      Wilmington, Delaware: Perry-Nalle Publishing, 1912; reprint
      ed., New York: Arno Press, 1972: 752.


MILDRED MARION COUGHLIN (1895-    )    Printmaker and Painter

American Art Annual, vol. 28. Washington, D.C.: American
      Federation of Arts, 1932.

American Prints in the Library of Congress: A Catalog of the
      Collection. Baltimore: Johns Hopkins Press, 1970.

A Selection of American Prints. A Selection of Biographies of
      Forty Women Artists Working Between 1904-1979. Santa Rosa,
      California: The Annex Galleries, 1987: 3.

Who's Who in American Art, vol. 5. Washington, D.C.: American
      Federation of Arts, 1953.


SARAH EAKIN(S) COWAN (1875-1958)    Painter

American Art Annual, vol. 28. Washington, D.C: American
      Federation of Arts, 1932.

A Century of Women Artists in Cragsmoor. Cragsmoor, New York:
      Cragsmoor Free Library, 1979.

Portraits by Distinguished American Artists. New York: Grand
      Central Art Galleries, New York, 1942: 52-53.


GENEVIEVE ALMEDA COWLES (b. 1871)    Painter

American Art Annual, vol. 28. Washington, D.C.: American
      Federation of Arts, 1932.

Fielding, Mantle. Dictionary of American Painters, Sculptors and
      Engravers. Enlarged ed. Greens Farms, Connecticut: Modern
      Books and Crafts, 1974.

Who's Who in American Art, vol. 1. Washington, D.C.: American
      Federation of Arts, 1935.

Woman's Who's Who of America. New York: American Commonwealth
    Co., 1914.


    MAUDE ALICE COWLES (1871-1905)    Painter and Illustrator

American Art Index, vol. 1.  Mew York:  Macmillan, 1899.

The American Personality:  The Artist-Illustrator of Life in the
    United States, 1860-1930.  Los Angeles:  The Grunwald Center
    for the Graphic Arts, University of California at Los Angeles,
    1976.

Clement, Clara Erskine.  Women in the Fine Arts from the Seventh
    Century B.C. to the Twentieth Century A.D.  Boston and New
    York:  Houghton, Mifflin and Co., 1904.


    LOUISE HOWLAND KING COX (1865-1945)    Painter

See volume 1 of this book.

American Art Annual, vol. 1.  New York:  Macmillan, 1899.

The Arts of the American Renaissance.  New York:  Hirschl and Adler
    Galleries, 1985.

Champney, Elizabeth.  "Woman in Art."  Quarterly Illustrator 2
    (April-June 1894):  111-24.

Clement, Clara Erskine.  Women in the Fine Arts.  Boston:
    Houghton, Mifflin and Co., 1904.

Elliott, Maud Howe, ed.  Art and Handicraft in the Woman's Building
    of the World's Columbian Exposition, Chicago, 1893.  Chicago:
    Rand, McNally and Co., 1894.

Hoeber, Arthur.  "Famous American Women Painters."  Mentor 2, no. 3
    (16 March 1914):  6-7.

"Louise Cox at the Art Students League, a Memoir."  Archives of
    American Art Journal 27, no. 1 (1987):  12-20.

Vose Winter 1987-88.  Boston:  Vose Galleries, 1987.


    NANCY COX-McCORMACK [CUSHMAN] (1885-1967)    Sculptor

See volume 1 of this book under Nancy Cox-McCormack Cushman.

American Art Annual, vol. 28.  Washington, D.C.:  American
    Federation of Arts, 1932.

Fielding, Mantle.  Dictionary of American Painters, Sculptors and Engravers.  Enlarged ed.  Greens Farms, Connecticut:  Modern Books and Crafts, 1974.


CAROLINE AMELIA CRANCH (1853-1931)   Painter

See volume 1 of this book.

American Paintings in the Metropolitan Museum of Art, vol. 3. Edited by Kathleen Luhrs.  New York:  Metropolitan Museum of Art in association with Princeton University Press, 1980.


RUTH CRAVATH (1902-1986)   Sculptor

California Art Research.  San Francisco:  Abstract form WPA Project 2874, 1937.

100 Years of California Sculpture.  Oakland:  The Oakland Museum, 1982.

"Ruth Cravath Dies--Noted San Francisco Sculptor."  San Francisco Chronicle, 2 December 1986.


JOSEPHINE CRAWFORD (1878-1952)   Painter

Eight Southern Women.  Greenville, South Carolina:  Greenville County Museum of Art, 1986.

Jordan, George E.  "The World of Art:  Crawford Bequest."  Times-Picayune, 2 April 1978:  2.

The World of Miss Josephine Crawford 1878-1952:  Paintings, Watercolors, Drawings.  New Orleans:  Isaac Delgado Museum of Art, 1965.


MARGARET FRENCH CRESSON (1889-1973)   Sculptor

See volume 1 of this book.

American Art Annual, vol. 28.  Washington, D.C.:  American Federation of Arts, 1932.

Obituary.  Who's Who in American Art, vol. 12.  Washington, D.C.: American Federation of Arts, 1976.

White, Nancy.  "Chesterwood."  Americana (July-August 1977): 18-23.

SUSAN CRILE (1942-    )    Painter

See volume 1 of this book.

Baker, Kenneth.  "Susan Crile:  Abstracting the Image."  Arts
      Magazine 50, no. 4 (December 1975):  54-55.

_____.  "Susan Crile at Fischbach."  Art in America 63, no. 5
      (September-October 1975):  104-105.

Field, Richard S., and Fine, Ruth E.  A Graphic Muse.  New York:
      Hudson Hills Press, 1987.

Frank, Elizabeth.  "Susan Crile at Droll/Kolbert."  Art in America
      68, no. 8 (October 1980):  130.

Kramer, Hilton.  "Susan Crile."  The New York Times, 5 May 1973.

_____.  "Susan Crile, Kornblee Gallery."  The New York Times, 20
      March 1971.

Mellow, James R.  "Susan Crile."  The New York Times, 13 March
      1972.

Philips, Deborah.  "Susan Crile."  Art News 80, no. 7 (September
      1981):  157.

Poling, Clark V.  Geometric Abstraction:  A New Generation.
      Boston:  Institute of Contemporary Art, 1981.

Raynor, Vivien.  "Susan Crile."  The New York Times, 28 February
      1987.

Russell, John.  "Susan Crile."  The New York Times, 1 June 1974.

Susan Crile:  Recent Paintings.  Essay by Elizabeth Frank.
      Cleveland:  Cleveland Center for Contemporary Art, 1984.

Westfall, Stephen.  "Susan Crile at Graham Modern."  Art in America
      73, no. 7 (July 1985):  131.

Works on Paper.  Richmond, Virginia:  Museum of Fine Arts, 1974.

CATHERINE CARTER CRITCHER (1868-1964)    Painter

See volume 1 of this book.

American Art Annual, vol. 28.  Washington, D.C.:  American
      Federation of Arts, 1932.

Cosentino, Andrew J., and Glassie, Henry H.  The Capital Image:
    Painters in Washington, 1800-1915.  Washington, D.C.:
    National Museum of American Art, 1983.

Eldredge, Charles C.; Schimmel, Julie; and Truettner, William H.
    Art in New Mexico, 1900-1945, Paths to Taos and Santa Fe.
    Washington, D.C.:  National Museum of American Art, 1986.

Kovinick, Phil.  The Woman Artist in the American West 1860-1960.
    Fullerton, California:  Muckenthaler Cultural Center, 1976.

Nelson, Mary Carroll.  "Catharine Critcher."  Southwest Profile
    (January-February 1986):  47-48.

_____.  The Legendary Artists of Taos.  New York:  Watson-Guptill,
    1980.

Samuels, Peggy and Harold.  The Illustrated Biographical
    Encyclopedia of Artists of the American West.  Garden City,
    New York:  Doubleday, 1976.

Tufts, Eleanor.  American Women Artists, 1830-1930.  Washington,
    D.C.:  National Museum of Women in the Arts, 1987.

Woman's Who's Who of America.  New York:  American Commonwealth
    Co., 1914.


        SALLY M. CROSS [BILL] (1874-1950)  Miniaturist

American Art Annual, vol. 28.  Washington, D.C.:  American
    Federation of Arts, 1932.  (under Bill).

Archives of American Art.  A Checklist of the Collection.
    Washington, D.C.:  Smithsonian Institution, 1975.

Fairbrother, Trevor J.  The Bostonians, Painters of an Elegant Age,
    1870-1930.  Boston:  Museum of Fine Arts, 1986.

Fielding, Mantle.  Dictionary of American Painters, Sculptors and
    Engravers.  Enlarged ed.  Greens Farms, Connecticut:  Modern
    Books and Crafts, 1974.

Who's Who in American Art, vol. 4.  Washington, D.C.:  American
    Federation of Arts, 1947.


        JOSEPHINE CULBERTSON (1852-1939)  Painter

American Art Annual, vol. 28.  Washington, D.C.:  American
    Federation of Arts, 1932.

Spangenberg, Helen. Yesterday's Artists on the Monterey Peninsula. Monterey, California: Monterey Peninsula Museum of Art, 1976.

Who's Who in American Art, vol. 2. Washington, D.C.: American Federation of Arts, 1937.


IMOGEN CUNNINGHAM (1883-1976)   Photographer

See volume 1 of this book.

The Art of California. Oakland: The Oakland Museum, 1984.

Szarkowski, John. Looking at Photographs: 100 Pictures from the Collection of the Museum of Modern Art. New York: The Museum of Modern Art, 1973.


LINDA CUNNINGHAM (1939-    )   Sculptor

Brenson, Michael. "Linda Cunningham." The New York Times, 29 November 1985.

Carl, Melinda. "Memorial on Display in City Park." The Sunday News (Lancaster, Pennsylvania), 4 May 1986: B15-16.

Galligan, Gregory. "Living Form: The New Sculpture of Linda Cunningham." Arts Magazine 61, no. 6 (February 1987): 34-35.

Heyman, Cheryl. "Linda Cunningham, 'War Memorial.'" Women Artists News 11, no. 2 (Spring 1986): 35.

Wallach, Alan. "Linda Cunningham." Arts Magazine 58, no. 6 (February 1984): 17.


ALICE MARION CURTIS (1847-1911)   Painter

See volume 1 of this book.

American Art Annual, vol. 1. New York: Macmillan, 1899.


LILY EMMET CUSHING (1909-1969)   Painter

Lily Cushing (1909-1969): A Retrospective View. New York: Hirshl and Adler Galleries, 1972.


NANCY CUSICK (1928-    )   Painter

See volume 1 of this book.

35th Annual Exhibition of Cumberland Valley Artists. Hagerstown, Maryland: Washington County Museum of Fine Arts, 1967.

Who's Who in American Art, 17th ed. New York: R. R. Bowker Co., 1986.


ELEANOR PARKE CUSTIS (1897-1983)   Painter and Photographer

American Art Annual, vol. 28. Washington, D.C.: American Federation of Arts, 1932.

Custis, Eleanor Parke. Composition and Pictures. Boston: Photographic Publishing Co., 1947.

Fielding, Mantle. Dictionary of American Painters, Sculptors and Engravers. Enlarged ed. Greens Farms, Connecticut: Modern Books and Crafts, 1974.

Groce, George C., and Wallace, David H. The New-York Historical Society's Dictionary of Artists in America 1564-1860. New Haven: Yale University Press, 1957.

1897--Eleanor Parke Custis--1983. Cambridge, Massachusetts: James R. Bakker Antiques, 1986.


VIRGINIA CUTHBERT (1908-    )   Painter

Annual Exhibition of Contemporary American Sculpture, Watercolors and Drawings. New York: Whitney Museum of American Art, 1944.

Annual Exhibition of Contemporary American Sculpture, Watercolors and Drawings. New York: Whitney Museum of American Art, 1953.

Exhibition of Paintings by Virginia Cuthbert. Pittsburgh: Carnegie Institute, Department of Fine Arts, 1938.

"No Straining for Effect." Art Digest 14, no. 4 (15 November 1939): 31.

O'Connor, John, Jr. "Exhibition of Thirty Paintings at the Carnegie Institute." Carnegie Magazine 12 (June 1938): 75-77.

Virginia Cuthbert and Philip Elliott: Paintings. Buffalo: Buffalo Fine Arts Academy, Albright Art Gallery.

Who's Who in American Art. New York: R. R. Bowker, Co., 1978.

92

JOYCE CUTLER-SHAW (1932-    )    Conceptual Artist

See volume 1 of this book.

Wingtrace/The Sign of Its Track Joyce Cutler-Shaw. Ithaca:
    Cornell University, Herbert F. Johnson Museum of Art, 1986.

Who's Who in American Art, 17th ed.  New York:  R.R. Bowker Co.,
    1986.


LOUISE DAHL-WOLFE (1895-    )    Photographer

Dahl-Wolfe, Louise.  Louise Dahl-Wolfe:  A Photographer's
    Scrapbook.  New York:  St. Martin's/Marek, 1984.

Eauclaire, Sally.  Louise Dahl-Wolfe, A Retrospective Exhibition.
    Washington, D.C.:  National Museum of Women in the Arts, 1987.

Gamarekian, Barbara.  "The Elegant Photography of Louise
    Dahl-Wolfe."  The New York Times, 28 September 1987:  Y22.

Mitchell, Margaretta K.  Recollections:  Ten Women of Photography.
    New York:  The Viking Press, 1979.

National Museum of Women in the Arts.  New York:  Harry Abrams,
    Inc., 1987:  74-75, 171.

Women of Photography.  An Historical Survey.  San Francisco:  San
    Francisco Museum of Art, 1975.


BETSY DAMON (1940-    )    Performance Artist

See volume 1 of this book.

Gadon, Elinor.  "Betsy Damon's 'A Memory of Clear Water.'"  Arts
    Magazine 61, no. 10 (Summer 1987):  76-77.


JOAN (SCHWARTZ) DANZIGER (1934-    )    Sculptor

The Animal Image:  Contemporary Objects and the Beast.  Washington,
    D.C.:  Renwick Gallery of American Art, Smithsonian
    Institution, 1981.

Nadelman, Cynthia.  "Joan Danziger."  Art News 79, no. 10 (December
    1980):  193.

A New Bestiary:  Animal Imagery in Contemporary Art.  Richmond,
    Virginia:  Institute of Contemporary Art of the Virginia
    Museum of Fine Arts, 1981.

New Sculpture: Baltimore, Washington, Richmond. Washington, D.C.:
    Corcoran Gallery of Art, 1970.

Pailla, Maryse. "A Portfolio of Regional Artists: Joan Danziger
    (Washington, D.C.)." Art Voices 4, no. 4 (July-August 1981):
    51.

Second Annual Exhibition of Washington Artists. Washington, D.C.:
    Phillips Collection, 1972.

Washington Sculptors. Philadelphia: Philadelphia Art Alliance,
    1973.

Watson-Jones, Virginia. Contemporary American Women Sculptors.
    Phoenix: Oryx Press, 1986.


JANE COOPER SULLY DARLEY (1807-1877)   Painter

Groce, George C., and Wallace, David H. The New-York Historical
    Society's Dictionary of Artists in America 1564-1860. New
    Haven: Yale University Press, 1957.

Wainwright, Nicholas B. Painting and Miniatures at The Historical
    Society of Pennsylvania. Philadelphia: Historical Society of
    Pennsylvania, 1974: 318.


ANN SOPHIA TOWNE DARRAH (1819-1881)   Painter

See volume 1 of this book.

National Collection of Fine Arts. Directory of the Bicentennial
    Inventory of American Paintings Executed Before 1914. New
    York: Arno Press, 1976.


HERMINIA BORCHARD DASSEL (d. 1857)   Painter

See volume 1 of this book.

Clement, Clara Erskine. Women in the Fine Arts. Boston and New
    York: Houghton, Mifflin and Co., 1904.

Fine, Elsa Honig. Women and Art. Montclair/London: Allanheld and
    Schram/Prior, 1978: 103.

Hanaford, Phebe A. Daughters of America. Augusta, Maine: True
    and Co., 1882: 276.

JUDY DATER (1941-    )   Photographer

See volume 1 of this book.

The Art of California. Oakland:  The Oakland Museum, 1984.

Enyeart, James L.  Judy Dater:  Twenty Years. Tucson:  University
    of Arizona Press, 1986.

Markowski, Gene.  The Art of Photography:  Image and Illusion.
    Englewood Cliffs, New Jersey:  Prentice-Hall, 1983:  82-83,
    102-103.

Phillips, Donna-Lee.  "Personas of Women."  Artweek 15, no. 13 (31
    March 1984):  15-16.

Witkin, Lee D., and London, Barbara.  The Photograph Collector's
    Guide.  Boston:  New York Graphic Society, 1979:  119-20,
    302-07.

CAROL KREEGER DAVIDSON (1931-    )   Sculptor

Connecticut Drawing, Painting and Sculpture 1978. Bridgeport:
    Carlson Art Gallery, University of Bridgeport; New Britain:
    New Britain Museum of American Art; New London:  Cummings Art
    Center, Connecticut College, 1978.

Contemporary Reflections 1974-1975. Ridgefield, Connecticut:
    Aldrich Museum of Contemporary Art, 1975.

Exhibition as Process. Hartford:  Wadsworth Atheneum, 1977.

Madoff, Steven Henry.  "Carol Kreeger Davidson at Terry
    Dintenfass."  Art in America 71, no. 3 (March 1983):  161.

Mann, Virginia.  "Carol Kreeger Davidson:  The Guardians."  Arts
    Magazine 54, no. 2 (October 1979):  118-19.

McHugh, Caril Dreyfuss.  "Carol Kreeger Davidson."  Arts Magazine
    57, no. 2 (October 1982):  15.

Painting and Sculpture Today 1978. Indianapolis:  Indianapolis
    Museum of Art, 1978.

Rohrer, Judith C.  "Carol Kreeger Davidson."  Arts Magazine 51,
    no. 101 (June 1977):  15.

Watson-Jones, Virginia.  Contemporary American Women Sculptors.
    Phoenix:  Oryx Press, 1986.

CORNELIA CASSIDY DAVIS (1868-1920)    Painter

See volume 1 of this book.

Dawdy, Doris Ostrander. Artists of the American West, vol. 1.
    Chicago:  Swallow Press, 1974.

Obituary. American Art Annual, vol. 18.  Washington, D.C.:
    American Federation of Arts, 1921.

Samuels, Peggy and Harold. The Illustrated Biographical
    Encyclopedia of Artists of the American West.  Garden City,
    New York:  Doubleday and Co., 1976.


GEORGIANA A. DAVIS (ca. 1852-1901)    Illustrator and Etcher

American Art Annual, vol. 1.  New York:  Macmillan, 1899.

One Hundred Years of Artist Activity in Wyoming 1837-1937.
    Laramie:  University of Wyoming Art Museum, 1976.

Peet, Phyllis.  American Women of the Etching Revival.  Atlanta:
    High Museum of Art, 1988.

Taft, Lorado.  Artists and Illustrators of the Old West, 1850-1900.
    New York:  Bonanza Books, 1953.

The Work of Women Etchers of America.  New York:  Union League
    Club, 1888.


GLADYS ROCKMORE DAVIS (1901-1967)    Painter

See volume 1 of this book.

Painters and Sculptors of Modern America.  Introduction by Monroe
    Wheeler.  New York:  Thomas Y.  Crowell Co., 1942.

Watson, Ernest W.  Color and Method in Paintings, As Seen in the
    Work of 12 American Painters.  New York:  Watson-Guptill
    Publications, 1942.


JANE ANTHONY DAVIS (1822-1855)    Painter

See volume 1 of this book.


LEILA DAW (1940-    )    Installation and Performance Artist

See volume 1 of this book.

96

Frueh, Hoanna. "St. Louis. Leila Daw at Atrium." Art in America
    75, no. 7 (July 1987): 133.

King, Mary. "St. Louis, Leila Daw, Atrium." Art News 86, no. 4
    (April 1987): 31.

Melf, Terry Hope. "Women's Autobiographical Artists' Books." New
    Art Examiner 15, no. 5 (January 1988): 64-65.


        BERTHA CORSON DAY [BATES] (1875-1968)    Illustrator

See Bertha Corson Day Bates.


            WORDEN DAY (1916-1986)    Woodcut Artist

Cole, Mary. "Calligraphy and Texture." Art Digest 25, no. 15 (1
    May 1951): 20.

Obituary. The New York Times, 3 February 1986.

Sawin, Martica. "Worden Day." Arts Magazine 33, no. 8 (May 1959):
    65.

A Selection of American Prints. A Selection of Biographies of
    Forty Women Artists Working Between 1904-1979. Santa Rosa,
    California: The Annex Galleries, 1987: 4.

"Worden Day [Bertha Schafer]." Art News 46, no. 11 (January 1948):
    43.

"Worden Day [Schafer]." Art News 50, no. 3 (May 1951): 44.

"Worden Day 'Debut.'" Art Digest 22, no. 7 (1 January 1948): 10.


            ELEANOR DE GHIZÉ (1896-    )    Painter

Contemporary Art of the United States. New York: World's Fair,
    IBM Building, 1940.

Who's Who in American Art, vol. 8. Washington, D.C.: American
    Federation of Arts, 1962.


            ADELAIDE DE GROOT (1876-    )    Painter

Bénézit, Emmanuel. Dictionnaire critique et documentaire des
    peintres, sculpteurs, dessinateurs et graveurs de tous
    les temps et de tous les pays. New ed. Paris: Librairie
    Grund, 1976.

D., M. "Adelaide de Groot." Art News 35, no. 14 (2 January 1937): 18.

Kospoth, B. J. Adélaïde de Groot. Paris: Editions des Quatre Chemins, 1932.

Who's Who in American Art, vol. 9. Washington, D.C.: American Federation of Arts, 1966.

D., H. "From the Decorative Angle." The New York Times, 18 December 1938, Section IX: 12.

DOROTHY DEHNER (1901-    ) Sculptor

See volume 1 of this book.

Dorothy Dehner/David Smith: Their Decades of Search and Fulfillment. New Brunswick: Jane Voorhees Zimmerli Art Museum, Rutgers University, 1984.

Dorothy Dehner: Sculpture and Watercolors. New York: Willard Gallery, 1957.

Watson-Jones, Virginia. Contemporary American Women Sculptors. Phoenix: Oryx Press, 1986.

Yau, John. "Dorothy Dehner At A.M. Sachs." Art in America 69, no. 4 (April 1981): 145-46.

ELAINE DE KOONING (1920-1989) Painter

See volume 1 of this book.

Brumer, Miriam. "Elaine de Kooning [Gruenebaum]." Art News 85, no. 8 (October 1986): 135-36.

Elaine De Kooning. Tyler, Texas: Tyler Museum of Art, 1972.

Field, Richard S., and Fine, Ruth E. A Graphic Muse. New York: Hudson Hills Press, 1987.

National Museum of Women in the Arts. New York: Harry N. Abrams, Inc., 1987: 96-97.

DEBORAH DE MOULPIED (1933-    ) Sculptor

See volume 1 of this book.

Burnham, Jack. Beyond Modern Sculpture. New York: George Braziller, 1968.

Newman, Thelma R. Plastics as an Art Form. Philadelphia: Chilton, 1964.

Sculptors Guild Annual Exhibition. New York: Lever House, 1983 and 1985.

Watson-Jones, Virginia. Contemporary American Women Sculptors. Phoenix: Oryx Press, 1986.

JILLIAN DENBY (1944-    )   Painter

See volume 1 of this book.

"Jillian Denby." The New York Times, 20 January 1985, Arts and Leisure Section:  44.

Who's Who in American Art, 15th ed. New York:  R.R. Bowker, Co., 1982.

AGNES DENES (1938-    )   Environmental Sculptor
and Graphic Artist

See volume 1 of this book.

Agnes Denes:  Perspectives. Washington, D.C.:  Corcoran Gallery of Art, 1974.

Agnes Denes:  Sculptures of the Mind, Philosophical Drawings. Berlin:  Amerika Haus, 1978.

"Environment. Amber Waves of Grime." Time Magazine, 23 August 1982):  63.

Selz, Peter.  "Agnes Denes:  The Visual Presentation of Meaning." Art in America 62, no. 2 (March-April 1974):  72-74.

Tuchman, Maurice, and Freeman, Judy. The Spiritual in Art: Abstract Painting 1890-1985.  Los Angeles:  Los Angeles County Museum of Art, 1986.

Who's Who in American Art, 17th ed. New York:  R.R. Bowker Co., 1986.

DONNA DENNIS (1942-    )   Sculptor

See volume 1 of this book.

Architectural Sculpture. Los Angeles:  Los Angeles Institute of Contemporary Art, 1980.

Armstrong, Richard.  "Reviews New York:  Donna Dennis, Holly
    Solomon Gallery; Joel Shapiro, Paula Cooper Gallery."
    Artforum 22, no. 2 (October 1983):  76-77.

Artists' Architecture.  London:  Institute of Contemporary Arts,
    1983.

Connections:  Bridges/Ladders/Ramps/Staircases/Tunnels.
    Philadelphia:  Institute of Contemporary Art of University of
    Pennsylvania,  1983.

Contemporary Reflections 1973-1974.  Ridgefield, Connecticut:
    Aldrich Museum of Contemporary Art, 1974.

Developments in Recent Sculpture.  New York:  Whitney Museum of
    American Art, 1981.

Directions.  Washington, D.C.:  Hirshhorn Museum, 1979.

Dwellings.  Philadelphia:  Institute of Contemporary Art of
    University of Pennsylvania; Purchase, New York:  Neuberger
    Museum, 1978.

4 Sculptors:  Maureen Conner, Donna Dennis, Irene Krugman, Eileen
    Spikol.  Stony Brook:  Art Gallery, State University of New
    York, 1982.

Jensen, Robert, and Conway, Patricia.  Ornamentalism:  The New
    Decorativeness in Architecture and Design.  New York:
    Clarkson N. Potter, 1982.

McGill, Douglas C.  "How Public Art is Changing New York City."
    The New York Times, 23 January 1988:  Y12.

New York.  San Francisco:  San Francisco Art Institute, 1978.

Les Nouveaux Fauves--Die Neuen Wilden.  Aachen, West Germany:  Neue
    Galerie Sammlung Ludwig, 1980.

Scale and Environment.  Minneapolis:  Walker Art Center, 1977.

Venice Biennale.  Venice, 1982.

Watson-Jones, Virginia.  Contemporary American Women Sculptors.
    Phoenix:  Oryx Press, 1986.

Westfall, Stephen.  "Donna Dennis at the Brooklyn Museum."  Art in
    America 76, no. 1 (January 1988):  131-32.

Who's Who in American Art, 17th ed.  New York:  R.R. Bowker Co.,
    1986.

DOROTHEA HENRIETTA DENSLOW  (1900-1971)  Sculptor

American Art Annual, vol. 28.  Washington, D.C.:  American
     Federation of Arts, 1932.

Fielding, Mantle.  Dictionary of American Painters, Sculptors and.
     Engravers.  Enlarged ed.  Greens Farms, Connecticut:  Modern
     Books and Crafts, 1974.

Throm, Judy.  "The Curator's Report."  Archives of American Art
     Journal 22, no. 3 (1982):  31.

MARIE OAKEY DEWING (1845-1927)  Painter

See volume 1 of this book.

American Art Annual, vol. 18.  Washington, D.C.:  American
     Federation of Arts, 1921.

A Circle of Friends:  Art Colonies of Cornish and Dublin.  Durham,
     New Hampshire:  University Art Galleries, University of New
     Hampshire, 1985.

Huber, Christine Jones.  The Pennsylvania Academy and Its Women.
     Philadelphia:  The Pennsylvania Academy of the Fine Arts,
     1974.

Rubinstein, Charlotte Streifer.  American Women Artists.  Boston:
     G. K. Hall, 1982.

Woman's Who's Who of America.  New York:  American Commonwealth
     Co., 1914.

GLADYS ROOSEVELT DICK  (1889-1926)  Painter

Fielding, Mantle.  Dictionary of American Painters, Sculptors and
     Engravers.  Enlarged ed.  Greens Farms, Connecticut:  Modern
     Books and Crafts, 1974.

"Forty-Six Works by Gladys Roosevelt Dick Shown."  Art Digest 7,
     no. 18 (July 1933):  14.

Obituary.  American Art Annual, vol. 24.  Washington, D.C.:
     American Federation of Arts, 1927.

Wolf, Amy J.  New York Society of Women Artists 1925.  New York:
     ACA Galleries, 1987.

ELEANOR CREEKMORE DICKINSON (1931-    )    Graphic Artist

See volume 1 of this book.

Epstein, Helga.  "Eleanor Dickinson, Social Historian and Artist."
    American Artist 44, no. 461 (December 1980):  80-83, 95-96.

Roth, Moira, ed.  Connecting Conversations:  Interviews with 28 Bay
    Area Women Artists.  Oakland, California:  Eucalyptus Press,
    Mills College, 1988.


        SARI CHYLINSKA DIENES (1898-    )    Assemblage Artist
                                             and Printmaker

See volume 1 of this book.

Miodoni, Cate.  "The Natural Order of Things:  Sari Dienes."
    Women Artists News 8, no. 1 (Fall 1982):  18-19.

Richards, M.C.  "The Bottle Gardens of Sari Dienes."  Craft
    Horizons 22 (September-October 1962):  24-25.

Van Baron, Judith.  "Sari Dienes."  Craft Horizons 34 (April
    1974):  48.

Who's Who in American Art, 17th ed.  New York:  R.R. Bowker Co.,
    1986.


        ANNIE BLANCHE DILLAYE (1851-1931)    Watercolorist and Etcher

American Prints in the Library of Congress:  A Catalog of the
    Collection.  Baltimore:  Johns Hopkins Press, 1970.

Clement, Clara Erskine.  Women in the Fine Arts.  Boston:  Houghton
    Mifflin, 1904.

Fielding, Mantle.  Dictionary of American Painters, Sculptors and
    Engravers.  Enlarged ed.  Greens Farms, Connecticut:  Modern
    Books and Crafts, 1974.

Memorial Exhibition of Watercolors and Etchings by Blanche Dillaye.
    Philadelphia:  Philadelphia Art Alliance, 1932.

Obituary.  American Art Annual, vol. 28.  Washington, D.C.:
    American Federation of Arts, 1932:  409.

Obituary.  The New York Times, 21 December 1931:  21.

Peet, Phyllis.  American Women of the Etching Revival.  Atlanta:
    High Museum of Art, 1988.

The Plastic Club. A Catalogue of Etchings, Pencil Sketches and Auto-Lithographs by Blanche Dillaye. Philadelphia: The Morris Press, 1902.

The Work of Women Etchers of America. New York: Union League Club, 1888.


JULIA McENTREE DILLON (1834-1919)   Painter

Gerdts, William H., and Burke, Russell. American Still-Life Painting. New York: Praeger, 1971.

Gerdts, William H. Women Artists of America 1707-1964. Newark: Newark Museum, 1965.

Kurtz, Charles M. World's Columbian Exposition, The Art Gallery. Philadelphia: George Barrie, 1893: 326.


EDITH DIMOCK [GLACKENS]   (1876-1955)   Painter

See volume 1 of this book.

Archives of American Art. Collection of Exhibition Catalogs. Boston: G.K. Hall and Co., 1979.


PAT DISKA (1924-    )   Sculptor

Meilach, Dona Z. Contemporary Stone Sculpture: Aesthetics, Method, Appreciation. New York: Crown, 1970.

Padovano, Anthony. The Process of Sculpture. New York: Doubleday, 1981.

La Part des Femmes dans l'Art Contemporain. Vitry-sur-Seine: Galerie Municipale, 1984.

Sculptors Guild Annual Exhibition. New York: Lever House, 1974-1985.

Watson-Jones, Virginia. Contemporary American Women Sculptors. Phoenix: Oryx Press, 1986.


EULABEE DIX (1878-1961)   Miniaturist

American Art Annual, vol. 28. Washington, D.C.: American Federation of Arts, 1932.

Catalogue DeLuxe of the Department of Fine Arts, Panama-Pacific
    International Exposition. Edited by John E. D. Trask and J.
    Nilsen Laurvik. San Francisco: Paul Elder and Co., 1915,
    vol. 2.

National Portrait Gallery, Permanent Collection Illustrated
    Checklist. Washington, D.C.: Smithsonian Institution Press,
    1982.

A Special Collection of Miniature Paintings by Miss Eulabee Dix.
    Saint Louis: Saint Louis Museum of Fine Arts, 1908.


            ANNA PARKER DIXWELL (1847-1885)    Painter and Etcher

See volume 1 of this book.

Exhibition of Pictures by Anna P. Dixwell. Boston: J. Eastman
    Chase's Gallery, 1884.

Peet, Phyllis. American Women of the Etching Revival. Atlanta:
    High Museum of Art, 1988.

The Work of Women Etchers of America. New York: Union League
    Club, 1888.


            LOIS DODD (1927-    )   Painter

See volume 1 of this book.

Koslow, Susan. "Lois Dodd [at Fischbach]." Arts Magazine 60, no.
    8 (April 1986): 117.

Turner, Norman. "Lois Dodd." Arts Magazine 52, no. 7 (March
    1978): 8.


            SARAH PAXTON BALL DODSON (1847-1906)    Painter

See volume 1 of this book.

The Brooklyn Museum American Paintings. Brooklyn: The Brooklyn
    Museum, 1979.


            ELIZABETH HONOR DOLAN (1887-1948)   Painter

American Art Annual, vol. 28. Washington, D.C.: American
    Federation of Arts, 1932.

104

Bucklin, Clarissa. Nebraska Art and Artists. Lincoln: University of Nebraska, 1932.

Geske, Norman A. Art and Artists in Nebraska. Lincoln: Sheldon Memorial Art Gallery, University of Nebraska, 1982: 35.

Ness, Zenobia B., and Orwig, Louise. Iowa Artists of the First Hundred Years. Des Moines: Wallace Homestead Co., 1939: 65.

Smith, Holmes. "Elizabeth Nolan's Habitat Backgrounds for the University of Nebraska." American Magazine of Art 20, no. 8 (August 1929): 460-62.

BLANCHE DOMBEK (1908-    )    Sculptor

Annual Exhibition: Contemporary Art. New York: Whitney Museum of American Art, 1947, 1948, 1950, 1952, and 1955.

Annual Exhibition of Painting and Sculpture. Philadelphia: Pennsylvania Academy of the Fine Arts, 1947.

Brumme, C. Ludwig. Contemporary American Sculpture. New York: Crown, 1948.

O'Hara, Frank. "Blanche Dombek." Art News 53, no. 6 (October 1954): 52.

Rood, John. Sculpture in Wood. Minneapolis: University of Minnesota Press, 1950.

Sculptors Guild Annual Exhibition. New York: Lever House, 1954-1985.

Seuphor, Michel. The Sculpture of This Century. New York: George Braziller, 1960.

_____. The World of Abstract Art. New York: George Wittenborn, 1957.

Watson-Jones, Virginia. Contemporary American Women Sculptors. Phoenix: Oryx Press, 1986.

KATHERINE SOPHIE DREIER (1877-1952)    Painter

See volume 1 of this book.

Blesh, Rudi. Modern Art USA. New York: Knopf, 1956.

Bohan, Ruth L. The Société Anonyme's Brooklyn Exhibition: Katherine Dreier and Modernism in America. Ann Arbor: UMI Research Press, 1982.

The Brooklyn Museum American Paintings. Brooklyn:  The Brooklyn
     Museum, 1979.

Davidson, Abraham A.  Early American Modernist Painting 1910-1935.
     New York:  Harper and Row, 1981.

1913 Armory Show 50th Anniversary Exhibition 1963.  Utica, New
     York:  Munson-Williams Proctor Institute, and New York:
     Armory of the Sixty-ninth Regiment, 1963.

Obituary.  The New York Times, 30 March 1952:  92.

Tufts, Eleanor.  American Women Artists, 1830-1930.  Washington,
     D.C.:  National Museum of Women in the Arts, 1987.


          ROSALYN DREXLER (1926-     )   Painter and Writer

See volume 1 of this book.

McGill, Douglas C.  "Painter, Novelist and . . . Wrestler?"  The
     New York Times, 16 August 1986:  Y11.

Rosalyn Drexler:  Intimate Emotions.  New York:  Grey Art Gallery,
     New York University, 1986.

Wilson, Judith.  "Rosalyn Drexler at Grey Art Gallery."  Art in
     America 74, no. 11 (November 1986):  163-164.


          ELSIE DRIGGS (1898-     )   Painter

See volume 1 of this book.

Davidson, Abraham A.  Early American Modernist Painting 1910-1935.
     New York:  Harper and Row, 1981.

First Biennial Exhibition of Contemporary American Sculpture,
     Watercolors and Prints.  New York:  Whitney Museum of American
     Art, 1933-34.

Goldberger, Paul.  "Art:  20th-Century Architectural Paintings."
     The New York Times, 30 October 1980:  Y23.

Loughery, John.  "Blending the Classical and the Modern:  The Art
     of Elsie Driggs."  Woman's Art Journal 7, no. 2 (Fall 1986-
     Winter 1987):  22-26 and cover.

Oresman, Janice C.  Twentieth-Century American Watercolor.  Albany:
     The Gallery Association of New York State, 1983.

Pemberton, Murdoch.  "As We Like It."  The New Yorker, 23 October
     1926.

106

Russell, John.  "Long Island Museum Celebrates Yankee Art."  The
    New York Times, 21 July 1978:  C1, C18.

Wilson, Richard Guy; Pilgrim, Dianne H.; and Tashjian, Dickran.
    The Machine Age in America 1918-1941.  New York:  Harry N.
    Abrams, Inc., and The Brooklyn Museum, 1986.

CATHERINE ANN DRINKER [JANVIER] (1841-1922)    Painter

See volume 1 of this book.

Fielding, Mantle.  Dictionary of American Painters, Sculptors and
    Engravers.  Enlarged ed.  Greens Farms, Connecticut:  Modern
    Books and Crafts, 1974.

Woman's Who's Who of America.  New York:  American Commonwealth
    Co., 1914.

ELLEN DRISCOLL (1953-    )    Sculptor

Glueck, Grace.  "Artists' artists."  Art News 81, no. 9 (November
    1982):  95-96.

Short, B. G.  "Short Reviews."  Women Artists News 12, no. 1
    (February-March 1987):  22.

Sturman, John.  "Ellen Driscoll, Strange Eloquence."  Art News 86,
    no. 5 (May 1987):  83-84.

Westfall, Stephen.  "Ellen Driscoll at Damon Vrandt."  Art in
    America 75, no. 3 (March 1987):  137.

SALLY HAZELET DRUMMOND (1924-    )    Painter

See volume 1 of this book.

Poirier, Maurice, and Necol, Jane.  "The '60s in Abstract:  13
    Statements and an Essay."  Art in America 71, no. 9 (October
    1983):  126-129.

Who's Who in American Art.  New York:  R.R. Bowker and Co., 1978.

LU DUBLE (1896-1970)    Sculptor

See volume 1 of this book.

"Guggenheim Fellows."  Art Digest 11, no. 13 (1 April 1937):  10.

Who's Who in American Art. New York:  R.R. Bowker Co., 1966.


MARY ANN DELAFIELD DuBOIS (1813-1888)   Sculptor

See volume 1 of this book.

Clark, Eliot. History of the National Academy of Design,
     1825-1953. New York:  Columbia University Press, 1954.

Ellet, Elizabeth. Women Artists in All Ages and Countries. New
     York:  Harper and Brothers, 1859.


YVONNE PENE Du BOIS [FURLONG] (1913-    )   Painter

"Du Bois' Daughter Exhibits." Art Digest 10, no. 18 (1 July 1936):
     27.

L., J. "Katherine Larkin; Yvonne du Bois & Elizabeth Colborne."
     Art News 37, no. 17 (21 January 1939):  13.

Who's Who in American Art, vol. 3. Washington, D.C.:  American
     Federation of Arts, 1940.

Yvonne Pene Du Bois:  Paintings from the Last Four Decades. New
     York:  Graham Gallery, 1985.


MABEL LISLE DUCASSE (1895-1976)   Painter

American Art Annual, vol. 28. Washington, D.C.:  American
     Federation of Arts, 1932.

American Art Notes. New York:  Jeffrey Alan Gallery, Autumn 1985.

A Century of Women Artists. Boston and New York:  Childs Gallery,
     1987.

Strauber, Susan, and Wilson, Kay. A View of Her Own:  Images of
     Women by Women Artists. Grinnell, Iowa:  Grinnell College,
     1987:  21.

Who's Who in American Art, vol. 4. Washington, D.C.:  American
     Federation of Arts, 1947.


RUTH (WINDMÜLLER) DUCKWORTH (1919-    )   Ceramic Sculptor

American Porcelain:  New Expressions in an Ancient Art.
     Washington, D.C.:  Renwick Gallery of National Museum of
     American Art, Smithsonian, 1980.

Clark, Garth. A Century of Ceramics in the United States 1878-1978. New York: E.P. Dutton, 1979.

Contemporary Ceramics: The Artist's Viewpoint. Kalamazoo: Kalamazoo Institute of Arts, 1977.

Hall, Julie. Tradition and Change: The New American Craftsman. New York: E.P. Dutton, 1977.

International Ceramics 1972. London: Victoria and Albert Museum, 1972.

Objects: USA. Washington, D.C.: Renwick Gallery of National Collection of Fine Arts, Smithsonian, 1969.

Ruth Duckworth, Claire Zeisler. Philadelphia: Moore College of Art, 1979.

"Ruth Duckworth Exhibition." Ceramics Monthly 28, no. 2 (February 1980): 48-51.

Watson-Jones, Virginia. Contemporary American Women Sculptors. Phoenix: Oryx Press, 1986.

Westphal, Alice. "The Ceramics of Ruth Duckworth." Craft Horizons 37, no. 4 (August 1977): 48-51.

Who's Who in American Art. New York: R.R. Bowker Co., 1978.

JOELLYN DUESBERRY (1944-    )    PAINTER

Birmelin, Blair T. "Joellyn Duesberry at Tatistcheff." Art in America 74, no. 2 (February 1986): 131, 132.

Bolt, Thomas. "Joellyn Duesberry." American Artist 50, no. 531 (October 1986): 48-53, 111, 113-115.

Brenson, Michael. "In the Arts: Critics' Choices." The New York Times, 13 November 1983, Section 2A: 3.

Doherty, M. Stephen. "Motifs for Landscape Painting." American Artist 48, no. 499 (February 1984): 54-55.

Hill, May Brawley. "Joellyn Duesberry." Arts Magazine 60, no. 2 (October 1985): 127.

Joellyn Duesberry. New Paintings. New York: Tatistcheff and Co., 1985.

Moorman, Peggy. "Joellyn Duesberry." Art News 83, no. 3 (March 1984): 223-24.

Raynor, Vivian. "Pooling of Resources Produces Stimulating
    Success." The New York Times, 7 February 1982, Section WC:  16.


MRS. E.B. DUFFEY (active 1856-1867)   Painter

Gerdts, William H. Women Artists of America 1707-1964. Newark:
    Newark Museum, 1965.

Huber, Christine Jones. The Pennsylvania Academy and Its Women.
    Philadelphia:  Pennsylvania Academy of the Fine Arts, 1974.


LORETTA DUNKELMAN (1937-     )   Painter

See volume 1 of this book.

Who's Who in American Art. New York:  R.R. Bowker Co., 1978.


EMELENE ABBEY DUNN (1859-1929)   Painter

Dunn, Emelene Abbey. Mediterranean Picture Lands. Rochester, New
    York:  Du Bois Press, 1929.

Obituary. American Art Annual, vol. 26.  Washington, D.C.:
    American Federation of Arts, 1929.


GRACE ANNETT DUPRÉ (1893/94-1984)   Painter

Falk, Peter Hastings. Who was Who in American Art. Madison,
    Connecticut:  Sound View Press, 1985.

Obituary. The New York Times, 4 June 1984.

Who's Who in American Art. New York:  R.R. Bowker Co., 1978.


CAROLINE DURIEUX (1896-     )   Printmaker

See volume 1 of this book.

Art, the Atom and LSU:  An Exhibition of Electron Prints by
    Caroline Durieux. Baton Rouge, Louisiana:  Louisiana State
    University Art Gallery, 1978.

Caroline Durieux:  Three Lifetimes in Printmaking--A Retrospective
    of Her Prints and Drawings. Bethlehem, Connecticut:  June 1
    Gallery, 1979.

110

Contemporary Art of the United States. New York: IBM Building
      World's Fair, 1940.

Jones, Howard Mumford.  "Lithographs of the Thirties and Forties by
      Caroline Durieux."  The New Republic, 4 March 1978:   34-35.

"She is 'Politely Cruel, Charmingly Venomous.'"  Art Digest 10, no.
      5 (1 December 1935)  14.

Zigrosser, Carl.  The Artist in America:  Twenty-Four Close-Ups of
      Contemporary Printmakers.  New York:  Alfred A. Knopf, 1942.


                    JEANNE DUVAL (1956-      )   Painter

Doherty, M. Stephen.  "Jeanne Duval."  American Artist 48, no. 500
      (March 1984):   46-50.

Lerman, Ora.  "Contemporary Vanitas."  Arts Magazine 62, no. 7
      (March 1988):   60-63.

O'Beil, Hedy.  "Jeanne Duval."  Arts Magazine 59, no. 7 (March
      1985):   40.



      ELIZABETH OTIS LYMAN BOOTT DUVENECK (1846-1888)   Painter

See volume 1 of this book.

Boime, Albert.  "Current and Forthcoming Exhibitions."  Burlington
      Magazine 112 (September 1970):   651 and fig. 140.

Clement, Clara Erskine.  Women in the Fine Arts.  Boston:  Houghton
      Mifflin, 1904.  (under "Boott")

Fielding, Mantle.  Dictionary of American Painters, Sculptors and
      Engravers.  Enlarged ed.  Greens Farms, Connecticut:  Modern
      Books and Crafts, 1974.  (under "Boott")

Frank Duveneck and Elizabeth Boott:  Paintings, Drawings, Prints
      and Memorabilia.  Stanford:  Art Gallery, Stanford University,
      1981.



                    JULIA S. DWIGHT (b. 1870)   Painter

American Art Annual, vol. 12.  Washington, D.C.:  American
      Federation of Arts, 1915.

American 19th and 20th Century Paintings, Drawings, Watercolors &
      Sculpture.  New York:  Sotheby Parke Bernet, 27 October 1978,
      Lot 36.

Bénézit, Emmanuel. Dictionnaire critique et documentaire des peintres, sculpteurs, dessinateurs, et graveurs de tous les temps et de tous les pays. New ed. Paris: Librairie Gründ, 1976.

Fielding, Mantle. Dictionary of American Painters, Sculptors and Engravers. Enlarged ed. Greens Farms, Connecticut: Modern Books and Crafts, 1974.

MABEL DWIGHT (1876-1955)    Printmaker

See volume 1 of this book.

First Biennial Exhibition of Contemporary American Sculpture, Watercolors and Prints. New York: Whitney Museum of American Art, 1933-34.

Print Annual, vol. 10. Boston: Childs Gallery, 1987.

Zigrosser, Carl. The Artist in America:  Twenty-Four Close-Ups of Contemporary Printmakers. New York: Alfred A. Knopf, 1942.

SUSAN HANNAH MACDOWELL EAKINS (1851-1938)    Painter

See volume 1 of this book.

Catalogue of the Exhibits of the State of Pennsylvania and of Pennsylvanians at The World's Columbian Exposition. [Harrisburg]: State Printer of Pennsylvania, 1893.

Davis, Douglas. "The Unknown Eakins." Newsweek, 28 May 1973:  80.

Foster, Kathleen A. "An Important Eakins Collection." Antiques 116 (December 1986):  1228-1237.

In This Academy. The Pennsylvania Academy of the Fine Arts, 1805-1976. Philadelphia: The Pennsylvania Academy of the Fine Arts, 1976.

Tufts, Eleanor. American Women Artists, 1830-1930. Washington, D.C.: National Museum of Women in the Arts, 1987.

SYBIL EASTERDAY (1876-1961)    Sculptor

See volume 1 of this book.

Dawdy, Doris Ostrander. Artists of the American West:  A Biographical Dictionary, vol. 2. Chicago: Sage Books, 1980.

112

*100 Years of California Sculpture*. Oakland:  The Oakland Museum, 1982.


DOROTHY EATON (1893-1960's)    Painter

*American Art Annual*, vol. 28.  Washington, D.C.:  American Federation of Arts, 1932.

Campbell, Lawrence.  "Dorothy Eaton."  *Art News* 68, no. 6 (October 1969):  16.

Ratcliff, Carter.  "Dorothy Eaton."  *Art International* 13 (November 1969) 76.

*Who's Who in American Art*, vol. 8.  Washington, D.C.:  American Federation of Arts, 1962.


MARY ABASTENIA ST. LEGER EBERLE (1878-1942)    Sculptor

See volume 1 of this book.

Casteras, Susan P.  "Abastenia St. Leger Eberle's *White Slave*."  *Woman's Art Journal* 7, no. 1 (Spring-Summer 1986):  32-36.

Conner, Janis c.  "American Women Sculptors Break the Mold."  *Arts and Antiques* 3, no. 3 (May-June 1980):  80-87.

*Famous Small Bronzes*.  New York:  The Gorham Co., 1928.

McIntyre, R. G.  "The Broad Vision of Abastenia Eberle, The Increasing Interest in Humanity Shown in this Sculptor's Recent Work."  *Arts and Decoration* 3, no. 10 (August 1913):  334-337.

Ness, Zenobia, and Orwig, Louise.  *Iowa Artists of the First Hundred Years*.  [Des Moines, Iowa]:  Wallace Homestead Co., 1939.

"Without Prejudice."  *International Studio* 73, no. 288 (March 1921):  III-V.

Tufts, Eleanor.  *American Women Artists, 1830-1930*.  Washington, D.C.:  National Museum of Women in the Arts, 1987.


EDRIS ECKHARDT (1910-    ) Ceramic Sculptor

*Annual Ceramic National Exhibition*.  Syracuse:  Syracuse Museum of Fine Arts, 1933-1952.

Beard, Geoffrey W. <u>International Modern Glass</u>. New York: Charles
    Scribner's Sons, 1976.

Clark, Garth. <u>A Century of Ceramics in the United States
    1878-1978</u>. New York: E.P. Dutton, 1979.

<u>The Diversions of Keramos: American Clay Sculpture from 1925-50</u>.
    Syracuse: Everson Museum of Art, 1984.

<u>Edris Eckhardt, Retrospective</u>. Syracuse: Everson Museum of Art,
    1983.

<u>The First Exhibition of Contemporary Ceramics of the Western
    Hemisphere</u>. Syracuse: Syracuse Museum of Fine Arts,
    traveling exhibition: Canada, South America, and United
    States, 1941.

<u>Golden Gate International Exposition</u>. San Francisco: San
    Francisco Museum of Art, 1939.

Grover, Ray and Lee. <u>Contemporary Art Glass</u>. New York: Crown,
    1975.

<u>Invitational Art Exhibition</u>. Cleveland: Cleveland Institute of
    Art, 1985.

Rothenberg, Polly. <u>The Complete Book of Creative Glass Art</u>. New
    York: Crown, 1974.

Watson-Jones, Virginia. <u>Contemporary American Women Sculptors</u>.
    Phoenix: Oryx Press, 1986.

SARAH J. EDDY (b. 1851)    Sculptor

Fielding, Mantle. <u>Dictionary of American Painters, Sculptors and
    Engravers</u>. Enlarged ed. Greens Farms, Connecticut: Modern
    Books and Crafts, 1957.

National Sculpture Society. <u>Contemporary American Sculpture</u>. San
    Francisco: California Palace of the Legion of Honor, 1929:
    86.

MARTHA EDELHEIT (1931-    )    Painter

See volume 1 of this book.

Edelman, Robet G. "Martha Edelheit at Soho 20." <u>Art in America</u>
    74, no. 11 (November 1986): 170 (repro. p. 168).

<u>Who's Who in American Art</u>. New York: R.R. Bowker Co., 1978.

114

MARY BETH EDELSON (20th Century)    Conceptual Artist

See volume 1 of this book.

Edelson, Mary Beth.  "Pilgramage/See for Yourself:  A Journey to a
    Neolithic Goddess Cave, 1977.  Grapceva, Hvar Island,
    Yugoslavia."  Heresies 2, no. 1 (Spring 1978):  96-99.

Lippard, Lucy.  "Caring:  Five Political Artists."  Studio
    International 193, no. 987 (March 1977):  197-207.

Who's Who in American Art.  New York:  R.R. Bowker Co., 1978.


            ESTHER EDMONDS (1888-1976)    Painter

Art in the United States Capitol.  Washington, D.C.:  U.S.
    Government Printing Office, 1976:  69.

Fielding, Mantle.  Dictionary of American Painters, Sculptors and
    Engravers.  Enlarged ed.  Greens Farms, Connecticut:  Modern
    Books and Crafts, 1974.


        KATE FLOURNOY EDWARDS (1877-1980)    Painter

American Art Annual, vol. 28.  Washington, D.C.:  American
    Federation of Arts, 1932.

Art of the United States Capitol.  Washington, D.C.:  U.S.
    Government Printing Office, 1976:  41.

Who's Who in American Art, vol. 12.  Washington, D.C.:  American
    Federation of Arts, 1915.


            SHIELA ELIAS (20th Century)    Painter

Brown, Betty.  "Sheila Elias."  Arts Magazine 57, no. 1 (September
    1982):  24.

Gill, Susan.  "Sheila Elias."  Art News 85, no. 5 (May 1986):
    131-132.

"Prints and Photographs Published."  Print Collectors News 15
    (September/October 1984):  143.

Shiela Elias.  New York:  Alex Rosenberg Gallery, 1986.

Who's Who in American Art, 17th ed.  New York:  R.R. Bowker Co.,
    1986.

ROWENA C. ELKIN (1917-    )    Sculptor

Fifth Texas Sculpture Symposium. Dallas: Connemara Conservancy,
     1985.

150 Works by Texas Women Artists. Dallas: Dallas Women's Caucus
     for   Art, 1986.

Texas Fine Arts Association Regional Winners Exhibition.   Austin:
     Laguna Gloria Art Museum, 1965.

Watson-Jones, Virginia.  Contemporary American Women Sculptors.
     Phoenix:  Oryx Press, 1986.


EDITH EMERSON (1888-1982)    Painter

See volume 1 of this book.

American Art Annual, vol. 28.  Washington, D.C.:  American
     Federation of Arts, 1932.

Clark, Edna.  Ohio Art and Artists.  Richmond, Virginia:  Garrett
     and Massie, 1932.

Edith Emerson:  A Retrospective Exhibition.  Philadelphia:
     Woodmere Art Gallery, 1969.

Fielding, Mantle.  Dictionary of American Painters, Sculptors and
     Engravers.  Enlarged ed.  Greens Farms, Connecticut:  Modern
     Books and Crafts, 1974.


LIN EMERY (1926-    )    Sculptor

See volume 1 of this book.

Annual Exhibition of Painting and Sculpture.  Philadelphia:
     Pennsylvania Academy of the Fine Arts, 1960.

Annual Exhibition of Painting and Sculpture.  Philadelphia:
     Pennsylvania Academy of the Fine Arts, 1964.

Art in Architecture:  General Services Administration Projects.
     Washington, D.C.:  National Museum of American Art, 1980.

Feldman, Edmund Burke.  Art as Image and Idea.  Englewood Cliffs,
     New Jersey:  Prentice-Hall, 1967.

Flint International.  Flint, Michigan:  Flint Institute of Arts,
     1966.

Glueck, Grace. "Lin Emery, Ju Ming (Max Hutchinson Gallery, 138 Green St.)" The New York Times, 21 December 1985, Section 3, p. 31.

Lin Emery. New York: Sculpture Center, 1962.

Redstone, Louis G., and Redstone, Ruth R. Public Art: New Directions. New York: McGraw-Hill, 1981.

Sculptors Guild Annual Exhibition. New York: Lever House, 1976.

Sculptors Guild Annual Exhibition. New York: Lever House, 1978.

Sculptors Guild Annual Exhibition. New York: Lever House, 1980.

Thalacker, Donald W. The Place of Art in the World of Architecture. New York: Chelsea House, 1980.

Watson-Jones, Virginia. Contemporary American Women Sculptors. Phoenix: Oryx Press, 1986.

Who's Who in American Art. New York: R.R. Bowker Co., 1978.

## E. LESLIE EMMET (b. 1877)   Painter

Archives of American Art. Collection of Exhibition Catalogs. Boston: G.K. Hall and Co., 1979.

Fielding, Mantle. Dictionary of American Painters, Sculptors Engravers. Enlarged ed. Greens Farms, Connecticut: Modern Books and Crafts, 1974.

Portraits of Americans by Americans. New York: National Association of Portrait Painters, 1945.

## LYDIA FIELD EMMET (1866-1952)   Painter

See volume 1 of this book.

American Art Annual, vol. 14. Washington, D.C.: American Federation of Arts, 1917.

Clement, Clara Erskine. Women in the Fine Arts. Boston: Houghton, Mifflin and Co., 1904.

Koke, Richard J. A Catalog of the Collection, Including Historical, Narrative, and Marine Art, vol. 2. Boston: G.K. Hall in association with The New-York Historical Society, 1982.

Lee, Cuthbert. Contemporary American Portrait Painters. New York: W.W. Norton and Co., 1929: 37-38.

"Lydia Emmet Dies; Won Art Awards." The New York Times, 18 August
    1952:  17.

Tufts, Eleanor.  American Women Artists, 1830-1930.  Washington,
    D.C.:  National Museum of Women in the Arts, 1987.


                ANGNA ENTERS (1907-1989)    Painter

"Angna Enters."  Art News 46, no. 1 (March 1947):  49.

"Angna Enters."  Art News 48, no. 1 (March 1949):  44.

Boswell, Helen.  "Angna Enters, Painter."  Art Digest 17, no. 7 (1
    January 1943):  19.

Brantome, Eugene.  "Review of First Person Plural."  Arts &
    Decoration 47, no. 6 (February 1938):  46.

Breunig, Margaret.  "Recent Paintings and Drawings by Angna
    Enters."  Art Digest 23, no. 11 (1 March 1949):  14, 18.

"A Dancer Remains a Mime in All Art Forms."  Art News 34, no. 22
    (29 February 1936):  9.

"Drawings by Angna Enters."  Minneapolis Institute of Art Bulletin
    24 (19 January 1935):  14.

"Drawings and Watercolors by Angna Enters."  Milwaukee Art
    Institute Bulletin 10 (October 1935):  3.

Enters, Angna.  Artist's Life.  New York:  Coward-McCann, 1958.

_____.  First Person Plural.  New York:  Stackpole Sons, 1937.

_____.  On Mime.  Middletown, Connecticut:  Wesleyan University
    Press, 1965.

_____.  Silly Girl, A Portrait of Personal Remembrance.  Cambridge,
    Massachusetts:  Houghton Mifflin, 1944.

Fourteen American Women Printmakers of the 30's and 40's.  South
    Hadley, Massachusetts:  Mount Holyoke College Art Museum,
    1973.

L[ansford, A[lonzo].  "Angna Enters Again."  Art Digest 21, no. 10
    (15 February 1947):  21, 3.

"Paintings on Display at Museum."  Portland Museum Bulletin 9
    (March 1948):  [2].

Schwartz, Jane.  "Around the Galleries."  Art News 33, no. 10 (8
    December 1934):  12.

"Spotlight! Famous Women in the Arts." Arts & Decoration 44, no. 7 (February 1936): 37.

Who's Who in American Art, vol. 2. Washington, D.C.: American Federation of Arts, 1937: 167.


MARTHA MAYER ERLEBACHER (1937-    )  Painter

See volume 1 of this book.

Cohen, Ronny. "'A Symbol in Some Way': New Paintings by Martha Mayer Erlebacher." Arts Magazine 59, no. 6 (February 1985): 122-123.

Martha Mayer Erlebacher. Essay by Ronny Cohen. Chicago: J. Rosenthal Fine Arts, 1987.

Martin, Alvin. American Realism, 20th Century Drawings and Watercolors From the Glenn C. Janss Collection. San Francisco: Museum of Modern Art, 1985.

Modern Myths. Boise, Idaho: Boise Gallery of Art, 1987.

Representational Drawing Today: A Heritage Renewed. Santa Barbara, California: University Art Museum, 1983.


FLORENCE ESTÉ (1860-1926)  Painter and Etcher

American Prints in the Library of Congress: A Catalog of the Collection. Johns Hopkins, 1970.

Clark, Edna. Ohio Art and Artists. Richmond, Virginia: Garrett & Massie, 1932.

Obituary. American Art Annual, vol. 4. Washington, D.C.: American Federation of Arts, 1926.

Peet, Phyllis. American Women of the Etching Revival. Atlanta: High Museum of Art, 1988.

Taylor, E.A. "The American Colony of Artists in Paris." The International Studio 45 (August 1911): 103-15.

The Work of Women Etchers of America. New York: Union League Club, 1988.

GRACE LYDIA EVANS (b. 1877)    Painter

An Exhibition of Women Students of William Merritt Chase. New
    York: Marbella Gallery, 1973.

Fielding, Mantle. Dictionary of American Painters, Sculptors and
    Engravers. Enlarged ed. Greens Farms, Connecticut: Modern
    Books and Crafts, 1974.


MINNIE JONES EVANS (1892-1987)    Folk Painter

Dewhurst, C. Kurt; MacDowell, Betty; and MacDowell, Marsha.
    Artists in Aprons. New York: E.P. Dutton, 1979.

Driskell, David C. Two Centuries of Black American Art. Los
    Angeles: Los Angeles County Museum of Art, 1976.

Kahan, Mitchell D. Heavenly Vision. The Art of Minnie Evans.
    Raleigh: North Carolina Museum of Art, 1986.

Meyer, Jon. "Minnie Evans (North Carolina Museum of Art)." Art
    News 85, no. 4 (April 1986):  144.

Minnie Evans. New York: Roko Gallery, 1977.

"Minnie Evans, 95, Folk Painter Noted for Visionary Work." The
    New York Times, 19 December 1987:  Y12.

Star, Nina Howell. Minnie Evans. New York: Whitney Museum of
    American Art, 1975.


ELIZABETH EYRE DE LANUX (1894-    )    Painter

Anscombe, Isabell. "Expatriates in Paris:  Eileen Gray Evelyn
    Wyld, and Eyre de Lanux." Apollo 115 (February 1982):
    117-18.

Bryant, Lorinda Munson. American Pictures and Their Painters. New
    York: Dodd Mead, 1925:  285-286.

Fahlman, Betsy. "Eyre de Lanux." Women's Art Journal 3, no. 2
    (Fall 1982/Winter 1983):  44-48.

Garland, Madge. "Interiors by Eyre de Lanux." Creative Art 6
    (April 1930):  263-265.

"A Spirited Revival of the Primitive Manner:  Painted Doors by Eyre
    de Lanux." Arts & Decoration 16 (January 1922):  198, 222.

NINA FAGNANI (ca. 1860?-after 1898)    Miniaturist

Bénézit, Emmanuel. Dictionnaire critique et documentaire des peintres, sculpteurs, dessinateurs et graveurs de tous les temps et de tous les pays. New ed. Paris: Librairie Gründ, 1976.

Falk, Peter Hastings, ed. Who Was Who in American Art. Madison, Connecticut: Sound View Press, 1985.

Havlice, Patricia Pate. Index to Artistic Biography, First Supplement. Metuchen, New Jersey: Scarecrow Press, 1981.

Johnson, Jane, and Greutzner, A., comps. Dictionary of British Artists, 1880-1940. Suffolk, England: Antique Collectors' Club, 1976.

Tufts, Eleanor. American Women Artists, 1830-1930. Washington, D.C.: National Museum of Women in the Arts, 1987.

HANNAH FAIRCHILD (active 1836-1839)    Painter

American Folk Art from the Collection of Peter Tillou, Litchfield, Connecticut. New York: Sotheby's, October 26, 1985, no. 77.

Dewhurst, C. Kurt; MacDowell, Betty; and MacDowell, Marsha. Artists in Apron: Folk Art by American Women. New York: E.P. Dutton, 1979.

Groce, George C., and Wallace, David H. The New-York Historical Society's Dictionary of Artists in America, 1564-1860. New Haven: Yale University Press, 1957.

ELIZABETH C. FALK (1941-    )    Sculptor

Recent Sculpture--Johnson Atelier: Workshop and Studio. Trenton: New Jersey State Museum, 1984.

Sculpture 1980. Baltimore: Maryland Institute College of Art, 1980.

Twenty-First Area Exhibition. Washington, D.C.: Corcoran Gallery of Art, 1978.

Watson-Jones, Virginia. Contemporary American Women Sculptors. Phoenix: Oryx Press, 1986.

CLAIRE FALKENSTEIN (1908-    )   Sculptor

See volume 1 of this book.

Annual Exhibition: Contemporary American Sculpture. New York:
    Whitney Museum of American Art, 1960.

Annual Exhibition: Contemporary American Sculpture. New York:
    Whitney Museum of American Art, 1964.

Artiste Objets. Paris:  Musée des Arts Decoratifs, 1962.

A Broad Spectrum: Contemporary Los Angeles Painters and Sculptors
    '84. Los Angeles:  Design Center, 1984.

Bullis, Douglas, ed. 50 West Coast Artists: A Critical Selection
    of Painters and Sculptors Working in California. Selected by
    Henry Hopkins.  San Francisco:  Chronicle Books, 1981.

Claire Falkenstein. In San Francisco, Paris, Los Angeles & Now.
    Palm Springs, California:  Palm Springs Desert Museum, 1980.

The Continuing Vision of Claire Falkenstein, 1947-84. Riverside,
    California:  University of California Art Gallery, 1984.

Fifty-Eighth Annual Exhibition of American Paintings and Sculpture:
    Abstract and Surrealist American Art. Chicago:  Art Institute
    of Chicago, 1947.

Mobiles and Articulated Sculpture. San Francisco:  California
    Palace of the Legion of Honor, 1948.

100 Years of California Sculpture: The Oakland Museum. Oakland:
    The Oakland Museum, 1982.

Painting and Sculpture in California: The Modern Era. San
    Francisco:  San Francisco Museum of Art and Washington, D.C.:
    National Collection of Fine Arts, 1976.

Pittsburgh International Exhibition of Painting and Sculpture.
    Pittsburgh:  Carnegie Institute Museum of Art, 1964.

Portraits and Palettes. Los Angeles:  Los Angeles County Museum of
    Art, 1980.

Roth, Moira, ed. Connecting Conversations: Interviews with 28 Bay
    Area Women Artists. Oakland, California:  Eucalyptus Press,
    Mills College, 1988.

Rubin, David S.  "Americans in Paris:  The 50s." Arts Magazine 54,
    no. 5 (January 1980):  19.

Watson-Jones, Virginia. Contemporary American Women Sculptors.
    Phoenix:  Oryx Press, 1986.


        SALLY JAMES FARNHAM (1876-1943)    Sculptor

See volume 1 of this book.

National Portrait Gallery, Permanent Collection Illustrated
    Checklist. Washington, D.C.:  Smithsonian Institution Press,
    1982.

Proske, Beatrice Gilman. Brookgreen Gardens Sculpture, vol. II.
    Brookgreen, South Carolina:  Brookgreen Gardens, 1955:  47-51.

"Six Women Sculptors at Work in Their Studios." Arts &
    Decoration 16 (November 1921):  26.


        HELEN FARR [SLOAN]  (1911-   )   Printmaker and Painter

Campbell, Larry.  "Reviews and Previews:  Farr." Art News 51, no.
    8 (December 1952):  45.

Fourteen American Women Printmakers of the 30's and 40's. South
    Hadley, Massachusetts:  Mount Holyoke College Art Museum,
    1973.

Who's Who in American Art, vol. 2. Washington, D.C.:  American
    Federation of Arts, 1937:  174.


        KATHERINE LEVIN FARRELL (1857-1951)    Painter and Etcher

American Art Annual, vol. 28. Washington, D.C.:  American
    Federation of Arts, 1932.

Fielding, Mantle. Dictionary of American Painters, Sculptors and
    Engravers. Enlarged ed.  Greens Farms, Connecticut:  Modern
    Books and Crafts, 1974.

Obituary. Who's Who in American Art, vol. 5.  Washington, D.C.:
    American Federation of Arts, 1953.

Peet, Phyllis. American Women of the Etching Revival. Atlanta:
    High Museum of Art, 1988.

The Work of Women Etchers of America. New York:  Union League
    Club, 1888.

CORNELIA ADELE STRONG FASSETT (1831-1898)   Painter

See volume 1 of this book.

Cosentino, Andrew J., and Glassie, Henry H.  The Capital Image:
    Painters in Washington, 1800-1915.  Washington, D.C.:
    National Museum of American Art, 1983.

Cowley, Charles.  "The Minority Report of the Electoral
    Commission."  Magazine of American History 27, no. 2 (February
    1892):  81-97.

Obituary.  American Art Annual, vol. 1.  New York:  Macmillan Co.,
    1899.

Rubinstein, Charlotte S.  American Women Artists.  Boston:  G.K.
    Hall and Co., 1982.

Tufts, Eleanor.  American Women Artists, 1830-1930.  Washington,
    D.C.:  National Museum of Women in the Arts, 1987.

Waters, Clara Erskine Clement, and Hutton, Laurence.  Artists of
    the Nineteenth Century and Their Works.  New York:  Arno Press
    reprint, 1969.

What is American in American Art (Intro. by Lloyd Goodrich;
    catalogue by Mary Black).  New York:  Knoedler, 1971.


CHRISTINE FEDERIGHI (1949-    )   Ceramic Sculptor

The Animal Image:  Contemporary Objects and the Beast.  Washington,
    D.C.:  Renwick Gallery of National Museum of American Art,
    Smithsonian, 1981.

Ceramic Echoes:  Historical References in Contemporary Ceramics.
    Kansas City, Missouri:  Nelson-Atkins Museum of Art, 1983.

Kash, Joanne.  "Profiles:  A Portfolio of Regional Artists,
    Christine Federighi (Miami, Florida)."  Art Voices 4, no. 3
    (May-June 1981):  71.

Kohen, Helen L.  "Forecast:  Bright Days for Art in South Florida."
    Art News 79, no. 10 (December 1980):  96-99.

Nigrosh, Leon I.  Low Fire:  Other Ways to Work in Clay.
    Worcester, Massachusetts:  Davis, 1980.

"Portfolio:  Christine Federighi."  American Craft 42, no. 1
    (February-March 1982):  36.

Watson-Jones, Virginia.  Contemporary American Women Sculptors.
    Phoenix:  Oryx Press, 1986.

124

Wechsler, Susan. "Interview: Views on the Figure." American
Ceramics 3, no. 1 (Spring 1984): 16-25.


BELLA TABAK FELDMAN (1940-    )   Mixed media

Bella Feldman. Geneva: Galerie Bernard Letu, 1975.

Boettger, Suzaan. "Exhibitions: Potent Allusions." Artweek 13,
no. 32 (2 October 1982): 4.

Feldman, Bella Tabak. "A View of Evolution Expressed in Sculpture:
A Reflection of Nuclear Angst." Leonardo 16, no. 4 (Autumn
1983): 259-64.

Frym, Gloria. Second Stories: Conversations with Women Whose
Artistic Careers Began After Thirty-Five. San Francisco:
Chronicle Books, 1979.

The Handmade Paper Object. Santa Barbara: Santa Barbara Museum of
Art, 1976.

The Presence of Light. Dallas: Meadows Gallery, Southern
Methodist University, 1984.

Scarborough, Jessica. "The Visual Language of Bella Feldman."
Fiberarts 11, no. 4 (July-August 1984): 30-33.

Watson-Jones, Virginia. Contemporary American Women Sculptors.
Phoenix: Oryx Press, 1986.

Workman, Andree M. "Sculpture in Search of Space." Artweek 11,
no. 28 (30 August 1984): 5-6.


OLIVE FELL (ca. 1900-1980)   Painter, Printmaker, and Sculptor

One Hundred Years of Artist Activity in Wyoming 1837-1937.
Laramie: University of Wyoming Art Museum, 1976.

Samuels, Peggy and Harold. The Illustrated Biographical
Encyclopedia of Artists of the American West. Garden City,
New York: Doubleday and Co., 1976.

A Selection of American Prints. A Selection of Biographies of
Forty Women Artists Working Between 1904-1979. Santa Rosa,
California: The Annex Galleries, 1987: 4.

ALMIRA T. FENNO-GENDROT (active 1871-1923)    Painter

American Art Annual, vol. 1.  New York:  Macmillan, 1899.

Fenno-Gendrot, Almira B.  Artists I Have Known.  Boston:  The
     Warren Press, 1923.

Hoppin, Martha J.  "Women Artists in Boston 1870-1900:  The Pupils
     of William Morris Hunt."  The American Art Journal 13, no. 1
     (Winter 1891):  22, 44.


BEATRICE FENTON (1887-1983)    Sculptor

See volume 1 of this book.

American Art Annual, vol. 28.  Washington, D.C.:  American
     Federation of Arts, 1932.

Fairmount Park Association, Philadelphia.  Sculpture of a City:
     Philadelphia's Treasures in Bronze and Stone.  New York:
     Walker Publishing Co., 1974.


KATHLEEN FERGUSON (1945-    )    Sculptor

Friedman, Jon R.  "Kathleen Ferguson."  Arts Magazine 54, no. 7
     (March 1980):  15.

Graham, William.  "Reviews Chicago:  Primitive Sources--
     Contemporary Visions, Jan Ciciero Gallery."  New Art Examiner
     8, no. 4 (January 1981):  20.

Kentucky Art 1983.  Lexington:  University of Kentucky Art Museum,
     1983.

1975 Biennial Exhibition:  Contemporary American Art.  New York:
     Whitney Museum of American Art, 1975.

Painting and Sculpture Today 1980.  Indianapolis:  Indianapolis
     Museum of Art, 1980.

Phillips, Deborah C.  "New York Reviews:  Group Show (Art Galaxy)."
     Art News 80, no. 7 (September 1981):  236.

Staniszewski, Mary Anne.  "New York Reviews:  Kathleen Ferguson (R.
     H. Oosterom)."  Art News 80, no. 3 (March 1981):  232.

Watson-Jones, Virginia.  Contemporary American Women Sculptors.
     Phoenix:  Oryx Press, 1986.

Yau, John. "Kathleen Ferguson at Nobé." Art in America 67, no. 3
      (May-June 1979):  141-142.


NANCY MAYBIN FERGUSON (1872-1967)    Painter

American Art Annual, vol. 28.  Washington, D.C.:  American
      Federation of Arts, 1932.

Huber, Christine Jones.  The Pennsylvania Academy and Its Women.
      Philadelphia:  Pennsylvania Academy of Fine Arts, 1974:  41.

Who's Who in American Art, vol. 9.  Washington, D.C.:  American
      Federation of Arts, 1966.


JACKIE FERRARA (1929-     )   Sculptor

See volume 1 of this book.

Architectural Sculpture.  Los Angeles:  Los Angeles Institute of
      Contemporary Art, 1980.

Biennial Exhibition:  Contemporary American Art.  New York:
      Whitney Museum of American Art, 1979.

Bourdon, David.  "Jackie Ferrara:  On the Cutting Edge of a New
      Sensibility."  Arts Magazine 50, no. 5 (January 1976):  90-91.

Ferrara, Lichtenstein, Nevelson, Ryman.  Bronxville, New York:
      Sarah Lawrence College, 1977.

Four Sculptors.  Williamstown, Massachusetts:  Williams College,
      1976.

Linder, Kate.  "Jackie Ferrara IL-Lusions."  Artforum 18, no. 3
      (November 1979):  57-61.

1970 Annual Exhibition:  Contemporary American Sculpture.  New
      York:  Whitney Museum of American Art, 1970.

Painting and Sculpture Today 1974.  Indianapolis:  Indianpolis
      Museum of Art, 1974.

See, Ingram.  "St. Louis Sculpture Park."  The New York Times, 22
      March 1987, Travel Section, p. 26.

Shepard, Ileen.  Sculpture of the 80's.  Essay by Lowery S. Sims.
      Queens, New York:  Queens Museum, 1987.

MAY ELECTA FERRIS [SMITH] (active 1880's-1890's)    Etcher

Peet, Phyllis. _American Women of the Etching Revival_. Atlanta:
     High  Museum of Art, 1988.

Weiman, Jeanne Madeline. _The Fair Women_. Chicago:  Academy
     Chicago, 1981:  306.

_The Work of Women Etchers of America_. New York:  Union League
     Club, 1888.


          BETTY W. FEVES (1918-    )   Ceramic Sculptor

_Annual Ceramic National Exhibition_.  Syracuse, New York:
     Everson Museum of Art, 1964.

_Fifth Annual International Exhibition of Ceramic Arts_. Washington,
     D.C.:  National Collection of Fine Arts, Smithsonian, 1955.

_International Exhibition of Contemporary Ceramic Art_.  Tokyo:
     National Museum, 1964.

Nichols, Ellen.  _Images of Oregon Women_.  Salem, Oregon:  Madison
     Press, 1983.

_Recent Sculpture U.S.A_.  New York:  The Museum of Modern Art, 1959.

Riegger, Hal.  "The Slab Sculpture of Betty Feves." _Ceramics
     Monthly_ 11, no. 1 (January 1963):  22-25, 32.

_Shirley Gittlesohn Paintings; Betty Feves, Ceramic Sculpture_.
     Portland, Oregon:  Fountain Gallery of Art, 1979.

Watson-Jones, Virginia.  _Contemporary American Women Sculptors_.
     Phoenix:  Oryx Press, 1986.


          JOSEFA FILKOSKY (1933-    )   Sculptor

Benton, Suzanne.  _The Art of Welded Sculpture_.  New York:  Van
     Nostrand Reinhold, 1975.

Evert, Marilyn, and Gay, Vernon.  _Discovering Pittsburgh's
     Sculpture_.  Pittsburgh:  University of Pittsburgh Press, 1983.

Glueck, Grace.  "New Sculpture Under the Sun, From Staten Island to
     the Bronx." _The New York Times_, 3 August 1979: C1, C15.

Miller, Donald.  "Sister Josefa's Pipe Dreams." _Art International_
     25, no. 10 (20 December 1971):  50-51.

128

Robinette, Margaret A. Outdoor Sculpture: Object and Environment. New York: Whitney Library of Design, 1976.

Sculptors Guild Annual Exhibition. New York: Lever House, 1983.

Sculptors Guild Annual Exhibition. New York: Lever House, 1984.

Watson-Jones, Virginia. Contemporary American Women Sculptors. Phoenix: Oryx Press, 1986.


JOAN FINE (1942-    )    Sculptor

Audobon Artists Annual Exhibition. New York: National Academy of Design, 1978.

Ehrlich, Robbie. "Joan Fine." Arts Magazine 53, no. 9 (May 1979): 40.
Fine, Joan. I Carve Stone. New York: Thomas Y. Crowell, 1979.

National Association of Women Artists: U.S.A. New York: American Cultural Center, 1981.

Watson-Jones, Virginia. Contemporary American Women Sculptors. Phoenix: Oryx Press, 1986.


PERLE FINE (1908-    )    Painter

See volume 1 of this book.

K., B. "Perle Fine (Parsons)." Art News 48, no. 4 (Summer 1949): 54.

Russo, Alexander. Profiles on Women Artists. Frederick, Maryland: University Publications of America, 1985.

Who's Who in American Art. New York: R.R. Bowker Co., 1978.


SHIRLEY FINK (1932-    )    Fiber Artist

Laury, Jean Ray. The Creative Woman's Getting-It-Together at Home Handbook. Cincinnati: Van Nostrand Reinhold, 1977.

Russell, Elfleda. Off-Loom Weaving: A Basic Manual. Boston: Little, Brown and Co., 1975.

Sauer, Dick. "'Fiberthing': Boston City Hall Gallery." Craft Horizons 33, no. 3 (June 1973): 41.

129

Znamierowski, Nell.  Fiber:  The Artist's View.  Greenvale, New
        York:  Hillwood Art Gallery, Long Island University, 1983.


                LEONDA F. FINKE (1922-    )    Sculptor

Annual Exhibition of Painting and Sculpture.  Philadelphia:
        Pennsylvania Academy of the Fine Arts, 1966.

Cleary, Fritz.  "Reality Reflected."  National Sculpture Review
        26, no. 1 (Spring 1977):  8-17, 25.

Meilach, Dona Z., and Kowal, Dennis.  Sculpture Casting.  New
        York:  Crown, 1972.

Proske, Beatrice Gilman.  "American Women Sculptors, Part II."
        National Sculpture Review 24, no. 4 (Winter 1975-76):  8-17,
        28.

Russell, Stella Pandell.  Art in the World.  New York:  Holt,
        Rinehart and Winston, 1984.

Sculptors Guild Annual Exhibition.  New York:  Lever House,
        1980-1985.

Shirey, David L.  "Art:  Epic Sculpture."  The New York Times, 25
        May 1980:  Long Island p. 19.

Watson-Jones, Virginia.  Contemporary American Women Sculptors.
        Phoenix:  Oryx Press, 1986.


                JANET FISH (1938-    )    Painter

See volume 1 of this book.

Arthur, John.  Realists at Work.  New York:  Watson-Guptill
        Publications, 1983.

Gardner, John.  "When Is a Painting Finished?"  Art News 84, no. 9
        (November 1985):  91-92.

Gill, Susan.  "Janet Fish."  Art News 86, no. 5 (May 1987):  148.

Henning, William T., Jr.  A Catalogue of the American Collection:
        Hunter Museum of Art.  Chattanooga, Tennessee:  Hunter Museum
        of Art, 1985:  257-258, pl. 42.

Henry, Gerrit.  "Fresh Flowerings, Janet Fish Brings New Life to
        Watercolor Still Life."  Art Today (Winter 1987-88):  34-37.

_____.  Janet Fish.  Geneva and New York:  Burton Skira and Co.,
        Ltd., 1987.

130

Kahn, Wolf. "Autocratic and Democratic Still-Life Painting."
American Artist 50, issue 523 (February 1986): 66-67.

Selections from The Frito-Lay Collection. Plano, Texas: Frito-
Lay, Inc., 1987: 40.

Smith, Heather. "Janet Fish, Marsh Gallery, University of
Richmond." New Art Examiner 15, no. 4 (December 1987): 54.


ELLEN THAYER FISHER (1847-1911)    Painter

American Cornucopia. Catalogue by John V. Brindle and Sally
Secrist. Introduction by William H. Gerdts. Pittsburgh:
Carnegie-Mellon University, 1976, p. 10.

McClinton, Katherine M. The Chromolithographs of Louis Prang. New
York: Crown, 1973.

Marlor, Clark S. "Ellen Thayer Fisher: Abbott's Sister." Journal
of Long Island History 12 (Fall 1975): 34-35.


LOUISE FISHMAN (1939-    )    Painter

Feinberg, Jean E. "Louise Fishman: New Paintings." Arts Magazine
54, no. 3 (November 1979): 105-107.

Fortieth Biennial Exhibition of Contemporary American Painting.
Washington, D.C.: Corcoran Gallery of Art, 1987.

Lancaster, Christa. "Louise Fishman." Arts Magazine 56, no. 9
(May 1982): 25.

Langlykke, Peter. Six Painters. Yonkers, New York: Hudson River
Museum, 1983.

McFadden, Sarah. "Expressionism Today: An Artists' Symposium."
Art in America 70, no. 11 (December 1982): 66.

1987 Biennial Exhibition. New York: Whitney Museum of American
Art, 1987.

Parke, Addison. "Louise Fishman." Arts Magazine 55, no. 4
(December 1980): 7.

Smith, Roberta. "Louise Fishman." The New York Times, 31 October
1986.

Storr, Robert. "Louise Fishman at Baskerville and Watson." Art in
America 73, no. 2 (February 1985): 139, 140-41.

GERTRUDE FISKE (1878-1961)    Painter

See volume 1 of this book.

Archives of American Art.  Collection of Exhibition Catalogues.
    Boston:  G.K.  Hall and Co., 1979.

Artists By Themselves.  New York:  National Academy of Design,
    1983.

Fairbrother, Trevor J.  The Bostonians, Painters of an Elegant Age,
    1870-1930.  Boston:  Museum of Fine Arts, 1986.

Gammell, R.H. Ives.  The Boston Painters 1900-1930.  Orleans,
    Massachusetts:  Parnassus Imprints, 1986.

Gertrude Fiske:  American Impressionist, 1878-1961.  Columbia,
    South Carolina:  Columbia Museum of Art, 1975.

Gertrude Fiske (1878-1928).  Boston:  Vose Galleries, 1987.

Gertrude Fiske Oil Paintngs, 1910-1928.  New York:  Robert
    Schoelkopf Gallery, 1969.

Mechlin, Leila.  "The Art of Today at Pittsburgh."  The American
    Magazine of Art 20, no. 12 (December 1929):  667.

Moore, Julia.  History of the Detroit Society of Women Painters and
    Sculptors, 1903-53.  River Rouge, Michigan:  Victory Printing
    Co., 1953.

Pierce, Patricia Jobe.  Edmund C.  Tarbell and the Boston School of
    Painting, 1889-1980.  Hingham, Massachusetts:  Pierce
    Galleries, 1980.

Women Pioneers in Maine Art 1900-1945.  Portland, Maine:  Joan
    Whitney Payson Gallery of Art, Westbrook College, 1985.


AUDREY FLACK (1931-    )    Painter

See volume 1 of this book.

Audrey Flack on Painting.  New York:  Harry N. Abrams, Inc., 1981.

Bass, Ruth.  "Audrey Flack."  Art News 83, no. 1 (January 1984):
    149.

Englehardt, Nina.  "Audrey Flack Portrays Man of the Year."  Women
    Artists News 3, no. 8 (February 1978).

Flack, Audrey.  Art and Soul.  New York:  E.P. Dutton, 1986.

Glueck, Grace. "The 20th Century Artists Most Admired by Other Artists." Art News 76, no. 9 (November 1977): 84.

Gouma-Peterson, Thalia. "Icons of Healing Energy: The Recent Work of Audrey Flack." Arts Magazine 58, no. 3 (November 1983): 136-141 and cover.

Henry, Gerrit. "Audrey Flack at Meisel." Art in America 72, no. 4 (April 1984): 184, 186.

Hills, Patricia, and Tarbell, Roberta K. The Figurative Tradition and the Whitney Museum of American Art: Paintings and Sculpture from the Permanent Collection. New York: Whitney Museum of American Art, 1980.

"Man of the Year." Time, 1 January 1978, cover.

National Museum of Women in the Arts. New York: Harry N. Abrams, Inc., 1987: 104-105.

Nemser, Cindy. "Conversation with Audrey Flack." Arts Magazine 48, no. 5 (February 1974): 34-37.

Raynor, Vivien. "Audrey Flack." The New York Times, 14 April 1978: C22.

Russo, Alexander. Profiles on Women Artists. Frederick, Maryland: University Publications of America, 1985.

Slatkin, Wendy. Women Artists in History from Antiquity to the 20th Century. Englewood Cliffs, New Jersey: Prentice-Hall, Inc., 1985.

Super-Realism from the Morton G. Neumann Family Collection. Kalamazoo, Michigan: Kalamazoo Institute of Arts, 1981.


LILLIAN H. FLORSHEIM (1896-    )  Sculptor

Bunch, Clarence. Acrylic for Sculpture and Design. New York: Van Nostrand Reinhold, 1972.

Chicago Area Artists. Des Moines, Iowa: Des Moines Art Center, 1967.

Krantz, Claire Wolf. "Reviews Chicago: Lillian Florsheim, Fairweather Hardin Gallery." New Art Examiner 10, no. 6 (March 1983): 16.

_____. "Lillian Florsheim: A Conversation with an Independent Abstractionist." New Art Examiner 10, no. 8 (May 1983): 12, 33.

<u>Lillian H. Florsheim</u>. Chicago: Museum of Contemporary Art, 1970.

Meilach, Dona Z. <u>Creative Carving: Materials, Techniques, Appreciation</u>. Chicago: Reilly and Lee, 1969.

<u>A Selection of Abstract Art 1912-1965: Lillian H. Florsheim Foundation for the Fine Arts</u>. Saint Louis: Washington University, New Orleans: Delgado Museum of Art, and Champaign, Illinois: Krannert Art Museum, 1967.

Watson-Jones, Virginia. <u>Contemporary American Women Sculptors</u>. Phoenix: Oryx Press, 1986.

MARGARET F. FOLEY (1827-1877)   Sculptor

See volume 1 of this book.

"Another American Sculptress. Miss Margaret Foley." <u>The Revolution</u>, 4 May 1871.

"Exhibition of the Society of Female Artists." <u>The Art-Journal</u> 10 (1871): 90-91.

H., M. "Art in Rome, 1872." <u>The Art-Journal</u> (1872): 131-132.

Hanaford, Phebe A. <u>Daughters of America</u>. Augusta, Maine.: True and Co., 1882: 303.

Swan, Mabel Munson. <u>The Athenaeum Gallery, 1827-1873</u>. Boston: The Boston Athenaeum, 1940: 182.

Tufts, Eleanor. <u>American Women Artists 1830-1930</u>. Washington, D.C.: National Museum of Women in the Arts, 1987.

JEAN F. FOLLETT (1917-    )   Sculptor

See volume 1 of this book.

Hess, Thomas B., and Baker, Elizabeth C., eds. <u>Art and Sexual Politics</u>. New York: Macmillan, 1973.

Kaprow, Allan. <u>Assemblage, Environments and Happenings</u>. New York: Harry N. Abrams, 1966.

<u>Pittsburgh International Exhibition of Painting and Sculpture</u>. Pittsburgh: Museum of Art, Carnegie Institute, 1958.

<u>Recent Acquisitions</u>. New York: The Museum of Modern Art, 1961.

Sandler, Irving. The New York School: The Painters and Sculptors of the Fifties. New York: Harper and Row, 1978.

Watson-Jones, Virginia. Contemporary American Women Sculptors. Phoenix: Oryx Press, 1986.

ELIZABETH A. FREEMAN FOLSOM (1812-1899)  Miniaturist

Bolton, Theodore. Early American Portrait Painters in Miniature. New York: F.F. Sherman, 1921.

Groce, George C., and Wallace, David H. The New-York Historical Society's Dictionary of Artists in America 1564-1860. New Haven: Yale University Press, 1957.

MARY FOOTE (1872-1968)  Painter

Archives of American Art. A Checklist of the Collection. Washington, D.C.: Smithsonian Institution, 1975; 2nd ed., rev., 1977.

National Association of Portrait Painters. Portraits of Americans by Americans. New York: The New-York Historical Society, 1945: 35-36.

National Portrait Gallery. Permanent Collection, Illustrated Checklist. Washington, D.C.: Smithsonian Institution Press, 1982: 45, 70.

MARY ANNA HALLOCK FOOTE (1847-1938)  Illustrator

See volume 1 of this book (and delete Portraits of Americans by Americans--wrong Foote!)

Clement, Clara Erskine. Women in the Fine Arts. Boston: Houghton Mifflin, 1904.

Hanaford, Phebe A. Daughters of America. Augusta, Maine: True and Co., 1882: 282.

135

Rubinstein, Charlotte S.  American Women Artists.  Boston:  G.K.
     Hall, 1982.

Samuels, Peggy and Harold.  The Illustrated Biographical
     Encyclopedia of Artists of the American West.  Garden City,
     New York:  Doubleday, 1976.

Who's Who in American Art, vol. 1.  Washington, D.C.:  American
     Federation of Arts, 1935.

Woman's Who's Who of America.  New York:  The American Commonwealth
     Co., 1914.


          HELEN KATHARINE FORBES (1891-1945)   Painter

American Art Annual, vol. 28.  Washington, D.C.:  American
     Federation of Arts, 1932.

Dawdy, Doris Ostrander.  Artists of the American West, vol. 1.
     Chicago:  Swallow Press, 1974.

Kovinick, Phil.  The Woman Artist in the American West 1860-1960.
     Fullerton, Califronia:  Muckenthaler Cultural Center, 1976.

A Woman's Vision:  California Painting into the 20th Century.  San
     Francisco:  Maxwell Galleries, 1983.


          BETTY DAVENPORT FORD (1924-    )   Ceramic Sculptor

Animals We Have Known.  Riverside, California:  Riverside Art
     Center and Museum, 1984.

Audubon Artists National Exhibition.  New York:  National Arts
     Club, 1953.

"Betty Davenport Ford."  American Artist 14, no. 7, issue 137
     (September 1950):  50-51, 78.

Los Angeles and Vicinity Artists.  Los Angeles:  Los Angeles County
     Museum of Art, 1955 and 1956.

Lovoos, Janice Penney.  "Betty Davenport Ford, Ceramic Sculpture."
     American Artist 22, no. 9, issue 219 (November 1958):  34-39,
     62-63.

_____.  "Sculptor Perfects Her Art."  Christian Science Monitor, 9
     August 1954:  4.

National Invitation Exhibition. Denver: Denver Art Museum, 1953.

Selections from the American Collection. Tempe, Arizona: Arizona
    State University, 1959.

Watson-Jones, Virginia. Contemporary American Women Sculptors.
    Phoenix: Oryx Press, 1986.


                MARGARET FORD (1941-    )    Ceramic Sculptor

Harrington, LaMar. Ceramics in the Pacific Northwest: A History.
    Seattle: University of Washington Press, 1979.

"News and Retrospect: Margaret Ford." Ceramics Monthly 27, no. 8
    (October 1979): 87, 89, 91, and cover.

"News and Retrospect: Margaret Ford." Ceramics Monthly 29, no. 9
    (November 1981): 77.

Pacific Currents/Ceramics 1982. San Jose, California: San Jose
    Museum of Art, 1982.

"Portfolio: Margaret Ford." American Craft 41, no. 6 (December
    1981-January 1982): 41.

Watson-Jones, Virginia. Contemporary American Women Sculptors.
    Phoenix: Oryx Press, 1986.

Weschsler, Susan. Low-Fire Ceramics: A New Direction in American
    Clay. New York: Watson-Guptil, 1981.


                E. CHARLTON FORTUNE (1885-1969)    Painter

"Art Today and Yesterday, Dealer's Choice: Underrated Artists."
    Art Today (Winter 1987-88): 46-47.

Impressionism, The California View, Paintings 1890-1930. Oakland:
    The Oakland Museum, 1981.

Orr-Cahall, Christina. The Art of California. Selected Works from
    the Collection of Oakland Museum. Oakland, California: The
    Oakland Museum, 1984, p. 96.

Porter, Bruce, et al. Art in California: A Survey of American Art
    with Special Reference to California Painting, Sculpture and
    Architecture, Past and Present, Particularly as Those Arts
    were Represented at The Panama-Pacific International
    Exposition. San Francisco: R.L. Bernier, 1916.

Spangenberg, Helen. Yesterday's Artists on the Monterey Peninsula.
    Monterey, California: Monterey Peninsula Museum of Art, 1976.

Westphal, Ruth. <u>Plein Air Painters of California:  The North</u>.
     Irvine:  Westphal Publishing, 1986.

<u>A Woman's Vision:  California Painting into the 20th Century</u>.  San
     Francisco:  Maxwell Galleries, 1983.


          MARION LAWRENCE FOSDICK (1888-1973)   Ceramicist

<u>Contemporary American Ceramics</u>.  Syracuse:  Syracuse Museum of Fine
     Arts, 1937.

Garth, Clark.  <u>A Century of Ceramics in the United States
     1878-1978</u>.  New York:  E.P. Dutton, 1979.

Fosdick, Marion L.  "Modeled Treatment of Pottery."  <u>American
     Ceramic Society Journal</u> 9 (1926).

Norwood, John Nelson.  <u>Fifty Years of Ceramic Education at State
     College of Ceramics, Alfred</u>.  New York:  Alfred, 1950.


          HARRIET CAMPBELL FOSS (1860-1938)   Painter

<u>American Art Annual</u>, vol. 10.  Washington, D.C.:  American
     Federation of Arts, 1913.

<u>American Still-Life Painting at Kennedy Galleries</u>.  New York:
     Kennedy Galleries, 1985.

<u>Catalogue of the Sixty-Second Annual Exhibition</u>.  Philadelphia:
     Pennsylvania Academy of the Fine Arts, 1892.

Johnson, Jane, and Greutzner, A.  <u>Dictionary of British Artists,
     1880-1940</u>.  Suffolk, England:  Antique Collectors' Club, 1976.

Naylor, Maria.  <u>National Academy of Design Exhibition Record
     1861-1900</u>.  New York:  Kennedy Galleries, 1973.

Thieme, U., and Becker, F.  <u>Allegemeines Lexikon der bildenden
     Künstler von der Antike bis zur Gegenwart</u>.  Leipzig:  W.
     Englemann, 1916.

Tufts, Eleanor.  <u>American Women Artists, 1830-1930</u>.  Washington,
     D.C.:  National Museum of Women in the Arts, 1987.


          MARGARET M. TAYLOR FOX (1857; active to 1941)   Painter,
                                        Illustrator, and Etcher

<u>American Art Annual</u>, vol. 28.  Washington, D.C.:  American
     Federation of Arts, 1932.

138

Fielding, Mantle. Dictionary of American Painters, Sculptors and Engravers. Enlarged ed. Greens Farms, Connecticut: Modern Books and Crafts, 1974.

Peet, Phyllis. American Women of the Etching Revival. Atlanta: High Museum of Art, 1988.

Who's Who in American Art, vol. 3. Washington, D.C.: American Federation of Arts, 1940.

The Work of Women Etchers of America. New York: Union League Club, 1888.

FRANCES M. FOY (1890-1963)    Painter

American Art Annual, vol. 28. Washington, D.C.: American Federation of Arts, 1932.

Jacobson, J.Z. Art of Today, Chicago--1933. Chicago: L.M. Stein, 1932.

Park, Marlene, and Markowitz, Gerald E. Democratic Vistas: Post Offices and Public Art in the New Deal. Philadelphia: Temple University Press, 1984.

Who's Who in American Art, vol. 3. Washington, D.C.: American Federation of Arts, 1940.

SUSAN STUART FRACKELTON (1848-1932)    Painter of Ceramics

Butts, Porter. Art in Wisconsin. Madison: Democratic Printing, 1936.

Clark, Garth. A Century of Ceramics in the United States 1878-1978. New York: E.P. Dutton, 1979.

Clement, Clara Erskine. Women in the Fine Arts. Boston: Houghton, Mifflin, 1904.

Frackelton, S. S. Tried by Fire: A Work on China-Painting. 1885. [Enlarged, 3rd. ed. revised, New York: D. Appleton and Co., 1895.]

Obituary. American Art Annual, vol. 29. Washington, D.C.: American Federation of Arts, 1932.

Prather-Moses, Alice Irma. The International Dictionary of Women Workers in the Decorative Arts. Metuchen, New Jersey: Scarecrow Press, 1981: 58.

Who's Who in American Art, vol. 4. Washington, D.C.: American
    Federation of Arts, 1947.

Willard, Frances E., and Livermore, Mary A. American Women.
    Detroit: Gale Research Co., 1973.

Woman's Who's Who of America. New York: American Commonwealth
    Co., 1914.


                EURILDA LOOMIS FRANCE (1865-1931)  Painter

American Art Annual, vol. 1. New York: Macmillan, 1899.

Bénézit, Emmanuel. Dictionnaire critique et documentaire des
    peintres, sculpteurs, dessinateurs et graveurs de tous les
    temps et de tous les pays. New ed. Paris: Librairie Gründ,
    1976.

Champney, Elizabeth W. "Woman in Art." Quarterly Illustrator 2
    (April-June 1894): 114-15.

Obituary. American Art Annual, vol. 28. Washington, D.C.:
    American Federation of Arts, 1932.


                JANE FRANK (1918-    )  SCULPTOR

American Artists of Renown. Gilmer, Texas: Wilson, 1981.

Busch, Julia M. A Decade of Sculpture: The 1960s. Philadelphia:
    Art Alliance Press, 1974.

Jane Frank. Philadelphia: Philadelphia Art Alliance, 1975.

Stanton, Phoebe B. The Sculptural Landscape of Jane Frank.
    Cranbury, New Jersey: A.S. Barnes, 1968.

Watson-Jones, Virginia. Contemporary American Women Sculptors.
    Phoenix: Oryx Press, 1986.


                MARY FRANK (1933-    )  Sculptor

See volume 1 of this book.

Armstrong, Richard. "Mary Frank." Artforum 21, no. 9 (May 1983):
    97.

Campbell, Lawrence. "Mary Frank at Zabriskie." Art in America 75,
    no. 3 (March 1987): 139-140.

140

Clark, Garth. A Century of Ceramics in the United States 1878-1978. New York: E.P. Dutton, 1979.

Hills, Patricia, and Tarbell, Roberta K. The Figurative Tradition and the Whitney Museum of American Art: Paintings and Sculpture from the Permanent Collection. New York: Whitney Museum of American Art, 1980.

Mary Frank: Sculpture and Monoprints. New York: Zabriskie Gallery, 1979.

Moorman, Margaret. "In a Timeless World." Art News 86, no. 5 (May 1987): 90-98 and cover.

Raynor, Vivien. "Sculptural Marvels of Mary Frank." The New York Times, 16 June 1978: C1, C23.

Shepard, Ileen. Sculpture of the 80's. Essay by Lowery S. Sims. Queens, New York: Queens Museum, 1987.

HELEN FRANKENTHALER (1928-    )    Painter

See volume 1 of this book.

Carmean, E.A., Jr. Helen Frankenthaler: A Painting Retrospective. Fort Worth: The Modern Art Museum of Fort Worth in conjunction with New York: Harry N. Abrams, Inc., 1988.

Elderfield, John. Helen Frankenthaler. New York: Harry N. Abrams, Inc., 1988.

Field, Richard S. and Fine, Ruth E. A Graphic Muse. New York: Hudson Hills Press, 1987.

"Frito-Lay Collection." Horizon (October 1985): 37.

Glueck, Grace. "The 20th Century Artists Most Admired by Other Artists." Art News 76, no. 9 (November 1977): 85.

A Guide to the Collection. Houston: Museum of Fine Arts, 1981.

Helen Frankenthaler: New Paintings. New York: Andre Emmerich Gallery, 1986.

Helen Frankenthaler: Prints 1961-1979. Essay by Thomas Krens. New York: Harper and Row in association with Williams College, 1980.

Kandel, Susan, and Hayt-Atkins, Elizabeth. "Helen Frankenthaler (Andre Emmerich)." Art News 87, no. 3 (March 1988): 189-90.

National Museum of Women in the Arts.  New York:  Harry N. Abrams,
     Inc., 1987.

Russell, John.  "Profusion of Good Art by Women."  The New York
     Times, 22 February 1985:  Y17, Y22.

Seiberling, Dorothy.  "Women Painters in Ascendance."  Life, 13
     May 1957:  74-77.

Smith, Roberta.  "Helen Frankenthaler."  The New York Times, 20
     December 1987:  Y36.

Zimmer, William.  "Helen Frankenthaler--From Studio to Ballet
     Stage."  The New York Times, 17 February 1985.

          MARY JETT FRANKLIN (1842-1928)   Painter and Etcher

American Art Annual, vol. 20.  Washington, D.C.:  American
     Federation of Arts, 1923.

19th Century American Women Artists.  New York:  Whitney Museum of
     American Art, Downtown Branch, 1976.

Peet, Phyllis.  American Women of the Etching Revival.  Atlanta:
     High Museum of Art, 1988.

The Work of Women Etchers of America.  New York:  Union League
     Club, 1888.

          LAURA GARDIN FRASER (1889-1934)   Sculptor

See volume 1 of this book.

Famous Small Bronzes.  New York:  The Gorham Co., 1928.

Proske, Beatrice Gilman.  Brookgreen Gardens Sculpture, vol. II.
     Brookgreen, South Carolina:  Brookgreen Gardens Sculpture,
     1955:  162-163.

Reiter, Ed.  "The Proposed Washington Commemorative:  Is the Time
     Finally Right for Laura Gardin Fraser's Design."  The
     Numismatist, May 1981:  1192-94.

          SONDRA FRECKELTON (1936-   )   Painter

See volume 1 of this book.

Bolt, Thomas.  "Reckless, Brave, or Both:  New Paintings by Sondra
     Freckelton."  Arts Magazine 60, no. 5 (January 1986):  52-53.

142

Field, Richard S., and Fine, Ruth E. A Graphic Muse. New York: Hudson Hills Press, 1987.

Freckelton, Sondra. "The Watercolor Page." American Artist 47, no. 492 (July 1983): 42-47, 97-98 and cover.

Freckelton, Sondra, and Doherty, M. Stephen. Dynamic Still Lifes in Watercolor. New York: Watson-Guptill, 1982.

Martin, Alvin. American Realism, 20th-Century Drawings and Watercolors From the Glenn C. Janss Collection. San Francisco: San Francisco Museum of Modern Art, 1985.

Mecklenburg, Virginia M. Modern American Realism: The Sara Roby Foundation Collection. Washington, D.C.: National Museum of American Art, 1987.


FLORENCE FREEMAN (1836-1876)    Sculptor

See volume 1 of this book.

Fielding, Mantle. Dictionary of American Painters, Sculptors and Engravers. Enlarged ed. Greens Farms, Connecticut: Modern Books and Crafts, 1974.

Rubinstein, Charlotte Streifer. American Women Artists. Boston: G. K. Hall, 1982.


JANE FREILICHER (1924-    )    Painter

See volume 1 of this book.

Berrigan, Ted. "Painter to the New York Poets." Art News 64 (November 1965): 44-47, 71-72.

Brenson, Michael. "Jane Freilicher Casts Her Landscape in a Special Light." The New York Times, 21 September 1986: Arts and Leisure Section, pp. 31, 34

Field, Richard S., and Fine, Ruth E. A Graphic Muse. New York: Hudson Hills Press, 1987.

Glueck, Grace. "Jane Freilicher." The New York Times, 11 March 1983.

Henry, Gerrit. "Jane Freilicher and the Real Thing." Art News 84, no. 1 (Janurary 1985): 78-83.

Hoelterhoff, Manuela. "Serious Painter in a Vanishing Landscape." The Wall Street Journal, 27 September 1983.

143

Jane Freilicher Paintings. Robert Doty, ed.  New York:  Taplinger
      Publishing Co., 1986.

Mathews, Margaret.  "Jane Freilicher."  American Artist 47 (March
      1983):  32-37.

Realism Now.  Poughkeepsie, New York:  Vassar College Art Gallery,
      1968.

Russell, John.  "Urban and Rural Vistas from Jane Freilicher."
      The New York Times, 8 April 1988:  Y16.

Russo, Alexander.  Profiles on Women Artists.  Frederick, Maryland:
      University Publications of America, 1985.

Stevens, Mark.  "Revival of Realism" Newsweek, 7 June 1982:
      66-67.


                VIOLA FREY (1933-   )   Ceramic Sculptor

Annual Ceramic National Exhibition.  Syracuse:  Everson Museum of
      Art, 1969.

Clark, Garth.  A Century of Ceramics in the United States 1878-1978.
      New York:  E.P.  Dutton, 1979.

_____.  Ceramic Art:  Comment and Review 1882-1978.  New York:
      Dutton Paperbacks, 1978.

Dunham, Judith L.  "Ceramic Bricolage:  The Protean Art of Viola
      Fey."  American Craft 41, no. 4 (August-September 1981):
      29-33.

Figurative Sculpture:  Ten Artists/Two Decades.  Long Beach:
      California State University Art Museum, 1984.

Kelly, Jeff.  "Viola Frey."  American Ceramics 3, no. 1 (Spring
      1984):  26-33 and cover.

Manhart, Marcia and Tom, eds.  The Eloquent Object.  Tulsa,
      Oklahoma:  Philbrook Museum of Art, 1987.

Roth, Moira, ed.  Connecting Conversations:  Interviews with 28 Bay
      Area Women Artists.  Oakland, California:  Eucalyptus Press,
      Mills College, 1988.

Viewpoint:  Ceramics, 1977.  El Cajon, California:  Grossmont
      College Gallery, 1977.

Viola Frey:  Paintings, Sculpture, Drawings.  San Francisco:  Quay
      Gallery, 1983.

144

Viola Frey Retrospective. Sacramento: Crocker Art Museum, 1981.

Watson-Jones, Virginia. Contemporary American Women Sculptors.
     Phoenix: Oryx Press, 1986.

Wechsler, Susan. Low-Fire Ceramics: A New Direction in American
     Clay. New York: Watson-Guptill, 1981.

Wenger, Lesley. "Viola Frey." Currant 1 (August 1975).


                NANCY FRIED (1945-   )   Sculptor

Brenson, Michael. "Nancy Fried." The New York Times, 15 March
     1986.

Cooper, Emmanuel. The Sexual Perspective. London: Routledge and
     Kegan Paul, 1986.

Heartney, Eleanor. "Nancy Fried at Graham Modern." Art in America
     76, no. 4 (April 1988):  210.

Moufarrege, Nicolas A. "Lavender: On Homosexuality and Art."
     Arts Magazine 57, no. 2 (October 1982):  81-82.


           HARRIET WHITNEY FRISHMUTH (1880-1979)   Sculptor

See volume 1 of this book.

American Art Annual, vol. 18. Washington, D.C.:  American
     Federation of Arts, 1921.

The Arts of the American Renaissance. New York:  Hirschl and Adler
     Galleries, 1985.

Famous Small Bronzes. New York:  The Gorham Co., 1928.

Henning, William T., Jr. A Catalogue of American Collection,
     Hunter Museum of Art. Chattanooga, Tennessee:  Hunter Museum
     of Art, 1985.

Obituary. Who's Who in American Art, vol. 14. Washington, D.C.:
     American Federation of Arts, 1980.

"Philadelphia's Outdoor Sculpture Show." International Studio 75,
     no. 302 (July 1922):  299.


             SARAH C. FROTHINGHAM (1821-1861)   Miniaturist

Bolton, Theodore. Early American Portrait Painters in Miniature.
     New York:  F. F. Sherman, 1921.

Clark, Eliot.  History of the National Academy of Design, 1825-
     1953.  New York:  Columbia University Press, 1954.

Fielding, Mantle.  Dictionary of American Painters, Sculptors and
     Engravers.  Enlarged ed.  Greens Farms, Connecticut:  Modern
     Books and Crafts, 1974.

Groce, George C., and Wallace, David H.  The New-York Historical
     Society's Dictionary of Artists in America 1564-1860.  New
     Haven:  Yale University Press, 1957.

LAURA ANNE FRY (1857-1943)    Ceramicist

Callen, Anthea.  Women Artists of the Arts and Crafts Movement
     1870-1914.  New York:  Pantheon Books, 1979.

Clark, Garth.  A Century of Ceramics in the United States
     1878-1978.  New York:  E.P. Dutton, 1979.

The Ladies, God Bless 'Em, The Women's Movement in Cincinnati in
     the Nineteenth Century.  Cincinnati:  Cincinnati Art Museum,
     1976.

Peck, Herbert.  The Book of Rookwood Pottery.  New York:  Crown
     Publishers, 1968.

LUCIA FAIRCHILD FULLER (1872-1924)    Painter

See volume 1 of this book.

A Circle of Friends:  Art Colonies of Cornish and Dublin.  Keene,
     New Hampshire:  Thorne-Sagendorph Art Gallery, and Durham, New
     Hampshire:  University Art Galleries, University of New
     Hampshire, 1985.

Fuller, Lucia Fairchild.  "Modern American Miniature Painters."
     Scribner's 67 (March 1920):  381-384.

Miller, Lucia.  "John Singer Sargent in the Diaries of Lucia
     Fairchild 1890 and 1891."  Archives of American Art Journal
     26, no. 4 (1986):  2-16.

Obituary.  American Art Annual, vol. 21.  Washington, D.C.:
     American Federation of Arts, 1924.

"Painters of Miniatures."  The New York Times, 2 February 1902:
     10.

Tufts, Eleanor.  American Women Artists, 1830-1930.  Washington,
     D.C.:  National Museum of Women in the Arts, 1987.

META WARRICK FULLER (1877-1968)    Sculptor

See volume 1 of this book.

Fine, Elsa Honig. The Afro-American Artist. New York:  Holt,
   Rinehart and Winston, 1973.

Harlem Renaissance:  Art of Black America. Introduction by Mary
   Schmidt Campbell. New York:  The Studio Museum in Harlem and
   Harry N. Abrams, Inc., 1987.

Kennedy, Harriet Forte. An Independent Woman:  The Life and Art of
   Meta Warrick Fuller (1877-1968). Framingham, Massachusetts:
   Danforth Museum, 1985.


SARAH E. FULLER (1829-1901)    Engraver

Fuller, S. E.  A Manual of Instruction in the Art of Wood Engraving.
   Boston:  Joseph Watson, 1867.

Groce, George C., and Wallace, David H.  The New-York Historical
   Society's Dictionary of Artists in America 1564-1860. New
   Haven:  Yale Unviersity Press, 1957.


SUE FULLER (1914-    )    Sculptor

See volume 1 of this book.

Glueck, Grace.  "Women at the Whitney." The New York Times, 19
   December 1970.

Jones, Stacy.  "Artist Devises a Three Dimensional Effect." The
   New York Times, 21 June 1969.

Kay, Jane H.  "Sue Fuller's Geometric Art." Christian Science
   Monitor, 17 September 1965.

Sue Fuller, Collages, Prints, String Compositions. Washington,
   D.C.:  Corcoran Gallery of Art, 1951.

Sue Fuller:  Prints, Drawings, Watercolors, Collages, String
   Compositions. San Antonio:  Marion Koogler McNay Art
   Institute, 1967.

Taylor, Robert.  "Sue Fuller's String Plexiglass Designs--
   Experiments in Space." Boston Sunday Herald, 19 September
   1965.

Watson-Jones, Virginia.  Contemporary American Women Sculptors.
   Phoenix:  Oryx Press, 1986.

SUZI GABLIK (1934-    )    Painter

See volume 1 of this book.

Mecklenburg, Virginia M.  Modern American Realism:  The Sara Roby
    Foundation Collection.  Washington, D.C.:  National Museum of
    American Art, 1987.

Ratcliff, Carter.  "Suzi Gablik at Dintenfass."  Art in America 67,
    no. 2 (March-April 1979):  149-150.


WANDA GAG (1893-1946)    Printmaker

See volume 1 of this book.

Cary, E. L.  "Peggy Bacon and Wanda Gag, Artists."  Prints 1 (March
    1931):  13-24.

First Biennial Exhibition of Contemporary American Sculptors,
    Watercolors and Prints.  New York:  Whitney Museum of American
    Art, 1933-34.


RETHA WALDEN GAMBARO (1917-    )    Sculptor

American Artists of Renown.  Gilmer, Texas:  Wilson, 1981.

Isberg, Emily.  "The Arts:  A Gallery of Modern Indian Art."
    Washington Post, 22 June 1978:  5.

Ohoyo One Thousand:  A Resource Guide of American Indian/Alaska
    Native Women.  Wichita Falls, Texas:  The Center, 1982.

Swift, Mary.  "Profiles Portfolio of Regional Artists:  Retha
    Walden Gambaro (Washington, D.C.)."  Art Voices South 3, no. 3
    (May-June 1980):  46.

Watson-Jones, Virginia.  Contemporary American Women Sculptors.
    Phoenix:  Oryx Press, 1986.


ELIZA DRAPER GARDINER (1871-1955)    Printmaker and Painter

American Art Annual, vol. 28.  Washington, D.C.:  American
    Federation of Arts, 1932.

Obituary.  Who's Who in American Art, vol. 6.  Washington, D.C.:
    American Federation of Arts, 1956.

A Selection of American Prints.  A Selection of Biographies of
    Forty Women Artists Working Between 1904-1979.  Santa Rosa,
    California:  The Annex Galleries, 1987:  5.

ELIZABETH JANE GARDNER (1837-1922)    Painter

See Elizabeth Jane Gardner Bouguereau.


CLARA PFEIFER GARRETT (b. 1882)    Sculptor

American Art Annual, vol. 28. Washington, D.C.: American
    Federation of Arts, 1932.

Fielding, Mantle. Dictionary of American Painters, Sculptors and
    Engravers. Enlarged ed. Greens Farms, Connecticut: Modern
    Books and Crafts, 1974.

Gardner, Albert TenEyck. American Sculpture: A Catalogue of the
    Collection of the Metropolitan Museum of Art. Greenwich: new
    York Graphic Society, 1965: 146.


CARMEN LOMAS GARZA (1948-    )    Printmaker

See volume 1 of this book.

Carmen Lomas Garza: Prints and Gouaches; Margo Humphrey:
    Monotypes. San Francisco: San Francisco Museum of Modern
    Art, 1980.


FRANCES H. GEARHART (1869-1958)    Printmaker

American Art Annual, vol. 28. Washington, D.C.: American
    Federation of Arts, 1932.

Fielding, Mantle. Dictionary of American Painters, Sculptors and
    Engravers. Enlarged ed. Greens Farms, Connecticut: Modern
    Books and Crafts, 1974.

Moure, Nancy D. Dictionary of Artists in Southern California
    Before 1950. Los Angeles: Dustin Publications, 1975.

A Selection of American Prints. A Selection of Biographies of
    Forty Women Artists Working Between 1904-1979. Santa Rosa,
    California: The Annex Galleries, 1987: 5.

Who's Who in American Art, vol. 3. Washington, D.C.: American
    Federation of Arts, 1940.


MAY GEARHART (1872-1951)    Etcher

American Art Annual, vol. 28. Washington, D.C.: American
    Federation of Arts, 1932.

Gearhart, May.  Sketches of a Late Etcher:  By and of May Gearhart.
     Chicago:  J.D. Schneider, 1939.

Moure, Nancy D.  Dictionary of Artists in Southern California
     Before 1950.  Los Angeles:  Dustin Publications, 1975.

Obituary.  Who's Who in American Art, vol. 5.  Washington, D.C.:
     American Federation of Arts, 1953.

A Selection of American Prints.  A Selection of Biographies of
     Forty Women Artists Working Between 1904-1979.  Santa Rosa,
     California:  The Annex Galleries, 1987:  6.


                    SONIA GECHTOFF (1926-     )   Painter

See volume 1 of this book.

Henry, Gerrit.  "Sonia Gechtoff [at Gruenebaum]."  Art News 86, no.
     10 (December 1987):  152.

Painting and Sculpture in California:  The Modern Era.  San
     Francisco:  San Francisco Museum of Art, 1976.

Sonia Gechtoff.  Essay by James R. Mellow.  New York:  Gruenebaum
     Gallery, 1980.

Younger American Painters.  New York:  Solomon R. Guggenheim
     Museum, 1954.


                    LILLIAN GENTH (1876-1953)   Painter

See volume 1 of this book.

American Art Annual, vol. 28.  Washington, D.C.:  American
     Federation of Arts, 1932.

Genth, Lillian.  "A Painting Trip in North Africa."  American
     Magazine of Art 28 (May 1927):  227-37.

Obituary.  Who's Who in American Art, vol. 6.  Washington, D.C.:
     American Federation of Arts, 1956.

Philadelphia Portraiture:  1740-1910.  Philadelphia:  Frank S.
     Schwarz and Son, 1982.

Sherman, Frederic Fairchild.  Landscape and Figure Painters of
     America.  New York:  priv. printed, 1917:  43-47.

Visages:  Persistence in Portraiture.  Fresno, California:  Fresno
     Metropolitan Museum, 1984.

EUGENIE GERSHOY (1902-    )    Sculptor

See volume 1 of this book.

First Biennial Exhibition of Contemporary American Sculpture,
    Watercolors and Prints.   New York:   Whitney Museum of American
    Art, 1933-34:   nos. 18,65, and 204.

Gardner, Albert TenEyck.  American Sculpture.  A Catalogue of the
    Collection of the Metropolitan Museum of Art.  Greenwich:  New
    York Graphic Society, 1965.

Woodstock's Art Heritage:  The Permanent Collection of the
    Woodstock Artists Association.  Essay by Tom Wolf.  Woodstock,
    New York:  Overlook Press, 1987.


EDITH LORING PEIRCE GETCHELL (1855-1940)   Etcher

American Art Annual, vol. 20.  Washington, D.C.:   American
    Federation of Arts, 1923.

"Another Exhibition of Etchings by Peirce and Dillaye at Williams &
    Everett's Gallery on Boylston Street."  The Art Interchange
    32 (16 January 1886):  6.

Exhibition of Etchings by Edith Loring Getchell. . . .   Worcester,
    Massachusetts:  Worcester Art Museum, 1908.

Fielding, Mantle.  Dictionary of American Painters, Sculptors and
    Engravers.  Enlarged ed.  Greens Farms, Connecticut:  Modern
    Books and Crafts, 1974.

Obituary.  The New York Times, 19 September 1940:   23.

Peet, Phyllis.  American Women of the Etching Revival.  Atlanta:
    High Museum of Art, 1988.

The Work of Women Etchers of America.  New York:  Union League
    Club, 1888.


JILL GIEGERICH (1952-    )    Painter

Brown, Betty Ann.  "Quotation, Illusion and Construction."
    Artweek 18, no. 14 (11 April 1984):  3.

Cotter, Holland.  "Eight Artists Interviewed."  Art in America 75,
    no. 5 (May 1987):  170-171.

Drohojowska, Hunter.  "Artists the Critics are Watching:  Los
    Angeles."  Art News 83, no. 9 (November 1984):  89-90.

Larsen, Susan C. "First Newport Biennial." Art News 84, no. 2 (February 1985): 111.

1985 Biennial. New York: Whitney Museum of American Art, 1985.

Princenthal, Nancy. "Jill Giegerich at David McKee." Art in America 75, no. 2 (February 1987): 146-47.

Singerman, Howard. "Los Angeles. Jill Giegerich." Artforum 22, no. 3 (November 1983): 85.

Wortz, Melinda. "Los Angeles. Jill Giegerich." Art News 82, no. 10 (December 1983): 117-18.

FRANCES ELLIOT GIFFORD (b. 1844)    Painter

American Art Annual, vol. 12. Washington, D.C.: American Federation of Arts, 1915.

Benjamin, S.G.W. Our American Artists. Boston, 1879. Reprint. New York: Garland Publishing, 1977.

Fielding, Mantle. Dictionary of American Painters, Sculptors and Engravers. Enlarged ed. Greens Farms, Connecticut: Modern Books and Crafts, 1974.

RUTH GIKOW (1915-1982)    Painter

See volume 1 of this book.

Ruth Gikow. New York: Kennedy Galleries, 1979.

Who's Who in American Art. New York: R.R. Bowker Co., 1978.

HELENA DE KAY GILDER (1848-1916)    Painter

See volume 1 of this book.

Clement, Clara Erskine. Women in the Fine Arts. Boston: Houghton, Mifflin and Co., 1904 (under De Kay).

19th Century American Women Artists. New York: Whitney Museum of American Art Downtown Branch, 1976.

DOROTHY GILLESPIE (1920-    )    Painter

See volume 1 of this book.

Breuning, Margaret. "Dorothy Gillespie." Arts Magazine 35, no. 1
     (October 1960): 57.

Dorothy Gillesplie. Fort Wayne, Indiana: Fort Wayne Museum of the
     Arts, 1979.

Martin, Richard. "Dorothy Gillespie." Arts Magazine 61, no. 2
     (October 1986): 107.

Pomphret, Margaret. "Dorothy Gillespie." Arts Magazine 52, no. 5
     (January 1978): 34.

Shirey, David L. "Dorothy Gillespie." Arts Magazine 52, no. 3
     (November 1977): 23.

Six South Florida Abstract Artists. Coral Gables: Lowe Museum,
     University of Miami, 1960.

Watson-Jones, Virginia. Contemporary American Women Sculptors.
     Phoenix: Oryx Press, 1986.

Weinstein, Ann. "Dorothy Gillespie." Arts Magazine 54, no. 2
     (October 1979): 17.

LAURA GILPIN (1891-1979)    Photographer

See volume 1 of this book.

Sandweiss, Martha A. Laura Gilpin: An Enduring Grace. Fort
     Worth: Amon Carter Museum, 1986.

_____. "Laura Gilpin and the Tradition of American Landscape
     Photography." The Desert Is No Lady, ed. by Vera Norwood and
     Janice Monk. New Haven: Yale University Press, 1987: 62-73.

LINNEA GLATT (1949-    )    Sculptor

Carlozzi, Annette. 50 Texas Artists. San Francisco: Chronicle
     Books, 1986.

Fire: One Hundred Texas Artists. Houston: Contemporary Arts
     Museum, 1979.

Fifth Texas Sculpture Symposium. Dallas: Connemara Conservancy,
     1985.

Freudenheim, Susan. "Art: Linnea Glatt's Sculpted Sanctuaries."
     Texas Homes 8, no. 6 (June 1984): 22-23, 25.

Hickey, Dave. "Linnea Glatt and Patricia Tillman: Post-Modern Options." Artspace 9, no. 3 (Summer 1985): 28-31.

Moore, Sylvia, ed. No Bluebonnets, No Yellow Roses: Essays on Texas Women in the Arts. New York: Midmarch Arts Press, 1988.

Raczka, Robert. "Linnea Glatt." Artspace 5, no. 3 (Summer 1981): 21-23.

Watson-Jones, Virginia. Contemporary American Women Sculptors. Phoenix: Oryx Press, 1986.

ANNA GLENNY (1888-    )   Sculptor

American Art Annual, vol. 12. Washington, D.C.: American Federation of Arts, 1932.

Devree, Howard. "Art and Democracy." Magazine of Art 32 (May 1939): 262-70.

First Biennial Exhibition of Contemporary American Sculpture, Watercolors and Prints. New York: Whitney Museum of American Art, 1933-34, no. 12.

Read, Helen A. "Portraits in Sculpture." Vogue 77, (1 February 1931): 36-37, 94.

Who's Who in American Art, vol. 3. Washington, D.C.: American Federation of Arts, 1940.

JUDITH WHITNEY GODWIN (1930-    )   Painter

Cohen, Ronny. "Judith Godwin." Art News 84, no. 2 (February 1985): 156.

Edgar, Natalie. "Judith Godwin." Arts Magazine 55, no. 10 (June 1981): 14.

Henry, Gerrit. "Judith Godwin (at Ingber)." Art News 79, no. 3 (March 1980): 196.

Nadelman, Cynthia. "Judith Godwin." Art News 80, no. 7 (September 1981): 242.

Who's Who in American Art. New York: R.R. Bowker, 1978.

154

BETTY GOLD (1935-    )    Sculptor

Ball, Maudette.  "Angles and Curves in Steel."  Artweek 11, no. 30
    (20 September 1980):  5.

Brown, Betty Ann.  "Harmonies of Duality."  Artweek 15, no. 7 (18
    February 1984):  5.

Watson-Jones, Virginia.  Contemporary American Women Sculptors.
    Phoenix:  Oryx Press, 1986.

Wortz, Melinda.  "Los Angeles:  Is There Any Way Out?"  Art News
    78, no. 6 (Summer 1979):  158, 160.


SHARON GOLD (1949-    )    Painter

Bell, Tiffany.  "Sharon Gold."  Arts Magazine 52, no. 4 (December
    1977):  36.

Cardozo, Judth Lopes.  "Sharon Gold, O.K. Harris."  Artforum 16,
    no. 4 (December 1977):  68-70.

Kuspit, Donald B.  "Existential Formalism; the Case of Sharon
    Gold."  Artforum 17, no. 7 (March 1979):  38-40.

Lieb, Vered.  "An Interview with Sharon Gold."  Arts Magazine 55,
    no. 9 (May 1981):  106-107.

Loughery, John.  "Three Aspects of Abstraction."  Arts Magazine 60,
    no. 8 (April 1986):  130.

Masheck, Joseph.  "Hard-Core Painting."  Artforum 16, no. 8 (April
    1978):  46-55.

Schwartz, Ellen.  "Sharon Gold (O.K. Harris)."  Art News 76, no. 9
    (November 1977):  261.

Stavitsky, Gail.  "Three Aspects of Abstraction."  Arts Magazine
    60, no. 8 (April 1986):  112.

Tatransky, Valentin.  "Sharon Gold."  Arts Magazine 53, no. 3
    (November 1978):  4.

Vernet, Gwynne.  "Drawing Invitational 1981."  Arts Magazine 56,
    no. 6 (February 1982):  25.

Westfall, Stephen.  "Sharon Gold at Stephen Rosenberg."  Art in
    America 76, no. 1 (January 1988):  139.

_____.  "The World Again:  Sharon Gold's New Paintings."  Arts
    Magazine 60, no. 5 (January 1986):  49-51.

Zimmer, William. "Sharon Gold." Arts Magazine 58, no. 10 (June
    1984): 6.


NAN GOLDIN (1953-    )   Photographer

Chabroudi, Martha. "Twelve Photographers Look at Us." Bulletin,
    Philadelphia Museum of Art 83, nos. 354-55 (Spring 1987):  6,
    16, and 17.

Goldin, Nan. The Ballad of Sexual Dependency. New York:
    Aperture Foundation, 1986.

Grundberg, Andy. "Nany Goldin's Bleak Diary of the Urban
    Subculture." The New York Times, 21 December 1986, Arts &
    Leisure Section:  33, 35.

Heartney, Eleanor. "Nan Goldin." Art News 86, no. 4 (April 1987):
    177, 179.

Holborn, Mark. "Nan Goldin's Ballad of Sexual Dependency."
    Aperture 103 (Summer 1986):  38-47.

Howell, John. "The Ballad of Sexual Dependency." Artforum 25, no.
    2 (October 1986):  8-10.

Kozloff, Max. "Photography. The Family of Nan." Art in America
    75, no. 11 (November 1987):  38-39, 41, and 43.

Liebmann, Lisa. "At the Whitney Biennial." Artforum 23, no. 10
    (Summer 1985):  61.

1985 Biennial. New York:  Whitney Museum of American Art, 1985.

Zelevansky, Lynn. "Innocence and Sophistication." Art News 83, no.
    8 (October 1984):  183, 185.


DEBORAH GOLDSMITH (1808-1836)   Painter

See volume 1 of this book.

Archives of American Art. A Checklist of the Collection.
    Washington, D.C.:  Smithsonian Institution, 1975.

Peterson, Karen, and Wilson, J.J. Women Artists. New York:
    Harper Colophon, 1976.

156

ANNE GOLDTHWAITE (1869-1944)    Painter

See volume 1 of this book.

American Art Annual, vol. 28.  Washington, D.C.:  American
    Federation of Arts, 1932.

Breeskin, Adelyn D.  Anne Goldthwaite.  A Catalogue Raisonné of the
    Graphic Work.  Montgomery, Alabama:  Montgomery Museum of Fine
    Arts, 1982.

Bundy, David S.  Painting in the South:  1564-1980.  Richmond,
    Virginia:  Virginia Museum, 1983:  291.

Chambers, Bruce W.  Art and Artists of the South:  The Robert P.
    Coggins Collection.  Columbia:  University of South Carolina
    Press, 1984:  124-25.

Eight Southern Women.  Greenville, South Carolina:  Greenville
    County Museum of Art, 1986.

First Biennial Exhibition of Contemporary American Sculpture,
    Watercolors and Prints.  New York:  Whitney Museum of American
    Art, 1933-34.

Gibbs, Josephine.  "Full-Dress Memorial for Anne Goldthwaite."
    Art Digest 19, no. 1 (1 October 1944):  10.

The Phillips Collection, A Summary Catalogue.  Washington, D.C.:
    The Phillips Collection, 1985.

Second Biennial Exhibition of Contemporary American Painting.  New
    York:  Whitney Museum of American Art, 1934:  no. 148.

The Springfield Museum of Fine Arts Handbook.  Springfield,
    Massachusetts:  Museum of Fine Arts, 1948:  45.

Wolf, Amy J.  New York Society of Women Artists 1925.  New York:
    ACA Galleries, 1987.


PATRICIA GONZALEZ (1958-    )  Painter

Beardsley, John, and Livingston, Jane.  Hispanic Art in the United
    States.  Houston:  Museum of Fine Arts, and New York:
    Abbeville Press, 1987.

Chulas Froneras:  An Exhibition of Contemporary Texas Hispanic Art.
    Houston:  The Midtown Art Center, 1986.

Everigham, Carol.  "Critic's Choice."  Houston Post, 30 March 1984:
    15D.

Fallon, Gretchen. "Artistic License." Houston Homes and Gardens 6
        (August 1984):  46, 105.

The 1985 Show:  Self Images. Houston:  Women's Caucus for Art,
        1985.


                ELIZA GOODRIDGE (1798-1882)   Miniaturist

Dresser, Louisa. "Portraits Owned by the American Antiquarian
        Society." Antiques 96 (November 1969):  725-26.

Gerdts, William H. Women Artists of America 1707-1964. Newark:
        Newark Museum, 1965.

Groce, George C., and Wallace, David H. The New-York Historical
        Society's Dictionary of Artists in America 1564-1860. New
        Haven:  Yale University Press, 1957.


                SARAH GOODRIDGE (1778-1853)   Miniaturist

See volume 1 of this book.

Dods, Agnes M. "Sarah Goodridge." Antiques 51 (May 1947):
        328-29.

Swan, Mabel Munson. The Athenaeum Gallery 1827-1873. Boston:  The
        Boston Athenaeum, 1940.

Tufts, Eleanor. American Women Artists, 1830-1930. Washington,
        D.C.:  National Museum of Women in the Arts, 1987.

Wharton, Anne Hollingsworth. Heirlooms in Miniature.
        Philadelphia:  J.B. Lippincott Co., 1898.


                BELLE GOODWIN (d. 1928)   Painter

American Still Lifes of the Nineteenth Century. New York:  Hirschl
        and Adler Galleries, 1971.

Fine 19th and 20th Century American and European Paintings.  Los
        Angeles:  Sotheby's, 17 and 18 November 1980, Lot 275.

Obituary. The New York Times, 17 August 1928:  19.


                SHIRLEY GORELICK (1924-    )   Painter

See volume 1 of this book.

158

Lubell, Ellen. "Shirley Gorelick." Arts Magazine 49, no. 10 (June 1976): 18-19.

Who's Who in American Art, 17th ed. New York: R.R. Bowker Co., 1986.


APRIL GORNIK (1953-    )    Painter

Cecil, Sarah. "April Gornik." Art News 84, no. 3 (March 1985): 144.

Cohrs, Timothy. "Hudson River Editions, Pelavin Editions--A Report Back from the Other-World of Printmaking." Arts Magazine 61, no. 3 (November 1986): 41-43.

Fisher, Jean. "April Gornik, Edward Thorp Gallery." Artforum 23, no. 7 (March 1985): 96.

Grimes, Nancy. "April Gornik (at Edward Thorp)." Art in America 87, no. 1 (January 1988): 153-54.

Parks, Addison. "April Gornik." Arts Magazine 60, no. 10 (June 1986): 116.

Pincus-Witten, Robert. "Entries--Analytical Pubism." Arts Magazine 59, no. 6 (February 1985): 89.

Selections from The Frito-Lay Collection. Plano, Texas: Frito-Lay, Inc., 1987: 30.

Sources of Light, Contemporary American Luminism. Seattle: Henry Art Gallery, University of Washington, [1953].

Westfall, Stephen. "April Gornik at Edward Thorp." Art in America 74, no. 10 (October 1986): 168.


FLORENCE WOLF GOTTHOLD (MRS. FREDERICK) (1858-1930)    Painter

Clark, Edna. Ohio Art and Artists. Richmond, Virginia: Garrett and Massie, 1932.

Cosentino, Andrew J., and Glassie, Henry H. The Capital Image, Painters in Washington, 1800-1915. Washington, D.C.: National Museum of American Art, Smithsonian, 1983.

Fielding, Mantle. Dictionary of American Painters, Sculptors and Engravers. Enlarged ed. Greens Farms, Connecticut: Modern Books and Crafts, 1974.

LORRIE GOULET (1925-    )    Sculptor

The American Tradition of Realism, Part II:  Painting and Sculpture
    of the 20th Century.  New York:  Kennedy Galleries, 1983.

Annual Exhibition.  New York:  National Academy of Design, 1966,
    1975, and 1977.

Annual Exhibition:  Contemporary American Sculpture, Watercolors
    and Drawings.  New York:  Whitney Museum of American Art,
    1948, 1949, 1950, 1953, 1955.

Annual Exhibition of Painting and Sculpture.  Philadelphia:
    Pennsylvania Academy of the Fine Arts, 1950-1962.

Audubon Artists Annual Exhibition.  New York:  National Arts Club,
    1967.

Collector's Choice.  Tulsa, Oklahoma:  Philbrook Art Center, 1964.

Eliscu, Frank.  Slate and Soft Stone Sculpture.  Philadelphia:
    Chilton, 1972.

Fifteenth Annual New England Exhibition.  New Cannan, Connecticut:
    Silvermine Guild of Artists, 1964.

Fort, Elene Susan.  "Lorrie Goulet."  Arts Magazine 55, no. 3
    (November 1980):   25-26.

Lorrie Goulet.  New York:  Sculpture Center, 1955.

Lorrie Goulet:  Sculpture.  New York:  Kennedy Galleries, 1971.

Lunde, Karl.  "Lorrie Goulet:  Themes of Woman."  Arts Magazine 50,
    no. 1 (September 1975):   82-83.

Mother and Child in Modern Art.  New York:  American Federation of
    Arts, 1963.

Recent Sculpture by Lorrie Goulet.  New York:  Kennedy Galleries,
    1973.

Sculptors Guild Annual Exhibition.  New York:  Lever House,
    1959-1974.

Sculpture:  Lorrie Goulet.  New York:  Sculptor's Gallery, Clay
    Club Sculpture Center, [1948].

Second Biennial of American Painting and Sculpture.  Detroit:
    Detroit Institute of Arts, 1960.

160

HENRIETTA AUGUSTA GRANBERY (1829-1927)    Painter

Gerdts, William, and Burke, Russell. American Still-Life Painting.
New York: Praeger, 1971.

Groce, George C., and Wallace, David H. The New-York Historical
Society's Dictionary of Artists in America, 1564-1860. New
Haven: Yale University Press, 1957.

Naylor, Maria. The National Academy of Design Exhibition Records
1861-1900, vol. 1. New York: Kennedy Galleries, 1973.

Rutledge, Anna Wells. The Pennsylvania Academy of the Fine Arts
1807-1870, Cumulative Record of Exhibition Catalogues.
Philadelphia: American Philosophical Society, 1955.

Tufts, Eleanor. American Women Artists, 1830-1930. Washington,
D.C.: National Museum of Women in the Arts, 1987.


VIRGINIA GRANBERY (1831-1921)    Painter

See volume 1 of this book.

Huber, Christine Jones. The Pennsylvania Academy and Its Women.
Philadelphia: Pennsylvania Academy of the Fine Arts, 1974.

Naylor, Maria, ed. National Academy of Design Exhibition Record
1861-1900, vol. 1. New York: Kennedy Galleries, 1973.

Rutledge, Anne Wells. The Pennsylvania Academy of the Fine Arts
1807-1870, Cumulative Record of Exhibition Catalogues.
Philadelphia: American Philosophical Society, 1955.


ELIZABETH GRANDIN (1889-1970)    Painter

American Art Annual, vol. 28. Washington, D.C.: American
Federation of Arts, 1932.

Fielding, Mantle. Dictionary of American Painters, Sculptors and
Engravers. Enlarged ed. Greens Farms, Connecticut: Modern
Books and Crafts, 1974.

Who's Who in American Art, vol. 1. (1936-37). Washington, D.C.:
American Federation of Arts, 1935.

Wolf, Amy J. New York Society of Women Artists, 1925. New York:
ACA Galleries, 1987.

BLANCHE CHLOE GRANT (1874-1948)    Illustrator and Painter

Abkemeier, Maryann, and Robertson, Laura.  Stand Against the Wind:
    A Biographical Sketchbook of New Mexico Women.  Albuquerque:
    Wahili Enterprises, 1977.

American Art Annual, vol. 28.  Washington, D.C.:  American
    Federation of Arts, 1932.

Dawdy, Doris Ostrandor.  Artists of the American West:  A
    Biographical Dictionary, vol. 1.  Chicago:  Swallow Press,
    1974.

Samuels, Peggy and Harold.  The Illustrated Biographical
    Encyclopedia of Artists of the American West.  Garden City,
    New York:  Doubleday, 1976.

NANCY GRAVES (1940-    )    Painter and Sculptor

See volume 1 of this book.

Amaya, Mario.  "Artist's Dialogue:  A Conversation with Nancy
    Graves."  Architectural Digest 39, no. 2 (February 1982):
    146, 150-51, 154-55.

Balken, Debra Bricker.  Nancy Graves:  Paintings, Sculpture,
    Drawing 1980-1985.  Poughkeepsie, New York:  Vassar College
    Art Gallery, 1986.

Berman, Avis.  "Nancy Graves' New Age of Bronze."  Art News 85, no.
    2 (February 1986):  56-64 and cover.

Brenson, Michael.  "Sculpture by Graves at Brooklyn Museum."  The
    New York Times, 18 December 1987:  Y19, Y23.

Carmean, E. A., Jr.; Cathcart, Linda L.; Hughes, Robert; and
    Shapiro, Michael Edward.  The Sculpture of Nancy Graves:  A
    Catalogue Raisonné.  New York:  Hudson Hills Press in
    conjunction with Fort Worth, Texas:  The Fort Worth Art
    Museum, 1987.

Field, Richard S., and Fine, Ruth E.  A Graphic Muse.  New York
    Hudson Hills Press, 1987.

Frank, Elizabeth.  "Her Own Way, The Daring and Inventive
    Sculptures of Nancy Graves."  Connoisseur 216, no. 889
    (February 1986):  54-61.

Galligan, Gregory.  "Between Nature and Culture:  The Nancy Graves
    Retrospective."  Arts Magazine 62, no. 6 (February 1988):
    66-67.

162

A Guide to the Collection. Houston: Museum of Fine Arts, 1981.

Heller, Nancy G. "Casting New Light on Sculpture." Museum & Arts Washington 3, no. 2 (March-April 1987): 21-24.

Kandel, Susan, and Hayt-Atkins, Elizabeth. "Nancy Graves (Brooklyn Museum, Knoedler, Associated American Artists)." Art News 87, no. 4 (April 1988): 135.

McGuigan, Cathleen. "Forms of Fantasy." The New York Times Magazine, 6 December 1987: 62-64, 92-95, 156-158.

Nancy Graves, Sculpture and Drawing 1970-1972. Cincinnati: Contemporary Arts Center, 1972.

Nancy Graves, A Survey 1969-1980. Essay by Linda L. Cathcart. Buffalo: Albright-Knox Art Gallery, 1980.

National Museum of Women in the Arts. New York: Harry N. Abrams, Inc., 1987.

Rose, Barbara. "Two American Sculptors: Louise Bourgeois and Nancy Graves." Vogue (January 1983): 222-23.

Russell, John. "Sculpture as a High-Wire Performance." The New York Times, 29 March 1987, Arts & Leisure Section: 33, 36.

Shapiro, Michael Edward. "Nature into Sculpture: Nancy Graves and the Tradition of Direct Casting." Arts Magazine 59, no. 3 (November 1984): 111-17.

_____. "Twentieth-Century American Sculpture." The Saint Louis Art Museum Bulletin 18, no. 2 (Winter 1986): 22.

Tuchman, Phyllis. Nancy Graves: Painting and Sculpture, 1978-1982. Santa Barbara: Santa Barbara Contemporary Arts Forum, 1983.

200 Years of American Sculpture. New York: Whitney Museum of American Art, 1976.

Watson-Jones, Virginia. Contemporary American Women Sculptors. Phoenix: Oryx Press, 1986.


(ELIZABETH) ELEANOR GREATOREX (1854-1897)    Painter and Etcher

A Century of Women Artists in Cragsmoor. Cragsmoor, New York: Cragsmoor Free Public Library, 1979: 7, 15.

Koehler, S. R. "Second Annual Exhibition of the Philadelphia Society of Artists." American Art Review 2 (1881): 103-15.

Peet, Phyllis. American Women of the Etching Revival. Atlanta:
    High Museum of Art, 1988.

The Work of Women Etchers of America. New York:  Union League
    Club, 1888.

W[right], M[argaret] B[ertha].  "Eleanor and Kathleen Greatorex."
    The Art Amateur 13 (September 1885):  69-70.

"The Year's Art as Received in the Quarterly Illustrator."  The
    Quarterly Illustrator 1 (January-March 1893):  26, 107, 115,
    201, and 285.


        ELIZA PRATT GREATOREX (1819-1897)   Painter and Etcher

See volume 1 of this book.

Artists By Themselves. New York:  National Academy of Design,
    1983.

A Century of Women Artists in Cragsmoor. Cragsmoor, New York:
    Cragsmoor Free Library, 1979.

Obituary.  The New York Daily Tribune, 11 February 1897:  11.

Obituary.  Boston Transcript, 11 February 1897:  7.

Old New York from the Battery to Bloomingdale:  Etchings by Eliza
    Greatorex. New York:  G.P. Putnam's Sons, 1875.

Peet, Phyllis. American Women of the Etching Revival. Atlanta:
    High Museum of Art, 1988.


        KATHLEEN HONORA GREATOREX (1851-1913)   Painter

See volume 1 of this book.

American Art Annual, vol. 12.  Washington, D.C.:  American
    Federation of Arts, 1915.

A Century of Women Artists in Cragsmoor. Cragsmoor, New York:
    Cragsmoor Free Library, 1979.

Woman's Who's Who in America. New York:  American Commonwealth
    Co., 1914.


        ELIZABETH SHIPPEN GREEN [ELLIOTT] (1871-1954)   Illustrator

See volume 1 of this book.

164

American Art Annual, vol. 28. Washington, D.C.: American
    Federation of Arts, 1932.

The American Personality: The Artist-Illustrator of Life in the
    United States, 1860-1930. Los Angeles: The Grunwald Center
    for Graphic Arts, University of California at Los Angeles,
    1976.

Goodman, Helen. "The Plastic Club." Arts Magazine 59, no. 7
    (March 1985): 100-103.

_____. "Women Illustrators of the Golden Age of American
    Illustration." Women's Art Journal 8, no. 1 (Spring-Summer
    1987): 13-22.

Reed, Walt, ed. The Illustrator in America 1900-1960s. New York:
    Reinhold Publishing Corp., 1966: 26.

Society of Illustrators. America's Great Women Illustrators 1850-
    1950. Chadds Ford, Pennsylvania: Brandywine River Museum,
    1985.

Woman's Who's Who of America. New York: American Commonwealth
    Co., 1914.

DOROTHEA SCHWARCZ GREENBAUM (1893-1986)   Sculptor

See volume 1 of this book.

Dorothea Greenbaum: Recent Sculpture--Bronze, Stone, Terra Cotta, A
    Selection of Drawings. New York: Hirschl and Adler
    Galleries, 1967.

First Biennial Exhibition of Contemporary American Sculpture,
    Watercolors and Prints. New York: Whitney Museum of American
    Art, 1933-34.

Obituary. The New York Times, 9 April 1986: Y45.

Proske, Beatrice Gilman. Brookgreen Gardens Sculpture, vol. II.
    Brookgreen, South Carolina: Brookgreen Gardens, 1955: 170.

ETHEL GREENE (1912-    )   Painter

Abblitt, Virginia, and Wasserman, Isabelle. Ethel Greene. San
    Diego: Jewish Community Center, 1983.

Granberry, Mike. "Ethel Greene is True to her Art." Los Angeles
    Times (San Diego County edition), 27 February 1987.

Hagberg, Marilyn. "Ethel Greene's Visual Puns." Artweek 4, no. 27 (18 August 1973): 5.

_____. "The Visual Puns of Ethel Greene." San Diego Magazine (July 1970): 74-77.

Jennings, Jan. "Ethel Greene Puts Paintings in Limbo." San Diego Tribune, 27 July 1973: E4.

_____. "Surrealist Show Opens." San Diego Tribune, 3 December 1971: C4.

Kietzmann, Armin. "An Artist's Perception: The Constant of Growth." San Diego Union, 28 May 1963: C7.

Miller, Elise. "This Surrealist Painter is Stingy with Surprises." Los Angeles Times (San Diego County edition), 20 November 1978: Part II: 6.

Miller, Marlan. "Exhibitions Spotlight Two Women Artists." Phoenix Gazette, 15 January 1972: 20.


GERTRUDE GLASS GREENE (1904-1956)    Sculptor

See volume 1 of this book.

Gertrude Greene: Constructions, Collages, Paintings. Text by Linda Hyman. New York: ACA Galleries, 1981.

Van Wagner, Judy Collischan. American Abstract Artists, 50th Anniversary Celebration. Hillwood Art Gallery, Long Island University, C. W. Post Campus, 1986: 35.


MARIE ZOE GREENE-MERCIER (1911-    )    Sculptor

Biennale Internazionale d'Arte 20 Premio del Fiorino. Florence: Palazzo Strozzi, 1971.

Elgar, Frank. Greene-Mercier. Paris: Le Musée de Poche, 1978.

Engelbrecht, Lloyd C. "Marie-Zoe Greene-Mercier: The Polyplane Collages." Art International 22, no. 6 (October 1978): 21-23, 52.

Fifty-Sixth Annual Exhibition by Artists of Chicago and Vicinity. Chicago: Art Institute of Chicago, 1952.

Fifty-Eighth Annual Exhibition of American Paintings and Sculpture: Abstract and Surrealist American Art. Chicago: Art Institute of Chicago, 1947.

Greene-Mercier, Marie Zoe. "The Role of Materials in my Geometric and Abstract Sculpture: A Memoir." Leonardo 15, no. 1 (January 1982) 1-6.

Mussa, Italo. Marie Zoe Greene-Mercier. Rome: Sifra, 1968.

Redstone, Louis G., and Redstone, Ruth R. Public Art: New Directions. New York: McGraw-Hill, 1981.

63$^e$ Exposition Société des Artistes Independants. Paris: Grand Palais des Champs Elysées, 1952.

Triennale de la Sculpture Européenne. Paris: Le Jardin du Palais Royal, 1978.

Watson-Jones, Virginia. Contemporary American Women Sculptors. Phoenix: Oryx Press, 1986.

ILSE GREENSTEIN (1929-1985)    Painter

See volume 1 of this book.

Brumer, Miriam. "Central Hall: Art Outside the Metropolis." The Feminist Art Journal 2, no. 3 (Fall 1973): 18.

MARION GREENWOOD (1909-1970)    Painter

See volume 1 of this book.

Painting America. Mural Art in the New Deal Era. Essay by Janet Marqusee. New York: Midtown Galleries, 1988.

Woodstock's Art Heritage: The Permanent Collection of the Woodstock Artists Association. Essay by Tom Wolf. Woodstock, New York: Overlook Press, 1987.

Zaidenberg, Arthur, compiled by. The Art of the Artist: Theories and Techniques of Art by the Artists Themselves. New York: Crown Publisher, 1951: 106-108.

ANGELA GREGORY (1903-    )    Sculptor

Agard, Walter Raymond. The New Architectural Sculpture. New York: Oxford University Press, 1935.

Cocke, Edward J. Monumental New Orleans. Jefferson, Louisiana: Hope Publications, 1974.

McInnes, V. Ambrose. Taste and See: Louisiana Renaissance,
    Religion and the Arts. New Orleans: Louisiana Renaissance,
    1977.

National Sculpture Society. San Francisco: California Palace of
    the Legion of Honor, 1929.

One Hundred and Thirty-Third Annual Exhibition of Painting and
    Sculpture. Philadelphia: Pennsylvania Academy of the Fine
    Arts, 1938.

Rose, Al. Born in New Orleans: Notables of Two Centuries.
    Tuscaloosa, Alabama: Portals Press, 1983.

Watson-Jones, Virginia. Contemporary American Women Sculptors.
    Phoenix: Oryx Press, 1986.

MARY GRIGORIADIS (1942-    )   Painter

See volume 1 of this book.

Kozloff, Max. "Mary Grigoriadis." Artforum 13 (March 1975):
    64-65.

Marter, Joan. "Mary Grigoriadis." Arts Magazine 59, no. 3
    (November 1984): 11.

FRANCES GRIMES (1869-1963)   Sculptor

See volume 1 of this book.

American Art Annual, vol. 28. Washington, D.C.: American
    Federation of Arts, 1932.

Clark, Edna. Ohio Art and Artists. Richmond, Virginia: Garrett
    and Massie, 1932.

A Circle of Friends: Art Colonies of Cornish and Dublin. Keene,
    New Hampshire: Thorne-Sagendorph Art Gallery, and Durham, New
    Hampshire: University Art Galleries, University of New
    Hampshire, 1985.

JAN GROOVER (1943-    )   Photographer

Andre, Linda. "A Knife is a Knife." Afterimage 11, no. 3 (October
    1983): 16-17.

Cooke, Susan. "The Photography of Jan Groover." Arts Magazine 57,
    no. 10 (June 1983): 80-81.

168

Ellis, Stephen. "Jan Groover at Robert Miller." Art in America
    74, no. 7 (July 1986): 115.

Groover, Jan. "The Medium is the Use." Artforum 12, no. 3
    (November 1973): 79-80.

Grundberg, Andy. "A New Breed Challenges the Illusion of Realism."
    The New York Times, 27 December 1987, Arts and Leisure: Y35,
    Y37.

_____. "Taming Unruly Reality." The New York Times, 15 March
    1987, Arts and Leisure: 36.

Hagen, Charles. "Jan Groover, Museum of Modern Art." Artforum 25,
    no. 10 (Summer 1987): 119-20.

Jan Groover. Washington, D.C.: Corcoran Gallery of Art, 1976.

Jan Groover Photographs. Essay by Alan Tractenburg. Purchase, New
    York: Neuberger Museum, State University of New York, 1983.

Karmel, Pepe. "Jan Groover at Sonnabend." Art in America 68, no.
    5 (May 1980): 152.

Kozloff, Max. "Jan Groover: Melancholy Modernist." Art in
    America 75, no. 6 (June 1987): 144-147.

Lifson, Ben. "Jan Groover's Embrace." Aperture 85 (1981): 34-43.

_____. "Still Lifes Run Deep." The Village Voice 25, no. 7 (18
    February 1980): 115.

Macmillan Biographical Encyclopedia of Photographic Artists and
    Innovators. New York: Macmillan, 1983.

Patton, Phil. "Jan Groover, Max Protetch Gallery." Artforum 14,
    no. 8 (April 1976): 68-69.

Perrone, Jeff. "Jan Groover: Degrees of Transparency." Artforum
    17, no. 5 (January 1979): 42-43 and cover.

Pincus-Witten, Robert. "Entries." Arts Magazine 50, no. 7 (March
    1976): 9-11.

Sturman, John. "Jan Groover (at Robert Miller)." Art News 85, no.
    1 (January 1986): 131.

Walsh, George; Naylor, Colin; and Held, Michael. Contemporary
    Photographers. New York: St. Martin's Press, 1982.

Witkin, Lee D., and London, Barbara. The Photograph Collector's
    Guide. Boston: New York Graphic Society, 1979.

Wooster, Ann-Sargent. "Jan Groover at the Neuberger Museum." Art in America 71, no. 11 (December 1983): 151-52.

Zucker, Barbara. "Jan Groover." Art News 75, no. 4 (April 1976): 118.


NANCY GROSSMAN (1940-    )    Sculptor

See volume 1 of this book.

A Celebration of American Women Artists, Part II: the Recent Generation. New York: Sidney Janis Gallery, 1984.

Kuspit, Donald B. "Nancy Grossman (Terry Dintenfass)." Artforum 23, no. 4 (December 1984): 85-86.

Mecklenburg, Virginia M. Modern American Realism: the Sara Roby Foundation Collection. Washington, D.C.: National Museum of American Art, 1987.

1968 Annual Exhibition: Contemporary American Sculpture. New York: Whitney Museum of American Art, 1968.

Painting and Sculpture Today 1974. Indianapolis: Indianapolis Museum of Art, 1974.

Watson-Jones, Virginia. Contemporary American Women Sculptors. Phoenix: Oryx Press, 1986.


AARONEL deROY GRUBER (1928-    )    Sculptor

Associated Artists of Pittsburgh Annual Exhibition. Pittsburgh: Carnegie Institute Museum of Art, 1958-1985.

Creative America: Forty-five Sculptors. Tokyo: American Art Center; Hong Kong: Hong Kong Museum of Art, 1973.

Curran, Ann. "Six Sculptors." Carnegie-Mellon Magazine 1, no. 1 (September 1982): 6, 12, 15-16.

Evert, Marilyn, and Gay, Vernon. Discovering Pittsburgh's Sculpture. Pittsburgh: University of Pittsburgh Press, 1983.

Miller, Donald. "Aaronel deRoy Gruber." Arts Magazine 52, no. 9 (May 1978): 21.

Mogelon, Alex, and Laliberté, Norman. Art in Boxes. New York: Van Nostrand Reinhold, 1974.

A Plastic Presence-Multiples. New York: The Jewish Museum, 1969.

170

Roukes, Nicholas. Sculpture in Plastic. New York: Watson-Guptill, 1978.

Seventy-Fifth Anniversary Associated Artists of Pittsburgh Exhibition. Pittsburgh: Carnegie Institute Museum of Art, 1985.

Twenty-Five Pennsylvania Women Artists. Loretto, Pennsylvania: Southern Alleghenies Museum of Art, 1979.

Watson-Jones, Virginia. Contemporary American Women Sculptors. Phoenix: Oryx Press, 1986.


FRIDA GUGLER (1874-1966)   Painter

American Art Annual, vol. 28. Washington, D.C.: American Federation of Arts, 1932.

Archives of American Art. Collection of Exhibition Catalogues. Boston: G.K. Hall and Co., 1979.

An Exhibition of Women Students of William Merritt Chase. New York: Marbella Galleries, 1973.

The Students of William Merritt Chase. Huntington, New York: Heckscher Museum, 1973.

Who's Who in American Art, vol. 5. Washington, D.C.: American Federation of Arts, 1953.


VIRGINIA GUNTER (1928-   )   Sculptor

Allusive Illusions. Norton, Massachusetts: Watson Gallery, Wheaton College, 1979.

Boston 1978. Brockton, Massachusetts: Brockton Art Center, 1978.

Kay, Jane Holtz. "Boston: Shaped in Situ." Art News 75, no. 9 (November 1976): 106, 112-114.

Mattera, Joanne. "Throbbing Needles II." Fiberarts 7, no. 2 (March-April 1980): 71-72.

_____. "Here Today, Gone Tomorrow: The Transitory Sculpture of Virginia Gunter." Fiberarts 8, no. 2 (March-April 1981): 18-19.

Taylor, Nora E. "N.E. Arts/Entertainment: Airy Forms Float Free in Science Museum." The Christian Science Monitor, 13 April 1977: 10.

Watson-Jones, Virginia. <u>Contemporary American Women Sculptors</u>.
    Phoenix:  Oryx Press, 1986.


MARCIA HAFIF (1929-    )   Painter

See volume 1 of this book.

Hafif, Marcia.  "Getting On with Painting."  <u>Art in America</u> 69, no.
    4 (April 1981):  132-139.

<u>Marcia Hafif</u>.  La Jolla:  Museum of Contemporary Art, 1975.

Poirier, Maurice, and Necol, Jane.  "The '60s in Abstract:  13
        Statements and an Essay."  <u>Art in America</u> 71, no. 9 (October
        1983):  127-29.

Wei, Lilly.  "Talking Abstract."  <u>Art in America</u> 75, no. 7 (July
        1987):  80-97.


NANCY HAGIN (1940-    )   Painter

Brown, Pamela.  "Nancy Hagin."  <u>Arts Magazine</u> 52, no. 5 (January
        1978):  4.

Henry, Gerrit.  "Nancy Hagin at Fishchbach."  <u>Art in America</u> 75,
        no. 10 (October 1987):  185-86.

Kahn, Wolf.  "Autocratic and Democratic Still-Life Painting."
        <u>American Artist</u> 50, no. 523 (February 1986):  68-9.

Miller, Marjorie.  "Nancy Hagin."  <u>Arts Magazine</u> 57, no. 5 (January
        1983):  7.


JOHANNA K. WOODWELL HAILMAN (b. 1871)   Painter

<u>American Art Annual</u>, vol. 28.  Washington, D.C.:  American
        Federation of Arts, 1932.

Archives of American Art.  <u>Collection of Exhibition Catalogs</u>.
        Boston:  G.K. Hall and Co., 1979.

<u>An Exhibition of Paintings by Six American Women</u>.  Saint Louis:
        Saint Louis City Art Museum, 1918.

Fielding, Mantle.  <u>Dictionary of American Painters, Sculptors and
        Engravers</u>.  Enlarged ed.  Greens Farms, Connecticut:  Modern
        Books and Crafts, 1974.

"Notes."  American Magazine of Art, March 1927:  158.

Who's Who in American Art, vol. 3.  Washington, D.C.:  American
     Federation of Arts, 1940.

Women's Who's Who of America.  New York:  American Commonwealth
     Co., 1914.


               ELLEN DAY HALE (1855-1940)   Painter

See volume 1 of this book.

American Art Annual, vol. 1.  New York:  Macmillan, 1899.

Cosentino, Andrew J., and Glassie, Henry H.  The Capital Image:
     Painters in Washington, D.C., 1800-1915.  Washington, D.C.:
     National Museum of American Art, Smithsonian, 1984.

Fairbrother, Trevor J.  The Bostonians, Painters of an Elegant
     Age, 1870-1930.  Boston:  Museum of Fine Arts, 1986.

Hanaford, Phebe A.  Daughters of America.  Augusta, Maine:  True
     and Co., 1882.

National Museum of Women in the Arts.  New York:  Harry N. Abrams,
     Inc., 1987.

Peet, Phyllis.  American Women of the Etching Revival.  Atlanta:
     High Museum of Art, 1988.

Tufts, Eleanor.  American Women Artists, 1830-1930.  Washington,
     D.C.:  National Museum of Women in the Arts, 1987.


               LILIAN WESTCOTT HALE (1881-1963)   Painter

See volume 1 of this book.

American Art Annual, vol. 28.  Washington, D.C.:  American
     Federation of Arts, 1932.

Artists by Themselves.  New York:  National Academy of Design,
     1983:  138.

"Drawings by Lilian Westcott Hale."  New York Herald Tribune, 2
     February 1936.

Fairbrother, Trevor J.  The Bostonians, Painters of an Elegant Age,
     1870-1930.  Boston:  Museum of Fine Arts, 1986.

Gammell, R.H. Ives.  The Boston Painters 1900-1930.  Orleans,
     Massachusetts:  Parnassus Imprints, 1986.

Neuhaus, Eugen. The Galleries of the Exposition, A Critical
Review of the Paintings, Statuary and the Graphic Arts in the
Palace of Fine Arts at the Panama-Pacific International
Exposition. San Francisco: Paul Elder and Co., 1915.

Next to Nature. Edited by Barbara Novak and Annette Blaugrund.
New York: National Academy of Design, 1980: 185-187.

Paintings and Drawings by Lilian Wescott Hale. New York:
Arlington Galleries, 1922.

Pierce, Patricia Jobe. Edmund C. Tarbell and the Boston School of
Painting, 1889-1980. Hingham, Massachusetts: Pierce
Galleries, 1980.

Troyon, Carol. The Boston Tradition. New York: American
Federation of Arts and Museum of Fine Arts, Boston, 1980:
198-99.

Tufts, Eleanor. American Women Artists, 1830-1930. Washington,
D.C.: Museum of Women in the Arts, 1987.

SUSAN HALE (1833-1910)    Painter

See volume 1 of this book.

Archives of American Art. A Checklist of the Collection. Boston:
G.K. Hall and Co., 1979.

Fielding, Mantle. Dictionary of American Painters, Sculptors and
Engravers. Enlarged ed. Greens Farms, Connecticut: Modern
Books and Crafts, 1974.

Obituary. The New York Times, 18 September 1910.

ANNE HALL (1792-1863)    Painter

See volume 1 of this book.

Ellet, Elizabeth Fries. Women Artists in All Ages and Countries.
New York: Harper Bros., 1859.

"The Fine Arts." The Knickerbocker 5 (1835): 554.

French, H. W. Art and Artists in Connecticut. Boston: Lee and
Shepard and New York: Charles T. Dillingham, 1879: 167-68.

Hanaford, Phebe A. Daughters of America. Augusta, Maine: True
and Co., 1882: 274.

174

Obituary. The New York Times, 14 December 1863: 8.

Perkins, Robert F., Jr., and Gavin, William J., III. The Boston
Athenaeum Art Exhibition Index 1827-1874. Boston: The
Library of the Boston Athenaeum, 1980.

Tufts, Eleanor. American Women Artists, 1830-1930. Washington,
D.C.: National Museum of Women in the Arts, 1987.

Wharton, Anne Hollingsworth. Heirlooms in Miniatures.
Philadelphia: J.B. Lippincott Co., 1898.


CHENOWETH HALL (1908-    )   Sculptor

Abbott, Berenice, and Hall, Chenowith. A Portrait of Maine. New
York: Macmillan, 1968.

New England Artists. Boston: Museum of Fine Arts, 1954.

Sculptors in Maine. Portland, Maine: Portland Museum of Art,
1956.

Watson-Jones, Virginia. Contemporary American Women Sculptors.
Phoenix: Oryx Press, 1986.


LEE HALL (1934-    )   Painter

See volume 1 of this book.

Getlein, Frank. "Lee Hall." Arts Magazine 58, no. 9 (May 1984):
5.

New Works by Lee Hall. New York: Betty Parsons Gallery, 1977.


NORMA BASSETT HALL (1889/90-1957)   Printmaker

American Art Annual, vol. 28. Washington, D.C.: American
Federation of Arts, 1931.

Kovinick, Phil. The Woman Artist in the American West 1860-1960.
Fullerton, California: Muckenthaler Cultural Center, 1976.

A Selection of American Prints. A Selection of Biographies of
Forty Women Artists Working Between 1904-1979. Santa Rosa,
California: The Annex Galleries, 1987: 6.

Who's Who in American Art, vol. 2. Washington, D.C.: American
Federation of Arts, 1937.

SUSAN HALL (1943-    )    Painter

Blumberg, Mark.  "Lighting up the Night."  <u>Artweek</u> 15, no. 25 (30
     June 1984):   7.

Clarke, John R.  "Visual and Conceptual Sturctures in Susan Hall's
     Paintings."  <u>Arts Magazine</u> 54, no. 1 (September 1979):   153-57
     and cover.

Cohen, Ronny H.  "Susan Hall, Hamilton Gallery."  <u>Artforum</u> 20, no.
     1 (September 1981):   81-82.

Curtis, Cathy.  "Banality's Provocative Edge."  <u>Artweek</u> 14, no. 31
     (34 September 1983):   16.

<u>Susan Hall:  New Prints</u>.  New York:  Hal Bromm Gallery, 1978.

<u>Susan Hall, Recent Work</u>.  New York:  Whitney Museum of American
     Art, 1972.


HELEN HAMILTON (1889-1970)   Painter

Love, Richard H.  <u>Helen Hamilton (1889-1970):  An American Post-
     Impressionist</u>.  Chicago:  R.H. Love Galleries, 1986.

Penfold, Saxby Vouler.  "Little Journeys to the Homes of Silver
     Mine Artists."  <u>New Canaan Advertiser</u>, 30 November 1933.


EDITH HAMLIN (1902-    )   Painter

See volume 1 of this book.

Collins, Jim, and Opitz, Glenn S.  <u>Women Artists in America</u>.
     Poughkeepsie, New York:  Apollo, 1980.

Kovinick, Phil.  <u>The Woman Artist in the American West 1861-1960</u>.
     Fullerton, California:  Muckenthaler Cultural Center, 1976:
     28.

Roth, Moira, ed.  <u>Connecting Conversations:  Interviews with 28 Bay
     Area Women Artists</u>.  Oakland, California:  Eucalyptus Press,
     Mills College, 1988.


GENEVIEVE KARR HAMLIN (1896-    )   Sculptor

<u>American Art Annual</u>, vol. 28.  Washington, D.C.:  American
     Federation of Arts, 1932.

National Sculpture Society and California Palace of the Legion of
Honor. Contemporary American Sculpture. New York, 1929.

Who's Who in American Art, vol. 8. Washington, D.C.: American
Federation of Arts, 1962.

Wood Sculpture by Genevieve Karr Hamlin. Sherburne, New York:
Rogers Conservation Art Center and Sherburne Art Society,
n.d. (ca. 1946).


BARBARA HAMMER (1939-    )    Filmmaker

See volume 1 of this book.

Kunst mit Eigen-Sinn. Aktuelle Kunst von Frauen. Vienna and
Munich: Löcher Verlag, 1985.


HARMONY HAMMOND (1944-    )    Painter and Sculptor

See volume 1 of this book.

Coker, Gylbert. "Harmony Hammond." Arts Magazine 58, no. 8 (April
1984): 2.

Cooper, Emmanuel. The Sexual Perspective. London: Routledge and
Kegan Paul, 1986.

Fabric Into Art. Old Westbury, New York: Amelie A. Wallace
Gallery, State University of New York, 1980.

Floored. Curated by John Perreault. Greenvale, New York:
Hillwood Art Gallery, Long Island University, 1983.

Harmony Hammond: Ten Years, 1970-1980. Essay by Lucy Lippard.
Minneapolis: Women's Art Registry of Minnesota, 1981.

Henry, Gerrit. "Harmony Hammond (at Bernice Steinbaum)." Art
News 85, no. 5 (May 1986): 130-31.

International Feminist Art. The Hague: Haags Gemeentemuseum,
1980.

Langer, Sandra L. "Harmony Hammond: Strong Affections." Arts
Magazine 57, no. 6 (February 1983): 122-23.

1987 Biennial Exhibition. New York: Whitney Museum of American
Art, 1987.

Princenthal, Nancy. "Harmony Hammond at A.I.R. and Luise Ross."
Art News 83, no. 6 (Summer 1984); 185.

Ratcliff, Carter.  "Harmony Hammond."  Arts Magazine 50, no. 7
    (March 1976):  7.

Raven, Arlene.  Crossing Over:  Feminism and Art of Social Concern.
    Ann Arbor:  U.M.I. Press, 1988.

Smith, Roberta Pancoast.  "Harmony Hammond."  Artforum 12, no. 6
    (February 1974):  88.

Traditional Conflict:  A Decade of Change 1963-1973.  New York:
    Studio Museum of Harlem, 1984.

Van Wagner, Judy Collischan.  "Harmony Hammond's Painted Spirits."
    Arts Magazine 60, no. 5 (January 1986):  22-25.

Watson-Jones, Virginia.  Contemporary American Women Sculptors.
    Phoenix:  Oryx Press, 1986.

CHARLOTTE HARDING (1873-1951)    Illustrator

See Charlotte Harding Brown.


ANNA ELIZABETH HARDY (1839-1934)    Painter

See volume 1 of this book.

Simpson, Corelli C. W.  Leaflets of Artists.  Bangor, Maine:  John
    H. Bacon, 1893.

MARY ANN HARDY (1809-1887)    Painter

Catalogue of American Portraits in the New-York Historical
    Society, vol. 1.  New Haven:  Yale University Press, 1974.

Gerdts, William H.  Women Artists of America 1707-1964.  Newark:
    Newark Museum, 1965.

Groce, George C., and Wallace, David H.  The New-York Historical
    Society's Dictionary of Artists in America 1564-1860.  New
    Haven:  Yale University Press, 1957.

Simpson, Corelli C.W.  Leaflets of Artists.  Bangor, Maine:  John
    H. Bacon, 1893.

MINNA R. HARKAVY (1895-1987)    Sculptor

See volume 1 of this book.

"Minna Harkavy, 101, Sculptor and Teacher." The New York Times, 5
    August 1987:  Y14.

Who's Who in American Art. New York:  R.R. Bowker, 1978.


                MAGS HARRIES (1945-    )  Sculptor

Allara, Pamela.  "Boston:  Shedding Its Inferiority Complex."
    Art News 78, no. 9 (November 1979):  98-101, 104-05.

_____.  "Mags Harries."  Art News 82, no. 3 (March 1983):  109.

Aspects of the 70s:  Directions in Realism.  Framingham,
    Massachusetts:  Danforth Museum, 1980.

Boston 1978.  Brockton, Massachusetts:  Brockton Art Center, 1978.

Collected Visions.  Women Artists at the Bunting Institute 1961-
    1986.  Cambridge:  Radcliffe College, 1986.

Eckardt, Wolf Von.  "Design:  Toward More Livable Cities."  Time,
    2 November 1981:  108, 110.

Faxon, Alicia, and Moore, Sylvia.  Pilgrims & Pioneers.  New York:
    Midmarch Arts Press, 1987:  84, 92-93.

Fleming, Ronald Lee, and Tscharner, Renata von, with Melrod,
    George.  Place Makers:  Public Art that Tells You Where You
    Art.  New York:  Hastings House, 1981.

New England Women.  Lincoln, Massachusetts:  DeCordova and Dan
    Museum, 1975.

Stapen, Nancy.  "Mags Harries."  Art New England 3, no. 9 (November
    1982):  3.

Twenty-Fourth Annual New England Exhibition.  New Canaan,
    Connecticut:  Silvermine Guild of Artists, 1973.

Watson-Jones, Virginia.  Contemporary American Women Sculptors.
    Phoenix:  Oryx Press, 1986.

Wolkomir, Richard.  "Sculpture in the Subways?  Is There a Better
    Place for It?"  Smithsonian April 1987:  114-127.


        HELEN MAYER HARRISON  (20th Century)  Conceptual Artist

See volume 1 of this book.

Auping, Michael.  Common Ground:  Five Artists in the Florida
    Landscape.  Sarasota:  The John and Mable Ringling Museum of
    Art, 1982.

Eisenman, Stephen F.  "Helen Mayer Harrison and Newton Harrison
    (Ronald Feldman)."  Arts Magazine 57, no. 6 (February 1983):
    43-44.

Leavitt, Thomas W.  The Lagoon Cycle:  Helen Mayer Harrison/Newton
    Harrison.  Ithaca:  Herbert F. Johnson Museum of Art, Cornell
    University, 1985.

Levin, Kin.  "Helen and Newton Harrison:  New Grounds for Art."
    Arts Magazine 52, no. 6 (February 1978):  126-29.

Lippard, Lucy R.  "Gardens:  Some Metaphors for a Public Art."
    Art in America 69, no. 9 (November 1981):  148-49.

MacDonald, Scott.  "Ithaca.  Helen Mayer Harrison and Newton
    Harrison (Herbert F. Johnson Museum of Art, Cornell)."
    Artforum 24, no. 2 (October 1985):  130-31.

Stiles, Kristine.  "Helen and Newton Harrison:  Questions."
    Arts Magazine 52, no. 6 (February 1978):  131-33.

Selz, Peter.  "Helen and Newton Harrison:  Art as Survival
    Instruction."  Arts Magazine 52, no. 6 (February 1978):
    130-31.

Schoenfeld, Ann.  "Helen Mayer Harrison and Newton Harrison."
    Arts Magazine 54, no. 10 (June 1980):  8.

Who's Who in American Art.  New York:  R.R. Bowker, 1978.

Wooster, Ann-Sargent.  "Helen Mayer Harrison and Newton Harrison at
    Ronald Feldman."  Art in America 71, no. 5 (May 1983):
    163-64.

Yard, Sally.  "Shadow of the Bomb."  Arts Magazine 58, no. 8 (April
    1984):  78-79.

GRACE HARTIGAN (1922-    )    Painter

See volume 1 of this book.

Campbell, Lawrence.  "To See the World Mainly Through Art:  Grace
    Hartigan's Great Queens and Empresses (1983)."  Arts Magazine
    (January 1984):  87-89.

Cohen, Ronny.  "Grace Hartigan."  Artforum 24, no. 8 (April 1986):
    106.

Glueck, Grace.  "Art:  Gestural Approach in Grey Gallery Show."
    The New York Times, 18 January 1985.

_____. "The 20th Century Artists Most Admired by Other Artists." Art News 76, no. 9 (November 1977): 87.

Mattison, Robert S. "Grace Hartigan: Painting Her Own History." Arts Magazine 59, no. 5 (January 1985): 66-72.

New Work by Grace Hartigan. New York: Tibor de Nagy Gallery, 1959.

Russo, Alexander. Profiles on Women Artists. Frederick, Maryland: University Publications of America, 1985.

Schimmel, Paul. Action Precision: The New Direction in New York, 1955-60. Newport Beach, California: Newport Harbor Museum, 1984.

Schoenfeld, Ann. "Grace Hartigan in the Early 1950s: Some Sources, Influences, and the Avant-Garde." Arts Magazine 60, no. 1 (September 1985): 84-88.

Simkins, Alice C. American Artists '76: A Celebration. San Antonio: Marion Koogler McNay Art Institute, 1976.

Thompson, Walter. "Grace Hartigan at Gruenebaum." Art in America 76, no. 5 (May 1988): 185.

WCA Honor Awards. Boston, Massachusetts: National Women's Caucus for Art, 1987.

Westfall, Stephen. "Then and Now: Six of the New York School Look Back." Art in America 73, no. 6 (June 1985): 118-20.


JOAN HARTLEY (1892-    )  Sculptor

Fiftieth Anniversary Exhibition 1889-1939. New York: National Association of Women Painters and Sculptors, 1939.

Proske, Beatrice Gilman. Brookgreen Gardens Sculpture. Brookgreen, South Carolina: Brookgreen Gardens, 1943.

Who's Who in American Art, vol. 3. Washington, D.C.: National Federation of Arts, 1940.


CLEO HARTWIG (1911-    )  Sculptor

American Painting and Sculpture from the Collection of the Museum. Newark: Newark Museum, 1944.

Annual Exhibition. New York: National Academy of Design, 1938-1983.

181

Annual Exhibition:  Contemporary American Sculpture, Watercolors
     and Drawings.  New York:  Whitney Museum of American Art,
     1948.

Bell, Enid.  "The Compatibles:  Sculptors Hartwig and Glinsky."
     American Artist 32, no. 6, issue 316 (June 1968):  44-49, 91.

Fifty-Third Annual Exhibition of American Paintings and Sculpture.
     Chicago:  Art Institute of Chicago, 1942.

Glinsky, Vincent, and Hartwig, Cleo.  "Direct Carving in Stone."
     National Sculpture Review (Summer 1965):  23-25.

Meilach, Dona Z.  Contemporary Stone Sculpture:  Aesthetics,
     Methods, Appreciation.  New York:  Crown, 1970.

Schnier, Jacques Preston.  Sculpture in Modern America.  Berkeley:
     University of California Press, 1948.

Sculptors Guild Annual Exhibition.  New York:  Lever House,
     1948-1985.

Watson-Jones, Virginia.  Contemporary American Women Sculptors.
     Phoenix:  Oryx Press, 1986.


                    MAREN HASSINGER (1947-    )   Sculptor

Bontemps, Arna Alexander, ed.  Forever Free:  Art by African-
     American Women 1862-1980.  Normal:  Illinois State University,
     1980.

East/West:  Contemporary American Art.  Los Angeles:  Museum of
     African American Art, 1984.

Mallinson, Constance.  "Maren Hassinger:  Nature Gone Mad."
     Images and Issues 3, no. 3 (November-December 1982):  53-54.

"Maren Hassinger."  The International Review of African American
     Art 6, no. 1 (Spring 1984):  34-41.

The Media, Style and Tradition of Ten California Artists.  Los
     Angeles:  Loker Gallery, California Museum of Science and
     Industry, 1981.

Stein, Mark.  "Steel Trees 'Grow' Along Freeways."  Los Angeles
     Times, 29 November 1979, Section IX:  1, 9.

Watson-Jones, Virginia.  Contemporary American Women Sculptors.
     Phoenix:  Oryx Press, 1986.

Wilson, William.  "Art Review:  Sculpture with a Poetic Fiber."
     Los Angeles Times, 16 August 1976, Section IV: 6.

182

_____. "Of Cables and Collages in Artists' Wonderland."
Los Angeles Times, 27 May 1981, Section VI: 1.


EMILY NICHOLS HATCH (1871-1959)   Painter

American Art Annual, vol. 28.  Washington, D.C.:  American
Federation of Arts, 1932.

Archives of American Art.  Collection of Exhibition Catalogs.
Boston:  G.K. Hall and Co., 1979.

An Exhibition of Women Students of William Merritt Chase.  New
York:  Marbella Gallery, 1973.

Fiftieth Anniversary Exhibition 1889-1939:  National Association of
Women Painters and Sculptors.  New York:  American Fine Arts
Building, 1939.

Obituary.  Who's Who in American Art, vol. 8.  Washington, D.C.:
American Federation of Arts, 1962.

Pisano, Ronald G.  The Students of William Merritt Chase.
Huntington, New York:  Heckscher Museum, 1973.


MARY CUMMINGS BROWN HATCH (active 1881-1920's)   Etcher

Peet, Phyllis.  American Women of the Etching Revival.  Atlanta:
High Museum of Art, 1988.

The Work of Women Etchers of America.  New York:  Union League
Club, 1888.


MARGARET FOOTE HAWLEY (1880-1963)   Miniaturist

Fortieth Annual Exhibition.  New York:  National Association of
Women Painters and Sculptors, 1931.

Fuller, Lucia Fairchild.  "Modern American Miniature Painters."
Scribner's 67, no. 3 (March 1920):  381-384.

Lounsberry, Elizabeth.  "American Miniature Painters."  The
Mentor 4, no. 23 (15 January 1917).

"Margaret Foote Hawley, Portrait Painter, 83, Dies."  The New York
Times, 19 December 1963:  33.

Obituary.  Who's Who in American Art, vol. 9.  Washington, D.C.:
American Federation of Arts, 1966.

Portraits of Americans by Americans. New York: The New-York
    Historical Society, 1945.


                MARION CAMPBELL HAWTHORNE (1870-1945)    Painter

American Art Annual, vol. 28. Washington, D.C.: American
    Federation of Arts, 1932.

Archives of American Art. Collection of Exhibition Catalogs.
    Boston: G.K. Hall and Co., 1979.

An Exhibition of Women Students of William Merritt Chase. New
    York: Marbella Gallery, 1973.

Obituary. Who's Who in American Art, vol. 4. Washington, D.C.:
    American Federation of Arts, 1947.

Pisano, Ronald G. The Students of William Merritt Chase.
    Huntington, New York: Heckscher Museum, 1973.


                SOPHIA PEABODY HAWTHORNE (1809-1871)   Painter

Groce, George C., and Wallace, David H. The New-York Historical
    Society's Dictionary of Artists in America 1564-1860. New
    Haven: Yale University Press, 1957.

Pearson, Norman Holmes. "Sophia Amelia Peabody Hawthorne."
    Notable American Women, vol. 2. Cambridge: Belknap Press of
    Harvard University Press, 1971.

Tharp, Louise Hall. The Peabody Sisters of Salem. Boston:
    Little, Brown and Co., 1950.

Withers, Josephine. "Artistic Women and Women Artists." Art
    Journal 35, no. 4 (Summer 1976): 330-36.


                MARY BREWSTER HAZELTON (1868-1953)    Painter

American Art Annual, vol. 1. New York: Macmillan, 1899.

Clement, Clara Erskine. Women in the Fine Arts. Boston: Houghton
    Mifflin, 1904.

Exhibition of Paintings by Mrs. Mary Brewster Hazelton. Boston:
    Rowlands Gallery, 1906.

Fielding, Mantle. Dictionary of American Painters, Sculptors and
    Engravers. Enlarged ed. Greens Farms, Connecticut: Modern
    Books and Crafts, 1974.

184

Pierce, Patricia Jobe. Edmund C. Tarbell and The Boston School of
Painting, 1889-1980. Hingham, Massachusetts: Pierce
Galleries, 1980.


BESSIE ELLA HAZEN (1862-1946)   Painter and Printmaker

American Art Annual, vol. 28. Washington, D.C.: American
Federation of Arts, 1932.

Moure, Nancy D. Dictionary of Artists in Southern California
Before 1950. Los Angeles: Dustin Publications, 1975.

Obituary. Who's Who in American Art, vol. 4. Washington, D.C.:
American Federation of Arts, 1947.

A Selection of American Prints. A Selection of Biographies of
Forty Women Artists Working Between 1904-1979. Santa Rosa,
California: The Annex Galleries, 1987: 7.


ANNE HEALY (1939-   )   Sculptor

See volume 1 of this book.

Beardsley, John. Art in Public Places: A Survey of Community-
Sponsored Projects Supported by the National Endowment for
the Arts. Washington, D.C.: Partners for Livable Spaces,
1981.

Monumenta, A Biennial Exhibition of Outdoor Sculpture. Newport,
Rhode Island, 1974.

Outdoor Environmental Art. Cleveland: New Gallery of Contemporary
Art, 1977.

Quintessence: Alternative Spaces Residency Program. Dayton, Ohio:
City Beautiful Council, and Wright State University
Art Department, 1980.

Robins, Corinne. "Anne Healy." Arts Magazine 56, no. 10 (June
1981): 21.

Sculpture Outdoors. Roslyn, New York: Nassau County Museum of
Fine Arts, 1975.

Southsite Project. Hempstead, New York: Emily Lowe Gallery, 1980.

Watson-Jones, Virginia. Contemporary American Women Sculptors.
Phoenix: Oryx Press, 1986.

Women Sculptors of the 1980's. Brooklyn: Pratt Institute, 1985.

MARY HEILMANN (1940-    )    Sculptor

Armstrong, Richard. "Mary Heilmann." Artforum 22, no. 7 (March 1984):  91.

Castle, Frederick Ted. "Mary Heilmann at The Clocktower." Art in America 72, no. 4 (April 1984):  185-86.

Fortieth Biennial Exhibition of Contemporary American Painting. Washington, D.C.:  Corcoran Gallery of Art, 1987.

Goldberg, Shellie R. "Mary Heilmann at Pat Hearn." Art News 86, no. 2 (February 1987):  153.

"Mary Heilmann." Ceramics Monthly 33, no. 3 (March 1985):  52.

Westfall, Stephen. "Mary Heilmann at Pat Hearn." Art in America 74, no. 12 (December 1986):  132, 134.

Wei, Lilly. "Talking Abstract." Art in America 75, no. 7 (July 1987):  80-89.

Zucker, Barbara. "Mary Heilmann (Holly Solomon Gallery)." Art News 75, no. 9 (November 1976):  144.


RIVA HELFOND (1910-    )    Printmaker and Painter

Greengard, Stephen Neil. "Ten Crucial Years:  A Panel Discussion by Six WPA Artists." Journal of Decorative and Propaganda Arts 1, no. 1 (Spring 1986):  46-48.

Riva Helfond. New York:  Serigraph Galleries, 1946.

Riva Helfond. New York:  Juster Gallery, 1959.


HELEN WEST HELLER (1885-1955)    Painter and Wood Engraver

American Art Annual, vol. 28. Washington, D.C.:  American Federation of Arts, 1932.

American Prints in the Library of Congress:  A Catalog of the Collection. Baltimore:  Johns Hopkins Press, 1970.

Harms, Ernst. "Helen West Heller--The Woodcutter." The Print Collector's Quarterly 29, no. 2 (April 1942):  250-71.

186

Heller, Helen West.  Woodcuts U.S.A.  New York:  Oxford University
    Press, 1947.

Obituary.  Who's Who in American Art, vol. 6.  Washington, D.C.:
    American Federation of Arts, 1956.

Reese, Albert.  American Prints of the Twentieth Century.  New
    York:  American Artists Group, 1949.


            PHOEBE HELMAN (1929-    )    Painter and Sculptor

Bell, Jane.  "Phoebe Helman."  Art News 77, no. 9 (November 1978):
    181, 183.

Kuspit, Donald.  "Phoebe Helman at Sculpture Now."  Art in America
    67, no. 3 (May-June 1979):  142-43.

Linker, Kate.  "Public Sculpture II:  Provisions for the Paradise."
    Artforum 19, no. 10 (Summer 1961):  37-42.

Robins, Corinne.  "American Urban Art Triumphant:  The Abstract
    Paintings of Arthur Cohen, Al Held, Phoebe Helman, and Frank
    Stella."  Arts Magazine 56, no. 9 (May 1982):  86-89.

Watson-Jones, Virginia.  Contemporary American Women Sculptors.
    Phoenix:  Oryx Press, 1986.


                HERA (1940-    )    Sculptor

See volume 1 of this book.

Who's Who in American Art, 17th ed.  New York:  R.R. Bowker and
    Co., 1986.


        ELLA SOPHONISBA HERGESHEIMER (1873-1943)    Painter

American Art Annual, vol. 18.  Washington, D.C.:  American
    Federation of Arts, 1921.

Art in the United States Capitol.  Washington, D.C.:  U.S.
    Government Printing Office, 1976.

In This Academy.  The Pennsylvania Academy of the Fine Arts
    1805-1976.  Philadelphia:  The Pennsylvania Academy of the
    Fine Arts, 1976:  71, 281.

Obituary.  Who's Who in American Art, vol. 4.  Washington, D.C.:
    American Federation of Arts, 1947.

Pisano, Ronald G.  The Students of William Merritt Chase.
    Huntington, New York:  Heckscher Museum, 1973.

Woman's Who's Who of America.  New York:  American Commonwealth
    Co., 1914.


            ELSIE WARD HERING (1874-1923)    Sculptor

See volume 1 of this book.

American Art Annual, vol. 18.  Washington, D.C.:  American
    Federation of Arts, 1921.

Colorado Women in the Arts.  Arvada, Colorado:  Arvada Center for
    the Arts and Humanities, 1979:  20-22.

Kohlman, Rena Tucker.  "America's Women Sculptors."  International
    Studio 76 (1922):  225, 228-29.

Proske, Beatrice G.  Brookgreen Gardens.  Brookgreen, South
    Carolina:  Brookgreen Gardens, 1943.


            HELENA HERNMARCK (1941-    )  Weaver

Freudenheim, Betty.  "Modern-Day Tapestries Give Warmth to
    Buildings."  The New York Times, 3 March 1988:  Y19.

Staroba, Kristin.  "Lia Cook and Helena Hernmarck."  Women Artists
    News 12, nos. 4 and 5 (Fall-Winter 1987):  14-15.

Von Eckardt, Wolf.  "Painting Pictures with Fabric."  Time, 28
    Janurary 1985:  89.


            LOUISE HERRESHOFF [EATON] (1876-1967)    Painter

See volume 1 of this book.

Tufts, Eleanor.  American Women Artists, 1830-1930.  Washington,
    D.C.:  National Museum of Women in the Arts, 1987.

CHRISTINE HERTER (1890-    )   Painter

American Art Annual, vol. 28.   Washington, D.C.:   American
    Federation of Arts, 1932.

Fielding, Mantle.   Dictionary of American Painters, Sculptors and
    Engravers.   Enlarged ed.   Greens Farms, Connecticut:   Modern
    Books and Crafts, 1974.

Fiftieth Anniversary Exhibition 1889-1939.   New York:   National
    Association of Women Painters and Sculptors, 1939.

Who's Who in American Art, vol. 3.   Washington, D.C.:   American
    Federation of Arts, 1940.


EVA HESSE (1933-1970)    Sculptor

See volume 1 of this book.

Kuspit, Donald.   "Eva Hesse (Pat Hearn Gallery)."   Artforum 26, no.
    8 (April 1988):   138-39.

Lorber, Richard.   "Eva Hesse."   Arts Magazine 51, no. 4 (December
    1976);   7.

National Museum of Women in the Arts.   New York:   Harry N. Abrams,
    Inc., 1987.

Rubinstein, Charlotte Streifer.   American Women Artists.   Boston:
    G.K. Hall and Co., 1982.

Sandler, Irving.   American Art of the 1960s.   New York:   Harper and
    Row, 1988.


LOUISE LYONS HEUSTIS (1865/78-1951)    Painter and Illustrator

American Art Annual, vol. 28.   Washington, D.C.:   American
    Federation of Arts, 1932.

Clement, Clara Erskine.   Women in the Fine Arts.   Boston:
    Houghton, Mifflin and Co., 1904:   159-60.

Fiftieth Anniversary Exhibition 1889-1939:   National Association of
    Women Painters and Sculptors.   New York:   American Fine Arts
    Building, 1939.

Pisano, Ronald G.   The Students of William Merritt Chase.
    Huntington, New York:   Heckscher Museum, 1973.

Woman's Who's Who of America. New York:  American Commonwealth
    Co., 1914.


            SHEILA HICKS (1934-    )    Fiber artist and Sculptor

Freudenheim, Betty.  "12,000 Men and a Woman:  U. S. Artist's
    Saudi Role."  The New York Times, 23 June 1986:  18.

Lévi-Strauss, Monique.  Sheila Hicks.  Paris:  Pierre Horay and
    Suzy Langlois, 1973; London:  Studio Vista, 1974.

Manhart, Marcia and Tom, eds.  The Eloquent Object.  Tulsa,
    Oklahoma:  Philbrook Museum of Art, 1987.

Munro, Eleanor.  Originals:  American Women Artists.  New York:
    Simon and Schuster, 1979:  362-69.


            ABBY WILLIAMS HILL (1861-1943)    Painter

Fields, Ronald.  Abby Wiliams Hill, 1861-1943.  Tacoma, Washington:
    University of Puget Sound, 1979.

_____.  "Abby Williams Hill:  Northwest Frontier Painter."
    Landmarks 2, no. 4 (1984):  2-7.

Kovinick, Phil  The Woman Artist in the American West 1860-1960.
    Fullerton:  Muckenthaler Cultural Center, 1976.

Tufts, Eleanor.  American Women Artists 1830-1930.  Washington,
    D.C.:  National Museum of Women in the Arts, 1987.

A Woman's Vision:  California Painting into the 20th Century.  San
    Francisco:  Maxwell Galleries, 1983.


            PAMELA E. HILL (1803-1860)    Miniaturist

Bolton, Theodore.  Early American Portrait Painters in Miniature.
    New York:  F.F. Sherman, 1921.

Groce, George C., and Wallace, David H.  The New-York Historical
    Society's Dictionary of Artists in America 1564-1860.  New
    Haven:  Yale University Press, 1957.

Swan, Mabel Munston.  The Athenaeum Gallery 1827-1873.  Boston:
    The Boston Athenaeum Gallery, 1940:  185-86.

190

ANNA ALTHEA HILLS (1882-1930)    Painter

Anna Althea Hills, 1882-1930. Long Beach, California:  California
     State University Art Galleries, 1976.

Clark, Edna. Ohio Art and Artists. Richmond, Virginia:  Garrett
     and Massie, 1932.

Moure, Nancy D. Dictionary of Artists in Southern California
     Before 1950. Los Angeles:  Dustin Publications, 1975.

Southern California Artists, 1890-1940. Laguna Beach, California:
     Laguna Beach Museum of Art, 1979.

Westphal, Ruth Lilly. Plein Air Painters of California, The
     Southland. Irvine, California:  Westphal, 1982.

A Woman's Vision:  California Painting into the 20th Century. San
     Francisco:  Maxwell Galleries, 1983.


LAURA COOMBS HILLS (1859-1952)    Painter

See volume 1 of this book.

American Art Annual, vol. 28. Washington, D.C.:  American
     Federation of Arts, 1932.

Clement, Clara Erskine. Women in the Fine Arts. Boston:
     Houghton, Mifflin and Co., 1904.

Duncan, Frances. "The Miniatures of Miss Laura Hills."
     International Studio 41, no. 162 (August 1910):  xlvi-xlviii.

Fairbrother, Trevor J. The Bostonians, Painters of an Elegant
     Age, 1870-1930. Boston:  Museum of Fine Arts, 1986.

Fuller, Lucia Fairchild. "Modern American Miniature Painters."
     Scribner's 67 (March 1920):  381-84.

Gammell, R.H. Ives. The Boston Painters 1900-1930. Orleans,
     Massachusetts:  Parnassus Imprints, 1986.

Obituary. Who's Who in American Art, vol. 5. Washington, D.C.:
     American Federation of Arts, 1953.


CLAUDIA RAGUET HIRST (1855-1942)    Painter

See volume 1 of this book.

American Art Annual, vol. 28.  Washington, D.C.:  American
    Federation of Arts, 1932.

Catalogue, First Exhibition of Original Paintings Held Under the
    Auspices of the Young Women's Christian Association.  Dallas,
    Texas:  Y.W.C.A., 1924.

Champney, Elizabeth.  "Women in Art."  Quarterly Illustrator 2
    (April-June 1894):  111-24.

Fiftieth Anniversary Exhibition 1889-1939:  National Association
    of Women Painters and Sculptors.  New York:  American Fine
    Arts Building, 1939.

Tufts, Eleanor.  American Women Artists, 1830-1930.  Washington,
    D.C.:  National Museum of Women in the Arts, 1987.

Wilmerding, John; Ayres, Linda; and Powell, Earl A.  An American
    Perspective:  Nineteenth-Century Art from the Collection of
    JoAnn and Julian Ganz, Jr.  Washington, D.C.:  National
    Gallery of Art, 1981.

KATHERINE THAYER HOBSON (1889-1982)   Sculptor

Obituary.  The New York Times, 23 September 1982:  Y23.

Who's Who in American Art.  New York:  R.R. Bowker Co., 1978.

MARGO HOFF (1912-    )   Painter

See volume 1 of this book.

Margo Hoff.  New York:  Banfer Gallery, 1968.

MALVINA HOFFMAN (1885-1966)   Sculptor

See volume 1 of this book.

American Art Annual, vol. 28.  Washington, D.C.:  American
    Federation of Arts, 1932.

Catalogue of American Portraits in The New-York Historical Society,
    vols. 1 and 2.  New Haven:  Yale University Press, 1974.

Conner, Janis C.  A Dancer in Relief, Works by Malvina Hoffman.
    Yonkers, New York:  Hudson River Museum, 1984.

Fiftieth Annual Exhibition.  New York:  National Association of
    Women Painters and Sculptors, 1942.

192

Henning, William T., Jr. A Catalogue of the American Collection, Hunter Museum of Art. Chattanooga, Tennessee: Hunter Museum of Art, 1985.

"Malvina Hoffman." Hammond's Illustrated Library World Atlas. New York: C.S. Hammond and Co., 1947: 273-96.

"Malvina Hoffman Uses Art to Present Characteristics of the Races." Art Digest 8, no. 9 (1 February 1934): 10 and cover.

Morton, Brian N. Americans in Paris, An Anecdotal Street Guide. Ann Arbor, Michigan: The Olivia and Hill Press, 1984.

National Museum of Women in the Arts. New York: Harry N. Abrams, Inc., 1987: 60-61.

"110 Statues." Art Digest 7, no. 8 (15 January 1933): 17.

Nochlin, Linda. "Malvina Hoffman: A Life in Sculpture." Arts Magazine 59, no. 3 (November 1984): 106-10.

Obituary. The New York Times, 11 July 1966: 1.

Temperley, Harold. "Malvina Hoffman in the East." The American Magazine of Art 20, no. 3 (March 1929): 132-37.

Tufts, Eleanor. American Women Artists, 1830-1930. Washington, D.C.: National Museum of Women in the Arts, 1987.

"Virginia Reviews Career of Malvina Hoffman." Art Digest 11, no. 12 (15 March 1937): 16.

Whiting, F.A., Jr. "Malvina Hoffman." Magazine of Art 30, no. 4 (April 1937): 246-47.

KATE CLIFTON OSGOOD HOLMES (1858-1925)    Painter

American Art Annual, vol. 18. Washington, D.C.: American Federation of Arts, 1932.

Cosentino, Andrew J., and Glassie, Henry H. The Capital Image: Painters in Washington, 1800-1915. Washington, D.C.: National Museum of American Art, Smithsonian, 1983.

McMahan, Virgil E. Washington, D.C. Artists Born Before 1900: A Biographical Directory. Washington, D.C., privately printed, 1976.

NANCY HOLT (1938-    )    Sculptor and Filmmaker

See volume 1 of this book.

Architectural Sculpture. Los Angeles:  Los Angeles Institute of
    Contemporary Art, 1980.

Artists in the American West. Reno:  Sierra Nevada Museum of Art,
    1980.

Artpark:  The Program in Visual Arts. Lewiston, New York:
    Artpark, 1974 and 1975.

Beardsley, John. Earthworks and Beyond:  Contemporary Art in the
    Landscape. New York:  Abbeville Press, 1984.

Castle, Ted. "Nancy Holt, Siteseer." Art in America 70, no. 3
    (March 1982):  84-91.

Content:  A Contemporary Focus 1974-1984. Washington, D.C.:
    Hirshhorn Museum and Sculpture Garden, 1984.

Lippard, Ludy R. Overlay:  Contemporary Art and the Art of
    Prehistory. New York:  Pantheon Press, 1983.

Lorber, Richard. "Nancy Holt, Whitney Museum of American Art."
    Artforum 16, no. 4 (December 1977):  71-72.

Marter, Joan. "Nancy Holt's Dark Star Park." Art Magazine 59, no.
    2 (October 1984):  637-39.

Natur-Skulptur, Nature-Sculpture. Stuttgart:  Württembergischer
    Kunstverein, 1981.

New Directions:  Contemporary American Art. New York:  Sidney
    Janis Gallery, 1981.

Painting and Sculpture Today 1974. Indianapolis:  Indianapolis
    Museum of Art, 1974.

Post-Minimalism. Ridgefield, Connecticut:  Aldrich Museum of
    Contemporary Art, 1982.

Probing the Earth:  Contemporary American Art. Washington, D.C.:
    Hirshhorn Museum and Sculpture Garden, 1977.

A Response to the Environment. New Brunswick:  Rutgers University,
    Douglass Collection, 1975.

A Sense of Reference. La Jolla:  Mandeville Center for the Arts,
    University of California, San Diego, 1975.

Shaffer, Diana. "Nancy Holt:  Spaces for Reflections or
    Projections." Art in the Land:  A Critical Anthology of
    Environmental Art. New York:  E.P. Dutton, 1983.

194

Storr, Robert. "Nancy Holt at John Wever." Art in America 72, no.
6 (Summer 1984): 168-69.

Time: The Fourth Dimension in Art. Brussels: Palais des
Beaux-Arts, 1984.

Watson-Jones, Virginia. Contemporary American Women Sculptors.
Phoenix: Oryx Press, 1986.


SARA HOLT (1946-    )   Sculptor

Expressions-Sculptures. Paris: Musée National des Monuments
Français, 1983.

Grandes Femmes, Petits Formats. Paris: Galerie Iris, 1974.

La Part des Femmes dans l'Art Contemporain. Vitry-sur-Seine:
Galerie Municipale, 1984.

"Plastics in Art, Sara Holt--Sculptor: Transparency in the Third
Dimension." Plastics 3, no. 9 (August 1977): cover, 4.

Popper, Frank. Art, Action and Participation. London: Studio
Vista, 1975.

Restany, Pierre. Plastics in Arts. New York: L. Amiel, 1974.

Schwartz, Ellen. "Paris Letter: November." Art International 16,
no. 1 (20 January 1972): 54-58.

Touraine, Liliane. "Paris." Art International 17, no. 6 (Summer
1873): 51-52.

Watson-Jones, Virginia. Contemporary American Women Sculptors.
Phoenix: Oryx Press, 1986.


JENNY HOLZER (1950-    )   Electric Sign Artist

Armstrong, Richard. "Jenny Holzer." Artforum 22, no. 6 (February
1984): 76.

Cotter, Holland. "Jenny Holzer at Barbara Gladstone." Art in
America 74, no. 12 (December 1986): 137-38.

Ferguson, Bruce. "Wordsmith: An Interview with Jenny Holzer."
Art in America 74, no. 12 (December 1986): 108-15, 153.

Foster, Hal. "Subversive Signs." Art in America 70, no. 10
(November 1982): 88-92.

Grimes, Nancy. "Jenny Holzer at Barbara Gladstone." Art News 86,
no. 2 (February 1987): 128, 130.

Handy, Ellen. "Jenny Holzer." Arts Magazine 63, no. 1 (September 1988): 91.

Howell, John. "The Message is the Medium." Art News 87, no. 6 (Summer 1988): 122-27 and cover.

Jones, Ronald. "Jenny Holzer's 'Under a Rock.'" Arts Magazine 61, no. 5 (January 1987): 42-43.

Kunst mit Eigen-Sinn. Aktuelle Kunst von Frauen. Vienna and Munich: Löcher Verlag, 1985.

Siegel, Jeanne. "Jenny Holzer's Language Games." Arts Magazine 60, no. 4 (December 1985): 64-68.

Simon, Joan. Jenny Holzer: Signs. Des Moines, Iowa: Des Moines Art Center, 1986.

Westerbeck, Colin. "Jenny Holzer." Artforum 25, no. 9 (May 1987): 154-55.

Zelevansky, Lynn. "Jenny Holzer." Art News 83, no. 1 (January 1984): 152.

HENRIETTA MARIA BENSON HOMER (1808-1884)   Watercolorist

See volume 1 of this book.

Groce, George C., and Wallace, David H. The New-York Historical Society's Dictionary of Artists in America 1564-1860. New Haven: Yale University Press, 1957.

Women Pioneers in Maine Art. Portland, Maine: Joan Whitney Payson Gallery of Art, Westbrook College, 1981.

DOROTHY HOOD (1919-    )   Painter

See volume 1 of this book.

Carlozzi, Annette. 50 Texas Artists. San Francisco: Chronicle Books, 1986.

Dorothy Hood. Washington, D.C.: Wallace Wentworth Gallery, 1986.

Everingham, Carol J. "Hood Exhibit Both Visual and Vocal." The Houston Post, 1 April 1984: 8F.

ffrench-frazier, Nina. "Dorothy Hood." Arts Magazine 52, no. 10 (June 1978): 28.

196

Hobbs, Robert. Dorothy Hood's Collages. Washington, D.C.:
    Wallace Wentworth Gallery, 1988.

Kalil, Susie, and Rose, Barbara. Fresh Paint. Houston: Museum of
    Fine Arts, 1985.

Vander Lee, Jana. A Sense of Spirit. Houston: Lawndale Annex,
    University of Houston, 1982.

Women's Caucus for Art Honor Awards. Houston: National Women's
    Caucus for Art, 1988.


ETHEL PAINTER HOOD (1908-1982)    Sculptor

Proske, Beatrice Gilman. Brookgreen Gardens Sculpture, vol. II.
    Brookgreen, South Carolina: Brookgreen Gardens, 1955:
    112-13.

Reed, Judith Kaye. "Heads by Hood." Art Digest 21, no. 9
    (1 February 1947):  18.

Who's Who in American Art. New York:  R.R. Bowker Co., 1978.


EDNA BOIES HOPKINS (1872-1937)    Printmaker

American Art Annual, vol. 28. Washington, D.C.:  American
    Federation of Arts, 1932.

Edna Boies Hopkins, Color Woodcuts 1900-1923. New York:  Mary Ryan
    Gallery, 1986.

Fielding, Mantle. Dictionary of American Painters, Sculptors and
    Engravers. Enlarged ed. Greens Farms, Connecticut:  Modern
    Books and Crafts, 1974.

Flint, Janet Altic. Provincetown Printers:  A Woodcut Tradition.
    Washington, D.C.:  National Museum of American Art, 1983.

Obituary. Who's Who in American Art, vol. 2. Washington, D.C.:
    American Federation of Arts, 1937.

A Selection of American Prints. A Selection of Biographies of
    Forty Women Artists Working Between 1904-1979. Santa Rosa,
    California:  The Annex Galleries, 1987:  7.


NELLIE MATHES HORNE (b. 1870)    Painter

Fielding, Mantle. Dictionary of American Painters, Sculptors and
    Engravers. Enlarged ed. Greens Farms, Connecticut:  Modern
    Books and Crafts, 1974.

McMahon, Virgil E.  Washington, D.C. Artists Born Before 1900; A
    Biographical Directory.  Washington, D.C., 1976.

Moure, Nancy D.  Dictionary of Artists in Southern California
    Before 1950.  Los Angeles:  Dustin Publications, 1975.

National Portrait Gallery, Permanent Collection Illustrated
    Checklist.  Washington, D.C.:  Smithsonian Institution Press,
    1982.


HARRIET HOSMER (1830-1908)   Sculptor

See volume 1 of this book.

Davies, Esther Payne.  "Harriet Hosmer.  When She Sculpted, She
    Broke the Mold."  Christian Science Monitor, 4 May 1988:
    30-31.

Hanaford, Phebe A.  Daughters of America.  Augusta, Maine:  True
    and Co., 1882:  300-03.

Harding, Jonathan P.  The Boston Athenaeum Collection.  Pre-
    Twentieth Century American and European Painting and
    Sculpture.  Boston:  Boston Athenaeum, 1984.

Surtees, Virginia.  The Ludovisi Goddess, The Life of Louisa Lady
    Ashburton.  Wilton, England:  Michael Russell, 1984.

Tufts, Eleanor.  American Women Artists, 1830-1930.  Washington,
    D.C.:  National Museum of Women in the Arts, 1987.

Withers, Josephine.  "Artistic Women and Women Artists."  Art
    Journal 35, no. 4 (Summer 1976):  330-36 and cover.


FRANCES C. LYONS HOUSTON (1851-1906)   Painter and Goldsmith

Archives of American Art.  Collection of Exhibition Catalogs.
    Boston:  G.K. Hall and Co., 1979.

A Circle of Friends:  Art Colonies of Cornish and Dublin.  Durham,
    New Hampshire:  University Art Galleries, and Keene, New
    Hampshire:  Thorne-Sagendorph Art Gallery, Keene State Collge,
    1985.

Clement, Clara Erskine.  Women in the Fine Arts.  Boston:
    Houghton, Mifflin and Co., 1904.

Fielding, Mantle.  Dictionary of American Painters, Sculptors and
    Engravers.  Enlarged ed.  Greens Farms, Connecticut:  Modern
    Books and Crafts, 1974.

MARION HOWARD (1883-1953)    Painter

Archives of American Art. Collection of Exhibition Catalogs.
    Boston:  G.K. Hall and Co., 1979.

Pierce, Patricia Jobe. Edmund C. Tarbell and the Boston School of
    Painting, 1889-1980. Hingham, Massachusetts:  Pierce
    Galleries, 1980.

_____. The Ten. Concord, New Hampshire:  Rumford Press, 1976.

Who's Who in American Art, vol. 3. Washington, D.C.:  American
    Federation of Arts, 1940.


FELICE WALDO HOWELL  (1897-1968)    Painter

American Art Annual, vol. 28. Washington, D.C.:  American
    Federation of Arts, 1932.

Archives of American Art. Collection of Exhibition Catalogs.
    Boston:  G.K. Hall and Co., 1979.

McMahan, Virgil E. Washington, D.C. Artists Born Before 1900:
    A Biographical Directory. Washington, D.C.:  1976.

Who's Who in American Art, vol. 8. Washington, D.C.:  American
    Federation of Arts, 1962.


ANNA GOODHART WHITTLETON HOWLAND (b. 1871)    Painter

American Art Annual, vol. 28. Washington, D.C.:  American
    Federation of Arts, 1932.

Fielding, Mantle. Dictionary of American Painters, Sculptors and
    Engravers. Enlgarged ed. Greens Farms, Connecticut:  Modern
    Books and Crafts, 1974.

First Annual Exhibition of Flower Paintings in Water-Color by
    Members of The Aquarelle Club of Washington. Washington,
    D.C.:  Woodward and Lothrop Galleries, 1904.

Who's Who in American Art, vol. 3. Washington, D.C.:  American
    Federation of Arts, 1940.


EDITH HOWLAND (1863-1949)    Sculptor

American Art Annual, vol. 28. Washington, D.C.:  American
    Federation of Arts, 1932.

National Sculpture Society. <u>Exhibition of American Sculpture</u>. New York, 1923.

National Sculpture Society and California Palace of the Legion of Honor. <u>Contemporary American Sculpture</u>. New York, 1929: 158.

Proske, Beatrice Gilman. <u>Brookgreen Gardens Sculpture</u>. Brookgreen, South Carolina: Brookgreen Gardens, 1943.

Obituary. <u>Who's Who in American Art</u>, vol. 5. Washington, D.C.: American Federation of Arts, 1953.

Weimann, Jeanne Madeline. <u>The Fair Women</u>. Chicago: Academy Chicago, 1981: 295.


ISABELLA HOWLAND (1895-1974)    Painter and Sculptor

Archives of American Art. <u>A Checklist of the Collection</u>. Washington, D.C.: Smithsonian Institution, 1975.

_____. <u>Collection of Exhibition Catalogs</u>. Boston: G.K. Hall and Co., 1979.

<u>Second Biennial Exhibition of Contemporary American Painting</u>. New York: Whitney Museum of American Art, 1934: no. 56.

<u>Who's Who in American Art</u>, vol. 3. Washington, D.C.: American Federation of Arts, 1940.

<u>Women Pioneers in Maine Art 1900-1945</u>. Portland, Maine: Joan Whitney Payson Gallery of Art, Westbrook College, 1985.


GRACE CARPENTER HUDSON (1865-1937)    Painter

See volume 1 of this book.

<u>The Art of California</u>. Oakland: Oakland Museum, 1984.

<u>A Woman's Vision: California Painting into the 20th Century</u>. San Francisco: Maxwell Galleries, 1983.


DAISY MARGUERITE HUGHES (1883-1968)    Painter

<u>American Art Annual</u>, vol. 28. Washington, D.C.: American Federation of Arts, 1932.

200

Archives of American Art.  Collection of Exhibition Catalogs.
    Boston:  G.K. Hall and Co., 1979.

Fine 19th and 20th Century European and American Paintings.  Los
    Angeles:  Sotheby's, 22 and 23 June 1981:  Lots 153, 154.

Moure, Nancy D.  Dictionary of Artists in Southern California
    Before 1950.  Los Angeles:  Dustin Publications, 1975.

Who's Who in American Art, vol. 8.  Washington, D.C.:  American
    Federation of Arts, 1962.


            MARIE ATKINSON HULL (1890-    )  Painter

American Art Annual, vol. 28.  Washington, D.C.:  American
    Federation of Arts, 1932.

Norwood, Malcolm M.; Elias, Virginia McGehee; and Haynie, William
    S.  The Art of Marie Hull.  Jackson:  University Press of
    Mississippi, 1975.

Who's Who in American Art.  New York:  R.R. Bowker Co., 1978.


            YVONNE TWINING HUMBER (1907-    )  Painter

Childs Gallery Painting Annual (Boston), vol. 3.  (n.d.):  20.

Who's Who in American Art, vol. 4.  Washington, D.C.:  American
    Federation of Arts, 1947.


            MARGO HUMPHREY (1942-    )  Printmaker

Carmen Lomas Garza:  Prints and Gouaches; Margo Humphrey:
    Monotypes.  San Francisco:  San Francisco Museum of Modern
    Art, 1980.

Cebulski, Frank.  "Phelan Awards."  Artweek 14, no. 28 (27 August
    1983):  4-5.

1938-1988:  The Work of Five Black Women Artists.  Atlanta:
    Atlanta College of Art Gallery, 1988.

"Prints and Photographs Published."  Print Collectors Newsletter 16
    (September-October 1985):  140.


            CLEMENTINE HUNTER (c. 1886-1988)  Painter

See volume 1 of this book.

Jones, Anne Hudson. "The Centennial of Clementine Hunter."
    Woman's Art Journal 8, no. 1 (Spring-Summer 1987): 23-27.


                    DEBORA HUNTER (1950-    )   Photographer

Directions 1981. Washington, D.C.:  Hirshhorn Museum and Sculpture
    Garden, 1981.

Hugunin, James. "Descriptions:  Home Hospice Series 1980-1985."
    New Art Examiner 13, no. 7 (March 1986):  50.

Kutner, Janet. "Dallas Exhibitions." Art News 79, no. 10
    (December 1980):  158.

The New Season. Nine Contemporary Photographers.  New York:
    Witkin Gallery, 1979.

Raczka, Robert. "Two Sides of Flatness:  Delahunty Gallery,
    Dallas." Artweek 11, no. 31 (27 September 1980):  16.

Rickey, Carrie. "Curatorial Conceptions, The Hirshhorn." Artforum
    19, no. 8 (April 1981):  49, 50.

Texas Photographers:  Four Directions. Amarillo, Texas:  Amarillo
    Art Center, 1980.

12. Dallas:  Dallas Museum of Art, 1979.

Who's Who in American Art, 17th ed.  New York:  R.R. Bowker Co.,
    1986.

Women See Women. New York:  Thomas Y. Crowell Co., 1976.


                    ISABEL HUNTER (1878-1941)   Painter

American Art Annual, vol. 18.  Washington, D.C.:  American
    Federation of Arts, 1921.

Dawdy, Doris Ostrander. Artists of the American West.  Chicago:
    Swallow Press, 1974.

Porter, Bruce, et  al. Art in California:  A Survey of American
    Art with Special Reference to California Painting, Sculpture
    and Architecture, Past and Present, Particularly as Those Arts
    were Represented at the Panama-Pacific International
    Exposition. San Francisco:  R.L. Bernier, 1916.

Spangenberg, Helen. Yesterday's Artists on the Monterey Peninsula.
Monterey, California: Monterey Peninsula Museum of Art, 1976.

A Woman's Vision: California Painting into the 20th Century. San
Francisco: Maxwell Galleries, 1983.


ANNA HYATT HUNTINGTON (1876-1973)    Sculptor

See volume 1 of this book.

American Art Annual, vol. 28. Washington, D.C.: American
Federation of Arts, 1932.

Caffin, Charles H. "Miss Hyatt's Statue of Joan of Arc." The
Century 92, no. 2 (June 1916): 308-11.

Catalogue: Exhibition of Sculpture by Anna Hyatt Huntington.
Foreword by Royal Cortissoz. Washington, D.C.: Corcoran
Gallery of Art, 1938.

Cook, Doris E. Woman Sculptor: Anna Hyatt Huntington (1876-1973).
Hartford, Connecticut: privately printed, 1976.

Famous Small Bronzes. New York: The Gorham Co., 1928.

Goodnough, Robert. "Anna Hyatt Huntington." Art News 51, no. 4
(June 1952): 97.

Humphries, Grace. "Anna Vaughn Hyatt's Statue." International
Studio 57 (December 1915): 47-50.

"The Maid of Orleans." Art Digest 12, no. 18 (1 July 1938): 34.

National Museum of Women in the Arts. New York: Harry N. Abrams,
Inc., 1987.

"Newark: Sculpture by A.H. Huntington." Art News 37, no. 35 (May
1939): 24-25.

Noble, Joseph Veach. "Anna Hyatt Huntington." Brookgreen
Bulletin 15, no. 4 (1985).

Payne, Frank Owen. "Noted American Sculptors at Work." Art and
Archaeology 21, no. 1 (March 1926): 124.

Proske, Beatrice Gilman. "Anna Hyatt Huntington." Brookgreen
Bulletin 13, no. 3 (1983).

Royère, Jean. Le Musicisme sculptural: Madame Archer Milton
Huntington: Trente-deux reproductions en photogravure.
Paris: Albert Messein, Editeur, 1933.

Schaub-Koch, Émile.  Hindu Art and the Art of Anna
    Hyatt-Huntington.  Lisbon:  International Institute of Arts
    and Letters, 1958.

Tufts, Eleanor.  American Women Artists, 1830-1930.  Washington,
    D.C.:  National Museum of Women in the Arts, 1987.


           MARGARET WENDELL HUNTINGTON (1867-1958)   Painter

American Art Annual, vol. 28.  Washington, D.C.:  American
    Federation of Arts, 1932.

C[lendenen], J[anet].  "Margaret Huntington at Barbizon."  Art
    Digest 20, no. 17 (1 June 1946):  19.

L., J.  "Margaret Huntington."  Art News 35, no. 14 (2 January
    1937):  18.

"Margaret Huntington Paints Nantucket."  Art Digest 8, no. 8 (15
    January 1934):  29.

"Watercolorist Amusingly Records the Fair's Sculpture."  Art News
    37 (16 September 1939):  15.

Who's Who in American Art, vol. 1.  Washington, D.C.:  American
    Federation of Arts, 1935.

Wolf, Amy J.  New York Society of Women Artists, 1925.  New York:
    ACA Galleries, 1987.


           HENRIETTE WYETH HURD (1907-    )   Painter

See volume 1 of this book.

Bell, David L.  "Santa Fe."  Art News 81, no. 10 (December 1982):
    92.

Doherty, M. Stephen.  "Eight Artists Open Their Studios."
    American Artist 51, no. 535 (February 1987):  48-49.

Exhibition of Paintings by Peter Hurd and Henriette Wyeth.
    Columbus, Ohio:  Columbus Gallery of Fine Arts, 1967.

Henriette Wyeth, Exhibition of Paintings.  Santa Fe:  Gerald Peters
    Gallery, 1982.

Period Gallery West.  Scottsdale, Arizona:  Period Gallery West,
    1979:  47.

HELEN HYDE (1868-1919)    Printmaker

See volume 1 of this book.

Obituary. American Art Annual, vol. 16.  Washington, D.C.:
American Federation of Arts, 1919.

Porter, Bruce, et al. Art in California:  A Survey of American Art
with Special Reference to California Painting, Sculpture and
Architecture, Past and Present. San Francisco:  R.L.
Bernier, 1916:  118 and pl. 269.

A Selection of American Prints. A Selection of Biographies of
Forty Women Artists Working Between 1904-1979.  Santa Rosa,
California:  The Annex Gallery, 1987:  8.

Sparrow, Walter Shaw. Women Painters of the World.  London:
Hodder and Stoughton, 1905.


BARONESS ANNE-MARGUERITE HENRIETTE HYDE DE NEUVILLE (ca. 1779-1849)
Painter

See volume 1 of this book.

Andrews, Wayne.  "Patience was her Reward:  The Records of the
Baroness Hyde de Neuville." Journal of the Archives of
American Art 4, no. 3 (July 1964):  1-8.

Baroness Hyde de Neuville:  Sketches of America, 1807-1822.  New
Brunswick, New Jersey:  Rutgers University and New York:  New-
York Historical Society, 1984.

Cosentino, Andrew J., and Glassie, Henry H.  The Capital Image:
Painters in Washington, 1800-1915. Washington, D.C.:
National Museum of American Art, Smithsonian Press, 1983.

Fenton, William N.  "The Hyde de Neuville Portraits of New York
Savages in 1807-1808." New-York Historical Society Quarterly
38 (April 1954):  119-37.


DAHLOV IPCAR (1917-    )    Painter

Exhibition of Paintings by Dahlov Ipcar. New York:  Passedoit
Gallery, 1943.

Paintings by Dahlov Ipcar. New York:  Bignou Gallery, 1940.

Who's Who in American Art, 17th ed.  New York:  R.R. Bowker Co.,
1986.

Women Pioneers in Maine Art 1900-1945. Portland, Maine: Joan
    Whitney Payson Gallery of Art, Westbrook College, 1985.


REA IRVIN (1881-1972)    Illustrator

American Art Annual, vol. 28. Washington, D.C.: American
    Federation of Arts, 1932.

Who's Who in American Art, vol. 10. Washington, D.C.: American
    Federation of Arts, 1970.


SHEILA EATON ISHAM (1927-    )    Painter

Fry, Edward F. Sheila Isham: Recent Work. Buffalo, New York:
    Buffalo Fine Arts Academy and Albright-Knox Art Gallery, 1981.

Kline, Katherine. "Reviews and Previews." Art News 69, no. 4
    (Summer 1970):  62.

Koethe, John. "Boston." Art News 70, no. 4 (Summer 1971):  18.

Russo, Alexander. Profiles on Women Artists. Frederick, Maryland:
    University Publications of America, 1985.

Stich, Sidra. "Five New Washington Artists." Art International 15
    (December 1971):  48-49.

Who's Who in American Art, 16th ed. New York: R.R. Bowker, Co.,
    1984.


MARGARET ISRAEL (1929-1987)    Potter and Painter

See volume 1 of this book.

Klein, Ellen Lee. "Margaret Israel." Arts Magazine 60, no. 5
    (January 1986):  128.

Obituary. Art in America 75, no. 6 (June 1987):  176.


MIYOKO ITO (1918-1983)    Painter

See volume 1 of this book.

Klement, Vera. "Miyoko Ito." Profile 4, no. 1 (January 1984).

Horsfield, Kate. "Interview with Miyoko Ito." Profile 4, no. 1
    (January 1984).

DIANE HEALY ITTER (1946-    )    Fiber Artist

Koplos, Janet.  "The Knot as Brush Stroke:  Diane Itter's Fiber
    Paintings."  American Craft 40, no. 1 (February-March 1980):
    20-23.

Malarcher, Patricia.  "Miniatures in Fiber."  Fiberarts 7
    (July-August 1980):  32-35.

Znamierowski, Nell.  Fiber:  The Artist's View.  Greenvale, New
    York:  Hillwood Art Gallery, Long Island University, 1983.


LOTTE JACOBI (1896-    )    Photographer

See volume 1 of this book.

National Portrait Gallery, Permanent Collection Illustrated
    Checklist.  Washington, D.C.:  Smithsonian Institution Press,
    1982.
Simson, Emily.  "Lotte Jacobi at Ledel."  Art News 83, no. 9
    (November 1984):  178, 183.

Sturman, John.  "Lotte Jacobi."  Art News 86, no. 6 (Summer 1987):
    215.


YVONNE JACQUETTE (1934-    )    Painter

See volume 1 of this book.

Berlind, Robert.  "Yvonne Jacquette at Brook Alexander."  Art in
    America 70, no. 9 (October 1982):  135-36.

Ellenzweig, Allen.  "Yvonne Jacquette."  Arts Magazine 51, no. 5
    (January 1977):  33-34.

Field, Richard S., and Fine, Ruth E.  A Graphic Muse.  New York:
    Hudson Hills Press, 1987.

Martin, Alvin.  American Realism, 20th Century Drawings and
    Watercolors from the Glenn C. Janss Collection.  San
    Francisco:  San Francisco Museum of Modern Art, 1985.

McGeevy, Linda.  "Yvonne Jacquette."  Arts Magazine 63, no. 1
    (September 1988):  92.

Nochlin, Linda.  "Some Women Realists:  Part I."  Arts Magazine 48,
    no. 5 (February 1974):  46-51.

Storr, Robert.  "Yvonne Jacquette at Brooke Alexander."  Art in
    America 74, no. 7 (July 1986):  118, 120.

Yvonne Jacquette: Paintings, Monotypes and Drawings. New York:
    Brooke Alexander Gallery, 1976.

Yvonne Jacquette: Tokyo Nightviews. Brunswick, Maine: Bowdoin
    College Museum of Art, 1986.


            REBECCA SALSBURY JAMES (1891-1968)    Painter

Dawdy, Doris Ostrander. Artists of the American West, vol. 1.
    Chicago: Swallow Press, 1974.

Samuels, Peggy and Harold. The Illustrated Biographical
    Encyclopedia of Artists of the American West. Garden City,
    New York: Doubleday and Co., 1976.


        BERTHA EVELYN CLAUSON JAQUES (1863-1941)    Printmaker

See volume 1 of this book.

American Art Annual, vol. 28. Washington, D.C.: American
    Federation of Arts, 1932.

American Prints in the Library of Congress: A Catalog of the
    Collection. Baltimore: Johns Hopkins Press, 1970.

Bertha E. Jaques. Houston: Gerhard Wurzer Gallery, 1982.

Bertha Jaques and the Chicago Society of Etchers. Bethlehem,
    Connecticut: June 1 Gallery, 1981.

"Chicago Etchers Honor Bertha Jaques." Art Digest 14, no. 2 (15
    October 1939): 25.

Clark, Edna. Ohio Art and Artists. Richmond, Virginia: Garrett
    and Massie, 1932.

Duncan, Virginia Hope. "Bertha E. Jaques." Prints 3 (January
    1933): 26-34.

Exhibition of Etchings, Aquatints, Drypoints and Drypoints in Color
    by Bertha E. Jaques. Chicago: Albert Roullier Art Galleries,
    1939.

"A Leader Retires." Art Digest 12, no. 1 (1 October 1937): 25.

Masters Prints and Drawings. Los Angeles: Marilyn Pink Gallery,
    1981.

Obituary. Chicago Tribune, 30 March 1941.

Obituary. Art Digest 15, no. 14 (15 April 1941).

A Selection of American Prints. A Selection of Biographies of
    Forty Women Artists Working Between 1904-1979. Santa Rosa,
    California: The Annex Galleries, 1987: 8.

Woman's Who's Who of America. New York: American Commonwealth
    Co., 1914.


                VIRGINIA JARAMILLO (1939-    )  Painter

¡Mira! The Canadian Club Hispanic Art Tour III. Farmington Hills,
    Michigan: Canadian Club, 1988.

1972 Annual Exhibition. New York: Whitney Museum of American Art,
    1972.

National Museum of Women in the Arts. Washington, D.C.: Harry N.
    Abrams, Inc., 1987.


                PENELOPE JENCKS (1936-    )  Sculptor

Birmelin, Blair. "Penelope Jencks: Sculpture." The Massachusetts
    Review 24, no. 2 (Summer 1983): 417-424.

Faxon, Alicia, and Moore, Sylvia. Pilgrims & Pioneers. New York:
    Midmarch Arts Press, 1987: 85-86, 96.

Fleming, Ronald Lee, and Tscharner, Renate von with Melrod, George.
    Place Makers: Public Art That Tells You Where You Art. New
    York: Hastings House, 1981.

Living American Artists and the Figure. University Park,
    Pennsylvania: Museum of Art, Pennsylvania State University,
    1974.

Parry, Marian. "An Interview with Penelope Jencks." American
    Artist 37, no. 373 (August 1973): 36-39, 64.

Spreight, Charlotte F. Images in Clay Sculpture: Historical and
    Contemporary Techniques. New York: Harper and Row, 1983.

Watson-Jones, Virginia. Contemporary American Women Sculptors.
    Phoenix: Oryx Press, 1986.

Who's Who in American Art. New York: R.R. Bowker Co., 1978.

PHOEBE A. PICKERING HOYT JENKS (1847-1907)    Painter

Bénézit, Emmanuel. Dictionnaire critique et documentaire des
    peintres, sculpteurs, dessinateurs et graveurs. New ed.
    Paris:  Librairie Gründ, 1976.

Clement, Clara Erskine. Women in the Fine Arts. Boston:
    Houghton, Mifflin and Co., 1904.

Fielding, Mantle. Dictionary of American Painters, Sculptors and
    Engravers. Enlarged ed. Greens Farms, Connecticut: Modern
    Books and Crafts, 1974.

ELIZABETH GILBERT JEROME (1824-1910)    Painter

Fielding, Mantle. Dictionary of American Painters, Sculptors and
    Engravers. Enlarged ed. Greens Farms, Connecticut: Modern
    Books and Crafts, 1974.

French, Henry. Art and Artists in Connecticut. Boston:  Lee and
    Shepard, 1879:  169.

Groce, George C., and Wallace, David H. The New-York Historical
    Society's Dictionary of Artists in America 1564-1860.  New
    Haven:  Yale University Press, 1957.

JOSEPHINE JESSUP (ca. 1858-1933)    Painter

"First Woman N.A. Dies." The Art Digest (1 October 1933):  12.

Obituary. American Art Annual, vol. 30.  Washington, D.C.:
    American Federation of Arts, 1934.

MAUDE SHERWOOD JEWETT (b. 1873)    Sculptor

American Art Annual, vol. 28.  Washington, D.C.:  American
    Federation of Arts, 1932.

American 19th and 20th Century Paintings, Drawings and Sculpture.
    New York:  Sotheby's, 21 October 1983:  Lot 332.

Famous Small Bronzes.  New York:  The Gorham Co., 1928.

Fielding, Mantle. Dictionary of American Painters, Sculptors and
    Engravers. Enlarged ed. Greens Farms, Connecticut: Modern
    Books and Crafts, 1974.

Kohlman, Rena Tucker.  "America's Women Sculptors." International
    Studio 76 (1922):  225-35.

210

National Sculpture Society. Exhibition of American Sculpture. New York: National Sculpture Society, 1923.

National Sculpture Society. Exhibition of American Sculpture. San Francisco: California Palace of the Legion of Honor, 1929.


PATRICIA JOHANSON (1940-      ) Sculptor and Environmental Artist

See volume 1 of this book.

Balken, Debra Bricker. Patricia Johanson: Drawings and Models for Environmental Projects, 1969-1986. Essay by Lucy Lippard. Pittsfield: Berkshire Museum, 1987.

Beyond the Monument. Text by Gary Garrels. Cambridge, Massachusetts: Hayden Gallery, M.I.T., 1983.

Campbell, Lawrence. "Patricia Johanson at Rosa Esman." Art in America 71, no. 11 (December 1983): 148.

Friedman, Jon R. "Patricia Johanson." Arts Magazine 53, no. 10 (June 1979): 31.

Graze, Sue. "Patricia Johanson: A Project for the Fair Park Lagoon." Dallas Museum of Fine Arts Bulletin (Fall 1982): [22].

Goossen, E. C. Eight Young Artists. Yonkers, New York: Hudson River Museum, 1964.

Henry, Gerrit. "Patricia Johanson at Twining." Art in America 76, no. 2 (February 1988): 147-48.

Marvel, Bill. "Signs of Life: After Decades of Inactivity, Fair Park is Coming Back--And so are the People." The Dallas Morning News, 23 August 1987: C1, 8, and 9.

Munro, Eleanor. "Earthwork Odyssey." The Christian Science Monitor, 25 March 1987: 30-31.

Patricia Johanson: Drawings for the Camouflage House and Orchid Projects. Introduction by Ellen H. Johnson. New York: Rosa Esman Gallery, 1979.

Patricia Johanson: Fair Park Lagoon, Dallas and Color-Gardens. Introduction by Lucy Lippard. New York: Rosa Esman Gallery, 1983.

Patricia Johanson: Interpretive Drawings for Architecture and Landscape. New York: Twining Gallery, 1987.

Restivo, Valerie. "Patricia Johanson: A Sculptor-Architect's Rare Perception Attracts a Guggenheim." Bennington College Quadrille 14, no. 1 (August 1980): 4, 7.

Shimizu, Tateo. "American Women Artists." The Asahi Shimbun (Tokyo), 19 January 1986.

Tasker, Georgia. "She Sculpts in Land, Water." The Miami Herald, 20 May 1984: H19.

Withers, Josephine. "In the World: An Art Essay." Feminist Studies 9, no. 2 (Summer 1983): 325-334 and cover.

Who's Who in American Art. New York: R.R. Bowker Co., 1986.

Zimmer, William. "In Stamford, Artists and Their Public Projects." The New York Times, 5 May 1985.

GRACE SPAULDING JOHN (1890-1972)    Painter

American Art Annual, vol. 28. Washington, D.C.: American Federation of Arts, 1932.

Moore, Sylvia. No Bluebonnets, No Yellow Roses: Essays on Texas Women in the Arts. New York: Midmarch Arts Press, 1988.

O'Brien, Esse Forrester. Art and Artists of Texas. Dallas: Tardy Publishing Co., 1935.

Samuels, Peggy and Harold. The Illustrated Biographical Encyclopedia of Artists of the American West. Garden City, New York: Doubleday and Co., 1976.

Who's Who in American Art. New York: R.R. Bowker Co., 1970.

ADELAIDE JOHNSON (1859-1955)    Sculptor

See volume 1 of this book.

American Art Annual, vol. 28. Washington, D.C.: American Federation of Arts, 1932.

Clement, Clara Erskine. Women in the Fine Arts. Boston: Houghton, Mifflin and Co., 1904: 380-81.

Who's Who in American Art, vol. 3. Washington, D.C.: American Federation of Arts, 1940.

Woman's Who's Who of America. New York: American Commonwealth Co., 1914.

BUFFIE JOHNSON (1912-    )    Painter

See volume 1 of this book.

Russo, Alexander. Profiles on Women Artists. Frederick, Maryland:
     University Publications of America, 1985.

Who's Who in American Art, 17th ed. New York: R.R. Bowker Co.,
     1986.


GRACE MOTT JOHNSON (1882-1967)    Sculptor

See volume 1 of this book.

American Art Annual, vol. 28. Washington, D.C.: American
     Federation of Arts, 1932.

Moore, Isabel. "A Sculptor of Animals." The American Magazine
     of Art 14, no. 2 (February 1923): 59-61.

Tarbell, Roberta K. "The Impact of the Armory Show on American
     Sculpture." Archives of American Art Journal 18, no. 2
     (1978): 2-11.

Who's Who in American Art, vol. 8. Washington, D.C.: American
     Federation of Arts, 1962.


MARIE JOHNSON-CALLOWAY (1920-    )    Painter

See "Marie Johnson" in volume 1 of this book.

Roth, Moira, ed. Connecting Conversations: Interviews with 28 Bay
     Area Women Artists. Oakland, California: Eucalyptus Press,
     Mills College, 1988.


FRANCES BENJAMIN JOHNSTON (1864-1952)    Photographer

See volume 1 of this book.

Cosentino, Andrew J., and Glassie, Henry H. The Capital Image,
     Painters in Washington, 1800-1915. Washington, D.C.:
     National Museum of American Art, Smithsonian, 1983.

Glenn, Constance W., and Rice, Leland. Frances Benjamin Johnston:
     Women of Class and Station. Long Beach, California: Art
     Museum and Galleries, California State University, 1979.

Gover, C. Jane. The Positive Image: Women Photographers in Turn
     of the Century America. Albany: State University of New York
     Press, 1988.

Hills, Patricia. Turn-of-the-Century America. New York: Whitney
    Museum of American Art, 1977.

Johnston, Frances Benjamin. "What a Woman Can Do With a Camera."
    The Ladies Home Journal, 1898: 7.

Szarkowski, John. Looking at Photographs: 100 Pictures in the
    Collection of the Museum of Modern Art. New York: The Museum
    of Modern Art, 1973.

HENRIETTA DEERING JOHNSTON (ca. 1670-1728/29)   Painter

See volume 1 of this book.

Keyes, Homer Eaton. "Coincidence and Henriette Johnston."
    Antiques 16 (December 1929): 490-94.

Selection from the Collection of the Carolina Art Association.
    Charleston, South Carolina: Carolina Art Association, 1977:
    46-48.

SARAH J. F. JOHNSTON (1850-1925)   Painter in Charcoal

See volume 1 of this book.


YNEZ JOHNSTON (1920-    )   Painter and Printmaker

See volume 1 of this book.

Bunce/Johnston/Mundt: New Talent Exhibition. New York: The
    Museum of Modern Art, 1950.

Graphics '71 West Coast, U.S.A. Lexington, Kentucky: University
    of Kentucky Art Gallery, 1970.

Painting and Sculpture in California: The Modern Era. San
    Francisco: San Francisco Museum of Modern Art, 1976.

III Bienal. São Paulo, Brazil: Museu de Arte Moderna, 1955.

Ynez Johnston: Graphic Work 1949-1966. San Francisco: San
    Francisco Museum of Art, 1967.

Ynez Johnston: Recent Paintings. Los Angeles: Paul Kantor
    Gallery, 1953.

AMY JONES (1899-    )   Painter

Archives of American Art. Collection of Exhibition Catalogs. Boston:  G.K. Hall and Co., 1979.

Park, Marlene, and Markowitz, Gerald E. Democratic Vista:  Post Offices and Public Art in the New Deal. Philadelphia:  Temple University Press, 1984.

Who's Who in American Art. Washington, D.C.:  American Federation of Arts, 1970.

JANE JONES (1907-    )   Painter

See volume 1 of this book.

Mallett, Daniel Trowbridge. Supplement to Mallett's Index of Artists. New York:  Peter Smith, 1948.

LOIS MAILOU JONES [PIERRE-NOEL] (1905-    )   Painter

See volume 1 of this book.

Atkinson, J. Edward, ed. Black Dimensions in Contemporary American Art. New York:  New American Library, 1971.

Campbell, Mary Schmidt. Tradition and Conflict:  Images of a Turbulent Decade, 1963-1973. New York:  The Studio Museum in Harlem, 1985.

Driskell, David C. Hidden Heritage:  Afro-American Art 1800-1950. Bellevue, Washington:  Bellevue Art Museum, 1985.

Gold, Allan R. "Exhibition for Black Artists Defended." The New York Times, 26 January 1988:  Y22.

Kelly, Mary Lou. "Lois Mailou Jones--Incisive Artist." Christian Science Monitor, 13 April 1973:  5-6.

Laduke, Betty. "Lois Mailou Jones:  The Grande Dame of African-American Art." Woman's Art Journal 8, no. 2 (Fall 1987-Winter 1988):  28-32.

Lois Mailou Jones Peintures 1937-1951. Tourcoing, France:  Presses Georges Frère, 1952.

Lois Mailou Jones:  Retrospective Exhibition 1932-1972. Washington, D.C.:  Howard University Gallery of Art, 1972.

Morrison, Keith.  Art in Washington and Its Afro-American Presence: 1940-1970.  Washington, D.C.:  Washington Project for the Arts, 1985.

Newfield, Marcia.  "Overdue Applause Greets Black Artists."  New Directions for Women  (March-April 1985):  4.

Women's Caucus for Art Honor Awards.  New York:  Women's Caucus for Art, 1986.

NELL CHOATE JONES (1879-1981)   Painter

Chambers, Bruce W.  Art and Artists of the South.  Columbia, South Carolina:  University of South Carolina Press, 1984.

Eight Southern Women.  Greenville, South Carolina:  Greenville County Museum of Art, 1986.

Paintings by Nell Choate Jones.  New York:  Marbella Gallery, 1979.

Who's Who in American Art, vol. 10.  Washington, D.C.:  American Federation of Arts, 1970.

JOHANNA JORDAN (1919-    )   Sculptor

Art Connections '84, Orange County Sculpture:  Source and Process.  Orange, California:  Guggenheim Gallery, Chapman College, 1984.

California Art Review.  Chicago:  Krantz, 1981.

Ewing, Richard.  "Reviews: Johanna Jordan at Abraxas Gallery."  Images and Issues 2, no. 3 (September-October 1982):  61.

Jordan, Johanna.  "Polychromed Multi-Positional, Sheet Aluminum Sculpture."  Leonardo 16, no. 1 (Winter 1983):  43-45.

Lewis, Roger.  "California Profiles:  Johanna Jordan (Laguna Beach)."  Art Voices 4, no. 1 (January-February 1981):  47.

Southern California 100.  Laguna Beach:  Laguna Beach Museum of Art, 1977.

Watson-Jones, Virginia.  Contemporary American Women Sculptors.  Phoenix:  Oryx Press, 1986.

216

MARY FRANCES JUDGE (1935-    )    Painter

See volume 1 of this book.

Who's Who in American Art. New York:  R.R. Bowker Co., 1986.


SYLVIA SHAW JUDSON (1897-1978)    Sculptor

American Art Annual, vol. 28.  Washington, D.C.:  American
    Federation of Arts, 1932.

Barrie, Dennis.  "Detroit."  Archives of American Art Journal 18
    (November 1978):  26.

Clark, Eliot.  History of the National Academy of Design, 1825-1953.
    New York:  Columbia University Press, 1954.

Fairmount Park Association, Philadelphia.  Sculpture of a City:
    Philadelphia's Treasures in Bronze and Stone.  New York:
    Walker Publishing Co., 1974.

Painting and Sculpture from 16 American Cities.  New York:  The
    Museum of Modern Art, 1933:  107.

Proske, Beatrice G.  Brookgreen Gardens.  Brookgreen, South
    Carolina:  Trustees, 1968.

Schnier, Jacques.  Sculpture in Modern America.  Berkeley:
    University of California Press, 1948:  64, 90.

Who's Who in American Art, vol. 1.  Washington, D.C.:  American
    Federation of Arts, 1935.


LUISE KAISH (1925-    )    Sculptor

See volume 1 of this book.

Annual Exhibition of Contemporary American Sculpture.  New York:
    Whitney Museum of American Art, 1962, 1964, 1966.

Annual Exhibition of Painting and Sculpture.  Philadelphia:
    Pennsylvania Academy of the Fine Arts, 1952, 1953, 1961, 1964.

Dash, Robert W.  "In the Galleries:  Luise Kaish."  Arts Magazine
    32, no. 7 (April 1958):  63.

Henry, Gerrit.  "Luise Kaish:  A Lyrical Essay."  Arts Magazine 62,
    no. 7 (March 1988):  86-88.

217

Kampf, Avram. Contemporary Synagogue Art: Developments in the United States, 1945-1965. New York: Union of American Hebrew Congregations, 1966.

_____. Jewish Experience in the Art of the Twentieth Century. South Hadley, Massachusetts: Bergin and Garvey, 1984.

Lipsey, Roger. "Luise Kaish's Small Worlds." Arts Magazine 56, no. 3 (November 1981): 158-60.

Luise Kaish. New York: Sculpture Center, 1958.

Martin, Richard. "Luise Kaish." Arts Magazine 59, no. 2 (October 1984): 11.

The New Decade: Thirty-Five American Painters and Sculptors. New York: Whitney Museum of American Art, 1955.

Sculptors Guild Annual Exhibition. New York: Lever House, 1960-1979.

Watson-Jones, Virginia. Contemporary American Women Sculptors. Phoenix: Oryx Press, 1986.


MARY KAUFMAN KARASICK (1888-1985)    Painter

Whelan, Anne. "Kent's Mary Karasick, Former Bridgeport Draftsman, a Distinguished Artist in the Academic Tradition." The Bridgeport Sunday Post 27 November 1949: B5.

Who's Who in American Art, vol. 3. Washington, D.C.: American Federation of Arts, 1940.


KAREN KARNES (1920-    )    Ceramicist

Clark, Garth. American Potters, The Work of Twenty Modern Masters. New York: Watson-Guptill, 1981.

_____. A Century of Ceramics in the United States 1878-1978. New York: E.P. Dutton, 1979.

Duberman, Martin. Black Mountain: An Exploration in Community. New York: E.P. Dutton, 1972.

Nordness, Lee. Objects: U.S.A. New York: The Viking Press, 1970.

Robertson, Seonaid. "Karen Karnes." Ceramic Review (March-April 1978).

218

Schwartz, Judith S. "The Essential Karnes." Karen Karnes: Works
1964-1977. New York: Hadler Gallery, 1977.

Smith, Dido. "Karen Karnes." Craft Horizons 18, no. 3 (May-June
1958).


GERTRUDE KÄSEBIER (1852-1934)   Photographer

See volume 1 of this book.

Gover, C. Jane. The Positive Image. Albany: State University of
New York, 1988.

Naef, Weston J. The Collection of Alfred Steiglitz. New York:
Viking Press, 1978.

National Museum of Women in the Arts. New York: Harry N. Abrams,
Inc., 1987: 72-73.

Slatkin, Wendy. Women Artists in History. Englewood Cliffs, New
Jersey: Prentice-Hall, 1985.

Szarkowski, John. Looking at Photographs: 100 Pictures from the
Collection of the Museum of Modern Art. New York: The Museum
of Modern Art, 1973.


DEBORAH KASS (20th Century)   Painter

Cameron, Dan. "Second Nature: New Paintings by Deborah Kass."
Arts Magazine 60, no. 8 (April 1986): 37-39.

Cohen, Ronny. "Deborah Kass." Artforum 24, no. 10 (Summer 1986):
128.

Dunn, Fontaine. "Deborah Kass." Arts Magazine 58, no. 5 (January
1984): 25.

Henry, Gerrit. "Deborah Kass." Art News 83, no. 4 (April 1984):
168.

Liebmann, Lisa. "Deborah Kass." Artforum 22, no. 8 (April 1984):
76.

Nadelman, Cynthia. "New Editions." Art News 86, no. 10 (October
1987): 135.

Westfall, Stephen. "Deborah Kass at Baskerville + Watson." Art in
America 74, no. 7 (July 1986): 123.

LILA PELL KATZEN (1932-    )    Sculptor

See volume 1 of this book.

Art:  A Woman's Sensibility.  Valencia, California:  California
      Institute of the Arts, 1975.

Floored.  Curated by John Perreault.  Greenvale, New York:
      Hillwood Art Gallery, Long Island University, 1983.

Henry, Gerrit.  "Sculpture Returns to the Garden."  Art News 82,
      no. 2 (February 1983):  143, 146.

Lila Katzen/Sculpture:  Ruins and Reconstructions.  Essay by Donald
      Kuspit.  New York:  Alex Rosenberg Gallery, 1985.

Morris, Diana.  "Lila Katzen, 'Dialogues.'"  Women Artists News 6,
      no. 5 (November 1980):  10.

O'Beil, Hedy.  "Lila Katzen."  Arts Magazine 59, no. 5 (January
      1985):  41.

Stevens, Elizabeth.  "Lila Katzen."  Arts Magazine 52, no. 10 (June
      1978):  23.

Watson-Jones, Virginia.  Contemporary American Women Sculptors.
      Phoenix:  Oryx Press, 1985.

Who's Who in American Art.  New York:  R.R. Bowker Co., 1986.

Zimmer, William.  "Mayan Themes in Stamford Sculpture Show."  The
      New York Times, 24 August 1986:  CN28.


                    JANE KAUFMAN (1938-    )    Painter

See volume 1 of this book.

One Man's Choice.  Dallas:  Dallas Museum of Fine Arts, 1969.

Who's Who in American Art.  Washington, D.C.:  American Federation
      of Arts, 1986.


                    LEE LUFKIN KAULA (1865-1957)    Painter

See volume 1 of this book.

American Art Annual, vol. 28.  Washington, D.C.:  American
      Federation of Arts, 1932.

Clement, Clara Erskine.  Women in the Fine Arts.  Boston:
      Houghton, Mifflin and Co., 1904.

Fielding, Mantle.  Dictionary of American Painters, Sculptors and
    Engravers.  Enlarged ed.  Greens Farms, Connecticut:  Modern
    Books and Crafts, 1974.


DORA WHEELER [KEITH]  (1857-1940)    Painter

See Dora Wheeler.


JULIE HART BEERS KEMPSON  (1835-1913)    Painter

Gerdts, William H.  Painting and Sculpture in New Jersey.
    Princeton:  Van Nostrand, 1964.

_____.  Women Artists of America 1707-1964.  Newark, New Jersey:
    Newark Museum, 1965.

_____ and Burke, Russell.  American Still-Life Painting.  New York:
    Praeger, 1971.

Groce, George C., and Wallace, David H.  The New-York Historical
    Society's Dictionary of Artists in America 1564-1860.  New
    Haven:  Yale University Press, 1957.


MARIE BOENING KENDALL  (1885-1953)    Painter

American Art Annual, vol. 28.  Washington, D.C.:  American
    Federation of Arts, 1932.

An Exhibition of Women Students of William Merritt Chase.  New
    York:  Marbella Gallery, 1973.

Fielding, Mantle.  Dictionary of American Painters, Sculptors and
    Engravers.  Enlarged ed.  Greens Farms, Connecticut:  Modern
    Books and Crafts, 1974.

Moure, Nancy D.  Dictionary of Artists in Southern California
    Before 1950.  Los Angeles:  Dustin Publications, 1975.


ADALINE KENT  (1900-1957)    Sculptor

See volume 1 of this book.

MacAgy, Jermayne; Kent, Alice C.; and Howard, Robert B., eds.
    Autobiography from the Notebooks and Sculpture of Adaline
    Kent.  Houston:  privately printed, 1958.

Mobiles and Articulated Sculpture.  San Francisco:  California
    Palace of the Legion of Honor, 1948.

100 Years of California Sculpture. Oakland, California:  The
    Oakland Museum, 1982.

Painting and Sculpture in California:  The Modern Era.  San
    Francisco:  California Palace of the Legion of Honor, 1976.

Ritchie, Andrew C.  Abstract Painting and Sculpture in America.
    New York:  The Museum of Modern Art, 1951:  152.

Ventura, Anita.  "Adaline Kent and Jeanne Miles (Betty Parsons
    Gallery)."  Arts Magazine 30, no. 8 (May 1956):  55.


                CORITA KENT (1918-1986)    Printmaker

See volume 1 of this book.

Obituary.  The New York Times, 20 September 1986:  14.


                MAURIE KERRIGAN (1951-    )   Sculptor

McFadden, Sarah.  "Report from Philadelphia."  Art in America 67,
    no. 3 (May-June 1979):  21-29.

Projects Made in Philadelphia.  Philadelphia:  Institute of
    Contemporary Art of University of Pennsylvania, 1982.

Return of the Narrative.  Palm Springs, California:  Palm Springs
    Desert Museum, 1984.

Silverthorne, Jeanne.  "Maurie Kerrigan."  Arts Magazine 54, no. 4
    (December 1979):  12.

Slatkin, Wendy.  "Maurie Kerrigan."  Arts Magazine 57, no. 9 (May
    1983):  12.

Seventy-Sixth Exhibition by Artists of Chicago and Vicinity.
    Chicago:  Art Institute of Chicago, 1977.

Watson-Jones, Virginia.  Contemporary American Women Sculptors.
    Phoenix:  Oryx Press, 1986.

Wooster, Ann-Sargent.  "Maurie Kerrigan at Touchstone."  Art in
    America 69, no. 10 (December 1981):  147, 149.


                KATHARINE KIMBALL (1866-1949)    Etcher

American Art Annual, vol. 28.  Washington, D.C.:  American
    Federation of Arts, 1932.

American Prints in the Library of Congress:  A Catalog of the
  Collection.  Baltimore:  Johns Hopkins Press, 1970.

Fielding, Mantle.  Dictionary of American Painters, Sculptors and
  Engravers.  Enlarged ed.  Greens Farms, Connecticut:  Modern
  Books and Crafts, 1974.

A Selection of American Prints.  A Selection of Biographies of
  Forty Women Artists Working Between 1904-1979.  Santa Rosa,
  California:  The Annex Galleries, 1987:  9.


YEFFE KIMBALL [SLATIN] (1914-1978)    Painter

See volume 1 of this book.

Who's Who in American Art.  New York:  R.R. Bowker Co., 1978.


ELEANORA KISSEL (1891-1966)    Painter

Dawdy, Doris Ostrander.  Artists of the American West:  A
  Biographical Dictionary, vol. 2.  Chicago:  Sage Books, 1980.

Samuels, Peggy and Harold.  The Illustrated Biographical
  Encyclopedia of Artists of the American West.  Garden City,
  New York:  Doubleday, 1976.

Who's Who in American Art, vol. 4.  Washington, D.C.:  American
  Federation of Arts, 1947.


THEO ALICE RUGGLES KITSON (1871-1932)    Sculptor

See volume 1 of this book.

Fielding, Mantle.  Dictionary of American Painters, Sculptors and
  Engravers.  Enlarged ed.  Greens Farms, Connecticut:  Modern
  Books and Crafts, 1974.

Freeman, Robert, and Lasky, Vivienne.  Hidden Treasures:  Public
  Sculpture in Providence.  Providence, Rhode Island:  Rhode
  Island Bicentennial Foundation, 1980.

"Kitson, Theo Alice Ruggles."  Encyclopedia Americana, vol. 16.
  New York and Chicago, 1950.

"Mrs. Kitson, Sculptor, Dies."  Art Digest (15 November 1932):  18.

Obituary.  American Art Annual, vol. 29.  Washington, D.C.:
  American Federation of Arts, 1933.

Woman's Who's Who of America. New York:  American Commonwealth
    Co., 1914.

World's Columbian Exposition, 1893, Official Catalogue.  Chicago:
    W. B. Conkey Co., 1893:  13.

BETTY KLAVUN (1916-     )   Sculptor

See volume 1 of this book.

Artpark:  The Program in Visual Arts.  Lewiston, New York:
    Artpark, 1977.

Bennetts, Leslie.  "Children Keep Sculpture Alive, and Also in Need
    of Repairs."  The New York Times, 28 May 1979:  A10.

Hoffman, Marilyn.  "Artist Designs Sturdy 'Sculpture' Playhouses
    for Children."  The Christian Science Monitor, 30 March 1981:
    18.

National Association of Women Artists Annual Exhibition.  New York:
    National Academy of Design, 1973.

National Association of Women Artists Annual Exhibition.  New York:
    National Academy of Design, 1975.

Watson-Jones, Virginia.  Contemporary American Women Sculptors.
    Phoenix:  Oryx Press, 1986.

VERA KLEMENT (1929-     )   Painter

See volume 1 of this book.

Ashton, Dore.  "Two Part Connection:  Vera Klement's Painting."
    Arts Magazine 58, no. 7 (March 1984):  78-79.

Dresner, Harold.  "Vera Klement, Roy Boyd Gallery."  New Art
    Examiner 14, no. 11 (Summer 1987):  44-45.

Moser, Charlotte.  "Chicago.  Vera Klement (Renaissance Society)."
    Art News 86, no. 6 (Summer 1987):  60, 62.

ORPHA KLINKER (1891-1964)   Painter

Moure, Nancy D.  Dictionary of Artists in Southern California
    Before 1950.  Los Angeles:  Dustin Publications, 1975.

Obituary.  Who's Who in American Art, vol. 9.  Washington, D.C.:
    American Federation of Arts, 1966.

224

Southern California Artists, 1890-1940. Laguna Beach, California: Laguna Beach Museum of Art, 1979.

A Woman's Vision: California Painting into the 20th Century. San Francisco: Maxwell Galleries, 1983.


                GEORGINA KLITGAARD (1893-1976)    Painter

See volume 1 of this book.

American Art Annual, vol. 28. Washington, D.C.: American Federation of Arts, 1932.

First Biennial Exhibition of Contemporary American Sculpture, Watercolors and Prints. New York: Whitney Museum of American Art, 1933-34.

Mechlin, Leila. "The Art of Today at Pittsburgh." The American Magazine of Art 20, no. 12 (December 1929): 685.

Who's Who in American Art, vol. 10. Washington, D.C.: American Federation of Arts, 1970.

Zaidenberg, Arthur, compiled by. The Art of the Artist: Theories and Techniques of Art by the Artists Themselves. New York: Crown Publishers, 1951: 148-49.


                GENE KLOSS (1903-    )    Painter and Printmaker

"Drypoints and Scenes of Southwest." Art News 47, no. 4 (April 1948): 8.

Kovinick, Phil. The Woman Artist in the American West, 1860-1960. Fullerton, California: Muckenthaler Cultural Center, 1976.

Morrow, B. F. "Highlights of Copper." Prints 7 (December 1936): 80-83.

Nelson, Mary Carroll. "Intaglios by Gene Kloss." American Artist 42, issue 427 (February 1978): 64-69, 86-91.

"New Aquatints." Art News 44, no. 2 (February 1946): 16.

Reese, Albert. American Prize Prints of the 20th Century. New York: American Artists Group, 1949.

A Selection of American Prints. A Selection of Biographies of Forty Women Artists Working Between 1904-1979. Santa Rosa, California: The Annex Galleries, 1987: 9.

225

Who's Who in American Art, 17th ed.  New York:  R.R. Bowker Co.,
    1986.


    SUZANNE KLOTZ-REILLY (1944-    )   Painter and Sculptor

Arizona Clay Sculpture.  Tucson:  Gross Gallery, University of
    Arizona, 1984.

Arizona Sculpture Invitational.  Flagstaff:  Museum of Northern
    Arizona, 1980, 1982.

Bush, Donald.  "Suzanne Klotz-Reilly at Phoenix Art Museum."
    Art Voices 4, no. 6 (November-December 1981):  59-60.

Collage and Assemblage.  Jackson:  Mississippi Museum of Art, 1981.

Donnell-Kotrozo, Carol.  "Profiles:  Suzanne Klotz-Reilly (Phoenix,
    Arizona)."  Art Craft Magazine 1, no. 2 (February-March 1980):
    37.

_____.  "Suzanne Klotz-Reilly at the Phoenix Art Museum."  Artspace
    5, no. 4 (Fall 1981):  59.

Levine, Melinda.  "Suzanne Klotz-Reilly at Jeremy Stone."
    Images and Issues 4, no. 2 (September-October 1983):  60-61.

Return of the Narrative.  Palm Springs, California:  Palm Springs
    Desert Museum, 1984.

"Roaring Forks Trailer Park."  Ceramics Monthly 30, no. 1 (January
    1982):  58-62.

Sculptors of the Southwest.  New York:  Sculpture Center, 1983.

Watson-Jones, Virginia.  Contemporary American Women Sculptors.
    Phoenix:  Oryx Press, 1986.


    ANNA ELIZABETH KLUMPKE (1856-1942)   Painter

See volume 1 of this book.

American Art Annual, vol. 20.  Washington, D.C.:  American
    Federation of Arts, 1923.

Clement, Clara Erskine.  Women in the Fine Arts.  Boston:
    Houghton, Mifflin and Co., 1904:  196-98.

Tufts, Eleanor.  American Women Artists, 1830-1930.  Washington,
    D.C.:  National Museum of Women in the Arts, 1987.

World's Columbian Exposition, 1893, Official Catalogue. Chicago: W.B. Conkey Co., 1893: 42.


GINA KNEE (1898-1982)   Painter

Eldredge, Charles; Schimmel, Julie; and Truettner, William H. Art in New Mexico, 1900-1945:  Paths to Taos and Santa Fe. Washington, D.C.:  National Museum of American Art, 1986.

Gerdts, William H. Women Artists of America 1707-1964.  Newark: Newark Museum, 1965.

Gina Knee. New York:  Willard Gallery, 1943.

"Gina Knee, 84, Artists Known For Semi-Abstract Works." The New York Times, 4 November 1982.

The Phillips Collection, A Summary Catalogue. Washington, D.C.: The Phillips Collection, 1985.

Samuels, Peggy and Harold. The Illustrated Biographical Encyclopedia of Artists of the American West. Garden City, New York:  Doubleday, 1976.


NELLIE AUGUSTA KNOPF (1875-1962)   Painter

See volume 1 of this book.

Women Pioneers in Maine Art 1900-1945. Portland, Maine:  Joan Whitney Payson Gallery of Art, Westbrook College, 1981.


GRACE KNOWLTON (1932-   )   Sculptor and Photographer

Auer, Michèle, and Auer, Michel. Encyclopédie international des Photographes de 1839 à nos jours. Hermance, Switzerland: Editions Camera Obscura, 1985.

Brenson, Michael. "The City as a Sculpture Garden:  Seeing the New and the Daring." The New York Times, 17 July 1987:  Y15, 18.

Brown, Carol Anderson. "Grace Knowlton." Arts Magazine 59, no. 5 (January 1985):  16.

Darami, Spencer. "Grace Knowlton." Arts Magazine 56, no. 1 (September 1981):  9.

Slivka, Rose. "Grace Knowlton at Twining." Art in America 73, no. 6 (June 1985):  139, 140-41.

Van Wagner, Judy Collischan.  Grace Knowlton.  Brookville, New
     York:  Hillwood Art Gallery, Long Island University, 1987.

_____.  "Grace Knowlton's 'Secret Spaces.'"  Arts Magazine 60, no.
     8 (April 1986):  74-75.


               HELEN MARY KNOWLTON (1832-1918)   Painter

See volume 1 of this book.

American Art Annual, vol. 10.  Washington, D.C.:  American
     Federation of Arts, 1913.

Archives of American Art.  Collection of Exhibition Catalogues.
     Boston:  G.K. Hall, 1979.

Who's Who in American Art, vol. 1.  Washington, D.C.:  American
     Federation of Arts, 1935.


               SUSAN RICKER KNOX (1875-1959)   Painter

American Art Annual, vol. 28.  Washington, D.C.:  American
     Federation of Arts, 1932.

American 19th and 20th Century Paintings, Drawings and Sculpture.
     New York:  Sotheby's, 23 June 1983, Lot 218.

Fielding, Mantle.  Dictionary of American Painters, Sculptors and
     Engravers.  Enlarged ed.  Greens Farms, Connecticut:  Modern
     Books and Crafts, 1974.

Samuels, Peggy and Harold.  Illustrated Biographical Encyclopedia
     of Artists of the American West.  Garden City, New York:
     Doubleday and Co., 1976.

Woman's Who's Who of America.  New York:  American Commonwealth
     Co., 1914.

Who's Who in American Art, vol. 1.  Washington, D.C.:  American
     Federation of Arts, 1935.


               FLORENCE CARY KOEHLER (1861-1944)   Painter and Jeweler

Callen, Anthea.  Women Artists of the Art and Crafts Movement,
     1870-1914.  New York:  Pantheon Books, 1979.

Cummins, Virginia R.  Rookwood Pottery Potpourri.  Silver Springs,
     Maryland:  Cliff R. Leonard and Duke Coleman, 1980.

Portrait of an Artist:  the Paintings and Jewelry of Florence
    Koehler, 1861-1944.  Providence:  Rhode Island School of
    Design Museum of Art, 1947.

Weiss, Peg.  "Florence Koehler and Mary Elizabeth Sharpe:  An
    American Saga of Art and Patronage."  Arts Magazine 53, no. 4
    (December 1978):  108-17.


                    IDA KOHLMEYER (1912-    )   Painter

See volume 1 of this book.

Green, Roger.  "Ida Kohlmeyer Month, New Orleans."  Art News 84,
    no. 6 (Summer 1985):  104-06.

Ida Kohlmeyer, Paintings and Sculpture.  New York:  Gimpel and
    Weitzenhoffer Gallery, 1984.

Ida Kohlmeyer:  Thirty Years.  Charlotte, North Carolina:  Mint
    Museum, 1983.


National Museum of Women in the Arts.  New York:  Harry N. Abrams,
    Inc., 1987:  206.

Watson-Jones, Virginia.  Contemporary American Women Sculptors.
    Phoenix:  Oryx Press, 1986.

Who's Who in American Art, 17th ed.  New York:  R.R. Bowker Co.,
    1986.

Wolff, Theodore F.  "Everyday Sculpture."  Christian Science
    Monitor, 2 May 1985:  46.


                    MARY KOLLOCK (1840-1911)   Painter

See volume 1 of this book.

Fielding, Mantle.  Dictionary of American Painters, Sculptors and
    Engravers.  Enlarged ed.  Greens Farms, Connecticut:  Modern
    Books and Crafts, 1974.


                MIRA EDGERLY KORZYBSKI (1872-1954)   Painter

American Art Annual, vol. 28.  Washington, D.C.:  American
    Federation of Arts, 1932.

Earle, Helen L.  Biographical Sketches of American Artists.
     Lansing:  Michigan State Library, 1912.

Who's Who in American Art, vol. 3.  Washington, D.C.:  American
     Federation of Arts, 1940.


               JOYCE KOZLOFF (1942-    )   Painter

See volume 1 of this book.

Field, Richard S., and Fine, Ruth E.  A Graphic Muse.  New York:
     Hudson Hills Press, 1987.

I-80 Series:  Joyce Kozloff.  Omaha, Nebraska:  Joslyn Art Museum,
     1982.

Johnston, Patricia.  Joyce Kozloff:  Visionary Ornament.  Boston:
     Boston University Art Gallery, 1986.

McGill, Douglas C.  "Art Enhances Region's Restored Train
     Stations."  The New York Times, 14 July 1985.

Robins, Corinne.  "Joyce Kozloff."  Arts Magazine 50, no. 10 (June
     1976):  5.

Stapen, Nancy.  "Joyce Kozloff."  Artforum 24, no. 10 (Summer
     1986):  130-31.

"Two Ethnics Sitting Around Talking About Wasp Culture, A
     Conversation between Joyce Kozloff and Jeff Perrone."  Arts
     Magazine 59, no. 7 (March 1985):  78-83.

Webster, Sally.  "Pattern and Decoration in the Public Eye."  Art
     in America 75, no. 2 (February 1987):  118-25.


               LINDA KRAMER (1937-    )   Sculptor

Alternative Spaces:  A History in Chicago.  Chicago:  Museum of
     Contemporary Art, 1984.

American Chairs:  Form, Function, and Fantasy.  Sheboygan,
     Wisconsin:  John Michael Kohler Arts Center, 1978.

Chicago and Vicinity, Painting and Sculpture.  Chicago:  The Art
     Institute of Chicago, 1977.

Chicago and Vicinity, Painting and Sculpture.  Chicago:  The Art
     Institute of Chicago, 1980.

Chicago and Vicinity, Painting and Sculpture.  Chicago:  The Art
     Institute of Chicago, 1984.

230

Elliot, David. "Chicago Enjoys Its Own Eclecticism." Art News 81, no. 5 (May 1982): 90-94.

_____. "Kramer's 'Current Energy' Lights Up Columbia Gallery." Chicago Sun-Times, 28 February 1982: 20.

Frueh, Joanna. "Linda Kramer and Claire Prussian at Artemisia." Art in America 65, no. 5 (September-October 1977): 121.

Koplos, Janet. "Linda Kramer." American Ceramics 2, no. 4 (Winter 1984): 14-19.

Kramer, Linda. "Natural and Cultural Energy: Installation Sculpture 1980-1985." Leonardo 20, no. 1 (1987): 23-26.

Meilach, Dona Z. Box Environments, with Assemblage and Construction. New York: Crown, 1975.

Painting and Sculpture Today 1978. Indianapolis: Indianapolis Museum of Art, 1978.

Taylor, Sue. "Ceramics break out of mold." Chicago Sun-Times, 13 March 1986: 78.

Thirty-Second Illinois Invitational. Springfield: Illinois State Museum, 1980.

Watson-Jones, Virginia. Contemporary American Women Sculptors. Phoenix: Oryx Press, 1986.

LEE KRASNER (1908-1984)    Painter

See volume 1 of this book.

Bell, Jane. "Lee Krasner." Art News 86, no. 3 (March 1987): 147.

Brenson, Michael. "Lee Krasner Pollock is Dead; Painter of New York School." The New York Times, 21 June 1984: Y25.

Cannell, Michael. "An Interview with Lee Krasner." Arts Magazine 59, no. 1 (September 1984): 87-89.

Glueck, Grace. "Art: Lee Krasner Finds Her Place in Retrospective at Modern." The New York Times, 21 December 1984: Section C: 31.

_____. "The 20th Century Artists Most Admired by Other Artists." Art News 76, no. 9 (November 1977): 89.

A Guide to the Collection. Houston: Museum of Fine Arts, 1981.

Hughes, Robert.  "Bursting Out of the Shadows."  Time, 14 November
    1983:  92-93.

Krasner/Pollock:  A Working Relationship.  Essay by Barbara Rose.
    New York:  Grey Art Gallery, New York University, 1981.

Landau, Ellen.  "Lee Krasner's Past Continuous."  Art News 83, no.
    2 (February 1984):  68-76.

Lee Krasner Collages.  Essay by Bryan Robertson.  Introduction by
    Robert Hughes.  New York:  Robert Miller Gallery, 1986.

Lee Krasner:  Recent Work.  New York:  Pace Gallery, 1981.

National Museum of Women in the Arts.  New York:  Harry N. Abrams,
    Inc., 1987:  92.

Rose, Barbara.  Lee Krasner:  A Retrospective.  New York:  The
    Museum of Modern Art, 1983.

Sill, Gertrude Grace.  "The Face in the Mirror."  Connoisseur (July
    1986):  51.

Vetrocq, Marcia E.  "An Independent Tack:  Lee Krasner."  Art in
    America 72, no. 5 (May 1984):  136-45.

Wallach, Amei.  "Krasner's Triumph."  Vogue, November 1983:
    442-45, 501-02.

Woodville, Louisa.  "Three Painters, Three Decades."  Arts Magazine
    59, no. 5 (January 1985):  19.

BARBARA KRUGER (1945-    )   Painter

Barbara Kruger:  Art of Representation.  London:  Institute of
    Contemporary Arts, 1983.

Barbara Kruger:  'We Won't Play Nature to Your Culture.'"  London:
    Institute of Contemporary Arts, 1983.

Brenson, Michael.  "Art:  Whitney Biennial's New Look."  The New
    York Times, 10 April 1987:  17.

Foster, Hal.  "Subversive Signs."  Art in America 70, no. 10
    (November 1982):  88-92.

Kunst mit Eigen-Sinn.  Aktuelle Kunst von Frauen.  Vienna and
    Munich:  Löcher Verlag, 1985.

Linker, Kate.  "Barbara Kruger."  Artforum 22, no. 1 (September
    1983):  77.

_____. "Barbara Kruger." Flash Art 121 (March 1985): 36-37.

McEvilley, Thomas. "Barbara Kruger." Artforum 24, no. 10 (Summer 1986): 122-23.

1973 Whitney Biennial. New York: Whitney Museum of American Art, 1973.

1983 Whitney Biennial. New York: Whitney Museum of American Art, 1983.

1987 Whitney Biennial. New York: Whitney Museum of American Art, 1987.

Owens, Craig. "The Medusa Effect of The Spectacular Ruse." Art in America 72, no. 1 (January 1984): 97-105.

Rice, Shelley. "Image-Making." Soho Weekly News, January 1979.

Siegel, Jeanne. "Barbara Kruger: Pictures and Words." Arts Magazine 61, no. 10 (Summer 1987): 17-21.

Squiers, Carol. "Diversionary (Syn)tactics, Barbara Kruger Has Her Way with Words." Art News 86, no. 2 (February 1987): 76-85, cover.

Sturken, Marita. "A Whitney Sampler." Afterimage 11, no. 3 (October 1983): 18.

LOUISE KRUGER (1924-    )   Sculptor

Annual Exhibition: Contemporary American Art. New York: Whitney Museum of American Art, 1960.

Annual Exhibition: Contemporary American Art. New York: Whitney Museum of American Art, 1961.

Annual Exhibition: Contemporary American Art. New York: Whitney Museum of American Art, 1962.

Glueck, Grace. "Art: Sculptured Figures of the 70's at Pratt Gallery." The New York Times, 7 November 1980: C19.

Henry, Gerrit. "Louise Kruger: Expressions in Wood." American Craft 40, no. 6 (December 1980-January 1981): 26-29.

Louise Kruger. New York: Robert Schoelkopf Gallery, 1968.

Mainardi, Patricia. "Louise Kruger." Arts Magazine 55, no. 7 (March 1981): 13.

O'Beil, Hedy. "Louise Kruger." Arts Magazine 52, no. 10 (June
1978): 48.

Sixty-Second Annual Exhibition of American Paintings and Sculpture.
Chicago: Art Institute of Chicago, 1957.

Watson-Jones, Virginia. Contemporary American Women Sculptors.
Phoenix: Oryx Press, 1986.


IRENE KRUGMAN (1925-1982)   Sculptor

Alloway, Lawrence. "Irene Krugman: An Obituary." Woman's Art
Journal 5, no. 2 (Fall 1984/Winter 1985): 53-54.

Brown, Gordon. "Irene Krugman." Arts Magazine 45, no. 6 (February
1971): 64.

Glueck, Grace. "Irene Krugman." The New York Times, 4 February
1977.

Malen, Lenore. "Irene Krugman." Arts Magazine 52, no. 8 (April
1978): 24.

Who's Who in American Art. New York: R.R. Bowker, 1978.

Works on Paper--Women Artists. (June Blum, Curator). Brooklyn:
Brooklyn Museum, 1975.


DIANA KURZ (1936-    )   Painter

Bard, Joellen. "Diana Kurz." Arts Magazine 51, no. 7 (March
1977): 12.

Campbell, Lawrence. "Diana Kurz at Alex Roxenberg." Art in
America 72, no. 5 (May 1984): 175, 177.

Diana Kurz: Figure Studies. Introduction by Lawrence Alloway.
Queens, New York: Queens College, 1977.

Langer, Sandra L. "Diana Kurz." Arts Magazine 58, no. 6 (February
1984): 14.

Morris, Diana. "Diana Kuraz, Recent Paintings." Women Artists
News 9, no. 4 (May-June 1984): 6.

O'Beil, Hedy. "Diana Kurz." Arts Magazine 58, no. 9 (May 1984):
41.

Selected Twentieth Century American Nudes. Introduction by John
Perreault. New York: Harold Reed Gallery, 1978.

234

Six Painters of the Figure. Introduction by Jean-Edith
    Weiffenbach. Boulder, Colorado: University of Colorado Art
    Gallery, 1979.


                KYRA [BELÁN SULLIVAN] (1947-    )    Painter

See volume 1 of this book.

Alioto, Susanne. "Kyra: Giving a Shape to Magic Realism." The
    Miami Herald, 11 February 1982.

Blaylock, Debbie. "Artist's Works Soar with Spirit of Freedom."
    Fort Lauderdale News/Sun Sentinel, 30 June 1985.

Erotica. Milwaukee: University of Wisconsin-Milwaukee Union Art
    Gallery, 1984.

Expressions! The 6th Annual Competition and Exhibition. (Judy
    Chicago, Juror). Hollywood, Florida: Art and Culture Center
    of Hollywood, 1986.

Kyra. "Censored: The Male Nude." Women Artists News 8, no. 2
    (Winter 1982-83): 26.

Kyra. "Profile." Hue Points 14, no. 1 (1986): 14.

Third Annual Miami Waves Experimental Film and Video Forum.
    (Sandra Langer, Juror). Miami: Miami-Dade Community College,
    1984.

30th Anniversary Gallery Exhibition. Fort Lauderdale: Broward Art
    Guild, 1982.

24th Annual M. Allen Hortt Memorial Exhibition. Fort Lauderdale:
    Museum of Art, 1982.


                SUZANNE LACY (1945-    )    Conceptual Artist

See volume 1 of this book.

"Political Performance Art: A Discussion by Suzanne Lacy and Lucy
    R. Lippard." Heresies 5, no. 1 (1984): 22-25.

Raven, Arlene. Crossing Over: Feminism and Art of Social Concern.
    Ann Arbor, Michigan: U.M.I. Press, 1988.

Roth, Moira. "Suzanne Lacy at the IDS Building (Minneapolis)."
    Art in America 76, no. 3 (March 1988): 162.

ANNA COLEMAN LADD (1878-1939)    Sculptor

See volume 1 of this book.

American Art Annual, vol. 28.  Washington, D.C.:  American
     Federation of Arts, 1932.

Archives of American Art.  A Checklist of the Collection.
     Washington, D.C.:  Smithsonian Institution, 1975.

Continental & Victorian.  Boston:  Robert W. Skinner, Copley Square
     Gallery, 1983:  Lots 301-346.

Ladd, Anna Coleman.  The Life of Anna Coleman Ladd.  Boston:
     Seaver Howland Press, 1920.

Proske, Beatrice G.  Brookgreen Gardens.  Brookgreen, South
     Carolina:  Brookgreen Gardens, 1943.

LILI LAKICH (1944-    )    Neon Artist

Askey, Ruth.  "Lili Lakich's Neon Portraits."  Artweek, 5 November
     1977:  5.

Donahue, Marlena.  "Neon Art Museum Exhibit; It's a Gas."  Los
     Angeles Times, 29 December 1984, Calendar Section:  1, 3.

Gable, Mona.  "The Neon Renaissance:  Recharging an Electric Art."
     The Wall Street Journal, 9 May 1985:  30.

Gamwell, Lynn.  "Approaches to Neon."  Artweek 9, no. 10 (11 March
     1978).

Lakich, Lili.  "What's New in Neon."  Los Angeles Times Magazine 2,
     no. 3 (19 January 1986):  cover, 15.

"Lili Lakich."  Artweek 5, no. 8 (23 February 1974):  6.

Moufarrege, Nicolas A.  "Lavender:  On Homosexuality and Art."
     Arts Magazine 57, no. 2 (October 1982):  85-86.

Neon Art from the West Coast.  Tokyo:  The Seibu Museum of Art,
     1984.

Neon Lovers Glow in the Dark, Lili Lakich.  Los Angeles:  Museum of
     Neon Art, 1986.

Plagens, Peter.  "Lili Lakich."  Artforum 13, no. 1 (September
     1974):  88-89.

Raven, Arlene.  "Your Goodbye Left Me with Eyes That Cry."
     Chrysalis 5 (1978):  53-57.

236

_____, and Iskin, Ruth. "Through The Peephole: Toward a Lesbian Sensibility in Art." Chrysalis 3 (October 1977): 19-31.

Wilson, William. Neon Signs and Symbols. Fullerton, California: Art Gallery, California State University, 1973.

Zone, Ray. "Spectral Psalms." Artweek 17, no. 9 (8 March 1986): 6.


JENNETT BRINSMADE LAM (1911-1983)    Painter

See volume 1 of this book.

Who's Who in American Art. New York: R.R. Bowker Co., 1978.


ELLA CONDIE LAMB (1862-1936)    Painter

See volume 1 of this book.

American Art Annual, vol. 28. Washington, D.C.: American Federation of Arts, 1932.

Fielding, Mantle. Dictionary of American Painters, Sculptors and Engravers. Enlarged ed. Greens Farms, Connecticut: Modern Books and Crafts, 1974.

Hoeber, Arthur. "Famous American Women Painters." Mentor 2, no. 3 (16 March 1914): 1, 6.

Obituary. Who's Who in American Art, vol. 2. Washington, D.C.: American Federation of Arts, 1937.

Woman's Who's Who of America. New York: American Commonwealth Co., 1914.


ROSE [ROSANNA] D. LAMB (1843-1927)    Painter

See volume 1 of this book.

Clement, Clara Erskine. Women in the Fine Arts. Boston: Houghton, Mifflin and Co., 1904.

Harding, Jonathan P. The Boston Athenaeum Collection Pre-Twentieth Century American and European Painting and Sculpture. Boston: Boston Athenaeum, 1984.

Washington University Gallery of Art, Illustrated Checklist. Saint Louis: Washington University, 1981: 51.

237

ELLEN LAMPERT (1948-    )    Painter

Ball, Maudette.  "Bitter Laughter."  Artweek 14, no. 34 (15 October
     1983):  4.

Ellen Lampert:  American Dreaming.  Santa Clara, California:
     Triton Museum of Art, 1983.

Ewing, Robert.  "Juicy Orange."  Artweek 14, no. 7 (19 February
     1983):  6.

Moore, Louise.  "Women's Worlds."  Artweek 14, no. 10 (12 March
     1983):  6.

Welles, Elenore.  "Continuing Generations."  Artweek 14, no. 14 (9
     April 1983):  4-5.

Who's Who in American Art, 17th ed.  New York:  R.R. Bowker Co.,
     1986.

Withers, Josephine.  "On the Inside Looking Out."  Feminist Studies
     11, no. 3 (Fall 1985):  559-68, cover.


          LOUISA LANDER (1826-1923)  Sculptor

See volume 1 of this book.

Clement, Clara Erskine.  Women in the Fine Arts.  Boston:  Houghton
     Mifflin Co., 1904.

Gollin, Rita K.  Portraits of Nathaniel Hawthorne.  DeKalb,
     Illinois:  Northern Illinois University Press, 1983.

Hanaford, Phebe A.  Daughters of America.  Augusta, Maine:  True
     and Co., 1882:  284-86.

Swan, Mabel Munson.  The Athenaeum Gallery 1827-1873.  Boston:  The
     Boston Athenaeum, 1940.


          KATHERINE WARD LANE (1899-    )    Sculptor

See volume 1 of this book and see "Weems" in volume 2.


          LOIS LANE (1948-    )    Painter and Printmaker

See volume 1 of this book.

Lawson, Thomas.  "Lois Lane at Willard."  Art in America 66, no. 2
     (March-April 1978):  136.

238

Who's Who in American Art, 17th ed.  New York:  R.R. Bowker Co.,
   1986.


SUSAN MINOT LANE (1832-1893)   Painter

Fielding, Mantle.  Dictionary of American Painters, Sculptors and
   Engravers.  Enlarged ed.  Greens Farms, Connecticut:  Modern
   Books, 1974.

Groce, George C., and Wallace, David H.  The New-York Historical
   Society's Dictionary of Artists in America 1564-1860.  New
   Haven:  Yale University Press, 1957.

Hoppin, Martha.  "Women Artists in Boston 1870-1900:  The Pupils of
   William Morris Hunt."  American Art 13, no. 1 (Winter 1981):
   17-46.


MARILYN LANFEAR (1930-   )   Sculptor and Performance Artist

American Women 1980.  São Paulo:  Museu de Arte Contemporanea da
   Universidade de São Paulo, 1980.

"A arte segundo as Norte-Americanas."  O Estado de São Paulo, 26
   October 1980.

"Artistas Americanas."  Folma de São Paulo, 26 October 1980.

Fawcett, Ruth.  "Lead Blouses:  Weighty Fashion."  San Antonio
   Express-News, 12 September 1982.

Moore, Sylvia, ed.  No Bluebonnets, No Yellow Roses:  Essays on
   on Texas Women in the Arts.  New York:  Midmarch Arts Press,
   1988.

Mum, Denise.  "Marilyn Lanfear (Philip Stansbury Gallery, New
   York)."  Women Artists News 12, nos. 4-5 (Fall-Winter 1987):
   41.

Neal, Patsy.  "Lead Blouses A Stunning Exhibit."  San Antonio Light,
   3 September 1982.

Paperworks:  An Exhibition of Texas Artists.  San Antonio:  San
   Antonio Museum Association, 1979.

Seiberling, Dorothy.  "A New Kind of Quilt."  The New York Times
   Magazine, 3 October 1982:  42-50.

Unaffiliated Artists 6.  Brookville, New York:  Hillwood Art
   Gallery, Long Island University, 1988.

ANNIE TRAQUAIR LANG (1885-1918)    Painter

See volume 1 of this book.

19th Century American Women Artists. New York:  Whitney Museum of
     American Art, Downtown Branch, 1976.

Obituary.  American Art Annual, vol. 16.   Washington, D.C.:
     American Federation of Arts, 1919.


DOROTHEA LANGE (1895-1965)    Photographer

See volume 1 of this book.

The Art of California. Oakland:  Oakland Museum, 1984.

Dorothea Lange:  Photographs of a Lifetime.  Essay by Robert Coles.
     Millerton, New York:  Aperture, 1982.

Fisher, Andrea. Let Us Now Praise Famous Women:  Women
     Photographers for the U. S. Government, 1935-1944.  London and
     New York:  Pandora Press, 1987.

Heyman, Therese Thau, et al. Celebrating a Collection, The Work of
     Dorothea Lange. Oakland:  The Oakland Museum, 1978.

Levin, Howard M., and Northrup, Katherine, eds.  Dorothea Lange:
     Farm Security Administration Photographs, 1935-1939, 2 vols.
     Glencoe, Illinois:  Text-Fiche Press, 1980.

Meltzer, Milton. Dorothea Lange:  A Photographer's Life.  New
     York:  Farrar, Straus, and Giroux, 1978.

Ohrn, Karin B. Dorothea Lange and the Documentary Tradition.
     Baton Rouge:  Louisiana State University Press, 1986.

Szarkowski, John. Looking at Photographs:  100 Pictures from the
     Collection of the Museum of Modern Art.  New York:  The Museum
     of Modern Art, 1973.

Taylor, Paul. On the Ground in the Thirties.  Salt Lake City:
     Smith, 1983.


FAY LANSNER (1921-    )   Painter and Tapestry Artist

See volume 1 of this book.

De Lallier, Alexandra.  "Fay Lansner:  Woman as Metaphor." Woman's
     Art Journal 7, no. 2 (Fall 1986-Winter 1987):  41-46.

Fay Lansner. Introduction by Barbara Guest. Swarthmore,
    Pennsylvania: AVA Books, 1977.

Russo, Alexander, ed. Profiles on Women Artists. Frederick,
    Maryland: University Publications of America, 1985: 145.

ELLEN LANYON (1926-    )    Painter

See volume 1 of this book.

Lanyon, Ellen. Strange Games. A 25 Year Retrospective.
    Urbana-Champaign, Illinois: University of Illinois, Krannert
    Art Museum, 1988.

_____, and Jacobi, Angela. "Starwort Phenomena." Woman's Art
    Journal 5, no. 1 (Spring-Summer 1984): cover.

Moehl, Karl. "Ellen Lanyon, Krannert Art Museum." New Art
    Examiner 14, no. 11 (Summer 1987): 54-55.

SYLVIA LARK (1947-    )    Painter

Boettger, Suzaan. "Sylvia Lark, Jeremy Stone Gallery." Artforum
    22, no. 6 (February 1984): 84-85.

Freuh, Joanna. "Chicago: Kathe Keller and Sylvia Lark at NAME."
    Art in America 67, no. 1 (January-February 1979): 148.

Sylvia Lark. San Francisco: Jeremy Stone Gallery, 1987.

Tamblyn, Christine. "Sylvia Lark." Art News 87, no. 2 (February
    1988): 155, 157.

Van Proyen, Mark. "Dissipating Lyricism." Artweek 16, no. 21 (25
    May 1985): 5.

HILDA KRISTINA GUSTAFSON LASCARI (1885-1937)    Sculptor

See volume 1 of this book.

Obituary. Who's Who in American Art, vol. 2. Washington, D.C.:
    American Federation of Art, 1937.

PAT LASCH (1944-    )    Painter

See volume 1 of this book.

Handy, Ellen.  "10th Anniversary Show."  Arts Magazine 61, no. 4
(December 1986):  121.

Lasch, Pat, and Lasch, Fred.  Art Book/Pastry Book.  If You Make a
Mistake Put a Rose On It.  New York:  privately printed, 1985.

Who's Who in American Art, 17th ed.  New York:  R.R. Bowker Co.,
1986.


BARBARA LATHAM (1896-    )   Painter

American Art Annual, vol. 30.  Washington, D.C.:  American
Federation of Arts, 1934.

Archives of American Art.  A Checklist of the Collection.
Washington, D.C.:  Smithsonian Institution, 1975; 2nd ed.,
rev., 1977.

Barbara Latham/Howard Cook.  Santa Fe:  Governors Gallery, 1977.

Eldredge, Charles C.; Schimmel, Julie; and Truettner, William H.
Art in New Mexico, 1900-1945, Paths to Taos and Santa Fe.
Washington, D.C.:  National Museum of American Art, and New
York:  Abbeville Press, 1986.

Samuels, Peggy and Harold.  The Illustrated Biographical
Encyclopedia of Artists of the American West.  Garden City,
New York:  Doubleday, 1976.


GERTRUDE KATHERINE LATHROP (1896-1986)   Sculptor

See volume 1 of this book.

American Art Annual, vol. 28.  Washington, D.C.:  American
Federation of Arts, 1932.

National Sculpture Society.  Exhibition of American Sculpture.  New
York, 1923.


SUSAN LAUFER (1950-    )   Painter

Bell, Tiffany.  "Susan Laufer."  Arts Magazine 59, no. 3 (November
1984):  2.

Heartney, Eleanor.  "Susan Laufer."  Art News 84, no. 10 (December
1985):  128.

Henry, Gerrit.  "Susan Laufer at Germans Van Eyck."  Art in
America 73, no. 1 (January 1985):  140-41.

242

Madoff, Steven Henry. "In the Deep of the Painting: New York by
    Susan Laufer." Arts Magazine 61, no. 1 (September 1986):
    78-79.

Sofer, Ken. "Susan Laufer." Art News 83, no. 10 (December 1984):
    152.

Westfall, Stephen. "Susan Laufer at Germans Van Eyck." Art in
    America 76, no. 1 (January 1988): 138.


EUGÉNIE ETIENETTE AUBANEL LAVENDER (1817-1898)    Painter

Groce, George C., and Wallace, David H. The New-York Historical
    Society's Dictionary of Artists in America 1564-1860. New
    Haven: Yale University Press, 1957.

O'Brien, Esse Forrester. Art and Artists of Texas. Dallas: Tardy
    Publishing Co., 1935.

Samuels, Peggy and Harold. The Illustrated Biographical
    Encyclopedia of Artists of the American West. Garden City,
    New York: Doubleday, 1976.


MARY LAWRENCE (1868-1945)    Sculptor

See Mary Lawrence Tonetti.


ADELAIDE J. LAWSON [GAYLOR] (1889-1986)    Painter

American Art Annual, vol. 28. Washington, D.C.: American
    Federation of Arts, 1932.

Braff, Phyllis. "An Adventurous Landscapist at 93." The New York
    Times, 12 September 1982, Long Island Section: 17.

Fielding, Mantle. Dictionary of American Painters, Sculptors and
    Engravers. Enlarged ed. Greens Farms, Connecticut: Modern
    Books and Crafts, 1974.

Who's Who in American Art, vol. 1. Washington, D.C.: American
    Federation of Arts, 1935.

Wolf, Amy J. New York Society of Women Artists 1925. New York:
    ACA Galleries, 1987.


KATHARINE STEWART LAWSON (b. 1885)    Sculptor

American Art Annual, vol. 28. Washington, D.C.: American
    Federation of Arts, 1932.

243

Burnet, Mary Q.  Art and Artists of Indiana.  New York:  Century
    Co., 1921.

National Sculpture Society.  Exhibition of American Sculpture.  San
    Francisco:  California Palace of the Legion of Honor, 1929.


                LOUISE LAWSON (b. 1861)   Sculptor

See volume 1 of this book.

Appleton's Cyclopaedia of American Biography, vol. 3.  New York:
    D. Appleton and Co., 1887.

              ELIZABETH LAYTON (1909-    )   Painter

Bonesteel, Michael.  "Elizabeth Layton at the Chicago Public
    Library Cultural Center."  Art in America 74, no. 7 (July
    1986):  125-26.

Cobb, Ann Kuckelman.  "Feminist Themes in the Art of Elizabeth
    Layton."  Kansas Quarterly 19, no. 4 (1987):  77-87.

Feldman, Edmund B.  The Artist.  Englewood Cliffs, New Jersey:
    Prentice-Hall, 1982.

National Museum of Women in the Arts.  New York:  Harry N. Abrams,
    Inc., 1987:  210.

Through the Looking Glass:  Drawings of Elizabeth Layton.
    Mid-American Arts Alliance Program, 1984.


              BLANCHE LAZZELL (1878-1956)   Painter

America Art Annual, vol. 18.  Washington, D.C.:  American
    Federation of Arts, 1921.

Campbell, Lawrence.  "Blanche Lazzell at Martin Diamond Fine Arts."
    Art in America 74, no. 7 (July 1986):  122-23.

Clarkson, John.  Blanche Lazzell.  Morgantown, Virginia:  West
    Virginia University Creative Arts Center Galleries, 1979.

Eight Southern Women.  Greenville, South Carolina:  Greenville
    County Museum of Art, 1986.

Flint, Janet Altic.  Provincetown Printers:  A Woodcut Tradition.
    Washington, D.C.:  National Museum of American Art, 1983.

Fort, Ilene Susan.  "Blanche Lazzell."  Arts Magazine 57, no. 2
    (October 1982):  20-21.

244

Obituary.  Who's Who in American Art, vol. 7.  Washington, D.C.:
American Federation of Arts, 1959.

Martin, Alvin.  American Realism, 20th-Century Drawings and
Watercolors From the Glenn C. Janss Collection.  San
Francisco:  San Francisco Museum of Modern Art, 1985.

Seckler, Doroth Gees.  Provincetown Painters, 1890s-1970s.
Syracuse, New York:  Everson Museum of Art, 1977.

Wolf, Amy J.  New York Society of Women Artists 1925.  New York:
ACA Galleries, 1987.


ALICE M. FRYE LEACH (1857-1943)    Painter

Harding, Jonathan P.  The Boston Athenaeum Collection.  Boston:
The Boston Athenaeum, 1984.

Obituary.  Who's Who in American Art, vol. 4.  Washington, D.C.:
American Federation of Arts, 1947.


ETHEL PENNIWELL BROWN LEACH (1878-1960)    Painter

American Art Annual, vol. 28.  Washington, D.C.:  American
Federation of Arts, 1932.

American Painters of the Impressionist Period Rediscovered.
Waterville, Maine:  Colby College Art Museum, 1975.

Fielding, Mantle.  Dictionary of American Painters, Sculptors and
Engravers.  Enlarged ed.  Greens Farms, Connecticut:  Modern
Books and Crafts, 1974.

Women Artists in the Howard Pyle Tradition.  Chadds Ford,
Pennsylvania:  Brandywine River Museum, 1975.


JUNE LEAF (1929-    )    Painter and Sculptor

See volume 1 of this book.

Who's Who in American Art, 17th ed.  New York:  R.R. Bowker Co.,
1986.


AMY FREEMAN LEE (1914-    )    Painter

Amy Freeman Lee.  New York:  Wellons Gallery, 1952.

Amy Freeman Lee:  Recent Watercolors.  Los Angeles:  Dalzell
     Hatfield Galleries, n.d. (ca. 1958).

Reverence for Life.  Austin, Texas:  University of Texas Art
     Museum, 1973.

Who's Who in American Art.  New York:  R.R. Bowker Co., 1978.


               CAROLINE LEE (1932-    )  Sculptor

Boudaille, Georges.  "Caroline Lee."  Cimaise, no. 107 (June-July-
     August 1972):  42-50.

Kenedy, R. C.  "Paris Letter."  Art International 11, no. 10
     (Christmas 1967):  80-84.

Kowal, Dennis, and Meilach, Dona Z.  Sculpture Casting:  Mold
     Techniques and Materials, Metals, Plastics, Concrete.  New
     York:  Crown, 1972.

La Part des Femmes dans l'Art Contemporain.  Vitry-sur-Seine:
     Galerie Municipale, 1984.

Schwartz, Ellen.  "Paris Letter:  November."  Art International 16,
     no. 1 (20 January 1972):  54-58.

Visions/Painting and Sculpture:  Distinguished Alumni 1945 to
     Present.  Chicago:  School of the Art Institute of Chicago,
     1976.

Watson-Jones, Virginia.  Contemporary American Women Sculptors.
     Phoenix:  Oryx Press, 1986.

Wentinck, Charles.  Modern and Primitive Art.  Oxford:  Phaidon,
     1978.


               DORIS EMRICK LEE (1905-1983)  Painter

See volume 1 of this book.

Doris Lee, 1905-1983.  (Alice Lewis, Curator).  Woodstock, New
     York:  Woodstock Artists Association, 1984.

Park, Marlene, and Markowitz, Gerald E.  Democratic Vistas:  Post
     Offices and Public Art in the New Deal.  Philadelphia:  Temple
     University Press, 1984.

Tufts, Eleanor.  American Women Artists, 1830-1930.  Washington,
     D.C.:  National Museum of Women in the Arts, 1987.

246

Woodstock's Art Heritage:  The Permanent Collection of the
     Woodstock Artists Association.  Essay by Tom Wolf.  Woodstock,
     New York:  Overlook Press, 1987.

Zaidenberg, Arthur, compiled by.  The Art of the Artist.  New York:
     Crown, 1951:  76-78.


          DORIS MARIE LEEPER (1929-    )   Painter and Sculptor

See volume 1 of this book.

Fifty National Women in Art.  Fort Myers, Florida:  Edison
     Community College, 1982.

Watson-Jones, Virginia.  Contemporary American Women Sculptors.
     Phoenix:  Oryx Press, 1986.

Who's Who in American Art, 17th ed.  New York:  R.R. Bowker Co.,
     1986.


          JULIETTE LEFF (1939-1987)   Painter

Klein, Ellen Lee.  "Juliette Leff."  Arts Magazine 62, no. 1
     (September 1987):  94.

Who's Who in American Art, 17th ed.  New York:  R.R. Bowker Co.,
     1986.


          MARY SWINTON LEGARÉ (b. 1792)   Painter

Ellet, Elizabeth.  Women Artists in All Ages and Countries.  New
     York:  Harper and Brothers, 1859:  301-12.

Groce, George C., and Wallace, David H.  The New-York Historical
     Society's Dictionary of Artists in America.  New Haven:  Yale
     University Press, 1987.

Hanaford, Phebe A.  Daughters of America.  Augusta, Maine:  True
     and Co., 1882:  275.


          CLARE LEIGHTON (1898-    )   Printmaker and Illustrator

See volume 1 of this book.

Hardin, Martin.  "Wood Engraving of Clare Leighton."  The Print
     Collector's Quarterly 22 (April 1935):  139-65.

Leighton, Clare.  Where Land Meets Sea:  The Tide Line of Cape Cod.
     New York:  Rinehart and Co., 1954.

_____. Wood-Engraving and Woodcuts. London and New York: Studio Publications, 1948.

A Selection of American Prints. A Selection of Biographies of Forty Women Artists Working Between 1904-1979. Santa Rosa, California: The Annex Galleries, 1987: 10.

Who's Who in American Art. New York: R.R. Bowker Co., 1978.

KATHRYN WOODMAN LEIGHTON (1876-1952)   Painter

American Art Annual, vol. 28. Washington, D.C.: American Federation of Arts, 1932.

Kovinick, Phil. The Woman Artist in the American West 1860-1960. Fullerton, California: Muckenthaler Cultural Center, 1976.

Moure, Nancy. Los Angeles Painters of the Nineteen Twenties. Claremont, California: Pomona College Gallery, 1972.

Samuels, Peggy and Harold. The Illustrated Biographical Encyclopedia of Artists of the American West. Garden City, New York: Doubleday, 1976.

Southern California Artists 1890-1940. Laguna Beach, California: Laguna Beach Museum of Art, 1979.

A Woman's Vision, California Painting into the 20th Century. San Francisco: Maxwell Galleries, 1983.

MATHILDE MUEDEN LEISENRING (ca. 1870-1949)   Painter

American Art Annual, vol. 28. Washington, D.C.: American Federation of Arts, 1932.

Cosentino, Andrew J., and Glassie, Henry H. The Capital Image, Painters in Washington, 1800-1915. Washington, D.C.: National Museum of American Art, 1893.

Fielding, Mantle. Dictionary of American Painters, Sculptors and Engravers. Enlarged ed. Greens Farms, Connecticut: Modern Books and Crafts, 1974.

Mathilde Mueden Leisenring: A Memorial Exhibition. Washington, D.C.: Corcoran Gallery of Art, 1950.

Who's Who in American Art, vol. 1. Washington, D.C.: American Federation of Arts, 1935.

BARBARA LEKBERG (1925-    )    Sculptor

Annual Exhibition. New York:  National Academy of Design, 1982,
    1984.

Annual Exhibition:  Contemporary American Art.  New York:  Whitney
    Museum of American Art, 1952-56.

Annual Exhibition of Painting and Sculpture.  Philadelphia:
    Pennsylvania Academy of the Fine Arts, 1950-64.

Andersen, Wayne.  American Sculpture in Process:  1930/1970.
    Boston:  New York Graphic Society, 1975.

Chapin, Louis.  "The Home Forum:  Dancing in Bronze."  The
    Christian Science Monitor, 19 July 1978:  20.

Hale, Nathan Cabot.  Welded Sculpture.  New York:  Watson-Guptill,
    1968.

Lynch, John.  Metal Sculpture:  New Forms, New Techniques.  New
    York:  Viking Press, 1974.

Raynor, Vivien.  "Art:  Noise in the Attic, Barbara Lekberg
    (Sculpture Center)."  The New York Times, 9 December 1977:
    C19.

Sculptors Guild Annual Exhibition.  New York:  Lever House,
    1973-85.

Watson-Jones, Virginia.  Contemporary American Women Sculptors.
    Phoenix:  Oryx Press, 1986.

ANNETTE LEMIEUX (1957-    )    Painter

Brooks, Rosetta.  "Remembrance of Objects Past."  Artforum 25
    (December 1986):  68-69.

Heartney, Eleanor.  "The Hot New Cool Art:  Simulationism."  Art
    News 86, no. 1 (January 1987):  136-37.

Indiana, Gary.  "Annette Lemeiux at Cash/Newhouse."  Art in America
    74, no. 7 (July 1986):  119-20.

Mahoney, Robert.  "Time After Time."  Arts Magazine 60, no. 10
    (June 1986):  126-27.

1987 Biennial Exhibition.  New York:  Whitney Museum of American
    Art, 1987.

Siegel, Jeanne.  "Annette Lemieux:  It's a Wonderful Life, or is
    it?"  Arts Magazine 61, no. 5 (January 1987):  78-81.

Solomon, Thomas.  A Brave New World:  A New Generation.
    Copenhagen:  Charlottenborg Exhibition Hall, 1985.


                TAMARA DE LEMPICKA (1898-1980)   Painter

Bojko, Szymon.  "Tamara de Lempicka."  Art and Artists 15 (June
    1980):  6-9.

Decker, Andrew.  "Tamara de Lempicka:  A Question of Style."
    Art News 86, no. 9 (November 1987):  27.

Gilot, Françoise.  "Tamara."  Art and Antiques (January 1986):
    64-69, 88.

Kizette de Lempicka-Foxhall, Baroness, as told to Charles Phillips.
    Passion by Design.  New York:  Abbeville Press, 1987.

Marmori, Giancarlo.  Tamara de Lempicka.  Translated by John
    Shepley.  London:  Idea Editions, 1978.

McKay, Gary.  "And the Baroness was an Artist, The Brushstrokes of
    Tamara de Lempicka."  Ultra (March 1988):  52-57.

Mechlin, Leila.  "The Art of Today at Pittsburgh."  The American
    Magazine of Art 20, no. 12 (December 1929):  669, 681.

Seiberling, Dorothy.  "Siren of a Stylish Era."  The New York
    Times Magazine, 1 January 1978:  14-15.

Vergine, Lea.  L'Altra Metà dell'Avanguardia 1910-1940.  Milan:
    Mazzotta, 1980.


                LUCY L'ENGLE (1889-1978)   Painter

American Art Annual, vol. 28.  Washington, D.C.:  American
    Federation of Arts, 1932.

Fielding, Mantle.  Dictionary of American Painters, Sculptors and
    Engravers.  Enlarged ed.  Greens Farms, Connecticut:  Modern
    Books and Crafts, 1974.

Wolf, Amy J.  New York Society of Women Artists 1925.  New York:
    ACA Galleries, 1987.


                JOANNE LEONARD (1940-    )   Photographer

Cohen, Joyce Tennyson, ed.  In/Sights, Self-Portraits of Women.
    Boston:  David R. Godine, 1978.

250

Connell, Evan S., ed. Women by Three. San Francisco: Pacific Coast Publishers, 1969.

Janson, H. W. History of Art. Revised and expanded by Anthony F. Janson. New York: Harry N. Abrams, Inc., 1986.: 781-83.

Lippard, Lucy. Inside and Beyond. Austin: Laguna Gloria Art Museum, 1980.

Lyons, Harriet. A Decade of Change. New York: Ms. Foundation Book Publication, 1980.

Photographers Encyclopaedia International 1839 to the Present. Hermance, Switzerland: Editions Camera Obscura, 1985.

"Photographs by Joanne Leonard." Creative Camera no. 103 (January 1973): 6-9.

Women of Photography. An Historical Survey. San Francisco: San Francisco Museum of Art, 1975.

Women See Woman. New York: Thomas Y. Crowell Co., 1976.

ORA LERMAN (1938-    )    Painter

See volume 1 of this book.

Campbell, Lawrence. "Ora Lerman at P.M. and Stein." Art in America 70, no. 10 (November 1982): 120-21.

Lerman, Ora. "Autobiographical Journey: Can Art Transform Personal and Cultural Loss?" Arts Magazine 59, no. 9 (May 1985): 103-05.

Who's Who in American Art, 17th ed. New York: R.R. Bowker Co., 1986.

ANNE [ANN] LESLIE (1792-after 1860)    Painter

Ellet, Elizabeth Fries Lummis. Women Artists in All Ages and Countries. New York: Harper Brothers, 1859.

Fielding, Mantle. Dictionary of American Painters, Sculptors and Engravers. Enlarged ed. Greens Farms, Connecticut: Modern Books and Crafts, 1974.

Groce, George C., and Wallace, David H. The New-York Historical Society's Dictionary of Artists in America 1564-1860. New Haven: Yale University Press, 1957.


        MARILYN ANNE LEVINE (1935-    )   Ceramic Sculptor

See volume 1 of this book.

Clark, Garth. A Century of Ceramics in the United States 1878-1978. New York: E.P. Dutton, 1979.

Cochran, Malcolm. Contemporary Clay: Ten Approaches. Hanover, New Hampshire: Dartmouth College, 1976.

Contemporary American Realism Since 1960. Philadelphia: Pennsylvania Academy of the Fine Arts, 1981.

A Decade of Ceramic Art: 1962-1972. Essay by Suzanne Foley. San Francisco: San Francisco Museum of Modern Art, 1972.

Donnell-Kotrozo, Carol. "Material Illusion: On the Issue of Ersatz Objects." Arts Magazine 58, no. 7 (March 1984): 88-91.

Homage to the Bag. Essay by Ruth Amdur Tanenhaus. New York: Museum of Contemporary Crafts, 1975.

Hyperrealisme et Trompe-L'Oeil: Réalités Objectives ou Réalités Illusoires. Maymac, Corrèze, France: Abbaye Saint-André, 1983.

Levin, Elaine. "Portfolio: Marilyn Levine." Ceramics Monthly 33, no. 3 (March 1985): 41-46.

Levin, Kim. "The Ersatz Object." Arts Magazine 48, no. 5 (February 1974): 52-55.

Manhart, Marcia and Tom, eds. The Eloquent Object. Tulsa, Oklahoma: Philbrook Museum of Art, 1987.

The Object as Poet. Essay by Rose Slivka. Washington, D.C.: Smithsonian Institution Press, 1977.

Painting and Sculpture Today 1972. Indianapolis: Indianapolis Museum of Art, 1972.

Sculpture in California 1975-1980. San Diego: San Diego Museum of Art, 1980.

Super Realism from the Morton G. Neumann Family Collection. Kalamazoo, Michigan: Kalamazoo Institute of Arts, 1981.

252

Watson-Jones, Virginia. Contemporary American Women Sculptors.
Phoenix: Oryx Press, 1986.


MARION LERNER LEVINE (1931-    )    Painter

See volume 1 of this book.

Who's Who in American Art, 17th ed. New York: R.R. Bowker Co.,
1986.


SHERRIE LEVINE (1947-    )    Painter

Cameron, Dan. "Absence and Allure: Sherri Levine's Recent Work."
Arts Magazine 58, no. 4 (December 1983): 84-87.

Grimes, Nancy. "Sherrie Levine [at] Mary Boone." Art News 86, no.
9 (November 1987): 191-92.

Hoy, Anne H. Fabrications: Staged, Altered, and Appropriated
Photographs. New York: Abbeville Press, 1987.

Linker, Kate. "Sherrie Levine." Artforum 25, no. 7 (March 1987):
123-24.

Marzorati, Gerald. "Art in the (Re)Making." Artnews 85, no. 5
(May 1986): 90-99, cover.

McGill, Douglas C. "An Original Slant on Originality." The New
York Times, 12 September 1987: Y12.

Morgan, Robert C. "Sherrie Levine: Language Games." Arts
Magazine 62, no. 4 (December 1987): 86-88.

Smith, Roberta. "Art: Sherrie Levine Mini-Retrospective." The
New York Times, 20 September 1987: Y36.

Wei, Lilly. "Talking Abstract." Art in America 75, no. 12
(December 1987): 112-14.


HELEN LEVITT (1913-    )    Photographer

Auer, Michèle and Auer, Michel. Encyclopédie International des
Photographes de 1839 à Nos Jours. Hermance, Switzerland:
Editions Camera Obscura, 1985.

Browne, Turner, and Partnow, Elaine. Macmillan Biographical
Encyclopedia of Photographic Artists and Innovators.
New York: Macmillan Publishing Co., 1983.

Edwards, Owen. "Her Eye is on the City." The New York Times
     Magazine, 5 April 1980.

Grundberg, Andy. "Finding Grace in the Awkward Humanity of
     People." The New York Times, 1 November 1987, Arts and
     Leisure Section: 41.

_____. "Helen Levitt at Carlton." Art in America 65, no. 4
     (July-August 1977): 98-99.

Helen Levitt Photographs. New York: Sidney Janis Gallery, 1980.

Hellman, Roberta, and Hoshino, Marvin. "The Photographs of Helen
     Levitt." Massachusetts Review, Winter 1978.

Levitt, Helen. A Way of Seeing. New York: Viking Press, 1965.

Livingston, Jane. Helen Levitt. Washington, D.C.: Corcoran
     Gallery of Art, 1980.

Lyons, Nathan. Photography in the Twentieth Century. New York:
     Horizon Press, 1967.

Munsterberg, Hugo. A History of Women Artists. New York:
     Clarkson N. Potter, 1975.

Szarkowski, John. Looking at Photographs: 100 Pictures from the
     Collection of the Museum of Modern Art. New York: The Museum
     of Modern Art, 1973.

_____. Mirrors and Windows: American Photography Since 1960. New
     York: The Museum of Modern Art, 1978.

Walsh, George; Naylor, Colin; and Held, Michael; eds. Contemporary
     Photographers. New York: Macmillan Press, 1982.

Witkin, Lee D., and London, Barbara. The Photograph Collector's
     Guide. Greenwich, Connecticut: New York Graphic Society,
     1979.

BEATRICE LEVY (1892-1974)    Painter and Printmaker

American Art Annual, vol. 28. Washington, D.C.: American
     Federation of Arts, 1932.

American Prints in the Library of Congress: A Catalog of the
     Collection. Baltimore: Johns Hopkins Press, 1970.

Fielding, Mantle. Dictionary of American Painters, Sculptors and
     Engravers. Enlarged ed. Greens Farms, Connecticut: Modern
     Books and Crafts, 1974.

254

A Selection of American Prints. A Selection of Biographies of
   Forty Women Artists Working Between 1904-1979. Santa Rosa,
   California: The Annex Galleries, 1987: 10.


ELLEN K. LEVY (20th Century)   Painter

Chambers, Karen S. "Ellen K. Levy." Arts Magazine 58, no. 7
   (March 1984): 8.

Grove, Nancy. "Interpretations of the Southwest." Arts Magazine
   60, no. 4 (December 1985): 100.

Marter, Joan. "Ellen K. Levy." Arts Magazine 58, no. 7 (February
   1987): 97.

Shoenfeld, Ann. "Ellen Levy." Arts Magazine 57, no. 2 (October
   1982): 13.


EDMONIA LEWIS (1844-ca. 1911)   Sculptor

See volume 1 of this book.

Driskell, David C. Hidden Heritage: Afro-American Art,
   1800-1950. Bellevue, Washington: Bellevue Art Museum and San
   Francisco: The Art Museum Association of America, 1985:
   27-29.

Hanaford, Phebe A. Daughters of America. Augusta, Maine: True
   and Co., 1882: 296-98.

Hartigan, Lynda Roscoe. Sharing Traditions, Five Black Artists in
   Nineteenth-Century America. Washington, D.C.: National
   Museum of American Art, 1985.

Richardson, Marilyn. "Vita: Edmonia Lewis." Harvard Magazine 88,
   no. 4 (March-April 1986): 40.

Tufts, Eleanor. American Women Artists, 1830-1930. Washington,
   D.C.: National Museum of Women in the Arts, 1987.


JOSEPHINE MILES LEWIS (1865-1959)   Painter

American Art Annual, vol. 28. Washington, D.C.: American
   Federation of Arts, 1932.

Fielding, Mantle. Dictionary of American Painters, Sculptors and
   Engravers. Enlarged ed. Greens Farms, Connecticut: Modern
   Books and Crafts, 1974.

Who's Who in American Art, vol. 3.  Washington, D.C.:  American
     Federation of Arts, 1940.


                LUCY LEWIS (1897-    )   Ceramicist

National Museum of Women in the Arts.  New York:  Harry N. Abrams,
     Inc., 1987.

Peterson, Susan.  Lucy M. Lewis, American Indian Potter.  Tokyo,
     New York, and San Francisco:  Kodansha International, 1984.


                LILIANE LIJN (1939-    )   Sculptor

Barret, Cyril.  "Art as Research:  The Experiments of Liliane
     Lijn."  Studio International 173 (June 1967):  314-16.

Beaumont, M. R.  "Liliane Lijn."  Arts Review 39 (13 March 1987):
     157.

Brett, Guy.  Kinetic Art.  London:  Studio Vista, 1968.

Burr, James.  "Around the Galleries."  Apollo 89 (April 1969):
     314.

Courtney, C.  "Liliane Lijn:  Headpieces Exhibited at the Venice
     Biennale."  Crafts 83 (November-December 1986):  57.


                EVA LLORÉNS (1921-    )   Painter

See volume 1 of this book.

Mon, Fernando.  Pintura Contemporanea en Galicia.  La Coruña:
     Caixa Galicia, 1987.


                SARA WORDEN LLOYD (b. 1853)   Painter

Fielding, Mantle.  Dictionary of American Painters, Sculptors and
     Engravers.  Enlarged ed.  Greens Farms, Connecticut:  Modern
     Books and Crafts, 1974.

Willard, Frances E., and Livermore, Mary A.  American Women.
     Reprint of 1897 ed., Detroit:  Gale Research, 1973 (under
     "Worden").

256

CARMEN LOMAS GARZA (1948-    )    Painter

Beardsley, John, and Livingston, Jane.  Hispanic Art in the United
    States.  Houston:  Museum of Fine Arts, and New York:
    Abbeville Press, 1987.

Carmen Lomas Garza.  Sacramento:  Galería Posada, 1985.

Carmen Lomas Garza, Prints and Gouaches; Margo Humphrey, Monotypes.
    San Francisco:  San Francisco Museum of Modern Art, 1980.

Chicano Expressions:  A New View of American Art.  New York:  INTAR
    Latin American Gallery, 1986.

Dále Gas:  Chicano Art of Texas.  Houston.  Houston:  Museum of
    Contemporary Art, 1977.

Hispanics U. S. A. 1982.  Bethlehem, Pennsylvania:  Ralph Wilson
    Gallery, Lehigh University, 1982.

McCombie, Mel.  "Hispanic Art in the United States, Houston MFA."
    Art News 86, no. 7 (September 1987):  156.

¡Mira!  The Tradition Continues.  New York:  El Museo del Barrio,
    1985.

Ofrendas.  Sacramento:  La Raza Bookstore and Galería Posada, 1984.

Raices y Visiones/Roots and Visions.  Washington, D.C.:  National
    Collection of Fine Arts, 1977.


        EVELYN BEATRICE LONGMAN (1874-1954)    Sculptor

See volume 1 of this book.

Adams, Adeline.  "Evelyn Beatrice Longman."  American Magazine of
    Art 19, no. 5 (May 1928):  237-49.

American Art Annual, vol. 28.  Washington, D.C.:  American
    Federation of Arts, 1932.

"A Longman Show."  The Art Digest 6, no. 8 (15 January 1932):  13.

National Museum of Women in the Arts.  New York:  Harry N. Abrams,
    Inc., 1987:  58-59.

National Portrait Gallery, Permanent Collection Illustrated
    Checklist.  Washington, D.C.:  Smithsonian Institution Press,
    1982.

Neuhaus, Eugen. The Art of the Exposition. San Francisco:  Paul
    Elder and Co., 1915:  89.

Tufts, Eleanor. American Women Artists, 1830-1930. Washington,
    D.C.:  National Museum of Women in the Arts, 1987.


        JENNETTE SHEPHERD HARRISON LOOP (1840-1909)   Painter

See volume 1 of this book.

Clark, Eliot. History of the National Academy of Design,
    1825-1953. New York:  Columbia University Press, 1954.

"Exhibition of the National Academy of Design." The Nation 22
    (1876):  235.

French, H. W. Art and Artists in Connecticut. Boston:  Lee and
    Shepard, and New York:  Charles T. Dillingham, 1879:  170-71.


            CAROLINE A. LORD (1860-1927)   Painter

American Art Annual, vol. 1. New York:  Macmillan Co., 1898.

Clark, Edna. Ohio Art and Artists. Richmond, Virginia:  Garrett
    and Massie, 1932:  475.

The Golden Age:  Cincinnati Painters of the 19th Century,
    Represented in the Cincinnati Art Museum. Cincinnati:
    Cincinnati Art Museum, 1979:  80.

Obituary. American Art Annual, vol. 26. Washington, D.C.:
    American Federation of Arts, 1929.


            ARLENE LOVE (1937-    )   Sculptor

Annual Exhibition of Painting and Sculpture. Philadelphia:
    Pennsylvania Academy of the Fine Arts, 1954.

Annual Exhibition of Painting and Sculpture. Philadelphia:
    Pennsylvania Academy of the Fine Arts, 1962.

Byrd, Joan Falconer. "Forms of Leather." American Craft 42, no. 3
    (June-July 1982):  26-29.

Goodman, Marilyn. "Arlene Love (Lawrence Oliver Gallery,
    Philadelphia)." New Art Examiner 14 (November 1986):  57.

Goodyear, Frank H., Jr. Contemporary Realism Since 1960. Boston:
    New York Graphic Society, 1981.

258

Hollander, Harry B. Plastics for Artists and Craftsmen. New York: Watson-Guptill, 1972.

LeMin, Robert. "F and M will uncover a new Ben Franklin." Intelligencer Journal (Lancaster, Pennsylvania), 22 October 1986: 1, 6.

McFadden, Sarah. "Report from Philadelphia." Art in America 67, no. 3 (May-June 1979): 21-27, 29, 31.

Newman, Thelma R. Plastics as an Art Form. Radnor: Chilton Book Co., 1974.

Recent Sculpture U. S. A. New York: Museum of Modern Art (traveling exhibition), 1959.

Roukes, Nicholas. Sculpture in Plastics. New York: Watson-Guptill, 1968.

Stein, Judith. "Arlene Love at Langman, Jenkintown." Art in America 62, no. 5 (September-October 1974): 115.

_____. "Arlene Love at Lawrence Oliver." Art in America 75, no. 2 (February 1987): 153-54.

Watson-Jones, Virginia. Contemporary American Women Sculptors. Phoenix: Oryx Press, 1986.


KATHERINE A. LOVELL (1877-1965)    Painter

American Art Annual, vol. 28. Washington, D.C.: American Federation of Arts, 1932.

An Exhibition of Women Students of William Merritt Chase. New York: Marbella Gallery, 1973.

Who's Who in American Art, vol. 6. Washington, D.C.: American Federation of Arts, 1956.


ELSIE MOTZ LOWDON (1883-1960)    Miniaturist

American Art Annual, vol. 28. Washington, D.C.: American Federation of Arts, 1932.

O'Brien, Esse Forrester. Art and Artists of Texas. Dallas: Tardy Publishing Co., 1935.

ANNA LOWNES (active 1884-1905)   Painter

American Art Annual, vol. 5.  New York:  Macmillan Co., 1905-06.

Catalogue of the Exhibits of the State of Pennsylvania and of
    Pennsylvanians at The World's Columbian Exposition.
    [Harrisburg?:]  State Printers of Pennsylvania, 1893:  118.

Sixtieth Annual Exhibition.  Philadelphia:  Pennsylvania Academy of
    the Fine Arts, 1890.

Tufts, Eleanor.  American Women Artists, 1830-1930.  Washington,
    D.C.:  National Museum of Women in the Arts, 1987.


                LEE LOZANO (1930-    )   Painter

Linville, Kasha.  "Lee Lozano, Whitney Museum."  Artforum 9, no. 6
    (February 1971):  81-82.

Poirier, Maurice, and Necol, Jane.  "The '60s in Abstract:  13
    Statements and an Essay."  Art in America 71, no. 9 (October
    1983):  129, 135.

Robins, Corinne.  "The Circle in Orbit."  Art in America 56, no. 6
    (November-December 1968):  69.

Waldman, Diane.  "Lee Lozano [Bianchini Gallery]."  Art News 65,
    no. 8 (December 1966):  13.


            MOLLY LUCE [BURROUGHS] (1896-1986)   Painter

See volume 1 of this book.

"Molly Luce Burroughs, 89, of Rhode Island, Noted Painter of the
    American Scene."  The Boston Herald, 17 April 1986:  53.

"Molly Burroughs, 89,  Painter."  The Boston Globe, 17 April 1986:
    64.

Second Biennial Exhibition of Contemporary American Painting.  New
    York:  Whitney Museum of American Art, 1934, no. 133.

Taylor, Robert.  "The Ordinary, the Fantastic."  The Boston Globe
    Magazine, 26 October 1980:  47.

Tufts, Eleanor.  American Women Artists, 1830-1930.  Washington,
    D.C.:  National Museum of Women in the Arts, 1987.

MARY LUCIER (1944-    )   Video Artist

Bonetti, David.  "American Beauties:  Grafting Masheck onto the Rose."  The Boston Phoenix, 4 February 1986:  5.

Festival Nacional de Video.  Madrid:  Circulo de Bellas Artes, 1986.

Glueck, Grace.  "Video Comes into Its Own at the Whitney Biennial." The New York Times, 24 April 1983.

Graze, Sue.  "Exhibition Concentrations 16:  Mary Lucier, Wilderness."  Dallas Museum of Art Bulletin 1, nos. 2-3 (Fall-Winter 1987-88):  26.

Hagen, Charles.  "Mary Lucier."  Artforum 22, no. 10 (summer 1984): 90.

Kutner, Janet.  "Monitoring Lucier's 'Wilderness'."  Dallas Morning News, 3 November 1987:  1C, 10C.

Lorber, Richard.  "Mary Lucier, The Kitchen."  Artforum 17, no. 1 (September 1978):  81.

The Luminous Image.  Amsterdam:  Stedelijk Museum, 1984.

Matrix 89.  Hartford:  Wadsworth Athenaeum, 1986.

Morse, Margaret.  "Mary Lucier:  Burning and Shining."  Video Networks 10, no. 5 (June 1986):  1, 6-7.

1983 Whitney Biennial.  New York:  Whitney Museum of American Art, 1983.

"Portrait of the Artist, 1987, Who Supports Him/Her."  Arts Review 4, no. 3 (Spring 1987):  29-30.

Rice, Shelley.  "Mary Lucier."  Women's Art Journal 5, no. 2 (Fall-Winter 1984-85):  41-44.

Russell, John.  "Why the Latest Whitney Biennial is More Satisfying."  The New York Times, 25 March 1983:  C1.

Schwan, Gary.  "Video Basks in the Light of Success."  The Post (Miami), 14 May 1985:  A10.

So There, Orwell.  New Orleans:  Louisiana World Exposition, 1984.

Sturken, Marita.  "A Whitney Sampler."  Afterimage 11, no. 3 (October 1983):  17.

10$^e$ Bienniale de Paris.  Paris:  Musée d'Art Moderne de la Ville,
    1977.

Wilderness.  Waltham, Massachusetts:  Rose Art Museum, Brandeis
    University, 1986.

Wooster, Ann-Sargent.  "Mary Lucier at the Whitney Museum."
    Art in America 70, no. 4 (April 1982):  138-39.

Zimmer, William.  "Mary Lucier."  The New York Times, 31 October
    1986.

_____.  "Wilderness at the Neuberger."  The New York Times, 31 May
    1987.


            BERTHA BOYNTON LUM (1879-1954)    Printmaker

See volume 1 of this book.

American Art Annual, vol. 28.  Washington, D.C.:  American
    Federation of Arts, 1932.

American Prints in the Library of Congress:  A Catalog of the
    Collection.  Baltimore:  Johns Hopkins Press, 1970.

Miller, Jo.  "America's Forgotten Printmakers."  Print Collector's
    Newsletter 4 (March-April 1973):  2-6.

Moure, Nancy D.  Dictionary of Artists in Southern California
    Before 1950.  Los Angeles:  Dustin Publications, 1975.

A Selection of American Prints.  A Selection of Biographies of
    Forty Women Artists Working Between 1904-1979.  Santa Rosa,
    California:  The Annex Galleries, 1987:  10.

A Woman's Vision:  California Painting into the 20th Century.  San
    Francisco:  Maxwell Galleries, 1983.


            HARRIET RANDALL LUMIS (1870-1953)    Painter

See volume 1 of this book.

American Art Annual, vol. 28.  Washington, D.C.:  American
    Federation of Arts, 1932.

Who's Who in American Art, vol. 5.  Washington, D.C.:  American
    Federation of Arts, 1953.

FLORENCE LUNDBORG (1871-1949)    Painter and Illustrator

See volume 1 of this book.

American Art Annual, vol. 28. Washington, D.C.: American
    Federation of Arts, 1932.

Neuhaus, Eugen. The Art of the Exposition. San Francisco: Paul
    Elder and Co., 1915:  89.

Obituary. Who's Who in America, vol. 5. Washington, D.C.:
    American Federation of Arts, 1953.

Porter, Bruce, et al. Art in California:  A Survey of American Art
    with Special Reference to California Painting, Sculpture and
    Architecture, Past and Present, Particularly as those Arts
    were Represented at the Panama-Pacific International
    Exposition. San Francisco: R.L. Bernier, 1916:  88.

Samuels, Peggy and Harold. The Illustrated Biographical
    Encyclopedia of Artists of the American West. Garden City,
    New York: Doubleday and Co., 1976.


HELEN LUNDEBERG (1908-    )   Painter

See volume 1 of this book.

The Art of California. Oakland: The Oakland Museum, 1984.

Butterfield, Jan. "Helen Lundeberg, A Poet Among Painters."
    Helen Lundeberg Since 1970. Palm Springs, California:  Palm
    Springs Desert Museum, 1983.

Helen Lundeberg. By Land and by Sea. Los Angeles: Tobey C. Moss
    Gallery, 1987.

Helen Lundeberg: Painting Through Five Decades. New York: Graham
    Galleries, 1982.

Helen Lundeberg. A Retrospective Exhibition. La Jolla:  La Jolla
    Museum of Contemporary Art, 1972.

Helen Lundeberg Still Life. Los Angeles: Tobey C. Moss Gallery,
    1985.

Hopkins, Henry. 50 West Coast Artists. San Francisco: Chronicle
    Books, 1981.

Nine Senior Southern California Painters. Los Angeles: Los
    Angeles Institute of Contemporary Art, 1974.

Painting and Sculpture in California:  The Modern Era.  San
    Francisco:  San Francisco Museum of Modern Art, 1976.

Schipper, Merle.  "Helen Lundeberg (at Tobey C. Moss)."  Art News
    85, no. 3 (March 1986):  121.

Seldis, Henry J.  Helen Lundeberg, A Retrospective Exhibition.
    La Jolla, California:  La Jolla Museum of Contemporary Art,
    1971.

A Woman's Vision:  California Painting into the 20th Century.  San
    Francisco:  Maxwell Galleries, 1983.

Wechsler, Jeffrey, and Berman, Greta.  Realism and Realities.  New
    Brunswick, New Jersey:  Rutgers University Art Gallery, 1981.


        FRANCES PLATT TOWNSEND LUPTON (active 1826-34)  Sculptor

Clark, Eliot.  History of the National Academy of Design,
    1825-1953.  New York:  Columbia University Press, 1954.

Ellet, Elizabeth.  Women Artists in All Ages and Countries.  New
    York:  Harper and Brothers, 1859.

Gardner, Albert TenEyck.  Yankee Stonecutters.  New York:  Columbia
    University Press, 1945.

Groce, George C.,  and Wallace, David H.  The New-York Historical
    Society's Dictionary of Artists in America, 1564-1860.  New
    Haven:  Yale University Press, 1957.


            MARILYN LYSOHIR (1950-    )  Ceramicist

Ceramic Echoes:  Historical References in Contemporary Ceramics.
    Kansas City:  Nelson-Atkins Museum of Art, 1983.

Okazaki, Arthur.  "Marilyn Lysohir."  American Ceramics 4, no. 1
    (Spring 1985):  60-67.

Pacific Currents/Ceramics 1982.  San Jose:  San Jose Museum of Art,
    1982.

Sculpture 1980.  Baltimore:  Maryland Institute College of Art,
    1980.

Speight, Charlotte F.  Images in Clay Sculpture:  Historical and
    Contemporary Techniques.  New York:  Harper and Row, 1983.

Thirtieth Spokane Annual Art Exhibition.  Spokane, Washington:
    Cheney Cowles Memorial Museum, 1978.

264

Watson-Jones, Virginia. Contemporary American Women Sculptors. Phoenix: Oryx Press, 1986.


MARY NICHOLENA MacCORD (1848-1909)   Painter

American Art Annual, vol. 28. Washington, D.C.: American Federation of Arts, 1932.

American Art Since 1850. San Francisco: Maxwell Galleries, 1968.

American Impressionism and 20th Century Paintings, Drawings and Sculpture. New York: Sotheby's, 20 December 1982: Lot 184.

American 19th and 20th Century Paintings, Drawings and Sculpture. New York: Sotheby's, 21 October 1983, Lot 285.


LOREN MacIVER (1909-   )   Painter

See volume 1 of this book.

Loren MacIver: An Exhibition of Early and Recent Paintings. Montclair: Montclair Art Museum, 1975.

Loren MacIver, Five Decades. Newport Beach: Newport Harbor Art Museum, 1983.

Loren MacIver: Paintings, Pastels, Drawings. New York: Pierre Matisse Gallery, 1966.

MacIver: Paintings. New York: Pierre Matisse Gallery, 1949.

The Phillips Collection, A Summary Catalogue. Washington, D.C.: The Phillips Collection, 1985.

Russell, John. "Loren MacIver." The New York Times, 24 April 1987: Y18.


LILIAN MacKENDRICK (1906-   )   Painter

Del Carlo, Omar, and Hall, Remy Inglis. "Lilian MacKendrick." The Connoisseur 186, no. 747 (May 1974).

Exhibition: Lilian MacKendrick. New York: Mortimer Levitt Gallery, 1949.

Exhibition: Lilian MacKendrick. Foreword by H. W. and Dora Jane Janson. New York: Hirschl and Adler Galleries, 1958.

Lilian MacKendrick. New York: Feigl Gallery, 1953.

*Lilian MacKendrick:  Recent Oil Paintings*.  New York:  Feigl
    Galleries, 1958.

*Who's Who in American Art*.  New York:  R.R. Bowker, 1978.


            FLORENCE MacKUBIN (1886-1918)    Painter

Champney, Elizabeth.  "Women in Art."  *Quarterly Illustrator* 2
    (April-June 1894):  111-24.

Clement, Clara Erskine.  *Women in the Fine Arts*.  Boston:  Houghton
    Mifflin Co., 1904.

Fielding, Mantle.  *Dictionary of American Painters, Sculptors and
    Engravers*.  Enlarged ed.  Greens Farms, Connecticut:  Modern
    Books and Crafts, 1924.

Obituary.  *American Art Annual*, vol. 15.  Washington, D.C.:
    American Federation of Arts, 1918.

*Woman's Who's Who in America*.  New York:  American Commonwealth
    Co., 1914.


        M. JEAN MacLANE [JOHANSEN] (1878-1964)    Painter

See volume 1 of this book (Jean MacLane).

*American Art Annual*, vol. 28.  Washington, D.C.:  American
    Federation of Arts, 1932.

"Art Museum has Interesting Summer Show."  *Toledo Times*, 18 August
    1935.

Caffin, Charles H.  "Some New American Painters in Paris."
    *Harper's Monthly Magazine* 118, no. 704 (January 1909):
    284-93.

Clark, Eliot.  *History of the National Academy of Design,
    1825-1953*.  New York:  Columbia University Press, 1954.

Eckford, Eugenia.  "'The Hilltop'--Jean MacLane."  *The Instructor*,
    May 1933:  15, 72, cover.

*Fifty Paintings by Jean MacLane*.  Pittsfield, Massachusetts:
    Berkshire Museum, 1979.

Lee, Cuthbert.  *Contemporary American Portrait Painters*.  New York:
    W.W. Norton and Co., 1929:  80-82.

Morrison, Dorothy. "Noted Painting Center of Attraction."
    Syracuse American, 17 January 1932:  15, 22.

Platt, Frederick.  Jean MacLane.  Charlottesville, Virginia:
    Balogh Gallery, 1984.

_____.  "The War Portraits."  Antiques 26, no. 1 (July 1984):
    142-53.

"Portraits Outstanding in Summer Exhibition at Museum of Art."
    The Toledo Sunday Times, 22 July 1928.

Ruthrauff, Florence Barlow.  "The Unfeminized Art of M. Jean
    MacLane."  Art and Decoration 3, no. 9 (July 1913):  299-301.

Tufts, Eleanor.  American Women Artists, 1830-1930.  Washington,
    D.C.:  National Museum of Women in the Arts, 1987.

MARY FAIRCHILD MacMONNIES [LOW] (1858-1946)    Painter

See volume 1 of this book.

American Art Annual, vol. 28.  Washington, D.C.:  American
    Federation of Arts, 1932.

Clement, Clara Erskine.  Women in the Fine Arts.  Boston:
    Houghton, Mifflin and Co., 1904.

Elliott, Maud Howe, ed.  Art and Handicraft in the Woman's Building
    of the World's Columbian Exposition, Chicago, 1893.  Chicago:
    Rand, McNally and Co., 1984:  60, 74-76.

Smart, Mary.  "Sunshine and Shade:  Mary Fairchild MacMonnies Low."
    Woman's Art Journal 4, no. 2 (Fall 1983-Winter 1984):  20-23.

CAROL BROOKS MacNEIL (1871-1944)    Sculptor

See volume 1 of this book.

American Art Annual, vol. 28.  Washington, D.C.:  American
    Federation of Arts, 1932.

Connor, Janis C.  "American Women Sculptors Break the Mold."  Art &
    Antiques 3 (May-June 1980):  80-87.

Obituary.  Who's Who in American Art, vol. 4.  Washington, D.C.:
    American Federation of Arts, 1947.

MARY L. MACOMBER (1861-1916)    Painter

See volume 1 of this book.

American Art Annual, vol. 1.  New York:  Macmillan, 1899.

Fielding, Mantle.  Dictionary of American Painters, Sculptors and
    Engravers.  Enlarged ed.  Greens Farms, Connecticut:  Modern
    Books and Crafts, 1924.

Hoeber, Arthur.  "Famous American Women Painters."  Mentor 2, no. 3
    (16 March 1914):  9.

Woman's Who's Who of America.  New York:  American Commonwealth
    Co., 1914.

EMMA FORDYCE MacRAE (1887-1974)    Painter

American Art Annual, vol. 28.  Washington, D.C.:  American
    Federation of Arts, 1932.

"Artists of All Sections in Revolving Show."  Art Digest 12, no. 18
    (1 July 1938):  17.

Bower, Nellie.  "Paintings Have Pleasing Qualities."  Miami Daily
    News, 24 June 1951.

Clark, Eliot.  History of the National Academy of Design,
    1825-1953.  New York:  Columbia University Press, 1954.

Emma Fordyce MacRae 1887-1974.  New York:  Richard York Gallery,
    1893.

Exhibition of Paintings by Dorothea M.  Litzinger and Emma F.
    MacRae.  New York:  The Anderson Galleries, 1914.

Exhibition of Paintings by Emma Fordyce MacRae.  New York:  Corona
    Mundi International Art Center of Roerich Museum, 1930.

Fiftieth Annual Exhibition.  New York:  National Association of
    Women Painters and Sculptors, 1942.

Fielding, Mantle.  Dictionary of American Painters, Sculptors and
    Engravers.  Enlarged ed.  Greens Farms, Connecticut:  Modern
    Books and Crafts, 1974.

"A Notable Exhibition in Gloucester."  American Magazine of Art 20,
    no. 10 (October 1929):  587.

Obituary.  The New York Times, 8 August 1974:  36.

268

*Paintings by Emma Fordyce MacRae*, A. N. A. Boston: Doll and Richards, 1935.

*Recent Paintings by Emma Fordyce MacRae* (Mrs. Homer F. Swift). New York: Grand Central Art Galleries, 1936.

Tufts, Eleanor. *American Women Artists, 1830-1930*. Washington, D.C.: National Museum of Women in the Arts, 1987.


ETHEL MAGAFAN (1916-    )    Painter

Breuning, Margaret. "Ethel Magafan." *Art Digest* 27, no. 8 (15 January 1953): 16.

Downes, Rackstraw. "Ethel Magafan [Midtown]." *Art News* 68, no. 2 (April 1969): 19.

"Ethel Magafan." *Arts Digest* 29, no. 3 (1 November 1954): 22-23.

"Fulbright Winners." *Art Digest* 26, no. 2 (15 October 1951): 18.

Goodnough, Robert. "Ethel and Jenne Magafan." *Art News* 49, no. 8 (December 1950): 60.

"Magafan Twins Together in New York Debut." *Art Digest* 15, no. 2 (15 October 1940): 21.

*Painting America. Mural Art in the New Deal Era.* Essay by Janet Marqusee. New York: Midtown Galleries, 1988.

Park, Marlene, and Markowitz, Gerald E. *Democratic Vistas: Post Offices and Public Art in the New Deal.* Philadelphia: Temple University Press, 1984.

Porter, Fairfield. "Ethel Magafan [Ganso]." *Art News* 53, no. 8 (December 1954): 53.

Reed, Judith Kaye. "Jenne and Ethel Magafan." *Art Digest* 25, no. 4 (15 November 1950): 21.

Sawin, Marticia. "Ethel Magafan." *Arts Magazine* 33, no. 7 (April 1959): 60.

Smith, Lawrence. "Ethel Magafan." *Arts Magazine* 35, nos. 8-9 (May-June 1961): 90.

Steiner, Raymond J. "Artist Brings Colorado Roots to Completed Canvases." *The Sunday Freeman*, 10 June 1984: 33.

Tufts, Eleanor. *American Women Artists, 1830-1930*. Washington, D.C.: National Museum of Women in the Arts, 1987.

Warren, Ron. "Ethel Magafan." Arts Magazine 58, no. 8 (April 1984): 39.

Watson, Ernest W. "Magafan and Mountains." American Artist 21, no. 10 (December 1957): 56-64.

Who's Who in American Art. New York: R.R. Bowker Co., 1978.

Zaidenberg, Arthur, compiled by. The Art of the Artist. Theories and Techniques of Art by the Artists Themselves. New York: Crown Publishers, 1951: 154-56.


JENNE MAGAFAN (1916-1952)    Painter

Devree, Howard. "Jenne Magafan." The New York Times, 1 March 1953, section 2: 8X.

Goodnough, Robert. "Ethel and Jenne Magafan." Art News 49, no. 8 (December 1950): 60.

"Identical Muralists." Newsweek, 15 May 1955: 94.

Jenne Magafan. Albany, New York: Albany Institute of History and Art, 1954.

"Magafan Twins Together in New York Debut." Art Digest 15, no. 2 (15 October 1941): 21.

"Miss Magafan to Paint Grafton Street Junior High Murals." Worcester Daily Telegram, 29 May 1947.

Obituary. Art Digest 27, no. 3 (1 November 1952): 9.

Obituary. The New York Times, 21 October 1952: 29.

"Twin Girls Score as Muralists." Los Angeles Times, 23 April 1944: Part III.

Woodstock's Art Heritage: The Permanent Collection of the Woodstock Artists Association. Essay by Tom Wolf. Woodstock, New York: Overlook Press, 1987.

Zaidenberg, Arthur, compiled by. The Art of the Artist: Theories and Techniques of Art by the Artists Themselves. New York: Crown Publishers, 1951: 133-34.


MURIEL MAGENTA (1932-    )    Filmmaker

See volume 1 of this book.

270

Donnell-Kotrozo, Carol. "Film: Defending Hair." Artweek 14, no.
25 (16 July 1983): 9.

_____. "Profiles: A Portfolio of Regional Artists, Muriel Magenta
(Scottscale, Arizona)." Art Voices 4, no. 6
(November-December 1981): 26.

_____. "Women and Art." Arts Magazine 55, no. 7 (March 1981):
11.

Magenta, Muriel. "Bride." New America, A Journal of American and
Southwestern Culture 4, no. 3 (1982): 86-90.

_____. "Video Cassette as Art World Traveller/Hair Raising in
Arizona." Women Artists News 12, no. 3 (Summer 1987): 16-17,
35.

Watson-Jones, Virginia. Contemporary American Women Sculptors.
Phoenix: Oryx Press, 1986.

GERTRUDE MAGIE (b. 1862)    Painter

American Art Annual, vol. 28. Washington, D.C.: American
Federation of Arts, 1932.

Fielding, Mantle. Dictionary of American Painters, Sculptors and
Engravers. Enlarged ed. Greens Farms, Connecticut: Modern
Books and Crafts, 1974.

EDITH M. MAGONIGLE (b. 1877)    Painter

American Art Annual, vol. 28. Washington, D.C.: American
Federation of Arts, 1932.

Fielding, Mantle. Dictionary of American Painters, Sculptors and
Engravers. Enlarged ed. Greens Farms, Connecticut: Modern
Books and Crafts, 1974.

Who's Who in American Art, vol. 3. Washington, D.C.: American
Federation of Arts, 1940.

CYNTHIA MAILMAN (1942-    )    Painter

See volume 1 of this book.

Frank, Peter. "Cynthia Mailman (Sotto 20)." Art News 77, no. 8
(October 1978): 181.

Who's Who in American Art, 17th ed. New York: R.R. Bowker Co.,
1986.

PATRICIA M. MAINARDI (1942-     )    Painter and Writer

See volume 1 of this book.

Burnside, Madeleine.  "Pat Mainardi (Ingber)."  Art News 78, no. 2
     (February 1979):  173.

Who's Who in American Art, 17th ed.  New York:  R.R. Bowker Co.,
     1986.


SYLVIA PLIMACK MANGOLD (1938-     )    Painter

See volume 1 of this book.

Field, Richard S., and Fine, Ruth E.  A Graphic Muse.  New York:
     Hudson Hills Press, 1987.

Florescu, Michael.  "Sylvia Plimack Mangold."  Arts Magazine 58,
     no. 7 (March 1984):  6.

Kramer, Hilton.  "Sylvia Mangold."  The New York Times, 2 March
     1974.

Mathews, Margaret.  "Sylvia Plimack Mangold."  American Artist 48,
     no. 500 (March 1984):  52-56, 84-88.

Nochlin, Linda.  "Some Women Realists:  Part I."  Arts Magazine 48,
     no. 5 (February 1974):  46-51.

Sylvia Plimack Mangold, Paintings 1965-1982.  Madison, Wisconsin:
     Madison Art Center, 1983.

Silverthorne, Jeanne.  "Sylvia Plimack Mangold."  Artforum 24, no.
     7 (March 1986):  117.


SALLY MANN (1951-     )    Photographer

Ellenzweig, Allen.  "Sally Mann at Marcuse Pfeiffer."  Art in
     America 75, no. 1 (January 1987):  139-40.

I shall save one land unvisited.  Eleven Southern Photographers.
     Essays by James Baker Hall and Jonathan Williams.  Frankfort,
     Kentucky:  Gnomon Press, 1978.

Livingston, Jane.  Sally Mann:  The Lewis Law Portfolio.
     Washington, D.C.:  Corcoran Gallery of Art, 1977.

_____.  Second Sight.  The Photographs of Sally Mann.  Boston:
     David Godine, 1983.

Orland, Ted. "Traces of Memory." Artweek 13 (6 November 1982): 11.

Sally Mann: Sweet Silent Thought. Introduction by Ted Orland. Durham, North Carolina: Center for Creative Photography, 1987.

Un/Common Ground: Virginia Artists 1988. Richmond, Virginia: Virginia Museum of Fine Arts, 1988.


ELSIE MANVILLE (1922-    )   Painter

Brown, P. S. "Elsie Manville." Arts Magazine 52, no. 8 (April 1978): 8.

Frank, Peter. "Elsie Manville." Art News 77, no. 8 (October 1978): 175.

Martin, Richard. "Elsie Manville." Arts Magazine 56, no. 6 (February 1982): 6.

Who's Who in American Art, 17th ed. New York: R.R. Bowker Co., 1986.


MARCIA MARCUS (1928-    )   Painter

See volume 1 of this book.

Derfner, Phyllis. "Marcia Marcus." Art in America 63, no. 3 (March 1975): 88-89.

Goodrich, Lloyd, and Bryant, Edward. Forty Artists Under Forty from the Collections of the Whitney Museum of American Art. New York: Frederick A. Praeger Publications, 1962.

Russo, Alexander. Profiles on Women Artists. Frederick, Maryland: University Publications of America, 1985.

Self-Portraits by Women Artists. Los Angeles: Gallery at the Plaza, Security Pacific National Bank, 1985.

Who's Who in American Art, 17th ed. New York: R.R. Bowker Co., 1986.


BERTA MARGOULIES [O'HARE] (1907-    )   Sculptor

See volume 1 of this book.

Berta Margoulies. New York: Forum Gallery, 1964.

Lowengrund, Margaret. "Elemental Form." Art Digest 23, no. 13 (1 April 1949): 13.

Rich, Jack C. The Materials and Methods of Sculpture. New York: Oxford University Press, 1947.

Roller, Marion. "The Challenge of Space." National Sculpture Review 31, no. 1 (Spring 1982): 8-13.

Watson-Jones, Virginia. Contemporary American Women Sculptors. Phoenix: Oryx Press, 1986.


                    MARISOL [ESCOBAR] (1930-    )    Sculptor

See volume 1 of this book.

Berman, Avis. "A Bold and Incisive Way of Portraying Movers and Shakers." Smithsonian 14, no. 11 (February 1984): 54-63.

Bernstein, Roberta. "Marisol's Self-Portraits: The Dream and the Dreamer." Arts Magazine 59, no. 7 (March 1985): 86-89.

Biennale 17. Antwerp: Middelheim, 12 June-2 October 1983.

Edelman, Robert G. "Marisol at Sidney Janis." Art in America 72, no. 9 (October 1984): 189.

Glueck, Grace. "The 20th Century Artists Most Admired by Other Artists." Art News 76, no. 9 (November 1977): 93.

Lippard, Ludy. Pop Art. New York: Praeger, 1966.

Marisol. Philadelphia: Moore College of Art, 1970.

Marisol. Worcester: Worcester Art Museum, 1973.

Marisol: Prints 1961-1973. New York: New York Cultural Center, 1973.

Mecklenburg, Virginia M. Modern American Realism: The Sara Roby Foundation Collection. Washington, D.C.: National Museum of American Art, 1987.

Raynor, Vivien. "Art: Marisol Sculpture from Leonardo Painting." The New York Times, 2 June 1984.

Shulman, Leon. Marisol. Worcester: Worcester Art Museum, 1971.

Watson-Jones, Virgina. Contemporary American Women Sculptors. Phoenix: Oryx Press, 1986.

274

Westfall, Stephen. "Marisol." Arts Magazine 59, no. 3 (November 1984): 38-39.


MARY ELLEN MARK (1940-    )   Photojournalist

Auer, Michèle and Auer, Michel. Encyclopédie Internationale des Photographes de 1839 à nos jours. Hermance, Switzerland: Editions Camera Obscura, 1985.

Johnstone, M. "A View of Santa Barbara." Artweek 16 (12 October 1985): 1.

Jordan, J. "Examining an Illness." Artweek 17 (17 May 1986): 10.

Mark, Mary Ellen. Falkland Roak. New York: Knopf, 1981.

_____. Passport. New York: Lustrum Press, 1974.

_____. Ward 81. New York: Simon and Schuster, 1979.

_____, and Leibovitz, Annie. The Photojournalist: Two Women Explore the Modern World and the Emotions of Individuals. New York: Thomas Y. Crowell, 1974.

Whelan, Richard. "Mary Ellen Mark (Castelli Photographs)." Art News 80, no. 9 (November 1981): 206.


AGNES MARTIN (1912-    )   Painter

See volume 1 of this book.

Agnes Martin. Paintings and Drawings, 1957-1975. London: Arts Council of Great Britain, 1977.

Grimes, Nancy. "New York Reviews. Agnes Martin [at] Pace." Art News 85, no. 10 (December 1986): 140.

Poirier, Maurice, and Necol, Jane. "The '60s in Abstract: 13 Statements and an Essay." Art in America 71, no. 9 (October 1983): 129, 132.

Sandler, Irving. American Art of the 1960s. New York: Harper and Row, 1988.

Stevens, Mark. "Mark Stevens on Art." The New Republic, 19 January 1987: 25-26.

MARIA MARTIN [BACHMAN]     (1796-1863)     Painter

See volume 1 of this book.

Groce, George C.,  and Wallace, David H.  The New-York Historical
     Society's Dictionary of Artists in America 1564-1860.  New
     Haven:  Yale University Press, 1957.


MARIA MARTINEZ (1884-1980)     Potter

See volume 1 of this book.

Clark, Garth.  A Century of Ceramics in the United States
     1878-1978.  New York:  E.P. Dutton, 1979.

Contemporary American Ceramics.  Syracuse:  Syracuse Museum of Fine
     Arts, 1937.

Hughto, Margie.  New Works in Clay by Contemporary Painters and
     Sculptors.  Syracuse:  Everson Museum of Art, 1976.

National Museum of Women in the Arts.  New York:  Harry N. Abrams,
     Inc., 1987.


ALICE TRUMBULL MASON (1904-1971)     Painter

See volume 1 of this book.

Alice Trumbull Mason:  Paintings from 1930 to 1950.  New York:
     Washburn Gallery, 1979.

Alice Trumbull Mason:  Paintings from 1929 to 1969.  New York:
     Washburn Gallery, 1988.

Cotter, Holland.  "Alice Trumbull Mason (Washburn)."  Art News
     87, no. 4 (April 1988):  145-46.

Van Wagner, Judy Collischen.  American Abstract Artists, 50th
     Anniversary Celebration.  Greenvale, New York:  Hillwood Art
     Gallery, Long Island University, C.W. Post Campus, 1986.

Westfall, Stephen.  "Alice Trumbull Mason:  Home-Grown
     Abstraction."  Art in America 73, no. 10 (October 1985):
     146-49.


EMILY MASON (1932-     )     Painter

See volume 1 of this book.

MARGRETHE MATHER (ca. 1885-1952)    Photographer

A Guide to the Collection.  Houston:  Museum of Fine Arts, 1981.

Justema, William.  "Memoir of Margrethe Mather."  Journal of
    Center for Creative Photography, University of Arizona, no. 11
    (1979).

Kramer, Hilston.  "Photographer Extraordinaire."  The New York
    Times, 23 December 1979, Arts and Leisure Section:  31.

Patterns in Photography.  San Francisco:  M.H. de Young Museum,
    1931.

Travis, David.  Photography Rediscovered.  New York:  Whitney
    Museum of American Art, 1979.

LUCIA KLEINHANS MATHEWS (1870-1955)    Painter

American Art Annual, vol. 28.  Washington, D.C.:  American
    Federation of Arts, 1932.

California Art in Retrospect:  1850-1915.  San Francisco:  Golden
    Gate International Exposition, 1940.

California Design 1910.  Pasadena, California:  Pasadena Center,
    1974.

Callen, Anthea.  Women Artists of the Arts and Crafts Movement,
    1870-1914.  New York:  Pantheon Books, 1979.

Jones, Harvey L.  Mathews:  Masterpieces of the California
    Decorative Style.  2nd ed.  Santa Barbara, California and Salt
    Lake City, Utah:  Perregrine Smith, Inc., 1980.

_____.  "Mathews--Renaissance People for a Renaissance Time."  The
    Museum of California, The Oakland Museum 8, no. 4
    (January-February 1985):  4-7.

Orr-Cahall, Christina.  The Art of California.  Oakland:  The
    Oakland Museum, 1985:  85.

Painting and Sculpture in California:  The Modern Era.  San
    Francisco:  San Francisco Museum of Modern Art, 1976.

Porter, Bruce, et al.  Art in California:  A Survey of American
    Art with Special Reference to California Painting, Sculpture
    and Architecture, Past and Present, Particularly as Those Arts
    were Represented at the Panama-Pacific International
    Exposition.  San Francisco:  R.L. Bernier, 1916.

Prather-Moses, Alice Irma.  The International Dictionary of Women
    Workers in the Decorative Arts.  Metuchen, New Jersey:
    Scarecrow Press, 1981:  110.

Spangenberg, Helen.  Yesterday's Artists on the Monterey Peninsula.
    Monterey, California:  Monterey Peninsula Museum of Art, 1976.

A Woman's Vision:  California Painting into the 20th Century.  San
    Francisco:  Maxwell Galleries, 1983.


PAT MATHIESEN (1934-    )  Sculptor

Goodman, John K.  "Pat Matheisen:  Akin to her Environment."
    Southwest Art 10, no. 10 (March 1981):  78-83.

Samuels, Peggy and Harold.  Contemporary Western Artists.  Houston:
    Southwest Art, 1982.

Watson-Jones, Virginia.  Contemporary American Women Sculptors.
    Phoenix:  Oryx Press, 1986.


ELEANOR MATLACK (active 1880's-90's)   Painter and Etcher

Peet, Phyllis.  American Women of the Etching Revival.  Atlanta:
    High Museum of Art, 1988.

The Work of Women Etchers of America.  New York:  Union League
    Club, 1888.


LOUISA MATTHIASDOTTIR (1917-    )   Painter

See volume 1 of this book.

Ashbery, John.  "North Light."  Art News 70, no. 10 (February
    1972):  44-45, 71-72.

_____.  "Louisa Matthiasdottir."  New York:  Robert Schoelkopf
    Gallery, 27 January 1982.

Diamond, Stuart.  "Louise Matthiasdottir."  Arts Magazine 58, no.
    10 (Summer 1984):  42-43.

Martin, Alvin.  American Realism, 20th Century Drawings and
    Watercolors, From the Glenn C. Janss Collection.  San
    Francisco:  San Francisco Museum of Modern Art, 1985.

Perl, Jed; Rosenthal, Deborah; and Weber, Nicholas Fox.  Louisa
    Matthiasdottir:  Small Paintings.  New York:  Hudson Hills
    Press, 1986.

278

Rosenthal, Deborah. "Louisa Matthiasdottir." Arts Magazine 50, no. 8 (April 1976): 12.

_____. "Louise Matthiasdottir at Robert Schoelkopf." Art in America 72, no. 10 (November 1984): 164-65.

Sawin, Martica. "Louise Matthiasdottir: A Painter of the Figure." Arts Magazine 36, no. 2 (November 1961): 26-33.

Tallmer, Jerry. "The Doctor's Daughter: Her Art is in the Stillness." New York Post, 9 January 1982.

### EMILY MAVERICK (1803-1850)    Engraver

Clark, Eliot. History of the National Academy of Design, 1825-1953. New York: Columbia University Press, 1954.

Fielding, Mantle. Dictionary of American Painters, Sculptors and Engravers. Enlarged ed. Greens Farms, Connecticut: Modern Books and Crafts, 1974.

Groce, George C., and Wallace, David H. The New-York Historical Society's Dictionary of Artists in America 1564-1860. New Haven: Yale University Press, 1957.

Stauffer, David M. American Engravers Upon Copper and Steel, 2 vols. New York: Burt Franklin, 1907.

### MARIA ANN MAVERICK (1805-1832)    Engraver and Lithographer

Clark, Eliot. History of the National Academy of Design, 1825-1953. New York: Columbia University Press, 1954.

Fielding, Mantle. Dictionary of American Painters, Sculptors and Engravers. Enlarged ed. Greens Farms, Connecticut: Modern Books and Crafts, 1974.

Groce, George C., and Wallace, David H. The New-York Historical Society's Dictionary of Artists in America 1564-1860. New Haven: Yale University Press, 1957.

Stauffer, David M. American Engravers Upon Copper and Steel, 2 vols. New York: Burt Franklin, 1907.

### LAURA WASSON MAXWELL (1877-1967)    Painter

Dawdy, Doris Ostrander. Artists of the American West, vol. 1. Chicago: Swallow Press, 1974.

Spangenberg, Helen.  Yesterday's Artists on the Monterey Peninsula. Monterey, California:  Monterey Museum of Art, 1976.


ROSEMARY MAYER (1943-    )   Sculptor

See volume 1 of this book.

Who's Who in American Art, 17th ed.  New York:  R.R. Bowker Co., 1986.


HARRIET HYATT MAYOR (1868-1960)   Sculptor

American Art Annual, vol. 28.  Washington, D.C.:  American Federation of Arts, 1932.

Clement, Clara Erskine.  Women in the Fine Arts.  Boston: Houghton, Mifflin and Co., 1904 (under Hyatt).

National Sculpture Society.  Exhibition of American Sculpture.  New York, 1923.

National Sculpture Society and California Palace of the Legion of Honor.  Contemporary American Sculpture.  New York, 1929.

Proske, Beatrice G.  Brookgreen Gardens.  Brookgreen, South Carolina:  Brookgreen Gardens, 1943.

Who's Who in American Art, vol. 3.  Washington, D.C.:  American Federation of Arts, 1940.


ILA McAFEE (1897-    )   Painter

Nelson, Mary C.  "Ila McAfee of the White Horse Studio."  American Artist 45 (January 1981):  64-69.

_____.  The Legendary Artists of Taos.  New York:  Watson-Guptill Publications, 1980.

Park, Marlene, and Markowitz, Gerald E.  Democratic Vistas:  Post Offices and Public Art in the New Deal.  Philadelphia:  Temple University Press, 1984.

Samuels, Peggy, and Harold.  The Illustrated Biographical Encyclopedia of Artists of the American West.  Garden City, New York:  Doubleday and Co., 1976.

FLORENCE McCLUNG (1894-     )     Painter

Fiftieth Annual Exhibition. New York:  National Association of
    Women Painters and Sculptors, 1942.

O'Brien, Esse Forrester.  Art and Artists of Texas.  Dallas:  Tardy
    Publishing Co., 1935.

Samuels, Peggy and Harold.  The Illustrated Biographical
    Encyclopedia of Artists of the American West.  Garden City,
    New York:  Doubleday, 1976.

Stewart, Rick.  Lone Star Regionalism.  Dallas:  Dallas Museum of
    Art, 1985:  13, 100, 179-80.

Who's Who in American Art, vol. 8.  Washington, D.C.:  American
    Federation of Arts, 1962.

M. EVELYN McCORMICK (1869-1948)     Painter

Dawdy, Doris Ostrander.  Artists of the American West:  A
    Biographical Dictionary, vol. 2.  Chicago:  Sage Books, 1980.

Porter, Bruce, et al.  Art in California:  A Survey of American
    Art with Special Reference to California Painting, Sculpture
    and Architecture, Past and Present, Particularly as Those Arts
    were Represented at the Panama-Pacific International
    Exposition.  San Francisco:  R. L. Bernier, 1916.

Spangenberg, Helen.  Yesterday's Artists on the Monterey Peninsula.
    Monterey, California:  Monterey Peninsula Museum of Art, 1976.

ANN McCOY (1946-     )     Painter

See volume 1 of this book.

Ann McCoy:  The Red Sea and the Night Sea.  Chicago:  The Arts Club
    of Chicago, 1979.

Bordeaux, Jean-Luc.  "The Silent World of Ann McCoy."  Art
    International 21, no. 1 (January-February 1977):  30-31, 63.

Brenson, Michael.  "They Seek Spiritual Meaning in an Age of
    Skepticism."  The New York Times, 11 May 1986, Arts and
    Leisure Section:  37, 41.

Kutner, Janet.  "Capturing Images of the Unknown."  Dallas Morning
    News, 6 August 1986:  1F, 3F.

McEvilley, Thomas. "Ann McCoy." Artforum 24, no. 8 (April 1986): 110.

Mecklenburg, Virgina M. Modern American Realism: The Sara Roby Foundation Collection. Washington, D.C.: National Museum of American Art, 1987.

Tuchman, Maurice, and Freeman, Judy. The Spiritual in Art: Abstract Painting, 1890-1985. Los Angeles: Los Angeles County Museum of Art, 1986.


GERALDINE McCULLOUGH (1922-    )   Sculptor

Adams, Russell L. Great Negroes, Past and Present. Chicago: Afro-American, 1969.

Bach, Ira J., and Gray, Mary Lackritz. A Guide to Chicago's Public Sculpture. Chicago: University of Chicago Press, 1983.

Bims, Hamilton. "A Sculptor Looks at Martin Luther King." Ebony 28, no. 6 (April 1973): 95-96, 98, 102, 104-05.

Canaday, John. "Art: Debutante and a Grand Old Man." The New York Times, 16 January 1964: L22.

Riedy, James L. Chicago Sculpture. Urbana: University of Illinois Press, 1981.

Watson-Jones, Virginia. Contemporary American Women Sculptors. Phoenix: Oryx Press, 1986.


KATHLEEN McENERY [CUNNINGHAM] (1885-1971)   Painter

Kathleen McEnery Cunningham. Rochester, New York: Memorial Art Gallery, University of Rochester, 1972.

1913 Armory Show, 50th Anniversary Exhibition 1963. Utica, New York: Munson-Williams-Proctor Institute, 1963.

Obituary. Democrat and Chronicle (Rochester, New York), 7 July 1971.

A Rochester Retrospective, Painting and Sculpture (1880-1950). Rochester, New York: Memorial Art Gallery, University of Rochester, 1980.

Tufts, Eleanor. American Women Artists, 1830-1930. Washington, D.C.: National Museum of Women in the Arts, 1987.

282

EUGENIE McEVOY (MRS. O'DELL) (d. 1975)   Painter

15th Biennial Exhibition. Washington, D.C.: Corcoran Gallery of
    Art, 1937.

"A Gallery-Goer's Week."  The New York Times, 7 May 1933.

Geerstsema, Tobie.  "From Famed Sharpshooter to Noted Artist--the
    Life and Times of Eugenie McEvoy O'Dell."  Woodstock Townsman,
    24 July 1975.

_____.  "The Late Eugenie McEvoy O'Dell."  The Daily Freeman,
    (Kingston, New York), 22 July 1975.

Paintings by Eugenie McEvoy. Albany, New York:  Albany Institute
    of History and Art, 1945.

7th Annual Artists Exhibition, Upper Hudson. Albany, New York,
    1942.


ISABEL McILVAIN (1943-   )   Sculptor

Bass, Ruth.  "New York Reviews:  Alive and Well in the '70s."
    Art News 80, no. 2 (February 1981):   214.

Glueck, Grace.  "Art:  Sculptured Figures of 70's at Pratt
    Gallery."  The New York Times, 7 November 1980:  C19.

Goodyear, Frank H.  Contemporary American Realism Since 1960.
    Boston:  New York Graphic Society, 1981.

"Model of Kennedy Statue Unveiled in Boston."  The New York Times,
    8 April 1988:  8Y.

Stolbach, Michael Hunt.  "Artists' Choice."  Arts Magazine 55, no.
    3 (November 1980):  23-24.

Watson-Jones, Virginia.  Contemporary American Women Sculptors.
    Phoenix:  Oryx Press, 1986.

Zimmer, William.  "Isabel McIlvain."  Arts Magazine 51, no. 10
    (June 1977):  37.


HENRIETTA FOXHALL McKENNEY (1825-87)   Painter

Groce, George C., and Wallace, David H.  The New-York Historical
    Society's Dictionary of Artists in America, 1564-1860.  New
    Haven:  Yale University Press, 1957.

Tufts, Eleanor. American Women Artists 1830-1930. Washington, D.C.: National Museum of Women in the Arts, 1987.


MARY LOUISE McLAUGHLIN (1847-1939)    Painter, Ceramicist, and
                                              Etcher

Callen, Anthea. Women Artists of the Arts and Crafts Movement, 1870-1914. New York: Pantheon Books, 1979.

Clark, Garth. A Century of Ceramics in the United States 1878-1978. New York: E.P. Dutton, 1979.

Contemporary American Ceramics. Syracuse: Syracuse Museum of Fine Arts, 1937.

Eidelberg, Martin. "Art Pottery." The Arts and Crafts Movement in America, 1876-1916. Edited by Robert J. Clark. Princeton: Princeton University Press, 1972.

Evans, Paul F. Art Pottery of the United States: An Encyclopedia of Producers and Their Marks. New York: Scribner's Sons, 1974.

Henzke, Lucile. American Art Pottery. Camden, New Jersey: Nelson, 1970.

Keen, Kirsten Hoving. American Art Pottery 1875-1930. Wilmington: Delaware Art Museum, 1978.

The Ladies, God Bless 'Em: The Women's Art Movement in Cincinnati in the 19th Century. Cincinnati: Cincinnati Art Museum, 1976.

McLaughlin, Mary Louise. China Painting: A Practical Manual for the Use of Amateurs in the Decoration of Hard Porcelain. Cincinnati: Robert Clarke and Co., 1877.

_____. Painting in Oil: A Manual for the Use of Students. Cincinnati: Robert Clarke and Co., 1888.

_____. Pottery Decoration Under the Glaze. Cincinnati: Clarke, 1880.

_____. Suggestion to China Painters. Cincinnati: Clarke, 1883.

Overglaze Imagery. Essays by Garth Clark, Judy Chicago, and Richard Shaw. Fullerton, California: California State University Art Gallery, 1977.

284

Peck, Herbert. The History of Rookwood Pottery. New York: Crown
    Publishers, 1968.

Peet, Phyllis. American Women of the Etching Revival. Atlanta:
    High Museum of Art, 1988.

Perry, Mrs. Aaron F. "Decorative Pottery of Cincinnati." Harper's
    New Monthly Magazine 62 (April-May 1881): 834-45.

Prather-Moses, Alice Irma. The International Dictionary of Women
    Workers in the Decorative Arts. Metuchen, New Jersey:
    Scarecrow Press, 1981: 105-06.

Weimann, Jeanne Madeline. The Fair Women. Chicago: Academy
    Chicago, 1981.


        BONNIE McLEARY (1890-    )   Sculptor

American Art Annual, vol. 26. Washington, D.C.: American
    Federation of Arts, 1929.

Clark, Eliot. History of the National Academy of Design,
    1825-1953. New York: Columbia University Press, 1954.

Famous Small Bronzes. New York: The Gorham Co., 1928.

Fielding, Mantle. Dictionary of American Painters, Sculptors and
    Engravers. Enlarged ed. Greens Farms, Connecticut: Modern
    Books and Crafts, 1974.

Gardner, Albert TenEyck. American Sculpture; A Catalogue of the
    Collection of the Metropolitan Museum of Art. Greenwich,
    Connecticut: New York Graphic Society, 1965: 163.

O'Brien, Esse Forrester. Art and Artists of Texas. Dallas: Tardy
    Publishing Co., 1935.

Who's Who in American Art, vol. 9. Washington, D.C.: American
    Federation of Arts, 1966.


        BLANCHE McMANUS [MANSFIELD] (b. 1870)   Painter and Illustrator

Clement, Clara Erskine. Women in the Fine Arts. Boston: Houghton
    Mifflin Co., 1904.

Fielding, Mantle. Dictionary of American Painters, Sculptors and
    Engravers. Enlarged ed. Greens Farms, Connecticut: Modern
    Books and Crafts, 1974 (under Mansfield).

Hills, Patricia. Turn-of-the-Century America. New York: Whitney
     Museum of American Art, 1977.

Keay, Carolyn. American Posters of the Turn of the Century. New
     York: St. Martin's, 1975: 29.

McManus, Blanche. The American Woman Abroad. New York: Dodd,
     Mead and Co., 1911.

Woman's Who's Who of America. New York: American Commonwealth
     Co., 1914.


NEYSA MORAN McMEIN (1890-1949)    Painter and Illustrator

American Art Annual, vol. 28. Washington, D.C.: American
     Federation of Arts, 1932.

Edmiston, Susan, and Cirino, Linda D. Literary New York. Boston:
     Houghton Mifflin Co., 1976.

Fielding, Mantle. Dictionary of American Painters, Sculptors and
     Engravers. Enlarged ed. Greens Farms, Connecticut: Modern
     Books and Crafts, 1974.

Obituary. Who's Who in American Art, vol. 5. Washington, D.C.:
     American Federation of Arts, 1953.

Reed, Walt, ed. The Illustrator in America, 1900-1960s. New York:
     Reinhold Publishing Co., 1966.

Who's Who in American Art, vol. 1. Washington, D.C.: American
     Federation of Arts, 1935.


HELEN FARNSWORTH MEARS (1872-1916)    Sculptor

See volume 1 of this book.

Fielding, Mantle. Dictionary of American Painters, Sculptors and
     Engravers. Enlarged ed. Greens Farms, Connecticut: Modern
     Books and Crafts, 1974.

Obituary. American Art Annual, vol. 13. Washington, D.C.:
     American Federation of Arts, 1916.

Obituary. The New York Sun, 18 February 1916: 1.

Statue of Miss Frances E. Willard. Proceedings in the Senate and
     House of Representatives on the Occasion of the Reception and
     Acceptance of the Statue from the State of Illinois.
     Washington, D.C.: Government Printing Office, 1905.

286

Woman's Who's Who of America. New York: American Commonwealth
    Co., 1914.


MARY ANN E. MEARS (1946-    )    Sculptor

Maryland Artists. College Park, Maryland: University of Maryland,
    1981.

Maryland Biennial '74. Baltimore: Baltimore Museum of Art, 1974.

1976 Biennial Exhibition. Baltimore: Baltimore Museum of Art,
    1976.

Sculpture 1980. Baltimore: Maryland Institute College of Art,
    1980.

Stevens, Elisabeth. "Baltimore Renovates, Rebuilds and
    Revitalizes." Art News 81, no. 8 (October 1982): 94-97.

Works by Maryland Artists for Hyatt Regency, Baltimore. Baltimore:
    Maryland State Arts Council, 1981.


LILLIAN BURK MEESER (1864-1943)    Painter

American Art Annual, vol. 28. Washington, D.C.: American
    Federation of Arts, 1932.

Bye, Arthur. Pots and Pans. Princeton: Princeton University
    Press, 1921: 226.

Fielding, Mantle. Dictionary of American Painters, Sculptors and
    Engravers. Enlarged ed. Greens Farms, Connecticut: Modern
    Books and Crafts, 1974.

Moore, Julia G. History of the Detroit Society of Women Painters
    and Sculptors, 1903-1953. River Rouge, Michigan: Victory
    Printing Co., 1953: 15.

Who's Who in American Art, vol. 3. Washington, D.C.: American
    Federation of Arts, 1940.


HILDRETH MEIÈRE (1892-1961)    Painter

Alexander, H.B. "Hildreth Meière's Work for Nebraska."
    Architecture 63 (June 1931): 34-38.

American Art Annual, vol. 28. Washington, D.C.: American
    Federation of Arts, 1932.

287

Lee, Anne. "Hildreth Meière: Mural Painter." Architectural
    Record 62 (August 1927): 103-12.

McCready, Eric S. "The Nebraska State Capitol: Its Design,
    Background and Influence." Nebraska History 55 (Fall 1974):
    393-403.

Meière, Hildreth. "The Question of Decoration." Architectural
    Forum 57 (July 1932): 1-8.

Obituary. The New York Times, 3 May 1961.

Watson, Ernest. "Hildreth Meière, Mural Painter." American
    Artists 5 (September 1941): 4-9.


                MARY B. MELLEN (19th Century)   Painter

Gerdts, William H., and Burke, Russell. American Still Life
    Painting. New York: Praeger, 1971.

Hanaford, Phebe A. Daughters of America. Augusta, Maine: True
    and Co., 1882: 289-90.

Sharf, Frederic A. "Fitz Hugh Lane Re-Considered." Essex
    Institute Historical Collections 96 (January 1960): 73-83.


            ELEANOR MARY MELLON (1894-1980)   Sculptor

American Art Annual, vol. 28. Washington, D.C.: American
    Federation of Arts, 1932.

National Sculpture Society. Exhibition of American Sculpture. New
    York, 1923.

National Sculpture Society and California Palace of the Legion of
    Honor. Contemporary American Sculpture. New York, 1929.

Proske, Beatrice Gilman. Brookgreen Gardens Sculpture, vol. II.
    Brookgreen, South Carolina: Brookgreen Gardens, 1955: 80-81.

Who's Who in American Art, vol. 8. Washington, D.C.: American
    Federation of Arts, 1962.


                ANA MENDIETA (1948-1985)   Sculptor

See volume 1 of this book.

Ana Mendieta, A Retrospective. Curated by Petra Barreras del Rio
    and John Perreault. New York: New Museum of Contemporary
    Art, 1987.

288

Brenson, Michael. "Art: Ana Mendieta Retrospective." The New
    York Times, 29 November 1987: Y40.

Buder, Leonard. "Sculptor Accused of Pushing Wife to Death."
    The New York Times, 10 September 1985.

"Further Public Art Notes." Art in America 73, no. 2 (February
    1985): 176.

Johnson, Ken. "Ana Mendieta at the New Museum of Contemporary
    Art." Art in America 76, no. 3 (March 1988): 153-54.

Latin American Art: A Woman's View. Miami: Frances Wolfson Art
    Gallery, Miami-Dade Community College, 1981.

Lippard, Lucy. "Ana Mendieta, 1948-1985." Hue Points 14, no. 1
    (Spring 1986): 54-55.

Morgan, Robert C. "Ana Mendiata (The New Museum of Contemporary
    Art)." Arts Magazine 62, no. 7 (March 1988): 111.

Obituary. Art in America 73, no. 11 (November 1985): 190.

KATHERINE MERRILL (b. 1876)    Painter and Etcher

American Art Annual, vol. 28. Washington, D.C.: American
    Federation of Arts, 1932.

Contemporary Art of the United States. Washington, D.C.: Corcoran
    Gallery of Art, 1940, no. 10.

Fielding, Mantle. Dictionary of American Painters, Sculptors and
    Engravers. Enlarged ed. Greens Farms, Connecticut: Modern
    Books and Crafts, 1974.

Theime, Ulrich, and Becker, Felix. Allgemeines Lexikon der
    Bildenden Kunstler.... Leipzig: E.A. Seemann, 1930.

Who's Who in American Art, vol. 3. Washington, D.C.: American
    Federation of Arts, 1940.

HELEN BIGELOW MERRIMAN (b. 1844)    Watercolorist

American Art Annual, vol. 28. Washington, D.C.: American
    Federation of Arts, 1932.

Fielding, Mantle. Dictionary of American Painters, Sculptors and
    Engravers. Enlarged ed. Greens Farms, Connecticut: Modern
    Books and Crafts, 1974.

Hoppin, Martha J.  "Women Artists in Boston, 1870-1900:  The Pupils
of William Morris Hunt."  The American Art Journal 13, no. 1
(Winter 1981):  17-46.


ANNA LEA MERRITT (1844-1930)  Painter

See volume 1 of this book.

Graham, Julie.  "American Women Artists' Groups:  1867-1930."
Woman's Art Journal 1, no. 1 (Spring-Summer 1980):  7-12.

Hanaford, Phebe A.  Daughters of America.  Augusta, Maine:  True
and Co., 1882:  279-280.

Merritt, Anna Lea.  "My Garden (A Hamlet in Old Hampshire)."
Century Magazine 62, no. 3 (July 1901):  342-51.

_____. "A Half-Time Boy and a Goat (A Hamlet in Old Hampshire)."
Century Magazine 62 (August 1901):  590-93.

_____. "A Hamlet in Old Hampshire." Century Magazine 62, no. 1
(May 1901):  3-14.

_____. "Making a Garden." Lippincott's 67 (March 1901):  353.

Nunn, Pamela Gerrish, ed.  Canvassing:  Recollections by Six
Victorian Women Artists.  London:  Camden Press, 1986.

Obituary.  American Art Annual, vol. 27.  Washington, D.C.:
American Federation of Arts, 1930.

Painting Women:  Victorian Women Artists.  Rochdale, England:
Rochdale Art Gallery, 1987.

Peet, Phyllis.  American Women of the Etching Revival.  Atlanta:
High Museum of Art, 1988.

Six Victorian Women Artists.  London:  Camden Press, 1986.


SALLY MICHEL (ca. 1900-    )  Painter

Hobbs, Robert.  "Sally Michel:  The Other Avery."  Woman's Art
Journal 8, no. 2 (Fall 1987-Winter 1988):  3-14.

The Milton Avery Family.  New Britain, Connecticut:  New Britain
Museum of American Art, 1968.

Nygren, Edward J., and Simmons, Linda Crocker. American Masters:
Works on Paper from the Corcoran Gallery of Art. Washington,
D.C.: Smithsonian Institution Traveling Exhibition Service
and Corcoran Gallery of Art, 1986.


MARY MICHIE (1922-    )  Sculptor

American Artists in Kenya. Nairobi:  New Stanley Gallery, 1969.

Ela, Janet. "Metallurgists Weld, Cast, Carve to Produce Art."
Wisconsin Academy Review 31, no. 2 (March 1985):  61-71.

Heddle, Lindo. "Wisconsin Women in the Arts; After Two Years."
Arts in Society 12, no. 2 (Summer-Fall 1975):  296-301.

Forty-Third Wisconsin Painters and Sculptors Annual Exhibition
of Wisconsin Art. Milwaukee:  Milwaukee Art Institute, 1957.

Michie, Mary. "Encounter with an African Potter." Ceramics
Monthly 25, no. 10 (December 1977):  32-35.

_____. "Travel:  Search for a Kenya Craftsman." The Christian
Science Monitor, 28 November 1978:  18.

Painting and Sculpture Midwest Biennial Exhibition. Minneapolis:
Walker Art Center, 1958.

Painting and Sculpture Midwest Biennial Exhibition. Minneapolis:
Walker Art Center, 1962.

Sixtieth Annual National April Salon. Springville, Utah:
Springville Museum of Art, 1984.

Wisconsin Painters and Sculptors, Annual Exhibition of Wisconsin
Art. Milwaukee:  Milwaukee Art Center, 1961.

Wisconsin Painters and Sculptors, Annual Exhibition of Wisconsin
Art. Milwaukee:  Milwaukee Art Center, 1963.

Wisconsin Painters and Sculptors, Annual Exhibition of Wisconsin
Art. Milwaukee:  Milwaukee Art Center, 1964.

Wisconsin Painters and Sculptors, Annual Exhibition of Wisconsin
Art. Milwaukee: Milwaukee Art Center, 1965.


EMILY WINTHROP MILES (1893-1962)   Sculptor

Emily W. Miles:  Sculpture and Drawings. New York:  Hudson D.
Walker Gallery, 1937.

Exhibition of Sculpture by Emily Winthrop Miles. New York: Wildenstein and Co., n.d. (ca. 1947).

Exhibition of Sculpture by Emily Winthrop Miles. New York: French and Co., Inc., 1948.

National Sculpture Society and California Palace of the Legion of Honor. Contemporary American Sculpture. New York: Kalkhoff Co., 1929: 230.

Sculpture and Drawings of Emily Winthrop Miles. Cambridge, Massachusetts: Fogg Art Museum, 1943.


JEANNE PATTERSON MILES (1908-    )   Painter and Sculptor

See volume 1 of this book.

Brooks, Perry. "Jeanne Miles." Arts Magazine 56, no. 8 (April 1982): 4.

Ventura, Anita. "Adaline Kent and Jeanne Miles (Betty Parsons Gallery)." Arts Magazine 30, no. 8 (May 1956): 55.

Who's Who in American Art. New York: R.R. Bowker Co., 1978.


HARRIETTE G. MILLER (1892-    )   Sculptor

American Art Annual, vol. 28. Washington, D.C.: American Federation of Arts, 1932.

First Biennial Exhibition of Contemporary American Sculpture, Watercolors and Prints. New York: Whitney Museum of American Art, 1933-34.

Who's Who in American Art, vol. 1. Washington, D.C.: American Federation of Arts, 1935.


LEE MILLER (1908-1977)   Photographer

Chadwick, Whitney. Women Artists and the Surrealist Movement. Boston: New York Graphic Society, 1985.

Krauss, Rosalind; Livingston, Jane; and Ades, Dawn. L'Amour Fou, Photography and Surrealism. New York: Abbeville Press, 1985.

Penrose, Antony. The Lives of Lee Miller. New York: Holt, Rinehart and Winston, 1985.

292

LEE ANNE MILLER (1938-    )    Painter and Printmaker

See volume 1 of this book.

Who's Who in American Art. New York:  R.R. Bowker Co., 1978.


MELISSA MILLER (1951-    )    Painter

Brenson, Michael. "In Melissa Miller's Wild Kingdom Lurks a World
of Wonder." The New York Times, 27 July 1986, Arts and
Leisure Section:  27, 29.

Carlozzi, Annette. 50 Texas Artists. San Francisco:  Chronicle
Books, 1986.

Cathcart, Linda L. Melissa Miller:  A Survey 1978-1986. Houston:
Contemporary Arts Museum, 1986.

Feinstein, Roni. "Melissa Miller:  The Uses of Enchantment."
Arts Magazine 58, no. 10 (Summer 1984):  70-72 and cover.

Greene, Alison de Lima. Twentieth-Century Art in the Museum's
Collection:  Direction and Diversity. Houston:  Museum of
Fine Arts, 1988.

Gregor, Katherine. "Melissa Miller's Animal Kingdom." Art News
85, no. 10 (December 1986):  106-15.

Kutner, Janet. "A Singular Vision of Animals." Dallas Morning
News, 22 November 1986, Section F:  1-2.

Loughery, John. "Melissa Miller." Arts Magazine 61, no. 2
(October 1986):  126.

"Portrait of the Artist, 1987, Who Supports Him/Her." Artsreview
4, no. 3 (Spring 1987):  17-18.


JEAN POND MINER (b. 1866)    Sculptor

Butts, Porter. Art in Wisconsin. Madison:  Democratic Printing,
1936.

Willard, Frances E., and Livermore, Mary A. American Women.
Reprint of 1897 ed., Detroit:  Gale Research, 1973.


NORMA MINKOWITZ (1937-    )    Fiber Artist

Marein, Shirley. Creating Rugs and Wall Hangings. New York:
Viking Press, 1975.

Minkowitz, Norma. "Norma Minkowitz." Fiberarts 13 (May-June 1986): 26.

Sommer, Elyse. Textile Collector's Guide. New York: Monarch Publishers, 1978.

_____. Wearable Art. New York: Crown Publishers, 1975.

Znamierowski, Nell. Fiber: The Artist's View. Greenvale, New York: Hillwood Art Gallery, Long Island University, 1983.


MARY MISS (1944-    )   Sculptor

See volume 1 of this book.

Alloway, Lawrence. New York Women Artists. Albany, New York: University Art Gallery, State University of New York, 1972.

Davies, Hugh M., and Onorato, Ronald J. Sitings: Alice Aycock, Richard Fleischner, Mary Miss, and George Trakas. La Jolla, California: La Jolla Museum of Contemporary Art, 1986.

Foote, Nancy. "Monument--Sculpture--Earthwork." Artforum 28, no. 2 (October 1979): 32-37.

Frank, Peter. "Mary Miss." Art News 75, no. 1 (January 1976): 122.

GEDOK American Women Artists. Hamburg, Germany: Kunsthaus, 1972.

Kardon, Janet. Connections: Bridges/Ladders/Staircases/Tunnels. Philadelphia: Institute of Contemporary Art, University of Pennsylvania, 1982.

Klien, Michael. Four Artists. Williamstown, Massachussetts: Williams College Museum of Art, 1976.

Linker, Kate. Mary Miss. London: Institute of Contemporary Arts, 1983.

Mary Miss Projects 1966-1987. London: Architectural Association, 1987.

McGill, Douglas C. "Sculpture Goes Public." The New York Times Magazine, 27 April 1986: 42-87.

Miss, Mary. "On a Redefinition of Public Sculpture." Perspecta 21: Yale Architectural Journal (1984): 52-70.

Onorato, Ronald J. "Illusive Spaces: The Art of Mary Miss." Artforum 17, no. 4 (December 1978): 28-33, cover.

Shepard, Ileen. Sculpture of the 80's. Essay by Lowery S. Sims. Queens, New York: Queens Museum, 1987.

"272 Guggenheim Fellowships For $5.9 Million Are Awarded." The New York Times, 13 April 1986.

Tuchman, Phyllis. Mary Miss, Interior Works 1966-1980. Providence, Rhode Island: Bell Gallery, Brown University, and Kingston, Rhode Island: Main Gallery, University of Rhode Island, 1981.

Vowinckel, Andreas, ed. Natur-Skulptur. Stuttgart, Germany: Württembergischer Kunstverein, 1981.

Watson-Jones, Virginia. Contemporary American Women Sculptors. Phoenix: Oryx Press, 1986.

JOAN MITCHELL (1926-    )    Painter

See volume 1 of this book.

Bernstock, Judith E. Joan Mitchell. New York: Hudson Hills Press, 1988.

Field, Richard S., and Fine, Ruth E. A Graphic Muse. New York: Hudson Hills Press, 1988.

Joan Mitchell: Paintings 1985-1986. New York: Xavier Fourcade, 1986.

Joan Mitchell: The Sixties. New York: Xavier Fourcade, 1985.

Kimmelman, Michael. "This American in Paris Kept True to New York." The New York Times, 17 April 1988, Art and Leisure section:  43.

Michaud, Yves. Joan Mitchell: La Grande Vallée. Paris: Galerie Jean Fournier, 1984.

_____. Joan Mitchell: River, Lille, Chord. Paris: Galerie Jean Fournier, 1987.

Moorman, Margaret. "Joan Mitchell [Xavier Fourcade]." Art News 85, no. 8 (October 1986):  129.

National Museum of Women in the Arts. New York: Harry N. Abrams, Inc., 1987:  98-99.

Piguet, Philippe. "Paris. Joan Mitchell." L'Oeil no. 383 (June 1987):  80-81.

Pleynet, Marcelin, and Rose, Barbara. Joan Mitchell: Choix de peintures (1970-1982). Paris: Musée d'Art Moderne de la Ville de Paris, 1982.

Sawin, Martica. "A Stretch of the Seine: Joan Mitchell's Paintings." Arts Magazine 62, no. 7 (March 1988): 29-31.

Westfall, Stephen. "Joan Mitchell at Fourcade." Art in America 73, no. 10 (October 1985): 156-57.

_____. "Then and Now: Six of the New York School Look Back." Art in America 73, no. 6 (June 1985): 113-14.

LISETTE MODEL (1906-1983)    Photographer

See volume 1 of this book.

Cravens, R.H. "Notes for a Portrait of Lisette Model." Aperture 86 (1982): 52-65.

A Guide to the Collection. Houston: Museum of Fine Arts, 1981.

Obituary. Art in America 71, no. 5 (May 1983): 224.

Szarkowski, John. Looking at Photographs: 100 Pictures from the Collection of the Museum of Modern Art. New York: The Museum of Modern Art, 1973.

Tighe, Mary Ann. "Lisette Model at Sander." Art in America 65, no. 1 (January-February 1977): 132.

TINA MODOTTI (1896-1942)    Photographer

See volume 1 of this book.

Rice, Shelley. "Tina Modotti at the Museum of Modern Art." Art in America 65, no. 4 (July-August 1977): 96.

Szarkowski, John. Looking at Photographs: 100 Pictures from the Collection of the Museum of Modern Art. New York: The Museum of Modern Art, 1973.

SABRA MOORE (1943-    )    Painter

See volume 1 of this book.

"A Fiesta of Women's Self-Expression." The New York Times, 25 January 1987, national edition: 30.

296

Olejarz, Harold. "Sabra Moore." Arts Magazine 53, no. 9 (May
    1979): 38.

"The Women's Movement in Art, 1986." Arts Magazine 61, no. 1
    (September 1986): 54-57.


        EMILY KELLEY MORAN (1850-1900)    Painter and Etcher

Peet, Phyllis. American Women of the Etching Revival. Atlanta:
    High Museum of Art, 1988.

Weimann, Jeanne Madeline. The Fair Women. Chicago: Academy
    Chicago, 1981: 306.

The Work of Women Etchers of America. New York:  Union League
    Club, 1888.


        MARY NIMMO MORAN (1842-1899)    Etcher and Painter

See volume 1 of this book.

Catalogue of the Complete Etched Works of Thomas Moran, N.A. and
    M. Nimmo Moran, S.P.E. New York:  Klackner Gallery, 1889.

Catalogue of The Work of the Women Etchers of America, April 12 to
    21, 1888. Introduction by M.G. van Rensselaer. New York:
    Union League Club, 1888.

Exhibition of The Work of the Women Etchers of America, November 1
    to December 31, 1887. Introduction by Sylvester Rosa Koehler.
    Boston:  Museum of Fine Arts, 1887.

Francis, Marilyn G. "Mary Nimmo Moran:  Painter-Etcher." Woman's
    Art Journal 4, no. 2 (Fall 1983-Winter 1984):  14-19.

Koehler, Sylvester R. "The Works of the American Etchers:  Mrs. M.
    Nimmo Moran." American Art Review 2 (1881).

O'Brien, Maureen C., and Mandel, Patricia C. F. The American
    Painter-Etcher Movement. Southampton, New York:  Parrish Art
    Museum, 1984.

Peet, Phyllis. American Women of the Etching Revival. Atlanta:
    High Museum of Art, 1988.

Prints of Nature--Poetic Etchings of Mary Nimmo Moran. Tulsa:
    University of Tulsa, 1984.

The Work of Women Etchers of America. New York:  Union League
    Club, 1888:  17-19.

INGE MORATH (1923-    )    Photographer

Aubier, Dominique. Fiesta in Pamplona. Translated by Deirdre
    Butler. London: Photography Magazine and Paris: Robert
    Delpire, 1956.

Auer, Michèle, and Auer, Michel. Encyclopédie International des
    Photographes de 1839 à nos Jours. Hermance, Switzerland:
    Editions Camera Obscura, 1985.

Browne, Turner, and Partnow, Elaine. Macmillan Biographical
    Encyclopedia of Photographic Artists and Innovators. New
    York: Macmillan, 1983.

Carlisle, Olga. Inge Morath. Lucerne: Burcher Verlag, 1975.

Morath, Inge, and Miller, Arthur. Chinese Encounters. New York:
    Farrar, Straus, Giroux, 1979.

_____. In Russia. New York: Studio Book, Viking Press, 1969.

Miller, Arthur. In the Country. New York: Studio Book, Viking
    Press, 1977.

Walsh, George; Naylor, Colin; and Held, Michael. Contemporary
    Photographers. New York: Saint Martin's Press, 1982.

Women See Woman. New York: Thomas Y. Crowell Co., 1976.

BARBARA MORGAN (1900-    )    Photographer

See volume 1 of this book.

Barbara Morgan. Photomontage. Dobbs Ferry, New York: Morgan and
    Morgan, 1980.

Kelley, Etna M. "Barbara Morgan: Painter Turned Photographer."
    Photography, September 1938.

Neugass, Fritx. "Great American Photographers: Barbara Morgan."
    Camera, February 1952.

Szarkowski, John. Looking at Photographs: 100 Pictures from the
    Collection of the Museum of Modern Art. New York: The Museum
    of Modern Art, 1973.

Women's Caucus for Art Honor Awards. New York: National Women's
    Caucus for Art, 1986.

298

MARY DE NEALE MORGAN (1868-1948)    Painter and Printmaker

American Art Annual, vol. 28. Washington, D.C.: American
    Federation of Arts, 1932.

Kovinick, Phil. The Woman Artist in the American West 1860-1960.
    Fullerton, California: Muckenthaler Cultural Center, 1976:
    42.

Porter, Bruce, et al. Art in California: A Survey of American Art
    with Special Reference to California Painting, Sculpture and
    Architecture, Past and Present, Particularly as those Arts
    were Represented at the Panama-Pacific International
    Exposition. San Francisco: R.L. Bernier, 1916.

A Selection of American Prints. A Selection of Biographies of
    Forty Women Artists Working Between 1904-1979. Santa Rosa,
    California: The Annex Galleries, 1987: 11.


MAUD MORGAN (1903-    )    Painter

Faxon, Alicia, and Moore, Sylvia. Pilgrims and Pioneers: New
    England Women in the Arts. New York: Midmarch Arts Press,
    1987: 118-19, 125.

Guiliano, Charles. "Viewing the Life Work of a Distinguished
    Artist." The Patriot Ledger (Boston), 25 February 1986.

Keyes, Norman, Jr. "Maud Morgan: A Life on Canvas." The Boston
    Globe, 6 February 1986, Calendar section.

"Maud Morgan." Art News 37 (19 November 1938): 13.

"Maud Morgan of Boston." Art Digest 13, no. 5 (1 December 1938):
    10.

"Maud Morgan Progresses." Art Digest 17, no. 3 (1 November 1942):
    16.

Maud Morgan: A Retrospective Exhibition, 1927-1977. Andover,
    Massachusetts: Addison Gallery of American Art, Phillips
    Academy, 1977.

"Maud Morgan: Woman with a Purpose." Art News 41 (15 October
    1942): 25.

1952 Annual. New York: Whitney Museum of American Art, 1952.

Painting and Sculpture Today. Indianapolis: Indianapolis Museum
    of Art, 1978.

299

Stapen, Nancy. "Women Artists Get Their Due." Boston Herald, 23
    January 1987: W6.

Women's Caucus for Art Honor Awards. Boston, Massachusetts:
    National Women's Caucus for Art, 1987.

Yau, John. "Maud Morgan at Betty Parsons." Art in America 70, no.
    8 (September 1982): 163.


            ALICE E. MORLEY (b. 1857)    Painter and Etcher

Peet, Phyllis. American Women of the Etching Revival. Atlanta:
    High Museum of Art, 1988.

The Work of Women Etchers of America. New York: Union League
    Club, 1888: 19.


            IMOGENE ROBINSON MORRELL (d. 1908)    Painter

Clement, Clara Erskine. Women in the Fine Arts. Boston:
    Houghton, Mifflin and Co., 1904.

Cosentino, Andrew J., and Glassie, Henry H. The Capital Image,
    Painters in Washington, 1800-1915. Washington, D.C.:
    National Museum of American Art, Smithsonian Institution,
    1983.

Hanaford, Phebe A. Daughters of America. Augusta, Maine: True
    and Co., 1882: 282-84.

"Probe Artist's Death." Washington Post, 23 November 1908.

Rubinstein, Charlotte Streifer. American Women Artists. Boston:
    G. K. Hall, 1982.

"Two Historical Paintings." Scribner's Monthly 11 (1876): 903.


            JULIE MORROW [DE FOREST] (ca. 1882-1979)    Painter

American Art Annual, vol. 28. Washington, D.C.: American
    Federation of Arts, 1932.

Clark, Edna. Ohio Art and Artists. Richmond, Virginia: Garrett
    and Massie, 1932.

Dawdy, Doris Ostrander. Artists of the American West: A
    Biographical Dictionary, vol. 2. Chicago: Sage Books, 1980.

Fielding, Mantle. Dictionary of American Painters, Sculptors and
    Engravers. Enlarged ed. Greens Farms, Connecticut: Modern
    Books and Crafts, 1974.

300

Gerdts, William H. American Impressionism. New York: Abbeville
    Press, 1984: 220.

Who's Who in American Art, vol. 1. Washington, D.C.: American
    Federation of Arts, 1935.


REE MORTON (1936-1977)    Sculptor

See volume 1 of this book.

Made in Philadelphia: Don Roger, Ree Morton, Italo Scanga,
    Phillips Simkin, Dennis Will. Philadelphia: Institute of
    Contemporary Art, 1973.

Obituary. Art in America 65, no. 4 (July-August 1977):  14.


ANNA MARY ROBERTSON MOSES ["GRANDMA"] (1860-1961)    Painter

See volume 1 of this book.

Armstrong, William. Barefoot in the Grass:  The Story of Grandma
    Moses. Garden City, New York: Doubleday and Co., 1970.

Grandma Moses, American Primitive. Introduction by Louis
    Bromfield. Edited by Otto Kallir. New York:  Doubleday and
    Co., 1947.

Who's Who in American Art, vol. 7. Washington, D.C.:  American
    Federation of Arts, 1959.


IRENE MOSS (20th Century)    Painter

See volume 1 of this book.

Who's Who in American Art. New York:  R.R.  Bowker Co., 1978.


JEANIE GALLUP MOTTET (1864-1934)    Painter

American Impressionists and 20th Century Paintings.... New York:
    Sotheby's, 2 December 1982:  nos. 34 and 46.

Fielding, Mantle. Dictionary of American Painters, Sculptors and
    Engravers. Enlarged ed. Greens Farms, Connecticut:  Modern
    Books and Crafts, 1974.

Obituary. Who's Who in American Art, vol. 1. Washington, D.C.:
    American Federation of Arts, 1935.

SUE BUCKINGHAM MOULTON (b. 1873)    Painter

American Art Annual, vol. 28.  Washington, D.C.:  American
     Federation of Arts, 1932.

Weber, Carl J.  Fore-Edge Painting.  Irvington-on-Hudson, New York:
     Harvey House, 1966:  147-48.

Who's Who in American Art, vol. 6.  Washington, D.C.:  American
     Federation of Arts, 1956.


ETHEL MUNDY (1876-1964)    Portraitist in Wax

American Art Annual, vol. 28.  Washington, D.C.:  American
     Federation of Arts, 1932.

Archives of American Art.  Collection of Exhibition Catalogs.
     Boston:  G.K. Hall and Co., 1979.

Fielding, Mantle.  Dictionary of American Painters, Sculptors and
     Engravers.  Enlarged ed.  Greens Farms, Connecticut:  Modern
     Books and Crafts, 1974.

Pyke, E. J.  A Biographical Dictionary of Wax Modelers.  Oxford:
     Clarendon Press, 1973.

Who's Who in American Art, vol. 8.  Washington, D.C.:  American
     Federation of Arts, 1962.


DORA LOUISE MURDOCH (1857-1933)    Watercolorist

American Art Annual, vol. 28.  Washington, D.C.:  American
     Federation of Arts, 1932.

Fielding, Mantle.  Dictionary of American Painters, Sculptors and
     Engravers.  Enlarged ed.  Greens Farms, Connecticut:  Modern
     Books and Crafts, 1974.

Obituary.  American Art Annual, vol. 30.  Washington, D.C.:
     American Federation of Arts, 1934.

Woman's Who's Who of America.  New York:  American Commonwealth
     Co., 1914.


ALICE MURPHY (1871-1909)    Painter

Loan Exhibition of Paintings by Alice Murphy (1871-1909).  New
     York:  Wally Findley Galleries, 1971.

National Cyclopaedia of American Biography. New York and Clifton,
    New Jersey: James T. White and Co., 1892-97.


ALICE HAROLD MURPHY (1896-1966)    Painter and Printmaker

American Prints in the Library of Congress:  A Catalog of the
    Collection. Baltimore:  Johns Hopkins Press, 1970.

Clark, Eliot.  History of the National Academy of Design.  New
    York:  Columbia University Press, 1954.

Obituary.  The New York Times, 12 April 1966:  35.

Reese, Albert.  American Prints of the Twentieth Century.  New
    York:  American Artists Group, 1949:  148, 250.


CATHERINE MURPHY (1946-    )    Painter

See volume 1 of this book.

Murphy, Catherine.  New Paintings and Drawings 1980-1985.  Text by
    Linda Nochlin.  New York:  Xavier Fourcade, 1985.

Silverthorne, Jeanne.  "Catherine Murphy."  Artforum 24, no. 6
    (February 1986):  103.

Stavitsky, Gail.  "Catherine Murphy."  Arts Magazine 60, no. 6
    (February 1986):  136-37.

Who's Who in American Art, 17th ed.  New York:  R.R. Bowker, 1986.


HARIETT ANDERSON STUBBS MURPHY (1851-1935)    Portraitist

Haifley, Julie Link.  "Washington, D.C."  Archives of American Art
    Journal 19, no. 1 (1979):  30.

National Portrait Gallery, Permanent Collection Illustrated
    Checklist.  Washington, D.C.:  Smithsonian Institution Press,
    1982.

Obituary.  Art Digest 10, no. 1 (1 October 1935):  11.


ELIZABETH MURRAY (1940-    )    Painter

Brenson, Michael.  "A Decade of Work from Elizabeth Murray."  The
    New York Times, 24 April 1988, Art & Leisure section:  24.

Cohen, Ronny H. "Elizabeth Murray's Colored Space." Artforum 21, no. 4 (December 1982): 51-55.

Field, Richard S., and Fine, Ruth E. A Graphic Muse. Hudson Hills Press, 1987.

Fortieth Biennial Exhibition of Contemporary American Painting. Washington, D.C.: Corcoran Gallery of Art, 1987.

Frank, Peter. "Elizabeth Murray." Art News 78, no. 1 (January 1979): 146, 148.

Galligan, Gregory. "Elizabeth Murray's New Paintings." Arts Magazine 62, no. 1 (September 1987): 62-66, cover.

Gardner, Paul. "Elizabeth Murray Shapes Up." Art News 83, no. 7 (September 1984): 46-55.

Gill, Susan. "Elizabeth Murray (at Paula Cooper)." Art News 86, no. 8 (October 1987): 168.

Graze, Sue, and Halbreich, Kathy. Elizabeth Murray: Paintings and Drawings. New York: Harry N. Abrams, Inc., 1987.

Hess, Elizabeth. "The Color of Murray." Ms. 16, no. 12 (June 1988): 34-37.

Images on Stone: Two Centuries of Artists' Lithographs. Houston: Sarah Campbell Blaffer Gallery, University of Houston, 1987.

Johnson, Ken. "Elizabeth Murray's New Paintings." Arts Magazine 62, no. 1 (September 1987): 67-69.

King, Elaine. Elizabeth Murray. Drawings, 1980-86. Pittsburgh: Carnegie Mellon University Art Gallery, 1986.

Kutner, Janet. "Dallas: Elizabeth Murray." Art News 86, no. 5 (May 1987): 45-46.

Lubell, Ellen. "Elizabeth Murray." Arts Magazine 51, no. 5 (January 1977): 36.

Murry, Jesse. "Quintet: The Romance of Order and Tension in Five Paintings by Elizabeth Murray." Arts Magazine 55, no. 9 (May 1981): 102-05.

Simon, Joan. "Mixing Metaphors: Elizabeth Murray." Art in America 72, no. 4 (April 1984): 140-46.

Smith, Roberta. "Elizabeth Murray at Paula Cooper." Art in America 67, no. 2 (March-April 1979): 150-51.

304

Tillim, Sidney. "Elizabeth Murray at Paula Cooper." Art in
America 75, no. 10 (October 1987): 177.

Wei, Lilly. "Talking Abstract." Art in America 75, no. 7 (July
1987): 80-93.


JUDITH MURRAY (1941-    )   Painter

Frank, Elizabeth. "Judith Murray at Pam Adler." Art in America
69, no. 4 (April 1981): 142-43.

Friedman, Jon R. "Judith Murray." Arts Magazine 53, no. 10 (June
1979): 31.

Stavitsky, Gail. "Judith Murray/Ursula Von Rydingsvard." Arts
Magazine 60, no. 5 (January 1986): 144.

Van Wagner, Judith Collischan. Judith Murray: Painting. Ursula
von Rydingsvard: Sculpture. Greenvale, New York: Hillwood
Art Gallery, Long Island University, 1985.

Who's Who in American Art, 17th ed. New York: R.R. Bowker Co.,
1986.


GWYNN MURRILL (1942-    )   Sculptor

Ballatore, Sandy. "Eight Los Angeles Artists." Artweek 7, no. 18
(1 May 1976): 1, 24.

Clothier, Peter. "Los Angeles. Gwynn Murrill at Asher Faure."
Art in America 71, no. 10 (November 1983): 235.

Contemporary Californians VIII: Gwynn Murrill and Martha Alf.
Laguna Beach: Laguna Beach Museum of Art, 1982.

Fellows Exhibition. Rome: American Academy, 1980.

McCloud, Mac. "The Rich Possibilities of Wood." Artweek 15, no.
10 (10 March 1984): 3-4.

Muchnic, Suzanne. "The Art Galleries: La Cinega Area." Los
Angeles Times, 26 April 1985, part VI: 4.

20 Years of Young Talent Winners. Los Angeles: Los Angeles County
Museum of Art, 1983.

Watson-Jones, Virginia. Contemporary American Women Sculptors.
Phoenix: Oryx Press, 1986.

Wortz, Melinda. "Los Angeles: Gwynn Murrill (at Asher Faure)."
    Art News 82, no. 9 (November 1983): 131-32.


            ETHEL KLINCK MYERS (1881-1960)    Sculptor

See volume 1 of this book.

Campbell, Lawrence. "Ethel Myers." Art News 65, no. 1 (March
    1966): 18.

Katz, Leslie. The Sculpture of Ethel Myers. New York: Robert
    Schoelkopf Gallery, 1963.

_____. The Sculpture and Drawings of Ethel Myers. New York:
    Robert Schoelkopf Gallery, 1966.

Who's Who in American Art, vol. 1. Washington, D.C.: American
    Federation of Arts, 1935: 304.

Wolf, Amy J. New York Society of Women Artists 1925. New York:
    ACA Galleries, 1987.


            ANNE TAYLOR NASH (1884-1968)    Painter

American Art Annual, vol. 30. Washington, D.C.: American
    Federation of Arts, 1934.

Chambers, Bruce W. Art and Artists of the South, the Robert P.
    Coggins Collection. Columbia, South Carolina: University of
    South Carolina Press, 1984: 133.

Who's Who in American Art, vol. 8. Washington, D.C.: American
    Federation of Arts, 1962.


            GERTRUDE NASON (1890-1969)    Painter

American Art Annual, vol. 28. Washington, D.C.: American
    Federation of Arts, 1932.

Fielding, Mantle. Dictionary of American Painters, Sculptors and
    Engravers. Enlarged ed. Greens Farms, Connecticut: Modern
    Books and Crafts, 1974.

Obituary. Who's Who in American Art, vol. 13. Washington, D.C.:
    American Federation of Arts, 1978.

Vose Winter 1987-88. Boston: Vose Galleries, 1987.

Who's Who in American Art, vol. 9. Washington, D.C.: American
Federation of Arts, 1966.


PHEBE (PHOEBE) DAVIS NATT (active 1870-1901)   Painter and Etcher

American Art Annual, vol. 1. New York: Macmillan, 1899.

Natt, Phebe D. "Paris Art-Schools." Lippincott's Monthly
Magazine 27 (March 1881): 269-76.

Peet, Phyllis. American Women of the Etching Revival. Atlanta:
High Museum of Art, 1988.

Weimann, Jeanne Madeline. The Fair Women. Chicago: Academy
Chicago, 1981: 308.

The Work of Women Etchers of America. New York: Union League
Club, 1888.


MARY SPENCER NAY (1913-    )   Painter

Contemporary Art of the United States. Washington, D.C.: Corcoran
Gallery of Art, 1940: no. 18.

Mary Spencer Nay. Louisville, Kentucky: J.B. Speed Art Museum,
1976.

Who's Who in American Art, 17th ed. New York: R.R. Bowker Co.,
1986.


MINNIE HARMS NEEBE (b. 1873)   Painter

American Art Annual, vol. 18. Washington, D.C.: American
Federation of Arts, 1932.

Jacobson, J.Z. Art of Today, Chicago--1933. Chicago: L.M. Stein,
1932.


ALICE NEEL (1900-1985)   Painter

See volume 1 of this book.

Alice Neel. New York: Graham Gallery, 1978.

Alice Neel Drawings and Watercolors. New York: Robert Miller
Gallery, 1986.

Johnson, Ellen. "Alice Neel's Fifty Years of Portrait Painting."
    Studio International 193, no. 987 (March 1977): 174-79.

Luvass, William. "Making It: An Interview with Alice Neel."
    Art Times, December 1986: 10-11.

National Museum of Women in the Arts. New York: Harry N. Abrams,
    Inc., 1987: 88-89.

Neel. Drawings & Watercolors. Address by Jack Baur. New York:
    Whitney Museum of American Art, 1985.

Nochlin, Linda. "Some Women Realists: Painters of the Figure."
    Arts Magazine 48, no. 8 (May 1974): 29-33.

Russo, Alexander. Profiles on Women Artists. Frederick, Maryland:
    University Publications of America, 1985.


                BARBARA NEIJNA (1937-    )   Sculptor

Annual Hortt Memorial Exhibition. Fort Lauderdale: Fort
    Lauderdale Museum of the Arts, 1973.

Edwards, Ellen. "South Florida: No Longer a Last Resort for Art."
    Art News 78, no. 10 (December 1979): 78-81.

Fundaburk, Emma Lila, and Davenport, Thomas G. Art in Public
    Places in the United States. Bowling Green: Bowling Green
    University Popular Press, 1975.

Kohen, Helen L. "Art Looks for a Place in the Sun." Art News 82,
    no. 2 (February 1983): 62-65.

Kuspit, Donald B. "Fort Lauderdale: Barbara Neijna at the Museum
    of Art." Art in America 69, no. 3 (March 1981): 133.

Thalacker, Donald W. The Place of Art in the World of
    Architecture. New York: Chelsea House, 1980.

Watson-Jones, Virginia. Contemporary American Women Sculptors.
    Phoenix: Oryx Press, 1986.


                LOUISE NEVELSON (1899-1988)   Sculptor

See volume 1 of this book.

Friedman, Martin. Nevelson: Wood Sculptures. New York: E.P.
    Dutton and Co., Inc., 1973.

308

Glueck, Grace. "The 20th Century Artists Most Admired by Other Artists." Art News 76, no. 9 (November 1977): 94.

Gordon, John. Louise Nevelson. New York: Whitney Museum of American Art, 1967.

Katz, William. "Dawns and Dusk." Arts Magazine 51, no. 5 (January 1977): 23.

Louise Nevelson. Houston: Museum of Fine Arts, 1969.

"Louise Nevelson, Sculptor, is Dead at 88." The New York Times, 19 April 1988: Y15.

McGill, Douglas C. "Sculptor's Life Related by Exhibition's Pieces." The New York Times, 11 January 1987: Y26.

Nevelson at Purchase: The Metal Sculptures. Purchase, New York: Neuberger Museum, State University of New York, 1977.

Watson-Jones, Virginia. Contemporary American Women Sculptors. Phoenix: Oryx Press, 1986.

Wilson, Laurie. Louise Nevelson: Iconography and Sources. New York: Garland Publishing, 1981.

BLANCHE NEVIN (1841-1925)    Sculptor

See volume 1 of this book.

Catalogue of the Exhibits of the State of Pennsylvania and of Pennsylvania at the World's Columbian Exposition. State Printer of Pennsylvania, 1893.

The Masterpieces of the Centennial Internationl Exhibition, vol. 1. Philadelphia, c. 1876. Reprint ed., New York: Garland Publishing, 1977.

HARRIOT B. NEWHALL (1874-1934)    Painter

American Art Annual, vol. 28. Washington, D.C.: American Federation of Arts, 1932.

Fielding, Mantle. Dictionary of American Painters, Sculptors and Engravers. Enlarged ed. Greens Farms, Connecticut: Modern Books and Crafts, 1974.

Pierce, Patricia. Edmund C. Tarbell and the Boston School of Painting, 1889-1980. Hingham, Massachusetts: Pierce Galleries, 1980.

WILLIE BETTY NEWMAN (1863-1935)    Painter

American Art Annual, vol. 28.  Washington, D.C.:  American
     Federation of Arts, 1932.

Fielding, Mantle.  Dictionary of American Painters, Sculptors and
     Engravers.  Enlarged ed.  Greens Farms, Connecticut:  Modern
     Books and Crafts, 1974.

Woman's Who's Who of America.  New York:  American Commonwealth
     Co., 1914.


MARILYN NEWMARK (1928-    )    Sculptor

Cleary, Fritz.  "Reality Reflected."  National Sculpture Review 26,
     no. 1 (Spring 1977):  8-17.

Dunwiddie, Charlotte.  "American Animaliers."  National Sculpture
     Review 26, no. 4 (Winter 1977-78):  8-19.

"Images of America, USIA Sends Exhibition Abroad."  National
     Sculpture Review 25, no. 1 (Spring 1976):  18-19.

Malmstrom, Margit.  "The Bronze Horses of Marilyn Newmark."
     American Artist 35, no. 4, issue 346 (April 1971):  28-33,
     80-81.

"Of Equines and Equestrians."  National Sculpture Review 33, no. 4
     (Winter 1984-85):  14-15.

Watson-Jones, Virginia.  Contemporary American Women Sculptors.
     Phoenix:  Oryx Press, 1986.


CLARA CHIPMAN NEWTON (1848-1936)    Ceramicist

Callen, Anthea.  Women Artists of the Art and Crafts Movement,
     1870-1914.  New York:  Pantheon, 1979.

Clark, Garth.  A Century of Ceramics in the United States
     1878-1978.  New York:  E.P. Dutton, 1979.

Cummins, Virginia R.  Rookwood Pottery Potpourri.  Silver Springs,
     Maryland:  Cliff R. Leonard and Duke Coleman, 1980.

The Ladies, God Bless 'Em:  The Women's Art Movement in Cincinnati
     In the 19th Century.  Cincinnati:  Cincinnati Art Museum,
     1976.

Peck, Herbert.  The Book of Rookwood Pottery.  New York:  Crown
     Publishers, 1968.

ELISABET NEY (1833-1907)   Sculptor

See volume of this book.

Cutrer, Emily Fourmy. The Art of the Woman: The Life and Work of
   Elizabet Ney. Lincoln: University of Nebraska Press, 1988.

Freudenheim, Susan. "Monumental Studio." Texas Homes, February
   1987: 68-71.

Moore, Sylvia, ed. No Bluebonnets, No Yellow Roses: Essays on
   Texas Women in the Arts. New York: Midmarch Arts Press,
   1988.


RHODA HOLMES NICHOLLS (1854-1930)   Painter

See volume 1 of this book.

American Art Annual, vol. 1. New York: Macmillan, 1899.

Elliot, Maud H. Art and Handicraft in the Woman's Building of the
   World's Columbian Exposition, Chicago, 1893. Chicago: Rand
   McNally and Co., 1894.

Fielding, Mantle. Dictionary of American Painters, Sculptors and
   Engravers. Enlarged ed. Greens Farms, Connecticut: Modern
   Books and Crafts, 1974.

Pisano, Ronald. Students of William Merritt Chase. Huntington,
   Long Island, New York: Heckscher Museum, 1973.

Woman's Who's Who of America. New York: American Commonwealth
   Co., 1914.


MARIA LONGWORTH NICHOLS (1849-1932)   Ceramicist

See Maria Longworth Nichols Storer.


MARY PLUMB NICHOLS (1836-after 1905)   Sculptor

American Art Annual, vol. 1. New York: Macmillan, 1899.

Groce, George C., and Wallace, David H. The New-York Historical
   Society's Dictionary of Artists in America 1564-1860. New
   Haven: Yale University Press, 1957.

Weimann, Jeanne Madeline. The Fair Women. Chicago: Academy
   Chicago, 1981: 295.

311

ELIZABETH NICHOLSON (1883-1926)   Painter

Burnet, Mary Q.  Art and Artists of Indiana.  New York:  Century
     Co., 1921.

Groce, George C., and Wallace, David H.  The New-York Historical
     Society's Dictionary of Artists in America 1564-1860.  New
     Haven:  Yale University Press, 1957.

Peat, Wilbur D.  Pioneer Painters of Indiana.  Chicago:  Lakeside
     Press, 1954.


LILLIE MAY NICHOLSON (1884-1964)   Painter

Berney, Charlotte.  "Lillie May Nicholson."  California Antiques &
     Fine Art, March 1986:  14-17.

Impressionism, The California View, Paintings 1890-1930.  Oakland:
     The Oakland Museum, 1981.

Nelson-Rees, Walter A.  Lillie May Nicholson, 1884-1964:  An Artist
     Rediscovered.  Oakland, California:  WIM, 1981.


GLADYS NILSSON (1940-    )   Painter

See volume 1 of this book.

Cohrs, Timothy.  "Gladys Nilsson."  Arts Magazine 61, no. 7 (March
     1987):  111.

Victor, Polly.  "Women Artists--Restoring the Balance."  Artweek
     18, no. 14 (11 April 1987):  1.

Who's Who in American Art, 17th ed.  New York:  R.R. Bowker Co.,
     1986.


ELEANOR NORCROSS (1854-1923)   Painter

See volume 1 of this book.

Archives of American Art.  Collection of Exhibition Catalogs.
     Boston:  G.K. Hall & Co., 1979.

Obituary.  American Art Annual, vol. 20.  Washington, D.C.:
     American Federation of Arts, 1923.

312

MARIA NORDMAN (1943-    )   Sculptor

Ayes, Anne.  "Tracking an Urban Spring."  Artweek 15 (9 June 1984):
    6.

Bijvoet, Marga.  "Maria Nordman:  Reflections of the Waves."
    Artweek 16, no. 10 (9 March 1985):  1.

Edgerton, Anne Carnegie, and Tuchman, Maurice.  "Modern and
    Contemporary Art Council, Young Talent Awards:  1963-1983."
    Bulletin, Los Angeles County Museum of Art 27 (1983):  37.

Nordman, Maria.  De Sculptura Works in the City.  Munich:
    Schirmer/Mosel, 1986.

Onorato, Ronald J.  Maria Nordman, Trabajos en la Ciudad de Ondas.
    La Jolla:  La Jolla Museum of Contemporary Art, 1985.

Plagens, Peter.  "Maria Nordman."  Artforum 12, no. 6 (February
    1974):  40-41.

Pohlen, Annelie.  "Munster.  Maria Nordman, Westfalischer
    Kunstverein."  Artforum 22, no. 7 (March 1984):  101.

Wortz, Melinda.  "Los Angeles.  Maria Nordman, 315 N. Alameda/166
    N. Central."  Artforum 22, no. 2 (October 1983):  82.

BARBARA NORFLEET (1926-    )   Photographer

Browne, Turner, and Partnow, Elaine.  Encyclopedia of Photographic
    Artists and Innovators.  New York:  Macmillan Co., 1983.

Norfleet, Barbara P.  All the Right People.  Boston:  New York
    Graphic Society, 1986.

Chahroudi, Martha.  "Twelve Photographers Look at Us."  Bulletin,
    Philadelphia Museum of Art 83, nos. 354-355 (Spring 1987):  6,
    20, 21.

ANN WEAVER NORTON (1910's-1982)   Sculptor

See volume 1 of this book.

Ann Norton:  "Gateways".  New York:  Max Hutchinson Gallery, 1980.

Obituary.  The New York Times, 4 February 1982.

ELIZABETH NORTON (b. 1887)    Sculptor and Printmaker

American Art Annual, vol. 28.  Washington, D.C.:  American
     Federation of Arts, 1932.

Archives of American Art.  Collection of Exhibition Catalogs.
     Boston:  G.K. Hall & Co., 1979.

Flint, Jane Altic.  Provincetown Printers:  A Woodcut Tradition.
     Washington, D.C.:  National Museum of American Art, 1983.

Library of Congress.  American Prints in the Library of Congress:
     A Catalog of the Collection.  Baltimore and London:  Johns
     Hopkins Press, 1970.

Who's Who in American Art, vol. 8.  Washington, D.C.:  American
     Federation of Arts, 1962.


PATSY NORVELL (1942-    )    Sculptor

See volume 1 of this book.

Brach, Paul.  "Patsy Norvell and Robert Zakanitch at Janis."  Art
     in America 71, no. 2 (February 1983):  130.

Jensen, Robert, and Conway, Patricia.  Ornamentalism:  The New
     Decorativeness in Architecture and Design.  New York:
     Clarkson N. Potter, 1982.

Painting and Sculpture Today, 1974.  Indianapolis:  Indianapolis
     Museum of Arts, 1974.

Van Wagner, Judy K. Collischan.  Reflections, New Conceptions of
     Nature.  Greenvale, New York:  Hillwood Art Gallery, Long
     Island University, 1984.

Watson-Jones, Virginia.  Contemporary American Women Sculptors.
     Phoenix:  Oryx Press, 1986.

Wood.  Roslyn, New York:  Nassau County Museum of Fine Arts, 1977.


ELIZABETH NOURSE (1859-1938)    Painter

See volume 1 of this book.

American Art Annual, vol. 28.  Washington, D.C.:  American
     Federation of Arts, 1932.

McChesney, Clara.  "An American Artist in Paris:  Elizabeth
     Nourse."  Monthly Illustrator, August 1986:  3-11.

314

Tufts, Eleanor. American Women Artists, 1830-1930. Washington,
    D.C.: National Museum of Women in the Arts, 1987.

Woman's Who's Who of America. New York: American Commonwealth
    Co., 1914.


BERTHA NOYES (1876-1966)   Painter

American Art Annual, vol. 28. Washington, D.C.: American
    Federation of Arts, 1932.

Catalogue of Paintings, Drawings,.... London: Christie, Manson &
    Woods, 2 July 1968.

Fielding, Mantle. Dictionary of American Painters, Sculptors and
    Engravers. Enlarged ed. Greens Farms, Connecticut: Modern
    Books and Crafts, 1974.

Who's Who in American Art, vol. 8. Washington, D.C.: American
    Federation of Arts, 1962.


MRS. A. T. OAKES (active 1852-1886)   Painter

Cowdrey, Mary Bartlett. National Academy of Design Exhibition
    Record, 1826-1860. New York: J.J. Little and Ives Co.,
    1943.

Groce, George C., and Wallace, David H. The New-York Historical
    Society's Dictionary of Artists in American 1564-1860. New
    Haven: Yale University Press, 1957.

Van Nostrand, Jeanne. The First Hundred Years of Painting in
    California 1775-1875. San Francisco: John Howell Books,
    1980.


ELLEN OAKFORD (active 1880's-1890's)   Etcher

Peet, Phyllis. American Women of the Etching Revival. Atlanta:
    High Museum of Art, 1988.

Weimann, Jeanne Madeline. The Fair Women. Chicago: Academy
    Chicago, 1981: 308.

The Work of Women Etchers of America. New York: Union League
    Club, 1888.

VIOLET OAKLEY (1874-1961)    Muralist and Illustrator

See volume 1 of this book.

Goodman, Helen. "The Plastic Club." Arts Magazine 59, no. 7
    (March 1985): 100-03.

_____. "Women Illustrators of the Golden Age of American
    Illustration." Woman's Art Journal 8, no. 1 (Spring-Summer
    1987): 13-22.

"Honored at the Pennsylvania Academy." Art Digest 14, no. 10 (15
    February 1940): 13.

M., E.D. "'The Opening of the Book of the Law' Mural Paintings by
    Violet Oakley A.N.A., for the Supreme Court Room in the
    Pennsylvania State Capitol at Harrisburg." American Magazine
    of Art 18, no. 1 (January 1927): 10-17.

Mills, Sally. Violet Oakley. The Decoration of the Alumnae House
    Living Room. Poughkeepsie, New York: Vassar College Art
    Gallery, 1984.


HENRIETTE AMIARD OBERTEUFFER (1878-1962)    Painter

See volume 1 of this book.

American Art Annual, vol. 28. Washington, D.C.: American
    Federation of Arts, 1932.


GERTRUDE O'BRADY (1901-    )    Painter

American Portraits: O'Brady. Paris: Georges Maratier, n.d.
    [1945].

"Art. Paris in the Spring." Time 47 (13 May 1946): 54-55.

C[ole], M[ary]. "Gertrude O'Brady." Art Digest 25, no. 17 (1
    June 1951): 19.

"Exhibition of Oils, Gouaches, and Pencil Drawings at Creative
    Gallery." Art News 50, no. 6 (June 1951): 51.

Gertrude O'Brady. New York: M. Knoedler and Co., Inc., 1949.

K., B. "Gertrude O'Brady [Knoedler]." Art News 48, no. 4 (Summer
    1949): 53.

L[owengrund], M[argaret]. "Portraits of Places." Art Digest 23,
    no. 17 (1 June 1949): 20.

316

NANCY O'CONNOR (1957-    )    Mixed Media Artist

Carlozzi, Annette.  50 Texas Artists.  San Francisco:  Chronicle
    Books, 1986:  76-77.

Selections from The Frito-Lay Collection.  Plano, Texas:
    Frito-Lay, Inc., 1987:  41.

Tennant, Donna.  "Nancy O'Connor (Contemporary Arts Museum,
    Houston)."  New Art Examiner 13, no. 6 (February 1986):  64.


SHEILA O'HARA (1953-    )    Weaver

Park, Betty.  "Sheila O'Hara, Wry Humor and Virtuoso Weaving."
    Fiberarts 10 (January-February 1983):  64-67.

"Portfolio."  American Craft 41, no. 5 (October-November 1981):
    41.

Znamierowski, Nell.  Fiber:  The Artist's View.  Greenvale, New
    York:  Hillwood Art Gallery, Long Island University, 1983.


GEORGIA O'KEEFFE (1887-1986)    Painter

See volume 1 of this book.

Asbury, Edith Evans.  "Georgia O'Keeffe Dead at 98; Shaper of
    Modern Art in U.S."  The New York Times, 7 March 1986:  1, 45.

Baker, Kenneth.  "What Went Wrong."  Connoisseur 217, no. 910
    (November 1987):  170-75.

_____.  "The World in a Drop of Water."  Artforum 24 (December
    1985):  56-59.

Brenson, Michael.  "How O'Keeffe Painted Hymns to Body and Spirit."
    The New York Times, 8 November 1987, Arts and Leisure Section:
    37, 43.

Breuning, Margaret.  "O'Keeffe's Latest."  Art Digest 19, no. 10
    (15 February 1945):  19.

Callaway, Nicholas, ed.  Georgia O'Keeffe:  One Hundred Flowers.
    New York:  Alfred A. Knopf, Callaway Editions, 1987.

Castro, Jan Garden.  The Art and Life of Georgia O'Keeffe.  New
    York:  Crown Publishers, 1985.

Cowart, Jack, and Hamilton, Juan. Georgia O'Keeffe. Art and
    Letters. Letters selected and annotated by Sarah Greenough.
    Washington, D.C.: National Gallery of Art and Boston: New
    York Graphic Society, Little, Brown and Co., 1987.

Decker, Andrew. "The Battle over Georgia O'Keeffe's
    Multimillion-Dollar Legacy." Art News 86, no. 4 (April 1987):
    120-27.

D'Emilio, Sandra, and Campbell, Suzan. Images of Spirit and
    Vision, Ranchos de Taos Church. Santa Fe: Museum of New
    Mexico, 1987.

Drohojowska, Hunter. "Georgia O'Keeffe 1887-1986." Art News 85,
    no. 6 (Summer 1986): 119-21.

Glueck, Grace. "The 20th Century Artists Most Admired by Other
    Artists." Art News 76, no. 9 (November 1977): 95.

A Guide to the Collection. Houston: Museum of Fine Arts, 1981.

Hoffman, Katherine. An Enduring Spirit. The Art of Georgia
    O'Keeffe. Metuchen, New Jersey: Scarecrow Press, 1984.

Hughes, Robert. "Loner in the Desert." Time, 12 October 1970:
    64, 67.

_____. "A Vision of Steely Finesse." Time, 17 March 1986: 83.

Langer, Cassandra L. "Beyond the Myth: The Unacknowledged Georgia
    O'Keeffe." Kansas Quarterly 19, no. 4 (1987): 11-23.

Lerman, Ora. "From Close-Up to Infinity: Reentering Georgia
    O'Keeffe's World." Arts Magazine 60, no. 9 (May 1986):
    80-83.

Messinger, Lisa Mintz. "Georgia O'Keeffe." Metropolitan Museum of
    Art Bulletin 42, no. 2 (Fall 1984): 3-63.

Mullan, Anthony P. "Georgia O'Keeffe in Washington: The Art and
    the Imagination." Arts Magazine 62, no. 7 (March 1988):
    32-33.

National Museum of Women in the Arts. New York: Harry N. Abrams,
    Inc., 1987: 80-81.

"O'Keeffe's Pineapple." Art Digest 14, no. 10 (15 February 1940):
    23.

The Phillips Collection, A Summary Catalogue. Washington, D.C.:
    The Phillips Collection, 1985.

318

Pollitzer, Anita. A Woman on Paper: Georgia O'Keeffe. New York: Touchstone/Simon and Schuster, 1988.

Reif, Rita. "Record Paid for an O'Keeffe." The New York Times, 4 December 1987: Y29.

Schimmel, Julie. "Georgia O'Keeffe, Museum Unveils Her Private Collection." New Mexico 65, no. 3 (March 1987): 28-35.

Scott, Nancy. "The O'Keeffe-Pollitzer Correspondence, 1915-1917." Source 3, no. 1 (Fall 1983): 34-41.

Second Biennial Exhibition of Contemporary American Painting. New York: Whitney Museum of American Art, 1934.

Stevens, Mark. "The Gift of Spiritual Intensity." Newsweek 17 March 1986: 77.

Tufts, Eleanor. American Women Artists, 1830-1930. Washington, D.C.: National Museum of Women in the Arts, 1987.

Turner, David, and Haskell, Barbara. Georgia O'Keeffe: Works on Paper. Santa Fe: Museum of New Mexico Press, 1985.

Yau, John. "O'Keeffe's Misfocus." Art News 87, no. 2 (February 1988): 114-19.

MINÉ OKUBO (1912-    )    Painter

The Art of California. Oakland: The Oakland Museum, 1984.

F[itzsimmons], J[ames]. "Miné-Okubo." Art Digest 26, no. 11 (1 March 1952): 25.

Holliday, Betty. "Miné Okubo [Levitt]." Art News 51, no. 1 (March 1952): 56.

"Miné Okubo." Art News 44, no. 6 (1 May 1945): 27.

Miné Okubo: An American Experience. Oakland, California: The Oakland Museum, 1972.

Okubo, Miné. Citizen 13660: Drawings and Text by Miné Okubo. New York: Columbia University Press, 1946.

Theil, Yvonne Greer. Artists and People. New York: Philosophical Library, 1959.

ELIZABETH OLDS (1896-    )    Painter and Printmaker

See volume 1 of this book.

American Prints in the Library of Congress:  A Catalogue of the
    Collection.  Baltimore and London:  Johns Hopkins Press, 1970.

C., R.  "Elizabeth Olds."  Art News 51, no. 2 (April 1952):  58.

Elizabeth Olds:  Exhibition of Oils and Watercolors.  New York:
    ACA Gallery, 1950.

Prescott, Kenneth W., and Arthur, Susan E.  Elizabeth Olds:
    Retrospective Exhibition.  Austin:  The R.G.K. Foundation,
    1986.


ELEANOR ONDERDONK (1884-1964)    Miniaturist

Moore, Sylvia, ed.  No Bluebonnets, No Yellow Roses:  Essays on
    Texas Women in the Arts.  New York:  Midmarch Arts Press,
    1988.

O'Brien, Esse Forrester.  Art and Artists of Texas.  Dallas:  Tardy
    Publishing Co., 1935.

Steinfeldt, Cecilia.  The Onderdonks:  A Family of Texas Painters.
    San Antonio, Texas:  Trinity University Press, 1976.

20th Century Women in Texas Art.  Austin, Texas:  Laguna Gloria Art
    Museum, 1974.


ROSE CECIL O'NEILL [WILSON] (1875-1944)    Illustrator

See volume 1 of this book.

American Art Annual, vol. 28.  Washington, D.C.:  American
    Federation of Arts, 1932 (under Wilson).

Browne, Edythe H.  "Rose O'Neill's Sculptured Drawings."
    International Studio 75, no. 299 (March 1922):  63-69.

Gibbons, Robert H., ed.  Sweet Monsters:  The Serious Art of Rose
    O'Neill.  (No city or publisher given), 1980.

Goodman, Helen.  "Women Illustrators of the Golden Age of American
    Illustration."  Woman's Art Journal 8, no. 1 (Spring-Summer
    1987):  13-22.

320

Obituary. Who's Who in American Art, vol. 4. Washington, D.C.:
American Federation of Arts, 1947.

Society of Illustrators. America's Great Women Illustrators
1850-1950. Chadds Ford, Pennsylvania: Brandywine River
Museum, 1985.

Turn-of-the-Century America: Paintings, Graphics, Photographs.
New York: Whitney Museum of American Art, 1977.


MARJORIE ORGAN (1886-1930)    Cartoonist and Caricaturist

American Art Annual, vol. 30. Washington, D.C.: American
Federation of Arts, 1934.

City Life Illustrated 1890-1940. Sloan, Glackens, Luks, Shinn--
Their Friends and Followers. Wilmington, Delaware: Delaware
Art Museum, 1980.

Fielding, Mantle. Dictionary of American Painters, Sculptors and
Engravers. Enlarged ed. Greens Farms, Connecticut: Modern
Books and Crafts, 1974.

Homer, William Innes. Robert Henri and His Circle. Ithaca, New
York: Cornell University Press, 1969.

Wolf, Amy J. New York Society of Women Artists 1925. New York:
ACA Galleries, 1987.


RUTH ORKIN (1921-1985)    Photographer

Auer, Michèle and Auer, Michel. Encyclopédie internationale des
Photographes de 1839 à nos jours. Hermance, Switzerland:
Editions Camera Obscura, 1985.

Browne, Turner, and Partnow, Elaine. Macmillan Biographical
Encyclopedia of Photographic Artists & Innovators. New York:
Macmillan Co., 1983.

Orkin, Ruth. More Pictures from My Window. New York: Rizzoli,
1983.

_____. A World Through My Window: Photographs by Ruth Orkin. New
York: Harper and Row, 1978.

A Photo Journal: Ruth Orkin. New York: Viking Studio Books,
1981.

"Ruth Orkin's New York." Horizon, March 1959.

Steichen, Edward, ed. The Family of Man. New York: The Museum of Modern Art, 1955.

Stevens, Nancy. "Ruth Orkin: Gravure Portfolio." Popular Photography, June 1977.

Walsh, George; Naylor, Colin; and Held, Michael. Contemporary Photographers. New York: Saint Martin's Press, 1982.

Witkin, Lee D., and London, Barbara. The Photograph Collector's Guide. Boston: New York Graphic Society, 1979.

Women See Woman. New York: Thomas Y. Crowell Co., 1976.

ELIZABETH OSBORNE (1936-    )    Painter

See volume 1 of this book.

Butera, Virginia Fabbri. "Elizabeth Osborne." Arts Magazine 56, no. 9 (May 1982): 31-32.

Martin, Alvin. American Realism, 20th Century Drawings and Watercolors From the Glenn C. Janss Collection. San Francisco: San Francisco Museum of Modern Art, 1985.

Scott, William P. "Elizabeth Osborne." Arts Magazine 62, no. 2 (October 1987): 99.

HARRIET FRANCES OSBORNE (1846-1913)    Painter and Etcher

Norton, Bettina A. Prints at the Essex Institute. Salem, Massachusetts: Essex Institute, 1978: 54-55.

Peet, Phyllis. American Women of the Etching Revival. Atlanta: High Museum of Art, 1988.

The Work of Women Etchers of America. New York: Union League Club, 1888.

SABINA OTT (20th Century)    Painter

Cotter, Holland. "Eight Artists Interviewed." Art in America 75, no. 5 (May 1987): 174-75.

French, David Stevens. "An Eclectic Selection." Artweek 16, no. 19 (11 May 1985): 5.

_____. "Reading the Images." Artweek 16, no. 22 (1 June 1985): 6.

322

Gardner, Colin. "Attack: Los Angeles." Arts Magazine 59, no. 7 (March 1985): 13.

Handy, Ellen. "Ron Nagle/Sabina Ott." Arts Magazine 60, no. 3 (November 1985): 139.


WINIFRED R. OWENS (1949-   )   Ceramic Sculptor

See volume 1 of this book.

Igoe, Lynn Moore, with James Igoe. 250 Years of Afro-American Art: An Annotated Bibliography. New York: R.R. Bowker Co., 1981.


JACK OX (1948-   )   Painter

Ox, Jack, with Peter Frank. "The Systematic Translation of Musical Composition into Paintings." Leonardo 17, no. 3 (1984): 152-58.

Ratcliff, Carter. "Looking at Sound." Art in America 68, no. 3 (March 1980): 87-95.

Who's Who in American Art, 17th ed. New York: R.R. Bowker Co., 1986.


MABEL PACKARD (1873-1938)   Miniaturist

American Art Annual, vol. 28. Washington, D.C.: American Federation of Arts, 1932.

Fielding, Mantle. Dictionary of American Painters, Sculptors, and Engravers. Enlarged ed. Greens Farms, Connecticut: Modern Books and Crafts, 1974.

Moure, Nancy D. Dictionary of Artists in Southern California Before 1950. Los Angeles: Dustin Publications, 1975.

Ness, Zenobia B., and Orwig, Louise. Iowa Artists of the First Hundred Years. [Des Moines, Iowa]: Wallace Homestead Co., 1939.


ETHEL LOUISE PADDOCK (b. 1887)   Painter

American Art Annual, vol. 28. Washington, D.C.: American Federation of Arts, 1932.

Fiftieth Anniversary Exhibition 1889-1939. New York: National Association of Women Painters and Sculptors, 1939.

Who's Who in American Art, vol. 1.  Washington, D.C.:  American
    Federation of Arts, 1935.

Wolf, Amy J.  New York Society of Women Artists 1925.  New York:
    ACA Galleries, 1987.


                BASHKA PAEFF (1893-1979)    Sculptor

See volume 1 of this book.

Dodd, Loring Holmes.  Golden Moments in American Sculpture.
    Cambridge, Massachusetts:  Dresser, Chapman and Grimes, 1967.

Fielding, Mantle.  Dictionary of American Painters, Sculptors and
    Engravers.  Enlarged ed.  Greens Farms, Connecticut:  Modern
    Books and Crafts, 1974.

Obituary.  The New York Times, 26 January 1979:  A23.


                MARIE DANFORTH PAGE (1869-1940)    Painter

See volume 1 of this book.

American Art Annual, vol. 28.  Washington, D.C.:  American
    Federation of Arts, 1932.

Fairbrother, Trevor J.  The Bostonians, Painters of an Elegant Age,
    1870-1930.  Boston:  Museum of Fine Arts, 1986.

Fielding, Mantle.  Dictionary of American Painters, Sculptors and
    Engravers.  Enlarged ed.  Greens Farms, Connecticut:  Modern
    Books and Crafts, 1974.

Mechlin, Leila.  "The Art of Today at Pittsburgh."  The American
    Magazine of Art 20, no. 12 (December 1929):  667.

Obituary.  Who's Who in American Art, vol. 3.  Washington, D.C.:
    American Federation of Arts, 1940.

Pierce, Patricia Jobe.  Edmund C. Tarbell and the Boston School of
    Painting, 1889-1980.  Hingham, Massachusetts:  Pierce
    Galleries, 1980.

Tufts, Eleanor.  American Women Artists, 1830-1930.  Washington,
    D.C.:  National Museum of Women in the Arts, 1987.

Woman's Who's Who of America.  New York:  American Commonwealth
    Co., 1914.

KATHARINE DUNN PAGON (1892-    )    Painter

American Art Annual, vol. 28. Washington, D.C.: American
    Federation of Arts, 1932.

Fielding, Mantle. Dictionary of American Painters, Sculptors and
    Engravers. Enlarged ed. Greens Farms, Connecticut: Modern
    Books and Crafts, 1974.

Who's Who in American Art, vol. 8. Washington, D.C.: American
    Federation of Arts, 1962.


SUSANNA PAINE (1792-1862)    Painter

Groce, George C., and Wallace, David H. The New-York Historical
    Society's Dictionary of Artists in America 1564-1860. New
    Haven: Yale University Press, 1957.

Paine, Susanna. Roses and Thorns or Recollections of an Artist.
    Providence, Rhode Island: B.T. Albro, 1854.

Women Pioneers in Maine Art. Portland, Maine: Joan Whitney Payson
    Gallery of Art, Westbrook College, 1981.


ADELAIDE C. PALMER (c. 1851-1928)    Painter

American Art Annual, vol. 28. Washington, D.C.: American
    Federation of Arts, 1932.

American Art Notes. New York: Jeffrey Alan Gallery, Autumn 1983.

Fielding, Mantle. Dictionary of American Painters, Sculptors and
    Engravers. Enlarged ed. Greens Farms, Connecticut: Modern
    Books and Crafts, 1974.

Painting Annual, vol. 4. Boston: Childs Gallery, 1986.

Woman's Who's Who of America. New York: American Commonwealth
    Co., 1914.


FANNY FLORA BOND PALMER (1812-1876)    Painter and Lithographer

See volume 1 of this book.

Brindle, John V., and Secrist, Sally. American Cornucopia, 19th
    Century Still Lifes and Studies. Pittsburgh: Hunt Institute
    for Botanical Documentation, Carnegie-Mellon University, 1976.

Mitchell, Peter. Great Flower Painters. Woodstock, New York:
    Overlook Press, 1973.

Rubinstein, Charlotte Streifer. "The Early Career of Frances Flora
    Bond Palmer (1812-1876)." American Art Journal vol. 17, no. 4
    (Autumn 1985): 71-94.


                JESSIE A. PALMER (1882-1956)   Painter

American Art Annual, vol. 28. Washington, D.C.: American
    Federation of Arts, 1932.

Fielding, Mantle. Dictionary of American Painters, Sculptors and
    Engravers. Enlarged ed. Greens Farms, Connecticut: Modern
    Books and Crafts, 1974.

O'Brien, Esse Forrester. Art and Artists of Texas. Dallas:   Tardy
    Publishing Co., 1935.

Who's Who in American Art, vol. 8. Washington, D.C.: American
    Federation of Arts, 1962.


                PAULINE PALMER (1867-1938)   Painter

American Art Annual, vol. 28. Washington, D.C.: American
    Federation of Arts, 1932.

Fielding, Mantle. Dictionary of American Painters, Sculptors and
    Engravers. Enlarged ed. Greens Farms, Connecticut: Modern
    Books and Crafts, 1974.

Obituary. Who's Who in American Art, vol. 3. Washington, D.C.:
    American Federation of Arts, 1940.

Pattison, James W. "Water-color Exhibition at the Art Institute."
    Brush and Pencil 4, no. 3 (1899): 149-58.

Woman's Who's Who of America. New York: American Commonwealth
    Co., 1914.


                ALICE MONROE PAPE (d. 1911)   Painter and Illustrator

Armstrong, Regina. "Representative American Women Illustrators:
    The Child Interpreters." Critic 36 (May 1900): 417-30.

326

Fielding, Mantle. *Dictionary of American Painters, Sculptors and Engravers.* Enlarged ed. Greens Farms, Connecticut: Modern Books and Crafts, 1974.

Obituary. *American Art Annual,* vol. 9. Washington, D.C.: American Federation of Arts, 1911.


DOROTHY PARIS (1899-    )    Painter

Campbell, Larry. "Dorothy Paris." *Art News* 50, no. 8 (December 1951): 49.

*Dorothy Paris.* New York: Barzansky Galleries, 1954.

*Dorothy Paris: Paintings of Portugal and North Africa.* New York: Van Deimern-Lilienfield Galleries, 1951.

F[itzsimmons], J[ames]. "Dorothy Paris." *Art Digest* 26, no. 2 (15 October 1951): 19.


MADELEINE FISH PARK (1891-1960)    Sculptor

*American Art Annual,* vol. 30. Washington, D.C.: American Federation of Arts, 1934.

Kovinick, Phil. *The Woman Artist in the American West 1860-1960.* Fullerton, California: Muckenthaler Cultural Center, 1976: 44.

Obituary. *Who's Who in American Art,* vol. 8. Washington, D.C.: American Federation of Arts, 1962.


CLARA WEAVER PARRISH (1861-1925)    Painter and Etcher

*American Art Annual,* vol. 1. New York: Macmillan, 1899.

Brown, C. Reynolds. *Clara Weaver Parrish.* Montgomery, Alabama: Museum of Fine Arts, 1980.

Champney, Elizabeth. "Woman in Art." *Quarterly Illustrator* 2 (April-June 1894): 111-24.

*Eight Southern Women.* Greenville, South Carolina: Greenville County Museum of Art, 1986.

Elliott, Maud Howe, ed. *Art and Handicraft in the Woman's Building of the World's Columbian Exposition, Chicago 1893.* Chicago: Rand, McNally and Co., 1894.

BETTY PARSONS (1900-1982)    Painter, Sculptor, and Art Dealer

See volume 1 of this book.

Mallinson, Constance.  "Objects and Abstraction."  Artweek 11, no. 20 (24 May 1980):  1, 16.

Obituary.  Art in America 70, no. 10 (November 1982):  174.

Perreault, John.  "Betty Parsons at Montclair Art Museum."  Art in America 62, no. 5 (September-October 1974):  115-116.

Russell, John.  "Betty Parsons and Elyssa Rundle, Armstrong Gallery."  The New York Times, 12 June 1987:  Y18.

_____.  "Betty Parsons:  Work from 1926 to 1980."  The New York Times, 12 April 1985.

EDITH BARRETTO PARSONS (1878-1956)    Sculptor

See volume 1 of this book.

Clement, Clara Erskine.  Women in the Fine Arts.  Boston:  Houghton Mifflin Co., 1904.

Famous Small Bronzes.  New York:  The Gorham Co., 1928.

Fielding, Mantle.  Dictionary of American Painters, Sculptors and Engravers.  Enlarged ed.  Greens Farms, Connecticut:  Modern Books and Crafts, 1974.

National Sculpture Society.  Exhibition of American Sculpture.  New York:  1923.

National Sculpture Society and California Palace of the Legion of Honor.  Contemporary American Sculpture.  New York, 1929.

GERTRUDE PARTINGTON (1883-1959)    Painter

See Gertrude Partington Albright.


SUZANNE PASCAL (1914-    )    Sculptor

Butler, Joseph T.  "The Glass Sculpture of Pascal."  Connoisseur 178, no. 715 (September 1971):  56-57.

Pascal:  Sculpture in Glass.  New York:  Bernard Danenberg Galleries, 1972.

Pascal:  Sculpture in Glass:  An Exhibition of 31 Chiseled Glass
Sculptures, 1978-79 [and] 5 Stainless Steel Sculptures, 1978-
79.  New York:  Alex Rosenberg Gallery, 1979.


PATRICIA PASSLOF (1928-    )   Painter

See volume 1 of this book.

Who's Who in American Art, 17th ed.  New York:  R.R. Bowker Co.,
1986.


ELSIE DODGE PATTEE (b. 1876)   Miniaturist

American Art Annual, vol. 30.  Washington, D.C.:  American
Federation of Arts, 1934.

Fuller, Lucia Fairchild.  "Modern American Miniature Painters."
Scribner's Magazine 67 (March 1920):  381-84.

Lounsbery, Elizabeth.  "American Miniature Painters."  Mentor 4,
no. 23 (5 January 1917).

Portraits by Distinguished American Artists.  New York:  Grand
Central Art Galleries, 1942.

Who's Who in American Art, vol. 8.  Washington, D.C.:  American
Federation of Arts, 1962.


MARGARET JORDAN PATTERSON (1869-1950)   Painter and Printmaker

American Art Annual, vol. 28.  Washington, D.C.:  American
Federation of Arts, 1932.

Fielding, Mantle.  Dictionary of American Painters, Sculptors and
Engravers.  Enlarged ed.  Greens Farms, Connecticut:  Modern
Books and Crafts, 1974.

Flint, Janet Altic.  Provincetown Printers:  A Woodcut Tradition.
Washington, D.C.:  National Museum of American Art, 1983.

Who's Who in American Art, vol. 3.  Washington, D.C.:  American
Federation of Arts, 1940.


HELEN SEARLE PATTISON (1830-1884)   Painter

See volume 1 of this book.

329

Clement, Clara Erskine. Women in the Fine Arts. Boston and New York: Houghton, Mifflin and Co., 1904.

Groce, George C., and Wallace, David H. The New-York Historical Society's Dictionary of Artists in America 1564-1860. New Haven: Yale University Press, 1957.

Probasco, Zane. An American Collection, The Hunter Museum of Art. Chattanooga, Tennessee: The Hunter Museum of Art, 1978.

Tufts, Eleanor. American Women Artists, 1830-1930. Washington, D.C.: National Museum of Women in the Arts, 1987.

Wilmerding, John; Ayres, Linda; and Powell, Earl A. An American Perspective, Nineteenth-Century Art from the Collection of JoAnn & Julian Ganz, Jr. Washington, D.C.: National Gallery of Art, 1981.


ETHEL KINNEY PAXSON (1885-    )    Painter

See volume 1 of this book.

An Exhibition of Women Students of William Merritt Chase. New York: Marbella Gallery, 1973.

Potter, Thomas F. "Meriden Artists Paxson." The Morning Record and Journal (Meriden, Connecticut), 21 May 1977: 7.

Sigler, Emily. "Essex Painter Recalls Her Long Life in Art." Hartford Courant, 29 May 1977: 7F.

Sullivan, Marianne. "Artist, 92, Prescribes Hard Work." The New Haven Registrar, 22 May 1977: 1D, 5D.


ELIZABETH VAUGHAN OKIE PAXTON (1877-1971)    Painter

Fairbrother, Trevor J. The Bostonians. Boston: Boston Museum of Fine Arts, 1986.

Fiftieth Annual Exhibition. New York: National Association of Women Painters and Sculptors, 1942.

Gammell, R.H. Ives. The Boston Painters 1900-1930. Orleans, Massachusetts: Parnassus Imprints, 1986.

Pierce, Patricia Jobe. Edmund C. Tarbell and the Boston School of Painting, 1889-1980. Hingham, Massachusetts: Pierce Galleries, 1980.

330

ELSIE PALMER PAYNE (1884-1971)   Watercolorist

American Art Annual, vol. 28.   Washington, D.C.:   American
Federation of Arts, 1932.

Moure, Nancy D.  Dictionary of Artists in Southern California
Before 1950.  Los Angeles:  Dustin Publications, 1975.

Who's Who in American Art, vol. 8.  Washington, D.C.:  American
Federation of Arts, 1962.


AMELIA PEABODY (1890-    )   Sculptor

American Art Annual, vol. 28.   Washington, D.C.:   American
Federation of Arts, 1932.

Archives of American Art.  Collection of Exhibition Catalogs.
Boston:  G.K. Hall and Co., 1979.

Fiftieth Annual Exhibition.  New York:  National Association of
Women Painters and Sculptors, 1942:  no. 86a.

National Sculpture Society.  Exhibition of American Sculpture.  San
Francisco:  California Palace of the Legion of Honor, 1929:
253.

Who's Who in American Art, vol. 10.  Washington, D.C.:  American
Federation of Arts, 1970.


HELEN LEE PEABODY (b. 1879)   Painter

American Art Annual, vol. 28.   Washington, D.C.:   American
Federation of Arts, 1932.

Pisano, Ronald G.  The Students of William Merritt Chase.
Huntington, New York:  Heckscher Museum, 1973.

Who's Who in American Art, vol. 4.  Washington, D.C.:  American
Federation of Arts, 1947.


MARION LAWRENCE PEABODY (b. 1875)   Painter and Sculptor

American Art Annual, vol. 28.   Washington, D.C.:   American
Federation of Arts, 1932.

Archives of American Art.  Collection of Exhibition Catalogs.
Boston:  G.K. Hall and Co., 1979.

National Sculpture Society.  Exhibition of American Sculpture.  San
   Francisco:  California Palace of the Legion of Honor, 1929:
   252, 253.


RUTH EATON COLBURN PEABODY (1898-1967)    Painter and Sculptor

American Art Annual, vol. 28.  Washington, D.C.:  American
   Federation of Arts, 1932.

Moure, Nancy D.  Dictionary of Artists in Southern California
   Before 1950.  Los Angeles: Dustin Publications, 1975.

Southern California Artists, 1890-1940.  Laguna Beach, California:
   Museum of Art, 1979.

Who's Who in American Art, vol. 5.  Washington, D.C.:  American
   Federation of Arts, 1953.


SOPHIA PEABODY (1809-1871)   Painter

See Sophia Peabody Hawthorne.


ELIZABETH PEAK (1952-    )   Printmaker

Elizabeth Peak:  Print and Drawings.  Brunswick, Maine:  Bowdoin
   College, 1982.

Lonman, Robin.  "Emerging Artists."  American Artist 48 [47], no.
   493 (August 1983):  40-41, 93-94.


ANNA CLAYPOOLE PEALE (1791-1878)   Painter

See volume 1 of this book.

In This Academy.  The Pennsylvania Academy of the Fine Arts, 1805-
   1976.  Philadelphia:  The Pennsylvania Academy of the Fine
   Arts, 1976:  94, 95, 284.

National Museum of Women in the Arts.  New York:  Harry N. Abrams,
   Inc., 1987:  42-43.

Philadelphia Portraiture:  1740-1910.  Philadelphia:  Frank S.
   Schwarz and Son, 1982.

332

Swan, Mabel Munson. *The Athenaeum Gallery 1827-1873*. Boston: The Boston Athenaeum, 1940: 188.

Tufts, Eleanor. *American Women Artists, 1830-1930*. Washington, D.C.: National Museum of Women in the Arts, 1987.

Wainwright, Nicholas B. *Painting and Miniatures at the Historical Society of Pennsylvania*. Philadelphia: The Historical Society of Pennsylvania, 1974.

Wharton, Anne Hollingsworth. *Heirlooms in Miniatures*. Philadelphia: J.B. Lippincott Co., 1898.


HARRIET CANY PEALE (ca. 1800-1869)    Painter

See volume 1 of this book.

Ellet, Elizabeth. *Women Artists in All Ages and Countries*. New York: Harper Bros., 1859.


MARGARETTA ANGELICA PEALE (1795-1882)    Painter

See volume 1 of this book.

*Four Generations of Commissions: The Peale Collection*. Baltimore: Maryland Historical Society, 1875.

Heller, Nancy G. *Women Artists*. New York: Abbeville, 1987.

*In This Academy. The Pennsylvania Academy of the Fine Arts, 1805-1976*. Philadelphia: The Pennsylvania Academy of the Fine Arts, 1976: 94, 97, 286.

Rubinstein, Charlotte Streifer. *American Women Artists*. Boston: G.K. Hall, 1982.

Tufts, Eleanor. *American Women Artists, 1830-1930*. Washington, D.C.: National Museum of Women in the Arts, 1987.


MARY JANE PEALE (1827-1902)    Painter

See volume 1 of this book.

Elam, Charles H. *The Peale Family: Three Generations of American Artists*. Detroit: Detroit Institute of Arts, 1967.

Huber, Christine Jones. *The Pennsylvania Academy and Its Women*. Philadelphia: The Pennsylvania Academy of the Fine Arts, 1974.

In This Academy.  The Pennsylvania Academy of the Fine Arts, 1805-
     1976.  Philadelphia:  The Pennsylvania Academy of the Fine
     Arts, 1976:  95, 286.

Tufts, Eleanor.  American Women Artists, 1830-1930.  Washington,
     D.C.:  National Museum of Women in the Arts, 1987.

Wainwright, Nicholas B.  Paintings and Miniatures at The Historical
     Society of Pennsylvania.  Philadelphia:  The Historical
     Society of Pennsylvania, 1974.


               SARAH MIRIAM PEALE (1800-1885)    Painter

See volume 1 of this book.

Heller, Nancy G.  Women Artists.  New York:  Abbeville, 1987.

In This Academy.  The Pennsylvania Academy of the Fine Arts, 1805-
     1976.  Philadelphia:  The Pennsylvania Academy of the Fine
     Arts, 1976:  94, 288.

King, Joan.  Sarah M. Peale:  America's First Woman Artist.
     Boston:  Branden Publishing Co., 1987.

Tufts, Eleanor.  American Women Artists, 1830-1930.  Washington,
     D.C.:  National Museum of Women in the Arts, 1987.


               HELEN S. PEARCE (b. 1895)    Painter

Eldredge, Charles C.; Schimmel, Julie; and Truettner, William.  Art
     in New Mexico, 1900-1945.  Paths to Taos and Santa Fe.
     Washington, D.C.:  National Museum of American Art, 1986.

Samuels, Peggy and Harold.  The Illustrated Biographical
     Encyclopedia of Artists of the American West.  Garden City,
     New York:  Doubleday, 1976.

Who's Who in American Art, vol. 8.  Washington, D.C.:  American
     Federation of Arts, 1962.


               MARGUERITE S. PEARSON (1898-1978)    Painter

"A Notable Exhibition in Gloucester."  American Magazine of Art 20,
     no. 10 (October 1929):  580, 586-87.

Directions in American Painting, 1875-1925.  Pittsburgh:  Carnegie
     Institute Museum of Art, 1982:  58.

"Marguerite S. Pearson." American Art Newsletter 3. Los Angeles: De Ville Galleries, 1985.

Marguerite S. Pearson, 1898-1978. Hingham, Massachusetts: Pierce Galleries, 1980.

Pierce, Patricia Jobe. Edmund Tarbell and the Boston School of Painting, 1889-1980. Hingham, Massachusetts: Pierce Galleries, 1980.

Who's Who in American Art, vol. 10. Washington, D.C.: American Federation of Arts, 1970.


CAROLINE PEART [BRINTON] (1870-1963)    Painter

American Art Annual, vol. 1. New York: Macmillan, 1899.

Brown, Ann Barton. "Can You Help Identify Some Sitters in Portraits by Caroline Peart?" Brandywine Catalyst 10, no. 3 (August 1982): 4.

CIGNA Collection Presents: Art in Pennsylvania from Franklin and Marshall College. Lancaster, Pennsylvania: Franklin and Marshall College, 1983.

Donohoe, Victoria. "A Neglected Career Emerges from Shadow." The Philadelphia Inquirer, 18 January 1986: 4-D.

Fielding, Mantle. Dictionary of American Painters, Sculptors and Engravers. Enlarged ed. Greens Farms, Connecticut: Modern Books and Crafts, 1974.


CLARA ELSENE WILLIAMS PECK (b. 1883)    Painter and Illustrator

American Art Annual, vol. 28. Washington, D.C.: American Federation of Arts, 1932.

Fielding, Mantle. Dictionary of American Painters, Sculptors and Engravers. Enlarged ed. Greens Farms, Connecticut: Modern Books and Crafts, 1974 (under Williams).

Mahony, Bertha E., and Whitney, Elinor. Contemporary Illustrators of Children's Books. Boston: Women's Educational and Industrial Union, 1930.

Reed, Walt, ed. The Illustrator in America, 1900-1960's. New York: Reinhold Publishing Corp., 1966.

Society of Illustrators. America's Great Women Illustrators 1850-1950. Chadds Ford, Pennsylvania: Brandywine River Museum, 1985.

Who's Who in American Art, vol. 8. Washington, D.C.: American Federation of Arts, 1962.

Yearbook of the Architectural League of New York and Catalogue of 34th Annual Exhibition. New York: Kalkhoff Co., 1920.


ROSALIE FRENCH PELBY (1793-1857)   Sculptor

Archives of American Art. Collection of Exhibition Catalogs. Boston: G.K. Hall and Co., 1979.

Groce, George C., and Wallace, David H. The New-York Historical Society's Dictionary of Artists in America, 1564-1860. New Haven: Yale University Press, 1957.


ELLA FERRIS PELL (1846-1922)   Painter and Sculptor

American Art Annual, vol. 10. Washington, D.C.: American Federation of Arts, 1913.

Bacon, Edgar Mayhew. "The Making of Masterpieces." The Quarterly Illustrator 1, no. 4 (1893): 302, 310.

Borak, Jeffrey. "Long Forgotten, The Lady is Now Remembered." Poughkeepsie Journal, 25 March 1973: 1D.

Champney, Elizabeth W. "Woman in Art." The Quarterly Illustrator 2, no. 2 (April-June 1894): 120.

Eldredge, Charles C. American Imagination and Symbolist Painting. New York: Grey Gallery, New York University, and Lawrence, Kansas: Spencer Art Museum, 1979.

Fielding, Mantle. Dictionary of American Painters, Sculptors and Engravers. Enlarged ed. Greens Farms, Connecticut: Modern Books and Crafts, 1974.

Gardner, Albert T. Yankee Stonecutters. New York: Columbia University Press, 1945: 74.

Trumble, Alfred. "Art's Summer Outings." The Quarterly Illustrator 2, no. 4 (1894): 388.

Tufts, Eleanor. American Women Artists, 1830-1930. Washington, D.C.: National Museum of Women in the Arts, 1987.

336

W., W.C. "Bread-Loaf Notes." Daily Evening Transcript (Boston),
19 August 1872: 1.

Woman's Who's Who of America. New York: American Commonwealth
Co., 1914.

"The Women Artists of New York and its Vicinity." The Evening
Post (New York), 24 February 1868: 2.


MARSHA PELS (1951-   )   Sculptor

Campbell, Lawrence. "Marsha S. Pels at Oscarsson Hood." Art in
America 72, no. 8 (September 1984): 213-14.

Lancaster, Christa. "Marsha Pels." Arts Magazine 56, no. 2
(October 1981): 3.

Nadelman, Cynthia. "Studio: Marsha Pels." Art News 85, no. 7
(September 1986): 65-66.


AGNES PELTON (1881-1961)   Painter

An American Gallery, vol. 3. New York: Richard York Gallery,
1987, no. 26.

The Art of California. Oakland: The Oakland Museum, 1984.

Contemporary Art. San Francisco: Golden Gate International
Exposition, 1939.

Exhibition of Paintings by Agnes Pelton. New York: Argent
Galleries, 1931.

Fielding, Mantle. Dictionary of American Painters, Sculptors and
Engravers. Enlarged ed. Greens Farms, Connecticut: Modern
Books and Crafts, 1974.

Fort, Ilene Susan. "Transcendental Painting Group." Arts
Magazine 56, no. 9 (May 1982): 30.

Fortieth Annual Exhibition. New York: National Association of
Women Painters and Sculptors, 1931.

International Exposition of Modern Art. New York: 69th Regiment
Armory, 1913.

Karlstrom, Paul J. "Regional Reports: West Coast." Archives of
American Art Journal 24, no. 3 (1984): 38.

Kovinick, Phil. The Woman Artist in the American West 1860-1960.
    Fullerton: Muckenthaler Cultural Center, 1976: 45.

1913 Armory Show 50th Anniversary Exhibition 1963. Utica, New
    York: Munson-Williams Proctor Institute, and New York:
    Armory of the Sixty-ninth Regiment, 1963.

Painting and Sculpture in California: The Modern Era. San
    Francisco: San Francisco Museum of Modern Art, 1977: 99,
    231.

Stainer, Margaret. "Agnes Pelton." Staying Visible: The
    Importance of Archives. Edited by Jan Rindfleisch.
    Cupertino, California: Helen Euphrat Gallery, De Anza
    College, 1981: 7-9.

Tufts, Eleanor. American Women Artists, 1830-1930. Washington,
    D.C.: National Museum of Women in the Arts, 1987.


    EDITH PENMAN (1860-1929)    Painter, Etcher, and Potter

Fielding, Mantle. Dictionary of American Painters, Sculptors and
    Engravers. Enlarged ed. Greens Farms, Connecticut: Modern
    Books and Crafts, 1974.

Fiftieth Anniversary Exhibition 1889-1939: National Association of
    Women Painters and Sculptors. New York: American Fine Arts
    Building, 1939.

Obituary. American Art Annual, vol. 26. Washington, D.C.:
    American Federation of Arts, 1929.

Obituary. Art Digest 3 (mid-January 1929): 12.

Peet, Phyllis. American Women of the Etching Revival. Atlanta:
    High Museum of Art, 1988.

Weimann, Jeanne Madeline. The Fair Women. Chicago: Academy
    Chicago, 1981: 308.

The Work of Women Etchers of America. New York: Union League
    Club, 1888.


    HELEN ALISON FRASER PENNIMAN (b. 1882)    Painter

American Art Annual, vol. 20. Washington, D.C.: American
    Federation of Arts, 1923.

338

Fielding, Mantle. *Dictionary of American Painters, Sculptors and Engravers.* Enlarged ed. Greens Farms, Connecticut: Modern Books and Crafts, 1974.

*Woman's Who's Who of America.* New York: American Commonwealth Co., 1914.


BEVERLY PEPPER (1924-    )   Sculptor

See volume 1 of this book.

Baker, Kenneth. "Interconnections: Beverly Pepper." *Art in America* 72, no. 4 (April 1984): 176-79.

Barnes, Helen. "Torre Olivola in Umbria: The Studio/Home of Sculptress Beverly Pepper." *Architectural Digest* 35, no. 8 (October 1978): 62-69.

Bell, Jane. "Beverly Pepper." *Art News* 84, no. 2 (February 1985): 135.

*Beverly Pepper: Private Scale Sculpture 1966-87.* New York: André Emmerich Gallery, 1987.

*Beverly Pepper: New Sculpture.* New York: André Emmerich Gallery, 1983.

Galligan, Gregory. "Beverly Pepper: Meditations out of Callous Steel." *Arts Magazine* 62, no. 2 (October 1987): 68-69.

Heller, Nancy G. *Women Artists.* New York: Abbeville, 1987.

Henry, Gerrit. "Beverly Pepper (André Emmerich)." *Art News* 83, no. 1 (January 1984): 158-59.

Kraus, Rosalind E. *Beverly Pepper, Sculpture in Place.* Buffalo: Albright-Knox Art Gallery, and New York: Abbeville Press, 1986.

Russell, John. "Art: Beverly Pepper, Sculptor and Painter, in 3 Shows at Once." *The New York Times*, 19 June 1987: Y17.

Solomon, Deborah. "Woman of Steel." *Art News* 86, no. 10 (December 1987): 112-17.

Thalacker, Donald W. *The Place of Art in the World of Architecture.* New York: Chelsea House, 1980.

Watson-Jones, Virginia. *Contemporary American Women Sculptors.* Phoenix: Oryx Press, 1986.

Welish, Marjorie.  "Beverly Pepper."  Arts Magazine 44, no. 4
        (February 1970):   54.


        ISABELLE CLARK PERCY (1882-1976)    Painter and Illustrator

American Art Annual, vol. 28.   Washington, D.C.:   American
        Federation of Arts, 1932.

Fielding, Mantle.  Dictionary of American Painters, Sculptors and
        Engravers.  Enlarged ed.  Greens Farms, Connecticut:  Modern
        Books and Crafts, 1974.

Who's Who in American Art, vol. 5.  Washington, D.C.:  American
        Federation of Arts, 1953.

Woman's Who's Who of America.  New York:  American Commonwealth
        Co., 1914.


        IRENE RICE PEREIRA (1907-1971)    Painter

See volume 1 of this book.

An Alumnus Salutes Dickinson College 200th Anniversary from the
        Collection of Meyer and Vivian Potamkin.  Harrisburg,
        Pennsylvania:  William Penn Memorial Museum, 1973, nos. 112,
        113.

I. Rice Pereira.  Washington, D.C.:  Corcoran Gallery of Art, 1956.

Second Biennial Exhibition of Contemporary American Painting.  New
        York:  Whitney Museum of American Art, 1934, no. 61.


        LUCY FITCH PERKINS (1865-1937)    Painter and Illustrator

American Art Annual, vol. 28.  Washington, D.C.:  American
        Federation of Arts, 1932.

Burnet, Mary Q.  Art and Artists of Indiana.  New York:  Century
        Co., 1921.

Mahony, Bertha E., and Whitney, Elinor.  Contemporary Illustrators
        of Children's Books.  Boston:  Women's Educational and
        Industrial Union, 1930.

McClinton, Katharine M.  The Chromolithographs of Louis Prang.  New
        York:  Crown Publishers, 1973.

340

Obituary. Who's Who in American Art, vol. 2. Washington, D.C.:
American Federation of Arts, 1937.

Woman's Who's Who of America. New York: American Commonwealth
Co., 1914.


SARAH PERKINS (1771-1831)   Pastelist

See volume 1 of this book.


CLARA GREENLEAF PERRY (1871-1960)   Painter

American Art Annual, vol. 30. Washington, D.C.: American
Federation of Arts, 1934.

Clara Greenleaf Perry: 1871-1960. Boston: James R. Bakker
Antiques, Inc., 1978.

Clement, Clara Erskine. Women in the Fine Arts. Boston: Houghton
Mifflin Co., 1904.

Field, Mantle. Dictionary of American Painters, Sculptors and
Engravers. Enlarged ed. Greens Farms, Connecticut: Modern
Books, 1974.

Woman's Who's Who of America. New York: American Commonwealth
Co., 1914.


LILLA CABOT PERRY (1848-1933)   Painter

See volume 1 of this book.

Birmingham, Doris. "The Black Hat by Lilla Cabot Perry." The
Currier Gallery of Art Bulletin (Fall 1986): 2-23, cover.

A Circle of Friends: Art Colonies of Cornish and Dublin, New
Hampshire. Durham, New Hampshire: University of New
Hampshire Art Galleries, 1985: 100-01.

De Kay, Charles. "The Quarter's Art." The Quarterly Illustrator
2 (April-June 1894): 208.

Fairbrother, TRevor J. The Bostonians, Painter of an Elegant Age
1870-1930. Boston: Museum of Fine Arts, 1986.

Gammell, R.H. Ives. The Boston Painters 1900-1930. Orleans,
Massachusetts: Parnassus Imprints, 1986..

Gerdts, William H. American Impressionism. New York: Abbeville,
1984.

Harding, Jonathan P. The Boston Athenaeum Collection. Pre-Twentieth Century American And European Painting and Sculpture. Boston: The Boston Athenaeum, 1986.

Harlow, Virginia. Thomas Sergeant Perry: A Biography. Durham, North Carolina: Duke University Press, 1950.

Henning, William T., Jr. A Catalogue of the American Collection, Hunter Museum of Art. Chattanooga, Tennessee: Hunter Museum of Art, 1985.

Lilla Cabot Perry. Essay by Lisa Ward. Chicago: Mongerson Gallery, 1984.

Morse, John T., Jr. Thomas Sergeant Perry, A Memoir. Boston and New York: Houghton Mifflin Co., 1929.

National Museum of Women in the Arts. New York: Harry N. Abrams, Inc., 1987: 50-51.

Obituary. American Art Annual, vol. 30. Washington, D.C.: American Federation of Arts, 1934.

Tufts, Eleanor. American Women Artists 1830-1930. Washington, D.C.: National Museum of Women in the Arts, 1987.

JANE PETERSON (1876-1965)    Painter

See volume 1 of this book.

Adventure & Inspiration, American Artists in Other Lands. New York: Hirschl and Adler Galleries, 1988.

American Art Annual, vol. 28. Washington, D.C.: American Federation of Arts, 1932.

Fiftieth Annual Exhibition. New York: National Association of Women Painters and Sculptors, 1942.

Jane Peterson: Paintings 1910-1920. New York: Robert Schoelkopf Gallery, 1968.

Jane Peterson, A Retrospective Exhibition. New York: Hirschl and Adler Galleries, 1970.

Obituary. The New York Times, 10 July 1966: 40.

Tufts, Eleanor. American Women Artists, 1830-1930. Washington, D.C.: National Museum of Women in the Arts, 1987.

342

Woman's Who's Who of America. New York:  American Commonwealth
     Co., 1914.


CAROLINE PETIGRU [CARSON] (1819-1894)   Painter

Groce, George C., and Wallace, David H.  The New-York Historical
     Society's Dictionary of Artists in America 1564-1860.  New
     Haven:  Yale University Press, 1957.

Wynne, George.  Early Americans in Rome.  Rome:  Daily American
     Printing, 1966:  viii (appendix) [under Carson].


MARY PETTY (1899-1976)   Illustrator and Cartoonist

America's Great Women Illustrators 1850-1950.  Chadds Ford,
     Pennsylvania:  Brandywine River Museum, 1985.

"Mary Petty."  The New Yorker 52 (12 April 1976):  144.

Obituary.  The New York Times, 11 March 1976:  40.

Petty, Mary.  This Petty Pace:  A Book of Drawings by Mary Petty.
     New York:  Alfred A. Knopf, 1945.


JUDY PFAFF (1946-    )   Sculptor

See volume 1 of this book.

Collings, Betty.  "Judy Pfaff."  Arts Magazine 55, no. 3 (November
     1980):  4.

Field, Richard S., and Fine, Ruth E.  A Graphic Muse.  New York:
     Hudson Hills Press, 1987.

Gill, Susan.  "Beyond the Perimeters.  The Eccentric Humanism of
     Judy Pfaff."  Arts Magazine 61, no. 2 (October 1986):  77-79.

Heller, Nancy G.  Women Artists.  New York:  Abbeville, 1987.

Karafel, Lorraine.  "Judy Pfaff [Holly Solomon]."  Art News 85, no.
     8 (October 1986):  129-30.

Kunst mit Eigen-Sinn.  Aktuelle Kunst von Frauen.  Vienna and
     Munich:  Löcher Verlag, 1985.

1987 Biennial.  New York:  Whitney Museum of American Art, 1987.

Russell, John. "Bright Young Talents: Six Artists with a Future." The New York Times, 18 May 1986, Arts & Leisure section: 1, 31.

Saunders, Wade. "Talking Objects: Interviews with Ten Younger Sculptors." Art in America 73, no. 11 (November 1985): 131, cover.

Shepard, Ileen. Sculpture of the 80's. Essay by Lowery S. Sims. Queens, New York: Queens Museum, 1987.

Smith, Roberta. Autonomous Objects. Charlotte, North Carolina: Knight Gallery/Spirit Square Arts Center, 1986.

Watson-Jones, Virginia. Contemporary American Women Sculptors. Phoenix: Oryx Press, 1986.

Yau, John. "On Location." Artforum 24, no. 10 (Summer 1986): 11-12.

ANN COLE PHILLIPS (1911-    )    Painter

Ann Cole Phillips: Recent Paintings. New York: Chase Gallery, 1958.

Ann Cole Phillips: Recent Paintings. New York: Bodley Gallery, 1965.

B[reuning], M[argaret]. "Ann Cole Phillips." Art Digest 27, no. 4 (15 November 1952): 20.

Campbell, Larry. "Ann Cole Phillips [Schaeffer]." Art News 51, no. 7 (November 1952): 58.

Levin, Kim. "Ann Cole Phillips [Bodley]." Art News 63, no. 2 (April 1964): 59-60.

MARJORIE ACKER PHILLIPS (1895-1985)    Painter

See volume 1 of this book.

American Art Annual, vol. 28. Washington, D.C.: American Federation of Arts, 1932.

Obituary. Art in America 73, no. 9 (September 1985): 166.

Phillips Collection, A Summary Catalogue. Washington, D.C.: The Phillips Collection, 1985.

Second Biennial Exhibition of Contemporary American Painting. New York: Whitney Museum of American Art, 1934, no. 81.

344

MARY WALKER PHILLIPS (1923-    )    Fiber Artist

Constantine, Mildred, and Larsen, Jack Lenor.  Wall Hangings.  New
    York:  The Museum of Modern Art, 1969.

Held, Shirley.  Weaving.  New York:  Holt, Rinehart and Winston,
    1973.

Phillips, Mary Walker.  Creative Knitting, an Art Form.  New York:
    Van Nostrand  Reinhold, 1971.

Znamierowski, Nell.  Fiber:  The Artist's View.  Greenvale, New
    York:  Hillwood Art Gallery, Long Island University, 1983.


LIL PICARD (1899-    )    Painter and Sculptor

See volume 1 of this book.

Who's Who in American Art.  New York:  R.R. Bowker Co., 1978.


HOWARDENA PINDELL (1943-    )    Painter

See volume 1 of this book.

Field, Richard S., and Fine, Ruth E.  A Graphic Muse.  New York:
    Hudson Hills Press, 1987.

Smith, Roberta Pancoast.  "Howardena Pindell."  Artforum 12, no. 6
    (February 1974):  88.

Who's Who in American Art, 17th ed.  New York:  R.R. Bowker Co.,
    1986.

Winerip, Michael.  "Computerized Billboard Brightens Up Times
    Square with Art-of-the-Month."  The New York Times, 26 August
    1983.


MARIANNA PINEDA [TOVISH] (1925-   )    Sculptor

See volume 1 of this book.

Collected Visions, Women Artists at the Bunting Institute 1961-
    1986.  Cambridge:  Radcliffe College, 1986.

Goldstein, Nathan.  The Art of Responsive Drawing.  Englewood, New
    Jersey:  Prentice-Hall, 1977.

Lerner, Abram. The Hirshhorn Museum and Sculpture Garden. New
     York: Harry N. Abrams, Inc., 1974.

Watson-Jones, Virginia. Contemporary American Women Sculptors.
     Phoenix: Oryx Press, 1986.

Who's Who in American Art, 17th ed. New York: R.R. Bowker Co.,
     1986.

EUNICE GRISWOLD PINNEY (1770-1849)  Painter

See volume 1 of this book.

Munsterberg, Hugo. A History of Women Artists. New York:
     Clarkson N. Potter, Inc., 1975.

Petersen, Karen, and Wilson, J.J. Women Artists. New York:
     Harper Colophon, 1976.

JODY PINTO (1942-    )   Sculptor

Architecture References. Los Angeles: Los Angeles Institute of
     Contemporary Art, 1980.

Dwellings. Philadelphia: Institute of Contemporary Art,
     University of Pennsylvania, 1978.

Land Marks. Annandale-on-Hudson, New York: Edith C. Blum Art
     Institute, Bard College, 1984.

Lavin, Maude. "Jody Pinto." Arts Magazine 55, no. 6 (February
     1981):  5.

Lippard, Lucy R. "Complexes: Architectural Sculpture in Nature."
     Art in America 67, no. 1 (January-February 1979):  86-97.

_____. Overlay: Contemporary Art and the Art of Prehistory. New
     York: Pantheon, 1983.

Nadelman, Cynthia. "Jody Pinto, Hal Bromm Gallery." Art News 82,
     no. 6 (Summer 1983):  200.

Schwendenwien, Jude. "Jody Pinto (at Hal Bromm)." Art News 87,
     no. 3 (March 1988):  200, 204.

Silverthorne, Jeanne. "Philadelphia. Jody Pinto at Marian Locks
     and Marian Locks East." Art in America 68, no. 3 (March
     1980):  127.

Staggs, Sam. "Pointing the Finger." Art News 86, no. 9 (November 1987): 16, 18.

Watson-Jones, Virginia. Contemporary American Women Sculptors. Phoenix: Oryx Press, 1986.


ADRIAN PIPER (1948-    )    Conceptual Artist and Photographer

Felshin, Nina. Disarming Images. Cincinnati: Contemporary Arts Center, 1984.

Interviews with Women in the Arts, part 2. New York: Tower Press, 1976: 24-27.

Kingsley, April. "Art Goes Underground." The Village Voice, 16 October 1978: 122.

Lippard, Lucy. "Caring: Five Political Artists." Studio International 193, no. 987 (March 1977): 197-207.

Matrix 56. Hartford: Wadsworth Atheneum, 1980.

Mayer, Rosemary. "Performance and Experience." Arts Magazine 47, no. 3 (December 1972): 33.

McEvilley, Thomas. "Adrian Piper (Alternative Museum)." Artforum 26, no. 1 (September 1987): 128-29.

Piper, Adrian. "Politics of Identity." Women Artists News 12, no. 2 (June 1987): 6.


JANE PIPER (1916-    )    Painter

Boyle, Richard J. Jane Piper. Philadelphia: Gross McCleaf Gallery, 1983.

Day, Larry, and Florescu, Michael. Jane Piper. New York: Bodley Gallery, 1981.

Florescu, Michael. "Jane Piper." Arts Magazine 55, no. 9 (May 1981): 18.

"Jane Piper." Art News 46, no. 2 (April 1947): 47.

"Jane Piper, Semi-Abstract." Art Digest 21, no. 13 (1 April 1947): 21.

Piper, Jane. "Remembering Arthur B. Charles." Arts Magazine 62, no. 7 (March 1988): 73-75.

Scott, William P. "Jane Piper." Arts Magazine 62, no. 3 (November 1987): 95.

_____. "Jane Piper at the Pennsylvania Academy of Fine Arts." Art in America 74, no. 12 (December 1986): 142-43.

Who's Who in American Art, 17th ed. New York: R.R. Bowker Co., 1986.


ALETHEA HILL PLATT (1861-1932)   Painter

American Art Annual, vol. 28. Washington, D.C.: American Federation of Arts, 1932.

Earle, Helen L., comp. Biographical Sketches of American Artists. Lansing: Michigan State Library, 1924.

Fielding, Mantle. Dictionary of American Painters, Sculptors and Engravers. Enlarged ed. Greens Farms, Connecticut: Modern Books and Crafts, 1974.

Woman's Who's Who of America. New York: American Commonwealth Co., 1914.


ELEANOR PLATT (1910-1974)   Sculptor

See volume 1 of this book.

Who's Who in American Art, vol. 4. Washington, D.C.: American Federation of Arts, 1947.


CORDELIA BUSHNELL PLIMPTON (1830-1886)   Potter

Clark, Edna. Ohio Art and Artists. Richmond, Virginia: Garrett and Massie, 1932.

Elliott, Maud H. Art and Handicraft in the Woman's Building of the World's Columbian Exhibition. New York: Goupil and Co., 1893.

The Ladies: God Bless 'Em. Cincinnati: Cincinnati Art Museum, 1976.

Weimann, Jeanne Madeline. The Fair Women. Chicago: Academy Chicago, 1981: 419.

348

CAROLYN GASSAN PLOCHMANN (1926-    )    Painter

Carolyn Plochmann, Recent Paintings. New York:  Kennedy Galleries,
    1973.

Fort, Ilene Susan.  "Carolyn Plochman."  Arts Magazine 57 (May
    1983):  62.

Hoving, Thomas.  "A Poetic and Quiet Painting."  Connoisseur 213
    (March 1983):  118.

The Paintings of Carolyn Plochmann. New York:  Kennedy Galleries,
    1983.

Who's Who in American Art, 17th ed.  New York:  R.R. Bowker Co.,
    1986.


ELIZABETH POE (1888-1947)    Painter

Archives of American Art.  Collection of Exhibition Catalogs.
    Boston:  G.K.  Hall and Co., 1979.

The Phillips Collection, A Summary Catalogue.  Washington, D.C.:
    The Phillips Collection, 1985.

Who's Who in American Art, vol. 4.  Washington, D.C.:  American
    Federation of Arts, 1947.


ANNE POOR (1918-    )    Painter

See volume 1 of this book.

Campbell, Lawrence.  "Anne Poor at Graham Modern."  Art in America
    75, no. 2 (February 1987):  152-53.

Hancock, Marianne.  "Anne Poor."  Arts Magazine 46, no. 2 (November
    1971):  66.

Who's Who in American Art, 17th ed.  New York:  R.R. Bowker Co.,
    1986.


MARION HOLDEN POPE (1872-1958)    Painter

American Art Annual, vol. 28.  Washington, D.C.:  American
    Federation of Arts, 1932.

Fielding, Mantle.  Dictionary of American Painters, Sculptors and
    Engravers.  Enlarged ed.  Greens Farms, Connecticut:  Modern
    Books and Crafts, 1974.

Moure, Nancy D.  Dictionary of Artists in Southern California
     Before 1950.  Los Angeles:  Dustin Publications, 1975.

Obituary.  Who's Who in American Art, vol. 7.  Washington, D.C.:
     American Federation of Arts, 1959.


                    KATHERINE PORTER (1941-    )   Painter

See volume 1 of this book.

Edelman, Robert G.  "Katherine Porter at Sidney Janis."  Art in
     America 75, no. 3 (March 1987):  135.

Krantz, Les, ed.  The New York Art Review.  New York:  Macmillan,
     1982.

Moorman, Margaret.  "Katherine Porter (Sidney Janis)."  Art News
     86, no. 4 (April 1987):  160.

Phillips, Deborah.  "Katherine Porter (David McKee)."  Art News 85,
     no. 2 (February 1985):  137.

Wadsworth, Susan M.  "Political and Moral Landscapes:  The Painting
     of Katherine Porter."  Arts Magazine 62, no. 1 (September
     1987):  84-87.


                    LILIANA PORTER (1941-    )   Painter

Collins, James.  "Liliana Porter, Hundred Acres Gallery."  Artforum
     12, no. 6 (February 1974):  74-75.

Frank, Peter.  "Reviews."  Art News 72, no. 4 (April 1973):  73.

Goldman, Shifra.  "Latin Americans Aqui/Here."  Artweek 15, (1
     December 1984):  3-4.

Heartney, Eleanor.  "Liliana Porter."  Arts Magazine 59, no. 3
     (November 1984):  36.

¡Mira!  The Canadian Club Hispanic Art Tour III.  Farmington Hills,
     Michigan:  Canadian Club, 1988.

"Prints & Photographs Published."  Print Collector's Newsletter 17,
     no. 3 (July-August 1986):  98.

Smith, Roberta Pancoast.  "Liliana Porter, Hundred Acres."
     Artforum 9, no. 8 (April 1973):  86.

MRS. S.C. PORTER (19th Century)    Painter

Fielding, Mantle. Dictionary of American Painters, Sculptors and
    Engravers. Enlarged ed. Greens Farms, Connecticut:  Modern
    Books and Crafts, 1974.

French, Henry W. Art and Artists in Connecticut. Boston:  Lee and
    Shepard, and New York:  Charles T. Dillingham, 1879:  172-73.

MARION SCOTT POST-WOLCOTT (1910-    )    Photographer

Contemporary Photographers. Editors George Walsh, Colin Naylor,
    and Michael Held. New York:  St. Martin's Press, 1982.

Elliot, James, and Westover, Marta.  "Marion Post Wolcott; FSA
    Photographs." University Art Museum Bulletin, Berkeley,
    California, April 1978.

Fisher, Andrea, ed. Let Us Now Praise Famous Women:  Women
    Photographers for the U.S. Government, 1935-1944.  London and
    New York:  Pandora Press, 1987.

Lifson, Ben.  "Not a Vintage Show--Post Wolcott." Village Voice,
    July 1979.

Murray, Joan.  "A Fight Against Complacency." Artweek 15, no. 31
    (22 September 1984):  13-14.

_____.  "Marion Post Wolcott." American Photographer (March 1980).

Palmer, Rebecca.  "A Continuing Concern." Artweek 17, no. 32 (4
    October 1986):  15.

Witkin, Lee D., and London, Barbara. The Photograph Collector's
    Guide. Boston:  New York Graphic Society, 1979.

JOANNA POUSETTE-DART (1947-    )    Painter

See volume 1 of this book.

Campbell, Lawrence.  "Joanna Pousette-Dart." Art in America 71,
    no. 9 (October 1983):  177.

Silverthorne, Jeanne.  "Joanna Pousette-Dart at Susan Caldwell
    Gallery." Artforum 22 (October 1983):  70-71.

AUDREY PREISSLER (1932-    )   Painter

Von Blum, Paul.  Audrey Preissler.  An American Humanist Artist of
    Today.  Harper's Ferry, West Virginia:  Helikon Design, 1980.

Who's Who in American Art, 15th ed.  New York:  R.R. Bowker Co.,
    1982.

EDITH MITCHELL PRELLWITZ (1865-1944)   Painter

American Art Annual, vol. 1.  New York:  Macmillan, 1899.

Artists By Themselves.  New York:  National Academy of Design,
    1983.

A Circle of Friends:  Art Colonies of Cornish and Dublin.  Durham,
    New Hampshire:  University Art Galleries, University of New
    Hampshire, 1985.

Exhibition of Forty Paintings by Henry Prellwitz and Edith
    Mitchell Prellwitz.  Brooklyn, New York:  Pratt Institute,
    Department of Fine Arts, 1899.

Obituary.  Who's Who in American Art, vol. 4.  Washington, D.C.:
    American Federation of Arts, 1947.

Woman's Who's Who of America.  New York:  American Commonwealth
    Co., 1914.

ELENA PRESSER (1940-    )   Painter

Blum, June.  Women's Art/Miles Apart.  New York:  Aaron Berman
    Gallery, Orlando:  Valencia Community College, 1982.

Collmer, Kathryn.  "Museum Notebook."  Southwest Art Magazine
    (March 1987):  91.

Cox, Petey.  "Elena Presser:  Marrying Painting and Music."  Miami
    Today, 11 April 1985:  19.

Digby, John, and Digby, Joan.  The Collage Handbook.  London:
    Thames and Hudson, 1985:  192-93.

Edwards, Ellen.  "Elena Presser."  Miami Herald, 9 March 1979.

Elena Presser:  Bach's Goldberg Variations.  Miami:  Frances
    Wolfson Art Gallery, Miami-Dade Community College, 1985.

Elena Presser: Transpositions: From the Goldberg Variations and Anna Magdalena Bach Notebooks. Philadelphia: Goldie Paley Gallery, Moore College of Art, 1988.

Goldthwaite, Thomas. "Artwork, Recital Prelude to Festival." Indianapolis Star, 16 June 1985: 1, 7.

Harper, Paula. "Presser's Goldberg Variations Transpose Bach's Music into Art." The Miami News, 12 April 1985: 2C.

Horowitz, Jeannie. "Exhibit, Harpsichord Concert Open in Gallery." Muhlenberg Weekly (Allentown, Pennsylvania), 4 October 1985: 2.

Kohen, Helen. "Presser's Variations in Harmony with Bach's Own." Miami Herald, 12 April 1985: 6D.

_____. "Working Mothers." Miami Herald, 14 October 1984.

Latin American Art: A Woman's View. Miami: Frances Wolfson Art Gallery, Miami-Dade Community College, 1981.

Maulfair, Jane. "Seeing Bach--Artist's Interpretation Set to Music." The Morning Call (Allentown, Pennsylvania), 27 October 1985, Section F: 1, 2.

McKenzie, Barbara. "Elena Presser's Art Tunes in on Bach." Atlanta Journal and Constitution, 4 May 1986: 2.


MAY WILSON PRESTON (1873-1949)    Illustrator

See volume 1 of this book.

American Art Annual, vol. 18. Washington, D.C.: American Federation of Arts, 1921.

Fielding, Mantle. Dictionary of American Painters, Sculptors and Engravers. Enlarged ed. Greens Farms, Connecticut: Modern Books and Crafts, 1974.

Five Women Impressionists. Santa Fe: Santa Fe East Gallery, 1982.

Memorial Exhibition: James Preston (1873-1962); May Wilson Preston 1873-1949). East Hampton, New York: Museum Section, Guild Hall, 1968.

353

Obituary. The New York Times, 19 May 1949.

Read, Walt, ed. The Illustrator in America, 1900-1960's. New
York: Reinhold Publishing Co., 1966.

Rubinstein, Charlotte Streifer. American Women Artists. Boston:
G.K. Hall and Co., 1982.

Woman's Who's Who of America. New York: American Commonwealth
Co., 1914.


M. ELIZABETH PRICE (1875-1960)    Painter

American Art Annual, vol. 28. Washington, D.C.: American
Federation of Arts, 1932.

American Watercolors and Drawings, Philadelphia Collection XI.
Philadelphia: Frank S. Schwarz and Son, 1981.

Fielding, Mantle. Dictionary of American Painters, Sculptors and
Engravers. Enlarged ed. Greens Farms, Connecticut: Modern
Books and Crafts, 1974.

Fiftieth Anniversary Exhibition 1889-1939: National Association of
Women Painters and Sculptors. New York: American Fine Arts
Building, 1939.

Who's Who in American Art, vol. 8. Washington, D.C.: American
Federation of Arts, 1962.


MARY PRINDIVILLE (b. 1876)    Painter

Archives of American Art. Collection of Exhibition Catalogs.
Boston: G.K. Hall and Co., 1979.

Second Biennial Exhibition of Contemporary American Painting. New
York: Whitney Museum of American Art, 1934, no. 82.


ELIZABETH PROPHET (1890-1960)    Sculptor

American Art Annual, vol. 28. Washington, D.C.: American
Federation of Arts, 1932.

Driskell, David C. Hidden Heritage: Afro-American Art, 1800-1950.
Bellevue, Washington: Bellevue Art Museum, and San Francisco:
The Art Museum Association of America, 1985.

Locke, Alain. "The American Negro as Artist." American Magazine
of Art 23, no. 3 (September 1931): 211-20.

354

Who's Who in American Art, vol. 1. Washington, D.C.: American
    Federation of Arts, 1935.


            DOROTHY PROVIS (1926-    )   Sculptor

Auer, James.  "Art Show at Neenah Trips the Furry, Light
    Fantastic."  The Milwaukee Journal, 20 March 1983,
    Entertainment Section:  6.

_____.  "Sculptor Finds Fuzzy Concept Fits Her Fine."  The
    Milwaukee Journal, 20 November 1977, Entertainment Section:
    4.

Buth-Furness, Christine.  "Dot Provis.  Concordia College Fine Arts
    Galleries."  New Art Examiner 12, no. 1 (October 1984):   62.

_____.  "Dot Provis--Textural Sculptor."  Women Artists News 9,
    nos. 5-6 (Summer 1984):  23, 27.

"Houses and Pillars, Mixed-Media Constructions at City College."
    The Fresno Bee, 24 August 1986, Section H:  15.

Myers, Trent.  1984 Wisconsin Biennial.  Madison:  Park Printing
    House, 1984.

Spencer, Mark J.  Wisconsin '85.  Stevens Point, Wisconsin:  Edna
    Carlsten Gallery, University of Wisconsin-Stevens Point, 1985.

Vance, Alex.  Preview.  Neenah, Wisconsin:  Bergstrom-Mahler
    Museum, 1983.

Wisconsin Women in the Arts Traveling Exhibition.  West Bend,
    Wisconsin:  West Bend Gallery of Fine Arts, 1988.


            MABEL PUGH (1891-    )   Painter and Illustrator

American Art Annual, vol. 28.  Washington, D.C.:  American
    Federation of Arts, 1932.

Archives of American Art.  A Checklist of the Collection.
    Washington, D.C.:  Smithsonian Institution, 1975.

Art in the United States Capitol.  Washington, D.C.:  U.S.
    Government Printing Office, 1976.

Mahony, Bertha E., and Whitney, Elinor.  Contemporary Illustrators
    of Children's Books.  Boston:  Women's Educational and
    Industrial Union, 1930.

355

Who's Who in American Art, vol. 8. Washington, D.C.: American
    Federation of Arts, 1962.


MARGARET McDONALD PULLMAN (d. 1892)    Painter and Illustrator

Burnet, Mary Q. Art and Artists of Indiana. New York: Century
    Co., 1921.

Peat, Wilbur D. Pioneer Painters of Indiana. Chicago: Lakeside
    Press, 1954.


ANN PURCELL (1941-    )    Painter

Cameron, Dan. "Ann Purcell." Arts Magazine 58, no. 3 (November
    1983): 18.

Livingston, Jane. Five Washington Artists. Washington, D.C.:
    Corcoran Gallery of Art, 1976.

Tannous, David. "'Five + One' at the Corcoran." Art in America
    65, no. 1 (January-February 1977): 131-32.

Who's Who in American Art, 17th ed. New York: R.R. Bowker, 1986.


REBECCA PURDUM (1959-    )    Painter

Henry, Gerrit. "Rebecca Purdum at Jack Tilton." Art in America
    74, no. 12 (December 1986): 134.

Moorman, Margaret. "Rebecca Purdam in a Mysterious Light." Art
    News 87, no. 3 (March 1988): 105-06.

Russell, John. "Bright Young Talents: Six Artists with a Future."
    The New York Times, 18 May 1986, Arts and Leisure Section: 1,
    31.

Seliger, Jonathan. "The Effect that Paint Produces: New Paintings
    by Rebecca Purdum." Arts Magazine 61, no. 6 (February 1987):
    78-79.


BRENDA PUTNAM (1890-1975)    Sculptor

See volume 1 of this book.

American Art Annual, vol. 28. Washington, D.C.: American
    Federation of Arts, 1932.

356

Fielding, Mantle. Dictionary of American Painters, Sculptors and Engravers. Enlarged ed. Greens Farms, Connecticut: Modern Books and Crafts, 1974.

"Kinswomen." Art Digest 7, no. 10 (15 February 1933): 32.

Obituary. The New York Times, 2 November 1975: 67.

Proske, Beatrice Gilman. Brookgreen Gardens Sculpture, vol. II. Brookgreen, South Carolina: Brookgreen Gardens, 1955: 160-61.

Woman's Who's Who of America. New York: American Commonwealth Co., 1914.

SARAH G. PUTNAM (late 19th-Century-early 20th-Century)
Portraitist

Archives of American Art. Collection of Exhibition Catalogs. Boston: G.K. Hall and Co., 1979.

Clement, Clara Erskine. Women in the Fine Arts. Boston and New York: Houghton, Mifflin and Co., 1904.

Huntsinger, Laura M. Harvard Portraits. Cambridge: Harvard University Press, 1936: 91, 110.

ELLEN BERNARD THOMPSON PYLE (1876-1936)    Painter and Illustrator

America's Great Women Illustrators 1850-1950. Chadds Ford, Pennsylvania: Brandywine River Museum, 1985.

Mayer, Anne E. Women Artists in the Howard Pyle Tradition. Chadds Ford, Pennsylvania: Brandywine River Museum, 1975.

Obituary. Who's Who in American Art, vol. 2. Washington, D.C.: American Federation of Arts, 1937.

KATHARINE PYLE (1863-1938)    Painter and Illustrator

American Watercolors and Drawings Philadelphia Collection XI. Philadelphia: Frank S. Schwarz and Son Gallery, 1981.

Mayer, Anne E. Women Artists in the Howard Pyle Tradition. Chadds Ford, Pennsylvania: Brandywine River Museum, 1975.

Schnessel, S. Michael. Jessie Willcox Smith. New York: Thomas Y. Crowell, [1977]: 83.

JOANNA QUINER (1796-1869)    Sculptor

Groce, George C., and Wallace, David H.  The New-York Historical
    Society's Dictionary of Artists in America 1564-1860.  New
    Haven:  Yale University Press, 1957.

Hanaford, Phebe A.  Daughters of America.  Augusta, Maine:  True
    and Co., 1882:  300.

Harding, Jonathan P.  The Boston Athenaeum Collection.  Boston:
    The Boston Athenaeum, 1984.


YVONNE RAINER (1934-    )    Filmmaker

Kaplan, E. Ann.  Women and Film.  New York:  Methuen, 1983.

Kruger, Barbara.  "Yvonne Rainer, 'The Man Who Envied Women.'"
    Artforum 24, no. 10 (Summer 1986):  124.

Kuhn, Annette.  Women's Pictures.  London:  Routledge and Kegan
    Paul, 1982.

Lippard, Lucy R.  "Yvonne Rainer on Feminism and her Film."
    Feminist Art Journal 4, no. 2 (Summer 1975):  5-11.

Michelson, Annette.  "Yvonne Rainer, Part Two 'Liver of
    Performers.'"  Artforum 12, no. 6 (February 1974):  30-35.

1987 Biennial Exhibition.  New York:  Whitney Museum of American
    Art, 1987.

Storr, Robert.  "The Theoretical Come-On."  Art in America 74, no.
    4 (April 1986):  158-65, cover.


ELLEN EMMET RAND (1876-1941)    Painter

See volume 1 of this book.

American Art Annual, vol. 28.  Washington, D.C.:  American
    Federation of Arts, 1932.

Curran, Grace Wickham.  "Ellen Emmet Rand, Portrait Painter."
    American Magazine of Art 19, no. 9 (September 1928):  471-79.

An Exhibition of Women Students of William Merritt Chase.  New
    York:  Marbella Gallery, 1973.

Lee, Cuthbert.  Contemporary American Portrait Painters.  New York:
    W.W. Norton and Co., 1929.

358

"Mrs. Ellen Rand, Noted Artist Dies." The New York Times, 19
December 1941: 25.

National Portrait Gallery, Permanent Collection Illustrated
Checklist. Washington, D.C.: Smithsonian Institution, 1982.

Neuhaus, Eugen. The Galleries of the Exposition. A Critical
Review of the Paintings, Sculpture and the Graphic Arts in the
Palace of Fine Arts at the Panama-Pacific International
-Exposition. San Francisco: Paul Elder and Co., 1915.

"Prize Winner at the Pennsylvania Academy." International Studio
75, no. 299 (March 1922): 79.

Richardson, Edgar P. American Paintings and Related Pictures in
the Henry Francis du Pont Winterthur Museum. Charlottesville:
University Press of Virginia, 1986.

Tufts, Eleanor. American Women Artists 1830-1930. Washington,
D.C.: National Museum of Women in the Arts, 1987.


LYNN RANDOLPH (1938-    )    Painter

Hill, Ed, and Bloom, Suzanne. "Lynn Randolph." Artforum 25, no. 7
(March 1987): 136-37.

Moore, Sylvia, ed. No Bluebonnets, No Yellow Roses: Essays on
Texas Women in the Arts. New York: Midmarch Arts Press,
1988.

The 1985 Show: Self-Images. Houston: Woman's Caucus for Art,
1985.


V.V. RANKINE (20th Century)    Sculptor

Frackman, Noel. "V.V. Rankine/Maria Gooding/John Cunningham."
Arts Magazine 52, no. 10 (June 1978): 37, 38.

Painting and Sculpture Today. Indianapolis: Indianapolis Museum
of Art, 1965.

Russo, Alexander. Profiles on Women Artists. Frederick, Maryland:
University Publications of America, 1985.

Thirtieth Biennial of Contemporary American Art. Washington, D.C.:
Corcoran Gallery of Art, 1967.

Who's Who in American Art. New York: R.R. Bowker Co., 1978.

CAROLINE L. ORMES RANSOM (1838-1910)    Painter

See volume 1 of this book.

Clark, Edna. Ohio Art and Artists. Richmond, Virginia:  Garrett &
    Massie, 1932.

Fielding, Mantle. Dictionary of American Painters, Sculptors and
    Engravers. Enlarged ed. Greens Farms, Connecticut:  Modern
    Books and Crafts, 1974.


ELLEN RAVENSCROFT (1876-1949)    Painter and Printmaker

American Art Annual, vol. 28.  Washington, D.C.:  American
    Federation of Arts, 1932.

Fielding, Mantle. Dictionary of American Painters, Sculptors and
    Engravers. Enlarged ed. Greens Farms, Connecticut:  Modern
    Books and Crafts, 1974.

Tradition. Washington, D.C.:  National Museum of American Art,
    1983.

Obituary. Who's Who in American Art, vol. 5.  Washington, D.C.:
    American Federation of Arts, 1953.

Wolf, Amy J. New York Society of Women Artists, 1925.  New York:
    ACA Galleries, 1987.


GRACE RAVLIN (1873-1956)    Painter

American Art Annual, vol. 28.  Washington, D.C.:  American
    Federation of Arts, 1932.

Archives of American Art. Collection of Exhibition Catalogs.
    Boston:  G.K. Hall and Co., 1979.

Dawdy, Doris Ostrander. Artists of the American West:  A
    Biographical Dictionary, vol. 2.  Chicago:  Sage Books, 1980.

Kovinick, Phil. The Woman Artist in the American West 1860-1960.
    Fullerton, California:  Muckenthaler Cultural Center, 1976:
    47.

Robertson, Edna, and Nestor, Sarah. Artists of the Canyons and
    Caminos, Santa Fe:  The Early Years. Layton, Utah:  Peregrine
    Smith, 1976.

Samuels, Peggy and Harold. The Illustrated Biographical
    Encyclopedia of Artists of the American West. Garden City,
    New York:  Doubleday and Co., 1976.

360

Who's Who in American Art, vol. 3. Washington, D.C.: American
Federation of Arts, 1940.


EVELYN RAYMOND (1908-    )    Sculptor

Annual Regional Sculpture Exhibition. Minneapolis:  Walker Art
Center, 1944.

Annual Regional Sculpture Exhibition. Minneapolis:  Walker Art
Center, 1945.

Annual Regional Sculpture Exhibition. Minneapolis:  Walker Art
Center, 1946.

Annual Regional Sculpture Exhibition. Minneapolis:  Walker Art
Center, 1947.

Art in the United States Capitol. Washington, D.C.:  U.S.
Government Printing Office, 1976.

Biennial of Painting, Prints, Sculpture--Upper Midwest.
Minneapolis:  Walker Art Center, 1956.

Paine, Sylvia. "Evelyn Raymond." WARM Journal (Autumn 1982):
4-7.

Watson-Jones, Virgina. Contemporary American Women Sculptors.
Phoenix:  Oryx Press, 1986.


GRACE R. RAYMOND (1876/77-1960's)    Painter

American Art Annual, vol. 28. Washington, D.C.:  American
Federation of Arts, 1932.

Clark, Edna. Ohio Art and Artists. Richmond, Virginia:  Garrett
and Massie, 1932.

Fielding, Mantle. Dictionary of American Painters, Sculptors and
Engravers. Enlarged ed. Greens Farms, Connecticut:  Modern
Books and Crafts, 1974.

Who's Who in American Art, vol. 1. Washington, D.C.:  American
Federation of Arts, 1935.


VINNIE REAM [HOXIE]    (1847-1914)    Sculptor

See volume 1 of this book.

Butts, Porter. Art in Wisconsin. Madison:  Democratic Printing,
1936.

Hall, Gordon Langley. *Vinnie Ream*. New York: Holt, Rinehart, Winston, 1963.

Heller, Nancy G. *Women Artists*. New York: Abbeville, 1987.

Jensen, James F. "Nineteenth-Century American Painting and Sculpture at the State Historical Society of Wisconsin." *Antiques* 110, no. 5 (November 1976): 1016-19.

Lemp, Joan A. "Vinnie Ream and Abraham Lincoln." *Woman's Art Journal* 6, no. 2 (Fall 1985-Winter 1986): 24-29.

Tufts, Eleanor. *American Women Artists, 1830-1930*. Washington, D.C.: National Museum of Women in the Arts, 1987.


HILLA REBAY (1890-1967)    Painter

Archives of American Art. *Collection of Exhibition Catalogs*. Boston: G.K. Hall and Co., 1979.

*Hilla Rebay: Paintings and Collages*. New York: French and Co. Gallery, 1962.

Lukach, Joan M. "Rebay, Hilla." *Notable American Women: The Modern Period*. Cambridge, Massachusetts: Belknap Press of Harvard University Press, 1980.

_____. *Hilla Rebay: In Search of the Spirit of Art*. New York: Braziller, 1983.

*Who's Who in American Art*, vol. 3. Washington, D.C.: American Federation of Arts, 1940.


JANE REECE (1869-1961)    Photographer

*'The Camera, the Paper, and I': a Collection of Photographs by Jane Reece*. Dayton, Ohio: Dayton Art Institute, 1952.

Pinckney, Helen L. "Jane Reece Memorial Exhibition: 'The Wonderful World of Photography.'" *Dayton Art Institute Bulletin* 21, no. 5 (March-April 1963): [1-8].

*Women of Photography. An Historical Survey*. San Francisco: San Francisco Museum of Art, 1975.

ETHEL REED (b. 1876)    Illustrator

The American Personality:  The Artist-Illustrator of Life in the
    United States, 1830-1960.  Los Angeles:  Grunwald Center for
    the Graphic Arts, University of California, 1976.

Hills, Patricia.  Turn-of-the-Century America.  New York:  Whitney
    Museum of American Art, 1977.

Keay, Carolyn.  American Posters of the Turn of the Century.  New
    York:  St. Martin's Press, 1975.

CLAUDIA REESE (1949-    )   Ceramic Sculptor

Carlozzi, Annette.  50 Texas Artists.  San Francisco:  Chronicle
    Books, 1986.

Kutner, Janet.  "Texas Clay."  American Ceramics 3, no. 3 (Fall
    1984):  36-43.

Theobald, Sharon A.  "Reviews Midwest, Indiana:  Claudia Reese and
    Margaret Prentice, Gallery 2, Purdue University."  New Art
    Examiner 8, no. 6 (May 1981):  23.

Watson-Jones, Virginia.  Contemporary American Women Sculptors.
    Phoenix:  Oryx Press, 1986.

EDNA REINDEL (1900-    )   Painter

American Art Annual, vol. 28.  Washington, D.C.:  American
    Federation of Arts, 1932.

Paintings and Mural Sketches.  New York:  MacBeth Gallery, 1937.

Second Biennial Exhibition of Contemporary American Painting.  New
    York:  Whitney Museum of American Art, 1934, no. 69.

DEBORAH REMINGTON (1935-    )   Painter

See volume 1 of this book.

L'Art Vivant aux Etats-Unis.  St. Paul de Vence, France:  Fondation
    Maeght, 1970.

Deborah Remington, A 20-Year Survey.  Essay by Dore Ashton.
    Newport Harbor, California:  Newport Harbor Art Museum, 1983.

Painting Endures.  Boston:  Institute of Contemporary Art, 1975.

363

Painting and Sculpture in California: The Modern Era. San
Francisco: San Francisco Museum of Modern Art, 1976.

Stiles, Knute. "The Mysterious Machine." Artforum 4, no. 6
(February 1966): 25-26.

Thompson, Walter. "Deborah Remington at Jack Shainman." Art in
America 75, no. 7 (July 1987): 126-27.

Who's Who in American Art, 17th ed. New York: R.R. Bowker Co.,
1986.


JEANNE REYNAL (1903-    )    Mosaicist

See volume 1 of this book.

Who's Who in American Art, 17th ed. New York: R.R. Bowker Co.,
1986.


BETSY GRAVES REYNEAU (1888-1964)    Painter

Bromley, Dorothy Dunbar. "Negro Portraits Used to Combat Racism in
U.S." New York Herald Tribune, 13 April 1947.

Dover, Cedric. American Negro Art. Greenwich, Connecticut: New
York Graphic Society, 1960.

National Portrait Gallery, Permanent Collection Illustrated
Checklist. Washington, D.C.: Smithsonian Institution Press,
1981.

Obituary. New York Herald Tribune, 21 October 1964.


VIRGINIA REYNOLDS (1866-1903)    Miniaturist

American Art Annual, vol. 1. New York: Macmillan, 1899.

Lounsbery, Elizabeth. "American Miniature Painters." Mentor 4,
no. 23 (15 January 1917): 5, 10.

Who's Who in America. Chicago: A.N. Marquis, 1903-05.

Who Was Who in America, vol. 1. Chicago: A.N. Marquis, 1942.

Williamson, George. History of Portrait Miniatures. London: G.
Bell, 1904.

KATHARINE NASH RHOADES (1885-1965)    Painter

"Art Notes."  The New York Times, 30 January 1915:  8.

Devree, Howard.  "A Reviewer's Notebook."  The New York Times, 17
   March 1935, Section viii:  7.

Homer, William Innes, et al.  Avant-Garde Painting and Sculpture in
   America 1910-25.  Wilmington, Delaware:  Delaware Art Museum,
   1975.

Meyer, Agnes Ernst.  Out of These Roots.  Boston:  Little, Brown
   and Co., 1953.

Vergine, Lea.  L'Altra Metà dell'Avanguardia 1910-1940.  Milan:
   Gabriele Mazzotta, 1980.

ANNE ESTELLE RICE (1879-1959)    Painter

Anne Estelle Rice (1879-1959):  Paintings, With a Biographical
   Study of the Artist by O. Raymond Drey.  Malcolm Easton, ed.
   Hull, England:  University of Hull, 1969.

Easton, Malcolm.  "The Art of Anne Estelle Rice."  Connoisseur 172,
   no. 694 (December 1969):  300-04.

The Letters of Katherine Mansfield.  John Middleton Murry, ed.  New
   York:  Alfred Knopf:  190, 304.

FRANCES RICH (1910-    )    Sculptor

The Sculpture of Frances Rich:  Frances Rich Retrospective
   Exhibition.  Palm Springs, California:  Palm Springs Desert
   Museum, 1969.

"Statue of St. Francis of Assisi and Three Small Bronze Studies."
   Liturgical Arts 20 (February 1952):  42.

"Three Recent Bronzes:  Pietà and Two Crucifixes."  Liturgical Arts
   21 (February 1953):  49.

Who's Who in American Art.  New York:  R.R. Bowker Co., 1978.

LUCY RICHARDS (Early 20th Century)    Sculptor

American Art Annual, vol. 28.  Washington, D.C.:  American
   Federation of Arts, 1932.

Famous Small Bronzes. New York:   The Gorham Co., 1928.

Fielding, Mantle.  Dictionary of American Painters, Sculptors and
    Engravers. Enlarged ed.  Greens Farms, Connecticut: Modern
    Books and Crafts, 1974.

Pattison, James William.  "Annual Exhibition of Painting and
    Sculpture, Art Institute, Chicago."  Fine Arts Journal 27, no.
    6 (December 1912):   791-99.


    CLARA VIRGINIA RICHARDSON (1855-1933)    Painter and Etcher

American Art Annual, vol. 28.  Washington, D.C.:  American
    Federation of Arts, 1932.

Fielding, Mantle.  Dictionary of American Painters, Sculptors and
    Engravers. Enlarged ed.  Greens Farms, Connecticut: Modern
    Books and Crafts, 1974.

Peet, Phyllis.  American Women of the Etching Revival.  Atlanta:
    High Museum of Art, 1988.

The Work of Women Etchers of America.  New York:  Union League
    Club, 1888.


    CONSTANCE COLEMAN RICHARDSON (1905-    )    Painter

See volume 1 of this book.

Barter, Judith A., and Springer, Lynn E.  Currents of Expansion:
    Painting in the Midwest, 1820-1940.  Saint Louis:  Saint Louis
    Art Museum, 1977:   no. 98.

Canaday, John.  "Art:  Contemporary Landscapist."  The New York
    Times, 20 January 1960.

Constance Richardson. New York:  Kennedy Galleries, 1960.

"A Modern Look at Distant Skies."  Art News 45, no. 3 (May 1946):
    35.

Paintings by Constance Richardson.  New York:  MacBeth Gallery,
    1944.

Paintings by Constance Richardson.  New York:  MacBeth Gallery,
    1946.

Tufts, Eleanor.  American Women Artists, 1830-1930.  Washington,
    D.C.:  National Museum of Women in the Arts, 1987.

6

Who's Who in American Art, 17th ed. New York: R.R. Bowker Co.,
1986.


MARGARET FOSTER RICHARDSON (1881-c. 1945)    Painter

See volume 1 of this book.

American 18th, 19th and 20th Century Paintings, Drawings and
Sculpture. New York: Sotheby's, 26 and 27 January 1984, Lot
512.

Fairbrother, Trevor J. The Bostonians: Painters of an Elegant
Age, 1870-1930. Boston: Museum of Fine Arts, 1986.

Pierce, Patricia Jobe. Edmund C. Tarbell and the Boston School of
Painting: 1889-1980. Hingham, Massachusetts: Pierce
Galleries, 1980.

Some Women Painters at the Syracuse Museum of Fine Arts. Syracuse,
New York: Museum of Fine Arts, 1914.

Tufts, Eleanor. American Women Artists, 1830-1930. Washington,
D.C.: National Museum of Women in the Arts, 1987.

Weber, Bruce. The Fine Line: Drawing with Silver in America.
West Palm Beach, Florida: Norton Gallery and School of Art,
1985.


MARY CURTIS RICHARDSON (1848-1931)    Painter

The Art of California. Oakland: The Oakland Museum, 1984.

California Art Research Monographs. Ed. Gene Hailey. San
Francisco: Works Progress Administration, vol. 5 (1937):
16-31.

Obituary. American Art Annual, vol. 28. Washington, D.C.:
American Federation of Arts, 1932.

Porter, Bruce, et al. Art in California: A Survey of American Art
with Special Reference to California Painting, Sculpture and
Architecture, Past and Present, Particularly as those Arts
were Represented at the Panama-Pacific International
Exposition. San Francisco: R.L. Bernier, 1916: 89, pl. 49.

Spangenberg, Helen.  <u>Yesterday's Artists on the Monterey
Peninsula</u>.  Monterey, California:  Monterey Peninsula Museum
of Art, 1976.

<u>A Woman's Vision:  California Painting Into the 20th Century</u>.  San
Francisco:  Maxwell Galleries, 1983.


MARY NEAL RICHARDSON (1859-1937)    Painter

<u>American Art Annual</u>, vol. 28.  Washington, D.C.:  American
Federation of Arts, 1932.

Archives of American Art.  <u>Collection of Exhibition Catalogs</u>.
Boston:  G.K. Hall and Co., 1979.

<u>Woman's Who's Who of America</u>.  New York:  American Commonwealth
Co., 1914.

<u>Women Pioneers in Maine Art</u>.  Portland, Maine:  Joan Whitney Payson
Gallery of Art, Westbrook College, 1981.


AGNES M. RICHMOND (1870-1964)    Painter

See volume 1 of this book.

<u>American Art Annual</u>, vol. 28.  Washington, D.C.:  American
Federation of Arts, 1932.

<u>American 18th, 19th and 20th Century Paintings, Drawings and
Sculpture</u>.  New York:  Sotheby's, 26 and 27 January 1984, Lot
582.

<u>American Impressionism:  The Second Generation</u>.  Washington, D.C.:
Taggart, Jorgensen and Putnam, [1983].

<u>American 19th and 20th Century Paintings, Drawings and Sculpture</u>.
New York:  Sotheby's, 21 October 1983, Lot 251.

<u>Fiftieth Anniversary Exhibition</u>.  New York:  National Association
of Women Painters and Sculptors, 1942, no. 321.

<u>Woman's Who's Who of America</u>.  New York:  American Commonwealth
Co., 1914.


ALICE RIDEOUT (b. ca. 1872)    Sculptor

See volume 1 of this book.

368

Elliott, Maud Howe, ed.  Art and Handicraft in the Woman's Building
    of the World's Columbian Exposition, Chicago, 1893.  Chicago:
    Rand, McNally and Co., 1894.


            WINIFRED SMITH RIEBER (1872-1963)    Painter

See volume 1 of this book.

Moure, Nancy D.  Dictionary of Artists in Southern California
    Before 1950.  Los Angeles:  Dustin Publications, 1975.


Porter, Bruce, et al.  Art in California:  A Survey of American Art
    with Special Reference to California Painting, Sculpture and
    Architecture, Past and Present, Particularly as Those Arts
    were Represented at the Panama-Pacific International
    Exposition.  San Francisco:  R.L. Bernier, 1916.


            FAITH RINGGOLD (1930-    )    Painter

See volume 1 of this book.

Faith Ringgold.  Change:  Painted Story Quilts.  New York:  Bernice
    Steinbaum Gallery, 1987.

Faith Ringgold:  Twenty Years of Painting, Sculpture, and
    Performance.  New York:  The Studio Museum in Harlem, 1983.

Galligan, Gregory.  "The Quilts of Faith Ringgold."  Art
    Magazine 61, no. 5 (January 1987):  62-63.

Gill, Susan.  "Faith Ringgold."  Arts Magazine 61, no. 7 (May
    1987):  96.

Gleuck, Grace.  "An Artist Who Turns Cloth into Social
    Commentary."  The New York Times, 29 July 1984, Arts and
    Leisure Section:  H24-25.

Gouma-Peterson, Thalia, and Zurko, Kathleen McManus.  Faith Ringgold:
    Painting, Sculpture, Performance.  Wooster, Ohio:  The College
    of Wooster Art Museum, 1985.

Henry, Gerrit.  "Faith Ringgold at the Studio Museum in Harlem."
    Art in America 72, no. 10 (November 1984):  154-55.

Johnson, William.  "Faith Ringgold."  Art News 69, no. 2 (April
    1970):  72.

Lippard, Lucy R.  "Faith Ringgold at Bernice Steinbaum."  Art in
    America 75, no. 5 (May 1987):  184-85.

Moorman, Margaret. "Faith Ringgold (Bernice Steinbaum)." Art News 86, no. 4 (April 1987): 159-60.

Perret, George A. "Faith Ringgold at Spectrum." Arts Magazine 44, no. 4 (February 1970): 61.

Ringgold, Faith. "Being My Own Woman." Women's Studies Quarterly XV, nos. 1-2 (Spring/Summer 1987): 31-34.

Rose, Barbara. "Black Art in America." Art in America 58, no. 5 (September 1970): 63.

Slatkin, Wendy. Women Artists in History from Antiquity to the 20th Century. Englewood Cliffs, New Jersey: Prentice-Hall, Inc., 1985.

LUCY PERKINS RIPLEY (d. 1949)    Sculptor

See volume 1 of this book.

American Art Annual, vol. 28. Washington, D.C.: American Federation of Arts, 1932.

CAROLINE EVERETT RISQUE (b. 1886)    Sculptor

American Art Annual, vol. 28. Washington, D.C.: American Federation of Arts, 1932.

Exhibition of American Sculpture. New York: National Sculpture Society, 1923.

Fielding, Mantle. Dictionary of American Painters, Sculptors and Engravers. Enlarged ed. Greens Farms, Connecticut: Modern Books and Crafts, 1974.

Perry, Stella George Stern. Little Bronze Playfellows. San Francisco: Paul Elder and Co., 1915.

Who's Who in American Art, vol. 1. Washington, D.C.: American Federation of Arts, 1935.

ELLEN ROBBINS (1828-1905)    Painter

See volume 1 of this book.

"Art in Boston." The Evening Post (New York), 26 January 1876: 1.

"Art Items." Daily Evening Transcript (Boston), 11 December 1867: 2.

370

Brindle, John V. American Cornucopia: 19th Century Still Life and
Studies. Pittsburgh: Hunt Institute for Botanical
Documentation, Carnegie Mellon University, 1976.

Fielding, Mantle. Dictionary of American Painters, Sculptors and
Engravers. Enlarged ed. Greens Farms, Connecticut: Modern
Books and Crafts, 1974.

Forshay, Ella M. Reflections of Nature: Flowers in American Art.
New York: Whitney Museum of American Art, 1984.

Gerdts, William H. Down Garden Paths: The Floral Environment in
Art. Rutherford, New Jersey: Fairleigh Dickinson University
Press, and London and Cranbury, New Jersey: Associated
University Presses, 1983.

McClinton, Katharine M. The Chromolithographs of Louis Prang. New
York: Crown Publishers, 1973.

"Notes." The Art Journal 3 (1877): 160.

Obituary. Watertown Tribune-Enterprise, 19 May 1905: 1.

"Sketchings." The Crayon (September 1860): 264.

Tufts, Eleanor. American Women Artists 1830-1930. Washington,
D.C.: National Museum of Women in the Arts, 1987.


ELIZABETH WENTWORTH ROBERTS (1871-1927)    Painter

American Art Annual, vol. 20. Washington, D.C.: American
Federation of Arts, 1923.

Archives of American Art. Collection of Exhibition Catalogs.
Boston: G.K. Hall and Co., 1979.

Fielding, Mantle. Dictionary of American Painters, Sculptors and
Engravers. Enlarged ed. Greens Farms, Connecticut: Modern
Books and Crafts, 1974.

National Collection of Fine Arts. Directory of the Bicentennial
Inventory of American Paintings Executed Before 1914. New
York: Arno Press, 1976.


MARY ROBERTS (d. 1761)    Miniaturist

Groce, George C., and Wallace, David H. The New-York Historical
Society's Dictionary of Artists in America 1564-1860. New
Haven: Yale University Press, 1957.

Horton, Frank L. "America's Earliest Woman Miniaturist."
    Journal of Early Southern Decorative Arts (November 1979):
    1-5.

Rutledge, Anna Wells. "Charleston's First Artistic Couple."
    Antiques 52 (August 1947): 100-02.

Severens, Martha R. The Miniature Portrait Collection of the
    Caroline Art Association. Charleston, South Carolina: Gibbes
    Art Gallery, 1984: 101-02.

Spruill, Julia Cherry. Women's Life and Work in the Southern
    Colonies. New York: Russell and Russell, 1969.


PRISCILLA ROBERTS (1916-    )  Painter

See volume 1 of this book.

Priscilla Roberts, Magic Realist: A Retrospective Exhibition;
    A Selection of Works from Public and Private Collections. New
    York: Grand Central Art Galleries, 1981.


ADELAIDE ALSOP ROBINEAU (1865-1929)   Ceramicist

Anscombe, Isabelle. A Woman's Touch. New York: Viking Penguin,
    1984.

The Art Deco Environment. Syracuse: Everson Museum of Art, 1976.

Barber, Edwin Atlee. Catalogue of American Potteries and
    Porcelain. Philadelphia: Pennsylvania Museum and School of
    Industrial Art, 1893.

Breck, Joseph. "A Memorial Exhibition." Metropolitan Museum
    Bulletin 24, no. 11 (November 1929): 279-80.

Callen, Anthea. Women Artists of the Arts and Crafts Movement,
    1870-1914. New York: Pantheon Books, 1979.

Clark, Garth. A Century of Ceramics in the United States 1878-
    1978. New York: E.P. Dutton, 1979.

Clark, Robert Judson. The Arts and Crafts Movement in America
    1876-1916. Princeton, New Jersey: Princeton University
    Press, 1972.

Eidelberg, Martin. "Art Pottery." The Arts and Crafts Movement in
    America 1876-1916. Ed. Robert Judson Clark. Princeton, New
    Jersey: Princeton University Press, 1972.

372

Evans, Paul F.  Art Pottery of the United States:  An Encyclopedia
    of Producers and Their Marks.  New York:  Scribner's Sons,
    1974.

Henzke, Lucile.  American Art Pottery.  Camden, New Jersey:
    Nelson, 1970.

Hull, William.  "Some Notes on Early Robineau Porcelains."
    Everson Museum of Art Bulletin 2 [1960].

Keen, Kirsten Hoving.  American Art Pottery 1875-1930.  Wilmington,
    Delaware:  Delaware Art Museum, 1978.

Kovel, Ralph, and Kovel, Terry.  Kovel's Collector's Guide to
    American Art Pottery.  New York:  Crown, 1974.

Levin, Elaine.  "Pioneers of Contemporary American Ceramics:
    Charles Binns, Adelaide Robineau."  Ceramics Monthly 23
    (November 1975):  22-27.

Overglaze Imagery.  Essays by Garth Clark, Judy Chicago, and
    Richard Shaw.  Fullerton, California:  California State
    University Art Gallery, 1977.

"Syracuse Gets  Robineau Memorial Group."  Art Digest 5 (15 January
    1931):  19.

Wise, Ethel Brand.  "Adelaide Alsop Robineau, American Ceramist."
    The American Magazine of Art 20, no. 12 (December 1929):
    687-91.

                CHARLOTTE ROBINSON (1924-     )    Painter

See volume 1 of this book.

Charlotte Robinson:  Paintings 1983-1985.  San Antonio, Texas:
    Marion Koogler McNay Art Museum, 1985.

Cooper, Kym.  "Artist's Hands Subject of New Exhibit."  The
    Washington Star 14 May 1981:  D2.

Marter, Joan.  Women Artists Series Year 8.  New Brunswick, New
    Jersey:  Douglas College, 1978.

Paul, Richard.  "Women in the Arts:  Charlotte Robinson, Worker-in-
    Trenches."  The Washington Post, 31 January 1979:  B-1, B-6.

Robinson, Charlotte, ed.  The Artist & The Quilt.  New York:
    Alfred A. Knopf, 1983.

Swift, Mary.  Hands of Artists.  Arlington, Virginia:  Arlington
    Art Center, 1981.

Tannous, David.  Tenth Juried Exhibition Works of Paper.
    Charlottesville, Virginia:  Second Street Gallery, 1982.

Vollmer, Cynthia.  "Artist Holds Paris Show."  San Antonio News, 14
    May 1963:  2-D.


                    IONE ROBINSON (1910-    )  Painter

Descargues, Pierre.  "La décoration internationale du Forum
    ex-mussolin; un projet de Ione Robinson."  Arts, 28 November
    1947:  3.

"Ione Robinson."  Art News 45, no. 10 (December 1946):  54.

Reed, Judith Kaye.  "Children of Europe."  Art Digest 21, no. 4 (15
    November 1946):  17.

Robinson, Ione.  A Wall to Paint On.  New York:  E.P Dutton and
    Co., 1946.


                    DOROTHEA ROCKBURNE (1934-    )  Painter

See volume 1 of this book.

Bell, Jane.  "Dorothea Rockburne at Xavier Fourcade."  Art News 84,
    no. 5 (May 1985):  115, 116.

Boettger, Suzaan.  "Dorothea Rockburne."  Artforum 24, no. 10
    (Summer 1986):  129-30.

Brenson, Michael.  "A Painter of Today, The Masters of the Past."
    The New York Times, 29 April 1988:  Y13, 18.

Dorothea Rockburne:  Painting and Drawing 1982-85.  New York:
    Xavier Fourcade, 1985.

Dorothea Rockburne.  A Personal Selection.  Paintings 1968-1986.
    New York:  Xavier Fourcade, 1986.

Field, Richard S., and Fine, Ruth E.  A Graphic Muse.  New York:
    Hudson Hills Press, 1987.

Gruen, John.  "Artist's Dialogue:  Dorothea Rockburne."
    Architectural Digest  (January 1987):  46.

374

_____. "Dorothea Rockburne's Unanswered Questions." Art News 85, no. 3 (March 1986): 97-101.

A Guide to the Collection. Houston: Museum of Fine Arts, 1981.

Loughery, John. "Dorothea Rockburne." Arts Magazine 62, no. 9 (May 1988): 92.

Lubell, Ellen. "Dorothea Rockburne." Arts Magazine 51, no. 5 (January 1977): 35.

National Museum of Women in the Arts. New York: Harry N. Abrams, Inc., 1987.

The Spiritual in Art: Abstract Painting 1890-1985. Los Angeles: Los Angeles County Museum of Art, 1986.

Stavitsky, Gail. "Dorothea Rockburne." Arts Magazine 60, no. 9 (May 1986): 104.


ANNETTE PERKINS ROGERS (1841-1920)    Painter

See volume 1 of this book.

Falk, Peter Hastings. Who Was Who in American Art. Madison, Connecticut: Sound View Press, 1985.


GRETCHEN ROGERS (1881-1967)    Painter

See volume 1 of this book.

American Art Annual, vol. 28. Washington, D.C.: American Federation of Arts, 1932.

Archives of American Art. Collection of Exhibition Catalogs. Bosotn: G.K. Hall and Co., 1979.

Fairbrother, Trevor J. The Bostonians: Painters of an Elegant Age, 1870-1930. Boston: Museum of Fine Arts, 1985.

Fielding, Mantle. Dictionary of American Painters, Sculptors and Engravers. Enlarged ed. Greens Farms, Connecticut: Modern Books and Crafts, 1974.

Gammell, R.H. Ives. The Boston Painters 1900-1930. Orleans, Massachusetts: Parnassus Imprints, 1986.

Pierce, Patricia Jobe. Edmund C. Tarbell and the Boston School of Painting. Hingham, Massachusetts: Pierce Galleries, 1980.

ADELHEID LANGE ROOSEVELT (1878-1962)    Sculptor

Homer, William Inness, et al.  Avant-Garde Painting and Sculpture
    in America 1910-25.  Wilmington, Delaware:  Delaware Art
    Museum, 1975.

Hyland, Douglas.  "Adelheid Lange Roosevelt:  American Cubist
    Sculptor."  Archives of American Art Journal 21, no. 4 (1981):
    10-17.

Tarbell, Roberta K.  "The Impact of the Armory Show on American
    Sculpture."  Archives of American Art Journal 18, no. 2
    (1978):  9.

LEATRICE ROSE (20th Century)    Painter

See volume 1 of this book.

Campbell, Lawrence.  "Leatrice Rose at Armstrong."  Art in America
    73, no. 10 (October 1985):  154-55.

Guest, Barbara.  "Leatrice Rose."  Arts Magazine 59, no. 10 (Summer
    1985):  13.

Who's Who in American Art, 17th ed.  New York:  R.R. Bowker Co.,
    1986.

RUTH STARR ROSE (1887-1965)    Painter and Printmaker

American Art Annual, vol. 28.  Washington, D.C.:  American
    Federation of Arts, 1932.

American Prints in the Library of Congress:  A Catalog of the
    Collection.  Baltimore:  Johns Hopkins Press, 1970.

Fiftieth Anniversary Exhibition 1889-1939.  New York:  National
    Association of Women Painters and Sculptors, 1939.

A Selection of American Prints.  A Selection of Biographies of
    Forty Women Artists Working Between 1904-1979.  Santa Rosa,
    California:  The Annex Galleries, 1987:  12.

DORIS ROSENTHAL [CHARASH] (1895-1971)    Painter and Printmaker

See volume 1 of this book.

American Art Annual, vol. 28.  Washington, D.C.:  American
    Federation of Arts, 1932.

376

Doris Rosenthal:  Paintings of Mexico.  New York:  Midtown
     Galleries, 1955.

Doris Rosenthal:  Paintings of Mexico.  New York:  Midtown
     Galleries, 1957.

Doris Rosenthal:  The West Indies.  New York:  Midtown Galleries,
     1952.

Second Biennial Exhibition of Contemporary American Painting.  New
     York:  Whitney Museum of American Art, 1934, no. 139.

"Shows Fruits of a Scholarship in Mexico."  Art Digest 8, no. 10
     (15 February 1934):  29.

Wolf, Amy J.  New York Society of Women Artists 1925.  New York:
     ACA Galleries, 1987.


          MARTHA ROSLER (1943-    )   Video Artist

Buchloh, Benjamin H.D.  "Allegorical Procedures:  Appropriation and
     Montage in Contemporary Art."  Artforum 21, no. 1 (September
     1982):  52-53.

_____.  "From Gadget Video to Agit Video:  Some Notes of Four
     Recent Video Works."  Art Journal 45, no. 3 (Fall 1985):
     217-27.

Gardner, Colin.  "Addressing Political Issues."  Artweek 14, no. 36
     (29 October 1983):  13.

Gever, Martha.  "An Interview with Martha Rosler."  Afterimage 9,
     no. 3 (October 1981):  10-17.

Kuspit, Donald B.  "The Art of Memory/The Loss of History."
     Artforum 24, no. 7 (March 1986):  120-21.

Lippard, Lucy.  "Caring:  Five Political Artists."  Studio
     International 193, no. 987 (March 1977):  197-207.

1979 Biennial.  New York:  Whitney Museum of American Art, 1979.

1983 Biennial.  New York:  Whitney Museum of American Art, 1983.

1987 Biennial.  New York:  Whitney Museum of American Art, 1987.

Rosler, Martha.  Martha Rosler, Three Works.  Halifax, Nova Scotia:
     The Press of the Nova Scotia College of Art and Design, 1981.

Sturken, Marita.  "A Whitney Sampler."  Afterimage 11, no. 3
     (October 1983):  17-18.

SUSAN ROTHENBERG (1945-    )    Painter

See volume 1 of this book.

Bell, Jane. "Susan Rothenberg." Art News 86, no. 5 (May 1987):
     147.

Grimes, Nancy. "Susan Rothenberg at Willard." Art in America 73,
     no. 11 (November 1985): 127.

A Guide to the Collection. Houston: Museum of Fine Arts, 1981.

Heller, Nancy G. Women Artists. New York: Abbeville, 1987.

Herrera, Hayden. "In a Class by Herself." Connoisseur (April
     1984): 112-17.

Hughes, Robert. "Spectral Light, Anxious Dancers." Time, 9
     November 1987: 109.

Malen, Lenore. "Susan Rothenberg." Art in America 87, no. 1
     (January 1988): 151.

Princenthal, Nancy. "Susan Rothenberg at Sperone Westwater." Art
     in America 76, no. 1 (January 1988): 129.

Schwabsky, Barry. "Susan Rothenberg." Arts Magazine 61, no. 8
     (April 1987): 107.

Susan Rothenberg. The Horse Paintings: 1974-80. New York:
     Gagosian Gallery, 1987.

SANDRA MENDELSOHN RUBIN (1947-    )    Painter

Clothier, Peter. "Sandra Mendelsohn Rubin at the Los Angeles
     County Museum." Art in America 73, no. 10 (October 1985):
     165.

Edgerton, Anne Carnegie, and Tuchman, Maurice. "Young Talent
     Awards: 1963-1983." Bulletin, Los Angeles County Museum of
     Art 27 (1983): 54.

Sandra Mendelsohn Rubin. Paintings and Drawings. New York:
     Claude Bernard Gallery, 1987.

ANDRÉE RUELLAN (1905-    )    Painter

See volume 1 of this book.

Andrée Ruellan. New York: Kraushaar Galleries, 1956.

378

"Andrée Ruellan Exhibits Her Action Paintings." Art Digest 14, no. 10 (15 February 1970): 17.

Breuning, Margaret. "Andrée Ruellan." Magazine of Art 30, no. 3 (April 1937): 258-59.

Collier, Alberta. "Paintings, Drawings Will Be Shown." The Times-Picayune, New Orleans, 1 February 1959.

Devree, Howard. "New York Exhibition Reviews." Magazine of Art 33, no. 2 (February 1940): 111-12.

First Biennial Exhibition of Contemporary American Sculpture, Watercolors and Prints. New York: Whitney Museum of American Art, 1933-34.

"The Gentle Humor of Andrée Ruellan." Art Digest 11, no. 12 (15 March 1937): 31.

Painting and Sculpture, 1957. Urbana: University of Illinois, 1957.

Park, Marlene, and Markowitz, Gerald E. Democratic Vistas: Post Offices and Public Art in the New Deal. Philadelphia: Temple University Press, 1984.

Pittsburgh International Exhibition. Pittsburgh: Carnegie Institute, 1943 through 1950.

Retrospective Exhibition of Paintings, Watercolors, Drawings, and Gouaches by Andrée Ruellan. Mountainville, New York: Storm King Art Center, 1966.

Seiberling, Frank J. "Ruellan's Painting of Spring Scene Has Universal Appeal." Toledo Sunday Times, 30 June 1940.

The Springfield Museum of Fine Arts Handbook. Springfield, Massachusetts: Springfield Museum of Fine Arts, 1948.

Watson, Ernest W. "An Interview with Andrée Ruellan." American Artist 7, no. 8 (October 1943): 8-13, cover.

_____. Twenty Painters. New York: Watson-Guptill, 1950.

Zaidenberg, Arthur, compiled by. The Art of the Artist. New York: Crown, 1951: 115-17.

MARGARET RUFF (b. 1847; active to 1897)    Painter and Etcher

"Landscapes and Portraits; The Grand Spring Display at the Academy of Fine Arts." Philadelphia Inquirer, 10 March 1887.

Peet, Phyllis. American Women of the Etching Revival. Atlanta: High Museum of Art, 1988.

The Work of Women Etchers of America. New York: Union League Club, 1888.


ESTELLE RUMBOLD-KOHN (Early 20th Century)    Sculptor

American Art Annual, vol. 28. Washington, D.C.: American Federation of Arts, 1932.

Kohlman, Rena Tucker. "America's Women Sculptors." International Studio 76, no. 307 (December 1922): 225-35.

National Sculpture Society and California Palace of the Legion of Honor. Contemporary American Sculpture. New York, 1929: 183-84.


OLIVE RUSH (1873-1966)    Painter

Burnet, Mary Q. Art and Artists of Indiana. New York: Century Co., 1921.

The Phillips Collection, A Summary Catalogue. Washington, D.C.: The Phillips Collection, 1985.

Samuels, Peggy and Harold. The Illustrated Biographical Encyclopedia of Artists of the American West. Garden City, New York: Doubleday, 1976.

Who's Who in American Art, vol. 1. Washington, D.C.: American Federation of Arts, 1935.

Woman's Who's Who of America. New York: American Commonwealth Co., 1914.

Women Artists in the Howard Pyle Tradition. Chadds Ford, Pennsylvania: Brandywine River Museum, 1975.


CLARISSA RUSSELL (b. 1809)    Miniaturist

Groce, George C., and Wallace, David H. The New-York Historical Society's Dictionary of Artists in America, 1564-1860. New Haven: Yale University Press, 1957.

Jackson, Emily N. Ancestors in Silhouette, Cut by August Edouart .... London and New York, 1921: 220.

380

Perkins, Robert F., Jr., and Gavin, William J., III. The Boston
   Athenaeum Art Exhibition Index, 1827-1874. Boston: The
   Library of the Boston Athenaeum, 1980: 123.

Tufts, Eleanor. American Women Artists 1830-1930. Washington,
   D.C.: National Museum of Women in the Arts, 1987.


ANNE RYAN (1889-1954)    Painter

See volume 1 of this book.

Anne Ryan: Collages 1948-1954. New York: André Emmerich Gallery,
   1979.

Anne Ryan: Color Wood Blocks, 1945-1949. New York: Kraushaar
   Galleries, 1977.

Archives of American Art. Collection of Exhibition Catalogs.
   Boston: G.K. Hall and Co., 1979.

A Guide to the Collection. Houston: Museum of Fine Arts, 1981.


MARGERY AUSTIN RYERSON (1886-1989)    Painter

See volume 1 of this book.

"Hospital Portraits." Art News 44 (September 1945):  26.

Portraits by Distinguished American Artists. New York:  Grand
   Central Art Galleries, 1942:  73-74.

"Prints of Children." Art Digest 7, no. 19 (August 1933):  22.

Ryerson, Margery. "Sketching Faces from the TV Screen." American
   Artist 33, no. 6 (Summer 1969):  68-70.

"Sketches of the Wounded." Art Digest 19, no. 20 (15 September
   1945):  15.

Who's Who in American Art, vol. 1. Washington, D.C.:  American
   Federation of Arts, 1935:  366.


ALISON SAAR (1956-    )    Painter

Brown, Betty Ann. "Theatrical Imagery." Arts Magazine 57, no. 2
   (October 1982):  24-25.

Bushyeager, Peter. "Alison Saar." New Art Examiner 13 (March
   1986):  56-57.

Cohen, Ronny.  "Alison Saar."  <u>Artforum</u> 23, no. 3 (November 1984):
105.

Klein, Ellen Lee.  "Alison Saar."  <u>Arts Magazine</u> 60, no. 8 (April
1986):  132.

Kuspit, Donald.  "Alison Saar (Monique Knowlton Gallery)."
<u>Artforum</u> 24, no. 8 (April 1986):  111-12.

"Portrait of the Artist, 1987, Who Supports Him/Her."  <u>Artsreview</u>
4, no. 3 (Spring 1987):  28-29.


BETYE SAAR (1926-    )    Assemblage and Collage Artist

See volume 1 of this book.

<u>Dimensions of Black</u>.  La Jolla:  La Jolla Museum of Art, 1970.

Hopkins, Henry.  <u>50 West Coast Artists</u>.  San Francisco:  Chronicle
Books, 1976.

<u>The Negro in American Art</u>.  Los Angeles:  UCLA Art Galleries,
University of California, 1966.

Rosing, Larry.  "Betye Saar."  <u>Arts Magazine</u> 50, no. 10 (June
1976):  7.

Shepard, Ileen.  <u>Sculpture of the 80's</u>.  Essay by Lowery S. Sims.
Queens, New York:  Queens Museum, 1987.

<u>Sixteen Los Angeles Women Artists</u>.  Norwalk, California:  Cerritos
College, 1982.

Slatkin, Wendy.  <u>Women Artists in History from Antiquity to the
20th Century</u>.  Englewood Cliffs, New Jersey:  Prentice-Hall,
Inc., 1985.

Slivka, Rose.  "The Object as Poet."  <u>Craft Horizons</u> 37, no. 1
(February 1977):  26-29, 62-63.

<u>30 Contemporary Black Artists</u>.  Minneapolis:  Minneapolis Institute
of Arts, 1969.

<u>West Coast '74/The Black Image</u>.  Sacramento:  Crocker Art Gallery,
1974.


KAY SAGE (1898-1963)    Painter

See volume 1 of this book.

382

382

Archives of American Art. Collection of Exhibition Catalogs.
    Boston: G.K. Hall and Co., 1979.

Chadwick, Whitney. Women Artists and the Surrealist Movement.
    Boston: New York Graphic Society, 1985.

Fine, Elsa Honig. Women and Art. Montclair/London: Allanheld &
    Schram/Prior, 1978.

Heller, Nancy G. Women Artists. New York: Abbeville Press, 1987.

Miller, Stephen. "The Surrealist Imagery of Kay Sage." Art
    International 26, no. 4 (September-October 1983): 32-56.

Wechsler, Jeffrey. Surrealism and American Art 1931-1947. New
    Brunswick: Rutgers University, 1977.

Your Move: Kay Sage. New York: Catherine Viviano Gallery, 1961.


        HELEN GERTRUDE SAHLER (1877-1950)   Sculptor

American Art Annual, vol. 28. Washington, D.C.: American
    Federation of Arts, 1932.

Fielding, Mantle. Dictionary of American Painters, Sculptors and
    Engravers. Enlarged ed. Greens Farms, Connecticut: Modern
    Books, 1974.

National Sculpture Society. Contemporary American Sculpture. San
    Francisco: California Palace of the Legion of Honor, 1929:
    276.

Obituary. Art Digest 25, no. 6 (15 December 1950): 33.

Obituary. The New York Times, 4 December 1950: 29.

Who's Who in American Art, vol. 4. Washington, D.C.: American
    Federation of Arts, 1947.


        MOTHER ST. CROIX (1854-1940)   Photographer

See volume 1 of this book.

Browne, Turner, and Partnow, Elaine. Macmillan Biographical
    Encyclopedia of Photographic Artists and Innovators. New
    York: Macmillan, 1983.

ANNETTA JOHNSON SAINT-GAUDENS (1869-1943)    Sculptor

American Art Annual, vol. 28.  Washington, D.C.:  American
    Federation of Arts, 1932.

A Circle of Friends:  Art Colonies of Cornish and Dublin.  Durham,
    New Hampshire:  University Art Galleries, University of New
    Hampshire, 1985:  106-07.

Clark, Edna.  Ohio Art and Artists.  Richmond, Virginia:  Garrett
    and Massie, 1932.

Fielding, Mantle.  Dictionary of American Painters, Sculptors and
    Engravers.  Enlarged ed.  Greens Farms, Connecticut:  Modern
    Books and Crafts, 1974.

National Sculpture Society.  Contemporary American Sculpture.  New
    York, 1929:  276.

Obituary.  Who's Who in American Art, vol. 4.  Washington, D.C.:
    American Federation of Arts, 1947.

Woman's Who's Who of America.  New York:  American Commonwealth
    Co., 1914.


CARLOTA DOLLEY SAINT-GAUDENS (1884-1927)    Painter

A Circle of Friends:  Art Colonies of Cornish and Dublin.  Durham,
    New Hampshire:  University Art Galleries, University of New
    Hampshire, 1985.

Fielding, Mantle.  Dictionary of American Painters, Sculptors and
    Engravers.  Enlarged ed.  Greens Farms, Connecticut:  Modern
    Books and Crafts, 1974.

Fuller, Lucia Fairchild.  "Modern American Miniature Painters."
    Scribner's Magazine 67 (March 1920):  381-84.

Obituary.  American Art Annual, vol. 24.  Washington, D.C.:
    American Federation of Arts, 1927.


NIKI DE SAINT PHALLE (1930-    )    Sculptor

See volume 1 of this book.

Matsumoto, Michiko.  Portrait of Niki de Saint Phalle.  Tokyo:
    Parco Co., Ltd., 1986.

Picard, Denis.  "Sur la Colline Embellie."  Connaissance des Arts,
    no. 431 (January 1988):  78-81.

384

Schulz-Hoffmann, Carla, et al.  Niki de Saint Phalle.  Munich:
Prestel-Verlag, 1987.


MARTHA SALEMME (1912-    )   Painter

B[ruening], M[argaret].  Husband & Wife--The Salemmes."  Art Digest
24, no. 4 (15 November 1949):  20.

Gendel, Milton.  "The Salemmes [Van Diemen-Lilienfeld]."  Art News
48, no. 8 (December 1949):  57.

L[owengrund], M[argaret].  "A Family Trait."  Art Digest 23, no. 5
(1 December 1948):  18.

Martha Salemme:  Watercolors.  New York:  Van Diemen Galleries,
1948.

Who's Who in American Art, 17th ed.  New York:  R.R. Bowker Co.,
1986.


LUCY ELLEN SALLICK (1937-    )   Painter

See volume 1 of this book.

Henry, Gerrit.  "Lucy Sallick at G.W. Einsten."  Art in America 71,
no. 2 (February 1983):  131, 135.

Russell, John.  "Lucy Sallick."  The New York Times, 23 September
1977.

Who's Who in American Art, 17th ed.  New York:  R.R. Bowker Co.,
1986.


HELEN ARNSTEIN SALZ (1883-1978)   Painter

Exhibition of Oils, Watercolors, Pastels by Alexander Nepote, Rubin
and Helen Salz.  Paris:  Rotunda Gallery, March 5-29, n.d.
(ca. 1946).

Who's Who in American Art, vol. 3.  Washington, D.C.:  American
Federation of Arts, 1940.

A Woman's Vision:  California Painting Into the 20th Century.  San
Francisco:  Maxwell Galleries, 1983.


ANNA M. SANDS (1860-after 1927)   Painter

American Art Annual, vol. 1.  New York:  Macmillan Co., 1899.

Cosentino, Andrew J., and Glassie, Henry H. The Capital Image:
    Painters in Washington, 1800-1915. Washington, D.C.:
    National Museum of American Art, Smithsonian Institution,
    1983.


HÉLÈNE SARDEAU (1899-1969)  Sculptor

Archives of American Art. Collection of Exhibition Catalogs.
    Boston:  G.K. Hall and Co., 1979.

First Biennial Exhibition of Contemporary American Sculpture,
    Watercolors and Prints. New York:  Whitney Museum of American
    Art, 1933-34.

Gardner, Albert TenEyck. American Sculpture. A Catalogue of the
    Collection of the Metropolitan Museum of Art. New York:
    Metropolitan Museum of Art, 1965:  173.

Obituary. The New York Times, 25 March 1969:  47.

Who's Who in American Art, vol. 9. Washington, D.C.:  American
    Federation of Arts, 1966.


MARGARET SARGENT [McKEAN] (1892-1978)  Painter and Sculptor

American Art Annual, vol. 28. Washington, D.C.:  American
    Federation of Arts, 1932.

The Feminine Gaze:  Women Depicted by Women 1900-1930. New York:
    Whitney Museum of American Art, Fairfield County, 1984.

Moore, Honor.  "My Grandmother Who Painted." The Writer on Her
    Work. Ed. Janet Sternburg. New York:  W.W. Norton and Co.,
    1980.  [Excerpt in Radcliffe Quarterly (March 1981):  18-21.]


EMILY SARTAIN (1841-1927)  Painter and Engraver

See volume 1 of this book.

Catalogue of the Exhibits of the State of Pennsylvania and
    Pennsylvanians at The World's Columbia Exposition.
    [Harrisburg?]:  State Printer of Pennsylvania, 1893.

Clement, Clara Erskine. Women in the Fine Arts. Boston:  Houghton
    Mifflin Co., 1904.

Fielding, Mantle. Dictionary of American Painters, Sculptors and
    Engravers. Enlarged ed. Greens Farms, Connecticut:  Modern
    Book and Crafts, 1974.

386

Goodman, Helen. "Emily Sartain: Her Career." Arts Magazine 61, no. 9 (May 1987): 61-65.

Hanaford, Phebe A. Daughters of America. Augusta, Maine: True and Co., 1882: 292-295.

In This Academy. The Pennsylvania Academy of the Fine Arts, 1805-1976. Philadelphia: The Pennsylvania Academy of the Fine Arts, 1976: 165, 170, 177, and 304.

Knauff, Theodore C. An Experiment in Training for the Useful and the Beautiful, A History. Philadelphia: Philadelphia School of Design for Women, 1922: 85-88.

Woman's Who's Who of America. New York: American Commonwealth Co., 1914.


HARRIET SARTAIN (b. 1873)    Painter

American Art Annual, vol. 28. Washington, D.C.: American Federation of Arts, 1932.

Fielding, Mantle. Dictionary of American Painters, Sculptors and Engravers. Enlarged ed. Greens Farms, Connecticut: Modern Books and Crafts, 1974.

Knauff, Theodore C. An Experiment in Training for the Useful and the Beautiful, A History. Philadelphia: Philadelphia School of Design for Women, 1922: 88-91.

Logan, Mary S. The Part Taken by Women in American History. New York: Arno Press reprint of 1912 book, 1972: 757.

Woman's Who's Who of America. New York: American Commonwealth Co., 1914.


JANE SAUER (1937-    )    Fiber Sculptor

Degener, Patricia. "Emotive Basketry." American Craft 46, no. 4 (August/September 1986): 42-47, 59.

Falconer, C.M. "The Knotted Sculpture of Jane Sauer." Fiberarts 13 (May-June 1986): 31-33, cover.

Malarcher, Patricia. "What Makes a Basket a Basket." Fiberarts 11 (January-February 1984): 38-39.

"Portfolio." American Craft 42, no. 1 (February-March 1982): 41.

Rice, Nancy N. "Jane Sauer." New Art Examiner 14, no. 1
    (September 1986): 60.


                HATTIE SAUSSY (1890-1978)   Painter

Chambers, Bruce W. Art and Artists of the South. Columbia, South
    Carolina: University of South Carolina Press, 1984.

Rush, Thetis B. Hattie Saussy, Georgia Painter. Spartanburg,
    South Carolina: Robert M. Hicklin, Jr., 1983.


            AUGUSTA CHRISTINE SAVAGE (1892-1962)   Sculptor

See volume 1 of this book.

Driskell, David C. Hidden Heritage: Afro-American Art, 1800-1950.
    Bellevue, Washington: Bellevue Art Museum, and San Francisco:
    The Art Museum Association of America, 1985.

Harlem Renaissance: Art of Black America. Intro. by Mary Schmidt
    Campbell. New York: The Studio Museum in Harlem and Harry N.
    Abrams, Inc., 1987.

Obituary. The New York Times, 27 March 1962.

Who's Who in American Art, vol. 1. Washington, D.C.: American
    Federation of Arts, 1935.


        HELEN ALTON SAWYER [FARNSWORTH] (1900-    )   Painter

American Art Annual, vol. 28. Washington, D.C.: American
    Federation of Arts, 1932.

Exhibition of Paintings by Wells M. Sawyer and Helen Alton Sawyer.
    New York: Babcock Galleries, 1921.

Watson, Ernest W. Twenty Painters. New York: Watson-Guptill,
    1950.


            LUCY WAY SISTARE SAY (1801-1886)   Illustrator

Burnet, Mary Q. Art and Artists of Indiana. New York: Century
    Co., 1921.

Groce, George C., and Wallace, David H. The New-York Historical
    Society's Dictionary of Artists in America 1564-1860. New
    Haven: Yale University Press, 1957.

388

Peat, Wilbur D. Pioneer Painters of Indiana. Chicago: Lakeside Press, 1954.


CONCETTA SCARAVAGLIONE (1900-1975)    Sculptor

See volume 1 of this book.

First Biennial Exhibition of Contemporary American Sculptors, Watercolors and Prints. New York: Whitney Museum of American Art, 1933.

Painters and Sculptors of Modern America. Autobiographical essays. Intro. by Monroe Wheeler. New York: Thomas Y. Crowell Co., 1942.

Park, Marlene, and Markowitz, Gerald E. Democratic Vistas:  Post Offices and Public Art in the New Deal. Philadelphia:  Temple University Press, 1984.

Wolf, Amy J. New York Society of Women Artists 1925. New York: ACA Galleries, 1987.


MIRIAM SCHAPIRO (1923-    )    Painter

See volume 1 of this book.

Daniels, Pamela, and Ruddick, Sara, eds. Working It Out. New York:  Pantheon, 1977.

Gill, Susan. "From 'Femmage' to Figuration." Art News 85, no. 4 (April 1986):  94-101.

Gouma-Peterson, Thalia. "The Theater of Life and Illusion in Miriam Schapiro's Recent Work." Arts Magazine 60, no. 7 (March 1986):  38-43, cover.

Heartney, Eleanor. "Miriam Schapiro at Bernice Steinbaum." Art in America 74, no. 7 (July 1986):  118-19.

Heller, Nancy G. Women Artists. New York:  Abbeville, 1987.

Henning, William T., Jr. A Catalogue of the American Collection, Hunter Museum of Art. Chattanooga, Tennessee:  Hunter Museum of Art, 1985:  259-60.

I'm Dancin' As Fast As I Can:  New Paintings by Miriam Schapiro. New York:  Bernice Steinbaum Gallery, 1986.

Loeb, Judy, ed. Feminist Collage:  Educating Women in the Visual Arts. New York:  Teachers College Press, Columbia University, 1979.

Lyons, Harriet. "The Art Biz." Ms., November 1985: 69-74, 108.

Miriam Schapiro: Femmages, 1971-1985. Saint Louis, Missouri: Brentwood Gallery, 1985.

Raven, Arlene. Crossing Over: Feminism and Art of Social Concern. Ann Arbor: U.M.I. Press, 1988.

Russell, John. "Miriam Schapiro (Bernice Steinbaum Gallery)." The New York Times, 1 April 1988: 22Y.

Sixteen Los Angeles Women Artists. Norwalk, California: Cerritos College, 1982.

Women's Caucus for Art Honor Awards. Houston: National Women's Caucus for Art, 1988.

Wortz, Melinda. "The New Woman's Royal Robes." Art News 82, no. 9 (November 1983): 131.

S. GERTRUDE SCHELL (1891-1970)    Painter

An Exhibition of Paintings by Susan Gertrude Schell. Philadelphia: Woodmere Art Gallery, 1962.

A Memorial Exhibition of Drawings by S. Gertrude Schell, 1891-1970. Philadelphia: Woodmere Art Gallery, 1972.

Who's Who in American Art, vol. 8. Washington, D.C.: American Federation of Arts, 1962.

ALICE SCHILLE (1869-1955)    Painter

See volume 1 of this book.

Alice Schille, A.W.S., 1869-1955: Watercolors. Boston: Vose Galleries, 1982.

Alice Schille Watercolors. Columbus, Ohio: Keny and Johnson Gallery, 1987.

American Art Annual, vol. 28. Washington, D.C.: American Federation of Arts, 1932.

Clark, Edna Maria. Ohio Art and Artists. Richmond, Virginia: Garrett and Massie, 1932.

Fortieth Annual Exhibition. New York: National Association of Women Painters and Sculptors, 1931.

390

Hammond, Lynn B. "Alice Schille--Everybody's Artist." The
    Columbus Dispatch Magazine, 29 March 1964.

Huber, Christine Jones. The Pennsylvania Academy and Its Women.
    Philadelphia: The Pennsylvania Academy of Fine Arts, 1974.

Obituary. Who's Who in American Art, vol. 6. Washington, D.C.:
    American Federation of Arts, 1956.

Owings, Edna. "The Art of Alice Schille." International Studio 50
    (August 1913): 31-33.

Portraits and Watercolors by Alice Schille. Columbus: Columbus
    Gallery of Fine Arts, 1931.

Trask, John E.D., and Laurvik, John Nilsen. Catalogue de Luxe of
    the Department of Fine Arts. San Francisco: Panama-Pacific
    International Exposition, 2 vols., 1915.

Tufts, Eleanor. American Women Artists 1830-1930. Washington,
    D.C.: National Museum of Women in the Arts, 1987.

Wells, Gary. "Alice Schille: Painters from the Midwest." Arts
    and Antiques 6 (September-October 1983): 64-71.


        MATHILDE GEORGINE SCHLEY (1864-1941)    Painter

American Art Annual, vol. 28. Washington, D.C.: American
    Federation of Arts, 1932.

Fielding, Mantle. Dictionary of American Painters, Sculptors and
    Engravers. Enlarged ed. Greens Farms, Connecticut: Modern
    Books and Crafts, 1974.

Who's Who in American Art, vol. 1. Washington, D.C.: American
    Federation of Arts, 1935.


        KATHERINE SCHMIDT [SHUBERT] (1898-1978)    Painter

See volume 1 of this book.

Baigell, Matthew, and Williams, Julia, eds. Artists Against War
    and Fascism, Papers of the First American Artists' Congress.
    New Brunswick, New Jersey: Rutgers University Press, 1986.

Goodrich, Lloyd and Sims, Patterson. The Katherine Schmidt Shubert
    Bequest & A Selective View of Her Art. New York: Whitney
    Museum of American Art, 1982.

Mecklenburg, Virginia M. <u>Modern American Realism:  The Sara Roby Foundation Collection</u>.  Washington, D.C.:  National Museum of American Art, 1987.

<u>The Neglected Generation of American Realist Painters:  1930-1948</u>. Wichita, Kansas:  Wichita Art Museum, 1981.

<u>Second Biennial Exhibition of Contemporary American Painting</u>.  New York:  Whitney Museum of American Art, 1934:  no. 110.

<u>Women Pioneers in Maine Art 1900-1945</u>.  Portland, Maine:  Joan Whitney Payson Gallery of Art, Westbrook College, 1985.

URSULA SCHNEIDER (1943-    )    Painter

French, Christopher.  "Pleasant Memories, Troubled Memories." <u>Artweek</u> 15, no. 44 (22 December 1984):  4.

Goldberg, Beth.  "Light in a Dark Time." <u>Artweek</u> 17, no. 31 (27 September 1986):  3.

<u>Ursula Schneider</u>.  Los Angeles:  California State University Fine Arts Gallery, 1979.

FLORA SCHOENFELD (1873-1960)   Painter

<u>American Art Annual</u>, vol. 28.  Washington, D.C.:  American Federation of Arts, 1932 (under "Schofield").

Fielding, Mantle.  <u>Dictionary of American Painters, Sculptors and Engravers</u>.  Enlarged ed.  Greens Farms, Connecticut:  Modern Books and Crafts, 1974.

Flint, Janet Altic.  <u>Provincetown Printers:  A Woodcut Tradition</u>. Washington, D.C.:  National Museum of American Art, 1983.

<u>Who's Who in American Art</u>, vol. 1.  Washington, D.C.:  American Federation of Arts, 1935.

Wolf, Amy J.  <u>New York Society of Women Artists 1925</u>.  New York: ACA Galleries, 1987.

BELLE KINNEY SCHOLZ (b. 1887)   Sculptor

See volume 1 of this book.

Burnet, Mary Q.  <u>Art and Artists of Indiana</u>.  New York:  Century Co., 1921:  421.

Who's Who in American Art, vol. 3. Washington, D.C.: American
    Federation of Arts, 1940.


CAROLEE SCHNEEMAN (1939-    )  Filmmaker and Performance Artist

See volume 1 of this book.

Kunst mit Eigen-Sinn. Aktuelle Kunst von Frauen. Vienna and
    Munich: Löcher Verlag, 1985.

Tuchman, Maurice, and Freeman, Judy. The Spiritual in Art:
    Abstract Painting 1890-1985. Los Angeles: Los Angeles County
    Museum of Art, 1986.

Who's Who in American Art, 17th ed. New York: R.R. Bowker Co.,
    1986.


            GRETE SCHULLER (1899 or 1900-1984)   Sculptor


Grete Schuller. New York: Sculpture Center, 1958.

Obituary. The New York Times, 18 June 1984.

Who's Who in American Art, vol. 14. Washington, D.C.:   American
    Federation of Arts, 1980.


            DONNA NORINE SCHUSTER (1883-1953)   Painter

American Art Annual, vol. 28. Washington, D.C.: American
    Federation of Arts, 1932.

Donna Norine Schuster (1883-1953). Downey, California: Downey
    Museum of Art, 1977.

Fielding, Mantle. Dictionary of American Painters, Sculptors and
    Engravers. Enlarged ed. Greens Farms, Connecticut: Modern
    Books and Crafts, 1974.

Gerdts, William H. American Impressionism. New York: Abbeville
    Press, 1984.

Impressionism, The California View, Painting 1890-1930. Oakland:
    The Oakland Museum, 1981.

393

Porter, Bruce, et al.  Art in California:  A Survey of American
    Art with Special Reference to California Painting, Sculpture
    and Architecture, Past and Present, Particularly as those
    Arts were Represented at the Panama-Pacific International
    Exposition.  San Francisco:  R.L. Bernier, 1916.

A Woman's Vision:  California Painting into the 20th Century.  San
    Francisco:  Maxwell Galleries, 1983.

Westphal, Ruth Lilly.  Plein Air Painters of California, The
    Southland.  Irvine, California:  Westphal, 1983.

Who's Who in American Art, vol. 1.  Washington, D.C.:  American
    Federation of Arts, 1935.


                ETHEL SCHWABACHER (1903-1984)    Painter

See volume 1 of this book.

Bass, Ruth.  "Ethel Schwabacher."  Art News 86, no. 10 (December
    1987):  162.

Berman, Greta, and Hadler, Mona.  Ethel Schwabacher.  New
    Brunswick, New Jersey:  Jane Voorhees Zimmerli Art Museum,
    Rutgers University, 1987.

Ethel Schwabacher:  Pastels and Oils.  New York:  Georgette
    Passedoit Gallery, 1947.

Nature in Abstraction.  New York:  Whitney Museum of American Art,
    1958.

1947 Annual Exhibition.  New York:  Whitney Museum of American Art,
    1947.

1949 Annual Exhibition.  New York:  Whitney Museum of American Art,
    1949.

1951 Annual Exhibition.  New York:  Whitney Museum of American Art,
    1951.

1952 Annual Exhibition.  New York:  Whitney Museum of American Art,
    1952.

1955 Annual Exhibition.  New York:  Whitney Museum of American Art,
    1955.

394

1956 Annual Exhibition. New York: Whitney Museum of American Art, 1956.

1957 Annual Exhibition. New York: Whitney Museum of American Art, 1957.

1958 Annual Exhibition. New York: Whitney Museum of American Art, 1958.

1961 Annual Exhibition. New York: Whitney Museum of American Art, 1961.

1963 Annual Exhibition. New York: Whitney Museum of American Art, 1963.

Schlossman, Jenni L. "Ethel Schwabacher: A Retrospective, 1945-1980." Women Artists News 13, no. 1 (Spring 1988): 16.

Schwabacher: Paintings and Glass Collages, 1951-1953. Foreword by Lloyd Goodrich. New York: Betty Parsons Gallery, 1953.

Twenty-Sixth Biennial Exhibition of Contemporary American Painting. Washington, D.C.: Corcoran Gallery of Art, 1959.

SUSAN SCHWALB (1944-    )    Silverpoint Artist

See volume 1 of this book.

Faxon, Alicia, and Moore, Sylvia. Pilgrims & Pioneers: New England Women in the Arts. New York: Midmarch Arts Press, 1987: 140-41.

Marter, Joan. "Women Artists." Arts Magazine 52, no. 6 (February 1978): 23.

Schwalb, Susan. "When a New York Artist Moves to Boston." Women Artists News 2, no. 1 (February-March 1987): 7.

Weber, Bruce. The Fine Line: Drawing with Silver in America. West Palm Beach: Norton Gallery of Art, 1985.

Who's Who in American Art, 17th ed. New York: R.R. Bowker, 1986.

BARBARA SCHWARTZ (1948-    )    Sculptor

See volume 1 of this book.

Campbell, Lawrence. "Barbara Schwartz." Art in America 72, no. 3 (March 1984): 161.

Gill, Susan. "Barbara Schwartz (Hirschl and Adler Modern)."
    Art News 86, no. 4 (April 1987): 169-71.

"Kips Bay '84." Interior Design 55 (September 1984): 236-37.

Phillips, Deborah C. "Barbara Schwartz." Art News 80, no. 10
    (December 1981): 176.

"Re-evaluated Art Currency: Barbara Schwartz, ASID, Replaces
    Famous Artists' Works with an Ephemeral Art Environment."
    Interior Design 51 (October 1980): 292-93.

Silverthorne, Jeanne. "Barbara Schwartz." Artforum 20, no. 5
    (January 1982): 76.

_____. "Barbara Schwartz." Artforum 22, no. 7 (March 1984): 94.

Skoggard, Ross. "Barbara Schwartz at Willard." Art in America 69,
    no. 10 (December 1981): 144, 146.

Zabel, Barbara. "Barbara Schwartz." Arts Magazine 58, no. 4
    (December 1983): 3.

THERESE SCHWARTZ (1928-    )    Painter

See volume 1 of this book.

Brumer, Miriam. "Therese Schwartz." Arts Magazine 44, no. 1
    (September-October 1969): 59.

Heartney, Eleanor. "Theresa [sic] Schwartz at Humphrey Fine Art."
    Art in America 75, no. 10 (October 1987): 182-83.

Knaus, David. "Therese Schwartz: Taking the Square." Helicon
    Nine, no. 8 (1983).

Who's Who in American Art, 17th ed. New York: R.R. Bowker Co.,
    1986.

EDITH A. SCOTT (1877-1978)    Painter

Fairbrother, Trevor J. The Bostonians, Painters of an Elegant Age
    (1870-1930). Boston: Museum of Fine Arts, 1986, no. 76 and
    colorplate: 163.

National Portrait Gallery. Permanent Collection, Illustrated
    Checklist. Washington, D.C.: Smithsonian Institution Press,
    1982.

JANET SCUDDER (1873-1940)    Sculptor

American Art Annual, vol. 28.  Washington, D.C.:  American
    Federation of Arts, 1932.

Burnet, Mary Q.  Art and Artists of Indiana.  New York:  Century
    Co., 1921.

Conner, Janis C.  "American Women Sculptors Break the Mold."  Art
    and Antiques 3 (May-June 1980):  80-87.

Fielding, Mantle.  Dictionary of American Painters, Sculptors and
    Engravers.  Enlarged ed.  Greens Farms, Connecticut:  Modern
    Books and Crafts, 1974.

Glueck, Grace.  "Garden Bronze of Past in Show."  The New York
    Times, 16 May 1985:  Y15, 18.

Morton, Brian N.  Americans in Paris, An Anectodal Street Guide.
    Ann Arbor, Michigan:  Olivia and Hill Press, 1984.

National Sculpture Society.  Contemporary American Sculpture.  San
    Francisco:  California Palace of the Legion of Honor, 1929.

Obituary.  Art Digest 14, no. 18 (1 July 1940):  24.

Obituary.  The New York Times, 11 June 1940:  25.

Proske, Beatrice Gilman.  Brookgreen Gardens Sculpture, vol. II.
    Brookgreen, South Carolina:  Brookgreen Gardens, 1955:
    144-45.

Tufts, Eleanor.  American Women Artists 1830-1930.  Washington,
    D.C.:  National Museum of Women in the Arts, 1987.

Van Wagner, Judy Collischan.  Long Island Estate Gardens.
    Greenvale, New York:  Hillwood Art Gallery, Long Island
    University, C.W. Post Campus, 1985.

Woman's Who's Who of America.  New York:  American Commonwealth
    Co., 1914.


HELEN SEARLE (1830-1884)    Painter

See Helen Searle Pattison.


SARAH CHOATE SEARS (1858-1935)    Painter

American Art Annual, vol. 28.  Washington, D.C.:  American
    Federation of Arts, 1932.

Clement, Clara Erskine. Women in the Fine Arts. Boston: Houghton Mifflin Co., 1904.

Elliott, Maud Howe, ed. Art and Handicraft in the Woman's Building of the World's Columbian Exposition, 1893. Chicago: Rand, McNally and Co., 1894: 58.

Naef, Weston J. The Collection of Alfred Stieglitz. New York: Viking Press, 1978.

Obituary. Who's Who in American Art, vol. 1. Washington, D.C.: American Federation of Arts, 1935.

Obituary. The New York Times, 28 September 1935.

Pierce, Patricia Jobe. Edmund C. Tarbell and the Boston School of Painting, 1889-1980. Hingham, Massachusetts: Pierce Galleries, 1980.

Woman's Who's Who of America. New York: American Commonwealth Co., 1914.

DIXIE SELDEN (1870-1935)   Painter

American Art Annual, vol. 28. Washington, D.C.: American Federation of Arts, 1932.

Clark, Edna. Ohio Art and Artists. Richmond, Virginia: Garrett and Massie, 1932.

Fielding, Mantle. Dictionary of American Painters, Sculptors and Engravers. Enlarged ed. Greens Farms, Connecticut: Modern Books and Crafts, 1974.

First Exhibition of Original Paintings Held Under the Auspices of the Young Women's Christian Association. Dallas, Texas: Y.W.C.A., 1924.

Obituary. Who's Who in American Art, vol. 2. Washington, D.C.: American Federation of Arts, 1937.

JOAN SEMMEL (1932-   )   Painter

See volume 1 of this book.

Henry, Gerrit. "Joan Semmel at 112 Green Street." Art in America 72, no. 10 (November 1984): 158, 159.

Marter, Joan. "Joan Semmel's Portrait: Personal Confrontations." Arts Magazine 58, no. 9 (May 1984): 104-06.

Westfall, Stephen. "Joan Semmel at Gruenebaum." Art in America
    76, no. 1 (January 1988): 137-38.

"The Women's Movement in Art, 1986." Arts Magazine 61, no. 1
    (September 1986): 54-57.


            SUSAN WATKINS SERPELL (1875-1913)   Painter

"Art Today and Yesterday, Dealer's Choice:  Underrated Artists."
    Art Today, Winter 1987-88:  49.

Clark, Eliot.  History of the National Academy of Design, 1825-1953.
    New York:  Columbia University Press, 1954.

Fielding, Mantle.  Dictionary of American Painters, Sculptors and
    Engravers.  Enlarged ed.  Greens Farms, Connecticut:  Modern
    Books and Crafts, 1974.

Woman's Who's Who of America.  New York:  American Commonwealth
    Co., 1914.


        (LYDIA) AMANDA BREWSTER SEWELL (1859-1926)   Painter

See volume 1 of this book.

Obituary.  American Art Annual, vol. 26.  Washington, D.C.:
    American Federation of Arts, 1929.

Rubinstein, Charlotte Striefer.  American Women Artists.  Boston:
    G.K. Hall and Co., 1982.


            DIANA SHAFFER (1951-    )   Sculptor

Cranbrook USA.  Bloomfield Hills, Michigan:  Cranbrook Academy of
    Art Museum, 1982.

Fifth Texas Sculpture Symposium.  Dallas:  Connemara Conservancy,
    1985.

Shaffer, Diana.  "Three Environmental Sculptures."  Leonardo 10;
    no. 3 (October 1977):  223-24.

Watson-Jones, Virginia.  Contemporary American Women Sculptors.
    Phoenix:  Oryx Press, 1986.


            MARY SHAFFER (1943-    )   Sculptor

Ballerini, Julia.  "Mary Shaffer's Glass."  Craft Horizons 34, no.
    1 (February 1979):  24-27.

Diamonstein, Barbaralee. Handmade in America: Conversations with Fourteen Craftmasters. New York: Harry N. Abrams, Inc., 1983.

Glass in the Modern World. Kyoto: National Museum of Modern Art, 1981.

Glass Roots. Lincoln, Massachusetts: DeCordova and Dana Museum, 1981.

Hunter-Stiebel, Penelope. "Contemporary Art Glass: An Old Medium Gets a New Look." Art News 80, no. 6 (Summer 1981): 130-35.

Kingsley, April. "Six Women at Work in the Landscape." Arts Magazine 52, no. 8 (April 1978): 108-12.

Robbins, Christine. "Sculptural Glass." American Craft 43, no. 4 (April-September 1983): 5-10.

Sculptural Glass. Tucson: Tucson Museum of Art, 1983.

Sculptures et Volumes de Verre. Annecy: Musée Château d'Annecy, and Tours: Galerie des Tanneurs, 1979.

Watson-Jones, Virginia. Contemporary American Women Sculptors. Phoenix: Oryx Press, 1986.

BERNARDA BRYSON SHAHN (1903- ) Painter

Barnett, Catherine. "The Writing on the Wall." Art and Antiques (March 1988): 90-99.

Bass, Ruth. "Bernarda Bryson Shahn." Arts Magazine 58, no. 4 (December 1983): 16.

Bernarda Bryson Shahn: The Continuing Creative Journey. New Brunswick, New Jersey: Mabel Smith Douglass Library, Douglass College, 1987.

First Detroit Exhibition of Selected Drawings by Bernarda Bryson. Detroit: Arwin Galleries, 1966.

Klemin, Diana. The Art of Art for Children's Books. New York: Clarkson N. Potter, 1966.

Loughery, John. "Three Figurative Artists." Arts Magazine 60, no. 7 (March 1986): 133.

Painting America. Mural Art in the New Deal Era. Essay by Janet Marqusee. New York: Midtown Galleries, 1988.

Rubin, Edward. "Bernarda Bryson Shahn." Art News 83, no. 1 (January 1984): 154.

ELLEN WALLACE SHARPLES (1769-1849)    Painter

See volume 1 of this book.

Bolton, Theodore. Early American Portrait Painters in Miniature.
New York:  F.F. Sherman, 1921.

Fielding, Mantle. Dictionary of American Painters, Sculptors and
Engravers. Enlarged ed. Greens Farms, Connecticut:  Modern
Books and Crafts, 1974.

Gahhart, Ann, and Broun, Elizabeth. "Old Mistresses, Women Artists
of the Past." Walters Art Gallery Bulletin 24 (April 1972).

Wilson, Arnold. "The Sharples Family of Painters." Antiques 100
(November 1971):  740-43.


ROLINDA SHARPLES (1793-1838)    Painter

See volume 1 of this book.

Heller, Nancy G. Women Artists. New York:  Abbeville, 1987.

Wilson, Arnold. "The Sharples Family of Painters." Antiques 100
(November 1971):  740-43.


HONORÉ SHARRER (1920-    )    Painter

See volume 1 of this book.

Baur, John. Revolution and Tradition in Modern American Art.
Cambridge:  Harvard University Press, 1951.

Fourteen Americans. Edited by Dorothy C. Miller. New York:
The Museum of Modern Art, 1946.

Gerdts, Abigail Booth, and Hills, Patricia. The Working American.
Washington, D.C.:  Smithsonian Institution, 1979.

Loucheim, Aline. "The Favored Few." Art News 45 (September 1946):
16.

Mecklenburg, Virginia. Modern American Realism:  Sara Roby
Foundation Collection. Washington, D.C.:  National Museum of
American Art, 1987.

Nadelman, Cynthia. "Honoré Sharrer." Art News 80, no. 9 (November
1981):  202, 206.

The New Decade. New York:  Whitney Museum of American Art, 1955.

WCA Honor Awards.  Boston, Massachusetts:  National Women's Caucus
     for Art, 1987.


                YOLANDA SHASHATY (20th Century)    Painter

Cohen, Ronny.  "Yolanda Shashaty."  Artforum 25, no. 2 (October
     1986):  131-32.

Grimes, Nancy.  "Yolanda Shashaty (at Sragow)."  Art News 87, no. 3
     (March 1988):  207, 210.

Potter, Everett.  "Yolanda Shashaty."  Arts Magazine 62, no. 5
     (January 1988):  94.


                SUSAN SHATTER (1943-    )   Painter

Cecil, Sarah.  "Susan Shatter."  Art News 83, no. 3 (March 1984):
     85-86.

Doherty, M. Stephen.  "Watercolor Today:  Ten Contemporary
     Artists."  American Artist 47 (February 1983):  84.

Field, Richard S., and Fine, Ruth E.  A Graphic Muse.  New York:
     Hudson Hills Press, 1987.

Henry, Gerrit.  "Susan Shatter's at Fishbach."  Art in America 75,
     no. 6 (June 1987):  155-57.

Kuspit, Donald B.  "Susan Shatter at Fischbach."  Art in America
     70, no. 9 (October 1982):  135.


                ANNIE CORNELIA SHAW (1852-1887)   Painter

Clement, Clara Erskine.  Women in the Fine Arts.  Boston:  Houghton
     Mifflin Co., 1904.

Fielding, Mantle.  Dictionary of American Painters, Sculptors and
     Engravers.  Enlarged ed.  Greens Farms, Connecticut:  Modern
     Books and Crafts, 1974.

Harding, Jonathan P.  The Boston Athenaeum Collection Pre-Twentieth
     Century American and European Painting and Sculpture.  Boston:
     The Boston Athenaeum, 1984.

Logan, Mary S.  The Part Taken by Women in American History.  New
     York:  Arno Press, reprint, 1972:  757.

Peet, Phyllis.  American Women of the Etching Revival.  Atlanta:
     High Museum of Art, 1988.

402

Special Exhibition and Sale of Works of Annie C. Shaw. Chicago:
    Art Institute of Chicago, 1887.

Willard, Frances E., and Livermore, Mary A., eds. American Women.
    Detroit: Gale Reprint, 1973.

The Work of Women Etchers of America. New York: Union League
    Club, 1888.


                    JUDITH SHEA (1948-    )  Sculptor

Artpark. Lewiston, New York: Artpark, 1974.

Cohen, Ronny. "Judith Shea." Artforum 23, no. 5 (February 1985):
    84-85.

Gill, Susan. "Judith Shea." Art News 86, no. 1 (January 1987):
    161.

Princenthal, Nancy. "Judith Shea." Art News 84, no. 2 (February
    1985): 141, 143.

Saunders, Wade. "Sculptors' Interview." Art in America 73, no. 11
    (November 1985): 134-35.

Van Wagner, Judy Collischan. "Judith Shea: A Personal Balance."
    Arts Magazine 61, no. 5 (January 1987): 76-77.

Westfall, Stephen. "Judith Shea at Willard." Art in America 73,
    no. 3 (March 1985): 158.


                    LAURA SHECHTER (1944-    )  Painter

See volume 1 of this book.

Fleminger, Susan. "Subtleties and Strengths: New Paintings by
    Laura Shechter." Arts Magazine 60, no. 2 (October 1985):
    48-49.

Weber, Bruce. The Fine Line: Drawing with Silver in America.
    West Palm Beach, Florida: Norton Gallery and School of Art,
    1985.


                    MARY GIVEN SHEERER (1865-1954)  Ceramicist

Clark, Garth. A Century of Ceramics in the United States
    1878-1978. New York: E.P. Dutton, 1979.

Henzke, Lucile. American Art Pottery. Camden, New Jersey: Nelson, 1970.

Keen, Kirsten Hoving. American Art Pottery 1875-1930. Wilmington, Delaware: Delaware Art Museum, 1978.

Kovel, Ralph, and Kovel, Terry. Kovel's Collector's Guide to American Art Pottery. New York: Crown, 1974.

Ormand, Suzanne, and Irvine, Mary E. Louisiana's Art Nouveau: The Crafts of the Newcomb Style. Gretna, Louisiana: Pelican Publishing, 1976.

Sheerer, Mary G. "The Development of the Decorative Processes at Newcomb." American Ceramic Society Journal 1 (August 1918).

_____. "Newcomb Pottery." Keramik Studio 1 (1899).

_____, and Cox, Paul E. "Newcomb Pottery." American Ceramic Society 1 (August 1918).

NAN JANE SHEETS (1885-    )   Painter

American Art Annual, vol. 28. Washington, D.C.: American Federation of Arts, 1932.

Dawdy, Doris Ostrander. Artists of the American West, vol. 1. Chicago: Swallow Press, 1974.

Kovinick, Phil. The Woman Artist in the American West 1860-1960. Fullerton, California: Muckenthaler Cultural Center, 1976: 50.

Samuels, Peggy, and Harold. The Illustrated Biographical Encyclopedia of Artists of the American West. Garden City, New York: Doubleday, 1976.

Who's Who in American Art, vol. 10. Washington, D.C.: American Federation of Arts, 1970.

CINDY SHERMAN (1954-    )   Photographer

Brenson, Michael. "Art: Whitney Shows Cindy Sherman Photos." The New York Times, 24 July 1987.

Cathcart, Linda L. Cindy Sherman: Photographs. Houston: Contemporary Arts Museum, 1980.

Cindy Sherman. Amsterdam: Stedelijk Museum, 1982.

404

Cindy Sherman. New York: Pantheon Books, 1984.

Cindy Sherman. Essays by Peter Schjeldahl and Lisa Phillips. New York: Whitney Museum of American Art, 1987.

Frascella, Larry. "Cindy Sherman's Tales of Terror." Aperture 103 (Summer 1986): 48-53.

Gambrell, Jamey. "Cindy Sherman, Metro Pictures." Artforum 20, no. 6 (February 1982): 85-86.

Grundberg, Andy. "Cindy Sherman: A Playful and Political Post Modernist." The New York Times, 22 November 1981.

_____. "The 80's Seen Through a Postmodern Lens." The New York Times, 5 July 1987: Arts and Leisure Section: 25, 29.

Haus, Mary Ellen. "Cindy Sherman, Metro Pictures. Whitney Museum of American Art." Art News 86, no. 8 (October 1987): 167-68.

Hoy, Anne H. Fabrications: Staged, Altered, and Appropriated Photographs. New York: Abbeville Press, 1987.

Iversen, Margaret. "Fashioning Feminine Identity." Art International 31, no. 2 (Spring 1988): 52-57.

Johnson, Ken. "Cindy Sherman and the Anti-Self: An Interpretation of Her Imagery." Arts Magazine 62, no. 3 (November 1987): 47-53.

Kunst mit Eigen-Sinn. Aktuelle Kunst von Frauen. Vienna and Munich: Löcher Verlag, 1985.

Liebman, Lisa. "Cindy Sherman." Artforum 22, no. 7 (March 1984): 95.

Marzorati, Gerald. "Imitation of Life." Art News 82, no. 7 (September 1983): 78-87, cover.

Melville, Stephen W. "The Time of Exposure: Allegorical Self-Portraiture in Cindy Sherman." Arts Magazine 60, no. 5 (January 1986): 17-21.

Morris, Diana. "Cindy Sherman." Women Artists News 10, no. 1 (Fall 1984): 18-19.

1983 Whitney Biennial. New York: Whitney Museum of American Art, 1983.

Perl, Jed. "Starring Cindy Sherman: Notes on the New Art World." The New Criterion, January 1986: 14-25.

Schjeldahl, Peter.  "Shermanettes."  Art in America 70, no. 3
     (March 1982):  110-11.

Self-Portraits by Women Artists.  Los Angeles:  Gallery at the
     Plaza, Security Pacific National Bank, 1985.

Sturken, Marita.  "A Whitney Sampler."  Afterimage 11, no. 3
     (October 1983):  18.

Tillim, Sidney.  "Cindy Sherman at Metro Pictures and the Whitney
     Museum."  Art in America 75, no. 12 (December 1987):  162-63.

Vitale, Robert.  "Cindy Sherman."  New Art Examiner 14, no. 11
     (Summer 1987):  53.


          SARAI SHERMAN (1922-    )    Painter and Sculptor

Apuleo, Vito.  "Sarai Sherman a La Nuova Pesa."  La Voce
     Republicana, 29 March 1961.

_____.  "La Voce di Sarai Sherman."  La Voce Republicana, 1 June
     1966.

Balestrieri, Elio.  "La Finestra dell-arte."  Il Secolo XIX, 2 July
     1963.

Barr, Alfred, Jr.  "Painting and Sculpture Acquisitions."  Museum
     of Modern Art Bulletin 28, nos. 2-4 (1960).

Breuning, Margaret.  "Sarai Sherman."  Art Digest 25, no. 13 (1
     April 1951):  19.

Burrows, Carlyle.  "More Good Solo Shows."  New York Herald
     Tribune, 21 February 1960.

The Changing Landscapes of the Italian South:  Human Landscapes,
     Urban and Rural.  Philadelphia:  Fleisher Art Memorial, 1983.

Contemporary American Painting and Sculpture.  Champaign:  Krannert
     Art Museum, University of Illinois, 1961.

De Santis, Giacomo.  "La Pittrice, Sherman."  Il Giornale di Lecco,
     18 March 1963.

Devree, Howard.  "Sarai Sherman."  The New York Times, 2 February
     1955.

Genauer, Emily.  "Sherman at the ACA."  New York Herald Tribune, 4
     February 1955.

406

Goodrich, Lloyd, and Bryant, Edward. Forty Artists Under Forty
from the Collections of the Whitney Museum of American Art.
New York: Praeger, 1962.

The Human Figure. Intro. by Alfred Barr, Jr. New York: The
Museum of Modern Art, 1962.

Innocenti, Mauro. "Sarai Sherman." La Nazione, 14 December 1966.

Lavagnino, Emilio. "Sarai Sherman." Il Messaggero, 24 February
1963.

Micacchi, Dario. "Roma: Sherman." L'Unità, 13 June 1964.

Minervino, Fiorella. "Sarai Sherman." Il Corriere della Sera, 30
May 1977.

Monteverdi, Mario. "La Pittrice Sherman." Corriere Lombardo, 12
March 1963.

Munson, Gretchen T. "Sarai Sherman." Art News 53, no. 10
(February 1955): 65.

O'Dougherty, Brian. "This Week Around the Galleries." The New
York Times, 8 December 1963.

163rd Annual Exhibition. New York: National Academy of Design,
1988.

"Openings: Sheep to Chevrons." Art & Antiques (April 1986): 35.

Parodi, Anton Giulio. "Sherman a La Polena." L'Unità, 21 June
1963.

Preston, Stuart. "New Talent." The New York Times, 13 May 1950.

Sala, Alberico. "Sarai Sherman." Il Giorno, 7 May 1977.

Sarai Sherman. Bay Harbor Islands, Florida: Gallery Ninety Nine,
1986.

Sarai Sherman, Ceramic Sculpture. Toronto: Canada: Madison
Gallery, 1986.

Stableford, Nancy. "Three Exhibitions in the Spotlight." Chicago
Tribune, 26 January 1964.

Terenzi, Claudia. "Sarai Sherman." Paese Sera, 19 February 1978.

Valsecchi, Marco. "Sherman." Il Giorno, 16 February 1961.

Venturoli, Marcello. <u>Sarai Sherman</u>. Notes by Edward Bryant.
    Rome:  Penelope, 1963.

<u>Who's Who in American Art</u>.  New York:  R.R. Bowker Co., 1978.


            MARY CLARE SHERWOOD (1869-1943)    Painter

<u>American Art Annual</u>, vol. 28.  Washington, D.C.:  American
    Federation of Arts, 1932.

<u>An Exhibition of Women Students of William Merritt Chase</u>.  New
    York:  Marbella Gallery, 1973.

Obituary.  <u>Who's Who in American Art</u>, vol. 4.  Washington, D.C.:
    American Federation of Arts, 1947.


            ROSINA EMMET SHERWOOD (1854-1948)    Painter

See volume 1 of this book.

<u>American Art Annual</u>, vol. 28.  Washington, D.C.:  American
    Federation of Arts, 1932.

Barrett, Patti.  "The Emmets:  A Family of Women Painters."  <u>The
    Berkshire Courier</u>, 5 August 1982:  1, 20.

Clement, Clara Erskine.  <u>Women in the Fine Arts</u>.  Boston:  Houghton
    Mifflin Co., 1904.

Fielding, Mantle.  <u>Dictionary of American Painters, Sculptors and
    Enravers</u>.  Enlarged ed.  Greens Farms, Connecticut:  Modern
    Books and Crafts, 1974.

McClinton, Katharine M.  <u>The Chromolithographs of Louis Prang</u>.  New
    York:  Crown Publishers, 1973.

Obituary.  <u>The New York Times</u>, 20 January 1948:  24.

Obituary.  <u>Who's Who in American Art</u>, vol. 5.  Washington, D.C.:
    American Federation of Arts, 1953.

Tufts, Eleanor.  <u>American Women Artists, 1830-1930</u>.  Washington,
    D.C.:  National Museum of Women in the Arts, 1987.

<u>Woman's Who's Who of America</u>.  New York:  The American Commonwealth
    Co., 1914.


            FLORENCE SCOVEL SHINN (1869-1940)    Illustrator

See volume 1 of this book.

408

American Art Annual, vol. 18. Washington, D.C.: American
    Federation of Arts, 1921.

A Circle of Friends: Art Colonies of Cornish and Dublin. Durham,
    New Hampshire: University of New Hampshire Art Galleries,
    1985: 115.

Turn-of-the-Century America: Paintings, Graphics, Photographs.
    New York: Whitney Museum of American Art, 1977: 101.

Woman's Who's Who of America. New York: American Commonwealth
    Co., 1914.


        EUGENIE FREDERICA SHONNARD (1886-1978)    Sculptor

See volume 1 of this book.

American Art Annual, vol. 28. Washington, D.C.: American
    Federation of Arts, 1932.

Bell, Enid. "The Sculpture of Eugenie Shonnard." American
    Artist 30 (June 1966): 62-67, 87-89.

Eugenie F. Shonnard. Santa Fe: Governor's Gallery, 1976.

Exhibition of American Sculpture. New York: National Sculpture
    Society, 1923: 227.

An Exhibition of Sculpture of Eugenie Shonnard. Santa Fe: Museum
    of New Mexico Art Gallery, 1954.

Samuels, Peggy and Harold. The Illustrated Biographical
    Encyclopedia of Artists of the American West. Garden City,
    New York: Doubleday, 1976.


        HENRIETTA MARY SHORE (1880-1963)    Painter and Printmaker

See volume 1 of this book.

American Art Annual, vol. 28. Washington, D.C.: American
    Federation of Arts, 1932.

Charlot, Jean. Art from the Mayans to Walt Disney. New York and
    London: Sheed and Ward, 1939.

Henrietta Shore, A Retrospective Exhibition: 1900-1963. Intro. by
    Jo Farb Hernandez. Monterey, California: Monterey Peninsula
    Museum of Art, 1986.

Porter, Bruce, et al. Art in California: A Survey of American Art with Special Reference to California Painting, Sculpture and Architecture, Past and Present, Particularly as those Arts were Represented at the Panama-Pacific International Exposition. San Francisco: R.L. Bernier, 1916.

Schipper, Marle. "Henrietta Shore (Laguna Art Museum)." Art News 86, no. 6 (Summer 1987): 66.

Spangenberg, Helen. Yesterday's Artists on the Monterey Peninsula. Monterey, California: Monterey Peninsula Museum of Art, 1976.

A Selection of American Prints. A Selection of Biographies of Forty Women Artists Working Between 1904-1979. Santa Rosa, California: The Annex Galleries, 1987: 13.

Wolf, Amy J. New York Society of Women Artists 1925. New York: ACA Galleries, 1987.

A Woman's Vision: California Painting into the 20th Century. San Francisco: Maxwell Galleries, 1983.


HARRIET SHORR (1939-    )   Painter

Bolt, Thomas. "Harriet Shorr's Chamber Music." Arts Magazine 61, no. 8 (April 1987): 69-71.

Kahn, Wolf. "Autocratic and Democratic Still-Life Painting," American Artist 50, issue 523 (February 1986): 68.

Martin, Alvin. American Realism, 20th-Century Drawings and Watercolors, From the Glenn C. Janss Collection. San Francisco: San Francisco Museum of Modern Art, 1985.

Oresman, Janice C. "Still Life Today." Arts Magazine 57, no. 4 (December 1982): 111-15.

Tannenbaum, Judith, ed. New York Art Yearbook, vol. 1, 1975-76. New York: Noyes Art Books, 1976.

Yourgrau, Barry. "Harriet Shorr." Arts Magazine 55, no. 5 (January 1981): 11.


ADA WALTER SHULZ (1870-1928)   Painter

American Art Annual, vol. 1. New York: Macmillan, 1899.

Burnet, Mary Q. Art and Artists of Indiana. New York: Century Co., 1921.

410

Fielding, Mantle. Dictionary of American Painters, Sculptors and
Engravers. Enlarged ed. Greens Farms, Connecticut: Modern
Books and Crafts, 1974.


ALBERTA REHM SHULZ (1892-    )   Painter

American Impressionism: The Second Generation. Washington, D.C.:
Taggart, Jorgensen and Putnam, [1983].

Who's Who in American Art, vol. 8. Washington, D.C.: American
Federation of Arts, 1962.


RUTH WHITTIER SHUTE (b. 1803)   Painter

Lipman, Jean, and Armstrong, Tom, eds. American Folk Painters of
Three Centuries. New York: Hudson Hills Press and Whitney
Museum of American Art, 1980.

Rubinstein, Charlotte Streifer. American Women Artists. Boston:
G.K. Hall, 1982.


CLAIRE SHUTTLEWORTH (1868-1930)   Painter

Archives of American Art. Collection of Exhibition Catalogs.
Boston: G.K. Hall and Co., 1979.

Catalogue of a Collection of Paintings, Sketchings, and Studies of
The Niagara River by Claire Shuttleworth. Buffalo, New York:
Albright Art Gallery, 1920.

Fielding, Mantle. Dictionary of American Painters, Sculptors and
Engravers. Enlarged ed. Greens Farms, Connecticut: Modern
Books and Crafts, 1974.

Obituary. American Art Annual, vol. 28. Washington, D.C.:
American Federation of Arts, 1932.

Shuttleworth, Claire. "Sketching Along the Niagara." Buffalo Arts
Journal, May 1925: 15-17.


HOLLIS SIGLER (1948-    )   Painter

Cecil, Sarah. "New Editions." Art News 82, no. 4 (April 1983):
86.

80th Exhibition by Artists of Chicago and Vicinity. Chicago: Art
Institute of Chicago, 1984.

411

Handy, Ellen. "Hollis Sigler." Arts Magazine 58, no. 4 (December
    1983): 39.

Hess, Elizabeth. "39th Corcoran Biennial." Art News 84, no. 6
    (Summer 1985): 107.

intimate/INTIMATE. Curated by Charles S. Mayer and Bert Brouwer.
    Terre Haute: Indiana State University, 1986.

Kirshner, Judith Russi. "Hollis Sigler, Dart Gallery." Artforum
    21, no. 8 (April 1983): 78.

Moser, Charlotte. "Hollis Sigler." Art News 85, no. 4 (April
    1986): 143.

1981 Biennial Exhibition. New York: Whitney Museum of American
    Art, 1981.

Thirty-ninth Corcoran Biennial of Contemporary American Painting.
    Washington, D.C.: Corcoran Gallery of Art, 1985.


SUZANNE SILVERCRUYS [FARNUM STEVENSON] (1898-1973)   Sculptor

See volume 1 of this book.

American Art Annual, vol. 28. Washington, D.C.: American
    Federation of Arts, 1932.

Fiftieth Annual Exhibition. New York: National Association of
    Women Painters and Sculptors, 1942, no. 85.


MARTHA SIMKINS (1869-1969)   Painter

American Art Annual, vol. 28. Washington, D.C.: American
    Federation of Arts, 1932.

Catalogue, First Exhibition of Original Paintings Held Under the .
    Auspices of the Young Women's Christian Association. Dallas,
    Texas: Y.W.C.A., 1924.

Church, Diana. Guide to Dallas Artists 1890-1917. privately
    printed, Plano, Texas: 1987.


NELL SINTON (1910-   )   Painter

Nell Sinton. Recent Paintings. San Francisco: San Francisco
    Museum of Art, 1970.

412

Raynor, Vivien. "Nell Sinton." Arts Magazine 36, no. 7 (April
    1962): 54.

Sandler, Irving. "Nell Sinton [Bolles]." Art News 61, no. 2
    (April 1962): 22.

Stiles, Knute. "San Francisco." Artforum 9, no. 3 (November
    1970): 93-94.

Ventura, Anita. "San Francisco." Arts Magazine 39, no. 1 (October
    1964): 24.

Who's Who in American Art. New York: R.R. Bowker, 1978.


            ELENA SISTO (1952-    )    Painter

Klein, Ellen Lee. "Elena Sisto." Arts Magazine 59, no. 1
    (September 1984): 38.

Pardee, Hearne. Inner Images: Paintings by Five Contemporary
    Artists. Waterville, Maine: Colby College Museum of Arts,
    1986.

_____. "Inner Images: Paintings by Five Contemporary Artists."
    Arts Magazine 61, no. 3 (November 1986): 64-65.

Westfall, Stephen. "Elena Sisto at Vanderwoude/Tananbaum." Art
    in America 75, no. 2 (February 1987): 150.


            HANNAH B. SKEELE (1829-1901)    Painter

See volume 1 of this book.

Fales, Martha Gandy. "Hannah B. Skeele, Maine Artist." Antiques
    122 (April 1982): 915-21, and "Addenda on Hannah B. Skeele."
    Antiques (November 1982): 1097.

Hannah B. Skeele. Kennebunk, Maine: The Brick Store Museum, 1982.

Women Pioneers in Maine Art. Portland, Maine: Joan Whitney Payson
    Gallery of Art, Westbrook College, 1981.


            SANDY SKOGLUND (1946-    )    Photographer

"Album: Sandy Skoglund." Arts Magazine 61, no. 5 (January 1987):
    116-17.

Degener, Patricia. "Sandy Skoglund's Uncuddly Babies." Saint
    Louis Post-Dispatch, 11 November 1983.

Edwards, Owen. "Flash-Maybe Babies: Sandy Skoglund's View of
    Pennies from Heaven." American Photographer Magazine 11, no.
    2 (August 1983): 59-61.

Eauclaire, Sally. The New Color. New York: Abbeville Press,
    1981.

Gagnon, Paulette. The Magic of the Image. Montreal: Museum of
    Contemporary Art, 1986.

Gauss, Kathleen McCarthy, and Grundberg, Andy. Photography and
    Art, 1946-86. New York: Abbeville Press, 1987.

Goldwater, Marge, and Armstrong, Liz. Cross-References: Sculpture
    into Photography. Minneapolis: Walker Art Center, 1987.

Hanson, Bernard. "A Plunge into the Surreal." The Hartford
    Courant, 23 May 1982.

Hoy, Anne H. Fabrications. New York: Abbeville Press, 1987.

Jacobs, Joseph. This is not a Photograph: Twenty Years of
    Large-Scale Photography, 1966-1986. Sarasota: John and Mable
    Ringling Museum of Art, 1987.

Moufarrege, Nicolas. Correspondences, New York Art Now. Tokyo:
    Laforet Museum Harajuko, 1985.

Points of View. Norman, Oklahoma: University of Oklahoma Museum
    of Art, 1982.

"Sandy Skoglund." Asahi Camera Magazine (November 1983): 132-36.

Saul, Julie M. Photography in America, 1910-Present. Tampa:
    Tampa Museum, 1983.

HAZEL BURNHAM SLAUGHTER (1888-1979)    Painter

Hazel Slaughter: Oil Paintings, Watercolors. New York: Feigh
    Gallery, 1946.

Hazel Slaughter: Recent Oil Paintings. New York: Feigh Gallery,
    1948.

Obituary. The New York Times, 5 September 1979: D21.

ARLENE SLAVIN (1942-   )   Painter

See volume 1 of this book.

"Fantasy Screens of Flora and Fauna."  Interior Design 55 (October
    1984):  126.

Henry, Gerrit.  "Arlene Slavin at Alexander Milliken."  Art in
    America 72, no. 2 (February 1984):  149-50.

Lichtenstein, Therese.  "Arlene Slavin."  Arts Magazine 58, no. 4
    (December 1983):  34.


SYLVIA SLEIGH (20th Century)   Painter

Frueh, Joanna.  "Chicago.  Sylvia Sleigh at Zaks."  Art in America
    74, no. 1 (January 1986):  143, 145.

Raynor, Vivien.  "Sylvia Sleigh."  The New York Times, 11 January
    1985.

Realism Now.  Poughkeepsie, New York:  Vassar College Art Gallery,
    1968.


JEANETTE PASIN SLOAN (1946-   )   Painter

See volume 1 of this book.

Bass, Ruth.  "Jeanette Pasin Sloan (G.W. Einstein).  Art News 78,
    no. 6 (Summer 1979):  188.

Henry, Gerrit.  "Jeanette Pasin Sloan at G.W. Einstein."  Art in
    America 73, no. 6 (June 1985):  143-44.

"Jeanette Pasin Sloan."  Print Collectors Newsletter 9, no. 6
    (January 1979):  195.

"Jeanette Pasin Sloan."  Print Collectors Newsletter, 17, no. 4
    (September/October 1986):  144.

A Just Temper Between Propensities:  New Still Life and Landscape
    Painting.  Foreword by David B. Lawall.  Charlottesville:
    University of Virginia Art Museum, 1987.

Lockhart, Anne I.  "Jeanette Pasin Sloan."  Arts Magazine 53, no. 8
    (April 1979):  3.

415

Midwest Realists. Oshkosh, Wisconsin: The Paine Art Center, 1985.

Prints and Multiples, 79th Exhibition by Artists of Chicago and
    Vicinity. Essay by Esther Sparks. Chicago: Art Institute of
    Chicago, 1981.

Seven Artists: Contemporary Drawings. Cleveland: Cleveland
    Museum of Art, 1978.

Vishny, Michele. "Notes on Still-Life Painting and the Art of
    Jeanette Pasin Sloan." Arts Magazine 57, no. 7 (March 1983):
    126-28.


                MARIANNE SLOAN (1875-1954)   Painter

American Art Annual, vol. 28. Washington, D.C.: American
    Federation of Arts, 1932.

Goodman, Helen. "The Plastic Club." Arts Magazine 59, no. 7
    (March 1985): 101.

Huber, Christine Jones. The Pennsylvania Academy and Its Women.
    Philadelphia: The Pennsylvania Academy of the Fine Arts,
    1974.

In Celebration of Fifty Years, 1930-1980. Philadelphia: Frank S.
    Schwarz and Son Gallery, 1980.

Obituary. Who's Who in American Art, vol. 6. Washington, D.C.:
    American Federation of Arts, 1956.


                ALICE RAVENEL HUGER SMITH (1876-1958)   Painter

American Art Annual, vol. 28. Washington, D.C.: American
    Federation of Arts, 1932.

Chambers, Bruce W. Art and Artists of the South. Columbia, South
    Carolina: University of South Carolina Press, 1984.

Eight Southern Women. Greenville, South Carolina: Greenville
    County Museum of Art, 1986.

Fielding, Mantle. Dictionary of American Painters, Sculptors and
    Engravers. Enlarged ed. Greens Farms, Connecticut: Modern
    Books and Crafts, 1974.

Kuhar, Kyra. Alice Ravenal Huger Smith of Charleston, South
    Carolina: An Appreciation on the Occasion of her 80th
    Birthday. Charleston, South Carolina: privately printed,
    1956.

416

Neff, Marietta. "A Painter of the Carolina Lowlands." American
  Magazine of Art 17, no. 8 (August 1926): 406-11.

Parris, Nina G. South Carolina Collection 1779-1985. Columbia,
  South Carolina: The Columbia Museum, 1985.

Sass, Herbert Ravenel. Adventures in Green Place with
  Reproductions of Seventeen Painting by Alice R. Huger Smith.
  New York: G.P. Putnam's Sons, 1935.

Smith, Alice Ravenel Huger. A Carolina Rice Plantation of the
  Fifties. New York: W. Morrow and Co., 1936.

_____, and Smith, Daniel Elliott Huger. The Dwelling Houses of
  Charleston, South Carolina. Philadelphia and London: J.B.
  Lippincott Co., 1917.

Who's Who in American Art, vol. 3. Washington, D.C.: American
  Federation of Arts, 1940.


GLADYS NELSON SMITH (1890-1980)   Painter

Paintings by Gladys Nelson Smith. Washington, D.C.: Veerhoff
  Galleries, 1979.

Simmons, Linda Crocker. Gladys Nelson Smith. Washington, D.C.:
  Corcoran Gallery of Art, 1984.


JESSIE WILLCOX SMITH (1863-1935)   Illustrator

See volume 1 of this book.

American Art Annual, vol. 28. Washington, D.C.: American
  Federation of Arts, 1932.

The American Personality: The Artist-Illustrator of Life in the
  United States, 1860-1930. Los Angeles: Grunwald Center for
  Graphic Art, University of California at Los Angeles, 1976.

Goodman, Helen. "The Plastic Club." Arts Magazine 59, no. 7
  (March 1985): 100-03.

_____. "Women Illustrators of the Golden Age of American
  Illustration." Woman's Art Journal 8, no. 1 (Spring-Summer
  1987): 13-22.

Obituary. Who's Who in American Art, vol. 1. Washington, D.C.:
  American Federation of Arts, 1935.

Reed, Walt, ed.  The Illustrator in America 1900-1960's.  New York: Reinhold Publishing Corp., 1966:  37.

Society of Illustrators.  America's Great Women Illustrators 1850-1950.  Chadds Ford, Pennsylvania:  Brandywine River Museum, 1985.

MARA SMITH (1945-    )   Sculptor

Brolin, Brent C., and Richards, Jean.  Sourcebook of Architectural Ornament:  Designers, Craftsmen, Manufacturers and Distributors of Custom and Ready-Made Exterior Ornament.  New York:  Van Nostrand Reinhold, 1982.

Fleming, Ronald Lee, and Von Tscharner, Renata, with Melrod, George.  Place Makers:  Public Art that Tells You Where You Art.  New York:  Hastings House, 1981.

Redstone, Louis G.  Masonry in Architecture.  New York:  McGraw-Hill, 1984.

Watson-Jones, Virginia.  Contemporary American Women Sculptors.  Phoenix:  Oryx Press, 1986.

MARY SMITH (1842-1878)   Painter

Artists of the Nineteenth Century.  Philadelphia:  Frank S. Schwarz and Son Gallery, 1980.

Groce, George C., and Wallace, David H.  The New-York Historical Society's Dictionary of Artists in American 1564-1860.  New Haven:  Yale University Press, 1957.

Huber, Christine Jones.  The Pennsylvania Academy and Its Women.  Philadelphia:  The Pennsylvania Academy of the Fine Arts, 1974.

PAMELA COLMAN SMITH (1877 or 1878-ca. 1950)   Painter and Illustrator

See volume 1 of this book.

Armstrong, Regina.  "Representative American Women Illustrators:  The Decorative Workers."  Critic 36 (June 1900):  520-29.

"Pamela Colman Smith."  Brush and Pencil 6 (June 1900):  135-41.

418

Smith, Pamela Colman. The Golden Vanity and the Green Bed: Words
and Music of Two Old English Ballads, with Pictures by Pamela
Colman Smith. New York: Doubleday and McClure Co., 1899.


JOAN SNYDER (1940-    )    Painter

See volume 1 of this book.

Brenson, Michael. "True Believers Who Keep the Flame of Painting."
The New York Times, 7 June 1987, Arts and Leisure section:
37.

Cannell, Michael. "Joan Snyder." Arts Magazine 57, no. 7 (March
1983): 4.

Field, Richard S., and Fine, Ruth E. A Graphic Muse. New York:
Hudson Hills Press, 1987.

Fortieth Biennal of Contemporary American Painting. Washington,
D.C.: Corcoran Gallery of Art, 1987.

Gardner, Paul. "When Is a Painting Finished?" Art News 84, no. 9
(November 1985): 92-93.

Gill, Susan. "Painting from the Heart." Art News 86, no. 4 (April
1987): 128-35.

Henry, Gerrit. "Joan Snyder: True Grit." Art in America 74, no.
2 (February 1986): 96-101.

Joan Snyder. Intro by J. Baker. New York: Hirschl and Adler
Modern Gallery, 1985.

Tarlow, Lois. "Profile: Joan Snyder." Art New England 8, no. 2
(February 1987): 14-15, 22.

"The Woman's Movement in Art, 1986." Arts Magazine 61, no. 1
(September 1986): 54-57.


ALICE RUGGLES SOHIER (b. 1880)    Painter

American Art Annual, vol. 28. Washington, D.C.: American
Federation of Arts, 1932.

Fielding, Mantle. Dictionary of American Painters, Sculptors and
Engravers. Enlarged ed. Greens Farms, Connecticut: Modern
Books and Crafts, 1974.

Gammell, R.H. Ives. The Boston Painters. 1900-1930. Orleans,
Massachusetts: Parnassus Imprints, 1986.

Who's Who in American Art, vol. 1.  Washington, D.C.:  American
     Federation of Arts, 1935.


              ROSALIND SOLOMON (1930-    )   Photographer

Auer, Michèle and Auer, Michel.  Encyclopédie International des
     Photographes de 1839 à Nos Jours.  Hermance, Switzerland:
     Editions Camera Obscura, 1985.

Hagen, Charles.  "Rosalind Solomon (Museum of Modern Art)."
     Artforum 25, no. 2 (October 1986):  133.

Kismaric, Susan.  American Children.  New York:  The Museum of
     Modern Art, 1981.

Sturman, John.  "Rosalind Solomon."  Art News 86, no. 3 (March
     1987):  159.

Szarkowski, John.  Mirrors and Windows, American Photography Since
     1960.  New York:  The Museum of Modern Art, 1978.

True, S.  "Rosalind Solomon, Corcoran Gallery of Art."  Afterimage
     8 (October 1980):  16.

Westerbeck, Colin L., Jr.  "Rosalind Solomon, The Corcoran Gallery
     of Art."  Artforum 18, no. 10 (Summer 1980):  89-90.


              EVE SONNEMAN (1946-    )   Photographer and Filmmaker

See volume 1 of this book.

Rosenblum, Naomi.  A World History of Photography.  New York:
     Abbeville, 1985.

Who's Who in American Art, 17th ed.  New York:  R.R. Bowker Co.,
     1986.

Zimmer, William.  "Eve Sonneman and the World in Color."  Arts
     Magazine 58, no. 10 (Summer 1984):  66-67.


              LILLY MARTIN SPENCER (1822-1902)   Painter

See volume 1 of this book.

An American Gallery, vol. 4.  New York:  Richard York Gallery,
     1988:  no. 6.

Bolton-Smith, Robin.  "The Sentimental Paintings of Lilly Martin
     Spencer."  Antiques 104, no. 1 (July 1973):  108-13.

Canaday, John. "The Resurrection of Lilly Martin Spencer." The New York Times, 29 July 1973, Arts and Leisure section.

Clark, Edna Maria. Ohio Art and Artists. Richmond, Virginia: Garrett and Massie, 1932: 106.

Edwards, Lee M. Domestic Bliss: Family Life in American Painting, 1840-1910. Yonkers, New York: Hudson River Museum, 1986.

Hadry, Henriette A. "Mrs. Lilly M. Spencer." Sartain's Magazine 9, no. 2 (1851): 152-54.

Hoopes, Donelson F., and Moure, Nancy Wall. American Narrative Painting. Los Angeles: Los Angeles County Museum of Art, 1974.

Pincus, Robert L. "A Woman's Place is in the Studio." Christian Science Monitor, 13 April 1988: 30.

Tufts, Eleanor. American Women Artists, 1830-1930. Washington, D.C.: National Museum of Women in the Arts, 1987.

NANCY SPERO (1926- ) Painter

See volume 1 of this book.

Adams, Brooks. "Spero's Muse: The Printed Paintings." The Print Collector's Newsletter 18, no. 1 (March-April 1986): 10-11.

Brenson, Michael. "Can Political Passion Inspire Great Art?" The New York Times, 28 April 1984, Arts and Leisure section.

_____. "Nancy Spero." The New York Times, 28 March 1986.

Craven, David. "Nancy Spero." Arts Magazine 61, no. 2 (October 1986): 113.

Dector, Joshua. "Nancy Spero." Arts Magazine 60, no. 10 (Summer 1986): 112.

Handy, Ellen. "Nancy Spero." Arts Magazine 61, no. 9 (May 1987): 105.

King, Elaine A. Nancy Spero, The Black Paris Paintings 1959-1966. Pittsburgh: Carnegie-Mellon University, 1985.

Kunst mit Eigen-Sinn. Aktuelle Kunst von Frauen. Munich: Löcher Verlag, 1985.

Kuspit, Donald B. "From Existence to Essence: Nancy Spero." Art in America 72, no. 1 (January 1984): 88-96.

Liebman, Lisa. "Nancy Spero, Willard Gallery." Artforum 22, no. 7 (March 1984): 94-95.

Lippard, Lucy. "Caring: Five Political Artists." Studio International 193, no. 987 (March 1977): 197-207.

_____. "Nancy Spero's 30 Years War." Village Voice, 19 April 1983.

Lyon, Christopher. "Nancy Spero." Art News 87, no. 5 (May 1988): 162.

McEvilley, Thomas. "Nancy Spero." Artforum 24, no. 10 (Summer 1986): 123-24.

Nahah, Dominique. Nancy Spero: Works since 1950. Syracuse: Everson Museum of Art, 1987.

Nancy Spero. London: Institute of Contemporary Arts, 1987.

Shottenkirk, Dena, and Spero, Nancy. "Dialogue: An Exchange of Ideas Between Dena Shottenkirk and Nancy Spero." Arts Magazine 61, no. 9 (May 1987): 34-35.

Siegel, Jeanne. "Nancy Spero: Woman as Protagonist." Arts Magazine 62, no. 1 (September 1987): 10-13.

Smith, Roberta. "Art: An Array of Styles and Trends in Galleries." The New York Times, 26 February 1988: 18Y.

ANN SPERRY (20th Century)    Sculptor

Ann Sperry/Barbara Zucker: A Decade of Work. Greenvale, New York: Hillwood Art Gallery, Long Island University, 1984.

Glueck, Grace. "Ann Sperry (Lerner-Heller Gallery)." The New York Times, 7 May 1982: C22.

Olson, J.M. Roberta. "Ann Sperry." Arts Magazine 49, no. 2 (October 1974): 68-69.

Painting and Sculpture Today 1978. Indianapolis: Indianapolis Museum of Art, 1978.

Shepard, Ileen. Sculpture of the 80's. Essay by Lowery S. Sims. Queens, New York: Queens Museum, 1987.

Sperry, Ann. "Conversations and Reminiscences." Heresies, Winter 1977-78: 84.

422

_____. "Emerging Forms, Steel Sculpture." Helicon Nine 1, no. 1 (Spring/Summer 1979): 26-29.

Stein, Judith. "Flowering: The Recent Sculpture of Ann Sperry." Arts Magazine 56, no. 8 (April 1982): 68-69.

Year of the Woman: Reprise. Bronx, New York: Bronx Museum of the Arts, 1976.


GAEL Z. STACK (1941-   )   Painter

Camfield, William. Works on Paper: Eleven Houston Artists. Houston: Museum of Fine Arts, 1985.

Carlozzi, Annette. 50 Texas Artists. San Francisco: Chronicle Books, 1986.

Greene, Alison de Lima. Twentieth-Century Art in the Museum Collection: Direction and Diversity. Houston: Museum of Fine Arts, 1988.

Hill, Ed, and Bloom, Suzanne. "Gael Stack." Artforum 24, no. 7 (March 1986): 125.

Moore, Sylvia, ed. No Bluebonnets, No Yellow Roses: Essays on Texas Women in the Arts. New York: Midmarch Arts Press, 1988.

Moser, Charlotte. "Artists the Critics are Watching." Art News 80, no. 5 (May 1981): 86-87.


ALICE STALLKNECHT (1880-1973)   Painter

A New England Town: A Portrait by Alice Stallknecht. Foreword by William C. Agee. Houston: Museum of Fine Arts, 1977.

Wight, Frederick. "Portrait of a New England Town." Art in America 65, no. 3 (May-June 1977): 106-07.


JANE CAROLINE MAHON STANLEY (1863-1940)   Painter

American Art Annual, vol. 28. Washington, D.C.: American Federation of Arts, 1932.

A Catalogue of the Collection of American Paintings in the Corcoran Gallery of Art. Washington, D.C.: Corcoran Gallery of Art, 1973.

Moore, Julia G.  History of the Detroit Society of Women Painters
    and Sculptors, 1903-1953.  River Rouge, Michigan:  Victory
    Publishing Co., 1953.

Obituary.  The New York Times, 1 November 1940:  25.

Who's Who in American Art, vol. 3.  Washington, D.C.:  American
    Federation of Arts, 1940.


            ELIZABETH CADY STANTON (1894-    )   Painter

American Art Annual, vol. 28.  Washington, D.C.:  American
    Federation of Arts, 1932.

Fielding, Mantle.  Dictionary of American Painters, Sculptors and
    Engravers.  Enlarged ed.  Greens Farms, Connecticut:  Modern
    Books and Craft, 1974.

Who's Who in American Art, vol. 8.  Washington, D.C.:  American
    Federation of Arts, 1962.


            LUCY MAY STANTON (1875-1931)   Painter

Art in the United States Capitol.  Washington, D.C.:  U.S.
    Government Printing Office, 1976:  51.

Fielding, Mantle.  Dictionary of American Painters, Sculptors and
    Engravers.  Enlarged ed.  Greens Farms, Connecticut:  Modern
    Books and Crafts, 1974.

Forbes, W. Stanton.  Lucy M. Stanton, Artist.  Atlanta, Georgia:
    Emory University, 1975.

Lounsbery, Elizabeth.  "American Miniature Painters."  Mentor 4,
    no. 23 (5 January 1917).

"Miss Lucy Stanton, Noted Artist, Dies."  The New York Times, 20
    March 1931.

National Portrait Gallery, Permanent Collection Illustrated
    Checklist.  Washington, D.C.:  Smithsonian Institution Press,
    1982.

Obituary.  American Art Annual, vol. 28.  Washington, D.C.:
    American Federation of Arts, 1932:  418.

Tufts, Eleanor.  American Women Artists, 1830-1930.  Washington,
    D.C.:  National Museum of Women in the Arts, 1987.

CORDELIA STANWOOD (1865-1958)    Photographer

Richmond, Chandler S. Beyond the Spring, Cordelia Stanwood of
    Birdsacre. Lamoine, Maine:  Latona Press, 1978.


ELIZA ALLEN STARR (1824-1901)    Painter and Illustrator

Groce, George C., and Wallace, David H. The New-York Historical
    Society's Dictionary of Artists in America 1564-1860. New
    Haven:  Yale University Press, 1957.

Starr, Eliza Allen. Pilgrims and Shrines, 2 vols. Chicago:   Union
    Catholic Publishing Co., 1883.

Weimann, Jeanne Madeline. The Fair Women. Chicago:  Academy
    Chicago, 1981.


EMMA STEBBINS (1815-1882)    Sculptor

See volume 1 of this book.

Clement, Clara Erskine. Women in the Fine Arts. Boston:
    Houghton Mifflin Co., 1904.

Crawford, John Stephens.  "The Classical Orator in Nineteenth
    Century American Sculpture." American Art Journal 6, no. 2
    (November 1974):  65-66.

Hanaford, Phebe A. Daughters of America. Augusta, Maine:  True
    and Co., 1882:  288-89.

Heller, Nancy G. Women Artists. New York:  Abbeville, 1987.


SANDY STEIN (1946-    )    Sculptor

Albritton, Jane.  "Reviews:  The Third Annual Sculpture Exhibition
    at Connemara Conservancy Near Dallas, Texas." Artspace 7, no.
    3 (Summer 1983):  66-69.

Annual Delta Art Exhibition. Little Rock:  Arkansas Arts Center,
    1979.

Ennis, Michael.  "Public Gestures." Texas Monthly (May 1985):
    172, 174-75.

Fifth Texas Sculpture Symposium. Dallas:  Connemara Conservancy,
    1985.

Watson-Jones, Virginia. Contemporary American Women Sculptors.
    Phoenix:  Oryx Press, 1986.

KATE TRAUMAN STEINITZ (1889-1975)    Painter and Printmaker

Glass, Judith Samuel. "Kate Steinitz Retrospective." Artweek 7 (1
      May 1976): 7.

Kate Steinitz: Art and Collection. San Bernardino, California:
      Art Gallery, California State College, 1982.

Who's Who in American Art, vol. 10. Washington, D.C.: American
      Federation of Arts, 1970.


PAT STEIR (1938-    )   Painter

See volume 1 of this book.

Baker, Kenneth. "Pat Steir." Arts Magazine 49, no. 8 (April
      1975): 21.

Broun, Elizabeth. Form, Illusion, Myth: Prints and Drawings of
      Pat Steir. Lawrence, Kansas: Spencer Museum of Art,
      University of Kansas, 1983.

Casademont, Joan. "Pat Steir (Max Protech Gallery)." Artforum 20,
      no. 6 (February 1982): 84.

Castle, Frederick Ted. "Pat Steir: Ways of Marking." Art in
      America 72, no. 6 (Summer 1984): 124-29.

Crary, Jonathan. "Pat Steir." Arts Magazine 50, no. 10 (June
      1976): 10.

Field, Richard S., and Fine, Ruth E. A Graphic Muse. New York:
      Hudson Hills Press, 1987.

Gardner, Paul. "Pat Steir: Seeing Through the Eyes of Others."
      Art News 84, no. 9 (November 1985): 80-88.

Gill, Susan. "Pat Steir." Art News 86, no. 6 (Summer 1987): 202,
      204.

Graze, Sue. "Concentrations 14: Pat Steir." Dallas Museum of Art
      Bulletin, Winter 1986-87: 10-11.

Images on Stone: Two Centuries of Artists' Lithographs. Houston:
      Sarah Campbell Blaffer Gallery, University of Houston, 1987.

Kutner, Janet. "Panels of Historic Importance." Dallas Morning
      News, 5 November 1986, section F: 1-2.

Princenthal, Nancy. "The Self in Parts." Art in America 75, no.
      11 (November 1987): 171, 173.

426

Ratcliff, Carter. "Pat Steir at Castelli Graphics." Art in America 74, no. 7 (July 1986): 113-14.

_____. Pat Steir Paintings. New York: Harry N. Abrams, 1986.

Selections form The Frito-Lay Collection. Plano, Texas: Frito-Lay Collection, Inc., 1987: 31.

Woodville, Louisa. "Three Painters, Three Decades." Arts Magazine 59, no. 5 (January 1985): 19.

Zelanski, Paul, and Fisher, Mary Pat. The Art of Seeing. Englewood Cliffs, New Jersey: Prentice-Hall, 1988: cover, back cover.


ALICE BARBER STEPHENS (1858-1932)    Illustrator

See volume 1 of this book.

Brown, Ann Barton. Alice Barber Stephens, A Pioneer Woman Illustrator. Chadds Ford, Pennsylvania: Brandywine River Museum, 1984.

Catalogue of the Exhibits of the State of Pennsylvania and of Pennsylvanians at The World's Columbian Exposition. [Harrisburg]: State Printer of Pennsylvania, 1893: 118, 161.

Goodman, Helen. "Alice Barber Stephens." American Artist 48, no. 50 (April 1984): 46-49, 98-100.

_____. "Alice Barber Stephens, Illustrator." Arts Magazine 58, no. 5 (January 1984): 126-29.

_____. "The Plastic Club." Arts Magazine 59, no. 7 (March 1985): 100-03.

_____. "Women Illustrators of the Golden Age of American Illustration." Woman's Art Journal 8, no. 1 (Spring-Summer 1987): 13-22.

In This Academy. The Pennsylvania Academy of the Fine Arts, 1805-1976. Philadelphia: Pennsylvania Academy of the Fine Arts, 1976: 64, 68, 278.

Reed, Walt, ed. The Illustrator in America 1900-1960's. New York: Reinhold Publishing Corp., 1966: 37.

Tufts, Eleanor. American Women Artists 1830-1930. Washington, D.C.: National Museum of Women in the Arts, 1987.

SUSANNE STEPHENSON (1935-    )    Ceramicist

Clark, Garth. American Potters, The Work of Twenty Modern Masters. New York: Watson-Guptill Publications, 1981.

_____. A Century of Ceramics in the United States 1878-1978. New York: E.P. Dutton, 1979.

Clay Today. Iowa City: School of Fine Arts, State University of Iowa, New Gallery, 1962.

Finkel, Marilyn. "Suzanne Stephenson." Craft Horizons 37, no. 6 (December 1977): 69-70.

HEDDA STERNE (1916-    )    Painter

See volume 1 of this book.

Ashton, Dore. Hedda Sterne: Forty Years. Flushing: Queens Museum, 1985.

Heartney, Eleanor. "Hedda Sterne at CDS." Art News 83, no. 6 (Summer 1984): 187.

Hedda Sterne: Portraits. New York: Lee Ault and Co., 1975.

Who's Who in American Art, 17th ed. New York: R.R. Bowker Co., 1986.

FLORINE STETTHEIMER (1871-1944)    Painter

See volume 1 of this book.

American Paintings. Brooklyn: The Brooklyn Museum, 1979.

Hartley, Marsden. "The Paintings of Florine Stettheimer." Creative Arts 9 (July 1931): 18-23.

Heins, Barbara. "Florine Stettheimer and the Avant-Garde American Portrait." New Haven: Yale University dissertation, 1986.

Obituary. The New York Times, 14 May 1944: 46.

Rubinstein, Charlotte Streifer. American Women Artists. Boston: G.K. Hall, 1982.

Tufts, Eleanor. American Women Artists, 1830-1930. Washington, D.C.: National Museum of Women in the Arts, 1987.

428

Tyler, Parker. "Stettheimer, Florine." Notable American Women, vol. 3. Edward T. James, ed. Cambridge, Massachusetts: Belknap Press of Harvard University Press, 1971.


MAY STEVENS (1924-    )    Painter

See volume 1 of this book.

American Herstory: Women and the U.S. Constitution. Curated by Eleanor Tufts. Atlanta: Atlanta College of Art, 1988.

Glueck, Grace. "May Stevens." The New York Times, 20 March 1981.

Knight, Christopher. "She Paints of Politics and Power." Los Angeles Herald Examiner, 21 April 1985: E2.

Lippard, Lucy. "Caring: Five Political Artists." Studio International 193, no. 987 (March 1977): 197-207.

May Stevens: Ordinary, Extraordinary, A Summation 1977-1984. Foreword by Patricia Hills. Essays by Donald Kuspit, Lucy Lippard, Moira Roth, and Lisa Tickner. Boston: Boston University, 1984.

Robinson, Hilary. Visibly Female, Feminism and Art: An Anthology London: Camden Press, 1987.

"272 Guggenheim Fellowships for $5.9 Million are Awarded." The New York Times, 13 April 1986.

Walker, John A. Rosa Luxemburg and Karl Liebknecht: Revolution, Remembrance, Representation. London: Pentonville Gallery, 1986.

Weisberg, Ruth. "Two Women Juxtaposed." Artweek 16, no. 19 (11 May 1985): 1.

Withers, Josephine. "Revising Our Forefathers: Reflections on the 'Ordinary Extraordinary' Art of May Stevens." Feminist Studies 13, no. 3 (Fall 1987): 485-512.

Zimmer, William. "Ten Major Women Artists." The New York Times, 22 March 1987.


HANNAH STEWART (1929-    )    Sculptor

Fuermann, George Melvin. The Face of Houston. Houston: Press of Premier, 1963.

A Marmac Guide to Houston and Galveston. Atlanta: Marmac
     Publishing, 1983.

Watson-Jones, Virginia. Contemporary American Women Sculptors.
     Phoenix: Oryx Press, 1986.


        LEORA KLAYMER STEWART (20th Century)   Fiber Artist

Gordon, Lillian. "Leora Stewart Manipulates Fiber to Her
     Advantage." Weaving and Fiber News 5, no. 2
     (November-December 1979).

Slesion, Suzanne. "Fiber Works on a Smaller Scale." The New York
     times, 17 May 1979:  C3.

Znamierowski, Nell. Fiber:  The Artist's View. Greenvale, New
     York:  Hillwood Art Gallery, Long Island University, 1983.


            HANNA STIEBEL (1923-    )   Sculptor

Fifty-Sixth Exhibition for Michigan Artists. Detroit:  Detroit
     Institute of Arts, 1966.

Michigan Collects Michigan Art. Pontiac:  Pontiac Art Center,
     1976.

Nawrocki, Dennis Alan, with Thomas J. Holleman. Art in Detroit
     Places. Detroit:  Wayne State University Press, 1980.

Redstone, Louis G. New Dimensions in Shopping Centers and Stores.
     New York:  McGraw-Hill, 1973.

_____, and Redstone, Ruth R. Public Art:  New Directions. New
     York:  McGraw-Hill, 1981.

Watson-Jones, Virgina. Contemporary American Women Sculptors.
     Phoenix: Oryx Press, 1986.


            MARGUERITE STIX (1907-1975)   Sculptor

See volume 1 of this book.

Campbell, Lawrence. "Marguerite Stix." Art News 57, no. 9
     (January 1959):  15.

Fitzsimmons, James. "Marguerite, Rennick and Schatz." Art
     Digest 26, no. 6 (15 December 1951):  20.

Marguerite. New York:  Bertha Schafer Gallery, 1953.

430

Marguerite Stix: Sculpture, Painting and Drawing. New York: Washington Irving Gallery, 1977.

Porter, Fairfield. "Marguerite." Art News 50, no. 8 (December 1951): 48.

Raynor, Vivien. "Marguerite Stix." Arts Magazine 35, nos. 8-9 (May-June 1961): 92.

ALICE KENT STODDARD (1884-1976)   Painter

American Art Annual, vol. 28. Washington, D.C.: American Federation of Arts, 1932.

Clark, Eliot. History of the National Academy of Design, 1825-1953. New York: Columbia University Press, 1954.

Huber, Christine. The Pennsylvania Academy and Its Women. Philadelphia: The Pennsylvania Academy of the Fine Arts, 1974.

Who's Who in American Art, vol. 1. Washington, D.C.: American Federation of Arts, 1935.

SYLVIA STONE (1928-   )   Sculptor

See volume 1 of this book.

Who's Who in American Art, 17th ed. New York: R.R. Bowker Co., 1986.

MARY STOPPERT (1941-   )   Sculptor

Abstract Art in Chicago. Chicago: Museum of Contemporary Art, 1976.

American Women Artists 1980. São Paulo, Brazil: Museu de Arte Contemporânea da Universidade de São Paulo, 1980.

Androgyny in Art. Hempstead, New York: Emily Lowe Gallery, 1982.

The Challenge of New Ideas: Contemporary Chicago Sculpture. Kalamazoo: Kalamazoo Institute of Arts, 1977.

Chicago: The City and Its Artists 1945-1978. Ann Arbor: University of Michigan, 1978.

Day, Holliday T. "Report from Chicago, Vital Signs: Drawing
    Invitational." Art in America 66, no. 6 (November-December
    1978): 38-39.

Morrison, C.L. "Reviews Chicago: . . . Mary Stoppert, Deson-Zaks
    Gallery." Artforum 14, no. 8 (April 1976): 78-79.

Schjeldahl, Peter. "Letter from Chicago." Art in America 64, no.
    4 (July-August 1976): 52-58.

Seventy-Fifth Exhibition by Artists of Chicago and Vicinity.
    Chicago: Art Institute of Chicago, 1974.

Seventy-Sixth Exhibition by Artists of Chicago and Vicinity.
    Chicago: Art Institute of Chicago, 1977.

Watson-Jones, Virginia. Contemporary American Women Sculptors.
    Phoenix: Oryx Press, 1986.


        MARIA LONGWORTH NICHOLS STORER (1849-1932)   Ceramicist

Anscombe, Isabelle. A Woman's Touch. New York: Viking Penguin,
    1984.

Barber, Edwin Atlee. Catalogue of American Potteries and
    Porcelain. Philadelphia: Pennsylvania Museum and School of
    Industrial Art, 1893.

Clark, Garth. A Century of Ceramics in the United States
    1878-1978. New York: E.P. Dutton, 1979.

Cummins, Virginia R. Rookwood Potpourri. Silver Springs,
    Maryland: Cliff R. Leonard and Duke Coleman, 1980.

Eidelberg, Martin. "Art Pottery." The Arts and Crafts Movement
    in America 1876-1916. Ed. Robert J. Clark. Princeton:
    Princeton University Press, 1972.

Elliot, Maud Howe, ed. Art and Handicraft in the Woman's Building
    of the Columbian Exposition, Chicago, 1843. Chicago: Rand
    McNally and Co., 1894: 103, 105.

Evans, Paul F. Art Pottery of the United States: An Encyclopedia
    of Producers and Their Marks. New York: Scribner's Sons,
    1974.

Henzke, Lucile. American Art Pottery. Camden, New Jersey:
    Nelson, 1970.

Keen, Kirsten Hoving. American Art Pottery 1875-1930. Wilmington,
    Delaware: Delaware Art Museum, 1978.

432

Kovel, Ralph, and Kovel, Terry. Kovel's Collector's Guide to
American Art Pottery. New York: Crown, 1974.

The Ladies, God Bless 'Em: The Women's Art Movement in Cincinnati
in the 19th Century. Cincinnati: Cincinnati Art Museum,
1976.

Logan, Mary S. The Part Taken by Women in American History.
Wilmington: Perry-Nalle Publishing Co., 1912; reprint ed.;
New York: Arno Press, 1972.

Peck, Herbert. The History of Rookwood Pottery. New York: Crown,
1968.

Perry, Mrs. Aaron F. "Decorative Pottery of Cincinnati." Harper's
New Monthly Magazine 62 (April-May 1881): 834-45.

Prather-Moses, Alice Irma. The International Dictionary of
Women Workers in the Decorative Arts. Metuchen, New Jersey:
Scarecrow Press, 1981: 121-22.

Storer, Maria Longworth (Nichols). History of the Cincinnati
Musical Festival and of the Rookwood. Paris, 1919.

Tanenhaus, Ruth A. "Rookwood: A Cincinnati Art Pottery." Art
and Antiques 3 (July-August 1980): 74-81.

Trapp, Kenneth R. "Japanese Influence in Early Rookwood Pottery."
Antiques 103, no. 1 (January 1973): 193-97.

Weimann, Jeanne Madeline. The Fair Women. Chicago: Academy
Chicago, 1981.


MARY CHASE PERRY STRATTON (1867-1961)   Ceramicist

Barber, Edwin Atlee. Catalogue of American Potteries and
Porcelain. Philadelphia: Pennsylvania Museum and School of
Industrial Art, 1893.

Bleicher, Fred, Hu, William C., and Uren, Marjorie E. Pewabic
Pottery: An Official History. Ann Arbor, Michigan: Arts
Ceramica, 1977.

Brunk, T. "Pewabic Pottery." Arts and Crafts in Detroit/1906-1976.
Detroit: Detroit Institute of Arts, 1976.

Callen, Anthea. Women Artists of the Arts and Crafts Movement.
New York: Pantheon, 1979.

Eidelberg, Martin. "Art Pottery." The Arts and Crafts Movement
in American 1876-1916. Ed. Robert J. Clark. Princeton:
Princeton University Press, 1972.

Evans, Paul F. Art Pottery of the United States: An Encyclopedia
of Producers and Their Marks. New York: Scribner's Sons,
1974.

Gibson, Athur H. Artists of Early Michigan.... Detroit: Wayne
State University Press, 1975 (under maiden name, Perry).

Henzke, Lucile. American Art Pottery. Camden, New Jersey:
Nelson, 1970.

Keen, Kirsten Hoving. American Art Pottery 1875-1930. Wilmington,
Delaware: Delaware Art Museum, 1978.

Kovel, Ralph, and Kovel, Terry. Kovel's Collector's Guide to
American Art Pottery. New York: Crown, 1974.

Moore, Julia G. History of the Detroit Society of Women Painters
and Sculptors, 1903-1953. River Rouge, Michigan: Victory
Printing Co., 1953.

Pear, Lillian Myers. The Pewabic Pottery: A History of Its
Products and People. Des Moines, Iowa: Wallace-Homestead
Book Co., 1976.

Robineau, Adelaide Alsop. "Mary Chase Perry--the Potter."
Keramik Studio 6, no. 10 (1905).

Stratton, Mary Chase. "Pewabic Records." American Ceramic Society
Bulletin 25 (15 October 1946).


                    MARIA JUDSON STREAN (1865-1949)  Miniaturist

American Art Annual, vol. 28. Washington, D.C.: American
Federation of Arts, 1932.

A Century of Women Artists in Cragsmoor. Cragsmoor, New York:
Cragsmoor Free Library, 1979.

Fielding, Mantle. Dictionary of American Painters, Sculptors and
Engravers. Enlarged ed. Greens Farms, Connecticut: Modern
Books and Crafts, 1974.

Fiftieth Anniversary Exhibition 1889-1939: National Association
of Women Painters and Sculptors. New York: American Fine
Arts Building, 1939.

434

Portraits by Distinguished American Artists. New York:  Grand
     Central Art Galleries, 1942:  78-79.

Woman's Who's Who of America. New York:  American Commonwealth
     Co., 1914.


          MARJORIE STRIDER (1939-    )   Sculptor

See volume 1 of this book.

Henry, Gerrit. "Marjorie Strider." Arts Magazine 59, no. 2
     (October 1984):  4.

Hunter, Sam. American Art of the 20th Century. New York:  Harry
     N. Abrams, 1972.

Saunders, Wade. "Hot Metal." Art in America 68, no. 6 (Summer
     1980):  87-95.

Van Wagner, Judith K.  Marjorie Strider:  10 Years 1970-1980.
     Greenvale, New York:  Hillwood Art Gallery, Long Island
     University, 1982.

Watson-Jones, Virginia. Contemporary American Women Sculptors.
     Phoenix:  Oryx Press, 1986.

Who's Who in America, 43rd ed.  Chicago:  Marquis, 1984.

Who's Who in American Art, 17th ed.  New York:  R.R. Bowker, 1986.


          LOUISA CATHERINE STROBEL (1803-1883)   Miniaturist

Groce, George C., and Wallace, David H.  The New-York Historical
     Society's Dictionary of Artists in America 1564-1860.  New
     Haven:  Yale University Press, 1957.

Severens, Martha R.  The Miniature Portrait Collection of the
     Carolina Art Association.  Charleston, South Carolina:  Gibbes
     Art Gallery, 1984:  110-14.


          GISELA-HEIDI STRUNCK (1945-    )   Sculptor

Fifth Texas Sculpture Symposium.  Dallas:  Connemara Conservancy,
     1985.

Kutner, Janet.  "Dallas:  Five Artists, Four Shows, Three
     Dimensions." Art News 76, no. 3 (March 1977):  95-98.

Tri-State Art Exhibition. Beaumont, Texas: Beaumont Art Museum, 1982.

Twenty-Seventh Annual Delta Art Exhibition. Little Rock: Arkansas Arts Center, 1984.

Watson-Jones, Virginia. Contemporary American Women Sculptors. Phoenix: Oryx Press, 1986.


JANE STUART (1812-1888)   Painter

See volume 1 of this book.

Fine, Elsa Honing. Women and Art. Montclair, New Jersey and London: Allanheld and Schram/Prior, 1978.

Harding, Jonathan P. The Boston Athenaeum Collection. Boston: The Boston Athenaeum, 1984.

19th Century American Women Artists. New York: Whitney Museum of American Art Downtown Branch, 1976.

Powel, Mary E. "Miss Jane Stuart." Bulletin of the Newport Historical Society 31 (January 1920): 1-16.


MICHELLE STUART (1938-    )   Sculptor and Painter

See volume 1 of this book.

Artner, Alan G. "Michelle Stuart." Chicago Tribune, 21 March 1986, Section 7: 52.

Beal, Graham. Michelle Stuart: Place and Time. Minneapolis: Walker Art Center, 1983.

Brenson, Michael. "Michelle Stuart." The New York Times, 18 April 1986.

Cavaliere, Barbara. "Michelle Stuart." Arts Magazine 53, no. 10 (June 1979): 30.

Contemporary Reflections. Ridgefield, Connecticut: Aldrich Museum of Contemporary Art, 1973.

Duvert, Elizabeth. "With Stone, Star, and Earth." The Desert Is No Lady. Ed. by Vera Norwood and Janice Monk. New Haven: Yale University Press, 1987: 197-222.

Forgey, Benjamin. "Michelle Stuart at Kornblatt." The Washington Post, 23 April 1988.

436

Hobbs, Robert. *Michelle Stuart*. Cambridge, Massachusetts:
Massachusetts Institute of Technology, 1977.

*I-80 Series: Michelle Stuart*. Omaha, Nebraska: Joslyn Art
Museum, 1981.

Januszczak, Waldemar. "Michelle Stuart." *The Guardian* (London),
25 September 1979.

Kent, Sarah. *Michelle Stuart/Paperwork*. London: Institute of
Contemporary Art, 1979.

Lippard, Lucy. *Ten Artists*. Fredonia, New York: State University
of New York, 1973.

Lipsey, Roger. "Michelle Stuart: A Decade of Work." *Arts
Magazine* 56, no. 8 (April 1982): 110-111.

Lubell, Ellen. "Michelle Stuart." *Arts Magazine* 49, no. 9 (May
1975): 12.

_____. "Michelle Stuart at Susan Caldwell." *Art in America* 70,
no. 5 (May 1982): 143-44.

Phillips, Patricia C. "A Blossoming of Cells." *Artforum* 25, no. 2
(October 1986): 116-17, cover.

Sandqvist, Tom. *Michelle Stuart*. Helsinki: Galeria Exit Krista
Mikkola, 1984.

Schjeldahl, Peter. "Michelle Stuart." *The New York Times*, 20
August 1972.

Sparks, Esther. *Michelle Stuart*. Chicago: The Arts Club of
Chicago, 1986.

Stoops, Susan L. *Ashes in Arcadia*. Waltham, Massachusetts: Rose
Art Museum, Brandeis University, 1988.

_____. *Silent Gardens*. Waltham, Massachusetts: Rose Art Museum
Brandeis University, 1988.

Tuchman, Maurice, and Freeman, Judy. *The Spiritual in Art:
Abstract Painting 1890-1985*. Los Angeles: Los Angeles County
Museum of Art, 1986.

Van Wagner, Judy Collischan. *Michelle Stuart*. Greenvale, New
York: Hillwood Art Gallery, Long Island University, 1985.

_____. *Reflections, New Conceptions of Nature*. Greenvale, New
York: Hillwood Art Gallery, Long Island University, 1984.

Westkott, Hanne.  "Michelle Stuart."  Kunstforum International,
     May-August 1981.

Westfall, Stephen.  "Melancholy Mapping."  Art in America 75, no. 2
     (February 1987):  104-09.

Winter, Peter.  "Kunstmarkt...Michelle Stuart in Hamburg."
     Frankfurter Allgemeine Zeitung, 31 May 1983.


               AUSTA DENSMORE STURDEVANT (1855-1936)   Painter

Buff, Barbara.  "Cragsmoor, an Early American Art Colony."
     Antiques 114 (November 1978):  1056-67.

A Century of Women Artists in Cragsmoor.  Cragsmoor, New York:
     Cragsmoor Free Public Library, 1979.

Obituary.  Who's Who in American Art, vol. 2.  Washington, D.C.:
     American Federation of Arts, 1937.


               SUSANNE SUBA (1913-    )   Illustrator

Frost, Rosamund.  "It Pays to Advertise."  Art News 42, no. 9
     (August-September 1943):  22.

Spots by Suba from the New Yorker.  New York:  E.P. Dutton and Co.,
     1944.

Who's Who in American Art.  New York:  R.R. Bowker, 1978.


               BETH AMES SWARTZ (1936-   )   Painter

See volume 1 of this book.

Donnell-Kotrozo, Carol.  "Beth Ames Swartz, Elaine Horwitch
     Galleries."  Artforum 22, no. 3 (November 1983):  84-85.

Nelson, Mary Carroll.  Connecting:  The Art of Beth Ames Swartz.
     Flagstaff, Arizona:  Northland Press, 1984.

Who's Who in American Art, 17th ed.  New York:  R.R. Bowker Co.,
     1986.


               ANNE TABACHNICK (1937-   )   Painter

See volume 1 of this book.

Collected Visions, Women Artists at the Bunting Institute
     1961-1986.  Cambridge:  Radcliffe College, 1986.

438

Henry, Gerrit. "Anne Tabachnick at Ingber." Art in America 73,
no. 3 (March 1985): 161.


ATHENA TACHA (1936-    )    Sculptor

See volume 1 of this book.

Lunde, Karl. "Art and the Environment." Arts Magazine 59, no. 7
(March 1985): 9.

"Perils of Public Sculpture." Art in America 76, no. 2 (February
1988): 176.

Rosen, Steven. "Women are Reshaping the Field of Public Art."
The New York Times, 8 November 1987): Y36.

Tacha, Athena. "Blair Fountain River Sculpture." Landscape
Architecture 74, no. 2 (March-April 1984): 72-74.

Watson-Jones, Virginia. Contemporary American Women Sculptors.
Phoenix: Oryx Press, 1986.

Wolff, Theodore F. "Artist Athena Tacha." The Christian Science
Monitor, 9 April 1981: 18.


AGNES TAIT [McNULTY] (1894-1981)    Painter

See volume 1 of this book.

Peña, Lydia M. "In the American Scene:  The Life and Times of
Agnes Tait." Woman's Art Journal 5, no. 1 (Spring-Summer
1984): 35-39.

_____. The Life and Times of Agnes Tait. Arvada, Colorado:
Arvada Center for the Arts and Humanities, and Roswell, New
Mexico: Roswell Museum and Art Center, 1984.


TOSHIKO TAKAEZU (1929-    )    Ceramicist

Brown, Conrad. "Toshiko Takaezu." Craft Horizons 19-20
(March-April 1959): 22-26.

Clark, Garth. American Potters, The Work of Twenty Modern Masters.
New York: Watson-Guptill Publications, 1981.

_____. A Century of Ceramics in the United States 1878-1978. New
York: E.P. Dutton, 1979.

Clay Today. Iowa City: School of Fine Arts, State University of Iowa, New Gallery, 1962.

Contemporary Ceramics: The Artist's Viewpoint. Kalamazoo, Michigan: Kalamazoo Institute of Art, 1977.

"Cranbrook 12: Portfolio." Ceramics Monthly 24 (June 1976).

A Decade of Ceramic Art: 1962-1972. Essay by Suzanne Foley. San Francisco: San Francisco Museum of Modern Art, 1972.

GRACE TALBOT (1901-    )    Sculptor

See volume 1 of this book.

American Art Annual, vol. 28. Washington, D.C.: American Federation of Arts, 1932.

MARY HARVEY TANNAHILL (1863-1951)    Painter

American Art Annual, vol. 28. Washington, D.C.: American Federation of Arts, 1932.

Eight Southern Women. Greenville, South Carolina: Greenville County Museum of Art, 1986.

Fiftieth Anniversary Exhibition 1889-1939. New York: National Association of Women Painters and Sculptors, 1939.

"Painters of Miniatures." The New York Times, 2 February 1902: 10.

Who's Who in American Art, vol. 1. Washington, D.C.: American Federation of Arts, 1935.

Wolf, Amy J. New York Society of Women Artists 1925. New York: ACA Galleries, 1987.

JOAN E. TANNER (1935-    )    Painter

Dills, Keith. "Risks and Declarations." Artweek 17, no. 26 (26 July 1986): 7.

Joan E. Tanner. California Viewpoints. Essay by Susan C. Larsen. Santa Barbara: Santa Barbara Museum of Art, 1986.

DOROTHEA TANNING (1910-    )    Painter

See volume 1 of this book.

Chadwick, Whitney. Women Artists and the Surrealist Movement. Boston:  New York Graphic Society, Little, Brown and Co., 1985.

Dorothea Tanning. Basel, Switzerland:  Galerie d'Art Moderne Marie-Suzanne Feigel, 1966.

Dorothea Tanning. On Paper, 1948-1986. New York:  Kent Fine Art, 1987.

Geldzahler, Henry. "Dorothea Tanning." Elle, April 1987:  116-18.

Gibson, Ann. "Dorothea Tanning:  The Impassioned Double Entendre." Arts Magazine 58, no. 1 (September 1983):  102-03.

Gruen, John. "Among the Sacred Monsters." Art News 87, no. 3 (March 1988):  178-82.

Heartney, Eleanor. "Dorothea Tanning." Art News 86, no. 6 (Summer 1987):  211-12.

Heller, Nancy G. Women Artists. New York:  Abbeville Press, 1987.

National Museum of Women in the Arts. New York:  Harry N. Abrams, Inc., 1987:  94-95.

Rian, Jeffrey. "Dorothea Tanning at Kent." Art in America 75, no. 4 (April 1987):  223.

Schwabsky, Barry. "Dorothea Tanning." Arts Magazine 61, no. 7 (March 1987):  106-07.

Tanning, Dorothea. Birthday. San Francisco:  Lapis Press, 1986.

Wechsler, Jeffrey. Surrealism and American Art 1931-1947. New Brunswick, New Jersey:  Rutgers University, 1977.

WALDINE TAUCH (1892-1986)    Sculptor

See volume 1 of this book.

American Art Annual, vol. 28. Washington, D.C.:  American Federation of Arts, 1932.

O'Brien, Esse Forrester. Art and Artists of Texas. Dallas:  Tardy Publishing Co., 1935.

LENORE TAWNEY (1925-    )    Fiber Artist

See volume 1 of this book.

An Exhibition of Collages, Constructions, Drawings, Objects and
    Weavings by Lenore Tawney. Philadelphia:  Peale Galleries of
    the Pennsylvania Academy of Fine Arts, 1970.

Henry, Gerrit.  "Cloudworks and Collage."  Art in America 74, no. 6
    (June 1986):  116-21.

Howard, Richard.  "Tawney."  Crafts Horizons 35, no. 1 (February
    1975):  46-47, 71-72, cover.

Manhart, Marcia and Tom, eds.  The Eloquent Object.  Tulsa,
    Oklahoma:  Philbrook Museum of Art, 1987.

The Presence of Light.  Curated by Dominique Mazeaud and Betty
    Park.  Dallas:  Meadows Gallery, Southern Methodist
    University, 1984.

Watson-Jones, Virginia.  Contemporary American Women Sculptors.
    Phoenix:  Oryx Press, 1986.

Winter, Amy.  "Lenore Tawney."  Arts Magazine 60, no. 5 (January
    1986):  108.

Znamierowski, Nell.  Fiber:  The Artist's View.  Greenvale, New
    York:  Hillwood Art Gallery, Long Island University, 1983.

ANNA HEYWARD TAYLOR (1879-1956)    Painter and Printmaker

American Art Annual, vol. 28.  Washington, D.C.:  American
    Federation of Arts, 1932.

Bellaman, Henry.  "The Work of Anna Heyward Taylor."  The State, 21
    December 1930.

Contemporary Art of the United States.  New York:  World's Fair,
    IBM Building, 1940.

Flint, Janet Altic.  Provincetown Printers:  A Woodcut Tradition.
    Washington, D.C.:  National Museum of American Art, 1983.

Obituary.  Who's Who in American Art, vol. 7.  Washington, D.C.:
    American Federation of Arts, 1959.

Parris, Nina G.  South Carolina Collection 1779-1985.  Columbia,
    South Carolina:  Columbia Museum, 1985.

Severens, Martha. Anna Heyward Taylor Printmaker. Greenville, South Carolina: Greenville County Museum of Art, and Charleston, South Carolina: Gibbes Art Gallery, 1987.

Taylor, Anna Heyward. "British Guiana Flowers." The Christian Science Monitor, 17 January 1921.

Women Printmakers. Philadelphia: Philadelphia Museum of Art, 1956.


JANE SIMON TELLER (1911-    ) Sculptor

Biennial Exhibition New Jersey Artists. Newark: Newark Museum, 1977.

Day, Worden. "Jane Teller." Art News 61, no. 1 (March 1962): 50.

DePaoli, Geri. "Jane Teller's Sculpture and Drawings: Powerful Presence in the 'Big Rhythm.'" Woman's Art Journal 8, no. 1 (Spring/Summer 1987): 28-32.

Merlach, Dona Z. Woodcraft: Basic Concepts and Skills. New York: Golden Press, 1976.

Miller, David. Jane Teller Retrospective. Sarasota Springs, New York: Skidmore College, 1986.

National Association of Women Artists Annual Exhibition. New York: National Academy of Design, 1960.

1962 Biennial Exhibition: Contemporary American Art. New York: Whitney Museum of American Art, 1962.

Powerful Presences/Tender Connections. Montclair, New Jersey: Montclair Art Museum, 1987.

Recent Sculpture U.S.A. New York: The Museum of Modern Art, 1959 (traveling exhibition).

Sculptors Guild Annual Exhibition. New York: Lever House, 1962-82.

Van Dommelen, David. Walls: Enrichment and Ornamentation. New York: Funk and Wagnalls, 1965.

Watson-Jones, Virgina. Contemporary American Women Sculptors. Phoenix: Oryx Press, 1986.

Women's Caucus for Art Honor Awards. Houston: National Women's Caucus for Art, 1988.

Wilson, Donald. <u>Wood Design</u>. New York: Watson-Guptill, 1968.


ALLIE VICTORIA TENNANT (1898-1971)    Sculptor

See volume 1 of this book.

O'Brien, Esse Forrester. <u>Art and Artists of Texas</u>. Dallas:    Tardy
      Publishing Co., 1935:    276-77.

Stewart, Rick. <u>Lone Star Regionalism</u>. Dallas:  Dallas Museum of
      Art, 1985.

<u>Texas Painting and Sculpture:  20th Century</u>. Dallas:  Southern
      Methodist University, 1971.


MADGE TENNENT (1889-1972)    Painter

Charlot, Jean. <u>The Donald Angus Collection of Oil Paintings by
      Madge Tennent</u>. Honolulu:  The Contemporary Art Center of
      Hawaii, 1968.

<u>Contemporary Art in the United States</u>. New York:  IBM Building,
      World's Fair, 1940.

Menton, Linda.  "Madge Tennent:  Artist of Hawaii." <u>Woman's
      Art Journal</u> 2, no. 1 (Spring/Summer 1981):  30-34.

Prithwish, Neogy. <u>Artists of Hawaii:  19 Painters and Sculptors</u>,
      vol. 1. Honolulu:  University Press of Hawaii, 1974.

Tennent, Arthur. <u>The Art and Writing of Madge Tennent</u>. Honolulu:
      Island Heritage, 1977.

_____. <u>Madge Tennent, My Mother</u>. Honolulu:  privately printed,
      1982.

Tennent, Madge. <u>Autobiography of an Unarrived Artist</u>. New York:
      Brentano's for Columbia University Press, 1949.

_____. <u>Hawaiian People; Drawings by Madge Tennent</u>. Honolulu:
      Advertiser Publishing Co., 1936.

<u>Who's Who in American Art</u>, vol. 3.  Washington, D.C.:  American
      Federation of Arts, 1940.


THEODORA W. THAYER (1868-1905)    Painter

<u>American Art Annual</u>, vol. 1.  New York:  Macmillan, 1899.

444

Fielding, Mantle. Dictionary of American Painters, Sculptors and Engravers. Enlarged ed. Greens Farms, Connecticut: Modern Books and Crafts, 1974.

Fuller, Lucia Fairchild. "Modern American Miniature Painters." Scribner's Magazine 67 (March 1920): 381-84.

Lounsbery, Elizabeth. "American Miniature Painting." The Mentor 4, no. 23 (5 January 1917): 8-9, 11.

"Painters of Miniatures." The New York Times, 2 February 1902: 10.

JULIA THECLA (1896-1973)   Painter

"Hoyer and Thecla, Painters with Imagination." Art Digest 18, no. 2 (15 October 1943): 9.

Lifton, Norma. "Julia Thecla." New Art Examiner 14, no. 1 (September 1986): 47.

Thwaites, J. and M. "Julia Thecla at the Rouillier Gallery, Chicago." Magazine of Art 30, no. 3 (March 1937): 178-79.

Wechsler, Jeffrey. Surrealism and American Art 1931-1947. New Brunswick: Rutgers University, 1977.

ALMA THOMAS (1891-1978)   Painter

See volume 1 of this book.

Alma W. Thomas: Recent Paintings 1975-1976. New York: Martha Jackson West Gallery, 1976.

Alma W. Thomas, A Retrospective Exhibition (1959-1966). Intro. by David C. Driskell. Washington, D.C.: Howard University Gallery of Art, 1966.

Atkinson, J. Edward, ed. Black Dimensions in Contemporary American Art. New York: New American Library, 1971.

Cavaliere, Barbara. "Alma W. Thomas." Arts Magazine 51, no. 5 (January 1977): 42.

Fine, Elsa Honig. The Afro-American Artist. New York: Holt Rinehart and Winston, 1973.

Fraser, C. Gerald. "Alma W. Thomas is Dead at 86; Widely Praised Abstract Painter." The New York Times, 25 February 1978, section C: 24.

Mellow, James R. "Expert Abstractions by Alma Thomas." The New York Times, 29 April 1972, section: L:   27.

North, Charles. "Alma Thomas at Martha Jackson." Art in America 65, no. 1 (January-February 1977):   125-26.

National Museum of Women in the Arts. New York:  Harry N. Abrams, Inc., 1987:   84-85, 235.

The Phillips Collection, A Summary Catalogue. Washington, D.C.: The Phillips Collection, 1985.

Richard, Paul. "Alma Thomas, 86, Dies; Washington Color Artist." Washington Post, 25 February 1978, section B:   6.

Schjeldahl, Peter. "Alma W. Thomas." The New York Times, 14 May 1972, section D:   23.

Shirley, David L. "At 77, She's Made It to the Whitney." The New York Times, 4 May 1972, section C:   52.

The Thirty-Fifth Biennial Exhibition of Contemporary American Painting. Washington, D.C.:  Corcoran Gallery of Art, 1977.

HANNE TIERNEY (c. 1941-    )   Performance Artist

Bass, Ruth. "Backstage at the Guggenheim." Art News 85, no. 6 (Summer 1986):   16, 18.

_____. "Hanne Tierney." Art News 81, no. 3 (March 1982):   218.

Cohen, Ronny H. "Hanne Tierney." Artforum 20, no. 8 (April 1982): 80.

Glueck, Grace. "Hanne Tierney." The New York Times, 14 December 1981.

Matrix 97. Hartford:  Wadsworth Atheneum, 1987.

Tierney, Hanne. Where's Your Baby Brother, Becky Bunting. Garden City, New York:  Doubleday, 1979.

PATRICIA TILLMAN (1954-    )   Sculptor

The Art Center 1983 Competition. Waco, Texas:  The Art Center, 1983.

Carlozzi, Annette. 50 Texas Artists. San Francisco:  Chronicle Books, 1986.

Freudenheim, Susan. "Patricia Tillman at Texas Christian
    University." Art in America 72, no. 10 (November 1984):   171,
    173.

Hickey, Dave. "Linnea Glatt and Patricia Tillman:  Post-Modern
    Options." Artspace 9, no. 3 (Summer 1985):   28-31.

Made-in-Texas. Austin:  University Art Museum, University of
    Texas, 1979.

Shreveport Art Guild National. Shreveport, Louisiana:  Meadows
    Museum of Art of Centenary College, 1980.


        MARY BRADISH TITCOMB (1856-1927)   Painter

Fielding, Mantle. Dictionary of American Painters, Sculptors and
    Engravers. Enlarged ed.  Greens Farms, Connecticut:  Modern
    Books and Crafts, 1974.

"Mary Bradish Titcomb." American Art Newsletter 3.  Los Angeles:
    De Ville Galleries, 1985.

Obituary. American Art Annual, vol. 26.  Washington, D.C.:
    American Federation of Arts, 1929.

"President Praises Boston Artist." Boston Advertiser, 15 February
    1915.

"Rises from Brockton Teacher to 'Painter for President'." Boston
    Evening Record, 18 February 1915.

Tufts, Eleanor. American Women Artists, 1830-1930. Washington,
    D.C.:  National Museum of Women in the Arts, 1987.


        BIANCA TODD (1889-    )   Painter

Exhibition of Oil Paintings and Mural Designs by Bianca Todd. New
    York:  Argent Galleries, n.d. [ca. 1932].

Fiftieth Anniversary Exhibition 1889-1939. New York:  National
    Association of Women Painters and Sculptors, 1939.

Who's Who in American Art, vol. 5.  Washington, D.C.:  American
    Federation of Arts, 1953.


        MARY LAWRENCE TONETTI (1868-1945)   Sculptor

American Art Annual, vol. 14.  Washington, D.C.:  American
    Federation of Arts, 1917.

447

Obituary.  Who's Who in American Art, vol. 4.  Washington, D.C.:
    American Federation of Arts, 1947.

Savell, Isabelle Keating.  The Tonetti Years at Snedens Landing.
    New City, New York:  Historical Society of Rockland County,
    1977.

Tharp, Louise Hall.  Saints-Gaudens and the Gilded Age.  Boston:
    Little, Brown, 1969.


                    HELEN TORR (1886-1967)   Painter

See volume 1 of this book.

Archives of American Art.  A Checklist of the Collection.
    Washington, D.C.:  Smithsonian Institution, 1975.

An Exhibition of Women Students of William Merritt Chase.  New
    York:  Marbella Gallery, 1973.

Henry, Gerrit.  "Helen Torr."  Art News 79, no. 7 (September 1980):
    25-26.


                    ROSA M. TOWNE (1827-1909)   Painter

See volume 1 of this book.

Groce, George C., and Wallace, David H.  The New-York Historical
    Society's Dictionary of Artists in America 1564-1860.  New
    Haven:  Yale University Press, 1957.


               ELIZABETH TRACY [MONTMINY] (1911-    )   Painter

Marling, Karal Ann.  Wall-to-Wall America.  Minneapolis:
    University of Minnesota Press, 1982.

Painting America.  Mural Art in the New Deal Era.  Essay by Janet
    Marqusee.  New York:  Midtown Galleries, 1988.

Park, Marlene, and Markowitz, Gerald E.  Democratic Vistas, Post
    Offices and Public Art in the New Deal.  Philadelphia:  Temple
    University Press, 1984.


               JOYCE WAHL TREIMAN (1922-    )   Painter

See volume 1 of this book.

448

Bloch, Maurice, and Holcomb, Grant.  Introduction by Selma Holo.
    Joyce Treiman:  Friends and Strangers.  Los Angeles:  Fisher
    Gallery, University of Southern California, 1988.

1951 Annual Exhibition of Contemporary American Painting.  New
    York:  Whitney Museum of American Art, 1951.

1952 Annual Exhibition of Contemporary American Painting.  New
    York:  Whitney Museum of American Art, 1952.

1953 Annual Exhibition of Contemporary American Painting.  New
    York:  Whitney Museum of American Art, 1953.

1958 Annual Exhibition of Contemporary American Painting. New
    York:  Whitney Museum of American Art, 1958.

Schulze, Franz.  "Straightforward Portraits."  Chicago Daily News,
    2 April 1962.

"Times Honors Women of the Year."  Los Angeles Times, 14 December
    1965.

"Treiman Retrospective Called Career of a Maverick."  Los Angeles
    Times, 5 February 1978, Calender.

A View of Her Own:  Images of Women by Women Artists.  Grinnell,
    Iowa:  Grinnell College, 1987:  30.

Wolff, Theodore F.  "Swimming Against the Contemporary Tide."  The
    Christian Science Monitor, 31 May 1988:  21-22.

Women's Caucus for Art Honors Award.  Los Angeles:  Women's Caucus
    for Art, 1985.


                SELINA TRIEFF (1934-    )   Painter

See volume 1 of this book.

"Album:  Selina Trieff."  Arts Magazine 60, no. 9 (May 1986):
    112-13.

Campbell, Lawrence.  "Selina Trieff at Graham Modern."  Art in
    America 74, no. 12 (December 1986):  138-40.

Marter, Joan.  "Confrontations:  The Paintings of Selina Trieff."
    Arts Magazine 60, no. 10 (Summer 1986):  51-53.

Mullarkey, Maureen.  "Selina Trieff."  Arts Magazine 58, no. 9 (May
    1984):  8.

Russell, John. "Selina Trieff, Graham Gallery." The New York
    Times, 12 June 1987: Y18.

Selina Trieff. Catalogue with introduction by Lawrence Alloway.
    New York: Graham Modern Gallery, 1986.


                  ANNE TRUITT (1921-    )  Sculptor

See volume 1 of this book.

Frank, Elizabeth. "Anne Truitt at Emmerich." Art in America 68,
    no. 5 (May 1980): 150-51.

Princenthal, Nancy. "Anne Truitt at André Emmerich." Art in
    America 75, no. 2 (February 1987): 142.

Russell, John. "New Sculpture by Anne Truitt." The New York
    Times, 7 March 1980: C19.

Russo, Alexander. Profiles on Women Artists. Frederick, Maryland:
    University Publications of America, 1985.

Truitt, Anne. Turn, The Journal of an Artist. New York: Viking,
    1986.

200 Years of American Sculpture. New York: Whitney Museum of
    American Art, 1976.

Watson-Jones, Virginia. Contemporary American Women Sculptors.
    Phoenix: Oryx Press, 1986.


                GRACE H. TURNBULL (1880-1976)  Sculptor

See volume 1 of this book.

American Art Annual, vol. 28. Washington, D.C.: American
    Federation of Arts, 1932.

Fiftieth Annual Exhibition. New York: National Association of
    Women Painters and Sculptors, 1942: no. 87.

"A Painter with a Literary Background." Art Digest 6 (15 October
    1931): 6.

Schnier, Jacques. Sculpture in Modern America. Berkeley:
    University of California Press, 1948.

HELEN M. TURNER (1858-1958)    Painter

See volume 1 of this book.

American Art Annual, vol. 28.  Washington, D.C.:  American
Federation of Arts, 1932.

Bryant, Lorinda Munson.  American Pictures and Their Painters.  New
York:  John Lane Co., 1917.

Buff, Barbara.  "Cragsmoor, an Early American Art Colony."
Antiques 114 (November 1978):  1056-67.

"Coral, A Painting by Helen Turner."  International Studio 76, no.
309 (March 1923):  441.

Eight Southern Women.  Greenville, South Carolina:  Greenville
County Museum of Art, 1986.

An Exhibition of Paintings by Six American Women.  Saint Louis:
City Art Museum, 1918.

Gerdts, William H.  American Impressionism.  New York:  Abbeville
Press, 1984:  230-31.

Heller, Nancy G.  Women Artists.  New York:  Abbeville Press, 1987.

Lee, Cuthbert.  Contemporary American Portrait Painters.  New York:
W.W. Norton and Co., 1929:  43-44.

The Phillips Collection, A Summary Catalogue.  Washington, D.C.:
The Phillips Collection, 1985.

Rabbage, Lewis Hoyer.  Helen M. Turner, N.A., A Retrospective
Exhibition.  Cragsmoor, New York:  Cragsmoor Free Library,
1983.

Tufts, Eleanor.  American Women Artists, 1830-1930.  Washington,
D.C.:  National Museum of Women in the Arts, 1987.


MARTHA (MATTIE) SCUDDER TWACHTMAN (1861-1936)    Painter and Etcher

Catalogue of the Eight Annual Exhibition of the School of Design
of the University of Cincinnati.  Cincinnati:  University of
Cincinnati, 1876.

Peet, Phyllis.  American Women of the Etching Revival.  Atlanta:
High Museum of Art, 1988.

The Work of Women Etchers of America.  New York:  Union League
Club, 1888.

ALICE KELLOGG TYLER (1864-1900)    Painter

Clarkson, Ralph. "Chicago Painters Past and Present." Art and
    Archaeology 12 (October 1921):   139.

Fraser, W. Lewis. "American Artists Series." Century
    Magazine 45, no. 3 (January 1893):   478 (and illus. p. 467).

Pattison, James W. "Water-color Exhibition at the Art Institute."
    Brush and Pencil 4, no. 3 (1899):   151-52.

Williams, Melissa Pierce. Alice Kellogg Tyler. Kansas City,
    Missouri:  Williams and McCormick, 1987.

_____. Alice Kellogg Tyler, Private Works. Columbia, Missouri:
    Williams and McCormick, 1986.

DORIS ULMANN (1884-1934)    Photographer

The Appalachian Photographs of Doris Ulmann. Text by John Jacob
    Niles and Jonathan Williams. Penland, South Carolina:  The
    Jargon Society, 1971.

The Darkness and the Light:  Photographs by Doris Ulmann. New
    York:  Aperture, 1974.

Eaton, Allen H. Handicrafts of the Southern Highlands. (50 photos
    by Doris Ullman). New York:  Russell Sage Foundation, 1937.

Featherstone, David. Doris Ulmann:  American Portraits.
    Albuquerque:  University of New Mexico Press, 1985.

Garland, Hamlin. "Doris Ulmann's Photographs." The Mentor, July
    1921:  42, 44.

Peterkin, Julia. Roll, Jordon, Roll. Illustrated by Doris Ulmann.
    London:  Jonathan Cape, 1934.

Thornton, Gene. "Ulmann Forces A New Look at Pictorialism." The
    New York Times, 12 January 1975, section D:   23.

Ulmann, Doris. "Among the Southern Mountaineers." The Mentor 18
    (August 1928):   23-32.

Women of Photography. An Historical Survey. San Francisco:  San
    Francisco Museum of Art, 1975.

LEILA USHER (1859-1955)    Sculptor

See volume 1 of this book.

American Art Annual, vol. 28.  Washington, D.C.:  American
    Federation of Arts, 1932.

Woman's Who's Who of America.  New York:  American Commonwealth
    Co., 1914.


ANNA M. VALENTIEN (1862-1947)    Potter

American Art Annual, vol. 28.  Washington, D.C.:  American
    Federation of Arts, 1932.

Cummins, Virginia R.  Rockwood Pottery Potpourri.  Silver Springs,
    Maryland:  Cliff R. Leonard and Duke Coleman, 1980.

Kamerling, Bruce.  "Anna and Albert Valentien:  The Arts and Crafts
    Movement in San Diego."  The Journal of San Diego History 24,
    no. 3 (Summer 1978):  343-66.

_____.  "Anna & Albert Valentien:  The Arts and Crafts Movement in
    San Diego."  Arts & Crafts Quarterly 1, no. 4 (July 1987):  1,
    12-20.

Ode to Nature:  Flowers and Landscapes of the Rookwood Pottery,
    1880-1940.  New York:  Jordan-Volpe Gallery, 1980.


ANNE GREGORY VAN BRIGGLE [RITTER] (1868-1929)    Painter and Potter

See volume 1 of this book.

American Art Annual, vol. 1.  New York:  Macmillan, 1899.

Bogue, Dorothy McGraw.  The Van Briggle Story.  Colorado Springs:
    Century One Press, 1976.

A Show of Color:  100 Years of Painting in the Pike's Peak Region.
    Colorado Springs:  Colorado Springs Fine Arts Center, 1971.

Van Briggle Pottery:  The Early Years.  Colorado Springs, Colorado
    Springs Fine Arts Center, 1975.


KATHERINE GIBSON VAN CORTLANDT (1895-    )    Sculptor

Proske, Beatrice G.  Brookgreen Gardens Sculpture.  Brookgreen
    Gardens, South Carolina:  Brookgreen Gardens, 1943.

Who's Who in American Art, vol. 3.  Washington, D.C.:  American
    Federation of Arts, 1940.


              BEATRICE WHITNEY VAN NESS (1888-1981)    Painter

American Art Annual, vol. 18.  Washington, D.C.:  American
    Federation of Arts, 1921.

Fielding, Mantle.  Dictionary of American Painters, Sculptors and
    Engravers.  Enlarged ed.  Greens Farms, Connecticut:  Modern
    Books, 1974.

National Museum of Women in the Arts.  New York:  Harry N. Abrams,
    Inc., 1987:  82-83.

Stahl, Elizabeth M.  Beatrice Whitney Van Ness 1888-1981.  Boston:
    Childs Gallery [1987].


              DOROTHY VARIAN (1895-1985)    Painter

See volume 1 of this book.

American Art Annual, vol. 28.  Washington, D.C.:  American
    Federation of Arts, 1932.

Archives of American Art.  Collection of Exhibition Catalogs.
    Boston:  G.K. Hall and Co., 1979.

Second Biennial Exhibition of Contemporary American Painting.  New
    York:  Whitney Museum of American Art, 1934, no. 102.


  ELIZABETH O'NEILL VERNER (1884-1979)    Painter and Illustrator

American Art Annual, vol. 28.  Washington, D.C.:  American
    Federation of Arts, 1932.

American Prints in the Library of Congress:  A Catalog of the
    Collection.  Baltimore:  Johns Hopkins Press, 1970.

Chambers, Bruce W.  Art and Artists of the South.  Columbia, South
    Carolina:  University of South Carolina Press, 1984.

Elizabeth O'Neill Verner, A Retrospective Exhibition on Her 80th
    Birthday.  Charleston, South Carolina:  Gibbes Art Gallery,
    1963.

Mirror of Time:  Elizabeth O'Neill Verner's Charleston.  Columbia,
    South Carolina:  McKissick Museums, University of South
    Carolina, 1983.

454

Obituary. Who's Who in American Art, vol. 14. Washington, D.C.: American Federation of Arts, 1980.

Parris, Nina G. South Carolina Collection 1779-1985. Columbia, South Carolina: The Columbia Museum, 1985.

Robinson, Bertram. "Etchings Done in Peacetime by Mrs. Verner at Plymouth Find Wartime Use." The Christian Science Monitor, 1 December 1942.

Verner, Elizabeth O'Neill. Mellowed by Time; A Charleston Notebook. Columbia, South Carolina: Bostick and Thornley, 1941.

_____. Other Places. Columbia, South Carolina: Bostick and Thornley, 1946.

_____. Prints and Impressions of Charleston. Forty-Eight Etchings by Elizabeth O'Neill Verner. Columbia, South Carolina: Bostick and Thornley, 1945.

_____. The Stonewall Ladies. Columbia, South Carolina: Tradd Street Press, 1963.


RUTH LANDSHOFF VOLLMER (1899-1982)   Sculptor

See volume 1 of this book.

Westfall, Stephen. "Preserving the Mystery: The Art of Ruth Vollmer." Arts Magazine 58, no. 6 (February 1984): 74-76.

Who's Who in American Art. New York: R.R. Bowker Co., 1978.


URSULA VON RYDINGSVARD (1942-    )   Sculptor

See volume 1 of this book.

Shepard, Ileen. Sculpture of the 80's. Essay by Lowery S. Sims. Queens, New York: Queens Museum, 1987.

Stavitsky, Gail. "Judith Murray/Ursula Von Rydingsvard." Arts Magazine 60, no. 5 (January 1986): 144.

Van Wagner, Judy Collischan. Judith Murray, Painting. Ursula von Rydingsvard, Sculpture. Greenvale, New York: Hillwood Art Gallery, Long Island University, 1985.

CHARMION VON WIEGAND (1899-1983)    Painter

See volume 1 of this book.

Birmelin, Blair T.  "Charmion von Wiegand at Marilyn Pearl."  Art in America 73, no. 10 (October 1985):  154.

Larsen, Susan C.  "Charmion Von Wiegand:  Walking on a Road with Milestones."  Arts Magazine 60, no. 3 (November 1985):  29-31.

National Museum of Women in the Arts.  New York:  Harry N. Abrams, Inc., 1987:  86-87.

Obituary.  The New York Times, 11 June 1983:  Y12.

Troy, Nancy.  Charmion Von Wiegand, Her Art and Life.  Miami Beach:  The Bass Museum of Art, 1982.

BESSIE POTTER VONNOH (1872-1955)    Sculptor

See volume 1 of this book.

American Art Annual, vol. 28.  Washington, D.C.:  American Federation of Arts, 1932.

Archives of American Art.  Collection of Exhibition Catalogs.  Boston:  G.K. Hall and Co., 1979.

Artists by Themselves.  New York:  National Academy of Design, 1983:  92.

Conner, Janis C.  "American Women Sculptors Break the Mold."  Art & Antiques 3 (May-June 1980):  80-87.

An Exhibition of Paintings by Robert Vonnoh and of Sculpture by Bessie Potter Vonnoh.  Saint Louis:  City Art Museum, 1916.

Fairmount Park Art Association, 50th Anniversary of the Fairmount Art Association 1871-1921.  Philadelphia:  Fairmount Park Art Association, 1922:  161, 237.

National Museum of Women in the Arts.  New York:  Harry N. Abrams, Inc., 1987:  59.

Obituary.  The New York Times, 9 March 1955:  27.

Tufts, Eleanor.  American Women Artists, 1830-1930.  Washington, D.C.:  National Museum of Women in the Arts, 1987.

Weimann, Jeanne Madeline.  The Fair Women.  Chicago:  Chicago Academy, 1981:  156, 165-66.

456

MARION KAVANAGH WACHTEL (1875-1954)    Painter

American Art Annual, vol. 28.  Washington, D.C.:  American
    Federation of Arts, 1932.

Kovinick, Phil.  The Woman Artist in the American West 1860-
    1960.  Fullerton, California:  Muckenthaler Cultural Center,
    1976.

Moure, Nancy Dustin Wall.  Dictionary of Art and Artists in
    Southern California Before 1930.  Los Angeles:  privately
    printed, 1975.

_____.  Los Angeles Painters of the Nineteen-Twenties.  Claremont,
    California:  Pomona College Gallery, 1972.

Porter, Bruce, et al.  Art in California:  A Survey of American Art
    with Special Reference to California Painting, Sculpture and
    Architecture, Past and Present, Particularly as those Arts
    were Represented at the Panama-Pacific International
    Exposition.  San Francisco:  R.L. Bernier, 1916:  67-68, pl.
    23.

Samuels, Peggy and Harold.  The Illustrated Biographical
    Encyclopedia of Artists of the American West.  Garden City,
    New York:  Doubleday, 1976.

A Woman's Vision:  California Painting into the 20th Century.  San
    Francisco:  Maxwell Galleries, 1983.

Westphal, Ruth Lily.  Plein Air Painters of California, The
    Southland.  Irvine, California:  Westphal, 1982.

ADELAIDE E. WADSWORTH (1844-1928)    Painter

See volume 1 of this book.

Fielding, Mantle.  Dictionary of American Painters, Sculptors and
    Engravers.  Enlarged ed.  Greens Farms, Connecticut:  Modern
    Books and Crafts, 1974.

Obituary.  American Art Annual, vol. 26.  Washington, D.C.:
    American Federation of Arts, 1929.

MARIA LOUISA WAGNER (ca. 1815-1888)    Painter

See volume 1 of this book.

American Still Lifes of the Nineteenth Century.  New York:  Hirschl
    and Adler Galleries, 1971:  34.

Obituary. Norwich (New York) Semi-Weekly Telegram, 24 October 1888.

Women: A Historical Survey of Works by Women Artists. Raleigh: North Carolina Museum of Art, 1972.


EMILY BURLING WAITE (b. 1887)    Painter

American Art Annual, vol. 28. Washington, D.C.: American Federation of Arts, 1932.

American 19th & 20th Century Paintings, Drawings and Sculpture. New York: Sotheby's, 21 October 1983, Lot 240.

American Prints in the Library of Congress: A Catalog of the Collection. Baltimore: Johns Hopkins Press, 1970.

Archives of American Art. Collection of Exhibition Catalogs. Boston: G.K. Hall and Co., 1979.

Fielding, Mantle. Dictionary of American Painters, Sculptors and Engravers. Greens Farms, Connecticut: Modern Books and Crafts, 1974.

Pierce, Patricia Jobe. Edmund C. Tarbell and the Boston School of Painting, 1889-1980. Hingham, Massachusetts: Pierce Galleries, 1980.

Who's Who in American Art, vol. 8. Washington, D.C.: American Federation of Arts, 1962.


ANNIE E.A. WALKER (1855-1929)    Painter

Bontemps, Arna Alexander, ed. Forever Free: Art by African-American Women 1862-1980. Alexandria, Virginia: Stephenson Inc., 1980.

Cederholm, Theresa Dickason, ed. Afro-American Artists, A Bio-bibliographical Directory. Boston: Boston Public Library, 1973.

Cosentino, Andrew J., and Glassie, Henry H. The Capital Image, Painters in Washington, 1800-1915. Washington, D.C.: National Museum of American Art, Smithsonian Institution, 1983.

NELLIE VERNE WALKER (1874-1973)    Sculptor

See volume 1 of this book.

American Art Annual, vol. 28.    Washington, D.C.:    American
    Federation of Arts, 1932.

Campbell, Margaret.    "The Lady was a Sculptress."    The Iowan 36,
    no. 3 (Spring 1988):    28-32, 40-43.

Chandler, Josephine C.    "Nelly Verne Walker:    An Appreciation."
    American Magazine 15 (July 1924):    366-70.

Ness, Zenobia B., and Orwig, Louise.    Iowa Artists of the First
    Hundred Years.    [Des Moines, Iowa]:    Wallace-Homestead Co.,
    1939.

Noun, Louise.    "Making Her Mark, Nellie Verne Walker."    The
    Palimpsest 68, no. 4 (Winter 1987):    160-73.

Woman's Who's Who of America.    New York:    American Commonwealth
    Co., 1914.


ABIGAIL B. WALLEY (b. 1845)    Painter

American Art Annual, vol. 28.    Washington, D.C.:    American
    Federation of Arts, 1932.

Archives of American Art.    Collection of Exhibition Catalogs.
    Boston:    G.K. Hall and Co., 1979.


MARTHA WALTER (1875-1976)    Painter

See volume 1 of this book.

American Art Annual, vol. 28.    Washington, D.C.:    American
    Federation of Arts, 1932.

Bénédite, Léonce.    Exposition, Tableaux par Miss Martha Walter.
    Paris:    Galeries Georges Petit, 1922.

The Children of Martha Walter.    Washington, D.C.:    The Arts Club
    and Philadelphia:    David David Gallery, 1985-86.

Sterling, William H.    Cassatt, Beaux, Walter.    Wilkes-Barre,
    Pennsylvania:    Sordoni Art Gallery, Wilkes College, 1980.

Tufts, Eleanor.    American Women Artists, 1830-1930.    Washington,
    D.C.:    National Museum of Women in the Arts, 1987.

459

PATTI WARASHINA (1940-    )    Ceramicist

A Century of Ceramics in the United States 1878-1978.  Syracuse:
    Everson Museum of Art, 1979.

Contemporary Clay:  Ten Approaches.  Hanover, New Hampshire:
    Dartmouth College, 1976.

Creative America:  Forty-Five Sculptors.  Tokyo:  American Art
    Center, 1973.

Glowen, Ron.  "Ceramic Metamorphosis."  Artweek 11, no. 33 (11
    October 1980):  16.

Guenther, Bruce.  50 Northwest Artists:  A Critical Selection of
    Painters and Sculptors Working in the Pacific Northwest.  San
    Francisco:  Chronicle Books, 1983.

Harrington, LaMar.  Ceramics in the Pacific Northwest:  A History.
    Seattle:  University of Washington Press, 1979.

Kangas, Matthew.  "Patti Warashina:  The Ceramic Self."  American
    Craft 39, no. 2 (April-May 1980):  2-8.

Manhart, Marcia and Tom, eds.  The Eloquent Object.  Tulsa,
    Oklahoma:  Philbrook Museum of Art, 1987.

Watson-Jones, Virginia.  Contemporary American Women Sculptors.
    Phoenix:  Oryx Press, 1986.

Weschsler, Susan.  Low-Fire Ceramics:  A New Direction in American
    Clay.  New York:  Watson-Guptill, 1982.


CATHERINE WEED BARNES WARD (b. ca. 1860's)    Photographer

Barnes, Catherine Weed.  "Photography from a Woman's Standpoint."
    Anthony's Photographic Bulletin 20 (1890):  41-42.

_____.  "Women as Photographers."  Anthony's Photographic
    Bulletin 22 (1891):  275-78.

_____.  "Women as Photographers."  Photographic Mosaics, 1891:
    117-22.

_____.  "Women as Professional Photographers."  Wilson's
    Photographic Magazine, 1891:  686-88.


Gover, C. Jane.  The Positive Image:  Women Photographers in Turn
    of the Century America.  Albany:  State University of New York
    Press, 1988.

460

ELSIE WARD (1874-1923)    Sculptor

See Elsie Ward Hering.


HILDA WARD (1878-1950)    Painter

American Art Annual, vol. 28.  Washington, D.C.:  American
    Federation of Arts, 1932.

Gerdts, William H.  Women Artists of America, 1707-1964.  Newark:
    Newark Museum, 1965.


LAURA WHEELER WARING (1887-1948)    Painter

American Art Annual, vol. 28.  Washington, D.C.:  American
    Federation of Arts, 1932.

Bontemps, Arna Alexander, ed.  Forever Free:  Art by African-
    American Women 1862-1980.  Alexandria, Virginia:  Stephenson,
    Inc., 1980.

Cederholm, Theresa D.  Afro-American Artists.  Boston:  Boston
    Public Library, 1973:  293-94.

Dover, Cedric.  American Negro Art.  Greenwich, Connecticut:  New
    York Graphic Society, 1960.

Driskell, David C.  Two Centuries of Black American Art.  Los
    Angeles:  Los Angeles County Museum of Art, 1976.

Igoe, Lynn Moore, with James Igoe.  250 Years of Afro-American Art:
    An Annotated Bibliography.  New York:  R.R. Bowker, 1981.

Tufts, Eleanor.  American Women Artists, 1830-1930.  Washington,
    D.C.:  National Museum of Women in the Arts, 1987.

Who's Who in American Art, vol. 4.  Washington, D.C.:  American
    Federation of Arts, 1947.


LEILA WARING (1876-1964)    Miniature Painter

American Art Annual, vol. 28.  Washington, D.C.:  American
    Federation of Arts, 1932.

Severens, Martha.  The Miniature Portrait Collection of the South
    Carolina Art Association.  Charleston, South Carolina:  Gibbes
    Art Gallery, 1984:  125-29.

DEBORAH WARNER (20th Century)    Fiber Artist

Poon, Vivian. "Deborah Warner's Visual Journal." Fiberarts 10
    (November-December 1983):  76-77.

Warner, Deborah. "From 'Four Corners Journal'." American Craft
    40, no. 4 (August-September 1980):  21-23.

Znamierowski, Nell. Fiber:  The Artist's View. Greenvale, New
    York:  Hillwood Art Gallery, Long Island University, 1983.

NELL WALKER WARNER (1891-1970)    Painter

American Art Annual, vol. 28. Washington, D.C.:  American
    Federation of Arts, 1932.

Bucklin, Clarissa. Nebraska Art and Artists. Lincoln:  University
    of Nebraska, 1932.

Moure, Nancy D. Dictionary of Artists in Southern California
    Before 1950. Los Angeles:  Dustin Publications, 1975.

Permanent Collection Catalogue. Springville, Utah:  Springville
    Museum of Art, 1972.

Who's Who in American Art, vol. 3. Washington, D.C.:  American
    Federation of Arts, 1972.

A Woman's Vision:  California Painting into the 20th Century. San
    Francisco:  Maxwell Galleries, 1983.

PECOLIA WARNER (1901-1983)    Quilt-maker

Ferris, William. "Pecolia Warner, Quilt Maker." Local Color:
    A Sense of Place in Folk Art. New York:  McGraw-Hill, 1982:
    175-191.

Thompson, Robert Farris. Flash of Spirit. New York:  Random
    House, 1983.

Wahlman, Maude Southwell, with John Scully. "Aesthetic Principles
    in Afro-American Quilts." Afro-American Folk Art and Crafts.
    Ed. William Ferris. Boston:  G.K. Hall, 1983:  79-97.

_____. Black Quilters. New Haven:  Yale University Art Gallery,
    1979.

Women's Caucus for Art Honor Awards. Philadelphia:  National
    Women's Caucus for Art, 1983.

462

CONSTANCE WHITNEY WARREN (1888-1948)    Sculptor

See volume 1 of this book.

American Bronze Sculpture, 19th and 20th Century. New York:
    Sanford and Patricia Smith Gallery, 1978.

Fisk, Frances Battaile. A History of Texas Artists and Sculptors.
    Abilene, Texas:  privately printed, 1928.

O'Brien, Esse Forrester. Art and Artists of Texas. Dallas:  Tardy
    Publishing Co., 1943.

Samuels, Peggy and Harold. The Illustrated Biographical
    Encyclopedia of Artists of the American West. Garden City,
    New York:  Doubleday, 1976.


JANE WASEY (1912-    )  Sculptor

See volume 1 of this book.

Who's Who in American Art, 17th ed. New York:  R.R. Bowker Co.,
    1986.


SUSAN C. WATERS (1823-1900)    Painter

See volume 1 of this book.

"New Discoveries in American Art." American Art Journal 19, no. 1
    (Winter 1987):  76-77.

19th Century American Women Artists. New York:  Whitney Museum of
    American Art Downtown Branch, 1976.


GENNA WATSON (1948-    )  Sculptor

The Animal Image:  Contemporary Objects and the Beast. Washington,
    D.C.:  Renwick Gallery of the National Museum of American Art,
    1981.

Forgey, Benjamin. "Galleries:  Beneath the Violence, Genna
    Watson's Poignant and Beautiful Sculptures." The Washington
    Post, 10 March 1984:  G9.

Images of the 70s:  9 Washington Artists. Washington, D.C.:
    Corcoran Gallery of Art, 1980.

Richard, Paul. "Galleries:  Women in Shadow, At Tartt, Watson's
    Haunting Sculptures." The Washington Post, 21 March 1987:
    B2.

Rubenfeld, Florence. "Reviews East Coast: Genna Watson, The Athenaeum." New Art Examiner 11, no. 8 (May 1984), section II: 4.

Twenty-First Area Exhibition: Sculpture. Washington, D.C.: Corcoran Gallery of Art, 1978.

Uncommon Visions. Rochester, New York: Memorial Art Gallery of University of Rochester, 1979.

The Washington Show. Washington, D.C.: Corcoran Gallery of Art, 1985.

Watson-Jones, Virginia. Contemporary American Women Sculptors. Phoenix: Oryx Press, 1986.

HELEN RICHTER WATSON (1926-    )    Ceramic Sculptor

Conrad, John W. Contemporary Ceramic Techniques. Englewood Cliffs, New Jersey: Prentice-Hall, 1979.

First Annual Distinguished Alumna Exhibition. Claremont, California: Humanities Gallery, Scripps College, 1978.

"Helen Richter Watson: Monumental Sculpture." Ceramics Monthly 28, no. 4 (April 1980): 56-57.

Nelson, Glenn C. Ceramics. New York: Holt, Rinehart and Winston, 1960.

Nigrosh, Leon I. Claywork: Form and Idea in Ceramic Design. Worcester, Massachusetts: Davis, 1975.

Petterson, Richard B., ed. Ceramic Art in America; A Portfolio. Columbus, Ohio: Professional Publications, 1969.

Twenty-Second Annual Ceramic National Exhibition. Syracuse, New York: Everson Museum of Art, 1962.

Watson-Jones, Virginia. Contemporary American Women Sculptors. Phoenix: Oryx Press, 1986.

[AGNES] NAN WATSON (1876-1966)    Painter

See volume 1 of this book.

American Art Annual, vol. 28. Washington, D.C.: American Federation of Arts, 1932.

464

Archives of American Art. Collection of Exhibition Catalogs.
Boston:  G.K. Hall and Co., 1979.

A Catalogue of the Collection of American Paintings in the Corcoran
Gallery of Art, vol. 2.  Washington, D.C.:  Corcoran Gallery
of Art, 1973.

National Portrait Gallery, Permanent Collection Illustrated
Checklist.  Washington, D.C.:  Smithsonian Institution, 1982.

Phillips Collection, A Summary Catalogue.  Washington, D.C.:
Phillips Collection, 1985.

Second Biennial Exhibition of Contemporary American Painting.  New
York:  Whitney Museum of American Art, 1934, no. 125.


EVA WATSON-SCHÜTZE (1867-1935)    Photographer

Block, Jean F.  Eva Watson-Schütze:  Chicago Photo-Secessionist.
Chicago:  University of Chicago Press, 1985.

Gover, C. Jane.  The Positive Image:  Women Photographers in Turn
of the Century America.  Albany:  State University of New York
Press, 1988.

Hills, Patricia.  Turn-of-the-Century America.  New York:  Whitney
Museum of American Art, 1977.

Holme, Charles, ed.  Art in Photography.  London, Paris, New York:
The Studio, 1905.

Jacobson, J.Z.  Art of Today, Chicago--1933.  Chicago:  L.M. Stein,
1932.

Keiley, Joseph T.  "Eva Watson-Schütze."  Camera Work, no. 9
(January 1905):  23-26.

National Museum of Women in the Arts.  New York:  Harry N. Abrams,
Inc., 1987.

Naef, Weston J.  The Collection of Alfred Stieglitz.  New York:
Viking Press, 1978.

Watson-Schütze, Eva.  "Portraits of Children."  The Photographer 1
(4 June 1904):  93.

Woodstock's Art Heritage:  The Permanent Collection of the
Woodstock Artists Association.  Essay by Tom Wolf.  Woodstock,
New York:  Overlook Press, 1987.

JUNE WAYNE (1918-    )    Printmaker and Painter

See volume 1 of this book.

Allen, Virginia. Tamarind:  Homage to Lithography. New York:  The
    Museum of Modern Art, 1969.

American Herstory:  Women and the U.S. Constitution. Curated by
    Eleanor Tufts. Atlanta:  College of Art, 1988.

Antreasian, Garo, and Adams, Clinton. The Tamarind Book of
    Lithography:  Art And Techniques. New York:  Harry N. Abrams,
    1971.

Images on Stone:  Two Centuries of Artists' Lithographs. Houston:
    Sarah Campbell Blaffer Gallery, University of Houston, 1987.

O'Beil, Hedy. "June Wayne." Arts Magazine 59, no. 6 (January
    1985):  41.

Raven, Arlene. "Cognitos:  June Wayne's New Paintings." Arts
    Magazine 59, no. 2 (October 1984):  119-21.

Women's Caucus for Art Honor Awards, 6th Annual Exhibition. Los
    Angeles:  Women's Caucus for Art, 1985.


                BEULAH BARNES WEAVER (1882-1957)    Painter

American Art Annual, vol. 28. Washington, D.C.:  American
    Federation of Arts, 1932.

The Phillips Collection, A Summary Catalogue. Washington, D.C.:
    The Phillips Collection, 1985.

Who's Who in American Art, vol. 5. Washington, D.C.:  American
    Federation of Arts, 1953.


                IDELLE WEBER (1932-    )    Painter

See volume 1 of this book.

Bass, Ruth. "Idelle Weber at Siegel Contemporary." Art News 83,
    no. 6 (Summer 1984):  190.

Henry, Gerrit. "Idelle Weber at Ruth Siegel." Art in America 74,
    no. 3 (March 1986):  151-52.

Idelle Weber:  Paintings and Works on Paper, 1982-1984. New York:
    Sigel Contemporary Art, 1984.

Klein, Ellen Lee. "Idelle Weber." Arts Magazine 60, no. 5 (January 1986): 127-28.

_____. "Idelle Weber." Arts Magazine 62, no. 6 (February 1988): 111.

Marter, Joan. "Idelle Weber." Arts Magazine 60, no. 3 (November 1985): 123.

Martin, Alvin. American Realism, 20th Century Drawings and Watercolors, From the Glenn C. Janss Collection. San Francisco: San Francisco Museum of Modern Art, 1985.

Widing, Eric P. "Idelle Weber." American Artist 48, issue 502 (May 1984): 46-51.

SARAH STILWELL WEBER (1878-1939)    Illustrator

American Art Annual, vol. 20. Washington, D.C.: American Federation of Arts, 1932.

The American Personality: The Artist-Illustrator of Life in the United States, 1830-1960. Los Angeles: Grunwald Center for the Graphic Arts, 1976.

Mayer, Anne E. Women Artists in the Howard Pyle Tradition. Chadds Ford, Pennsylvania: Brandywine River Museum, 1975.

Obituary. The New York Times, 6 April 1939.

Reed, Walt, ed. The Illustrator in America, 1900-1960's. New York: Reinhold Publishing Corp., 1966: 37.

_____, and Reed, Roger. "The Brandywine Heritage: Howard Pyle and His Students." The Illustrator Collector 14, no. 1 (1988): 10.

KATHARINE WARD LANE WEEMS (1899-    )    Sculptor

See volume 1 of this book under "Lane."

Ambler, Louise Todd. Katharine Lane Weems, Sculpture and Drawings. Boston: The Boston Athenaeum, 1987.

American Art Annual, vol. 28. Washington, D.C.: American Federation of Arts, 1932 (under "Lane").

Greenthal, Kathryn; Kozol, Paula M.; and Ramirez, Jan Seidler. American Figurative Sculpture in the Museum of Fine Arts, Boston. Boston: Museum of Fine Arts, 1986.

Weems, Katharine Lane, as told to Edward Weeks.  Odds Were Against
    Me:  A Memoir.  New York:  Vantage Press, 1985.


        AGNES WEINRICH (1873-1946)    Painter and Printmaker

"Art Today and Yesterday, Dealer's Choice:  Underrated Artists."
    Art Today, Winter 1987-88:  45-46.

Flint, Janet Altic.  Provincetown Printers:  A Woodcut Tradition.
    Washington, D.C.:  National Museum of American Art, 1983.

Newman, Sasha.  "Agnes Weinrich."  Women Artists in Washington
    Collections.  Edited by Josephine Withers.  College Park:
    University of Maryland Art Gallery and Women's Caucus for Art,
    1979.

The Phillips Collection, A Summary Catalogue.  Washington, D.C.:
    The Phillips Collection, 1985.

Wolf, Amy J.  New York Society of Women Artists 1925.  New York:
    ACA Galleries, 1987.


        RUTH WEISBERG (1942-    )    Printmaker

See volume 1 of this book.

A Broad Spectrum:  Contemporary Los Angeles Painters and Sculptors
    '84.  Los Angeles:  The Design Center, 1984.

A Circle of Life, Ruth Weisberg.  Essay by Selma Holo.  Los
    Angeles:  Fisher Gallery, University of Southern California,
    1986.

Clothier, Peter.  "Ruth Weisberg at USC."  Art in America 74, no. 4
    (April 1986):  197-98 and illus. p. 199.

Gouma-Peterson, Thalia.  "Passages in Cyclical Time:  Ruth
    Weisberg's Scroll."  Arts Magazine 62, no. 6 (February 1988):
    56-59.

Hirsch, Gilah Yelin.  "Ruth Weisberg:  Transcendence of Time
    Through Persistence of Imagery."  Woman's Art Journal 6, no.
    2 (Fall 1985-Winter 1986):  41-45.

Isenberg, Barbara.  "Cradled in Legacy of the Holocaust."  Los
    Angeles Times, 5 October 1985, Part V:  4.

Lerman, Ora.  "Autobiographical Journey:  Can Art Transform
    Personal and Cultural Loss?"  Arts Magazine 59, no. 9 (May
    1985):  103-07.

Ruth Weisberg, Paintings, Drawings, Prints, 1968-1988. Curated by
    Marion E. Jackson. Essay by Thalia Gouma-Peterson. New York:
    The Feminist Press, 1988.

Self-Portraits by Women Artists. Los Angeles: Gallery at the
    Plaza, Security Pacific National Bank, 1985.

Spectrum Los Angeles. Berlin: Hartje Gallery, 1985.

Wortz, Melinda. "Ruth Weisberg." Art News 83, no. 1 (January
    1984): 112-13.

MABEL WELCH (d. 1959)    Painter

American Art Annual, vol. 28. Washington, D.C.: American
    Federation of Arts, 1932.

Fiftieth Anniversary Exhibition 1889-1939. New York: National
    Association of Women and Sculptors, 1939.

Lounsbery, Elizabeth. "American Miniature Painters." Mentor 4,
    no. 23 (5 January 1917): 11.

Portraits by Distinguished American Artists. New York: Grand
    Central Art Galleries, 1942: 82-83.

Rucker, Kathryn. "Some Miniatures by Mabel Welch." Art and
    Decoration 3, no. 9 (July 1913): 305.

Who's Who in American Art, vol. 1. Washington, D.C.: American
    Federation of Arts, 1935.

JULIA BRACKEN WENDT (1871-1942)    Sculptor

See volume 1 of this book.

American Art Annual, vol. 28. Washington, D.C.: American
    Federation of Arts, 1932.

Clement, Clara Erskine. Women in the Fine Arts. Boston:
    Houghton, Mifflin, 1904.

Fielding, Mantle. Dictionary of American Painters, Sculptors and
    Engravers. Enlarged ed. Greens Farms, Connecticut: Modern
    Books and Crafts, 1974.

100 years of California Sculpture. Oakland, California: The
    Oakland Museum, 1982.

469

Porter, Bruce, et al.  Art in California:  A Survey of American
    Art with Special Reference to California Painting, Sculpture
    and Architecture, Past and Present, Particularly as those Arts
    were Represented at the Panama-Pacific International
    Exposition.  San Francisco:  R.L. Bernier, 1916.

Who's Who in American Art, vol. 1.  Washington, D.C.:  American
    Federation of Arts, 1935.


                CAROL D. WESTFALL (1938-    )  Fiber Artist

Schlossman, Betty L.  "Review:  Clay, Fiber, Metal by Women
    Artists."  Art Journal 37, no. 4 (Summer 1978):  330-32.

7th International Biennial of Tapestry.  Lausanne, Switzerland:
    Musée Cantonal des Beaux-Arts, 1975.

Westfall, Carol, and Glashausser, Suellen.  Plaiting, Step by Step.
    New York:  Watson Guptill, 1976.

Who's Who in American Art.  New York:  R.R. Bowker Co., 1986.

Znamierowski, Nell.  Fiber:  The Artist's View.  Greenvale, New
    York:  Hillside Art Gallery, Long Island University, 1983.


                MARY PILLSBURY WESTON (1817-1894)   Painter

Bolton, Theodore.  Early American Portrait Painters in Miniature.
    New York:  F.F. Sherman, 1921:  172.

Ellet, Elizabeth.  Women Artists in All Ages and Countries.  New
    York:  Harper Bros., 1859:  332-42.

French, Henry W.  Art and Artists in Connecticut.  Boston:  Lee and
    Shepard, 1879:  175-76.

Groce, George C., and Wallace, David H.  The New-York Historical
    Society's Dictionary of Artists in America, 1564-1860.  New
    Haven:  Yale University Press, 1957.

Hanaford, Phebe A.  Daughters of America.  Augusta, Maine:  True
    and Co., 1982:  287.

Lipman, Jean, and Winchester, Alice.  Primitive Painters in
    America, 1750-1950.  Freeport, New York:  Books for Libraries,
    1971:  182.

MARGARET WHARTON (1943-    )    Sculptor

Artemisia:  Ten Years 1973-1983.  Chicago:  Artemisia Gallery,
     1984.

Glauber, Robert.  "Chairs as Metaphor:  The Sculpture of Margaret
     Wharton."  Arts Magazine 56, no. 1 (September 1981):  84-87.

Hoffeld, Jeffrey.  "Chairperson Margaret Wharton."  Arts Magazine
     53, no. 3 (November 1978):  160.

Kirshner, Judith Russi.  "Reviews Chicago:  Margaret Wharton,
     Museum of Contemporary Art."  Artforum 20, no. 5 (January
     1982):  85-86.

Lubell, Ellen.  "Margaret Wharton."  Arts Magazine 51, no. 10 (June
     1977):  45.

100 Artists:  100 Years.  Chicago:  Art Institute of Chicago, 1979.

Painting and Sculpture Today.  Indianapolis:  Indianapolis Museum
     of Art, 1976.

Painting and Sculpture Today.  Indianapolis:  Indianapolis Museum
     of Art, 1980.

Seventy-Fifth Exhibition by Artists of Chicago and Vicinity.
     Chicago:  Art Institute of Chicago, 1974.

Seventy-Sixth Exhibition by Artists of Chicago and Vicinity.
     Chicago:  Art Institute of Chicago, 1977.

Tully, Judd.  "Vita Breva, Chaise Lounge:  The Art of Margaret
     Wharton."  Arts Magazine 57, no. 10 (June 1983):  114-15.

Watson-Jones, Virginia.  Contemporary American Women Sculptors.
     Phoenix:  Oryx Press, 1986.

CANDACE WHEELER [THURBER] (1827-1923)    Textile Designer

See volume 1 of this book.

Anscombe, Isabelle.  A Woman's Touch:  Women in Design from 1860
     to the Present Day.  New York:  Viking Penguin, 1984.

Callen, Anthea.  Women Artists of the Arts and Crafts Movement
     1870-1914.  New York:  Pantheon Books, 1979.

Wheeler, Candace.  The Development of Embroidery in America.  New
     York and London:  Harper and Bros. Publishers, 1921.

\_\_\_\_\_. Principles of Home Decoration, with Practical Examples. New York: Doubleday, Page and Co., 1903.


DORA WHEELER [KEITH] (1857-1940)    Painter

See volume 1 of this book.

American Art Annual, vol. 28.  Washington, D.C.:  American Federation of Arts, 1932.

Elliott, Maud Howe, ed.  Art and Handicraft in the Woman's Building of the World's Columbian Exposition, Chicago, 1893.  Chicago: Rand, McNally and Co., 1894:  53, 55, 90.

Fielding, Mantle.  Dictionary of American Painters, Sculptors and Engravers.  Enlarged ed.  Greens Farms, Connecticut:  Modern Books and Crafts, 1974.

Woman's Who's Who of America.  New York:  American Commonwealth Co., 1914.


MARY WHEELER (1846-1920)    Painter

See volume 1 of this book.

Obituary.  American Art Annual, vol. 18.  Washington, D.C.: American Federation of Arts, 1921.


VERA M. WHITE (1888-1966)    Painter

Philadelphia Collection XXIV.  Philadelphia:  Frank S. Schwarz, 1984.

Who's Who in American Art, vol. 8.  Washington, D.C.:  American Federation of Arts, 1962.


MARY URSULA WHITLOCK (d. 1944)    Painter

American Art Annual, vol. 1.  New York:  Macmillan Co., 1899.

Fielding, Mantle.  Dictionary of American Painters, Sculptors and Engravers.  Enlarged ed.  Greens Farms, Connecticut:  Modern Books and Crafts, 1974.

Obituary.  Who's Who in American Art, vol. 4.  Washington, D.C.: American Federation of Arts, 1947.

SARAH WYMAN WHITMAN (1842-1904)    Painter and Stained Glass
                                   Designer

See volume 1 of this book.

American Art Annual, vol. 1.  New York:  Macmillan Co., 1899.

Elliott, Maude Howe, ed.  Art and Handicraft in the Women's
    Building of the World's Columbian Exposition, Chicago, 1893.
    Chicago:  Rand, McNally and Co., 1894:  93, 97.

Hoeber, Arthur.  "Famous American Women Painters."  Mentor 2, no. 3
    (16 March 1914).

Sarah Whitman.  Record of the Memorial Service.  Boston:
    Merrymount Press, 1904.

Tonalism:  An American Experience.  Phoenix:  Phoenix Art Museum,
    1982.

Whitman, Sarah W.  The Making of Pictures:  Twelve Short Talks with
    Young People.  Chicago:  Interstate Publishing Co., [1886].


ANNE WHITNEY (1821-1915)    Sculptor

See volume 1 of this book.

National Portrait Gallery, Permanent Collection Illustrated
    Checklist.  Washington, D.C.:  Smithsonian Institution Press,
    1982.

Obituary.  American Art Annual, vol. 12.  Washington, D.C.:
    American Federation of Arts, 1915.

Petersen, Karen, and Wilson, J.J.  Women Artists.  New York:
    Harper and Row, 1976.

Tufts, Eleanor.  American Women Artists, 1830-1930.  Washington,
    D.C.:  National Museum of Women in the Arts, 1987.

"World's Oldest Sculptor Gone."  Boston Sunday Globe, 14 February
    1915:  32.


GERTRUDE VANDERBILT WHITNEY (1875-1942)    Sculptor

See volume 1 of this book.

American Art Annual, vol. 18.  Washington, D.C.:  American
    Federation of Arts, 1921.

Boswell, Peyton. "Whitney Obituary." Art Digest 16, no. 15 (1 May 1942): 3, 6.

Calder, A. Stirling. The Sculpture and Mural Decorations of the Exposition, A Pictorial Survey of the Art of the Panama-Pacific International Exposition. San Francisco: Paul Elder and Co., 1915.

DuBois, Guy Pène. "Mrs. Whitney's Journey in Art." International Studio 76, no. 308 (January 1923): 351-54.

First Biennial Exhibition of Contemporary American Sculpture, Watercolors and Prints. New York: Whitney Museum of American Art, 1933.

Heller, Nancy G. Women Artists. New York: Abbeville Press, 1987.

"Mrs. H.P. Whitney, Sculptor, is Dead." The New York Times, 18 April 1942: 15-16.

"Mrs. Whitney's Cody Rides in Dallas." Art Digest 10, no. 17 (1 June 1936): 19.

"Mrs. Whitney Exhibits Her New Sculpture." Art Digest 10, no. 13 (1 April 1936): 6.

Obituary. Who's Who in American Art, vol. 4. Washington, D.C.: American Federation of Arts, 1947.

ISABEL LYDIA WHITNEY (1884-1962)   Painter

American Art Annual, vol. 28. Washington, D.C.: American Federation of Arts, 1932.

Gerdts, William H. Women Artists of America 1707-1964. Newark: Newark Museum, 1965.

Watercolors and Drawings: Memorial Exhibition--Isabel Lydia Whitney. New York: Pen and Brush Gallery, 1962.

Who's Who in American Art, vol. 3. Washington, D.C.: American Federation of Arts, 1940.

MARY HUBBARD WHITWELL (1847-1908)   Painter

Hoppin, Martha J. "Women Artists in Boston, 1870-1900: The Pupils of William Morris Hunt." The American Art Journal 13, no. 1 (Winter 1891): 22, 44.

HANNAH WILKE (1940-    )    Sculptor and Performance Artist

See volume 1 of this book.

Bass, Ruth. "Hannah Wilke, Ronald Feldman Fine Arts." Art News
    84, no. 3 (March 1985):  139-40.

Who's Who in American Art, 17th ed.  New York:  R.R. Bowker Co.,
    1986.


CLARA ELSENE WILLIAMS (b. 1883)    Painter and Illustrator

See Clara Elsene Williams Peck.


EDITH CLIFFORD WILLIAMS (c. 1880-1971)    Painter

Homer, William Innes, et al.  Avant-Garde Painting and Sculpture in
    America 1910-25.  Wilmington:  Delaware Art Museum, 1975.


MARGARET LINDSAY WILLIAMS (1887-1960)    Painter

Bénézit, Emmanuel.  Dictionnaire critique et documentaire des
    peintres, sculpteurs, dessinateurs et graveurs de tous les
    temps et de tous les pays.  New ed.  Paris:  Librarie Gründ,
    1976.

National Portrait Gallery, Permanent Collection Illustrated
    Checklist.  Washington, D.C.:  Smithsonian Institution, 1982.

Thieme, U., and Becker, F.  Allgemeines Lexikon der bildenden
    Künstler.  Leipzig:  E.A. Seeman, 1947.


ADA CLENDENIN WILLIAMSON (1880-1958)    Painter

American Art Annual, vol. 28.  Washington, D.C.:  American
    Federation of Arts, 1932.

Fielding, Mantle.  Dictionary of American Painters, Sculptors and
    Engravers.  Enlarged ed.  Greens Farms, Connecticut:  Modern
    Books and Crafts, 1974.

Obituary.  Who's Who in American Art, vol. 7.  Washington, D.C.:
    American Federation of Arts, 1959.

Robinson, Mary E.G., and McCreesh, Carolyn D.  Ada Clendenin
    Williamson 1880-1958:  Glimpses of the Artist Through Her
    Diaries, Letters and Scrapbooks.  West Chester, Pennsylvania:
    Chester County Historical Society, 1982.

CLARA McDONALD WILLIAMSON (1875-1976)    Painter

See volume 1 of this book.

Graves, John.  "Aunt Clara's Luminous World."  *American Heritage*
    21, no. 5 (August 1970):  46-56.

*Texas Painting and Sculpture:  20th Century*.  Dallas:  Southern
    Methodist University, 1971.

*20th Century Women in Texas Art*.  Austin, Texas:  Laguna Gloria Art
    Museum, 1974.

*Who's Who in American Art*, vol. 12.  Washington, D.C.:  American
    Federation of Arts, 1976.


MARY ANN WILLSON (active 1810-1825)    Painter

See volume 1 of this book.

DePauw, Linda Grant, and Hunt, Conover.  *Remember the Ladies, 1750-
    1815:  Women in America*.  New York:  Viking Press, 1976.

*Miss Willson's Watercolors, 1800-1825*.  New York:  Harry Stone
    Gallery, 1944.

Peterson, Karen, and Wilson, J.J.  *Women Artists*.  New York:
    Harper and Row, 1976.


HELEN MIRANDA WILSON (1948-    )    Painter

See volume 1 of this book.

"Album:  Helen Miranda Wilson."  *Arts Magazine* 60, no. 6 (February
    1986):  114-15.

Moorman, Margaret.  "Helen Miranda Wilson:  Places for the Hungry
    Heart."  *Art News* 86, no. 2 (February 1987):  71-72.

Pardee, Hearne.  *Inner Images:  Paintings by Five Contemporary
    Artists*.  Waterville, Maine:  Colby College Museum of Art,
    1986.


JANE WILSON (1924-    )    Painter

See volume 1 of this book.

Gardner, Paul.  "Jane Wilson's Weather Eye."  *Art News* 84, no. 10
    (December 1985):  56-60.

476

Novak, Barbara, and Blangrund, Annette. Next to Nature. New York:
National Academy of Design, 1980.

Who's Who in American Art, 17th ed. New York: R.R. Bowker Co.,
1986.


MAY WILSON (1905-1986)  Sculptor

1970 Sculpture Annual. New York: Whitney Museum of American Art,
1970.

Obituary. Art in America 75, no. 1 (January 1987): 160.

Wilson, Bill. "Grandma Moses of the Underground." Art & Artists,
May 1968.

Who's Who in American Art. New York and London: R.R. Bowker Co.,
1978.


ARLINE WINGATE (1906-   )  Sculptor

Russo, Alexander. Profiles on Women Artists. Frederick, Maryland:
University Publications of America, 1985.

Who's Who in American Art. New York and London: R.R. Bowker Co.,
1978.


NINA WINKEL (1905-   )  Sculptor

Annual Exhibition. New York: National Academy of Design, 1945-85.

Annual Exhibition: Contemporary American Sculpture. New York:
Whitney Museum of American Art, 1950.

Brummé, C. Ludwig. Contemporary American Sculpture. New York:
Crown, 1948.

Dryfoos, Nancy. "Nina Winkel...her Copper Sculpture." National
Sculpture Review 20, no. 4 (Winter 1971-72): 18-19.

Edgar G. Barton and Nina Winkel Sculpture. Plattsburgh, New York:
Myers Fine Arts Gallery, State University of New York, 1983.

Hale, Nathan Cabot. Welded Sculpture. New York: Watson-Guptill,
1968.

National Sculpture Society Annual Exhibition. New York: National
Sculpture Society, 1946-83.

Nina Winkel: Sculpture. New York: Clay Club Gallery, 1944.

Proske, Beatrice Gilman. "American Women Sculptors, Part II."
    National Sculpture Review 24, no. 4 (Winter 1975-76): 8-17,
    28.

Schnier, Jacques Preston. Sculpture in Modern America. Berkeley:
    University of California Press, 1948.

Watson-Jones, Virginia. Contemporary American Women Sculptors.
    Phoenix: Oryx Press, 1986.

Who's Who in American Art. New York: R.R. Bowker, 1978.

JACKIE WINSOR (1941-    )    Sculptor

See volume 1 of this book.

Decter, Joshua. "Jackie Winsor." Arts Magazine 60, no. 9 (May
    1986): 118-19.

Gill, Susan. "Jackie Winsor [at Paula Cooper]." Art News 85, no.
    6 (Summer 1986): 144.

Lippard, Lucy R. "Jackie Winsor." Artforum 12, no. 6 (February
    1974): 56-58, cover.

"Portrait of the Artist, 1987, Who Supports Him/Her." Artsreview
    4, no. 3 (Spring 1987): 80.

Silverthorne, Jeanne. "Jackie Winsor." Artforum 24, no. 9 (May
    1986): 132.

Watson-Jones, Virginia. Contemporary American Women Sculptors.
    Phoenix: Oryx Press, 1986.

Westfall, Stephen. "Jackie Winsor at Paula Cooper." Art in
    America 74, no. 5 (May 1986): 153-54.

Who's Who in American Art, 17th ed. New York: R.R. Bowker Co.,
    1986.

ETHEL BRAND WISE (1888-1933)    Sculptor

Obituary. American Art Annual, vol. 30. Washington, D.C.:
    American Federation of Arts, 1934.

478

JOAN WITEK (1943-    )   Painter

Bell, Jane. "Joan Witek [at] Rosa Esman." Art News 83, no. 8
    (October 1984):   177-78.

Caldwell, John. Joan Witek. Pittsburgh:   Carnegie Institute,
    1984.

Carrier, David. "Joan Witek at John Davis." Art in America 75,
    no. 7 (July 1987):   131, 132.

Sims, Lowery Stokes. "Joan Witek." Arts Magazine 59, no. 1
    (September 1984):   4.


CAROLINE WITHERS (1830-1906)    Miniature Painter

Ellet, Elizabeth Fries Lummins. Women Artists in All Ages and
    Countries. New York:   Harper Bros., 1859.

Groce, George C., and Wallace, David H. The New-York Historical
    Society's Dictionary of Artists in America 1564-1860. New
    Haven:   Yale University Press, 1957.

Severens, Martha R. The Miniature Portrait Collection of the
    Carolina Art Association. Charleston, South Carolina:   Gibbes
    Art Gallery, 1984:   130.


EVELYN ALMOND WITHROW (1858-1928)    Painter

Dawdy, Doris Ostrander. Artists of the American West, vol. 1.
    Chicago:   Swallow Press, 1974.

A Woman's Vision:   California Painting into the 20th Century. San
    Francisco:   Maxwell Galleries, 1983.


DEE WOLFF (1948-    )   Painter

Camfield, William. Works on Paper:   Eleven Houston Artists.
    Houston:   Museum of Fine Arts, 1985.

Carlozzi, Annette. 50 Texas Artists. San Francisco:   Chronicle
    Books, 1986.

Hauser, Reine. "Artists the Critics are Watching:   Houston."
    Art News 83, no. 9 (November 1984):   88-89.

A Sense of Spirit. Houston:   Lawndale Annex, University of
    Houston, 1982.

Moore, Sylvia, ed. No Bluebonnets, No Yellow Roses: Essays on Texas Women in the Arts. New York: Midmarch Arts Press, 1988.

Paperworks: An Exhibition of Texas Artists. San Antonio: San Antonio Museum Association, 1979.


BEATRICE WOOD (1893-    )  Ceramicist

Avant-Garde Painting and Sculpture in America 1910-25. Wilmington: Delaware Art Museum, 1975.

Beatrice Wood, Retrospective. Fullerton: California State University, 1983.

Bryan, Robert. "The Ceramics of Beatrice Wood." Craft Horizons 30, no. 2 (March-April 1970): 28-33.

Clark, Garth. A Century of Ceramics in the United States 1878-1978. New York: E.P. Dutton, 1979.

Frankel, Robert H. Beatrice Wood, A Retrospective. Phoenix: Phoenix Art Museum, 1973.

Hapgood, Elizabeth Reynolds. "All the Cataclysms: A Brief Survey of the Life of Beatrice Wood." Arts Magazine 52, no. 7 (March 1978): 107-09.

Hare, Denise. "The Lustrous Life of Beatrice Wood." Craft Horizons 38, no. 3 (June 1978): 26-31, 69-70.

Homer, William Innes, et al. Avant-Garde Painting and Sculpture in America 1910-25. Wilmington: Delaware Art Museum, 1975.

Levin, Elaine. "Women in Clay. Ceramics Review 91 (January-February 1985): 31.

Manhart, Marcia and Tom, eds. The Eloquent Object. Tulsa, Oklahoma: Philbrook Museum of Art, 1987.

Naumann, Francis M. "Beatrice Wood and the Dada State of Mind." Beatrice Wood and Friends: From Dada to Deco. New York: Rosa Esman Gallery, 1978.

_____. "The Drawings of Beatrice Wood." Arts Magazine 57, no. 7 (March 1983): 108-11.

Nin, Anaïs. "Beatrice Wood." Artforum 3 (January 1965): 4, 47.

Seigel, Judy. "Beatrice Wood." Women Artists News 12, nos. 4-5 (Fall-Winter 1987): 9-11.

480

WCA Honor Awards. Boston, Massachusetts: National Women's Caucus
for Art, 1979.

Wood, Beatrice. The Autobiography of Beatrice Wood: I Shock
Myself. Ojai, California: Dillingham Press, 1985.

_____. "I Shock Myself: Excerpts from the Autobiography
of Beatrice Wood." Arts Magazine 51, no. 9 (May 1977):
134-39.


JEAN WOODHAM (1925-    )    Sculptor

Annual Exhibition of Painting and Sculpture. Philadelphia:
Pennsylvania Academy of the Fine Arts, 1950-54.

Annual New England Exhibition. New Canaan, Connecticut:
Silvermine Guild of Artists, 1955-60.

Benton, Suzanne. The Art of Welded Sculpture. New York: Van
Nostrand Reinhold, 1975.

Charles, Eleanor. "Sculpture Moves Outdoors." The New York Times,
25 July 1982: CN1, CN21.

Eight Connecticut Sculptors. Waterbury, Connecticut: Mattatuck
Museum, 1969.

Fundaburk, Emma Lila, and Davenport, Thomas G. Art in Public
Places in the United States. Bowling Green, Ohio: Bowling
Green University Popular Press, 1975.

National Association of Women Artists Annual Exhibition. New York:
National Academy of Design, 1951-74.

Padovano, Anthony. The Process of Sculpture. New York:
Doubleday, 1981.

Schnier, Jacques Preston. Sculpture in Modern America. Berkeley:
University of California Press, 1948.

Watson-Jones, Virginia. Contemporary American Women Sculptors.
Phoenix: Oryx Press, 1986.


ETHELYN HURD WOODLOCK (1907-    )    Painter

Exhibition of Paintings by Ethelyn Hurd Woodlock. Midland Park,
New Jersey: The Wyckoff Colony of New England Women, 1964.

Who's Who in American Art. New York: R.R. Bowker, 1978.

BETTY WOODMAN (1930-    )   Potter

Clark, Garth.  American Potters, The Work of Twenty Modern Masters.
    New York:  Watson-Guptill Publications, 1987.

_____.  A Century of Ceramics in the United States 1878-1978.
    New York:  E.P. Dutton, 1979.

DeVore, Richard.  "Ceramics of Betty Woodman."  Craft Horizons 38,
    no. 1 (February 1978):  28-31, 66-67.

Eight Independent Production Potters.  Kansas City:  Kansas City
    Art Institute, 1976.

"Eight Independent Production Potters."  Craft Horizons 37, no. 1
    (February 1977):  49.

Fiber, Metal and Clay.  Ann Arbor, Michigan:  Slusser Gallery,
    1977.

The Fred and Mary Marer Collection.  Claremont, California:
    Scripps College Art Gallery, 1974.

"Portrait of the Artist, 1987, Who Supports Him/Her."  Artsreview
    4, no. 3 (Spring 1987):  40.


MABEL MAY WOODWARD (1877-1945)   Painter

See volume 1 of this book.

American Art Annual, vol. 28.  Washington, D.C.:  American
    Federation of Arts, 1932.

American Impressionism:  The Second Generation.  Washington, D.C.:
    Taggart, Jorgensen and Putnam, [1983].

A Century of American Painting, 1850-1950.  Columbus, Ohio:  Keny
    and Johnson Gallery, 1981.

Fielding, Mantle.  Dictionary of American Painters, Sculptors and
    Engravers.  Enlarged ed.  Greens Farms, Connecticut:  Modern
    Books and Crafts, 1974.

Important American Paintings, Drawings and Sculpture.  New York:
    Sotheby's, 31 May 1984:  Lot 187 and 201.

Women Pioneers in Maine Art 1900-1945.  Portland, Maine:  Joan
    Whitney Payson Gallery of Art, Westbrook College, 1985.

NANCY WORTHINGTON (1947-    )    Sculptor

Dryer, Dianne. "Nancy Worthington's Social Commentaries."
    Artweek 8, no. 12 (19 March 1977):  4.

XVIII Bienal Internacional de São Paulo.  São Paulo, Brazil:  Museu
    de Arte Moderna, 1985.

The Exchange Show:  San Francisco/Bay Area--Berlin.  Berlin:
    Galerie Franz Mehring, 1981.

Jan, Alfred. "Exhibitions:  Polemics Through Art." Artweek 15,
    no. 15 (14 April 1984):  3.

MacDonald, Robert. "Forms of Figuration." Artweek 10, no. 11 (17
    March 1979):  7.

Malone, Mollie. "Exhibitions:  Judging Our Society." Artweek 14,
    no. 7 (19 February 1983):  16.

Watson-Jones, Virginia. Contemporary American Women Sculptors.
    Phoenix:  Oryx Press, 1986.

Weeks, H.J. "Reviews of the Exhibitions.  California:  Nancy
    Worthington at Zara, San Francisco." Art Voices/South 2, no.
    3 (May-June 1979):  65-66.

MARY WRENCH (18th Century)    Miniaturist

Bolton, Theodore.  Early American Portrait Painters in Miniature.
    New York:  F.F. Sherman, 1921.

Foster, J.J.  Miniature Painters, British and Foreign:  With Some
    Account of Those Who Practiced in America in the 18th
    Century.  New York:  E.P. Dutton and Co., 1903.

Groce, George C., and Wallace, David H.  The New-York Historical
    Society's Dictionary of Artists in America 1564-1860.  New
    Haven:  Yale University Press, 1957.

Sellers, Charles Coleman.  Charles Willson Peale.  New York:
    Scribner, 1969:  101-03.

ALICE MORGAN WRIGHT (1881-1975)  Sculptor

See volume 1 of this book.

American Art Annual, vol. 28.  Washington, D.C.:  American
    Federation of Arts, 1932.

Fahlman, Betsy. Sculpture and Suffrage, The Art and Life of Alice Morgan Wright (1881-1975). Albany, New York: Albany Institute of History and Art, 1978.

Fiftieth Annual Exhibition. New York: National Association of Women Painters and Sculptors, 1942: no. 107.

Sculpture, Alice Morgan Wright. New York: Marie Sterner Galleries, 1937.

Tarbell, Roberta K. "The Impact of the Armory Show on American Sculpture." Archives of American Art Journal 18, no. 2 (1978): 9.

Wright, Alice Morgan. "Sculpture and Suffrage." New York State Business and Professional Women 14 (December 1947): 7-9.

CATHERINE MORRIS WRIGHT (1899-    )   Painter

See volume 1 of this book.

American Art Annual, vol. 28. Washington, D.C.: American Federation of Arts, 1932.

C.M. Wright, A.N.A.: Retrospective Exhibition 1915-1951. Newport, Rhode Island: Newport Art Association, 1952.

Catharine Morris Wright Retrospective Exhibition 1915-1953. Philadelphia: Woodmere Art Gallery, 1954.

Watts, Harvey M. "The Art of Catherine Morris Wright." Art and Archaeology 32 (July-August 1931): 17-27.

MARGARET HARDON WRIGHT (1869-1936)   Printmaker

American Art Annual, vol. 28. Washington, D.C.: American Federation of Arts, 1932.

American Prints in the Library of Congress: A Catalog of the Collection. Baltimore: Johns Hopkins Press, 1970.

"Margaret Hardon Wright." Alumnae Bulletin, Randolph Macon Woman's College 76 (Spring 1983): 17, 18.

Obituary. Who's Who in American Art, vol. 2. Washington, D.C.: American Federation of Arts, 1937.

484

PATIENCE LOVELL WRIGHT (1725-1786)    Sculptor

See volume 1 of this book.

Clement, Clara Erskine. Women in the Fine Arts. Boston:
Houghton, Mifflin, 1904.

Ellet, Elizabeth. Women Artists in All Ages and Countries. New
York: Harper and Bros., 1859.

McClelland, Elizabeth. "Patience Lovell Wright: Sculptor."
Early American Life 7 (April 1976): 72-75.

Pyke, E.J. A Biographic Dictionary of Wax Modelers. Oxford:
Clarendon Press, 1973.

Taft, Lorado. "Women Sculptors of America." The Mentor 6 (1
February 1919): 23.


LOUISE HEUSER WUESTE (1803-1875)    Painter

Dawdy, Doris Ostrander. Artists of the American West, vol. 1.
Chicago: Swallow Press, 1974.

Groce, George C., and Wallace, David H. The New-York Historical
Society's Dictionary of Artists in America 1564-1860. New
Haven: Yale University Press, 1957.

Moore, Silvia, ed. No Bluebonnets, No Yellow Roses: Essays on
Texas Women in the Arts. New York: Midmarch Arts Press,
1988.

O'Brien, Esse Forrester. Art and Artists of Texas. Dallas: Tardy
Publishing Co., 1935.

Pinckney, Pauline A. Painting in Texas, The Nineteenth Century.
Austin: University of Texas Press, 1967.


CAROLYN WYETH (1909-    )    Painter

See volume 1 of this book.


LILLA YALE (1859-1929)    Painter

An Exhibition of Women Students of William Merritt Chase. New
York: Marbella Gallery, 1973.

19th Century American Women Artists. New York: Whitney Museum of
American Art Downtown Branch, 1976.

Pisano, Ronald.  The Students of William Merritt Chase.
Huntington, Long Island, New York:  Heckscher Museum, 1973.


ENID YANDELL (1870-1934)    Sculptor

See volume 1 of this book.

American Art Annual, vol. 28.  Washington, D.C.:  American
Federation of Arts, 1932.

Clement, Clara Erskine.  Women in the Fine Arts.  Boston:
Houghton, Mifflin, 1904.

Enid Yandell and the Branstock School.  Providence:  Rhode Island
School of Design Museum, 1947.

Tennessee Centennial and International Exposition (Catalogue).
Nasvhille, 1897:  236.

Yandell, Enid, Loughborough, Jean, and Hayes, Laura.  Three Girls
in a Flat.  Chicago:  Knight, Leonard and Co., 1892.


JULIE CHAMBERLAIN NICHOLLS YATES (d. 1929)    Sculptor

Famous Small Bronzes.  New York:  The Gorham Co., 1928:  79, 93.

Obituary.  American Art Annual, vol. 27.  Washington, D.C.:
American Federation of Arts, 1930.

Proske, Beatrice C.  Brookgreen Gardens.  Brookgreen, South
Carolina:  Trustees, 1943:  290-91.


RUTH YATES (1896-1969)    Sculptor

Proske, Beatrice G.  Brookgreen Gardens Sculpture.  Brookgreen,
South Carolina:  Brookgreen Gardens, 1943.

Schnier, Jacques.  Sculpture in Modern America.  Berkeley:
University of California Press, 1948.

Who's Who in American Art, vol. 8.  Washington, D.C.:  American
Federation of Arts, 1962.


CONNIE ZEHR (1938-    )    Sculptor

See volume 1 of this book.

Sixteen Los Angeles Women Artists.  Norwalk, California:  Cerritos
College, 1982.

486

EVA ZEISEL (1907-    )    Porcelain Designer

Eidelberg, Martin, ed. Eva Zeisel: Designer for Industry.
    Chicago: University of Chicago Press, 1984.

"International Style." Apollo 121 (April 1985):  271.

Lessard, Suzannah. "Profiles (Eva Zeisel)." The New Yorker 63,
    no. 8 (13 April 1987):  36-59.

Wright, N. "Zeisel Sets the Table." Industrial Design 32
    (January-February 1985):  85.


CLAIRE ZEISLER (1903-    )    Fiber Artist

See volume 1 of this book.

"Claire Zeisler. "'Grand Dame of the Threads' to Show in
    Scottsdale." Art-Talk, November 1987:  27.

Glueck, Grace. "Claire Zeisler (Whitney Museum of American Art)."
    The New York Times, 4 January 1985:  C15.

Manhart, Marcia and Tom, eds. The Eloquent Object. Tulsa,
    Oklahoma: Philbrook Museum of Art, 1987.

Upshaw, Reagan. "Claire Zeisler at the Whitney." Art in America
    73, no. 6 (June 1985):  137.


HARRIET ZEITLIN (1929-    )    Printmaker and Painter

American Herstory: Women and the U.S. Constitution. Curated by
    Eleanor Tufts. Atlanta: Atlanta College of Art Gallery,
    1988.

Bicentennial Suite: Twelve Original Intaglio and Relief Prints.
    Los Angeles: Zeitlin, 1975.

Harriet Zeitlin, A Survey 1966-1984. Long Beach, California:  The
    Senior Eye Gallery, 1984.

Johnson, Beverly Edna. "Graphics that Go Beyond." The Los Angeles
    Times Home Magazine, 16 November 1975:  14.

_____. "Happenings." The Los Angeles Times Home Magazine, 6 July
    1975:  22.

L.A. Nine. Palm Springs, California:  Palm Springs Desert Museum,
    1980.

Larsen, Dave. "Recasting the Ancient Art of Making Faces." The Los Angeles Times, 11 June 1982, View section: 1.

Pincus, Robert L. "The Galleries." The Los Angeles Times, 11 June 1982, Calendar section: 15.

Power. Curated by Mary Jane Jacobs. Los Angeles: Southern California Women's Caucus for Art, 1987.

75th Anniversary Exhibit. Long Beach, California: The Senior Eye Gallery, 1984.

Taking Liberties. Los Angeles: Southern California Women's Caucus for Art, 1988.

Who's Who in America, 17th ed. New York: R.R. Bowker Co., 1986.

Wilson, Barbara. "Harriet Zeitlin: Interview." Currant (San Francisco) 1, no. 2 (June-July 1975): 41.

LAURA ZIEGLER (1927-    )  Sculptor

See volume 1 of this book.

Brown, Gordon. "David Levine/Laura Ziegler." Arts Magazine 49, no. 6 (February 1975): 18.

Cochran, Diane. "Laura Ziegler: Portraits in Terra Cotta." American Artist 39, issue 395 (June 1975): 30-35, 68-69.

Who's Who in American Art. New York: R.R. Bowker Co., 1978.

ELYN ZIMMERMAN (1945-    )  Sculptor

Day, Holliday T. Elyn Zimmerman, Images of the City: Photographs & Sculptures. Omaha, Nebraska: Joslyn Art Museum, 1985.

Frueh, Joanna. "Reviews Chicago: Elyn Zimmerman, Museum of Contemporary Art." Artforum 18, no. 6 (February 1980): 103-04.

Gopnik, Adam. "Elyn Zimmerman's Marabar." Arts Magazine 59, no. 2 (October 1984): 78-79.

Lubell, Ellen. "Elyn Zimmerman at Hudson River Museum." Art in America 70, no. 5 (May 1982): 139-40.

Scardino, Albert. "Let a Thousand Flowers Bloom." The New York Times, 1 February 1987, Business section: 23.

Silverthorne, Jeanne. "Reviews. 'Directions 1983' Hirshhorn Museum." Artforum 22, no. 2 (October 1983): 79-80.

Tsai, Eugenie. "Elyn Zimmerman: Palisades Project." Arts Magazine 56, no. 8 (April 1982): 138-39.

Varnedoe, Kirk. "Site Lines: Recent Work by Elyn Zimmerman." Arts Magazine 53, no. 4 (December 1978): 148-51.

Watson-Jones, Virginia. Contemporary American Women Sculptors. Phoenix: Oryx Press, 1986.

Who's Who in American Art, 17th ed. New York: R.R. Bowker Co., 1986.

MARGUERITE ZORACH (1887-1968)    Painter

See volume 1 of this book.

"Album: Marguerite Zorach." Arts Magazine 58, no. 5 (January 1984): 62-63.

American Paintings. Brooklyn, New York: Brooklyn Museum, 1979: 127.

Archives of American Art. A Checklist of the Collection. Washington, D.C.: Smithsonian Institution, 1975.

A Circle of Friends: Art Colonies of Cornish and Dublin. Keene, New Hampshire: Keene State College of Art Gallery, 1985.

Davidson, Abraham A. Early American Modernist Painting 1910-1935. New York: Harper and Row, 1981.

Fine, Elsa Honig. Women and Art. Montclair/London: Allanheld and Schram/Prior, 1978.

Flint, Janet Altic. Provincetown Printers: A Woodcut Tradition. Washington, D.C.: National Museum of American Art, 1983.

Henry, Gerrit. "Marguerite Zorach." Art News 83, no. 4 (April 1984): 175.

Mannes, Marya. "The Embroideries of Marguerite Zorach." International Studio 95 (March 1930): 29-33.

Marguerite Zorach. Waterville, Maine: Colby College Art Museum, 1968.

Marter, Joan M.  "Three Women Artists Married to Early Modernists:
    Sonia Delaunay-Terk, Sophie Tauber-Arp, and Marguerite
    Thompson Zorach."  Arts Magazine 54, no. 1 (September 1979):
    88-95.

National Museum of Women in the Arts.  New York:  Harry N. Abrams,
    1987:  78-79.

Tarbell, Roberta K.  William and Marguerite Zorach:  The Maine
    Years.  Rockland, Maine:  William A. Farnsworth Art Museum,
    1980.

Tufts, Eleanor.  American Women Artists, 1830-1930.  Washington,
    D.C.:  National Museum of Women in the Arts, 1987.

Wolf, Amy J.  New York Society of Women Artists 1925.  New York:
    ACA Galleries, 1987.

Women Pioneers in Maine Art 1900-1945.  Portland, Maine:  Joan
    Whitney Payson Gallery of Art, Westbrook College, 1985.

BARBARA ZUCKER (1940-    )  Sculptor

See volume 1 of this book.

Anne Sperry/Barbara Zucker:  A Decade of Work.  Greenvale, New
    York:  Hillwood Gallery, Long Island University, 1984.

Artpark:  The Program in Visual Arts.  Lewiston, New York:
    Artpark, 1978.

A Celebration of American Women Artists Part II:  The Recent
    Generation.  New York:  Sidney Janis Gallery, 1984.

Cohen, Ronny.  "Barbara Zucker at Pam Adler."  Art News 84, no. 6
    (Summer 1985):  121.

Donadio, Emmie.  "'Coming Alive at a Certain Time':  An Interview
    with Barbara Zucker on the Role of Historical Models."  Arts
    Magazine 59, no. 10 (Summer 1985):  78-81, cover.

I-80 Series:  Barbara Zucker.  Omaha, Nebraska:  Joslyn Art Museum,
    1981.

Rickey, Carrie.  "Conduits of a Feather Flocked Together:  Barbara
    Zucker's New Sculptures."  Arts Magazine 52, no. 10 (June
    1978):  106-07.

Russell, John.  "Profusion of Good Art by Women."  The New York
    Times, 22 February 1985:  22.

490

Shepard, Ileen. Sculpture of the 80's. Essay by Lowery S. Sims. Queens, New York: Queens Museum, 1987.

Silverthorne, Jeanne. "Barbara Zucker, Pam Adler Gallery." Artforum 22, no. 3 (November 1983): 83.

Van Wagner, Judy Collischan. "Barbara Zucker's Activated Objects." Arts Magazine 59, no. 10 (Summer 1985): 82-84.

Watson-Jones, Virginia. Contemporary American Women Sculptors. Phoenix: Oryx Press, 1986.

Who's Who in American Art, 17th ed. New York: R.R. Bowker Co., 1986.

Women's Art--Women's Lives: Invitational Exhibition of Vermont Women Artists. Brattleboro: Brattleboro Museum and Art Center, 1982.

ADDENDUM

MARILYN LERNER (1942-    )    Painter

Cohen, Ronny.  "Marilyn Lerner."  Artforum 25, no. 10 (Summer
     1987):  121-22.

Cotter, Holland.  "Marilyn Lerner at John Good."  Art in America
     75, no. 7 (July 1987):  131, 132-33.

Downes, Rackstraw.  "Marilyn Lerner."  Art News 68, no. 3 (May
     1969):  69.

Frank, Peter.  "Marilyn Lerner."  Art News 76, no. 2 (February
     1977):  121.

Loughery, John.  "Marilyn Lerner."  Arts Magazine 61, no. 10 (June
     1987):  110.

1971 Biennial Exhibition.  New York:  Whitney Museum of American
     Art, 1971.

Wasserman, Emily.  "Marilyn Lerner, Zabriskie Gallery."  Artforum
     7, no. 9 (May 1969):  66-67.

Who's Who in American Art.  New York:  R.R. Bowker Co., 1978.